MW01027896

AN
EXEGETICAL
COMMENTARY

HAGGAI,
ZECHARIAH,
MALACHI

AN
EXEGETICAL
COMMENTARY

HAGGAI, ZECHARIAH, MALACHI

Eugene H. Merrill

MOODY PRESS
CHICAGO

HAGGAI

In a day of profound discouragement and misplaced priorities following the return of the Jews from Babylonian exile, the prophet Haggai sounded a clarion call of rebuke, exhortation, and encouragement to his contemporaries. They had begun to rebuild their own homes and businesses and to establish their statehood as a Jewish community but had been derelict in tending to the construction of the temple and making the Lord the central focus of all their hopes and dreams. The message of Haggai, so effective in shaking the Jews of 520 B.C. from their lethargy, has an abiding relevance for all who fail to seek first the Kingdom of God and His righteousness.

ZECHARIAH

Whereas Haggai's vision encompassed, for the most part, his immediate, temporal situation, the range of his contemporary and colleague was much more expansive; for Zechariah not only shared Haggai's burden about the inertia of the postexilic community, but by vision and dream saw the unfolding of Divine purpose for all of God's people and for all the ages to come. Rich in apocalyptic imagery and packed with messianic prediction and allusion, Zechariah's writings became a favorite of the New Testament evangelists and apostles. The glorious hope expounded by the prophet was viewed by them as being fulfilled in the saving work and witness of Jesus Christ. No Minor Prophet excels Zechariah in the clarity and triumph by which he looks to the culmination of God's program of redemption.

MALACHI

The burden of this, the last of the Old Testament prophets, was the glaring inconcinnity between the identity of the Jewish community as the people of God and the living out of all that this required of them. Theirs was not the problem of rebuilding the Temple and holy city, for that had long been done by Malachi's day; rather, it was the issue of holy living and holy service in the aftermath of all the external accomplishments. Malachi, though dead, yet speaks to the modern world about the need to bring performance into line with profession. His message, therefore, is current, especially in light of the coming of the One of whom the prophet so eloquently spoke.

Table of Contents

Preface

The books of Haggai, Zechariah, and Malachi—composed as they were in the postexilic period of Israel's history—were intended, among other purposes, to bring hope to a people whose national and even personal lives had been shattered by the Babylonian destruction of Jerusalem and the Temple and the subsequent deportation of much of the Jewish population. That hope centered not only on the return of the exiles and restoration of their religious and political community but pre-eminently in the eschatological promise of a messianic redeemer and ruler.

The foregoing reasons make these brief prophetic writings particularly relevant and beneficial to modern Christians, for they can see in them the covenant faithfulness of God to His ancient people—a faithfulness exhibited in the coming of Jesus Christ—and they can take heart in the realization that the God who restored Israel long ago can also restore them in times of spiritual decline and personal tragedy. This has been my experience, at least, as I have been confronted with the power and presence of the God of Israel and Father of our Lord Jesus Christ. The undertaking of a commentary on these books has proven to be more than a mere task. Instead, it has turned into an opportunity to be reminded in a fresh way of the perfection of God's eternal purposes.

The successful completion of a project of this nature is dependent on many others besides the author. I wish first to thank Bruce Winter, David DeBoys, Iain Hodgins, and other staff members and colleagues at Tyndale House, Cambridge, for their hospitality and invigorating fellowship in the year 1989-90. Also, I thank the administration and faculty of Dallas Theological Seminary for a year's sabbatical that offered the time and resources to pursue the project. These resources include Amy Hall and Sue Knepp, whose patient word processing—always done with competence and cheerfulness—contributed more than words can say. Finally, I stand in gratitude to my wife Janet and to family and friends who have encouraged me along the way. To all who have been a part, this work is affectionately dedicated.

Abbreviations

The following abbreviations supplement the list adopted by the *Journal of Biblical Literature*:

Akk.   Akkadian
Arab.   Arabic
BWAT   *Beitrage zur Wissenschaft von Alten Testament*
CTR   *Criswell Theological Review*
EB   English Bible
EBC   *The Expositor's Bible Commentary*
GTJ   *Grace Theological Journal*
HB   Hebrew Bible
IndTS   *Indian Theological Studies*
ITC   International Theological Commentary
JTh   *The Journal of Theology*
KHAT   *Kurzer Hand-Kommentar zum Alten Testament*
NKJV   New King James Version
OTWSA   *Ou-Testamentiese Werkgemeenskap van Suid-Afrika*
RTR   *Reformed Theological Review*
SMA   Studies in Mediterranean Archaeology
SoJT   *Southwestern Journal of Theology*
SP   Samaritan Pentateuch
Syr   Syriac
TAPS   Transactions of the American Philosophical Society

THAT	Theologisches Handworterbuch zum Alten Testament
ThEv	Theologia Evangelica
TOTC	Tyndale Old Testament Commentary
WEC	Wycliffe Exegetical Commentary

Selected Bibliography

General Works

Ackroyd, Peter R. *Exile and Restoration*. Philadelphia: Westminster, 1968.

_____. *Israel Under Babylon and Persia*. Oxford: Oxford Univ., 1970.

Archer, Gleason L., Jr. *A Survey of Old Testament Introduction*. Rev. ed. Chicago: Moody, 1985.

Bright, John. *A History of Israel*. 3d ed. Philadelphia: Westminster, 1981.

Childs, Brevard S. *Introduction to the Old Testament As Scripture*. Philadelphia: Fortress, 1979.

Cathcart, Kevin J., and Robert P. Gordon. *The Targum of the Minor Prophets*. Vol. 14. Edinburgh: T. & T. Clark, 1989.

Davies, W. D., and Louis Finkelstein, eds. *The Cambridge History of Judaism*. Vol. 1, *Introduction: The Persian Period*. Cambridge: Cambridge Univ., 1984.

De Vaux, Roland. *Ancient Israel, Its Life and Institutions*. London: Darton, Longman & Todd, 1961.

Driver, S. R. *An Introduction to the Literature of the Old Testament*. Edinburgh: T. & T. Clark, 1913.

Eissfeldt, Otto. *The Old Testament, An Introduction*. Oxford: Basil Blackwell, 1965.

Fishbane, Michael. *Biblical Interpretation in Ancient Israel*. Oxford: Clarendon, 1985.

Fohrer, Georg. *Introduction to the Old Testament*. London: SPCK, 1970.

France, R. T. *Jesus and the Old Testament*. London: Tyndale, 1971.

Hanson, Paul. *The Dawn of Apocalyptic*. Philadelphia: Fortress, 1975.

Harrison, R. K. *Introduction to the Old Testament*. Grand Rapids: Eerdmans, 1969.

Kaiser, Otto. *Introduction to the Old Testament*. Oxford: Basil Blackwell, 1975.

Kirkpatrick, A. F. *The Doctrine of the Prophets*. London: Macmillan, 1901.

Koch, Klaus. *The Rediscovery of Apocalyptic*. SBT 22. London: SCM, 1972.

Merrill, Eugene H. *Kingdom of Priests: A History of Old Testament Israel*. Grand Rapids: Baker, 1987.

Olmstead, A. T. *History of the Persian Empire*. Chicago: Univ. of Chicago, 1948.

Parker, Richard A., and Waldo H. Dubberstein. *Babylonian Chronology 626 B.C.–A.D. 75*. Providence, R.I.: Brown Univ., 1956.

Pritchard, James B., ed. *Ancient Near Eastern Texts Relating to the Old Testament*. Princeton, N.J.: Princeton Univ., 1950.

Russell, D. S. *The Method and Message of Jewish Apocalyptic*. London: SCM, 1964.

Soggin, J. Alberto. *Introduction to the Old Testament*. London: SCM, 1989.

Weiser, Artur. *Introduction to the Old Testament*. London: Darton, Longman & Todd, 1961.

Westermann, Claus. *Basic Forms of Prophetic Speech*. Philadelphia: Westminster, 1967.

Wiseman, D. J. *Chronicles of Chaldaean Kings (625–556 B.C.) in the British Museum*. London: British Museum, 1956.

Yamauchi, Edwin M. *Persia and the Bible*. Grand Rapids: Baker, 1990.

Haggai

Commentaries and Special Studies

Amsler, Samuel. *Aggée, Zacharie 1-8, Zacharie 9-14*. CAT. Neuchatel: Delachaux & Niestlé, 1981.

Baldwin, Joyce G. *Haggai, Zechariah, Malachi*. London: Tyndale, 1972.

Beuken, W. A. M. *Haggai–Sacharja 1-8*. Assen: Van Gorcum, 1967.

Coggins, R. J. *Haggai, Zechariah, Malachi*. Sheffield: JSOT, 1987.

Elliger, Karl. *Das Buch der zwölf kleinen Profeten*. Göttingen: Vandenhoeck & Ruprecht, 1982.

Horst, F. *Die zwölf kleinen Propheten Nahum bis Maleachi*. Tübingen: J. C. B. Mohr, 1964.

Mason, Rex. *The Books of Haggai, Zechariah, and Malachi*. CBC. Cambridge: Cambridge Univ., 1977.

Meyers, Carol L., and Eric M. Meyers. *Haggai, Zechariah 1-8*. AB. Garden City, N.Y.: Doubleday, 1987.

Mitchell, H. G. *A Commentary on Haggai and Zechariah*. ICC. Edinburgh: T. & T. Clark, 1912.

Petersen, David L. *Haggai and Zechariah 1-8*. London: SCM, 1985.

Rudolph, Wilhelm. *Haggai–Sacharja 1-8–Sacharja 9-14–Maleachi*. KAT. Gütersloh: Gerd Mohn, 1976.

Sellin, D. Ernst. *Das Zwölfprophetenbuch*. KAT. Leipzig: Deichert, 1922.

Smith, Ralph L. *Micah–Malachi*. WBC. Waco, Tex.: Word, 1984.

Stuhlmueller, Carroll. *Haggai & Zechariah*. ITC. Grand Rapids: Eerdmans, 1988.

Verhoef, Pieter A. *The Books of Haggai and Malachi*. NICOT. Grand Rapids: Eerdmans, 1987.

Wolff, Hans Walter. *Dodekapropheten 6. Haggai*. BKAT. Neukirchen-Vluyn: Neukirchener, 1986.

Articles

Ackroyd, Peter R. "The Book of Haggai and Zechariah 1-8," *JJS* 3 (1952): 151-56.

———. "Studies in the Book of Haggai," *JJS* 2 (1951): 163-76; *JJS* 3 (1952): 1-13.

———. "Two Old Testament Historical Problems of the Early Persian Period," *JNES* 17 (1958): 13-27.

Carroll, Robert P. "Eschatological Delay in the Prophetic Tradition," *ZAW* 94 (1982): 47-58.

Christensen, Duane L. "Impulse and Design in the Book of Haggai," *JETS* 35 (1992): 445-56.

Clark, David J. "Problems in Haggai 2:15-19," *BT* 34 (1983): 432-39.

Dumbrell, W. J. "Kingship and Temple in the Post-Exilic Period," *RTR* 37 (1978): 33-42.

Eybers, I. H. "The Rebuilding of the Temple According to Haggai and Zechariah," *OTWSA* 13-14 (1970-71): 15-26.

Hamerton-Kelly, R. G. "The Temple and the Origins of Jewish Apocalyptic," *VT* 20 (1976): 1-15.

Japhet, Sara. "Sheshbazzar and Zerubbabel Against the Background of the Historical and Religious Tendencies of Ezra-Nehemiah," *ZAW* 94 (1982): 66-98.

Kessler, John A. "The Shaking of the Nations: An Eschatological View," *JETS* 30 (1987): 159-66.

Koch, Klaus. "Haggai's unreines Volk," *ZAW* 79 (1967): 52-66.

Lust, J. "The Identification of Zerubbabel with Sheshbassar," *ETL* 63 (1987): 90-95.

McCarthy, Dennis J. "An Installation Genre?" *JBL* 90 (1971): 31-41.

Mason, R. A. "The Purpose of the 'Editorial Framework' of the Book of Haggai," *VT* 27 (1977): 413-21.

May, Herbert G. "'This People' and 'This Nation' in Haggai," *VT* 18 (1968): 190-97.

North, Francis S. "Critical Analysis of the Book of Haggai," *ZAW* 68 (1956): 25-46.

Petersen, David L. "Zerubbabel and Jerusalem Temple Reconstruction," *CBQ* 36 (1974): 366-72.

Pierce, Ronald W. "Literary Connectors and a Haggai/Zechariah/Malachi Corpus," *JETS* 27 (1984): 277-89.

_____. "A Thematic Development of the Haggai/Zechariah/Malachi Corpus," *JETS* 27 (1984): 401-11.

Radday, Yehuda T., and Moshe A. Pollatschek. "Vocabulary Richness in Post-exilic Prophetic Books," *ZAW* 92 (1980): 333-46.

Rainey, Anson. "The Satrapy 'Beyond the River,'" *AJBA* 1/2 (1969): 51-78.

Siebeneck, Robert T. "The Messianism of Aggeus and Proto-Zacharias," *CBQ* 19 (1957): 312-28.

Steck, Odil H. "Zu Haggai 1:2-11," *ZAW* 83 (1971): 355-79.

Van Rooy, H. F. "Eschatology and Audience: The Eschatology of Haggai," *Old Testament Essays* 1/1 (1988): 49-63.

Wessels, W. J. "Haggai from a Historian's Point of View," *Old Testament Essays* 1/2 (1988): 47-61.

Wolf, Herbert. "'The Desire of all Nations' in Haggai 2:7: Messianic or Not?" *JETS* 19 (1976): 97-102.

Zechariah

Commentaries and Special Studies

Amsler, Samuel. *Aggée, Zacharie 1-8, Zacharie 9-14*. CAT. Neuchatel: Delachaux & Niestlé, 1981.

Baldwin, Joyce G. *Haggai, Zechariah, Malachi*. London: Tyndale, 1972.

Barker, Kenneth L. "Zechariah." In *EBC*, vol. 7. Edited by Frank E. Gaebelein. Grand Rapids: Zondervan, 1985.

Chary, Theophane. *Aggée-Zacharie-Malachie*. Paris: Librairie Lecoffre, 1969.

Deissler, A. *Zwölf Propheten III. Zefanja, Haggai, Sacharja, Maleachi*. Würzburg: Echter, 1988.

Elliger, Karl. *Die Propheten Nahum, Habakuk, Zephanja, Haggai, Sacharja, Maleachi*. ATD. Göttingen: Vandenhoeck & Ruprecht, 1982.

Horst, F. *Die zwölf kleinen Propheten, Nahum bis Maleachi.* HAT 14. Tübingen: J. C. B. Mohr, 1964.

Jansma, Taeke. *Inquiry into the Hebrew Text and the Ancient Versions of Zechariah IX-XIV.* Leiden: Brill, 1949.

Jeremias, Christian. *Die Nachtgesichte des Sacharja.* Göttingen: Vandenhoeck & Ruprecht, 1977.

Keil, C. F. *The Twelve Minor Prophets.* Edinburgh: T. & T. Clark, 1871.

Lacocque, André. *Zacharie 9-14.* CAT. Neuchatel: Delachaux & Niestlé, 1981.

Lamarche, Paul. *Zacharie IX-XIV. Structure Littéraire et Messianisme.* Paris: Librairie Lecoffre, 1961.

Leupold, H. C. *Exposition of Zechariah.* Grand Rapids: Baker, 1971.

Mason, Rex. *The Books of Haggai, Zechariah, and Malachi.* CBC. Cambridge: Cambridge Univ., 1977.

Meyers, Carol, and Eric M. Meyers. *Haggai, Zechariah 1-8.* AB. Garden City, N.Y.: Doubleday, 1987.

Mitchell, H. G. *A Commentary on Haggai and Zechariah.* ICC. Edinburgh: T. & T. Clark, 1912.

Nowack, W. *Die kleinen Propheten.* HAT. Göttingen: Vandenhoeck & Ruprecht, 1903.

Otzen, Benedikt. *Studien über Deuterosacharja.* ATD 6. Copenhagen: Prostand Apud Munksgaard, 1964.

Petersen, David L. *Haggai and Zechariah 1-8.* London: SCM, 1985.

Petitjean, Albert. *Les Oracles du Proto-Zacharie.* Paris: J. Gabalda, 1969.

Rignell, L. G. *Die Nachtgesichte des Sacharja.* Lund: Gleerup, 1950.

Rothstein, J. W. *Die Nachtgesichte des Sacharja.* BWAT 8. Leipzig: J. C. Hinrichs, 1910.

Rudolph, Wilhelm. *Haggai-Sacharja 1-8–Sacharja 9-14–Maleachi.* KAT. Gütersloh: Gerd Mohn, 1976.

Saebø, Magne. *Sacharja 9-14. Untersuchungen von Text und Form.* Neukirchen-Vluyn: Neukirchener Verlag, 1969.

Sellin, D. Ernst. *Das Zwölfprophetenbuch.* Leipzig: A. Deichert, 1922.

Seybold, Klaus. *Bilder zum Tempelbau. Die Visionen des Propheten Sacharja.* Stuttgart: KBW, 1974.

Stuhlmueller, Carroll. *Haggai and Zechariah.* ITC. Grand Rapids: Eerdmans, 1988.

Unger, Merrill F. *Zechariah.* Grand Rapids: Zondervan, 1963.

Van Hoonacker, A. *Les douze petits Prophètes.* Paris: Librairie Victor Lecoffre, 1908.

Articles

Allan, Nigel. "The Identity of the Jerusalem Priesthood During the Exile," *HeyJ* 23 (1982): 259-69.

Barker, Margaret. "The Evil in Zechariah," *HeyJ* 19 (1978): 12-27.

_____. "The Two Figures in Zechariah," *HeyJ* 18 (1977): 38-46.

Bartnicki, Roman. "Das Zitat van Zack IX, 9-10 und die Tiere im Bericht van Matthäus über dem Einzug Jesu in Jerusalem (Mt XXI, I-II)," *NovT* 18 (1976): 161-66.

Carroll, Robert P. "Twilight of Prophecy or Dawn of Apocalyptic?" *JSOT* 14 (1979): 3-35.

Chernus, Ira. "'A Wall of Fire Round About': The Development of a Theme in Rabbinic Midrash," *JJS* 30 (1979): 18-84.

Clark, David J. "The Case of the Vanishing Angel," *BT* 33 (1982): 213-18.

_____. "Discourse Structure in Zechariah 7:1-8:23 (Comparison with Haggai; Appendix: Structural Layout)," *BT* 36 (1985): 328-35.

Crossan, John Dominic. "Redaction and Citation in Mark 11:9-10 and 11:17," *BR* 17 (1972): 33-50.

Dahood, Mitchell. "Zachariah 9:1 *'ên 'ādām*," *CBQ* 25 (1963): 123-24.

Delcor, Matthias. "Les Allusions à Alexandre le Grand dans Zach 9:1-8," *VT* 1 (1951): 110-24.

_____. "Deux Passages Difficiles: Zach 12:11 et 11:13," *VT* 3 (1953): 67-77.

_____. "Hinweise auf das Samaritanische Schisma in Alten Testament," *ZAW* 74 (1962): 281-91.

_____. "Un Probleme de Critique Textuelle et d'Exegese: Zach 12:10," *RB* 58 (1951): 189-99.

_____. "Les Sources du Deutero-Zacharie et Ses Procedes d'Emprunt," *RB* 59 (1952): 385-411.

Draper, J. A. "The Heavenly Feast of Tabernacles: Revelation 7:1-17," *JSNT* 19 (1983): 133-47.

Driver, G. R. "Old Problems Re-examined," *ZAW* 80 (1968): 174-83.

Duff, Paul Brooks. "The March of the Divine Warrior and the Advent of the Greco-Roman King: Mark's Account of Jesus' Entry into Jerusalem," *JBL* 111 (1992): 55-71.

Eichrodt, Walther. "Vom Symbol zum Typos: Ein Beitrag zur Sacharja-Exegese Zech 1:7—6:9," *TLZ* 13 (1957): 509-22.

Feigin, Samuel. "Some Notes on Zechariah 11:4-17," *JBL* 44 (1925): 203-13.

Finley, Thomas J. "The Sheep Merchants of Zechariah 11," *GTJ* 3 (1982): 31-65.

Galling, Kurt. "Die Exilswende in der Sicht des Propheten Sacharja," *VT* 2 (1952): 18-36.

Good, Robert M. "Zechariah's Second Night Vision," *Bib* 63 (1982): 56-59.

Gordon, R. P. "The Targum to the Minor Prophets and the Dead Sea Texts: Textual and Exegetical Notes," *RQum* 8 (1974): 425-29.

_____. "Targum Variant Agrees with Wellhausen!" *ZAW* 87 (1975): 218-19.

Greenfield, Jonas C. "The Aramean God Rammān/Rimmōn," *IEJ* 26 (1976): 195-98.

Halpern, Baruch. "The Ritual Background of Zechariah's Temple Song," *CBQ* 40 (1978): 167-90.

Hamerton-Kelly, R. B. "The Temple and the Origins of Jewish Apocalyptic," *VT* 20 (1970): 1-15.

Hanson, Paul D. "Zechariah 9 and the Recapitulation of an Ancient Ritual Pattern," *JBL* 92 (1973): 37-59.

Harrelson, Walter. "The Trial of the High Priest Joshua: Zechariah 3," *ErIsr* 16 (1982): 116*-24*.

Hartle, James A. "The Literary Unity of Zechariah," *JETS* 35 (1992): 145-57.

Hill, Andrew E. "Dating Second Zechariah: A Linguistic Reexamination," *HAR* 6 (1982): 105-34.

Japhet, Sara. "Sheshbazzar and Zerubbabel," *ZAW* 95 (1983): 218-29.

Jones, Douglas R. "A Fresh Interpretation of Zechariah IX-XI," *VT* 12 (1962): 241-59.

Joubert, W. H. "The Determination of the Contents of Zechariah 1:7–2:17 Through a Structural Analysis," *OTWSA* 20-21 (1977-78): 66-82.

Kline, Meredith G. "The Structure of the Book of Zechariah," *JETS* 34 (1991): 179-93.

Kloos, Carola J. L. "Zech. II 12: Really a Crux Interpretum?" *VT* 25 (1975): 729-36.

Le Bas, Edwin E. "Zechariah's Climax to the Career of the Corner-Stone," *PEQ* 83 (1951): 139-55.

_____. "Zechariah's Enigmatical Contribution to the Corner-Stone," *PEQ* 82 (1950): 102-22.

Lipiński, E. "Recherches sur le livre de Zacharie," *VT* 20 (1970): 25-55.

Luke, K. "The Thirty Pieces of Silver (Zch. 11:12f.)," *Indian Theological Studies* 19 (1982): 15-32.

Malamat, A. "The Historical Settings of Two Biblical Prophecies of the Nations," *IEJ* 1 (1950-51): 149-59.

Mason, Rex A. "The Relation of Zech 9-14 to Proto-Zechariah," *ZAW* 88 (1976): 227-39.

_____. "Some Echoes of the Preaching in the Second Temple?: Tradition Elements in Zechariah 1-8," *ZAW* 96 (1984): 221-35.

May, Herbert G. "A Key to the Interpretation of Zechariah's Visions," *JBL* 57 (1938): 173-84.

North, Robert. "Zechariah's Seven-spout Lampstand," *Bib* 51 (1970): 183-206.

Oswalt, John N. "Recent Studies in Old Testament Eschatology and Apocalyptic," *JETS* 24 (1981): 289-301.

Patsch, H. "Der Einzug Jesu in Jerusalem," *ZTK* 68 (1971): 1-26.

Petersen, David L. "Zerubbabel and Jerusalem Temple Reconstruction," *CBQ* 36 (1974): 366-72.

_____. "Zechariah's Visions: A Theological Perspective," *VT* 34 (1984): 195-206.

Portnoy, Stephen L., and David L. Petersen. "Biblical Texts and Statistical Analysis: Zechariah and Beyond," *JBL* 103 (1984): 11-21.

Radday, Yehuda T., and Dieter Wickmann. "The Unity of Zechariah Examined in the Light of Statistical Linguistics," *ZAW* 87 (1975): 30-55.

Richter, Hans-Friedemann. "Die Pferde in Den Nachtgesichten des Sacharja," *ZAW* 98 (1986): 96-100.

Ringgren, Helmer. "Behold Your King Comes," *VT* 24 (1974): 207-11.

Robinson, Donald F. "Suggested Analysis of Zechariah 1-8," *ATR* 33 (1951): 65-70.

Ruethy, Albert E. "'Sieben Augen auf Einem Stein,' Sach 3:9," *TLZ* 13 (1957): 522-29.

Saebø, Magne. "Die deuterosacharjanische Frage," *ST* 23 (1969): 115-40.

Sinclair, Lawrence A. "Redaction of Zechariah 1-8," *BR* 20 (1975): 36-47.

Strand, Kenneth A. "An Overlooked Old Testament Background to Revelation 11:1," *AUSS* 22 (1984): 317-25.

_____. "The Two Olive Trees of Zechariah 4 and Revelation 11," *AUSS* 20 (1982): 257-61.

Thomas, D. Winton. "Zechariah 10:11a," *ExpTim* 66 (1955): 272-73.

Tidwell, N. L. A. "*Wā 'ōmar* (Zech 3:5) and the Genre of Zechariah's Fourth Vision," *JBL* 94 (1975): 343-55.

Torrey, C. C. "The Foundry of the Second Temple at Jerusalem," *JBL* 55 (1936): 247-60.

_____. "The Messiah Son of Ephraim," *JBL* 66 (1947): 253-77.

Tournay, R. "Zacharie XII-XIV et l'histoire d'Israël," *RB* 81 (1974): 355-94.

Treves, Marco. "Conjecture Concerning the Date and Authorship of Zechariah IX-XIV," *VT* 13 (1963): 196-207.

Tuell, Steven S. "The Southern and Eastern Borders of Abar-Nahara," *BASOR* 284 (1991): 51-57.

VanderKam, James C. "Joshua the High Priest and the Interpretation of Zechariah 3," *CBQ* 53 (1991): 553-70.

van Zijl, P. J. "A Possible Interpretation of Zech. 9:1 and the function of 'the eye' (*ayin*) in Zechariah," *JNSL* 1 (1971): 59-67.

Villalón, José R. "Sources Vetero-Testamentaires de la Doctrine Qumranienne des Deux Messies," *RevQ* 8 (1972): 53-63.

Zolli, Eugenio. " Eyn Adam," *VT* 5 (1955): 90-92.

Malachi

Commentaries and Special Studies

Alden, Robert L. "Malachi." In *EBC*, vol. 7. Edited by Frank E. Gaebelein. Grand Rapids: Zondervan, 1985.

Baldwin, Joyce G. *Haggai, Zechariah, Malachi*. London: Tyndale, 1972.

Chary, Theophane. *Aggée-Zacharie-Malachie*. Paris: Librairie Lecoffre, 1969.

Deissler, A. *Zwölf Propheten III. Zefanja, Haggai, Sacharja, Maleachi*. Wurzburg: Echter, 1988.

Deutsch, Richard R. *Calling God's People to Obedience. A Commentary on the Book of Malachi*. ITC. Grand Rapids: Eerdmans, 1987.

Elliger, Karl. *Die Propheten Nahum, Habakuk, Zephanja, Haggai, Sacharja, Maleachi*. ATD 25. Göttingen: Vandenhoeck & Ruprecht, 1982.

Glazier-McDonald, Beth. *Malachi, The Divine Messenger*. SBL Diss. Series 98. Atlanta: Scholars Press, 1987.

Hitzig, F. *Die zwölf kleinen Propheten*. Leipzig: S. Hirzel, 1881.

Horst, F. *Die zwölf kleinen Propheten, Nahum bis Maleachi*. HAT 14. Tübingen: J. C. B. Mohr, 1964.

Kaiser, Walter C., Jr. *Malachi. God's Unchanging Love*. Grand Rapids: Baker, 1984.

Laetsch, Theodore. *Minor Prophets*. St. Louis: Concordia, 1956.

Marti, Karl. *Das Dodekapropheten*. KHAT XIII. Tübingen: J. C. B. Mohr, 1904.

Mason, Rex. *The Books of Haggai, Zechariah, and Malachi*. CBC. Cambridge: Cambridge Univ., 1977.

Nowack, W. *Die kleinen Propheten*. HAT. Göttingen: Vandenhoek & Ruprecht, 1903.

Orelli, C. von. *The Twelve Minor Prophets*. Edinburgh: T. & T. Clark, 1893.

Rudolph, Wilhelm. *Haggai–Sacharja 1-8–Sacharja 9-14–Maleachi*. KAT. Gütersloh: Gerd Mohn, 1976.

Smith, John M. P. *A Critical and Exegetical Commentary on the Book of Malachi*. ICC. Edinburgh: T. & T. Clark, 1912.

Smith, Ralph L. *Micah-Malachi*. WBC. Waco, Tex.: Word, 1984.

Van Hoonacker, A. *Les Douze Petits Prophètes*. Paris: Librairie Victor Lecoffre, 1908.

Verhoef, Pieter A. *The Books of Haggai and Malachi*. NICOT. Grand Rapids: Eerdmans, 1987.

Vuilleumier, René. *Malachie*. CAT. Neuchatel: Delachaux & Niestlé, 1981.

Articles

Baldwin, J. G. "Malachi 1:11 and the Worship of the Nations in the Old Testament," *TynBul* 23 (1972): 117-24.

Braun, Roddy. "Malachi—A Catechism for Times of Disappointment," *CurTM* 4 (1977): 297-303.

Clendenen, E. Ray. "The Structure of Malachi: A Textlinguistic Study," *CTR* 2 (1987): 3-17.

Drinkard, Joel F., Jr. "The Socio-Historical Setting of Malachi," *RevEx* 84 (1987): 383-90.

Dumbrell, William J. "Malachi and the Ezra-Nehemiah Reforms," *RTR* 35 (1976): 42-52.

Fischer, James A. "Notes on the Literary Form and Message of Malachi," *CBQ* 34 (1972): 315-20.

Fitzmyer, Joseph A. "More About Elijah Coming First," *JBL* 104 (1985): 295-96.

Freedman, David B. "An Unnoted Support for a Variant to the MT of Mal 3:5," *JBL* 98 (1979): 405-06.

Fuller, Russell. "Text-Critical Problems in Malachi 2:10-16," *JBL* 110 (1991): 47-57.

Harrison, George W. "Covenant Unfaithfulness in Malachi 2:1-16," *CTR* 2 (1987): 63-72.

Jones, David Clyde. "A Note on the LXX of Malachi 2:16," *JBL* 109 (1990): 683-85.

Kaiser, Walter C., Jr. "Divorce in Malachi 2:10-16," *CTR* 2 (1987): 73-84.

_____. "The Promise of the Arrival of Elijah in Malachi and the Gospels," *GTJ* 3 (1982): 221-33.

Keown, Gerald L. "Messianism in the Book of Malachi," *RevEx* 84 (1987): 443-51.

Klein, George L. "An Introduction to Malachi," *CTR* 2 (1987): 19-37.

McKenzie, Steven L., and Howard N. Wallace, "Covenant Themes in Malachi," *CBQ* 45 (1983): 549-63.

Ogden, Graham S. "The Use of Figurative Language in Malachi 2:10-16," *BT* 39 (1988): 223-30.

Robinson, Alan. "God, the Refiner of Silver," *CBQ* 11 (1949): 188-90.

Rudolph, W. "Zu Mal 2:10-16," *ZAW* 93 (1981): 85-90.

Scalise, Pamela. "To Fear or not to Fear: Questions of Reward and Punishment in Malachi 2:17–4:2," *RevEx* 84 (1987): 409-18.

Schreiner, Stefan. "Mischehen-Ehebruch-Ehescheidung," *ZAW* 91 (1979): 207-28.

Smith, Ralph. "The Shape of Theology in the Book of Malachi," *SWJT* 30 (1987): 22-27.

Snyman, S. D. "Antitheses in the Book of Malachi," *JNSL* 10 (1990): 173-78.

Swetnam, James. "Malachi 1:11: An Interpretation," *CBQ* 31 (1969): 200-209.

Tate, Marvin E. "Questions for Priests and People in Malachi 1:2–2:16," *RevEx* 84 (1987): 391-407.

Thomas, D. Winton. "The Root *SN'* in Hebrew, and the Meaning of QDRNYT in Malachi 3:14," *JJS* 1 (1948-49): 182-88.

Van Selms, A. "The Inner Cohesion of the Book of Malachi," *OTWSA* 13-14 (1970-71): 27-40.

Verhoef, P. A. "Some Notes on Malachi 1:11," *OTWSA* 9 (1966): 163-72.

Watts, J. D. W. "Introduction to the Book of Malachi," *RevEx* 84 (1987): 373-81.

Wendland, Ernst. "Linear and Concentric Patterns in Malachi," *BT* 36 (1985): 108-21.

Haggai

Introduction to Haggai

HISTORICAL CONTEXT

The prophets Haggai and Zechariah were contemporaries and therefore shared a common historical setting—Jerusalem at the end of the sixth century B.C. That setting may be precisely identified, for no other biblical authors, with the exception of Ezekiel, tied their ministries and messages more closely to a chronological framework.

Haggai dates his first recorded revelation to the first day of the sixth month of the second year of the Persian king Darius Hystaspes (522-486 B.C.). This is the month Elul, equivalent to Ulu of the Babylonian/Persian calendar and corresponding in the Julian calendar to August-September. Prior to the Exile the calendar year began in autumn, but by the Exile the Jews adopted the Babylonian calendar, thus locating new year's day in the spring.[1] Haggai's precise date therefore is August 29, 520 B.C.[2] He next refers to the response of Zerubbabel and Joshua to the message of Yahweh, dating that to the twenty-fourth day of the same month, or September 21 (Hag. 1:15). The prophet then assigns his second oracle to the twenty-first day of the seventh month (i.e., Tishri), or October 17 (2:1). Finally, he

---

1. Jack Finegan, *Handbook of Biblical Chronology* (Princeton, N.J.: Princeton Univ., 1964), 38-40.
2. For the establishment of the Julian dates here and elsewhere, see Richard A. Parker and Waldo H. Dubberstein, *Babylonian Chronology 626 B.C.–A.D. 75* (Providence: Brown Univ., 1956), 30.

3

cites the twenty-fourth day of the ninth month (Kislev), December 18 (2:10, 20).

Zechariah dates his first vision to the eighth month (Marcheshwan) of Darius's second year, that is, October-November 520 B.C. (Zech. 1:1). Then, more specifically, he ties his night visions to the twenty-fourth day of the eleventh month of the same year (1:7), February 15, 519 B.C., according to modern calendars. Thus, all the ministry of Haggai and the first two oracles of Zechariah fall between the sixth and eleventh months of Darius's second year. Zechariah provides one more date, however, the fourth day of the ninth month (Kislev) of the fourth year of Darius, December 7, 518 B.C. This marked the occasion of his interview with Sharezer, Regem-melek, and other leaders from Bethel (7:1).

The strict attention to matters of chronology exhibited by Haggai and Zechariah is characteristic of the annalistic style of history writing employed in Neo-Babylonian and Persian times. The famous "Babylonian Chronicles" with its insistence on documenting every royal achievement to the month and day is a case in point.[3] Peter Ackroyd's opinion is that the dating formulae of Haggai may be artificial, with no other purpose than to "give a fuller expression to the conviction that the word of the Lord is operative and known in the precise situations of history."[4] No difficulties, however, exist in them sufficient to justify their being taken in any but a prima facie manner. Interestingly, in another place the same scholar argues that "clearly the onus of proof must rest on anyone who disputes the dates [in Haggai]."[5]

As noted already, Ezekiel, an older contemporary of Haggai and Zechariah, took pains to establish the chronological parameters of his ministry (Ezek. 1:1-2; 8:1; 20:1; 24:1; 26:1; 29:1, 17; 30:20; 31:1; 32:1, 17; 33:21; 40:1). Daniel, also of the same period, did likewise, though he was content to speak only of the years in which something significant occurred (Dan. 1:1; 2:1; 7:1; 8:1; 9:1, 10:1). Ezra and Nehemiah, both a half century or more later than Haggai and Zechariah, reflect the same interest in chronological precision (Ezra 1:1; 3:1, 6, 8; 4:24; 6:15; 8:31; 10:9, 17; Neh 1:1; 2:1; 5:14; 6:15; 7:73-8:2; 9:1; 13:6). David Petersen draws attention to the fact that dates now must be in reference to Persian kings since there no longer were kings of Judah to provide that framework.[6]

---

3. D. J. Wiseman, *Chronicles of Chaldaean Kings (625-556 B.C.) in the British Museum* (London: Trustees of the British Museum, 1961).
4. Peter R. Ackroyd, "Two Old Testament Historical Problems of the Early Persian Period," *JNES* 17 (1958): 22.
5. Peter R. Ackroyd, "Studies in the Book of Haggai," *JJS* 2 (1951): 173.
6. David L. Petersen, *Haggai and Zechariah 1-8* (London: SCM, 1985), 43; cf.

The chronological cross-referencing by the biblical authors suggests they were aware they were part of an international community. The experience of Exile under Babylonia and the continuing subservience to Persia made it crystal clear that tiny Judah was inextricably involved in the affairs of the surrounding world, no matter how distasteful that might be. It was only natural, then, for her spokesmen, statesmen, and prophets to give account of themselves in terms of the larger geopolitical environment. The history of God's people would no longer be recorded and recounted in isolation from the remainder of the civilized world. Pieter Verhoef also makes the point that dating of prophetic oracles emphasized the authenticity of the message. However this may be true of the postexilic prophets, it does not account for the absence of such data in earlier prophetic writing.[7]

That world must now be addressed briefly in order that the message of the postexilic prophets might find contextual moorings.[8] They spoke, after all, not abstractly or existentially, but to a people who struggled to find meaning in a chaotic world that threatened to overwhelm them with its political and military might.[9] As men of God, they desired to share a word from God that would address the exigencies of a remnant community that was struggling to reestablish itself on the holy soil of Palestine against what must have appeared to be insuperable obstacles. What forces had brought them to the present hour, and what hope did they have for a renewal of the ancient covenant promises and glory? In what kind of world did they live? What were the prospects in light of present realities and in anticipation of future divine intervention?

Less than four decades after the fall of Jerusalem to the Babylonians in 586 B.C., it was evident that the balance of power in the Eastern world was beginning to shift. As early as the accession of Nabo-polassar as king of the Neo-Babylonian empire, Cyaxares (625-585) had become ruler of Media and all of northern Mesopota-

---

Pieter A. Verhoef, *The Books of Haggai and Malachi*, NICOT (Grand Rapids: Eerdmans, 1987), 46-47.

7. Pieter A. Verhoef, "Notes on the Dates in the Book of Haggai," in *Text and Context: Old Testament and Semitic Studies for F. C. Fensham*, ed. A. Claassen, JSOTSup Series 48 (Sheffield: Sheffield Academic Press, 1988), 263-64.

8. For a good survey of the Middle Eastern world of the sixth-fifth centuries B.C., see A. T. Olmstead, *History of the Persian Empire* (Chicago: Univ. of Chicago, 1948); Peter R. Ackroyd, *Exile and Restoration* (Philadelphia: Westminster, 1968); G. Buchanon Gray, "The Foundation and Extension of the Persian Empire," in *CAH* 4:1-25; G. B. Gray and M. Cary, "The Reign of Darius," *CAH* 4:173-228; Edwin M. Yamauchi, *Persia and the Bible* (Grand Rapids: Baker, 1990).

9. Peter R. Ackroyd, "Studies in the Book of Haggai," *JJS* 3 (1952): 11-12.

mia. He then conquered Persia (in southwest Iran), placing Cambyses over it as governor. Upon the death of Cyaxares, his son Astyages (585-550) succeeded him. The daughter of Astyages was the mother of Cyrus II, vassal of Astyages and ruler of the Persian province of An-shan. Cyrus soon antagonized his grandfather by making an alliance with Nabonidus, king of Babylonia and Astyages's bitter enemy. The result was a rupture between Astyages and Cyrus and the eventual conquest of Media by the young Persian upstart in 550 B.C.

Meanwhile, Nebuchadnezzar II (605-562), who had conquered and destroyed Jerusalem and deported its leading citizens in July of 586 B.C., had passed from the scene to be followed by Amel-Marduk (562-560), Neriglissar (560-556), and Labashi-Marduk (556). Naboni-dus (556-539), whose north Mesopotamian roots and devotion to the moon god Sin were to alienate him from his Babylonian subjects, then took over. Preoccupied as he was by his cult and by foreign travel and trade, Nabonidus left the responsibility of government largely in the hands of his son Belshazzar. It was the latter, as the Bible clearly intimates (Dan. 5:1-31), who fell to Cyrus when Babylon finally capit-ulated to the Persians on October 12, 539 B.C.

Beginning in 555, the year Cyrus defeated his Median grand-father, he had incorporated Media, Lydia, and Babylonia into his rapidly expanding Persian empire. At last only the city of Babylon itself remained. Its surrender to Cyrus was a foregone conclusion since, according to the so-called "Verse Account of Nabonidus" and other texts,[10] Nabonidus had so offended Marduk, chief deity of Baby-lon, by his impious devotion to Sin that Marduk had determined to turn his estate over to a "shepherd" who would better tend it. That shepherd, of course, was Cyrus.

The biblical version of the rise of Cyrus is quite different, for it is Yahweh, not Marduk, who raised him up (Isa. 44:24–45:7) and who called him to deliver His captive people from Babylonian bondage. That Cyrus was indeed called to do so is clear from the famous Cylin-der of Cyrus.[11] That it was Yahweh who provided the impulse is attested to in the OT by both the Chronicler (2 Chron. 36:22-23) and Ezra (1:1-4).

In 538 B.C. Cyrus issued his decree that the Jews and all other captive peoples could return to their respective homelands. He had begun to organize his vast domain into a system of satrapies, further subdivided into provinces,[12] and the satrapy of special relevance to

---

10. James B. Pritchard, ed., *Ancient Near Eastern Texts Relating to the Old Testament* (Princeton, N.J.: Princeton Univ., 1950), 312-16.
11. *ANET*, 315.
12. Gray and Cary, "The Reign of Darius," *CAH* 4:194-201.

the Jewish community was known as *Bābili eber nāri* ("Babylon beyond the river"), a huge jurisdiction between the Euphrates River and the Mediterranean Sea.[13] Within that satrapy were entities such as Galilee, Samaria, Ashdod, Ammon, and especially Yehud (or Judah).[14] Each of these was under a governor who reported directly to the satrap, or administrator, of the district of *eber nāri*.

The picture is not entirely clear, but it seems that Yehud, though weak and impoverished compared to provincial neighbors such as Samaria, was independent of them and not a subdivision. Thus, the various Jewish governors could carry their case directly to the satrap in times of difficulty. The first of these governors was Sheshbazzar, leader of the first return from Babylon to Jerusalem (Ezra 1:5-11; 5:14). It is likely that he is the same as Shenazzar, a son of Jehoiachin, the last surviving king of Judah (1 Chron. 3:18).[15] He held his position for only a brief time, for already in the second year after Cyrus's decree (536 b.c.) Zerubbabel appears as the governor (Ezra 3:2, 8; cf. Hag. 1:1).

The relationship of Zerubbabel to Sheshbazzar and to the Davidic dynasty is somewhat obscure.[16] He is usually described as the "son of Shealtiel" (Ezra 3:2, 8; Neh. 12:1; Hag. 1:1, 12, 14; 2:2, 23; Matt. 1:12), but in the Chronicler's genealogy he is the son of Pedaiah (1 Chron. 3:19). Both Shealtiel and Pedaiah were sons of Jehoiachin— along with Shenazzar (= Sheshbazzar?)—so either Zerubbabel was the levirate son of Pedaiah on behalf of Shealtiel[17] or (more likely) Shealtiel had died before he could become governor, his younger brother Sheshbazzar taking that role instead.[18] Zerubbabel, son of Shealtiel and nephew of Sheshbazzar, then succeeded Sheshbazzar

13. Anson Rainey, "The Satrapy 'Beyond the River,'" *AJBA* 1/2 (1969): 51-78; Ephraim Stern, "The Persian Empire and the Political and Social History of Palestine in the Persian Period," in *The Cambridge History of Judaism*, vol. 1, *Introduction: The Persian Period*, eds. W. D. Davies and Louis Finkelstein (Cambridge: Cambridge Univ., 1984), 78-87.
14. The province is called *yĕhûdâ* in Haggai but *yĕhûd* in the Aramaic of Ezra 7:14 and in extrabiblical bullae and seals. See Carol L. Meyers and Eric M. Meyers, *Haggai, Zechariah 1-8*, AB (Garden City, N.Y.: Doubleday, 1987), 13-14.
15. Thus John Bright, *A History of Israel*, 3d ed. (Philadelphia: Westminster, 1981), 362. For a presentation of various views, see Sara Japhet, "Sheshbazzar and Zerubbabel Against the Background of the Historical and Religious Tendencies of Ezra-Nehemiah," *ZAW* 94 (1982): 71-72.
16. For various views, see Roddy Braun, *1 Chronicles*, WBC (Waco, Tex.: Word, 1986), 52-53.
17. Wilhelm Rudolph, *Haggai-Sacharja 1-8–Sacharja 9-14–Maleachi*, KAT (Gütersloh: Gütersloher: Verlaghaus Gerd Mohn, 1976), 31.
18. Meyers and Meyers, *Haggai, Zechariah 1-8*, 11.

upon his death. Pedaiah possibly served as foster father for Zerub-babel until he reached his maturity.

Sara Japhet argues that Sheshbazzar was the first governor of Judah but denies that he was related to Zerubbabel or, indeed, to the royal family at all.[19] F. C. Fensham says that it is not acceptable to identify Sheshbazzar with the Shenazzar of 1 Chron. 3:18 and that his identification as "prince" (הַנָּשִׂיא, *hannāśî*) in Ezra 1:8 proves nothing more than that he was a person raised to a position of authority.[20] This is the view also of Joseph Blenkinsopp who admits that Shesh-bazzar's title would be unassailable evidence of his Davidic lineage were it possible to connect Sheshbazzar with Shenazzar. With most modern scholars he concludes that nothing can be known of Shesh-bazzar's identity.[21]

What is important is that Zerubbabel was a grandson of Jehoia-chin and therefore the legitimate heir of the Davidic throne. His ap-pointment as governor allowed his Judean royal descent to coincide with his Persian political appointment. How long he served in that capacity cannot be determined, but he was still governor by 520 B.C. The recent discovery of bullae and seals bearing the names of Judean governors suggests that Zerubbabel may be dated to c. 510, Elnathan c. 510-490, Yehoʻezer c. 490-470, and Ahzai c. 447-445.[22] Nehemiah, of course, commenced his governorship then and continued on to 433 B.C.

Little is known of the period between the decree of Cyrus (538 B.C.) and the ministry of Haggai and Zechariah (520 B.C.). Evidently Cyrus had laid down a firm political and social foundation, and until his death in 530 B.C. the Persian Empire, including Yehud, enjoyed tranquillity and prosperity. Ezra provides the information that in the seventh month of the first year back in Jerusalem (537 B.C.) the peo-ple, under the leadership of Zerubbabel and Joshua the priest, built an altar on the Temple ruins and celebrated the Feast of Tabernacles (Ezra 3:1-7). In the second month of the next year (536) the founda-tions of the new Temple were laid (3:8-10). After this the record is virtually silent except for the statement that the adversaries of the Jews began a campaign of harassment, seeking to prevent reconstruc-tion of the house of the Lord. This continued throughout the reign of Cyrus and Cambyses (530-522) into the time of Darius (522-486).

---

19. Japhet, "Sheshbazzar and Zerubbabel," 94-98.
20. F. C. Fensham, *The Books of Ezra and Nehemiah*, NICOT (Grand Rapids: Eerdmans, 1982), 46.
21. Joseph Blenkinsopp, *Ezra-Nehemiah* (Philadelphia: Westminster, 1988), 78-79.
22. These approximate dates follow the suggestions of N. Avigad, *Bullae and Seals from a Post-Exilic Judean Archive. Qedem* (Jerusalem: Hebrew Univ., 1976), 4:35.

Cambyses, son of Cyrus, was noted particularly for his conquest of Egypt and its absorption into the Persian hegemony. Cambyses also left a negative legacy of mismanagement that left the Empire in a near shambles. His mysterious death was followed by an attempted usurpation of the Persian throne by Gaumata, an official who claimed to be a brother of Cambyses hitherto thought to be dead. Before Gaumata could seize control he was assassinated by Darius Hystaspes and some collaborators, and Darius placed himself in power on September 29, 522.[23]

The chaotic reign of Cambyses without doubt contributed to the ability of the Jews' enemies to interdict their work and otherwise make life miserable for them. The succession of Darius changed all that, however, for after he put down various rebellions attendant to his rise to power, he implemented far-ranging and effective political and fiscal policies that brought stability throughout his realm. Within two years all was at peace, except for Egypt. Darius, therefore, made plans to invade that intractable satrapy and bring it into line, an action that took place in 519-518 B.C.[24]

Meanwhile, Judah's foes, including even Tattenai, governor of the entire *eber nāri* province, hoped to capitalize on Darius's newness to office by sending a letter warning him about Jewish rebellion (Ezra 5:6-17). Darius immediately made a search of the archives of Cyrus at Ecbatana and verified that the Jewish claims that reconstruction of the Temple and city was authorized by Cyrus himself were true. Without further ado the work was resumed and completed by 515 B.C. (6:15). The anticipated march of Darius through Palestine on his way to Egypt in 519 may have done as much as anything to encourage the Jews and frustrate the evil intentions of their neighbors.

This, then, is the setting of the ministries of Haggai and Zechariah. First appearing in the biblical record in 520 B.C., two years after Darius's accession, they took advantage of the Pax Persiaca to urge their compatriots on to the noble task of Temple building (Hag. 1:2; cf. Ezra 5:1-2). Joyce Baldwin is correct in asserting (contrary to many scholars) that Haggai's exhortation to build was not a sign of rebellion against a Persian government in disarray, for he was already many months too late for that; rather, he was taking advantage of the peace that ensued after Darius was established.[25] From a political standpoint the prospects were never more bright and, said the prophets, never were times more propitious to reestablish the theocratic

---

23. There is a lacuna in the calendars at the time of Darius's accession, but A. Poebel and W. Hinz make a case for this date. Cf. Ackroyd, "Two Old Testament Historical Problems," 14 n. 9.
24. Olmstead, *History of the Persian Empire*, 141.
25. Joyce G. Baldwin, *Haggai, Zechariah, Malachi* (London: Tyndale, 1972), 16.

community so that Yahweh's ancient covenant promises to His people could find fulfillment.

The biblical texts, though scanty, make it quite clear that the restoration community was small and demoralized. Ezra reckons the number of returnees under Sheshbazzar (or Zerubbabel) to have been 42,360 in addition to 7,337 slaves and 200 singers (2:64-65). The number of indigenous Jews is unknown but could not have numbered more than that. John Bright argues that the total population of Judah in 522 B.C. could not have exceeded 20,000, but his estimate is based on a denial that the list of returnees in Ezra 2 and Nehemiah 7 refers to the return under Sheshbazzar and Zerubbabel, a denial that is without foundation.[26] That it is an account of early return (between 538 and 522) is put beyond dispute by H. G. M. Williamson.[27] Some rebuilding must have been undertaken in the Judean towns and villages since their destruction at Babylonian hands, but Jerusalem remained mostly in ruins (5:3, 9).

The repopulation of the land, at least outside Jerusalem, gave rise to the rebuilding of houses and storage buildings and to the clearing and cultivation of the farmlands. In fact, it was the rapidity and conviction with which this was done that caused Haggai to lament that, by comparison, the house of the Lord was neglected. His burden then was that this inequity be redressed and that the people do all they could in spite of their still rather limited resources to erect a house of the Lord that could provide a suitable expression of His presence among them. Until this was done the restoration would remain incomplete and the gracious promises of the Lord unfulfilled.

LITERARY CONTEXT

The book of Haggai is only one composition among a rather rich corpus of Hebrew literature of the sixth and fifth centuries B.C., including Zechariah, Esther, 1 and 2 Chronicles, Ezra-Nehemiah, and Malachi. The transmission of the text, with all the redactional and editorial touches that inevitably attended that process, makes it impossible to recover the *ipsissima verba* of the prophet with absolute certainty, but clearly there is no reason to think that there were any more than cosmetic changes in the product that left his hands. Haggai, then, can be regarded as an authentic document of the sixth century, whose provenience it professes.[28]

26. Bright, *A History of Israel*, 365.
27. H. G. M Williamson, *Ezra, Nehemiah*, WBC (Waco, Tex.: Word, 1985), 30-32.
28. Samuel Amsler, *Aggée, Zacharie 1-8*, CAT (Paris: Neuchatel, 1981), 14. An

LANGUAGE AND STYLE

Unanimous tradition assigns the book of Haggai to the prophet whose name it bears, but since he wrote no other canonical literature, this work is *sui generis* in terms of a "Haggai corpus." It is possible, however, to compare Haggai to contemporary literature, especially to Zechariah, and to draw certain conclusions about language and style, both that which is unique to Haggai and that shared by him with others.

Scholars have long debated whether Haggai is composed in only prose. BHK renders it as such, whereas BHS identifies 1:4-6, 7b-11; 2:3b-9, 14b-19, 21-23 as poetry. The matter is not easily decided since elevated prose differs little from "ordinary" Hebrew poetry.[29] Driver says that Haggai "lacks the imagination and poetical power possessed by most of the prophets; but his style is not that of pure prose: his thoughts, for instance, not unfrequently shape themselves into parallel clauses such as are usual in Hebrew poetry."[30]

Driver's assessment appears to be borne out by the stylistic devices that appear with regularity: the parallelism of 1:6; the metric rhythm[31] of 1:3-6, 8; 2:4-5, 21-23; the use of chiastic framing in 1:4, 9, 10; 2:23; a "dialogue style"[32] like that of Malachi in 1:4, 5, 9; 2:11-13; and paronomasia in 1:4 (חָרֵב, *ḥārēb*, "ruin") and 1:11 (חֹרֶב, *ḥōreb*, "drought"). Haggai does not rise to the literary heights of his colleague Zechariah, but Zechariah deals much more with the lofty themes of apocalyptic, which tends toward colorful imagery and fantastic symbolism.[33] Yet Haggai is a delightful piece, one that betrays an author of unusual literary sensitivity.[34]

---

extreme position that views virtually nothing as original to Haggai may be found in Francis S. North, "Critical Analysis of the Book of Haggai," *ZAW* 68 (1956): 25-46.

29. It is probably impossible to make a sharp distinction between these two modes of speech. Thus R. J. Coggins, *Haggai, Zechariah, Malachi* (Sheffield: JSOT, 1987), 36.

30. S. R. Driver, *An Introduction to the Literature of the Old Testament* (Edinburgh: T. & T. Clark, 1913), 344. Ackroyd ("Studies in the Book of Haggai," *JJS* 2, 164) suggests that the oracles of the book were originally couched in poetic form. In a recent study, Christensen not only affirms that Haggai was a poetical (even musical) text, but he sets forth an elaborate prosodic analysis demonstrating this. He concludes that the book consists of three cantos (1:1-14; 1:15-2:9; 2:10-23), all displaying similar concentric architectural design. Duane L. Christensen, "Impulse and Design in the Book of Haggai," *JETS* 35 (1992): 445-46.

31. Petersen, *Haggai and Zechariah 1-8*, 32.

32. Verhoef, *The Books of Haggai and Malachi*, 18.

33. D. S. Russell, *The Method and Message of Jewish Apocalyptic* (London: SCM, 1964), 90, 122-27.

34. From the standpoint of genre criticism Petersen's description (*Haggai and Zechariah 1-8*, 35) of Haggai as "a brief apologetic historical narrative" is quite apposite.

LITERARY INTEGRITY

Scholarly consensus maintains that the book of Haggai was written by its attributive author except, perhaps, for editorial frameworks and minor later interpolations. The delimitation of such frameworks has been most thoroughly carried out by W. A. M. Beuken and Rex A. Mason. Mason, in a sympathetic treatment of Beuken's work (though he plays down Beuken's suggestion about a "Chronistic" influence on Haggai), identifies the "editorial framework" as 1:1, 3, 12, 13*a*, 14, 15; 2:1, 2 (probably), 10, 20.[35] Haggai himself is unknown except for his writing and two references to him in Ezra (5:1; 6:14). His name in Hebrew (חַגַּי, *ḥaggay*) means "my feast" or the like, possibly because he was born on a festival day (חַג, *ḥag*). Though he is the only Haggai of the Bible, related forms such as Haggi (Gen. 46:16), Haggit (2 Sam. 3:4), and Haggiah (1 Chron. 6:30) suggest that it was a popular name. In addition, it is attested in Hebrew seals of the postexilic period and in Phoenician, South Arabic, and Aramaic sources. Names associated with festival days as propitious occasions for birth finds parallels in Egyptian and Akkadian texts as well.[36]

The book of Haggai consists of four addresses of the prophet (Hag. 1:1-15; 2:1-9, 10-19, 20-23), the first of which has two parts (1:1-11, 12-15). This structure will receive attention presently, but for now it is important to consider various viewpoints as to the origin and growth of the composition.

First, it is generally agreed that Haggai himself is responsible for the bulk of the material and that he arranged it according to four addresses set off by chronological notations (1:1, 15; 2:1, 10, 20). But a difficulty already emerges since the second oracle, 1:12-15, is followed and not preceded by the chronological datum, as is the case with the other three. To resolve this anomaly, some scholars have proposed that 1:15 should be divided, with 15*b* joined to 2:1, to create the full formula of year, month, and day.[37] Thus 1:15*b*–2:1 precedes what then becomes the second oracle (1:15*b*–2:9). The remainder of

---

35. W. A. M. Beuken, *Haggai-Sacharja 1-8* (Assen: van Gorcum, 1967), 28-83; Rex A. Mason, "The Purpose of the 'Editorial Framework' of the Book of Haggai," *VT* 27 (1977): 414. A strong case for the unity of the book, especially in response to the arguments of T. André (*Le Prophete Aggée*, 1895) to the contrary, may be found in H. G. Mitchell, *A Commentary on Haggai and Zechariah*, ICC (Edinburgh: T. & T. Clark, 1912), 28-30. For evidence of the homogeneity of Haggai from a profile of vocabulary frequency, see Yehuda T. Radday and Moshe A. Pollatschek, "Vocabulary Richness in Post-Exilic Prophetic Books," *ZAW* 92 (1980): 333-46.
36. Hans Walter Wolff, *Dodekapropheton 6. Haggai*, BKAT (Neukirchen-Vluyn: Neukirchener Verlag, 1986), 2.
37. So already the LXX, VL, Vg, and Syriac, followed by BHK.

1:15 would be left suspended unless it is recognized that 2:10-19 consists of two fundamentally different messages, 2:10-14 and 2:15-19. J. W. Rothstein, on the basis of Ezra 4:1-5, identified "this people" of Hag. 2:14 with the Samaritans, supporting a date three months after the laying of the Temple foundations (2:10). Haggai 2:15-19, however, seems to fit the subject matter of 1:1-11, a period before or at the very beginning of the construction. The chronology of 1:15a should then introduce 2:15-19, requiring a transposition of 2:15-19 and 2:10-14 (and 2:1-9).[38] Eissfeldt[39] proposes that the twenty-fourth day of 2:18 resulted from carelessness on the part of the redactor who placed that day in the ninth month, in line with 2:10, rather than in the sixth month as the chronological introduction of 1:15a required.

The issues raised in this analysis will receive detailed attention in the commentary, but it is important that the linchpin of the difficulty, the apparent dislocation of 1:15, be explained now since discussion of the arrangement of the book depends on it. The following points should be considered.

(1) Haggai 1:1-15 is one long address subdivided into 1:1-11 and 1:12-15. In light of this, the prophet clearly would want to avoid interrupting his discourse with a chronological note before the second part; hence, he placed it at the end as a kind of inclusio with 1:1 (both second year, sixth month).

(2) The absence of a reference to a year in 2:1 leads one to suspect that the "second year" of 1:15b is doing double duty.[40] It provides a year for 1:12-15 and one for 2:1-9 at the same time. The structure is day, month, year (1:15), month, day (2:1).

(3) There is no ancient manuscript variation from the traditional order. The scroll of the minor prophets from the caves of Murabba'at, which contains 1:15, shows no evidence of a different tradition.[41] The LXX does combine 1:15 with 2:1, separating v. 15 from the section 1:12-15, but this only leads to a confusing blending of mutually exclu-

---

38. J. W. Rothstein, *Juden und Samaritaner: Die grundlegende Scheidung von Judentum und Heidentum*, BWANT 3 (Leipzig: Hinrichs, 1908), cited by Verhoef, *The Books of Haggai and Malachi*, 112. The demarcation and sequence of the sections accepted by most critical scholars are those of F. Horst: 1:1-14; 1:15a-2:15-19; 1:15b-2:9; 2:10-14; 2:20-23. See F. Horst, *Die zwölf kleinen Propheten Nahum bis Maleachi* (Tübingen: Verlag von J. C. B. Mohr, 1964), 204-9.
39. Otto Eissfeldt, *The Old Testament. An Introduction* (Oxford: Basil Blackwell, 1965), 427.
40. Thus A. S. van der Woude, *Haggai, Maleachi* (Nijkerk: Callenbach, 1982), cited by Verhoef, *The Books of Haggai and Malachi*, 93.
41. P. Benoit, J. T. Milik, and R. de Vaux, *Discoveries in the Judaean Desert*. II. *Les Grottes de Murabba'at*. Texte (Oxford: Clarendon 1960), 203-5.

sive data. The second oracle (2:1-9) could not have been delivered on both the twenty-fourth day of the sixth month and the twenty-first day of the seventh month. This, of course, is one reason that most scholars separate 1:15 into two parts to begin with, connecting v. 15*a* to 2:15-19 and allowing v. 15*b* to provide the year as part of the regular formula for 2:1.

Recently H. W. Wolff has dealt with the composition of Haggai by proposing three "growth rings" in the transmission of the accounts.[42] The center he calls the "prophetic proclamation" delivered on the prophet's five appearances (1:4-11; 2:15-19; 2:3-9; 2:14; 2:21*b*-23). These, he says, were probably collected by a circle of disciples and placed within "sketches of scenes." The second ring of material consists of such matters as the history of Haggai's effect on his listeners (1:12*b*-13), the history that preceded his addresses (2:11-13), and the opposition he elicited (1:2). The outer ring, created by the "Haggai chronicler," provides introductory information such as setting and chronology (1:1-3; 1:15*a*; 1:15*b*–2:2; 2:10; 2:20-21*a*). In addition, Wolff sees other accretions to the work of the chronicler: the interpolations of 2:5α, 17; the last two words of 2:18; the first four words of 2:19aβ; and LXX expansions at the end of 2:9, 14, 21, 22bα.[43]

Though justification for seeing different hands at work between the Haggai core and the contribution of the "chronicler" must await detailed treatment in the commentary, Wolff is no doubt correct in his general view of some redactionary process, but his efforts to isolate its stages and the specific contributions of each hand smack of the kind of special pleading inherent in source analysis of any kind. There is nothing in the style, form, vocabulary, and content of the book of Haggai that precludes it from having come entirely as it stands from the prophet himself.[44]

In his insistence on such a pattern of growth, Wolff is in line with much recent critical scholarship that posits two major ideological traditions in Haggai—that of the oracles and that of the editorial framework. The message of the former (i.e., of Haggai himself) is that the blessing of God depends on the building of the Temple. The message of the (later) framework is in line with the theocratic emphasis

---

42. Wolff, *Haggai*, 3-4.
43. As suggested above, the hypothesis of a "Chronistic Milieu" for Haggai and Zechariah 1-8, stressing strong affinities between the books of Chronicles and Ezra-Nehemiah and these two prophets, was developed especially by Beuken, (*Haggai-Sacharja 1-8*). For a brief review of his analysis see Coggins, *Haggai, Zechariah, Malachi*, 27-29.
44. Thus essentially Eissfeldt, *The Old Testament, An Introduction*, 428-29.

of P on the continuation of the covenant community in the present and future with little or no eschatological element. Such bifurcation of traditions (and of the composition of the book itself) has little or no objective basis but has been developed primarily as a reflex of an alleged division in postexilic Judaism between a visionary eschatological party and a practical hierocratic party, a view which itself has no clear-cut warrant in the biblical accounts.[45]

LITERARY STRUCTURE

Each of the four addresses (1:1-15; 2:1-9, 10-19, 20-23), the first of which is subdivided into two sections (1:1-11, 12-15), is introduced by a chronological datum except for 1:12-15, where the chronological note follows the pericope. The reason for this, as already proposed, was to avoid a break in what is essentially one message—Haggai's exhortation to rebuild (vv. 2-11) and the people's response (vv. 12-14).

In addition, there are the usual formulae of address and transition. Thus, 1:1*b* notes the reception of the word of Yahweh by Haggai the prophet, a word to be delivered to Zerubbabel the governor and Joshua the priest. Verse 12 reports the reaction of the officials and people, v. 13*a* introduces the second message, v. 13*b* is that message, and v. 14 is the response to the second message. Following the closing and opening statements about chronology (1:15; 2:1*a*) is the formula of reception of revelation (2:1*b*-2). The third message (2:3-9) follows and then the next chronological note (v. 10*a*) and reception of revelation (v. 10*b*). Finally, in reverse order, the word about revelation (v. 20*a*) and the last statement of chronology (v. 20*b*) introduce the fifth oracle (2:21-23).

The literary form of the prophetic messages is difficult to categorize. The standard patterns typical of preexilic prophets seem to have broken down,[46] resulting in a rather eclectic assemblage of cliches and characteristics. Baldwin,[47] however, observes an equal division between the "judgment speech" and the "announcement of salvation" and points out the repeated order of accusation (1:1-11; cf. 2:10-17), response (1:12-14; cf. 2:18, 19), and assurance of God's triumph (2:1-9; cf. 2:20-23).

---

45. For a survey of the matter see Rex Mason, "The Prophets of the Restoration," *Israel's Prophetic Tradition*, ed. R. Coggins, A. Phillips, M. Knibb (Cambridge: Cambridge Univ., 1982), 140-45. See also Introduction to Zechariah in this volume.
46. Petersen, *Haggai and Zechariah 1-8*, 36-37.
47. Baldwin, *Haggai, Zechariah, Malachi*, 31.

The following outline indicates the structure of Haggai to be followed in the commentary.

I. Rebuilding the Temple (1:1-15)
   A. Introduction and Setting (1:1)
   B. The Exhortation to Rebuild (1:2-11)
     1. The Indifference of the People (1:2-6)
     2. The Instruction of the People (1:7-11)
   C. The Response of God's People (1:12-15)
     1. Their Attitude (1:12)
     2. Their Confidence (1:13)
     3. Their Work (1:14-15)
II. The Glory to Come (2:1-9)
   A. A Reminder of the Past (2:1-3)
   B. The Presence of the Lord (2:4-5)
   C. Outlook for the Future (2:6-9)
III. The Promised Blessing (2:10-19)
   A. Present Ceremonial Defilement (2:10-14)
     1. Righteousness Is Not Contagious (2:10-12)
     2. Wickedness Is Contagious (2:13-14)
   B. Present Judgment and Discipline (2:15-19)
     1. The Rebuke of the People (2:15-17)
     2. The Prospects of the People (2:18-19)
IV. Zerubbabel the Chosen One (2:20-23)
   A. Divine Destruction (2:20-22)
   B. Divine Deliverance (2:23)

DISTINCTIVE TEACHING

At the heart of the book of Haggai is the prophet's urgent insistence that the postexilic Jewish community get to the work of rebuilding the Temple. As Childs points out, the first (1:1-15) and third (2:10-19) oracles relate the present poverty of the people to the disregard of God's Temple, whereas in the second (2:1-9) and fourth (2:20-23) the promise is reiterated that Israel's eschatological hope is still valid.[48] Though these two great themes may not be viewed in a cause-and-effect manner, Haggai nevertheless makes clear that present rebuilding is prerequisite to future glory.

Haggai's distinctiveness lies in his single-mindedness. No other prophecy is so fixed on a specific objective, nor is it likely that any other was so successful in its accomplishment (1:12, 14; cf. Ezra

48. Brevard S. Childs, *Introduction to the Old Testament As Scripture* (Philadelphia: Fortress, 1979), 469.

5:1-2). With his feet firmly planted in the world of the sixth century B.C., Haggai lifted up his eyes and those of his people to the eschaton as well—to the day when the Lord would fill His house with His glory and peace (Hag. 2:7-9). Faithfulness in the comparatively little details of today will yield incalculable dividends in the tomorrows to come.

Robert Chisholm draws attention to Haggai's emphasis on God's continuing love for His people, a love associated with His demand that they rebuild the Temple and otherwise demonstrate their faithfulness. The problems they have encountered are directly attributable to their failures in these respects, for by their neglect the community has borne witness to their covenant disobedience. But, as Chisholm shows, adherence to the prophetic injunction to covenant loyalty would issue in such blessings as the enriching of the eschatological Temple, its being filled with the glory of God, and the restoration of the Davidic dynasty.[49]

TRANSMISSION OF THE TEXT

Well-informed students of Scripture are aware that the original texts of the Bible have long since disappeared. In the case of the Hebrew manuscripts of the OT, what survive are copies of copies multiplied several times over. Complicating matters further are the varying readings attested in ancient versions such as the Greek Septuagint, the Aramaic Targums, Syriac, Old Latin, and many others. Although these frequently agree with the Hebrew Masoretic tradition, sometimes they do not, therefore presupposing a different, non-Masoretic line of transmission. All of these witnesses, Hebrew and non-Hebrew alike, must be consulted in an effort to recover the original text of the biblical composition.

The study of Haggai is largely unencumbered by the problem of textual variation since the ancient manuscripts and versions differ little from the Masoretic tradition. The Dead Sea Murabba'Jat scroll of the minor prophets of A.D. 150, for example, offers no improvement on the MT Haggai. In fact, the Mur differs from the MT in only two minor points: in 2:1 (*'el* for *bĕyad*) and in 2:3 (*'ittô* for *'ōtô*).[50]

The LXX and its generally dependent offspring such as the Pesh. and Vg, do offer some deviations from the MT, particularly by expansions of the MT (2:9, 14, 21, 22), arrangements of verses (LXX 1:9-10 = MT 1:9; LXX 2:1-2 = MT 1:15 + 2:1; LXX 2:15 (last clause) + 2:16

---

49. Robert B. Chisholm, Jr. "A Theology of the Minor Prophets," in *A Biblical Theology of the Old Testament*, ed. Roy B. Zuck (Chicago: Moody, 1991), 418-22.
50. Benoit et al., *Les Grottes de Murabba'at*, 184.

= MT 2:15), and differences of rendering (cf. 1:1, 14; 2:2, and other examples in the commentary). The principal versions generally support the MT and argue strongly, as Verhoef shows,[51] against the many alterations of the MT suggested by both BHK and BHS. That this is the case will be demonstrated point by point in the commentary.

51. Verhoef, *The Books of Haggai and Malachi*, 19-20.

1
Rebuilding the Temple (1:1-15)

A. Introduction and Setting (1:1)

This note of introduction provides the setting for the first oracle of the prophet (1:2-11 [+12-15]) and identifies him and the immediate recipients of his message. For the date of the oracle and the identification and historical role of Darius, see Introduction to Haggai under Historical Context.

Translation

¹In the second year of Darius the king, on the first day of the sixth month, the word of YHWH came *through the prophet Haggai to Zerubbabel the son of Shealtiel, governor of Judah, and to Joshua son of Jehozadak, the high priest, as follows:

Exegesis and Exposition

Haggai, whose name means something like "festive" or "festival," appears (apart from self-references in this treatise) only in Ezra 5:1 and 6:14. Most scholars claim that because Haggai's name appears in the book he could not be its author.[1] There are, however, no grounds for such a supposition, which, if held consistently, would deny all self-

---

1. So, e.g., Carol L. Meyers and Eric M. Meyers, *Haggai, Zechariah 1-8*, AB (Garden City, N.Y.: Doubleday, 1987), 5.

references to the biblical writers as coming from their own pens.[2] Since the oracle was transmitted on the first day of the month, a festival day (Num. 10:10; cf. 28:11), the prophet's name itself was revelatory of the occasion. Some scholars suggest that, because Haggai refers to the glory of the preexilic Temple of Solomon (Hag. 2:3), he must have been quite aged at the time he delivered his word to Zerubbabel and Joshua in 520 B.C.[3] His very question in 2:3 ("who among you saw this Temple in its former glory?") suggests if anything, however, that he was not among them, having perhaps been born in the Diaspora.

Zerubbabel son of Shealtiel (see Introduction to Haggai under Historical Context) bears a name clearly attesting to his Babylonian origins (Akkadian *zēr bābili*, "descendant of Babylon"). As grandson of the last legitimate king of Judah, Jehoiachin (1 Chron. 3:17-19), Zerubbabel, the chosen "signet" (Hag. 2:23), was qualified in every way to succeed as Davidic king even though under Persian dominion he had to settle for the office of governor. If in the biblical record Sheshbazzar is the same as Shenazzar (again see discussion in the Introduction; 1 Chron. 3:18), Zerubbabel was the second of a line of Jewish governors culminating in Nehemiah.

The term "governor" (Heb. פֶּחָה, *peḥâ*) is an Akkadian loan-word (*pāḥatu/pīḥatu*) suggesting an office perhaps not precisely what "governor" conveys but simply an overseer of a jurisdiction within the Persian imperial structure.[4] Regardless, his appointment to high position as a Davidide stands in ironic contrast to the humiliation of his grandfather Jehoiachin who, having been the "signet" upon Yahweh's right hand (Jer. 22:24), was removed and cast aside, none of his sons succeeding him on the throne.

Joshua the son of Jehozadak, here designated the high priest, is mentioned outside Haggai in Ezra 3:2, 8; 5:2; 10:18; Neh. 12:26; Zech. 6:11. The Jehozadak of 1 Chron. 6:14-15 is without doubt Joshua's father, a fact that establishes Joshua's Aaronic lineage through Zadok (1 Chron. 6:1-5). Thus, the Davidic royal descent as well as that of the Aaronic priests meet in the postexilic age as common recipients of God's word of hope and promise through Haggai and Zechariah. This dyarchic structure in postexilic Judaism, spelled out in Zechariah, has profound messianic and post-biblical ramifications.[5]

---

2. Cf. Otto Eissfeldt, *The Old Testament: An Introduction*, (Oxford: Basil Blackwell, 1965), 428.
3. So, e.g., Joyce G. Baldwin, *Haggai, Zechariah, Malachi* (London: Tyndale, 1972), 28.
4. F. C. Fensham, *The Book of Ezra and Nehemiah*, NICOT (Grand Rapids: Eerdmans, 1982), 125.
5. See Meyers and Meyers, *Haggai, Zechariah 1-8*, 17.

Additional Notes

1:1 The translation "through the prophet Haggai" reflects the Hebrew phrase בְּיַד־חַגַּי הַנָּבִיא, a formula that occurs also in 1:3; 2:1 (cf. Mal. 1:1) and means literally "by the hand of the prophet Haggai." Mason suggests, correctly it seems, that the use of this phrase three times in the framework of Haggai's brief work signifies either history viewed as linked cause and effect or a concern to draw a parallel between the establishment of the first Temple and that of the second.[6] The use of Haggai as any instrument certainly favors the view that it is YHWH Himself who is effecting the revelation and results.[7]

B. The Exhortation to Rebuild (1:2-11)

1. THE INDIFFERENCE OF THE PEOPLE (1:2-6)

Translation

²Thus says *YHWH of hosts, "These people have said, *'The time has not come, the time for rebuilding the house of YHWH.'" ³Therefore, the word of YHWH came through the prophet Haggai saying, ⁴"Is it the time for you yourselves to live in your *paneled houses while this house is in ruins?" ⁵Now here is what YHWH of hosts says: "Think carefully on your ways. ⁶You have sown much but have little harvest, eating with no satisfaction. You have drunk but are not satiated, clothed but without warmth. *He who earns wages does so (only to end up) with a purse with holes." (1:2-6)

Exegesis and Exposition

In his first oracle—to be classified, perhaps, as a dispute and judgment speech—the prophet chides the returned exiles and their fellow countrymen for putting their own interests ahead of the Lord and the Temple.[8] The result, he says, has been calamitous, for the more they sought self-satisfaction the less they achieved it.

To refer to the Jews as "these people" (v. 2) is to imply an alienation, certainly at least in their attitude toward the Lord and holy things (cf. 2:14).[9] Never once does the Lord call them "My people," the

---

6. Rex A. Mason, "The Purpose of the 'Editorial Framework' of the Book of Haggai," *VT* 27 (1977): 414-16.
7. Meyers and Meyers, *Haggai, Zechariah 1-8*, 7.
8. J. William Whedbee correctly sees 1:2-11 as a single text and identifies it rhetorically as a disputation in a question-answer schema. For his excellent analysis, see "A Question-Answer Schema in Haggai 1: The Form and Function of Haggai 1:9-11," in *Biblical and Near Eastern Studies*, ed., G. A. Tuttle (Grand Rapids: Eerdmans, 1978), 184-94.
9. H. G. May, "'This People' and 'This Nation' in Haggai," *VT* 18 (1968): 193. Cf. Isa. 6:9, 10; Hos. 1:9.

normal designation for the nation in covenant fellowship with Him. The displeasure of the Lord finds its immediate source in the fact that the restored community, now well established after eighteen years in the land (from 538 to 520 B.C.; cf. Introduction to Haggai), has postponed any work on the Temple except for the laying of its foundations sixteen years earlier (Ezra 3:8-13). It is true that the work had been impeded by opposition from without (4:1-5, 24), but the real cause for delay was an insistence that "the time has not come" (v. 2). F. G. Hamerton-Kelly, with other scholars, attributes the delay in building the Temple to the visionary school of Ezekiel, which saw the rebuilding as sinful because it was not done by God Himself, a view that suggests a distinct possibility.[10]

The speciousness of the people's excuse is apparent from the fact that, while the Temple work was halted, they had undertaken their own construction activities apace. Not only so, but the houses they built were, in some cases at least, luxurious in their appointments. With obvious irony, the prophet speaks of the rich paneling they have installed, using a term (סָפַן, *sāpan*, "to cover, panel") that otherwise describes the interior of the glorious Temple of Solomon (1 Kings 6:9) and his own magnificent palace buildings (2 Kings 7:3, 7; cf. Jer. 22:14).[11] However, Joyce Baldwin's point, that paneling may not mean luxury but only completion of construction, is certainly cogent, especially in view of the poverty to which the people have been reduced on the whole (cf. Hag. 1:6).[12] The real issue, nonetheless, is clear. Members of the postexilic community, far from articulating their faith in the Lord's gracious restoration and covenant renewal by erecting a place where He might once more dwell among them (cf. 2:4-9), were concerned only for their own well-being. The time for the Lord had not come because the time they needed for their own interests was uppermost in their minds.[13]

---

10. R. G. Hamerton-Kelly, "The Temple and the Origins of Jewish Apocalyptic," *VT* 20 (1970): 12. For further discussion of this conflict between the alleged "visionary" and "hierocratic" elements of Jewish postexilic life, see the Introduction to Zechariah under Historical Context.
11. "Paneling" or "paneled" (with David L. Petersen, *Haggai and Zechariah 1-8*, [London: SCM, 1985], 48) is preferable to "roof" (Otto Steck, "Zu Haggai 1:2-11", *ZAW* 83 [1971]: 362).
12. Baldwin, *Haggai, Zechariah, and Malachi*, 40; cf. Rex Mason, *The Books of Haggai, Zechariah, and Malachi*, CBC (Cambridge: Cambridge Univ., 1977), 16.
13. Thomas suggests that the time to which the people refer is the end of the seventy years predicted by Jeremiah (25:11). This may well be the case if the terminus ad quem is the destruction of the Temple in 586 B.C., for the "time" then would be 516, still four years away; D. Winton Thomas, "Haggai," in *IB*, ed. G. A. Buttrick et al. (New York: Abingdon, 1956), 6:1041.

It is precisely at this point that Haggai raises his first interrogation (v. 4) and issues his first challenge (v. 5). The prophet shifts his attention from Zerubbabel and Joshua to the people at large, a fact that explains the second introductory formula of v. 3.[14] Using their own word for "time" (עֵת, *ēt*), suggesting an appropriate or suitable moment (BDB, 773), Haggai turns around the argument of the people by asking whether indeed it was appropriate for them to build their own houses even though they have protested that it was not appropriate to build the house of Yahweh. How could they have so perverted their priorities that the dwelling place of the Lord of hosts (v. 2) could take second place to those of His servant people?

The challenge to them is expressed in the strongest terms: "Think carefully on your ways," the prophet commands (v. 5). Literally he says, "Set your heart upon your ways," an injunction calling for the utmost degree of reflection and attention. The same idiom occurs in v. 7 and without an object (such as "ways") in 2:15, 18. That it is a formula nearly unique to Haggai is clear from the very few attestations elsewhere (Job 1:8; Isa. 41:22). The demand for attention is called for in order that the people might understand the connection between their negligence of God's house and their total lack of success in everyday life (Hag.1:6). It is a classic case of cause and effect.

To make his point, Haggai gives four examples of the futility of selfish effort. The people have planted abundantly but for very little return. There may be metaphorical overtones to this statement, but that it should be taken quite literally as well is evident from the next observation by the prophet: They eat and drink but never to the full. Evidently the crops have failed badly and now at the end of August (1:1; cf. Introduction to Haggai under Historical Context), just when the fall harvest ought to be shortly underway, the prospects are gloomy indeed. Even their clothing is inadequate to keep them warm, perhaps because the animals whose hides and hairs were the principal source of raw material were themselves scarce or unproductive.[15] Finally, whatever profits did come their way were lost through the holes in their purses. It is entirely possible that these purses were actually pockets or other pouches in the garments, especially if coinage was in circulation by then in Judah, but more likely they were merely bags whose purpose was to carry not only precious metals but other commodities as well (cf. Gen. 42:35; Prov. 7:20).[16] The language

---

14. Cf. Pieter A. Verhoef, *The Books of Haggai and Malachi*, NICOT (Grand Rapids: Eerdmans, 1987), 53-54.
15. For this and other possible causes, see ibid., 61-62.
16. Raphael Loewe, "The Earliest Biblical Allusion to Coined Money?" *PEQ*, 1955, 147-50.

may be figurative; that is, the more income the people earned the more they lost through inflation and otherwise. A literal use, however, is quite in line with the poverty induced by crop failure and other natural disasters (cf. Hag. 1:10-11). The same inferior or worn-out clothing that failed to warm the body would easily become threadbare and develop holes through which their liquid assets could escape.

The indifference of the people toward holy things has thus been exposed, attested most eloquently by the dire effects of unproductive labor and an economy in shambles. Failure to address their highest priority—the building of an earthly dwelling place for their God—has reduced them to poverty. But Coggins is correct in pointing out that the cause and effect was not mechanistic. Rebuilding the Temple would not per se bring God's blessing. There must be genuine restoration of worship and service by the people.[17] These prophetic reminders should give them reason to pay the closest attention to what God is about to communicate.

Additional Notes

1:2 The epithet "Lord of hosts" (יְהוָה צְבָאוֹת) is a favorite of Haggai, occurring elsewhere in 1:5, 7, 9, 14; 2:4, 6, 7, 8, 9, 11, 23 (*bis*). Here it refers not so much to the armies of YHWH as to YHWH himself.[18] He is the Almighty, a description particularly important to the postexilic prophets (Zechariah, 53 times, and Malachi, 24 times) who must encourage tiny and defenseless Judah in the face of the enormous might of imperial Persia.

For the MT עֶת־בֹּא ("a time comes") with the verb in the infinitive, the LXX reads ἥκει ("has come") reflecting either an original בָּא ("has come") or, more likely, a translation of the infinitive into a finite rendering. That is unnecessary because the infinitive absolute can function as a finite verb (GKC, 113y). The LXX (with Vg) also takes עֵת ("time") as the adverb (ה)עַתָּה ("now"), thus rendering the whole phrase "it has not come, the time. . . ." Although this avoids repeating "time," the repetition itself is arresting with its staccato effect (cf. the same word in v. 4).

1:4 The grammatical structure בְּבָתֵּיכֶם סְפוּנִים ("your paneled houses"), is irregular because—as some LXX MSS., the Targums, and

---

17. R. Coggins, *Haggai, Zechariah, Malachi*, 34. Verhoef (*The Books of Haggai and Malachi*, 63) shows that the judgments here are those associated with covenant disobedience (cf. Lev. 26:26; Deut. 6:11; 28:38, 39).
18. Verhoef, *The Books of Haggai and Malachi*, 52; cf. Kenneth L. Barker, "YHWH Sabaoth: 'The Lord Almighty,'" in *The NIV: The Making of a Contemporary Translation*, ed. Kenneth L. Barker (Grand Rapids: Zondervan, 1986), 109-10.

the Vg suggest—one would expect בְּבָתִים, without the suffix, in apposition to the following passive participle. There is no need for emendation of the participle, because it can function adverbially after the suffixed noun (GKC, 118p; 131h, n. 1).

1:6 Both BHK and BHS, on the basis of a few MSS, suggest יִשְׂתַּכֵּר ("earns wages") for מִשְׂתַּכֵּר (lit. "one earning wages"). The result would be, "he who earns wages, earns wages . . ." as opposed to "he who earns wages is one who earns wages. . . ." The meaning is the same in either case, but the juxtaposition of the identical hithpael participles has a pleasing alliterative effect.

THE INSTRUCTION OF THE PEOPLE (1:7-11)

Translation

⁷Thus says YHWH of hosts, "Think carefully on your ways. ⁸Go up to the hill country and bring back timber to build the Temple; I will delight in it and *be glorified," says YHWH. ⁹"You looked for much but instead there was little, and when you brought it home I blew upon it. Why?" says YHWH of hosts. "Because of my house, which is in ruins since each of you runs to his own house. ¹⁰*Therefore, because of you the skies have withheld their dew and the earth its produce. ¹¹Moreover, I have called for a drought upon the field, the hill country, the grain, the new wine, the fresh oil, and everything that springs from the ground; also upon man and animal and everything they produce."

Exegesis and Exposition

The urgent exhortation of v. 5 is repeated exactly in v. 7, minus the introductory עַתָּה ('attâ, "now"). That particle suggests a cause-and-effect relationship—in light of the preceding indictment (vv. 2-6), the people need to reflect on their ways. Though 'attâ is lacking here in the formula, the sentiment is the same. The indifference of the people (Haggai's thrust in vv. 2-6) must lead to instruction so that the impasse might be resolved and the work of Temple building begun. There is, in fact, a great deal of repetition between the two sections of the oracle, particularly between vv. 4, 6 and 9-11.[19] Whereas in v. 6 the prophet pointed out that the people had sown much (הַרְבֵּה, harbê) but brought on little (מְעָט, mě 'āṭ), in v. 9 he says they looked for much (הַרְבֵּה, harbê) but instead there was little (מְעָט, mě 'āṭ). Furthermore, they suffered from a lack of food, drink, clothing, and resources (v. 6),

---

19. For two important form-critical studies that see vv. 2-8 and 9-11 as complementary or even parallel units, see Klaus Koch, "Haggais unreines Volk," *ZAW* 79 (1967): 58; Steck, "Zu Haggai 1:2-11," 368-72.

a condition attributed to the drought the Lord had brought upon the land (vv. 10-11), the effects of which are again listed in precisely the same order: food, drink, protection, and productivity.

The fundamental cause for this disastrous condition, hinted at in v. 4, is clearly articulated in v. 9: "Because of my house, which is in ruins" (חָרֵב, *ḥārēb*, in both places). It is the ruin (*ḥārēb*) of the Temple that has elicited the drought (חֹרֶב, *ḥōreb*, v. 11) with its punitive and devastating results. The command to rebuild (v. 8) is in strong antithesis to the malingerers of Judah, who insisted that the time for rebuilding the house of YHWH had not yet come (v. 2). By argument, by literary structure, and by repetitive and paronomastic vocabulary, the prophet sets the two parts of his exhortation side by side with brilliant effect.[20]

After the normal introductory formula, "Thus says YHWH of hosts" (v. 7*a*; cf. 1:2, 5; 2:6, 11), Haggai once more urges upon Zerubbabel, Joshua, and presumably the people as well (note the plural pronouns and community participation throughout) that they take to heart in the most serious way their failures in the past and the remedy for those failures about to be announced (v. 7). It is really very simple. They must go up to the hill country (a place of heavy forestation until relatively recent times)[21] and bring back timber with which to build the Temple. Lack of any reference to stone or other materials does not demand the hypothesis that the Temple was a wooden structure, for quite clearly there was abundant stone from the demolished Temple of Solomon lying all about. Meyers and Meyers propose that wood was indeed scarce and was probably used for scaffolding rather than as building material.[22] Ezra records the letter of Tattenai, governor of *eber nāri*, who complains to King Darius that the Jews, thanks to Haggai and Zechariah, were already rebuilding the Temple "with great stones and timber" (Ezra 5:8; cf. 6:4).

Compliance with the command to rebuild the house of YHWH would turn the Lord's displeasure (implied in the reversals of Hag. 1:6) into pleasure. The verb expressing this reaction, רָצָה (*rāṣâ*, "be pleased," v. 8), conveys the more refined idea of acceptance, of conformity to the mind and will of God (cf. Pss. 147:10; 149:4).[23] He would delight in it because it would be an accomplishment of His own will and purposes. What that purpose is may be disclosed in the epex-

---

20. Whedbee, "A Question-Answer Schema," 188.
21. Thomas, "Haggai," in *IB*, 6:1041; Baldwin, *Haggai, Zechariah, Malachi*, 41.
22. Meyers and Meyers, *Haggai, Zechariah 1-8*, 28.
23. W. A. M. Beuken, *Haggai–Sacharja 1-8* (Assen: Van Gorcum, 1967), 185-86.

egetical statement that follows: "and I will . . . be glorified." This Niphal form of כָּבֵד (kābēd) appears to bear a reflexive nuance; that is, it suggests the idea that YHWH, whose will is accomplished by the building of the Temple, thereby gets glory for Himself (BDB, 457; GKC 51c). The glory (כָּבוֹד, kābôd) of God is a circumlocution for His own Person and presence, a truth abundantly attested in the OT (Ex. 16:10; 24:16, 17; 33:18, 22; 40:34, 35; Lev. 9:6, 23; Num. 14:10; Ezek. 1:28; 3:12, 23; etc.) The destruction of the Temple had brought the departure of His glory (Ezek. 11:23), but its reconstruction would allow His glory once more to inhabit its sacred precincts (Hag. 2:7, 9; cf. Zech. 2:5, 10, 11).

As though to reinforce His point that the promised glory has been frustrated by Judah's indolence and self-centeredness, YHWH reiterates that the people had sought much for themselves but with meager results (Hag. 1:9). In fact, what little they did manage to bring home[24] He "blew upon." The verb נָפַח (nāpaḥ) is used elsewhere without the preposition בְּ (b) to speak of destruction and judgment (Ezek. 22:20, 21).[25] A similar idea (but with the verb נָשַׁב, nāšab) occurs in Isa. 40:7, where the prophet says that the grass and flower wither away because YHWH has blown upon them.

Anticipating their question as to why all these dreadful things have happened, YHWH attributes them to the unfinished state of the second Temple (Hag. 1:9d), a dereliction on the part of the community compounded by their running to their own houses while His is unsuitable for habitation (v. 9e). That this is not just a community concern, in which the individual bears no responsibility, is contradicted by the blunt language of the text: lit. "you are running, each of you, to his own house." Amsler is correct in suggesting that "running" figuratively describes the zeal of the people who rush to achieve their own glory before that of YHWH.[26] Whereas they should have been about the business of Temple building with all due speed, they moved with alacrity to take care of themselves first.

In a brief chiastic pattern of "judgment (v. 9a-b)–cause for judgment (v. 9c-e)–judgment (vv. 10-11)," the Lord amplifies the reasons and means for the setbacks the postexilic generation has experienced.

---

24. הֲבֵאתֶם הַבַּיִת ("when you brought it home") should be understood as bringing the produce to one's home rather than to the Temple, for, as Petersen (*Haggai and Zechariah 1-8*, 52) suggests, the Temple was not yet built. For the opinion that the Temple is in view, see Friedrich Peter, "Zu Haggai 1,9" *TZ* 7 (1951): 150-51.
25. Verhoef, *The Books of Haggai and Malachi*, 70-71.
26. Samuel Amsler, *Aggée, Zacharie 1-8, Zacharie 9-14*, CAT (Neuchatel: Delachaux & Niestlé, 1981), 26.

All nature has collaborated with Him in withholding its bounties (v. 10), resulting in the grievous drought that has decimated the land and induced the most severe deprivation and despair. W. J. Dumbrell points out the language of covenant curse in v. 11. Only covenant obedience can turn that around.[27] The instruction to rebuild, then, culminates with a most persuasive inducement to do so. As long as the task remains unfinished, the people can continue to expect poverty and lack of fulfillment.

Additional Notes

1:8 The defectively written cohortative אֶכָּבְדָ (cf. Qere) suggests the idea of purpose, such as "that I may be glorified." The missing ה may be explained, with Mitchell, as due to the following א.[28] The close connection between this verb and the preceding indicative אֶרְצֶה makes it most likely that this apparent cohortative is indeed to be construed as indicative, as suggested already by Rudolph: "Die Sinn ist hier vom Imperfekt nicht verschieden."[29] Meyers and Meyers take the ending as an old subjunctive, a reading that does not change the meaning in any case.[30]

1:10 The alleged dittography (double writing of עַל־כֵּן) proposed by both BHK and BHS and supported by the LXX is not orthographically a dittograph, nor does its presence detract from the sentence. In fact, it is much in line with the prophet's thought that it is precisely because of the people's sins that the ensuing calamities have occurred.

C. THE RESPONSE OF GOD'S PEOPLE (1:12-15)

Scholarship is divided as to whether 1:12-15 belongs to 1:2-11 as Haggaic material or should be construed as a separate unit. The argument turns primarily on the question of the editorial framework (see Introduction to Haggai under Literary Integrity for fuller discussion). Rothstein, followed by many other scholars, proposed that v. 15 should be divided, with v. 15*a* serving as a chronological introduction to 2:5-19, which in the present text is dislocated. This leaves v. 15*b* to complete the formula for 2:1-9, which otherwise lacks reference to a year. Once this is done, 1:12-14 is allowed to remain part of 1:2-11 because it no longer has a date formula at the end.

---

27. W. J. Dumbrell, "Kingship and Temple in the Post-Exilic Period," *RTR* 37 (1978): 38.

28. H. G. Mitchell, *A Commentary on Haggai and Zechariah*, ICC (Edinburgh: T. & T. Clark, 1912), 52.

29. "The sense here is not different from the imperfect." Wilhelm Rudolph, *Haggai-Sacharja 1-8–Sacharja 9-14–Maleachi*, KAT (Gütersloh: Verlaghaus Gerd Mohn, 1976), 29.

30. Meyers and Meyers, *Haggai, Zechariah 1-8*, 28.

It is true that all the other oracles of Haggai are preceded by information as to date (1:1; 2:1; 2:10; 2:20), so that such information at the end of a pericope would appear to be anomalous. And if Rothstein is correct that a new oracle begins at 2:15, one should expect it to have a date, perhaps that of 1:15*a*. This kind of argument, however, overlooks such literary considerations as inclusio or double duty, both of which appear to be involved here.[31] The first oracle (1:2-15) thus begins and ends with the date formula, thereby enveloping the passage. The reason is not hard to find. The first date marks the occasion of Haggai's exhortation and the last its successful outcome. Twenty-three days expired between word and deed, a period bracketed by the dating formulae.

Also to be considered in favor of the unity of 1:15 is the fact that it contains day–month–year in that order and that 2:1 has only month and day, thus lacking the normal pattern. If one observes that the year of 1:15 serves also as the year of 2:1, however, the matter of both the unity of 1:15 and its relationship to 2:1 is resolved. As to the matter of 2:15-19 being a separate pericope in need of an introductory date, the view lacks any convincing objective evidence, as comment on that passage will show.

The position taken here is that the first oracle consists of an address (1:2-11) and a response (1:12-14), bracketed by an introductory (1:1) and concluding (1:15) date formula. This allows the text to make eminent sense as it stands and precludes the need to look for a dislocated oracle on which to append a chronological datum that admittedly looks out of place but on closer examination is very much at home. H. G. Mitchell denies vv. 12-15 to Haggai precisely because they are an account of the reaction to the oracle of vv. 2-11.[32] This line of reasoning would deny to the prophets all narrative that refers to themselves in the writings attributed to them, a manifestly unsupportable contention. As Eissfeldt explains, however, "It is only that this prophet, in order to enhance the impression of the complete objectivity of his report, has chosen not the first person but the third person form."[33]

1. THEIR ATTITUDE (1:12)

Translation

12Then Zerubbabel son of Shealtiel, Joshua son of Jehozadak, the high priest, and all the remnant of the people obeyed YHWH their God *according to the words of Haggai the prophet, just as YHWH

31. Ibid., 36-37.
32. Mitchell, *A Commentary on Haggai and Zechariah*, 27, 40, 42.
33. Eissfeldt, *The Old Testament: An Introduction*, 428.

*their God had sent him; and the people became fearful before YHWH.

Exegesis and Exposition

The stern rebuke and urgent appeal of the prophet Haggai to the leaders and citizens of the remnant community had the desired effect, for they began at once to resume the work of Temple construction, a task that had been set aside for sixteen years. The motivation was more than that of fear, though that was a factor to be sure (v. 12). More important was the pledge of YHWH to be with them (v. 13) and the supernatural stirring of their spirits to carry out His mandate (v. 14). Within a month they organized themselves, made their plans, marshaled their labor force, and set about the work (v. 15).

Although Haggai is the only biblical author to refer to Zerubbabel as governor (1:1, 14; 2:2, 21), he fails to do so here and in 2:4, 23. Since he is called "servant" in 2:23, the extra title "governor" would not, of course, be appropriate anyway. The LXX and Vg supply פֶּחַת (*paḥat*, "governor of") in 1:12 and 2:4, though such insistence on uniformity is clearly too rigid. Moreover, the fact that Zerubbabel is not called governor by Ezra-Nehemiah, the Chronicler, or (especially) Zechariah does not call into question the accuracy of Haggai's description. He also is virtually the only author to describe Joshua always as high priest (see otherwise only Zech. 3:1, 8; 6:11), but clearly he held that office (cf. Neh. 12:10). The reason for Haggai's practice of referring to the titles of both Zerubbabel and Joshua lies in the fact that he was addressing them as leaders and through them the people.[34] Their leadership credentials must therefore be emphasized.

The people here are called שְׁאֵרִית הָעָם (*šĕ'ērît hā 'ām*), "the remnant of the people." The notion of a chosen few who would survive both apostasy and judgment to become the nucleus of a restored covenant nation is pervasive in the OT (especially Ezra 9:14; Isa. 10:20-22; 11:11, 16; 28:5; 37:4, 31, 32; 46:3; Jer. 23:3; 31:7; Mic. 2:12; 5:6, 7; 7:18; Zeph. 2:7, 9; 3:13; Zech. 8:6, 11, 12). Though it may not bear that technical sense here (or in Hag. 1:14; 2:2), it certainly anticipates it.[35] Stuhlmueller goes so far as to identify the remnant here with the exiles as opposed to the local people who had not gone into exile. He therefore accuses Haggai of siding with Ezekiel against Second Isaiah

---

34. Sara Japhet, "Sheshbazzar and Zerubbabel Against the Background of the Historical and Religious Tendencies of Ezra-Nehemiah," *ZAW* 94 (1982): 82, 84.
35. Mason, "The Purpose of the 'Editorial Framework,'" 417-18; Meyers and Meyers, *Haggai, Zechariah 1-8*, 34.

in promoting the construction of a Temple as fulfillment of the eschatological hope.[36] The evidence he adduces is scarcely persuasive.

Additional Notes

1:12 This rendering of the preposition עַל, which is difficult here (cf. the SP, Tg. Ps.-J. reading לְ ["to"]), takes the preposition in the sense of "in accordance with," a clearly attested meaning (BDB, 754; GKC, 119aa, n. 3).[37]

The LXX presupposes אֲלֵיהֶם ("to them") rather than אֱלֹהֵיהֶם ("their God"), but other LXX MSS, Syr, Tg. Ps.-J., and Vg read both ("their God to them"). This latter would smooth out the passage by providing an object to whom (or which) the prophet is sent. As to the former point—the emendation of "their God" to "to them," thus leaving the Tetragrammaton to stand by itself—this would be most irregular in Haggai (cf. in this same verse). In any case, the MT poses no difficulty as it stands.

2. THEIR CONFIDENCE (1:13)

Translation

[13]Then Haggai, *the messenger of YHWH bearing YHWH's message, spoke to the people: "'I am with you,' says YHWH."

Exegesis and Exposition

Though many scholars argue that v. 13 is an interpolation here[38] or is otherwise out of place, the assurance of God's presence among the people is a most appropriate response to the statement at the end of v. 12 that "the people became fearful before YHWH."[39] Overwhelmed by both the awesomeness of the task that lay before them and the sense that YHWH's judgment was tantamount to His absence from them in a covenantal sense, they needed to know that their confidence could lie in Him, the one who lived among them.[40] The same sentiment is expressed by the prophet in 2:4.

Additional Notes

1:13 Haggai's self-predication, מַלְאַךְ יְהוָה ("messenger of YHWH"), occurs only here in the book as opposed to his usual חַגַּי הַנָּבִיא ("Hag-

---

36. Carroll Stuhlmueller, *Haggai & Zechariah*, ITC (Grand Rapids: Eerdmans, 1988), 22-23.
37. Cf. Peter R. Ackroyd, "Studies in the Book of Haggai," *JJS* 2 (1951): 167.
38. So Mitchell, *A Commentary on Haggai and Zechariah*, 55.
39. Ackroyd, "Studies in the Book of Haggai," 168.
40. Beuken, *Haggai–Sacharja 1-8*, 37-42, notes the terminology of covenant renewal in v. 13.

gai the prophet"). It is this fact, more than any other, that suggests to many scholars that the verse is non-Haggaic. Besides the use here, however, the phrase occurs as a prophetic epithet in 2 Chron. 36:15, 16; Isa. 42:19; 44:26. To deny Haggai variation of terminology is highly arbitrary and subjective. Moreover, one should note the combination and wordplay (מַלְאַךְ, "messenger"; מַלְאֲכוּת, "message"), which in itself would explain the epithet.[41] For the consistent use of מַלְאָכָא in Tg. Ps.-J. for heavenly beings alone, see Kevin J. Cathcart and Robert P. Gordon, *The Targum of the Minor Prophets* (Edinburgh: T. & T. Clark, 1989), 178 n. 17.

3. THEIR WORK (1:14-15)

Translation

¹⁴So YHWH stirred up the spirit of Zerubbabel son of Shealtiel, governor of Judah, and the spirit of Joshua son of Jehozadak, the high priest, and the spirit of all the remnant of the people so that they came and worked on the house of YHWH of hosts, their God, ¹⁵on the twenty-fourth day of the month, in the sixth *(month), in the second year of Darius the king.

Exegesis and Exposition

YHWH's assurance that He was with His people finds expression in His supernatural movement among them. Governor, priest, and people alike experienced His gracious intervention and responded to the kindling of their dormant spirits by setting to the work. The occurrence of the verb עוּר (*ûr*) here in the hiphil stem places the initiative for the reawakening of the people in the will and purpose of YHWH himself.[42] To be with them is to empower them to work (cf. also 2 Chron. 36:22-23; Isa. 41:2, 25; 45:13 with reference to the motivation of Cyrus to serve YHWH).

The date here reveals that there was a twenty-three day interval between the time the message to rebuild was first proclaimed (Hag. 1:1) and the time of its execution. Various explanations for this delay are offered, the most likely being that the intervening three weeks were right in the midst of harvest time when every hand was needed to bring in the crops, especially in this year of unusual drought (1:11).[43]

41. Petersen, *Haggai and Zechariah 1-8*, 56.
42. Stuhlmueller, *Haggai & Zechariah*, 24.
43. Verhoef, *The Books of Haggai and Malachi*, 88.

Additional Notes

1:15 The word "month" (חֹדֶשׁ) is lacking here, but such an omission, particularly when the day of the month has just been cited, is not unusual (cf. 2:1, 10, 18). Those scholars who divide this verse, assigning v. 15a to the following (2:1-9 or 2:15-19), usually suggest that בַּשִּׁשִּׁי ("in the sixth") is a clumsy interpolation[44] and should be dropped, thereby rounding off the first message with a reference only to the day. If, however, v. 15 be retained as a unit, the reference to the month is necessary to balance that of 2:1, where the month clearly is indispensable to the formula.

---

44. D. Ernst Sellin, *Das Zwölfprophetenbuch*, KAT (Leipzig: Deichert, 1922), 405-6; and many scholars since.

2
The Glory to Come (2:1-9)

Virtually all students of Haggai agree that 2:1-9 (or 1:15b–2:9) constitutes a single and undivided oracle, though there is difference of opinion as to its placement in the book. Those who regard 1:15 as a unit belonging to the pericope 1:1-15 follow the traditional sequence, whereas those who view 1:15a as the dating formula for the misplaced separate oracle of 2:15-19 usually place 1:15a + 2:15-19 before 1:15b–2:9. The rationale for this is discussed in the introduction to chap. 3.

The oracle as a whole contains markedly eschatological language, especially in vv. 6-9. The prophet thus is burdened to show that the unpromising beginning of a second Temple will someday give way to one whose magnificence and glory far transcend those of Solomon's. YHWH is with His people, he says, and will, in line with His ancient covenant promises, re-enact the Exodus and restoration to such a degree that the Temple will become a place of pilgrimage for all nations and the depository of their tribute. The ferment and war of the nations in their own day will desist, and YHWH will bring in the day of peace.

A. A REMINDER OF THE PAST (2:1-3)

Translation

¹In the seventh (month), on the twenty-first day of the month, the word of YHWH came *through the prophet Haggai as follows: ²"Say

now to Zerubbabel son of Shealtiel, governor of Judah, to Joshua son of Jehozadak, the high priest, and to the remnant of the people, ³'Who among you who survive saw this Temple in its former glory? How do you see it now? Is it not like nothing to you?'"

Exegesis and Exposition

The introductory date formula, as suggested above, depends for completeness on the last phrase of 1:15 ("the second year of Darius the king"), which serves as an axis between day-month (1:15*b*) and month-day (2:1*a*). Significantly enough, this word of YHWH came on the twenty-first of Tishri (October 17), which was precisely the seventh day of the Feast of Tabernacles (cf. Num. 29:32-34). Exactly 440 years earlier (Tishri, 960 B.C.) Solomon had finished and dedicated his Temple (1 Kings 6:38; 8:2), to which the prophet is about to compare the one under present construction. Twenty-six days had passed since construction began, and already the differences were becoming painfully evident.

No one would be more aware of the contrast between the respective structures than those old enough to have remembered the Solomonic Temple so ruthlessly destroyed by the Babylonians 66 years earlier. To these Haggai addresses his question, which is not, therefore, altogether rhetorical: "Who among you . . . saw this Temple in its former glory?" That there probably were some survivors is plain from Ezra's account of the laying of the foundation 16 years earlier (Ezra 3:8-13). Having clearly recalled the Temple of old, many of the elderly burst into tears when they saw its humble replacement (3:12). Now the reaction of those same survivors who were still alive was evidently much the same, for Haggai concludes that they viewed the new building as inconsequential compared to the old.

Additional Notes

2:1 The MT preserves the same prophetic formula here as in 1:1 and 1:3 but the Murabbaʿat fragment of Haggai (*DJD*, 2, 184) reads אֶל ("to") for בְּיַד ("through"). The difference is not significant except that the following imperative (Hag. 2:2), which is addressed *to* Haggai, would seem to favor אֶל. Lack of versional difference from the MT, on the other hand, suggests that בְּיַד may have become a stereotyped synonym for אֶל.

B. THE PRESENCE OF THE LORD (2:4-5)

Translation

⁴"'Even so, be strong, Zerubbabel,' says YHWH, 'and be strong, Joshua son of Jehozadak, the high priest, and *all you people of the

land,' says YHWH, 'and work. For I am with you,' says YHWH of
hosts. ⁵ *'(In light of) the word which I covenanted with you when
you came from Egypt and my Spirit, who even now abides among
you, do not fear.'"

Exegesis and Exposition

Once more Haggai speaks a word of encouragement to the leaders
and the people, urging them to be strong. He is, of course, not referring to physical strength, for that cannot be commanded. What is in
view is an exhortation to boldness and confidence, the kind of charge
Moses made to Joshua (Deut. 31:6, 7, 23; Josh. 1:6, 7, 9, 18).[1] That can
be possible because YHWH will be with them just as He was with
Moses and Joshua.

The somewhat veiled allusion to Moses and Joshua (most appropriate in view of the name of the present high priest) becomes more
transparent in v. 5 with its reference to the Exodus, covenant, and
Tabernacle. The syntax of the text as it stands in the MT is difficult,
but the meaning is quite clear. Just as YHWH had been with His
people in the ancient days of redemption and election, so much so
that they triumphed gloriously over their foes, so He would be with
them now. For this reason they had every cause to be encouraged and
to "not fear." The same injunction אַל־תִּירָא (*'al tîrā*) infuses the language of Isaiah in his anticipation of the second exodus of the restoration from Babylon and the ultimate deliverance of the nation in the
eschaton (Isa. 40:9; 41:10, 13, 14; 43:1, 5; 44:2; 54:4). Haggai thus
harks back to the past but also, with Isaiah, anticipates future redemption and glory. That provides an entrée into the eschatological
message of vv. 6-9.

Additional Notes

2:4 The phrase "all you people" as opposed to his usual "all the
remnant of the people" (cf. 1:12, 14; 2:2) lends support to the observation already made that Haggai does not use "remnant" (שְׁאֵרִית) in its
technical sense of an elect community but rather to describe the
insignificant population that survived the Babylonian captivity (see
Exegesis and Exposition on 1:12). By NT times עַם הָאָרֶץ ("people of the
land") had come to refer to the peasantry, but in the OT it generally
speaks of the free citizens.[2]

2:5 The proposed translation views the truncated beginning of
the verse as an elliptical *casus pendens*, requiring something similar

---

1. Carroll Stuhlmueller, *Haggai & Zechariah*, ITC (Grand Rapids: Eerdmans,
   1988), 26.
2. Roland de Vaux, *Ancient Israel: Its Life and Institutions* (London: Darton,
   Longman & Todd, 1961), 70-72.

to the phrase in parentheses. This seems preferable to the excision of everything up to and including "Egypt" as proposed by the the LXX. BHS suggests emending אֶת־הַדָּבָר ("the word") to זֹאת הַבְּרִית ("this covenant"), but that does not improve the sense and has no textual support. Michael Fishbane understands this use of אֵת as "formulaic." He regards it as a substantive or explicative introduction to the regular nominative הַדָּבָר and offers the following interpretive translation of vv. 4-5: "For I am with you . . . namely/that is to say, [in accordance with] the promise which I made with you when you left Egypt." Thus, the אֵת is a scribal gloss, a conclusion for which Fishbane finds support in the omission of the particle in the LXX.[3] The *lectio difficilior*, though problematic, should nevertheless stand as is. For the accusative particle אֵת, as due to attraction to the following relative pronoun אֲשֶׁא, cf. GKC, 117l.[4] Meyers and Meyers propose that "the word" is the object of the verb עֲשׂוּ in v. 4, resulting in the translation, "do . . . the word." The "word" then becomes synonymous with the covenant that follows.[5]

C. OUTLOOK FOR THE FUTURE (2:6-9)

Translation

⁶"Thus says YHWH of hosts: *'It is but a little time until once more I shake the heavens, the earth, the sea, and the dry ground. ⁷I will also shake all the nations, and the *precious things of all the nations will come; then I will fill this house with glory,' says YHWH of hosts. ⁸The gold and silver belong to Me,' says YHWH of hosts. ⁹'The latter glory of this house will be greater than its former glory,' says YHWH of hosts, 'and in this place I will give peace,' says YHWH of hosts."

Exegesis and Exposition

In this first extended eschatological vision of the book, Haggai, in clearly apocalyptic terms,[6] describes the tremendous upheavals that will attend the epiphany of YHWH in the last days. When nature and the nations suffer convulsion, the peoples of the earth will come to

---

3. Michael Fishbane, *Biblical Interpretation in Ancient Israel* (Oxford: Clarendon, 1985), pp. 49-50.
4. For further discussion of this accusative, see Peter R. Ackroyd, "Some Interpretive Glosses in the Book of Haggai," *JJS* 7 (1956): 163.
5. Carol L. Meyers and Eric M. Meyers, *Haggai, Zechariah 1-8*, AB (Garden City, N.Y.: Doubleday, 1987), 51.
6. H. F. Van Rooy draws attention to at least eight examples of eschatological terms in this brief passage. See his "Eschatology and Audience: The Eschatology of Haggai," *Old Testament Essays* (NS) 1, no. 1 (1988), 59.

recognize the sovereignty of YHWH and render the homage due Him. That will take the form particularly of tribute brought to the new Temple of YHWH, which, in that day of His coming, will be filled with a glory far surpassing that of the Temple of Solomon. Climaxing it all will be the peace of YHWH centered in that glorious place.

Building on the allusions to Exodus, covenant, and divine presence in v. 5, this passage continues the typological parallels introduced there and found in other prophetic language as well, particularly in Isaiah. In fact, the whole panorama of Israel's history from the Exodus to the first Temple provides the backdrop against which the eschatological revelation of how YHWH will accomplish His redemptive work in the ages to come should be viewed.

Though the phrase עוֹד אַחַת מְעַט הִיא (*'ôd 'aḥat mĕ 'aṭ hî'*) in v. 6 is difficult (lit., "yet once, it is a little"), the objects of the shaking—heavens, earth, sea, and land—appear beyond doubt to draw attention to YHWH's violent intervention in the past and to suggest that He will do so once more, and in just a little while (cf. Heb. 12:27-28). One particularly thinks of the Exodus-Sinai complex of events. Psalm 68:8 (HB 68:9) describes it as follows:

The earth shook,
The heavens poured down rain,
Before God, the One of Sinai,
Before God, the God of Israel.

Referring to the crossing of the Red Sea, Ps. 77:16-18 (HB 77:17-19) declares:

The waters saw You, O God;
The waters saw You and were in pain;
The depths also trembled.
The clouds poured out water;
The skies sent out a sound;
Your arrows went abroad.
The voice of Your thunder was in the whirlwind,
The lightnings lightened the world;
The earth trembled and shook.

Though the verb רָעַשׁ (*rā'aš*), used by Haggai to describe the shaking (vv. 6, 7), does not occur in reference to the reaction of the nations to God's redemptive acts of the past, the narratives do make clear that they were shaken by what they heard and saw. The Song of Moses relates, "The peoples have heard, they tremble" (רָגַז, *rāgaz*, a synonym of *rā'aš*) (Ex. 15:14). As for the leaders of Edom and Moab, "trembling (רַעַד, *ra'ad*) has seized them," and "all the inhabitants of Canaan have melted" (מוּג, *mûg*; Ex. 15:15; cf. Deut. 2:25; Josh. 2:9).

These phenomena will accompany the new exodus and new covenant as well, as both Haggai (2:6-7) and other prophets attest. There will be a shaking of the natural structures (Jer. 4:24; Ezek. 38:20) and of men and nations (Isa. 64:2; Ezek. 38:20; Mic. 7:17). That is clearly eschatological language as Meyers and Meyers point out.[7] Verhoef suggests that the terminology here is that of holy war, particularly seen in the hiphil form of the verb.[8] These cataclysmic events will cause the peoples to bring their "precious things" to the holy city and Temple. Once this has come to pass, YHWH will fill the Temple with His glory.

One immediately recalls the occasion of the filling of the completed Mosaic Tabernacle with the glory of YHWH (Ex. 40:34-35), a filling that climaxed the construction of the edifice and its furnishing with precious objects of gold and silver (25:1-9). Much of this material, it seems, came to the Israelites from their Egyptian neighbors whom they despoiled on their way out of Egypt (3:21, 22; 11:2, 3; 12:35).[9] In this respect, at least, "precious things" from the nations contributed to the worship of YHWH.

More conclusive of the parallel being drawn here—especially since our passage specifically refers to it—is the means by which the Temple of Solomon was largely furnished, namely, the tribute of the nations.[10] David gained dominion over the surrounding states and from them extracted revenues, particularly in the form of gold and silver (2 Sam 8:7-8, 10-11). These he "dedicated to YHWH" (v. 11). Solomon later used them to beautify the Temple at Jerusalem (1 Kings 7:51; cf. 1 Chron. 29:3-5) preparatory to YHWH's taking up residence there and filling the place with His glory (1 Kings 7:51– 8:11). Thus the "precious things" of the nations came to the Temple, even if not entirely voluntarily, establishing a prototype for that time when they would do so in the even more glorious age to come.

That age in which "the latter glory of this house will be greater than its former glory" (Hag. 2:9) finds description in other prophets as well (see, e.g., Ezek. 44:4; Zech. 2:5; 14:9-15) but nowhere more· extensively parallel to Hag. 2:6-9 than in Isa. 60:4-14. The prophet there describes the coming of the riches of the nations to Zion (v. 5; cf. 61:6; Mic. 4:13),[11] riches that include gold and are accompanied by praise to YHWH (v. 6). In that day the kings of the nations will serve

---

7. Meyers and Meyers, *Haggai, Zechariah 1-8*, 52-53.
8. Pieter A. Verhoef, *The Books of Haggai and Malachi*, NICOT (Grand Rapids: Eerdmans, 1987), 102-3.
9. Herbert Wolf, "'The Desire of All Nations' in Haggai 2:7: Messianic or Not?" *JETS* 19 (1976): 97-98.
10. Stuhlmueller, *Haggai & Zechariah*, 30.
11. Wolf, "'The Desire of All Nations' in Haggai 2:7," 98. Wolf draws attention to the occurrence of הָפַךְ ("turn") in Isa. 60:5, the very verb that occurs in Hag. 2:22 to speak of the overthrow of the nations.

YHWH (v. 10), and they and their wealth will be brought captive to Him (v. 11). One result of all this is the beautification of the house of YHWH (v. 7), the place He will glorify with the gifts of the nations (v. 13). Wolf suggests that both "treasure" and "glory" have a twofold meaning—material splendor and personal appearance, the latter here referring to the coming Messiah.[12] Elliger combines treasures with glory by proposing that it was the submission of the nations that would glorify God.[13] This alone cannot explain the glory of the Temple, however. Verhoef denies that the glory of God is in view at all here, seeing a reference only to the glory of material things.[14] This is inconsistent with v. 9, however, where even Verhoef interprets the glory as the presence of YHWH.

The real glory of the eschatological Temple will not consist of material things, not even silver and gold. This may, in fact, be the primary thrust of v. 8, which otherwise appears somewhat disjointed. Rather than suggesting that the new Temple will be full of silver and gold, since it all belongs to YHWH anyway, the point may well be that because all such things are His and are therefore not of value to Him, His own glory is what is central.[15] This view gains strength in light of the fact that the Zerubbabel Temple, a meagerly and sparsely furnished house of worship to be sure, is nonetheless what is first in view in the eschatological promise. YHWH, after all, said, "I will delight in it and be glorified" (Hag. 1:8). Haggai affirms that its glory will consist not of silver and gold but of His presence (2:4-5), and the glory of that to come will also be His presence in it and among His people (2:7). The essence of that divine habitation and its universal expression will be peace or wholeness (v. 9; cf. Isa. 9:7; 66:12).[16]

Additional Notes

2:6 Many scholars conclude that this difficult phrase is corrupt. They read with the LXX ἔτι ἅπαξ ("yet/still once"), presupposing only עוֹד אַחַת as original.[17] That, however, omits half the statement the

---

12. Ibid., 101.
13. Karl Elliger, *Das Buch der zwolf kleinen Profeten*, (Gottingen: Vandenhoeck & Ruprecht, 1982), 2:92-93.
14. Verhoef, *The Books of Haggai and Malachi*, 104.
15. R. T. Siebeneck sees this promise as being messianic but, rightly, only in the sense of the messianic kingdom and not the Messiah Himself; see "The Messianism of Aggeus and Proto-Zacharias," *CBQ* 19 (1957): 315-16. Stuhlmueller (*Haggai & Zechariah*, 28) flatly states that "this text will receive its fulfillment when the Messiah enters the temple."
16. "Peace in this place" (Jerusalem) would yield an implied play on words in Hebrew (*šālôm* in *Yěrūsālāyim*), that is, "peace in the city of peace."
17. H. G. Mitchell, *A Commentary on Haggai and Zechariah*, ICC (Edinburgh: T. & T. Clark, 1912), 65.

prophet is trying to make. Haggai is concerned to point out not only that there will be another shaking of all things but that it is imminent. Meyers and Meyers propose that the feminine pronoun הִיא at the end of the phrase is a copula going with אַחַת, which in turn intrudes into the familiar idiom עֹד מְעַט. This, they conclude, was for the purpose of stressing the imminence of the event.[18]

2:7 The Hebrew vocable here (חֶמְדָּה>חֶמְדַּת) is singular and in the absolute means "desire" (BDB, 326). The predicate is plural, however, so the plain intent of the author is to render "the desired (things) of all nations." For the singular as representing collectives, cf. GKC, 145b, though the grammar suggests reading here חֲמֻדֹת with the LXX. This may, in fact, be a preferable option because חֲמוּדָה means "precious things."[19]

---

18. Meyers and Meyers,*Haggai, Zechariah 1-8*, 52.
19. Thus Wolf, "'The Desire of All Nations' in Haggai 2:7," 98; Meyers and Meyers, *Haggai, Zechariah 1-8*, 53.

3
The Promised Blessing (2:10-19)

Many scholars follow J. W. Rothstein in dividing the third oracle (2:10-19) into two sections—2:10-14 and 2:15-19 (see introduction to 1:12-15 in chap. 1).[1] They do this because of the assumption that "this people" of v. 14 refers not to Judah but to Judah's enemies in the land and because of the need to find a pericope to which 1:15*a* can serve as an introductory dating formula. Since 2:10-14 has such a formula, these scholars argue that 2:15-19 is independent of 2:10-14 and should follow 1:15*a*.[2] The order of the material is, therefore, 1:1-14; 1:15*a* + 2:15-19; 1:15*b*–2:9; 2:10-14; 2:20-23. The unity of 1:15 has already been addressed (see introduction to 1:12-15); no need exists for it to be divided once its connection to 2:1 is properly understood.

As to the problem of "this people" of v. 14, Rothstein's suggestion that it refers to the Samaritans and their allies is wholly without foundation.[3] He proposes that 2:10-14 is referring to the opposition to

---

1. So, e.g., Wilhelm Rudolph, *Haggai-Sacharja 1-8–Sacharja 9-14–Maleachi,* *KAT* (Gutersloher: Verlaghaus Gerd Mohn, 1976), 49-51.
2. For these arguments and a strong rebuttal, see Herbert G. May, "'This People' and 'This Nation' in Haggai," *VT* 18 (1968): 190-91.
3. For detailed arguments that "this people" refers to the Jews themselves, see Klaus Koch, "Haggais unreines Volk," *ZAW* 79 (1967): 52-66; David L. Petersen, *Haggai and Zechariah 1-8,* (London: SCM, 1985), 81-82; R. J. Coggins, *Samaritans and Jews* (Oxford: Basil Blackwell, 1975), 46-52.

Temple building encountered by the Jews as recorded in Ezra 3:8–
4:5, a passage whose setting he dates to 520 B.C. rather than to 536 as
Ezra 3:8 demands. Tying Hag. 2:15-19 to 1:15a, he dates that section
to the sixth month of the second year despite the fact that the dating
formula of 2:10-14 explicitly records the ninth month of the second
year. As for the troublesome "ninth month" of 2:18, it is treated either
as a gloss or emended to "sixth" in line with 1:15a.

Close scrutiny of these arguments reveals that they have no real
substance, nor is there any need to rearrange the text in such a high-
handed manner. The following brief points should be considered:

(1) The alleged introduction to 2:15-19, 1:15a, is, as has been
argued repeatedly, a necessary part of 1:15b and 2:1.

(2) "This people" is a perfectly appropriate description of the
Jews, especially since the term עָם (ʿām) has already been used by
Haggai to describe them (1:2).[4] The use of גּוֹי (gôy), though frequently
descriptive of foreigners, is also suitable here because it forms part of
a poetic couplet and serves as a synonym to ʿām. Dumbrell argues
that "this people" refers to the Jews who had never gone into exile,
and it is from these that the remnant of the return are to keep their
distance.[5] There is no evidence, however, that Haggai ever made such
a distinction within the community. Stuhlmueller goes still further
and suggests that the ʿam hā ʾāreṣ ("people of the land"; cf. 2:4) are
identical to "this people" of 2:14, both terms describing the despised
indigenous Jews who became Samaritans.[6] Again, there is no evidence for such a connection.

(3) The section 2:10-19 reveals a literary unity similar to 1:2-11
and 2:3-9. All three units have a present situation (1:2-4; 2:3; 2:10-14),
an exhortation introduced by עַתָּה (ʿattâ; 1:5; 2:4; 2:15), and a promise
for the future (1:8; 2:5-9; 2:19b). Form-critically, a strong case can be
made for a clear parallel between these sections, one that is hopelessly broken if 2:15-19 is displaced.

(4) There is no support for emending "ninth" (2:18) to "sixth" or
for excising it altogether except as an exercise in *petitio princeps*.
Moreover, there is no textual or versional evidence whatsoever in
favor of Rothstein's dislocation hypothesis as a whole. Murabbaʿat
and all other ancient witnesses agree with the MT throughout as far
as the overall structure of the book is concerned.

---

4. May, "'This People' and 'This Nation' in Haggai," 193.
5. W. J. Dumbrell, "Kingship and Temple in the Post-Exilic Period," *RTR* 37
   (1978), 39.
6. Carroll Stuhlmueller, *Haggai & Zechariah*, ITC (Grand Rapids: Eerdmans,
   1988), 36.

A. PRESENT CEREMONIAL DEFILEMENT (2:10-14)

1. RIGHTEOUSNESS IS NOT CONTAGIOUS (2:10-12)

Translation

[10]On the twenty-fourth day of the ninth month, in the second year of Darius, the word of YHWH came to Haggai the prophet saying, [11]"Thus says YHWH of hosts, 'Ask now the priests concerning the law whether, if [12]one carries holy flesh in the corner of his garment and his (garment) corner touches bread, a boiled dish, wine, oil, or any other food, the thing will become holy.'" The priests answered, "No."

Exegesis and Exposition

The third oracle, constituting 2:10-19, is dated on the twenty-fourth of Kislev (or December 18, 520 B.C.), about three months after the work on the Temple had begun again in earnest (1:15) and two months after its pitifully modest prospect was beginning to become apparent (2:1, 3). A promise of great eschatological blessing has been given (2:6-9), but there is need now for hope for the present hour, for this time forward (v. 19*d*). Such hope has not been realized up to this point, however, because the restoration community has not met the prerequisites for blessing.[7] They have deluded themselves into thinking that holiness is gained merely by association with holy things (vv. 11-12) and have failed to consider that unholy associations render one unclean (vv. 13-14). The bitter experiences of drought and shortage (vv. 16-17; cf. 1:6, 10, 11) should have alerted the people to their sinfulness, but they had not, at least until recent days (v. 17*c*). Now, however, things will be different, for a spirit of confession and renewal has brought the people to the place of divine favor (v. 19*d*).

The specific occasion for the oracle is unclear, but it could well have been delivered as a warning against cooperation with the Samaritans and others in the work of the Temple building and participation in the cultus. A hint of this may appear in the account of Ezra (6:6-15), who notes that after the rebuilding had commenced (cf. 5:1-2) it met with severe opposition from Tattenai the satrap and his friends (5:13-17). When the matter came to Darius's attention, he directed Tattenai not only to desist (6:7), but to provide building materials and even sacrificial animals to the Jews for their disposal (6:8-10). Though this gesture of the king was made in good faith and

---

7. I. H. Eybers, "The Rebuilding of the Temple According to Haggai and Zechariah," *OTWSA* 13-14 (1970-71): 23; Pieter A. Verhoef, *The Books of Haggai and Malachi*, NICOT (Grand Rapids: Eerdmans, 1987), 115.

no doubt was so received by the Jews, its use by them would unquestionably be contrary to Mosaic law.

This suggestion clarifies the hypothetical set of questions posed by YHWH to the priests. Eric Meyers makes a convincing case for seeing in Haggai's appeal to the priests for a *tôrâ* on the matter at hand a request for a priestly ruling (cf. Mal. 2:7). This would thus be the predecessor of the later rabbinic *pĕsaq dîn*.[8] Can one, merely by laying holy hands on unholy things, make them holy (Hag. 2:12)? The answer obviously is negative. The ruling here is based on Leviticus 6:20 (EB 6:27), which teaches that a person can become consecrated by touching consecrated meat. However, there is no teaching there or elsewhere to the effect that anything that touches something else that has become secondarily consecrated is consecrated thereby. Thus, unless the foods mentioned here contacted the meat directly, they would remain profane.[9] Even so, the gifts of pagan kings, no matter the spirit in which they are given, cannot become clean and acceptable to YHWH just because they come in contact with the sacred sites and rituals of the covenant people. Such gifts should, therefore, be politely refused. To fail to do so is to render the people themselves unclean (v. 14).

2. WICKEDNESS IS CONTAGIOUS (2:13-14)

Translation

13Then Haggai said, "If one who is *unclean because of death touches one of these things, will it become unclean?" And the priests answered, "It will be unclean." 14Then Haggai responded, "'Thus is this people, this nation, before Me,' says YHWH. 'And thus is every work of their hands; everything they offer there is unclean.'"

Exegesis and Exposition

The second hypothetical case pertains to the converse of the first. Granted, unclean things cannot be rendered clean by virtue of their association with the clean. However, will things that are already clean become contaminated by the unclean? The answer is an unqualified yes. The case specifically in mind is the corruption brought about by contact with a corpse, a state of affairs addressed in Lev. 7:19; 22:4-6 and Num. 19:11-13, 22. Whether one should attempt to

8. Eric M. Meyers, "The Use of *tôrâ* in Haggai 2:11 and the Role of the Prophet in the Restoration Community," in *The Word of the Lord Shall Go Forth*, ed. Carol L. Meyers and M. O'Connor (Winona Lake, Ind.: Eisenbrauns, 1983), 71. See also Petersen, *Haggai and Zechariah 1-8*, 73-76.
9. See Michael Fishbane, *Biblical Interpretation in Ancient Israel* (Oxford: Clarendon, 1985), 297.

link this dead body to someone or something in the immediate context of the passage is questionable and certainly unnecessary. The point is crystal clear that God's people can pollute and have polluted themselves because of ungodly associations.

All doubt of this is dispelled by YHWH's indictment that the people are טָמֵא (*ṭāmē'*, "ritually unclean"), as are their deeds and even their sacrifices (Hag. 2:14). The three are linked together, of course, for a sinful man cannot do good works or offer acceptable sacrifices, nor can a righteous man commit evil works and offer improper tribute to YHWH and remain in holiness before Him.

Again, it is impossible to know precisely what called forth these words of denunciation. The context of the book itself would favor the view that it is the people's self-centeredness and inverted priorities that are in mind (1:2-4, 9), but the language of cult and worship might favor the idea already expressed, that the community had been too tolerant and accepting of the assistance granted to them by their pagan neighbors, assistance that involved even the presentation of sacrificial animals.

Additional Notes

2:13 The translation "unclean because of death" is an expansion of טְמֵי־נֶפֶשׁ ("unclean of a person"). This rather euphemistic phrase is an abbreviation of טָמֵא (נֶפֶשׁ מֵת) ("[unclean] because of a dead person"; cf. Lev. 21:11; Num. 6:6). The translation proposed here seeks to focus on the uncleanness and not on the particular object by which it is incurred. Fishbane suggests that the prophet asks the rhetorical question in order to establish an analogy between the hypothetical ritual case and the actual situation of the Jews. Moreover, Fishbane says, "For reasons not stated, the people, like those touching a corpse, are impure in the first degree; so that whatever they do or sacrifice is thereby defiled."[10]

B. PRESENT JUDGMENT AND DISCIPLINE (2:15-19)

1. THE REBUKE OF THE PEOPLE (2:15-17)

Translation

¹⁵"'Now therefore consider carefully from today and *backward, before stone was laid on stone in the Temple of YHWH. ¹⁶*From that time on, when one came to a heap of twenty (measures), there were only ten; when he came *to the wine vat to draw out fifty from it,

---

10. Ibid., 297-98.

there were only twenty. ¹⁷I struck with blight, mildew, and hail all the work of your hands, but *you brought nothing to Me,' says YHWH."

Exegesis and Exposition

The moral and spiritual defilement of the community described in the previous passage (vv. 10-14) called for divine retribution and discipline. From the very beginning of their postexilic life, before the foundations of the Temple itself were laid some 16 years earlier, the people had suffered YHWH's wrath because of their egoistic self-serving (vv. 16-17; cf. 1:6, 9-11). This chastening marked their whole life until Haggai, called by God, urged them to forsake their short-sighted materialism and resume the work of building a house for YHWH.

The language of failed expectation here is very much like that of Haggai 1. They had sown much and reaped little (1:6) and had looked for much but found little (1:9). All this was because YHWH visited them with drought (1:11), a generic term fleshed out in the blight, mildew, and hail of the present passage (2:17). Until Haggai came with his convicting word of repentance, there was no change of heart toward YHWH (v. 17*b*).

Haggai introduces his rebuke with the same sharp adverbial conjunction עַתָּה, *'attâ*) as he did his adjuration of 1:5 and his word of encouragement in 2:4. It marks a turning point in this third oracle, one that shifts the scene from the present to the past. The prophet asks his hearers to review the span of time from the present moment to the time preceding the laying of the first foundation stones. Though some interpreters maintain that the reference is only back to the resumption of construction three months earlier (2:10; cf. 1:15), the phrase מִן־הַיּוֹם הַזֶּה וָמָעְלָה (*min-hayyôm hazzê wāma'ĕlâ*, "from this day and beyond"), followed by the parallel and intensifying אֶל־אֶבֶן מִטֶּרֶם שׂוֹם־אֶבֶן (*miṭṭerem śûm-'eben 'el-'eben*, "before stone was placed on stone"), gives the impression of the passing of much more than three months.[11] Moreover, the shortages that came about because of the Jews' dereliction antedated the first oracle of Haggai and also therefore the resumption of the building.

These shortages reduced the harvests and food-stores by 50 percent or more (v. 16). The labor of plowing, sowing, cultivating, and harvest, "all the work at your hands" (כָּל־מַעֲשֵׂה יְדֵיכֶם, *kol-ma'ăśê yĕdêkem*; cf. the similar phrase in 1:11, כָּל־יְגִיעַ כַּפָּיִם, *kol-yĕgîa' kappāyîm*), was to no avail because of YHWH's intervention in the form of natural forces of destruction. But neither were YHWH's strokes of

11. For defense of the earlier (536) date, see (if equivocally) Peter R. Ackroyd, "Studies in the Book of Haggai," *JJS* 3 (1952): 2 n. 1.

discipline effective, for the people through all those years refused to reciprocate and return anything to Him. This understanding of the difficult phrase וְאֵין־אֶתְכֶם אֵלָי (lit. "and there was not you to Me") is preferable in the context where the issue is the people's stinginess in withholding their produce from YHWH (2:16-19; cf. 1:9-11). Though many scholars draw attention to Amos 4:9, where a similar formula occurs, the resemblance is only superficial, particularly since there is no verb in our Haggai passage.[12] Meyers and Meyers draw attention to the chiastic structure of Hag. 2:17, in which the omission of the verb in the fourth colon is a deliberate device to emphasize the pronouns אֶתְכֶם and אֵלָי, which complement the pronouns אֶחְכֶם and (יְדֵי)כֶם in the previous line. More important is their linkage of 2:17 with 1:13: lit. "'I am with you!'—Oracle of Yahweh," as compared to "'nothing [brought] you to Me'—Oracle of Yahweh."[13] On balance it seems best to view the prophet's condemnation as one having to do not with returning to YHWH but refusing to offer appropriate gifts to Him.

Additional Notes

2:15 מָעְלָה: the translation "backward," depends on the overall sense of the passage to establish the meaning, because by itself it means "upward" (BDB, 751). Verhoef suggests ultimately that vv. 16-17 must be considered parenthetical to vv. 15, 18-19, the whole passage taking the form of an inclusio in which the opening and closing occurrences of the formula "from this day and forward" serve as brackets. He sees a pattern, then, of looking forward (15a), looking backward (15b-17), looking forward (18). This has the advantage of taking מָעְלָה in its usual sense, but, as Verhoef concedes, it plays havoc with מִטֶּרֶם (15b), which means lit. "from before." In other words, 15a and 15b cannot be divided; therefore, מָעְלָה, parallel to מִטֶּרֶם, must also refer to the past. Verhoef's explanation—that this is an antithetical parallelism—is forced.[14] The vantage point here is clearly from the present to the past.

2:16 The problematic מִהְיוֹתָם (a qal infinitive construct with 3 m. p. suffix and prefixed preposition, lit. "from their being") is idiomatic for something like "from the time they were then." The LXX reads τίνες ἦτε ("how was it with you?"), based on a Heb. מַה־הֱיִיתֶם. The sheer difficulty of the MT is presumptive evidence in its favor.

The phrase אֶל־הַיֶּקֶב לַחְשֹׂף חֲמִשִּׁים פּוּרָה literally reads "to the wine vat to draw out fifty (from) the winepress." Evidently the wine-

---

12. Hans W. Wolff, *Haggai* (Minneapolis: Augsburg, 1988), 65.
13. Carol L. Meyers and Eric M. Meyers, *Haggai, Zechariah 1-8* (Garden City, N.Y.: Doubleday, 1987), 61-62.
14. Verhoef, *The Books of Haggai and Malachi*, 120-24.

making apparatus consisted of both the press (פּוּרָה) and vat (יֶקֶב), פּוּרָה, here an adverbial accusative, specifies only the part of the apparatus from which the wine was being taken.[15] This is expressed in more general terms in the chosen translation "from it."

2:17 For the MT וְאֵין־אֶתְכֶם ("and there was not with you" [for Me]), the LXX (cf. Pesh.) reads, καὶ οὐκ 'επεστρέψατε ("and you would not turn" [to Me]). Whereas this clarifies an otherwise obscure phrase, the suggested "you brought nothing to Me" seems to express the sentiment well.

2. THE PROSPECTS OF THE PEOPLE (2:18-19)

Translation

¹⁸"'Consider carefully from today and backward, from the twenty-fourth day of the ninth month, *from the day the Temple of YHWH was founded—think about it. ¹⁹Is the seed yet in the storehouse? Indeed, even the vine, fig tree, pomegranate, and olive tree have not produced. Yet from today on I will bless you.'"

Exegesis and Exposition

Throughout most of this section the prophet continues to assess the spiritual profligacy of the nation. This time, however, he does not begin with the initial groundbreaking for the Temple in 536 B.C. (v. 15), but with the renewal of construction exactly three months earlier (v. 18; cf. 1:15). Again, the conclusion is that YHWH has disciplined His wayward people by withholding the blessing of abundant harvest.[16]

Because it seems unlikely that judgment would continue after the people had obeyed the call of the prophet to repentance and renewal (cf. 1:14), many scholars prefer to emend "ninth (month)" of v. 18 to "sixth (month)." This allows the reference to the laying of the foundation to pertain to the original work of many years earlier in agreement with vv. 15 and following. Once 2:15-19 is separated from 2:10-14 and 1:15*a* becomes the dating formula for 2:15-19 (see Introduction to Haggai under Literary Context), the transition from 1:14 to 1:15*a* + 2:15-19 seems most apparent.

All this makes excellent sense if one can be allowed to emend "ninth" to "sixth" or to view it as an interpolation. There is, however, no warrant for that in any MS or version, all of which uniformly read

---

15. Oded Borowski, *Agriculture in Iron Age Israel* (Winona Lake, Ind.: Eisenbrauns, 1987), 111-12.
16. Robert P. Carroll, "Eschatological Delay in the Prophetic Tradition?" *ZAW* 94 (1982): 56. Carroll suggests that here and elsewhere in Haggai the promise is inviolable, but its fulfillment is dependent on the obedience of the people.

"ninth." It seems best to understand the phrase "stone upon stone" of
v. 15 as an allusion to the preparatory work described in Ezra 3:8-13
and "founded" (יָסַד, *yāsad*) as referring to the resumption of work
recounted in 5:1-5. This is admittedly somewhat arbitrary inasmuch
as *yāsad* is the very word used by Ezra in his record of the earliest
work on the Temple (3:6, 11). But one must remember that there are
no separate Hebrew verbs to distinguish between build and rebuild
or even found and refound.[17]

The phrase *min hayyôm hazzê wāmā'elâ* in Hag. 2:18 is an exact
replication of the wording in v. 15, and here as well as there must
point to the past: "from today and backward."[18] This may appear to
suggest that the twenty-fourth day of the ninth month is identical to
the day the foundation of the Temple was laid (or relaid), but this
cannot be the case because that occurred on the twenty-fourth day of
the sixth month (1:14-15). Petersen proposes that this day was the day
of the ritual rededication of the Temple, a rededication involving "the
ritual manipulation of a foundation deposit." If this is correct, it
would explain nicely the problematic laying of the foundation in the
ninth month.[19] The better resolution of the difficulty lies in a close
reading of Haggai's prose in v. 18. The passage seen in this light not
only is clarified in meaning, but many of the alleged textual difficulties likewise disappear. The following pattern—a somewhat loose
chiasm—is suggested:

A שִׂימוּ־נָא לְבַבְכֶם (*śîmû-nā' lĕbabĕkem*)

  B מִן־הַיּוֹם הַזֶּה וָמָעְלָה (*min hayyôm hazze wāmā'ĕlâ*)

    C מִיּוֹם עֶשְׂרִים (*miyyôm 'eśrîm . . .*)

  B' לְמִן־הַיּוֹם אֲשֶׁר־יֻסַּד הֵיכַל יְהוָה (*lĕmin-hayyôm 'ăšer-yussad hêkal YHWH*)

A' שִׂימוּ לְבַבְכֶם (*śîmû lĕbabĕkem*)

Lines A and A' envelope the passage with an appeal to give attention, whereas line C, the dating formula ("from the twenty-fourth day

---

17. Eybers, "The Rebuilding of the Temple According to Haggai and Zechariah," 19. Eybers cites B. Gemser to the effect that *yāsad* means not only to
lay a foundation but to commence to build or to rebuild (cf. Zech. 8:9).
18. Nearly all commentators understand the formula here to be pointing to
the future, but, as the present approach is proposing, that presents difficulties in understanding the grammar of v. 19. See, e.g., Joyce G. Baldwin,
Haggai, Zechariah, Malachi, (London: Tyndale, 1972), 52; H. G. Mitchell, *A
Commentary on Haggai and Zechariah*, ICC (Edinburgh: T. & T. Clark,
1912), 71: "The construction in this case is the same [as in v. 15*b*] and the
connection perfectly analogous. The passage should therefore be rendered, 'from the time when the temple hath been founded.'"
19. David L. Petersen, "The Prophetic Process Reconsidered," *Iliff Review* 41
(1984):17.

of the ninth month"), serves as the axis. Lines B and B' are clearly paired, "from this day and backward" paralleling "from the day the Temple of YHWH was founded." The glimpse backward is to the day of the (re)founding. The problematic לְמִן (*lĕmin*) of line B' rather than לְ (*lĕ*) alone, which one might expect, is because of the parallelism to מִן (*min*) in line B. It might even be preferable to render the line "to the day. . . ."

Richard D. Patterson[20] offers an attractive alternative analysis of vv. 15-19 in which the thrice occurring introductory phrase לְבַבְכֶם שִׂימוּ . . . provides the structure:

שִׂימוּ־נָא לְבַבְכֶם (15a)	שִׂימוּ־נָא לְבַבְכֶם (18a)	הַזֶּה אֲבָרֵךְ + 19a-b
		מִן הַיּוֹם (19c)
מִן הַיּוֹם הַזֶּה וָמָעְלָה (15b) + 15c-17	מִן־הַיּוֹם הַזֶּה וָמָעְלָה (18b) + 18 c-d	שִׂימוּ לְבַבְכֶם (18e)

It is clear that lines 15b and 18b are identical and 19c similar to them both (all but the last word). Patterson further observes that a contrast is set up with (1) past days before work was begun on the Temple (vv. 15-17) and (2) the statement concerning the significance of the day of the "founding ceremony" to transforming present conditions into future blessings (vv. 18-19), a significance underscored by the repetition of the introductory formula, the second occurrence of which is formed so as to create an inclusio:

שִׂימוּ־נָא לְבַבְכֶם מִן הַיּוֹם הַזֶּה וָמָעְלָה	(15a-b)
מִיּוֹם עֶשְׂרִים . . .	(18c)
לְמִן הַיּוֹם . . .	(18d)
שִׂימוּ לְבַבְכֶם . . .	(18e)

Either approach supports the view that *mā'ĕlâ* refers to a backward glance, one focused on the refounding of the Temple and subsequent events.

Support for this interpretation appears in v. 19, which indicates that the produce of the land has not yet been forthcoming even though the work on the Temple has been underway for some time. This, of course, would not be at all surprising because the harvest was virtually over by the sixth month, the date of the commencement of the work, so one would have no expectation of crops afterward. The interpretation that vv. 15-19 have a future orientation ("from this day forward") generally holds that there is a backward glance in v. 15b ("one stone on another") and in vv. 16-17, but understands vv. 18-19 to

---

20. Richard D. Patterson, private communication, January 8, 1991.

be present and future. The idea, then, is that the date of the laying of the foundation is the date of the oracle, the twenty-fourth day of the ninth month (v. 18), and that the seed has already been sown and the fruit trees give promise of rich production in the season to come.[21] However, it is now at the end of December, and, because of the withholding of God's provision in the year just past, there is little on which to subsist. Nevertheless, things will be different now says YHWH, for "from today on I will bless you" (v. 19). The people have submitted to the word of YHWH through Haggai the prophet, and even though the vestiges of their previous disobedience remain to make their existence most uncomfortable, all this will change. God will begin a new age of prosperity.

Additional Notes

2:18 Though the sense of the passage appears to require a preposition לְ, meaning "to" or "till," the text has לְמִן, regularly translated "from" (BDB, 583). It is entirely possible that the form should be split into its separate prepositions and rendered "to (the time) from" or something similar. Thus, "Consider carefully from today and backward . . . to (the time) from the day the Temple of YHWH was founded (until now)." This would yield a pattern: today—backward, the past—the present. More simply, the לְ may only be explicative, to be rendered "that is" or the like.

---

21. For a full discussion, see David J. Clark, "Problems in Haggai 2.15-19," *BT* 34 (1983): 432-39.

4
Zerubbabel the Chosen One (2:20-23)

A. DIVINE DESTRUCTION (2:20-22)

This fourth and final message of Haggai, an oracle of salvation,[1] was received and delivered on the very same day as the third, but to Zerubbabel alone. The language of the passage is unmistakably apocalyptic, as the shaking, the universalism ("the heavens and the earth," "kingdoms of the nations"), and the overthrow of all human structures attest. It is also the language of holy war[2] in which YHWH vanquishes all competing princes and powers and sits enthroned above them on behalf of His own people.

Translation

20Then the word of YHWH came a second time to Haggai on the twenty-fourth day of the month, saying, 21"Speak to Zerubbabel governor of Judah as follows: 'I am about to shake the heavens and the earth. 22I will overthrow the royal thrones and shatter the strength of the *kingdoms of the nations. I will overthrow chariots and those who ride them, and the horses and their riders will fall, each man by his own brother's sword.'"

---

1. Ralph L. Smith, *Micah-Malachi*, WBC (Waco, Tex.: Word, 1984), 162. For an excellent literary analysis of the section, see Pieter A. Verhoef, *The Books of Haggai and Malachi* NICOT (Grand Rapids: Eerdmans, 1987), 139-40.
2. Gerhard von Rad, *Der Heilige Krieg im alten Israel* (Zurich: Zwingli Verlag), 1951, 65-66.

Exegesis and Exposition

This passage focuses on the destruction of all things hostile to the rule of YHWH, a destruction that cannot be separated from the last clause of 2:19 and that explains the abruptness of that clause in its own context. The promise to bless from that very day (v. 19) finds its expression, in other words, in the eschatological hope outlined in vv. 20-23. In terms reminiscent of his second oracle, the prophet speaks of a shaking of heaven and earth (cf. 2:6) and the overthrow and shattering of human kingdoms (cf. 2:7*a*). Petersen draws attention to the linkage between this passage and the overthrow of kingdoms in the royal (Davidic) Psalms (2, 110) and the destruction of the Egyptian hosts by YHWH in the Red Sea (Ex. 14:23; 15:5). Haggai's picture, then, is a mosaic drawn from many traditions.[3] Though the promise to fill His house with the precious things of the nations and with His own glory (2:7*b*) is lacking here, it is certainly implied in v. 23.

This, however, points up a major difference in the two addresses, for the shaking of the nations in 2:7 results in their bringing tribute to YHWH in His Temple. Here, it is more than a shaking—it is a shattering and defeat of the nations so severe in its results that no one and no thing remains but YHWH and His own sovereign rule.

Additional Notes

2:22 The LXX presupposes מְלָכִים ("kings") here for מַמְלָכוֹת ("kingdoms"). This is unsatisfactory, because in the eschaton it is the kingdoms of the world that are overthrown as enemies of the kingdom of God (cf. Isa. 13:9; Dan. 2:44-45), not the kings themselves.

B. DIVINE DELIVERANCE (2:23)

Translation

23"'In that day,' says YHWH of hosts, 'I will take you, Zerubbabel son of Shealtiel, My servant,' says YHWH, 'and I will appoint you like a signet, for I have chosen you,' says YHWH of hosts."

Exegesis and Exposition

Continuing with his focus on the future, the prophet introduces the climax of his message by relating it to "that day" (בַּיּוֹם הַהוּא, *bayyôm hahû'*), a favorite phrase in eschatological speech (cf. Isa. 2:11, 17, 20; 3:7, 18; Amos 8:3, 9; Hos. 2:18, 21; and many others). He

---

3. David L. Petersen, *Haggai and Zechariah 1-8*, (London: SCM, 1985), 100-101. So also Carroll Stuhlmueller, *Haggai & Zechariah*, ITC (Grand Rapids: Eerdmans, 1988), 37.

directs his remarks specifically to Zerubbabel, whom he no longer identifies as governor but as servant.[4] The shift is extremely significant, for "servant" in these kinds of settings is loaded with salvific, even messianic, nuances.[5] One immediately recalls such usage with respect to David (1 Kings 11:34; Ezek. 34:23), Israel (Isa. 41:8, 9; 44:21; 49:3; Jer. 30:10; 46:27, 28) and the suffering servant (Isa. 42:1; 49:5, 6, 7; 52:13–53:12). When the verb בָּחַר (*bāḥar*, "chosen") accompanies עֶבֶד (*'ebed*, "servant"), the redemptive role of the person so designated is enhanced all the more (cf. Isa. 41:8; 42:1; 44:4; 49:7).[6]

As servant of YHWH, Zerubbabel will be chosen to serve as a signet (חוֹתָם, *ḥôtām*), that is, as a seal whose purpose is to reflect and represent the person whose name it bears. Zerubbabel, like a seal inscription, will be the instrument of YHWH who will serve as His vice-regent[7] on the earth and attest to His ownership of all upon which He places His signature.[8]

Since the context indisputably is eschatological in nature, the Zerubbabel of the text cannot be the governor whom Haggai has so frequently addressed. Rather, one must see Zerubbabel as a prototype of one to come who will be YHWH's servant and chosen vessel. Yet the use of the name Zerubbabel (to the exclusion, one should note, of Joshua) is not without importance, for the point is made thereby that the signet will be of the line of which Zerubbabel is the most visible figure in Haggai's own generation.[9]

Of crucial importance is the message of Jer. 22:24-30 regarding the matter. Here the very word *ḥôtām* occurs again, this time as a ring seal upon the right hand of YHWH. In a hypothetical word of judgment YHWH addresses Coniah (i.e., Jehoiachin; cf. 2 Kings 24:6), the last king of Judah, and says that even if Coniah were His signet (which was not the case) He would remove Him from His hand (Jer. 22:24). As it is, the king is a rejected vessel, one who will be cast out and who might as well be childless, since none of his seed will succeed him on David's throne (v. 30).

---

4. Sara Japhet ("Shesbazzar and Zerubbabel Against the Background of the Historical and Religious Tendencies of Ezra-Nehemiah." *ZAW* 94 [1982]: 77) points out the interesting fact that "this is the only place in the Bible where a prophecy of the End of Days is focused upon an historical figure of the present identified by name."
5. Rex Mason, *The Books of Haggai, Zechariah, and Malachi*, CBC (Cambridge: Cambridge Univ., 1977), 25.
6. Georg Sauer, "Serubbabel in der Sicht Haggais und Sacharjas," *Das Ferne und Nahe Wort*, ed. F. Maass (Berlin: Töpelmann, 1967), 203-4.
7. D. Winton Thomas, "Haggai," *IB*, ed. G. A. Buttrick et al. (New York: Abingdon, 1956), 6:1049.
8. See G. L. Knapp, "Signet," *ISBE* 4:508.
9. Verhoef, *The Books of Haggai and Malachi*, 147.

Zerubbabel the governor was a descendant of Jehoiachin, most likely his grandson (1 Chron. 3:17-19; Matt. 1:12). Neither he nor any other immediate descendant of Jehoiachin sat on the throne of David, so to that extent the curse on Jehoiachin remained in effect. In what sense, then, can eschatological Zerubbabel serve as the chosen signet of YHWH?

The answer lies in understanding Zerubbabel as a link between the Davidic monarchy that had come to an inglorious end in Jehoiachin and that which would be revived in ages to come.[10] When it became apparent that Jehoiachin was banished to Babylon, never to return, hope for the revival of the Davidic rule centered first on his sons and, failing that, on his grandsons. At last, when one of them, Zerubbabel, became governor of Judah, it must have seemed to the restored community that God's ancient covenant promise—that there would never fail to be a son of David on the throne (2 Sam. 7:16; Ps. 89:24-37)—had come to pass.

Hope in Zerubbabel was intensified and confirmed by the message of Haggai's contemporary prophet Zechariah. He spoke of the servant of YHWH as a branch (3:8) and then of the fact that Zerubbabel, who had begun the work of Temple rebuilding, would finish it (4:9).[11] Then, in a remarkable combination of these motifs, Zechariah described one to come who would be named "Branch," who would build the Temple of YHWH, and who would serve as both king and priest upon the throne (6:12-13). This same Branch is identified in eschatological texts as a descendant of David (Jer. 23:5; 33:15), the shoot from the stock of Jesse (Isa. 11:1) who will attract all nations to Himself (Isa. 11:10). Because biblical theology identifies this one as Jesus Christ (Acts 13:22-23), Zerubbabel becomes a code name for the promised Messiah.[12] The despair following Jehoiachin's rejection is turned to hope in the proclamation of Zerubbabel as the chosen signature of YHWH Himself.

---

10. So Japhet, "Sheshbazzar and Zerubbabel," 78.
11. W. J. Dumbrell, "Kingship and Temple in the Post-Exilic Period," *RTR* 37 (1978): 33.
12. Herbert Wolf, "The Desire of All Nations in Haggai 2:7: Messianic or Not?" *JETS* 19 (1976): 101-2; cf. R. T. Siebeneck, "The Messianism of Aggeus and Proto-Zacharias," *CBQ* 19 (1957): 318; Ralph L. Smith, *Micah-Malachi*, 163.

Zechariah

Introduction to Zechariah

HISTORICAL CONTEXT

Zechariah commenced his ministry, so far as his own account is concerned, in the eighth month of the second year of the Persian king Darius Hystaspes (Zech. 1:1). He does not specify the day, but the eighth month (Julian calendar) would be between late October and late November, 520 B.C.[1] The final two oracles of Haggai were delivered on the twenty-fourth day of that same month and year (or December 18, 520),[2] so Zechariah's public ministry overlapped that of Haggai by approximately one month.

Before the implications of that fact are explored, it is necessary to examine other chronological data of the book of Zechariah. Like Haggai, Zechariah is concerned to pinpoint the major turning points of his ministry by attaching them to a sequential, chronological framework. Thus, after the general introduction, dated in the eighth month of Darius's second year (Zech. 1:1-6), Zechariah assigns the night visions (1:7–6:15) to the twenty-fourth day of the eleventh month (1:7), February 15, 519 B.C. His final chronological reference is to the fourth year of Darius and the fourth day of the ninth month (7:1). This is December 7, 518. If one accepts the unity of the whole book (a posi-

---

1. Richard A. Parker and Waldo H. Dubberstein, *Babylonian Chronology 626 B.C.-A.D. 75* (Providence: Brown Univ., 1956), 30.
2. See commentary on Haggai above, 3-4, 45.

tion accepted here and defended), this last date presumably marks the occasion for all the oracles and other messages of chapters 7-14.

It is difficult to determine what role Zechariah may have played in connection with the public ministry of Haggai, a ministry that commenced only two months before his own (Hag. 1:1). When they are mentioned together (Ezra 5:1; 6:14), Haggai's name is always first, suggesting either his leadership or his prophetic and canonical priority. In any case, the two men of God together encouraged the resumption of Temple construction after it had lain dormant for 18 years (from 536 to 520 B.C.; cf. Ezra 3:8-10; 5:1-2). With Haggai, Zechariah provided the leadership to enable their compatriots to bring the building task successfully to completion by about March 13, 515 B.C. (Ezra 6:14-15).[3]

An integration of the chronological data of Haggai and Zechariah might yield further clues as to their relationship, though admittedly such clues would be deduced with some measure of speculation. The most critical part of Haggai's appeal seems to occur in Hag. 2:1-9, for there he addresses the profound pessimism that had begun to envelop the people a few weeks after Temple reconstruction began. They saw the new building as nothing compared to the glorious Temple of Solomon, so they needed the assurance that YHWH was with them (2:4) and that eventually the glory of the second Temple would exceed that of the first (2:7-9). Within weeks (or even days) Zechariah followed this up with a reminder of God's displeasure with their fathers' attitudes and actions in the past (Zech. 1:2) and assured them that, if they turned to YHWH, He would turn to them (1:3). Both prophets thus contrast the past with the present and future, with Haggai stressing the rebuilt Temple as a sign and source of God's blessing and Zechariah emphasizing the role of repentance and renewal in achieving that end. The two prophets worked hand in glove, complementing each other's message.

The general historical background of these early years of Darius has been reviewed in the Introduction to Haggai (pp. 3-10), so there is no need to do more here than to consider briefly the two years of Zechariah's ministry that postdated Haggai's. Unfortunately, little can be said, for both biblical and extrabiblical sources are virtually silent. The OT witness is limited to the book of Ezra, which, though composed some 60 or 70 years after the last date in Zechariah, must be considered reliable.[4] As just suggested, Ezra recounts the leader-

---

3. Parker and Dubberstein, *Babylonian Chronology*, 30.
4. H. G. M. Williamson, *Ezra, Nehemiah*, WBC (Waco, Tex: Word, 1985), xxviii-xxxii.

ship of Haggai and Zechariah in the Temple project (Ezra 5:1-2) and relates in some detail the opposition to the work from Tattenai, governor of the satrapy *eber-nāri*, and his allies (Ezra 5:13-17). Once Darius the king settled the matter of the legitimacy of the operation and authorized the work to continue (6:1-12), the Jews, under Haggai and Zechariah, brought it to an end (6:13). Apparently Darius's edict forestalled any further interdiction of the work and allowed it to be finished. For Ezra is clear, in reviewing the whole history of the restoration, that the antagonism of the Jews' enemies continued only until the reign of Darius, that is, until 520 B.C. (Ezra 4:5). Not until Xerxes came to power (486) did serious opposition begin again (Ezra 4:6). It is safe to assume, therefore, that the work went on unimpeded in the two years of Zechariah's ministry (520-518).

Persian texts record a western campaign by Darius in the winter of 519-518 B.C., an itinerary that included Palestine. Many scholars propose that Zerubbabel, governor of Yehud (i.e., Judah), was deposed by Darius at that time, allegedly for rebellion or for having the misfortune of having been designated by Haggai (2:23) as successor to the Davidic throne.[5] The only basis for such a view is the disappearance from the biblical record of any reference to Zerubbabel after 520. This *argumentum e silentio* is hardly conclusive of the deposition hypothesis, however.

What is clear is that Darius continued on to Egypt where he put down incipient rebellions by the end of November 518 B.C. and then returned home. The last date of Zechariah, December 7, follows or perhaps even generally coincides with Darius's return trip through Judah. What effect this contact by the Persian king had on the message of Zechariah in chapters 7 through 14 cannot be determined. The commentary to follow offers some suggestions.

Kenneth Barker and other scholars account for some of the differences between Zechariah 1-8 and 9-14 by suggesting that the prophet may have lived well into the fifth century, possibly into the reign of the Persian king Artaxerxes I (465-424 B.C.).[6] This can be supported by the reference to Zechariah in the genealogy of Neh. 12:10-16. The passing of at least 30 or 40 years from the time of Zechariah's earlier oracles can easily explain the allegedly later historical references (such as to Greece in 9:13) and the clearly more eschatological perspective of the last six chapters.

---

5. A. T. Olmstead, *History of the Persian Empire* (Chicago: Univ. of Chicago, 1948), 142.
6. Kenneth L. Barker, "Zechariah," in *EBC*, ed. Frank E. Gaebelein (Grand Rapids: Zondervan, 1985), 7:597; cf. Gleason L. Archer, Jr., *A Survey of Old Testament Introduction*, rev. ed. (Chicago: Moody, 1985), 437.

LITERARY CONTEXT

This commentary will proceed on the assumption that the book of Zechariah as it appears in its traditional and canonical form is a literary unity composed by the ascribed author, the prophet Zechariah. What is necessary now, before literary unity is defended, is to address matters of language and style through careful form-critical and literary analyses. Those that mark off the peculiar characteristics of the composition will be specially noted.

LANGUAGE AND STYLE

Students of Zechariah have for years recognized that the predominant genres of the book are visions and oracles, the former contained in chapters 1-6 (1:8-15; 2:1-4 [EB 1:18-21]; 2:5-9 [EB 2:1-5]; 3:1-7; 4:1-6a, 10b-14; 5:1-4; 5:5-11; 6:1-8.[7] The latter is found in both 1-6 (1:16-17; 2:10-17 [EB 2:6-13]; 3:8-10; 4:6b-10a; 6:9-15) and 7-14 (7:4-14; 8:1-23; 9:1–11:17; 12:1–14:21).[8] In addition there is the oracular introduction to the whole collection (1:1-6 [+7]). One will note that the oracles are of two kinds functionally: those that introduce or flow from visions (chaps. 1-6) and those that stand independently. How they function will be discussed throughout the commentary.

For now it is important to understand that prophetic visions, though lacking in Haggai, were not the invention of Zechariah. Indeed, visions were the stock in trade of all the prophets, beginning with Amos.[9] The oracle likewise, whatever its particular form or genre, is the essence of prophetic communication. What has to be understood then is the way Zechariah relates and makes use of the particular speech forms that constitute his argument. For the sake of convenience, the visions and oracles will be considered separately and in that order.

Modern studies of the visions of Zechariah began with the important work of J. W. Rothstein, *Die Nachtgesichte des Sacharja (BWAT* 8), published in 1910.[10] Major subsequent works on the subject include those by L. G. Rignell (1950), Kurt Galling (1952), Klaus Seybold (1974), Christian Jeremias (1977), Gerhard Wallis (1978), and Baruch

7. Klaus Seybold, *Bilder zum Tempelbau. Die Visionen des Propheten Sacharja* (Stuttgart: KBW Verlag, 1974), 24-30.
8. Albert Petitjean, *Les Oracles du Proto-Zacharie* (Paris: Librairie Lecoffre, 1969), viii.
9. Christian Jeremias, *Die Nachtgesichte des Sacharja* (Göttingen: Vandenhoeck & Ruprecht, 1977), 88-106.
10. J. W. Rothstein, *Die Nachtgesichte des Sacharja, BWAT* 8 (Leipzig: J. C. Hinrichs'sche Buchhandlung, 1910).

Halpern (1978).[11] Ranging from Rothstein's view that the visions are collections of phrases and glosses gathered over a period of time[12] to that of contemporary scholars who see the visions as homogeneous and unified messages received by the prophet in one nocturnal revelation,[13] these studies share in common the notion that the visions serve, among various purposes, the aim of bringing about the restoration of Temple and cult.

The book of Zechariah as it stands makes plain that the eight visions of chapters 1-6 came to the prophet in the course of one night, on the twenty-fourth day of the eleventh month (1:7). Whereas the question of the significance (if any) of the vision's sequence must await later attention, for now it is important to look at the structures of the vision texts themselves to see if there is a discernible pattern.

Carol L. and Eric M. Meyers, in their commentary *Haggai, Zechariah 1-8*, have recently broken new ground in their analysis of the components of the Zechariah visions and the pattern of their sequence.[14] They draw attention to common formulaic language such as "I raised my eyes," "I looked/saw," "(and) behold," "again," and others (p. lvii). Also common to the visions is extensive use of symbolism; the role of mediating beings, especially angels; a more transcendant view of God than in earlier prophecy; and an emphasis on the universal sovereignty of God.

David L. Petersen (*Haggai and Zechariah 1-8*) views the matter of kinship of the vision texts somewhat differently. He posits their commonality around the notions of "in betweenness," motion, and the motif "the whole earth."[15] The first of these refers to Zechariah's stance between "purely mundane concerns and a utopian vision of renewal." This separates Zechariah from other exilic and postexilic

---

11. L. G. Rignell, *Die Nachtgesichte des Sacharja* (Lund: Gleerup, 1950); Kurt Galling, "Die Exilswende in der Sicht des Propheten Sacharja," *VT* 2 (1952): 18-36 (reprinted in *Studien zur Geschichte Israels im Persischen Zeitalter* [Tübingen: J. C. B. Mohr, 1964], 109-26); Klaus Seybold (see n. 7 above); Christian Jeremias (see n. 9 above); Gerhard Wallis, "Die Nachtgesichte des Propheten Sacharja: zur Idee einer Form," Congress Volume, Göttingen, 1977, ed. W. Zimmerli et al. (Leiden: Brill, 1978), 377-91; Baruch Halpern, "The Ritual Background of Zechariah's Temple Song," *CBQ* 40 (1978): 167-90.
12. Rothstein, *Die Nachtgesichte des Sacharja*, 3-7.
13. Georg Fohrer, *Introduction to the Old Testament* (London: SPCK, 1970), 463.
14. Carol L. Meyers and Eric M. Meyers, *Haggai, Zechariah 1-8*, AB (Garden City, N.Y.: Doubleday, 1987).
15. David L. Petersen, *Haggai and Zechariah 1-8*, (Philadelphia: Westminster, 1984), 113-14.

prophets, such as Ezekiel and Haggai, but also betrays the content of his visions—he views reality as suspended somewhere between heaven and earth.

By motion is meant simply that all the visions are filled with activity, with earthly and heavenly figures alike on the go. Even visions one and two, which appear to be static, provide the occasion for responsive action. Finally, the "whole earth" theme, similar to the universalism noted by the Meyers and others, is a common unifying bond.

In answering the question why these motifs prevail in the visions, Petersen suggests the twofold response that Zechariah is doing theology and that the visions "comprise Zechariah's experientially based responses to these problems of a community attempting to reorganize itself" (p. 115). The theology he is doing is attempting to explain why and how YHWH will deal with iniquity, how He will be present in Jerusalem, how the community's leadership will be organized, and other such matters.

Although one might disagree in details with the two analyses just set forth, they do draw attention correctly to the use by the prophet of a literary vehicle that addresses the needs of a community in a specific historical context but in a way that transcends that context and opens the door to the cosmic, universal sovereignty of YHWH. They also agree in maintaining that the elements shared commonly by the visions give them a unity in themselves and a coherence among them. This aspect will be dealt with below.

The oracles, as a second major literary category in Zechariah, have also received a great deal of attention, particularly by W. A. M. Beuken (1967), Albert Petitjean (1969), Joyce Baldwin (1972), and D. L. Petersen (1984).[16] Again, however, it was Rothstein who first showed that Zechariah 1-6 was a composite of visions and discourses. The latter he divided by form into two basic groups: those that were preceded by a formula of introduction in the first person (4:8-10*a*; 6:9-15) and those without any introductory statement (1:16-17; 2:10-17 [EB 2:6-13]; 3:8-10).[17]

Petitjean and other scholars have followed up on Rothstein's early labors and have noted the function of oracles intertwined among the visions of chapters 1-6 as well as independent oracles pertaining to fasting (7-8) and eschatological matters (9-11; 12-14). Petersen agrees with Petitjean's pattern as a whole, but his analysis differs in detail as

---

16. W. A. M. Beuken, *Haggai-Sacharja 1-8* (Assen: van Gorcum, 1967); Albert Petitjean (see n. 8 above); Joyce Baldwin, *Haggai, Zechariah, Malachi* (London: Tyndale, 1972); David L. Petersen (see n. 15 above).
17. Cited by Petitjean, *Les Oracles*, viii.

the accompanying table shows. Both have provided a most plausible analysis of the delimitation and function of the various oracular units in Zechariah 1-6. According to Petersen, 1:14-17 is an oracular response to the first vision (1:8-13), one consisting in fact of two separate oracles (vv. 14-15, 16-17). Similarly, 2:10-17 (EB 2:6-13) responds to vision three (2:5-9 [EB 2:1-5]), 3:8-10 (so Petitjean; Petersen, 3:6-10) responds to vision four (3:1-7 [or 1-5]), 4:6b-10a (thus Petitjean; Petersen, 4:6-7, 8-10, 12) appears within and is relevant to vision five (4:1-6a, 10b-14 [Petitjean; Petersen, 4:1-5, 11]), and 6:9-15 (Petitjean; Petersen, 6:10-11, 14; 6:12-13) follows the eighth vision (Petitjean 6:1-8 [Petersen, 6:1-9, 15]).[18]

The Visions and Oracles of Zechariah 1-6

	Albert Petitjean	David L. Petersen
Vision One	1:8-13	1:8-13
Oracle One	1:14-17	1:14-17
Vision Two	2:1-4 (EB 1:18-21)	2:1-4
Vision Three	2:5-9 (EB 2:1-5)	2:5-9
Oracle Two	2:10-17 (EB 2:6-13)	2:10-17
Vision Four	3:1-7	3:1-5
Oracle Three	3:8-10	3:6-10
Vision Five	4:1-6a, 10b-14	4:1-5, 11
Oracle Four	4:6b-10a	4:6-7, 8-10, 12
Vision Six	5:1-4	5:1-4
Vision Seven	5:5-11	5:5-11
Vision Eight	6:1-8	6:1-8, 15
Oracle Five	6:9-15	6:10-11, 14; 6:12-13

It is obvious that Petersen does not follow Petitjean exactly in his literary boundaries for the oracular material and, indeed, there is very little agreement on the matter across the spectrum of contemporary scholarship. This, however, little affects the near consensus that the oracles of Zechariah are, in the first section (chaps.1-6) at least, designed to introduce, clarify, or otherwise aid and assist in the proclamation of the visionary message.

The linkage between the visions and their complementary oracles extends to shared imagery and themes such as personified Zion, the cities of Judah, the nations coming to Zion, Zion shouting for joy, and others derived ultimately from Isaiah especially. As Petersen observes, "such continuities between oracle, vision, and Isaiah suggest that despite certain differences in perspective, there is shared discourse between the prophetic traditionists of the Isaianic circle, the

---

18. Petersen, *Haggai and Zechariah 1-8*, 121.

prophet Zechariah, and those preserving Zechariah's visions and oracles."[19] Even though the latter phrase implies redactionary work for which there is no evidence in the text, Petersen's general point is well taken.

The oracles of Zechariah 7-8 are quite different from those of chapters 1-6 in that they stand independent of visions, coming rather in response to questions posed to the prophet by certain of his fellow citizens (7:1-3). Though they deal with the common theme of fasting, they do take the form of separate addresses marked usually by some kind of speech formula (thus 7:4-7, 8-14; 8:1-8, 9-13, 14-17, 18-23).

Despite the clear distinctions brought about by setting and function, these oracles partake of the standard oracular elements and show marked affinity with those in chapters 1-6. Such matters as the 70 years (1:12; 7:5), Jerusalem to be inhabited (2:8; 7:7), divine anger/wrath (2:15; 7:12), "Thus spoke YHWH of Hosts" (1:14, 17; 2:12; 3:7; 6:12; 7:9; 8:2, 3, 4, 6, 7, 9, 14, 19, 20, 23), and the return to Zion/Jerusalem (1:16; 8:3) bear this out. In addition to strengthening the case for the unity of 1-6 and 7-8 (a matter reserved for later discussion), such points are useful in delineating the prophet's language and style.

It is a nearly unanimous conviction among critical scholars that Zechariah 9-14 is not original to the book. This commentary will later show the untenableness of that position, but for now it is necessary to say something about that last section in terms of its literary character.

Paul Lamarche, about whose work more will be said later, divides these chapters into the traditional sections 9-11 and 12-14.[20] The first he then subdivides into an oracle concerning neighboring nations (9:1-8); the arrival and description of the king (9:9-10); the victorious war of Israel, return, and prosperity (9:11–10:1); the sin of idolatry and chastisement (10:2-3*a*); the restoration of Judah and Ephraim, return and prosperity, chastisement of enemies (10:3*b*–11:3); and the rejected shepherd (11:4-17).[21] One can see the faint outlines of a chiastic structure here and, indeed, Lamarche's analysis depends upon the chiasmus of which chapters 9-11 are the first part. This receives detailed treatment below.

As for chapters 12-14, Lamarche, again in line with an overall chiastic analysis, delimits the material into the following units: victorious war of Israel (12:1-9); the Lord's agent slain, repentance,

---

19. Ibid., 122.
20. Paul Lamarche, *Zacharie IX-XIV. Structure Littéraire et Messianisme* (Paris: Librairie Lecoffre, 1961), 34.
21. Ibid., 35.

mourning, and purification (12:10–13:1); the rejection of idols (13:2-6); the shepherd smitten, purification, reconciliation with God (13:7-9); victorious war of Israel (14:1-15); and the nations obligated to go up to Jerusalem (14:16-21).[22]

Although this approach has more to say about structure than it does about language and style, one can hardly separate them. But more to the point of the latter, it is important to note the differences between chapters 1-8 and 9-14 in these respects. As has already been argued, the first part, except for chapters 7-8, is largely dominated by the vision genre with all that this implies in terms of literary criticism. The oracle sections of those chapters as well as the oracles of 7 and 8 ("sermon material" in the words of Baldwin[23]) relate to the visions and reinforce their eschatological thrust. With the visions they also share some basic ingredients of apocalypticism. Chapters 9-14 move beyond the mere use of apocalyptic devices, however, and become full-blown apocalyptic treatises. This partly explains why many critics seek to divorce these chapters from the Zechariah corpus and why this material, when interpreted according to hermeneutical canons appropriate to the first eight chapters, remains so difficult to comprehend.

It is therefore necessary that some attention be given to the history and characteristics of apocalyptic language and literature, for Zechariah, more than any other OT prophet, employs it in his message to the second Temple community. The subject as a whole is vast and has been the object of so many comprehensive and adequate publications in recent years that there is no need here to do more than briefly summarize the apocalyptic as literary genre, as it relates to Zechariah.[24]

As recently as 1972 Klaus Koch[25] lamented that "there are as yet no form-critical investigations of the apocalyptic writings," a situation that has changed little since then. As a result, the best one can do is to try to develop a typological model on the basis of writings commonly regarded as apocalyptic and judge individual composi-

---

22. Ibid., 72-73.
23. Baldwin, *Haggai, Zechariah, Malachi*, 70.
24. For important surveys, see Michael A. Knibb, "Prophecy and the Emergence of the Jewish Apocalypses," *Israel's Prophetic Tradition*, eds. Richard Coggins, Anthony Phillips, and Michael Knibb (Cambridge: Cambridge Univ., 1982), 155-80; John N. Oswalt, "Recent Studies in Old Testament Eschatology and Apocalyptic," *JETS* 24 (1981): 289-301. For Zechariah's special contribution to apocalyptic, see Samuel Amsler, "Zacharie et L'Origin de L'Apocalyptique," Congress Volume, Uppsala, 1971, ed. H. Nyberg (Leiden: Brill, 1972), 227-31.
25. Klaus Koch, *The Rediscovery of Apocalyptic*, SBT 22 (London: SCM, 1972), 24.

tions, such as Zechariah, against that model. This is a kind of circular method to be sure. At the same time one must, as Paul Hanson has warned, avoid viewing apocalytpicism as a rigid, frozen form that always and under all circumstances exhibits common characteristics.[26] Older scholarship (and some modern as well) maintained that apocalypticism was a late development, certainly postexilic, so that apocalyptic texts in purportedly preexilic writings had to be viewed as secondary to them.[27] This is no longer a credible position in light of recent studies that show the roots of apocalyptic reaching deep into preexilic times. The corollary to the notion that apocalyptic was late, namely, that it was shaped by non-Jewish (primarily Zoroastrian) influences, has also come under attack and has been largely abandoned.[28] It is somewhat surprising, then, to read in John J. Collins that Jewish apocalypticism, as found at least in 1 Enoch and Daniel, "was essentially a new creation, designed for the needs of a new age." Though he distinguishes between the pure apocalypticism of Daniel and apocalyptic elements in works such as Isa. 24-27, Zech. 9-14, and Joel, Collins still largely reverts to an earlier position regarding the origin of apocalyptic.[29]

Zechariah, then, stood in an already ancient apocalyptic tradition from which he drew heavily and to which he made an enormously significant contribution, one particularly observable in the NT book of Revelation. Having said that, however, it is important to point out that apocalyptic did receive an incalculable impetus from the trauma of the Exile, for that calamity shook not only the social and political structures of Judah to their very foundations but was in danger of undermining the covenant faith itself. With no Temple and with Zion in wreck and ruin, on what basis could the eternal promises of YHWH to His people find fulfillment?

The answer lay in the shift of focus from the present to the future, from the local to the universal, from the earthly to the cosmic or heavenly. Even the restoration hardly changed the equation, for Judah was an insignificant client state of a mighty empire, there was no

---

26. Paul D. Hanson, *The Dawn of Apocalyptic* (Philadelphia: Fortress, 1975), 4-8.
27. S. R. Driver, *An Introduction to the Literature of the Old Testament* (Edinburgh: T. & T. Clark, 1913), 219-23. See also William R. Millar, *Isaiah 24-27 and the Origin of Apocalyptic* (Missoula, Mont.: Scholars Press, 1976). Millar traces apocalyptic to Isaiah 24-27, which he dates to the last half of the sixth century B.C., about the time of Zechariah (p. 120).
28. D. S. Russell, *The Method and Message of Jewish Apocalyptic* (London: SCM, 1964), 264-71.
29. John J. Collins, "The Place of Apocalypticism in the Religion of Israel," in *Ancient Israelite Religion*, eds. Patrick D. Miller, Jr., Paul D. Hanson, S. Dean McBride (Philadelphia: Fortress, 1987), 549-58.

scion of David on her throne, and there were no signs that this dismal state of affairs would change in the normal course of events. Haggai had suggested that part of the problem was the indifference of the people who must rebuild the Temple if they expected a reversal of their circumstances. Even he, however, saw that a final and total change must await the eschaton when the glory of YHWH would fill His Temple (Hag. 2:6-9) and a descendant of David would rule from Zion (2:20-23).

Zechariah, even more than Haggai, lifted his gaze to horizons above and beyond his own age, though clearly much of his effort and message was directed to the immediate concerns of restoration of the community and cult. Apocalyptic was the vehicle by which this eschatological concern could be best articulated, the same vehicle that other prophets had employed when addressing the same issues (cf. Isa. 24-27; Ezek. 1:4–3:15; 38-39; Joel 3). Only apocalyptic could express the utter transcendence involved in the radical transformations that would accompany the irruption of the kingdom of YHWH and the consequent shattering of all human and earthly systems in its wake.

The typological model adduced above becomes such by virtue of certain literary and conceptual features that give it coherence. Koch is helpful in suggesting some of these. In the first place, apocalyptic as literary genre is characterized by "discourse cycles,"[30] frequently described as visions and revealing matters formerly concealed as mysteries and now understood only by an interpreter such as an angel. Another element is the spiritual turmoil into which the prophet is thrown as a result of his visual or auditory experience. A third is the paraenesis that accompanies the revelation report, the "sermon material" to use Baldwin's terminology.[31] The purpose obviously is to make application of the vision to the hearer/reader. Still another literary hallmark, one typical of late, postbiblical apocalyptic, is pseudonymity, a phenomenon some scholars apply to Zechariah 9-14 (without warrant in our view). Finally, Koch includes the use of "mythical images rich in symbolism" (p. 26) by means of which historical and terrestrial events are cast in the grotesque language of metaphor, a kind of encoding into a literary form that was common currency in late Jewish and early Christian times.

Apocalyptic as a conceptual, intellectual movement gives evidence, first of all, of understanding history in terms of an imminent overthrow of all earthly conditions. Moreover, that end of history appears as a vast cosmic catastrophe, one that inexorably follows the

---

30. Koch, *The Rediscovery of Apocalyptic*, 24-33.
31. Baldwin, *Haggai, Zechariah, Malachi*, 70.

course of history that itself is perceived in a segmented, epochal manner. There are thus units of fours, sevens, or twelves, all marking eras and periods within which historical events take place. These events are predetermined by a sovereign God who often administers them through angelic subordinates. Following the great, final cataclysm a new salvation, paradisaical in character, arises in which all nations participate, though the covenant people continue to play a central role. The principal feature of this is the establishment of the kingdom of God in which He or His messianic agent sits enthroned. Overarching all is the glory of YHWH, which not only expresses His presence but marks the whole creation as a regenerated entity.

These general observations of Koch find more specific application to Zechariah in the superb study by Joyce Baldwin on the literary genre of the book.[32] She sees apocalyptic as a principal unifying factor in the entire composition, a device characterized by visions of the submission of nations (1:21; 2:9; 8:20-23), the exaltation of Jerusalem (1:17; 2:4, 5, 10-12; 7:3), and the work of the Branch (3:8; 6:12). These same elements, with a note of conflict (11:4-14), appear in chapters 9-14 as well.

The apocalyptic visions of Zechariah, though filled with symbolism, are not as complicated and bizarre as those of Ezekiel, but do require angelic interpreters, at least in chapters 1-6. He goes beyond Ezekiel and other earlier apocalyptists, however, in his declarations that what he envisions is as good as done, for it is only an earthly reflection of what has in fact come to pass in heaven. The future is certain because of the inexorable pattern already revealed. This heavenly model is painted in symbolic imagery in the form of animals, numbers, objects, and persons.

Baldwin goes on to show that even the non-visionary parts of Zechariah (chaps. 7-14) reveal apocalyptic overtones. There is the historical retrospect of chapters 7 and 8 which, by demonstrating the patterning of Israel's history, blends the historical past with the eschatological future. The whole is permeated by apocalyptic allusions to earthquake (14:4-6), miraculous intervention by YHWH (9:14; 12:3-4), eschatological battle (12:1-9; 14:1-15), divine deliverance of Jerusalem (9:8; 12:7; 14:1-8), and bitter mourning (12:10-14) but ultimate joy (9:9; 14:16). In short, the entire work, if not apocalyptic as a whole, is permeated with apocalyptic life and spirit.

Finally, a brief word must be said about Zechariah's use of apocalyptic and his role within that tradition. Beginning especially with

---

32. Ibid., 7-74.
33. Otto Plöger, *Theokratie und Eschatologie*, WMANT 2 (Neukirchen: Neukircher-Vluyn), 1959.

the work of Otto Ploger in 1959[33] there has developed the hypothesis that postexilic Judaism consisted of two major and conflicting parties, each of which was attempting to gain political and ideological control of the restoration community. These were the hierocratic element, whose agenda was the implementation of the priestly rule over the covenant people in line with Ezekiel, P, and the Chronicler, and the idealistic element, which viewed the present restoration efforts as so much wasted, humanistic enterprise and awaited the coming of the true theocracy to be set up by YHWH himself. The idealistic adherents' inspiration was the second exodus message of "Second" Isaiah.

Paul Hanson, in his influential book *The Dawn of Apocalyptic* (1975), takes his point of departure from Ploger (though he curiously mentions him only once)[34] but carries his central thesis much further. He maintains that the hierocratic sector was composed of the Zadokite priesthood, which was in conflict with the Levites for domination of the cult. It also opposed the visionary element that, in the tradition of Deutero-Isaiah, awaited an apocalyptic breakthrough of divine sovereignty. Prophetic support for these movements, according to Hanson, revolves around Haggai and Zechariah particularly, both of whom championed the hierocratic cause. Deutero-Zechariah (i.e., chaps. 9-14), on the other hand, favored the idealists, expressing its message in the strong apocalyptic terms characteristic of that composition. Hanson does not deny apocalyptic to the hierocratic faction, arguing in fact that apocalyptic was common to both schools, but he sharply distinguishes between heirocratic apocalypticism, which viewed the end as already present, and visionary apocalpticism, which still awaited the eschaton.

The historical turning point that marked the victory of the hierocrats was the accession of Darius to the throne and his support of Temple construction and Jewish nationhood, even to the extent of allowing a Davidic offspring, Zerubbabel, to occupy high office. This apparent fulfillment of the earlier prophetic promises made it clear beyond question (so Hanson) that the long-awaited eschatological kingdom had come and the priests were at least its co-administrators. With the disappearance of Zerubbabel shortly thereafter, Joshua alone was in control, a turn of events that henceforth guaranteed to the priesthood the place of political as well as cultic dominance. Apart from the feeble ex post facto efforts of Deutero-Zechariah, especially, the hierocratic view of reality remained in place until the

---

34. Hanson, *The Dawn of Apocalyptic*, 278.
35. Ibid., 410.

second century when new struggles revived the visionaries once more along with their particular brand of apocalypticism.[35]

Although there is much to commend in Hanson's approach, his assumption of party strife with its accompanying notion of antithetical apocalyptic schools is totally without foundation, as many critics of his book have pointed out.[36] The alleged differences between the Deutero-Isaiah tradition and that of Trito-Isaiah, Ezekiel, Haggai, Zechariah, and the Chronicler can be sustained only by positing the hypothesis in the first place and then reading the various texts accordingly.[37] In point of fact, there is a univocal message from apocalyptic and non-apocalyptic prophet alike that the present systems and structures of the Jew's life—political, social, and religious—are short-lived and are to be replaced wholesale by the eschatological rule and domain of YHWH their God. Haggai, Zechariah, and the others do indeed exhort their countrymen to rebuild and restore, but they insist nevertheless that what they build is only anticipatory of something far more glorious in the age to come. History to them and to all the prophets is the threshold opening up to the kingdom of God, but it is not synonymous with it.

LITERARY INTEGRITY

Much of the previous discussion of the language and style of Zechariah has alluded to and indeed been informed by questions of its unity, date, authorship, and structure. This last point will be addressed separately below, but it cannot be avoided altogether in this section. It is hoped that many of the issues raised in the previous pages will also find clarification and support here.

A random check of commentaries on Zechariah reveals that few address the whole book and, if they do, they approach it as two separate works, each in need of its own commentary. Even more surprising, and indeed dismaying, is the lack of justification for this bifurcation of the book, except for such desultory comments as those of D. L. Petersen in his otherwise fine work on Zechariah 1-8: "In this commentary I follow the critical judgment of scholars over the years who have discerned a fundamental division between Zechariah 1-8 and 9-14."[38] Then, citing only Eissfeldt (1965) and Otzen (1964) for support, he proceeds to deal with Zechariah 1-8 as though that were

---

36. See, e.g., P. R. Ackroyd, *Int* 30 (1976): 414; Robert P. Carroll, *JSOT* 14 (1979): 19-20; Alden Thompson, *AUSS* 15 (1977): 78; Ina Willi-Plein, *VT* 29 (1979): 124-25.
37. Carroll, *JSOT*, 14, 25.
38. Petersen, *Haggai and Zechariah 1-8*, 109.

the end of the matter, totally ignoring the fruit of twenty years of labor that has called the bifurcation of the book into question again.

Similarly, in their massive recent commentary on Haggai and Zechariah 1-8 (1987), Carol L. and Eric M. Meyers defend the limits of their work not only for reasons of length, but because "it is our present contention that these two works [Zechariah 9-14 and Malachi] emanate from the latter part of the first half of the fifth century."[39] Presumably a stronger defense for the division of Zechariah will appear in their forthcoming commentary on Zechariah 9-14 and Malachi.

There is, then, a consensus in critical scholarship that Zechariah is a composite of two or even three major works, Zechariah (1-8), Deutero-Zechariah (9-11), and Trito-Zechariah (12-14). This consensus is so deep-rooted and taken for granted that most modern commentaries, as just observed, take it as a given. Even standard introductions repeat the arguments for division raised many years ago. While this is perhaps to be lamented, it is incumbent on those who adhere to the book's unity to provide some kind of credible rationale in light of this solid wall of contrary opinion.

Ironically enough, the first crack in the structure of unity of composition came at the devout hands of the seventeenth-century English scholar Joseph Mede, who noted that Matt. 27:9a attributed the following quotation (vv. 9b-10) to Jeremiah when in fact it appears to be based on Zech. 11:12-13. He took this to mean that the Holy Spirit was attempting in this manner to correct the tradition of authorship by attributing chapters 9-11 of Zechriah to Jeremiah instead.[40]

Subsequent investigation revealed that chapters 12-14 also must be denied to Zechariah, for this section too was incompatible with the chronological parameters of Zechariah.[41] Specifically, chapters 9-11, with their references to Ephraim (i.e., Israel) and Assyria, must antedate 722 B.C., the year Samaria fell and Ephraim no longer existed. Chapters 12-14, on the other hand, depict Judah as still existing but seem to view Josiah as having already died (12:11). A date for this section between 609 and 586 thus seemed reasonable. In both cases, these sections were many decades earlier than Zechariah.

There remained the question as to why chapters 9-11 were allotted to Zechariah at all if he was indeed not their author. One answer

---

39. Meyers and Meyers, *Haggai, Zechariah 1-8*, ix.
40. Benedikt Otzen, *Studien über Deuterosacharia* (Copenhagen: Prostand Apud Munksgaard, 1964), 11-13. This study contains a full history of research on this matter (pp. 11-34); see also Magne Saebø, "Die deuterosacharjanische Frage," *ST* 23 (1969): 115-40.

was that a Zechariah in fact did write this section, but he was Zechariah son of Jeberechiah, a contemporary of Isaiah (Isa. 8:2). The ascription in Zech. 1:1, "Zechariah the son of Berechiah, the son of Iddo," was assumed to be a conflation of the name of the early Zechariah and that of the author of the first eight chapters, known elsewhere (Neh. 12:16) simply as the son of Iddo. As a result, Zechariah son of Jeberechiah became confused with Zechariah son of Iddo and the first eleven chapters at least were ascribed to Zechariah son of Berechiah, son of Iddo, making the author the grandson rather than the son of Iddo.[42]

Apart from the distinct difference between the names Berechiah and Jeberechiah, this thesis falls apart when it is recognized that the contents of chapters 9-14 are much later than the period of Isaiah, the extreme views of some scholars in that direction notwithstanding. This point was first elaborated systematically by Bernhard Stade (1881) who maintained the unity of 9-14 but insisted that it must be dated long after Zechariah, probably as late as the latter part of the wars of Alexander's successions, the Diadochi (ca. 280 B.C.). The reason for this was the reference to Greece in Zechariah 9:13 and to what appears to be a series of conflicts involving either Alexander, the Diadochi, or even the Ptolemies of the third century B.C. (Zech 9:1-10).[43]

Once the lateness of the second part of the book had been conceded, it was an easy matter for some scholars to search for a Maccabean or even later milieu for its origin. The parable of the shepherds (11:4-17), for example, was thought to be based on three actual kings, ranging from the Israelite kings Zechariah, Shallum, and Menahem (the preexilic view)[44] to the Jewish priests Simon, Menelaus, and Lysimachus of the second century.[45] The very latitude of interpretation suggested by these extreme positions on just one pericope is typical of the manner in which the whole section is dealt with. There is little wonder that attempts to date the various oracles on the basis of perceived historical settings have met with such little favor.

A little more moderation prevails in contemporary study of the matter of the unity of Zechariah but, as already indicated, virtually no critical scholar accepts the authorship of all the book by

---

41. This view was popularized especially by Leonhard Bertholdt. See Otzen, *Studien über Deuterosacharia*, 20-22.
42. Otto Eissfeldt, *The Old Testament: An Introduction* (Oxford: Basil Blackwell, 1965), 435.
43. Otzen, *Studien über Deuterosacharia*, 27-29.
44. So F. Hitzig, cited by Otzen, *Studien über Deuterosacharia*, 24.
45. So Willy Staerk, cited by Otzen, *Studien über Deuterosacharia*, 29.

Zechariah. Some, such as Hill[46] and Hanson,[47] come close by at least dating the two parts at about the same time. Others admit the close dependence of 9-14 on 1-8, attributing it to an early "Zechariah school," or something of that sort.[48] There are a few who still regard 9-14 as essentially a hodge-podge collection of originally independent pieces, a collection whose organization and coherence, if any, are to be attributed to sensitive and creative editorializing. Artur Weiser, who embraces this position, does admit that "it is not absolutely necessary to conjecture this since the discrepancies can also be explained by the author being dependent on earlier materials."[49]

The remainder of the proponents of a Deutero-Zechariah position hold tenaciously either to a preexilic setting for some of the material, with the rest in the era of Zechariah or later,[50] or to a late, post-Zechariah date, even as late as the Maccabean period.[51] Those views are, however, dwindling in support for reasons to be adduced next and in the following section.

In his important critical commentary H. G. Mitchell, though a staunch advocate of a multiple authorship thesis, marshaled some strong support in favor of the unity of Zechariah, if only for the purpose of exposing its weakness.[52] He particularly cited G. L. Robinson, *The Prophecies of Zechariah* (1896), who compiled an exhaustive list of items that he believed betrayed common authorship. Many of these, upon closer examination, are doubtless of little value because of their generalities, but the following appear to be noteworthy and to have elicited from Mitchell some rather unconvincing rebuttal.

Robinson points out five major areas of comparison. First of all, the two parts, he says, contain the same fundamental ideas such as "an unusually deep spiritual tone"; a similar attitude of hope and expectation regarding the return of the nation, the habitation of Jerusalem, the building of the Temple, a messianic hope, and God's uni-

---

46. Andrew E. Hill, "Dating Second Zechariah: A Linguistic Reexamination," *HAR* 6 (1982): 132.
47. Hanson, *The Dawn of Apocalyptic*, 27.
48. Carroll Stuhlmueller, *Haggai & Zechariah*, ITC (Grand Rapids: Eerdmans, 1988), 47; Rex. A. Mason, "The Relation of Zech 9-14 to Proto-Zechariah," *ZAW* 88 (1976): 227-39.
49. Artur Weiser, *Introduction to the Old Testament* (London: Darton, Longman & Todd, 1961), 274. For suggestions as to these "earlier materials," see M. Delcor, "Les Sources du Deutéro-Zacharie et Ses Procedes D'Emprunt," *RB* 59 (1952): 385-411. Delcor does, however, view 9-14 as a unity, a work composed by a single author/editor (p. 411).
50. Otzen, *Studien über Deuterosacharia*.
51. Marco Treves, "Conjectures Concerning the Date and Authorship of Zechariah IX-XIV," *VT* 13 (1963): 196-207.
52. H. G. Mitchell, *A Critical and Exegetical Commentary on Haggai and Zechariah*, ICC (Edinburgh: T. & T. Clark, 1912), 242-44.

versal providence; the prophet's attitude toward Judah; and his attitude toward the nations.

Second, Robinson notes common "peculiarities of thought." Specifically he lists "the habit of dwelling on the same thought," the tendency to expand a fundamental thought into five parallel clauses (cf. 1:17; 3:8; 6:13; etc.), the use made of the cardinal number two, the resort to symbolic actions, and the habit of drawing lessons from the past.

He next cites "certain peculiarities of diction and style" and offers an extensive list, many of which, to be sure, are questionable. That many others are significant is tacitly admitted by Mitchell, who has to resort to assuming interpolations in a few of the passages that Robinson adduces, fewer examples of other types than Robinson lists, and the possibility that many of the similarities may be accounted for by copyists' mistakes.

The last compelling comparison Robinson draws is the citation by both parts of Zechariah of the same earlier prophets. This Mitchell dismisses by observing that "although most of the books with which parallels may be found are the same, the number of coincidences with some of them is very different."[53] He fails to give any specific examples that would support his objection.[54]

Joyce Baldwin offers many of the same evidences for unity as propounded by Robinson, as well as a few more.[55] She draws attention to similarity of phraseology between 2:10 and 9:9 and between 7:14 and 9:8, for example. Other fruitful comparisons are in 6:10, 11, 13; 8:4, 5; 14:5; and 14:9 where, in each case, there is repetition of a key idea. The predilection for the vocative is common to both parts as well.

Though the arguments for divided authorship are quite substantial, as the previous survey shows, they are not insuperable and, in fact, even at the level of vocabulary, style, motifs, and themes a strong case can be made for the contrary and traditional persuasion that the entire book originated from the pen of one man, its attributive author, and from the last quarter of the sixth century. Recent studies of a more rhetorical-literary kind are even more devastating to the prevailing source-critical approaches, threatening even to dismantle them entirely, at least in the form in which they have appeared in the

---

53. Ibid., 244.
54. Other scholars have also drawn attention to connections between Zechariah 1-8 and 9-14. In addition to those mentioned by Robinson, B. S. Childs provides several others in his *Introduction to the Old Testament As Scripture* (London: SCM, 1979), 482-83.
55. Baldwin, *Haggai, Zechariah, Malachi*, 68-69.

past two centuries. It is appropriate now to turn to some of these newer analyses.

It is impossible here to do more than focus on two or three recent studies of the form and structure of Zechariah and/or its major sections. This will be accomplished by looking first at Zechariah 1-8 as addressed by Meyers and Meyers, 9-14 by Lamarche, and the synthesis of the whole proposed by Baldwin.

The very first sentence of the lengthy section of their introduction to Haggai-Zechariah 1-8 entitled "Literary Considerations" reveals the position of Meyers and Meyers (hereafter, the Meyers) concerning the relationship of Haggai to Zechariah and the unity of Zechariah 1-8: "Haggai and the first eight chapters of the canonical book of Zechariah belong together as a composite work."[56] They then proceed to build their case by first of all citing common themes, such as reorganization of national life and institutions, common casts of characters, and common sets of questions and answers addressed to and responded to by the respective prophets.

The unity goes beyond this in their view, however, for the Meyers suggest a time close after the last date in Zechariah (Dec. 7, 518 B.C.) when a redaction of the whole collection took place. This must have preceded the Temple dedication of 516 or 515, because that event is not mentioned, but the completion of the Temple, on the other hand, may have given the prophets the sanction that would allow their works to be rounded off and combined as one publication. This redactionary work explains, in their opinion, the mixing of genres within and between the books so as to produce an unmistakable coherence and pattern.

Though admitting that the redactor's identity can never be known for certain, the Meyers are quite comfortable in attributing the final work to Zechariah himself (cf. Zech. 7:4; 8:1). The interlocking of the chronological data of both books was a device he used to provide a unifying structure, and it is of interest to note that, though there are eight date formulae, there are only seven dates, two in Haggai being the same (Hag. 2:19, 20). This repeated date is in the center of the list of dates, and it marks the Temple refoundation

---

56. Meyers and Meyers, *Haggai, Zechariah 1-8*, p. xliv. To show how far modern scholarship has come in 40 years in terms of an essentially unified view of Zechariah's composition of chaps. 1-8, see Donald F. Robinson, "A Suggested Analysis of Zechariah 1-8," *ATR* 33 (1951): 65-70. Robinson limits the "authentic" material to 1:1-7, 14b-17; 2:6-13; 3:7-10; 4:6b-10a; 6:9–8:23 (pp. 67-68).

ceremony. Moreover, the pattern 7 + 1 for the dates establishes a pattern followed throughout the collection. For example, seven of the date formulae have month/day/year, whereas an eighth (Zech. 1:1) omits it; seven dates are in Darius's second year and an eighth is in his fourth; and seven dates precede the unit for which they provide information, whereas one (Hag. 1:15) follows. The pattern 7 + 1 has other applications, to be noted later.

The Meyers next point out correspondences between Haggai and Zechariah 7-8, beginning with the date formula in Haggai 1:1 and Zechariah 7:1, the only two in which the regnal year of the Persian king is the first item. Then in a chart they list 17 more features shared by Haggai 1-2 and Zechariah 7-8.[57] Some of these may not be significant (e.g., "be strong" or "blessing"), but the cumulative effect is quite impressive.

As for Zechariah 1-8 itself, the Meyers admit the threefold division of 1:1-6, 1:7–6:15, and 7:1–8:23 but see interconnections of style and subject matter that bind the whole together. Thus, part one is introductory narrative, part two is primarily vision material, and part three oracular. The three parts appear to reflect chronological development as well, as the date formulae make clear. Though narration dominates in part one, however, there is also oracle; visions are central in part two, but there are also oracles; and oracles prevail in part three, but not without narration.[58]

Phraseology and vocabulary also are distributed repetitively among the three sections. Thus between parts one and three are such words as "word of YHWH came to" (1:1 and 7:1, 4; 8:1, 8), "earlier prophets" (1:4, 5, 6 and 7:7, 12), "proclaim" (1:4 and 7:7, 13), ancestors (1:4-6 and 7:11-12), divine anger/wrath (1:2 and 7:12), "Thus spoke YHWH of Hosts" (1:3, 4 and 7:9; 8:2, 3, 4, 6, 7, 9, 14, 19, 20, 23), and "decided to" (1:6 and 8:14, 15). The list of commonalities between parts two and three is even more impressive. A few (out of 14 listed by the Meyers) are: "seventy years" (1:12 and 7:5), Jerusalem inhabited (2:8 and 7:7), holy mountain (2:17 and 8:3), "They will be my people" (2:15 and 8:8), and Yehud as holy land (2:16 and 8:22-23).

Within part two (1:7–6:15) the Meyers have observed a further 7 + 1 pattern in the distribution of the visions. As is well known, there are eight of these arranged (so the Meyers) in three subsets: three (1-3) at the beginning, three (5-7) at the end, and two ("prophetic" vision and number 4) in the middle. This arrangement is defended by

---

57. Meyers and Meyers, *Haggai, Zechariah 1-8*, xlix. For further support of the Haggai-Zechariah 7-8 connection, see David J. Clark, "Discourse Structure in Zechariah 7.1–8.23," *BT* 36 (1985): 334-35.
58. Meyers and Meyers, *Haggai, Zechariah 1-8*, li, chart 4.

the parallels drawn between the first three and the last three visions, namely, subject matter (e.g., horses in 1 and 7), internal structure, and language. Moreover, the units of visions 5-7 are in inverse order to those same units in visions 1-3. This focuses attention on the two middle visions which become, for that reason, the heart of the discourse.

That central point becomes clear also by considering the purview of the visions. By means of concentric circles the Meyers graphically demonstrate that the outer circle (visions 1 and 7) is universal in its outlook, with number 1 emphasizing God's omniscience and number 7 His omnipotence. The next circle (visions 2 and 6) is international, stressing Judah and the empires (2) and Yehud and Persia (6). The third circle (visions 3 and 5) is national in character, dealing with Jerusalem's territory (3) and the self-rule of Yehud (5). The center then (prophetic vision + 4) is Jerusalem, specifically the Temple and leadership.

In an admittedly arbitrary way, the Meyers have not included Zech. 3:1-7 as one of the numbered visions, though they offer reasons for the omission. Primarily it is because this vision lacks the standard formulaic language of the others and because of the 7 + 1 pattern that seems to be a dominant element of Zechariah's composition. Yet, it is clearly a vision and, in fact, is complementary to vision 4. Therefore it cannot be eliminated entirely.

As for part three (7:1–8:23), the Meyers point out the literary integrity of these two chapters by themselves and also their relationship to Haggai as framework for Zechariah 1-6. They have their own date formula (7:1) but lack visions, clear signs of their independence of part two, but with part one (1:1-6) they share a retrospective interest and with part two (1:7–6:15) common oracular language. There can be no question therefore of the unity of the third part and of its intrinsic connection to both part one and part two.

All in all, the Meyers have made a bold and creative statement concerning the unity of Zechariah 1-8 and its relationship to Haggai. Whether their analysis will stand the test of rigid criticism remains to be seen, but its general position is likely to prove correct.

It is unfortunate that they fail to follow up their own method by applying it both to Zechariah 9-14 (which they may indeed do in their forthcoming commentary) and to the whole matter of the unity of 1-14, something they have almost dismissed out of hand.[59] Happily, however, Paul Lamarche has redressed the first lack in his revolutionary study, *Zacharie IV-XIV: Structure Litteraire et Messianisme* (1961).[60]

---

59. Ibid., ix.
60. See note 20 above.

Of particular interest here is his rhetorical-critical analysis of this section, an analysis that has led him to conclude that these chapters are all of one piece, a unity designed and composed in such an intricate manner as to leave no doubt as to its integrity.[61] The method employed or, better, discovered in the composition itself, is that of chiasmus, an arrangement by which a pattern of inverse relationships forms the organization of the piece in question.[62]

To illustrate his approach Lamarche turns first to Zechariah 14:1-15.[63] He then finds the structure a, b, c, d, e, d', c', b', a', with vv. 1-2*a* and 12-15 forming the outer envelope, 2*a-b* and 10*b*-11 the next inner, 3-5 and 9-10*a* the next, 6 and 7*b*-8 next, and finally 7*a* in the center. That focal point is the unique day of YHWH, around which the entire passage revolves.

After reviewing earlier approaches (pp. 20-23), Lamarche presents his own method (pp. 23-33) before applying it to each of the pericopes of the section (pp. 34-104) and setting out his conclusions in terms of both structure and meaning (pp. 105-23). It is clearly impossible to do more than consider the former of these—the literary structure—at this point, though some of the exegetical insights will receive due attention in the commentary.

Lamarche begins by noting chiastic structures in the last part of the section, chapters 12-14. He suggests a parallelism between 12:1-9 and 14:1-15, one confirmed by several verbal correspondences (12:3 and 14:2; 12:6 and 14:10; 12:9 and 14:12). Next, there clearly is an inclusio surrounding 12:10–13:1 and 13:7-9 (cf. 12:10 and 13:7; 13:1 and 13:9; 12:10 and 13:9). As for 13:7-9, which most critics say is misplaced here, belonging rather to the shepherd text of chapter 11, Lamarche replies that it is perfectly in place here, both text-critically and literary-critically, as his chiasm shows beyond question.[64]

Turning to chapters 9-11, Lamarche cites the pairing of 9:1-8 with

---

61. Lamarche, *Zacharie IX-XIV*, 154-55.
62. For an important but unpublished critique of Lamarche's chiastic approach, see G. Michael Butterworth, "The Structure of the Book of Zechariah" (diss. for King's College, London, 1989), esp. 165-94. See also the book reviews by F. Buck, *CBQ* 24 (1962): 319-20; J. A. Emerton, *JTS* 14 (1963): 113-16; W. Harrelson, *JBL* 82 (1963): 116-17; R. Tournay, *RB* 69 (1962): 588-92. Meredith Kline ("The Structure of the Book of Zechariah," *JETS* 34 [1991]: 192-93) has also suggested a structural interlocking on the basis of what he describes as "an intricate triple-hinge mechanism." So sophisticated is this arrangement that there is no doubt, he says, that the entire book must be "attributed to an original master for the whole work."
63. Lamarche, *Zacharie IX-XIV*, 11.
64. Ibid., 108.

14:16-21; 9:9-10 with 11:4-17; and 9:11–10:1 with 10:3*b*–11:3. The brief "idol-oracle" of 10:2-3*a* is left as the centerpiece.

Lamarche has clearly made his point about the unity of 9-11 and 12-14 respectively, but he goes beyond that to show the unity between them established through a remarkable integration of the two chiastic structures. As pointed out above, he has linked 9:1-8 and 14:16-21, providing thereby a bracket around the whole of the material. Both pericopes deal with the nations, the neighboring and the distant as well. 9:9-10 (arrival and description of the king) and 11:4-17 (rejection of the shepherd by the people) correspond within 9-11 but also with a matched pair in 12-14, namely, 12:10–13:1 (the piercing of the representative of YHWH) and 13:7-9 (the smiting of the shepherd). Whereas this second element (9:9-10) immediately follows the first in chapters 9-11, in 12-14 it (12:10–13:1) is third; i.e., there is an inversion of the second and third components. It follows, then, that the third element in 9-11 (9:11–10:1) and its companion (10:3*b*–11:3) correspond to the second element in 12-14 (12:1-9 and 14:1-15). The middle text of 12-14 concerns the suppression of idols and false prophets (13:2-6), precisely the message of the centerpoint of 11-13 (10:2-3*a*).

The chart of the preceding (without the content labels) is as follows:

A 9:1-8			A' 14:16-21		
B 9:9-10	B' 11:4-17		C" 12:1-9	C‴ 14:1-15	
C 9:11–10:1	C'10:3*b*–11:3		B" 12:10–13:1	B‴ 13:7-9	
D 10:2-3*a*			D' 13:2-6		

It is readily apparent that a cohesive structure exists in which nothing is omitted and to which nothing need be added. As Lamarche concludes, one can hardly account for such symmetry and integration apart from single authorship.[65]

Between them the Meyers and Lamarche appear to have made redoubtable cases for the unity of Zechariah 1-8 and 9-14, respectively. But what may be said of the unity of the entire book? To our knowledge no one has yet attempted a full-scale investigation of the problem along rhetorical-critical lines, though some efforts have been made in the area of linguistic and statistical analyses.[66] An

---

65. Ibid., 106.
66. See, e.g., Yehuda T. Radday and Dieter Wickmann, "The Unity of Zechariah Examined in the Light of Statistical Linguistics," *ZAW* 87 (1975): 30-55; Andrew E. Hill (see n. 46 above); Stephen L. Portnoy and David L. Petersen, "Biblical Texts and Statistical Analysis: Zechariah and Beyond," *JBL* 103 (1984): 11-21; James A. Hartle, "The Literary Unity of Zechariah," *JETS* 35 (1992): 145-57.

exception is the brief statement of Joyce Baldwin in her commentary,[67] but her remarks are quite preliminary and need considerable testing and elaboration.

Baldwin draws attention to chiastic patterns within Zechariah 1-6, suggesting that the eight visions are arranged abbccbba, with the theological climax in the middle, the fourth and fifth (so also the Meyers). Moreover, the introductory call of 1:1-6 is repeated in the sermons of 7:4-14 and 8:9-17, themselves part of a chiastic pattern. The climax of 1-8, Baldwin shows, is the flocking of the nations to Jerusalem (8:20-23), a theme repeated in 14:16-21. Other chiasms she adduces are in 1:14-17; 8:9-13; 10:10, 11; and 14:1-15, where the misfortunes of vv. 1-6 are balanced by the joys of vv. 7-14. On the whole, when linguistic, literary, and theological aspects are given careful and sympathetic consideration, there is more to favor the unity of the book than its division.

As far as literary form is concerned, the same confusion in the matter as has marked the study of Haggai also prevails in the study of Zechariah. A glance at the two major editions of the MT will show that BHK regards all of Zechariah as prose, whereas BHS takes the following to be poetic: 1:3*b*, 5-6, 14*b*-17; 2:8*b*-14; 3:7-10; 4:6*b*-10*a*; 5:4; 6:12*b*-13; 7:5, 9-10; 8:2-13, 20-22; 9:9-10, 11-17; 10:1-12; 11:1-3, 17; 14:1-19. The distinction between Hebrew prose and poetry is notoriously difficult to make, so one ought not be dogmatic, especially when the major hallmarks of poetry, such as parallelism, are either missing or poorly developed.

Andrew Hill has examined the matter to some extent, especially in chapters 9-14, and concludes on the basis of the "prose-particle" method of Andersen and Freedman that "Haggai, Zechariah 1-8, and Malachi are representative of Hebrew prose, while Second Zechariah appears to be a mixture of poetry (chapter 9) and prose (chapters 10-14)."[68] Portnoy and Petersen basically concur,[69] though they broaden the range of poetry to include most of chapters 9-11. It seems, then, that though poetic elements do occur sporadically throughout the book, especially in the great eschatological oracles of chapters 9-11, Zechariah has composed his message primarily in prose.

As a result of the literary/rhetorical analyses just surveyed, it is apparent that several modes of outlining the material come to mind. For the purpose of dealing with the units in a manageable way, how-

---

67. Baldwin, *Haggai, Zechariah, Malachi*, 80-81.
68. Hill, "Dating Second Zechariah: A Linguistic Reexamination," 108.
69. Portnoy and Petersen, "Biblical Texts and Statistical Analysis: Zechariah and Beyond," 20.

ever, some of the interlocking patterns that appear to be plausible cannot be followed in the format of a commentary. The following outline will therefore reveal the structure around which the exposition proceeds.

Part One: The Night Visions (1:1–6:15)

1. Introduction (1:1-6)

Visions (1:7–6:8)

2. Vision One: The Four Horsemen (1:7-17)
   A. Introduction to the Visions (1:7)
   B. Content of the Vision (1:8)
   C. Interpretation of the Vision (1:9-15)
   D. Oracle of Response (1:16-17)
3. Vision Two: The Four Horns (1:18-21 [HB 2:1-4)])
   A. Content of the Vision (1:18, 20 [HB 2:1, 3])
   B. Interpretation of the Vision (1:19, 21 [HB 2:2, 4])
4. Vision Three: The Surveyor (2:1-13 [HB 2:5-17])
   A. Content of the Vision (2:1-2 [HB 2:5-6])
   B. Interpretation of the Vision (2:3-5 [HB 2:7-9])
   C. Oracle of Response (2:6-13 [HB 2:10-17])
      1. Warning to Babylon (2:6-9 [HB 2:10-13])
      2. Blessing for Judah (2:10-13 [HB 2:14-17])
5. Vision Four: The Priest (3:1-10)
   A. Content of the Vision (3:1-5)
   B. Interpretation of the Vision (3:6-7)
   C. Oracle of Response (3:8-10)
6. Vision Five: The Menorah (4:1-14)
   A. Content of the Vision (4:1-3)
   B. Interpretation of the Vision (4:4-6, 11-14)
   C. Oracle of Response (4:7-10)
7. Vision Six: The Flying Scroll (5:1-4)
   A. Content of the Vision (5:1-2)
   B. Interpretation of the Vision (5:3-4)
8. Vision Seven: The Ephah (5:5-11)
   A. Content of the Vision (5:5-7)
   B. Interpretation of the Vision (5:8-11)
9. Vision Eight: The Chariots (6:1-8)
   A. Content of the Vision (6:1-4)
   B. Interpretation of the Vision (6:5-8)
10. Concluding Oracle (6:9-15)
    A. The Selection of the Priest (6:9-12*a*)
    B. The Significance of the Priest (6:12*b*-15)

Part Two: Oracles Concerning Hypocritical Fasting (7:1–8:23)

1. Introduction and Concern (7:1-3)
2. Hypocrisy of Fasting (7:4-14)
   A. Criticism of Fasting (7:4-7)
   B. Instruction Concerning Fasting (7:8-14)
      1. Basis for Genuine Fasting (7:8-10)
      2. Rebellion Against YHWH's Word (7:11-12)
      3. Judgment Because of Rebellion (7:13-14)
3. Blessing of True Fasting (8:1-23)
   A. Restoration of Jerusalem (8:1-8)
   B. Prosperity of Jerusalem (8:9-13)
   C. Expectations for Jerusalem (8:14-17)
   D. Pilgrimage to Jerusalem (8:18-23)

Part Three: Oracle Concerning YHWH'S Sovereignty (9:1–11:17)

1. Coming of the True King (9:1-17)
   A. Historical and Eschatological Preparation for His Coming (9:1-8)
   B. Historical and Eschatological Event of His Coming (9:9-10)
   C. Deliverance and Conquest of His People (9:11-17)
2. Restoration of the True People (10:1-12)
   A. Rejection of Judah's Wicked Leadership (10:1-3*a*)
   B. Selection of Judah's Righteous Leadership (10:3*b*-7)
   C. Judah and the Second Exodus (10:8-12)
3. History and Future of Judah's Wicked Kings (11:1-17)
   A. Summation of Their Judgment (11:1-3)
   B. The Prophet as a Shepherd(-king) (11:4-14)
      1. His Charge Because of Judah's Wicked Kings (11:4-6)
      2. His Enactment of YHWH's Rejection of the Wicked Kings (11:7-11)
      3. His Fee for Serving as the Shepherd (11:12-14)
   C. The Evil Shepherd(-king) to Come (11:15-17)

Part Four: Oracle Concerning Israel (12:1–14:21)

1. Repentance of Judah (12:1-14)
   A. Security of God's People (12:1-9)
   B. Mourning of God's People (12:10-14)
2. Refinement of Judah (13:1-9)
   A. Cleansing of God's People (13:1-6)
   B. Preservation of God's People (13:7-9)

3. Sovereignty of YHWH (14:1-21)
   A. Deliverance of His People (14:1-8)
      1. Their Tribulation (14:1-2)
      2. Their Salvation (14:3-8)
   B. Exaltation of His People (14:9-21)
      1. Their Security (14:9-11)
      2. Their Victory over Enemies (14:12-15)
      3. Their Place as a Center of Pilgrimage (14:16-21)

DISTINCTIVE TEACHING

The overall message of Zechariah, though occasionally obscure, is largely clear and plain. The prophet is concerned to comfort his discouraged and pessimistic compatriots, who are in the process of rebuilding their Temple and restructuring their community but who view their efforts as making little difference in the present and offering no hope for the future. With his eye on both the temporal task at hand and the eschatological day to come, he challenges members of the restored remnant to go to work with the full understanding that what they do, feeble as it appears, will be crowned with success when YHWH, true to His covenant word, will bring to pass the fulfillment of His ancient promises to the fathers.

The media through which he communicates this word of encouragement and triumph are those of apocalyptic vision and interwoven and separately articulated oracles of eschatological salvation. Thus, horses and horns, measuring lines and menorahs, communicate symbolically that YHWH's house will be built (Zech 1:16), His cities made prosperous (1:17) and secure (7:5). The nations will join in pilgrimage to them (2:11), a pilgrimage that will lead to the dwelling place of YHWH, which He will bring to completion by His own might and power (4:6-10). Evil will be removed from the land (5:8-11), so that the son of David might reign in peace as priest and king (6:8, 12-13).

The hypocrisy of the present day (7:6) will become a thing of the past, for YHWH will first judge His people (7:14), then bring them back to the land (8:8) so that they might worship Him in truth and righteousness (8:14-17). So mighty will be His display of grace to His people that many nations will take note and desire to become one with them (8:20-23). Johan A. Burger sees two levels of meaning in Zechariah, the particularistic and the universalistic. He sees them, however, in contradiction to each other, with the latter the only appropriate one for the Christian. These bipolar themes are, indeed, the central foci of the book, but that they are in contradiction is without theological basis. Zechariah views Israel as the special object of

YHWH's saving grace, but in the development of eschatological hope Israel becomes the vehicle by which the nations come to faith as well. Thus the particularistic gives way to the universalistic.[70]

Those who do not respond to YHWH's call will be like His enemies of old, whom He reduced to ignominy and disgrace (9:1-7). Led by their conquering king, the armies of YHWH will establish universal peace (9:9-10). Their ability to do this will be predicated on YHWH's mighty arm. For as in days of old when He brought His redeemed people out of Egypt, He will repeat this act so that they might once more enter the land of promise over which they exercise dominion (10:8-12). The wicked rulers of the past (chap. 11) will be replicated in the future, but not for long, for they will be replaced by the godly house of David (12:7-8). From that house one figure will stand out, a pierced One who will be a nexus of repentance and forgiveness (12:10). YHWH Himself will purify His people (13:1) and restore them to covenant oneness with Himself (13:9). Then He Himself will come to deliver His beleagured people once and for all and to rule over them and over all nations that in that day will make pilgrimage to Jerusalem and offer homage to His sovereignty (14:9, 16).

This is not the message of either a "hierocratic realist" or an "apocalyptic idealist." It is, rather, that of a man of God who has his feet firmly planted in both worlds—that of the struggling, disappointed, disillusioned, postexilic Jewish community and that of the glorious redeemed kingdom of YHWH yet to come.[71] The one, important as it is in the here and now, will give way to the other. It is sufficient for the people of the remnant to know this and, motivated by it, to be about the business of serving their God in the day in which He placed them.

TRANSMISSION OF THE TEXT

The text of Zechariah is in excellent repair, there being but few places (to be noted in the commentary) where the MT may be improved from the versions or other Hebrew traditions. In no case does the material appear to be dislocated, either from text-critical or internal considerations.

---

70. Johan A. Burger, "Two Levels of Meaning in the Book of Zechariah," *ThEv* 14 (1981): 12-17.
71. Zechariah represents a position described by Patterson as "emergent apocalyptic." See Richard D. Patterson, *Nahum, Habbakuk, Zephaniah*, WEC (Chicago: Moody, 1991), 288.

H. G. Mitchell has provided an exhaustive list[72] of textual mod-
ifications on the basis of "additions, omissions and distortions
through the fault of careless or ignorant transcribers."[73] For the most
part the items he lists rest on purely conjectural emendations, an
approach that enjoys little favor today, though some must and will be
given serious consideration in the commentary.

Taeke Jansma has made a comprehensive study of all the textual
data of Zechariah 9-14, something that sorely needs to be done for the
first eight chapters as well.[74] Again, his evidence would tend to support the conclusion stated above that the MT is in a remarkably good
state of preservation and that only in extremely superficial (and
probably, in most cases, tendentious) ways do the manuscripts and
versions depart from it. In conclusion, Jansma's observation about
the relative role and significance of text-criticism in general is worth
noting: "Judging and weighing is the work of exegesis. Every text-
critical work only goes part of the way. It may find its completion by
an exegetical study."[75] To that task we must now turn our attention.

---

72. Mitchell, *A Critical and Exegetical Commentary on Haggai and Zechariah*,
    86-97, 222-31.
73. Ibid., 85.
74. Taeke Jansma, *Inquiry into the Hebrew Text and the Ancient Versions of
    Zechariah IX-XIV* (Leiden: Brill, 1949).
75. Ibid., 59.

PART 1
The Night Visions (1:1–6:15)

1
Introduction (1:1-6)

This rather lengthy introduction is clearly intended to serve as a preface to all the night visions of chapters 1–6, if not to the entire book. This is evident from the fact that 1:7 is also an introduction, either to the first vision (1:8-17) or, more likely, to all eight because none of the others has a typical introductory statement.[1] As for the occasion and purpose of the entire complex of visions, Halpern suggests that they have to do primarily with the foundation of the second Temple.[2] On the whole this is most plausible, though Zechariah's intention clearly goes beyond this to include major eschatological themes, such as messianic rule and universal salvation. In fact, Siebeneck goes so far as to say that this section (with chaps. 7-8) "is devoted almost exclusively to the messianic promise,"[3] perhaps also an overstatement. Nolting proposes that the overriding theme of the vision section is the coming of the King. This seems to be a more accurate assessment.[4] Petersen maintains that the visions "stand somewhere between utopian social vision and concrete physical and social detail." Zechariah provides through the visions, according to

---

1. Theophane Chary, *Aggée-Zacharie, Malachie* (Paris: Librairie Lecoffre, 1969), 53.
2. Baruch Halpern, "The Ritual Background of Zechariah's Temple Song," *CBQ* 40 (1978): 169.
3. Robert T. Siebeneck, "The Messianism of Aggeus and Proto-Zacharias," *CBQ* 19 (1957): 318.
4. Paul F. Nolting, "The Eight Night Visions of Zechariah," *JTh* 26 (1986): 18.

Petersen, "a theological perspective relevant to a new situation, that of a Yahwism without independent territorial state."[5] This is probably too much a "this-worldly" interpretation.

Translation

¹In the eighth month of the second year of Darius the Word of YHWH came to the prophet *Zechariah, son of Berechiah son of Iddo, saying, ²"YHWH was very angry with your fathers. ³Therefore say to them, 'Thus says YHWH of hosts, "Turn to Me," *says YHWH of hosts, "and I will turn to you," says YHWH of hosts.' ⁴Do not be like your fathers, to whom the former prophets called out, saying, 'Thus says YHWH of hosts, "Turn now *from your evil ways and deeds," but they would not listen or obey Me,' says YHWH. ⁵As for your fathers, where are they? And do the prophets live forever? ⁶But did My words and statutes which I commanded my servants the prophets not overtake *your fathers?" Then they turned, saying, "As YHWH of hosts decided to do to us in accordance with our ways and deeds, thus He has done."

Exegesis and Exposition

The second year of Darius Hystaspes was 520 B.C., and the eighth month, translated into the Julian/Gregorian calendar, was October-November (see Introduction to Zechariah, p. 61). This vision came to Zechariah about a month before the prophet Haggai received his final vision on the twenty-fourth day of the ninth month, December 18, 520 (Hag. 2:10, 20). Why the prophet failed to include the day of the month in his dating formula is unclear because he does so in his other two uses of the formula (1:7; 7:1). It may be, as Carol and Eric Meyers suggest, that it is because this is the only date of Zechariah that falls within Haggai's chronology and that greater specificity was not required.[6]

Zechariah, here identified as the son of Berechiah and grandson of Iddo, is referred to otherwise only in Ezra (5:1; 6:14) and Nehemiah (12:16) in the OT. Both Ezra and Nehemiah imply that the prophet is the son of Iddo, neither one mentioning Berechiah, father of Zechariah. It is likely that Berechiah died young and that Zechariah was reared by his grandfather. Zechariah was brought by his grandfather from Babylonian exile and succeeded him in the office of priest (Neh. 12:16).[7] Since Iddo was a contemporary of Zerubbabel at the time of

5. David L. Petersen, "Zechariah's Visions: A Theological Perspective," *VT* 34 (1984): 198, 206.
6. Carol L. Meyers and Eric M. Meyers, *Haggai, Zechariah 1-8*, AB 25 B (Garden City, N.Y.: Doubleday, 1987), 90-91.
7. Merrill F. Unger, *Zechariah* (Grand Rapids: Zondervan, 1963), 19-20.

the "first return" (538 B.C.), Zechariah was likely quite young in 520, being, in fact, a contemporary of Joiakim, son of the first postexilic priest Joshua (Neh. 12:10, 12-16). Joiakim's own son Eliashib was high priest in the time of Nehemiah (Neh. 3:1; cf. 13:4), about 445 B.C., so Joiakim's priesthood (and thus Zechariah's ministry) very likely lasted well after 520, perhaps as late as the end of the first quarter of the fifth century.[8]

A more perplexing and serious problem regarding Zechariah is the possibility of his being identified by Jesus in the gospels (Matt. 23:35; Luke 11:51) as the "Zechariah son of Berachiah" who was slain between the sanctuary and the altar. The only OT reference to such a martyrdom appears to refer to a prophet Zechariah who was a son of Jehoiada the priest, a story to be dated no later than 800 B.C. (2 Chron. 24:20-22). A further complication is that there was also a Zechariah son of Jeberechiah who was an acquaintance of the prophet Isaiah (Isa. 8:2). Though he is not described in Isaiah as a prophet, it is likely that he was, particularly because he served as a witness, along with Uriah the priest, to the message YHWH was delivering to Isaiah. The name Jeberechiah is clearly not a difficulty, being but a fuller writing of Berechiah. It may be this man, then, to whom Jesus referred.

The problem with this explanation, of course, is that there is no record of the violent death of this Zechariah. One might suppose that Jehoiada the priest had a son Berechiah, no longer known apart from the NT, and that it was his son Zechariah who was murdered. The great age of Jehoiada at his death (130 years; 2 Chron. 24:15) would suggest that Zechariah was his grandson and not son, particularly if the Zechariah of 2 Chron. 24:21 is the same as the prophet who tutored young Uzziah around 800 B.C. (2 Chron. 26:5). As Matthew suggests, Jesus is referring to the first (Abel) and last (Zechariah) prophetic martyrs in terms of their canonical appearance, Gen. 4 and 2 Chron. 24 respectively, and not as the first and last chronologically.[9]

The only other explanation that avoids the assumption of pure error is that Zechariah the prophet of our book was martyred eventually and that this fact went unrecorded in either the OT or subsequent Jewish tradition. This obviously is most unlikely.

8. Cross argues that papponymy (naming after one's grandfather) was at work in the lists of postexilic priests, so that Eliashib of Nehemiah's time was actually the great-grandson of Joiakim and not his son. Cross nevertheless dates Joiakim's birth ca. 545 B.C., in line with my own proposal; Frank M. Cross, "A Reconstruction of the Judean Restoration," *JBL* 94 (1975): 4-18.
9. Wilhelm Rudolph, *Haggai-Sacharja 1-8—Sacharja 9-14—Maleachi*, KAT (Gütersloh: Gütersloher Verlagshaus Gerd Mohn, 1976), 68.

The first part of the prophet's message is a solemn exhortation to learn from history. One can almost describe Zechariah's remarks in 1:2-6 as a sermon, for, as Mason has shown, it bears the characteristics of the *Gattung* "sermon," as do other passages in the book (e.g., 7:4-7, 11-14; 8:1-8, 9-13, 14-17).[10] YHWH had been extremely displeased with the generations past (v. 2), for they had stubbornly refused to heed the appeal of the prophets of old who had in vain pleaded with them to turn to YHWH that he might turn to them (vv. 3-4). The verb שׁוּב (*šûb*, "turn"), used three times in vv. 3-4, has a strong covenant connotation.[11] This is confirmed by the technical terms דָּבָר (*dābār*, "word") and חֹק (*ḥōq*, "statute") of v. 6. These nouns refer regularly to the stipulations of the covenant made with Israel at Sinai (cf. Deut. 4:1-2; 17:19; 27:8, 10; Neh. 9:8, 13, 14).[12]

To turn from YHWH, therefore, is to break covenant with Him and to turn to evil ways and deeds (v. 4). In a covenant context "ways" and "deeds" refer not just to incidental sins but to a whole pattern of rebellion and disloyalty. The reference to the former prophets and their cry of repentance echoes the verdict of the history of the northern tribes following the collapse of Samaria under the Assyrians in 722 B.C. The defeat of Israel, the historian had said, came about because Israel had sinned against YHWH by "fearing other gods" and "walking in the statutes" (חֻקִּים, *ḥuqqîm*) of the nations (2 Kings 17:7-8). This act of treason was denounced by the prophets who had urged the nation to "turn" (שׁוּב) from her "evil ways" (דַּרְכֵיכֶם הָרָעִים, *darĕkêkem hārāʿîm*), the very language of Zechariah 1:4, and to keep the commandments, statutes (*ḥuqqîm*), and law YHWH had given her (2 Kings 17:13). The connection with the covenant is made directly in 2 Kings 17:15 with the juxtaposition of *ḥuqqîm* and בְּרִית (*bĕrît*, "covenant").

Zechariah next turns his attention to the calamity that overcame the ancestors because of their failure to heed. Both they and the prophets who warned them had long since passed away (v. 5), but the Word had come to pass. The wicked nation had been overthrown according to the terms of the covenant, and those who lived to see it had had to admit that what YHWH had threatened He had brought to pass (v. 6). There is an ironic twist to the reaction of the people who

---

10. Whether or not such sermonic texts were, in fact, first preached orally and were typical of postexilic preaching cannot, I believe, be determined; cf. Rex Mason, "Some Echoes of the Preaching in the Second Temple?" *ZAW* 96 (1984): 221-35.
11. William L. Holladay, *The Root Šûbh in the Old Testament* (Leiden: Brill, 1958), 141.
12. Peter C. Craigie, *The Book of Deuteronomy*, NICOT (Grand Rapids: Eerdmans, 1976), 129.

"turned," Zechariah says (v. 6), in response to their calamity, but not in repentance.

This is the best understanding of שׁוּב here, for otherwise there appears to be a contradiction with v. 4, which says that the warnings of the prophets were to no avail. Most commentators, however, view the subject of v. 6 as the fathers of the exilic period, whereas that of v. 4 is the unrepentant fathers of the preexilic era. This seems arbitrary.[13]

The message of Zechariah is precisely the same as that of his prophetic forebears. His people must turn to YHWH in covenant affirmation if they expect YHWH to reciprocate (v. 3). The rupture in covenant that seems so obvious in Haggai (1:4-6, 9-11; 2:14-17) must be addressed and redressed, says Zechariah. Perhaps that is the explanation for the integration of his message with that of his contemporary prophet.

Additional Notes

1:1 The name *Zechariah* reflects the Hebrew זְכַרְיָה (*zĕkaryâ*), "he whom YHWH remembers." It is thus of a type known as a theophoric name, one containing part or all of a divine name, in this case YHWH.

1:3 The phrase "says YHWH of hosts," occurring three times in this verse, is lacking in some of the LXX codices in the last two instances. The heaping up of this epithet is clearly rare but on the other hand most striking. Haggai employs it 14 times in only 38 verses, Zechariah 53 times, and Malachi 24 times. Its abundant use in postexilic times ought not be surprising, for in light of the emergence of universal empires Judah needs to know that YHWH is indeed almighty, the "Lord of Hosts," Lord even of those mighty powers.

1:4 For the clearly mispointed Kethib מַעֲלִילֵיכֶם read with Qere מַעַלְלֵיכֶם or perhaps with many versions מִמַּעַלְלֵיכֶם ("from your deeds"), though עֲלִילָה (fem.) is attested as a noun meaning "deed."

1:6 BHS reads אֶתְכֶם for אֲבֹתֵיכֶם in order to avoid contradiction with v. 4. Thus, the prophet addresses the fathers in v. 4 and his own postexilic audience ("you") in v. 6. It is his own generation, then, that repents.

---

13. For שׁוּב in the ordinary sense of "turn about," see Gen. 14:7; Ex. 14:2; Josh. 8:21; 1 Chron. 21:20.

2
Vision One: The Four Horsemen (1:7-17)

A. INTRODUCTION TO THE VISIONS (1:7)

This second introduction in the book embraces all the visions to follow (1:8–6:16), as is clear from the absence of another until chapter 7. It is also the mark of a subdivision of the book following the general introduction of 1:1-6. In the strict sense, the first vision itself consists of vv. 8-15, with v. 7 providing the introduction and vv. 16-17 the interpretive oracle.[1] Petitjean more precisely ends the vision at v. 14*a*, but in doing so he includes (incorrectly in my view) vision material, such as the angelic discourse, in the oracle, which is not visionary.[2]

Translation

7On the twenty-fourth day of the eleventh month, the month Shebat, in the second year of Darius, the Word of YHWH came to Zechariah the prophet, the son of Berechiah the son of Iddo, saying,

Exegesis and Exposition

The twenty-fourth day of the eleventh month, Shebat, is February 15, 519 B.C., in the modern calendar (see Introduction to Zechariah, p.

---

1. J. W. Rothstein, *Die Nachtgesichte des Sacharja* (Leipzig: Hinrichs, 1910), 12-13, 55.
2. Albert Petitjean, *Les Oracles du Proto-Zacharie* (Paris: J. Gabalda, 1969), 53.

61). This is approximately three months after the initial call of Zechariah (1:1) and two months after Haggai's last revelation (Hag. 2:10, 20). It is quite possible that the vision introduced first on that date was prompted by the need to affirm Haggai's endorsement of Zerubbabel as the signet of YHWH (Hag. 2:23), the one who would rule on his behalf. That notion of dominion is central in the first vision. The return of Darius to Persia from Egypt, through Palestine, may also have given rise to elements of the vision, particularly the horsemen. H. G. May, with some plausibility, argues that the New Year ritual of coronation may be in view. New Year's day was coming shortly, a time when Zerubbabel could be crowned as the Davidic successor. When May suggests, however, that the horses in visions one and eight indicate Zechariah's dependence on Babylonian mythological motifs, he goes beyond the evidence.[3]

B. CONTENT OF THE VISION (1:8)

Translation

⁸I saw in the night and look, a man riding a red horse who stood among some myrtle trees in the ravine. And behind him were red, *sorrell, and white horses.

Exegesis and Exposition

Though the technical terms for *vision*, such as חָזוֹן (*ḥāzôn*) and מַרְאֶה (*ma'rê*), and for *dream*, such as חֲלוֹם (*ḥălôm*), are lacking here and throughout the whole vision section, it is most obvious that the prophet is recounting a series of dream-visions that he saw all in one night. But these dreams were not random and from his own imagination, for they appear to be in a kind of historical and chronological sequence, on the one hand, and in an interlocking literary pattern, on the other. For now, it is worth noting that vision eight (6:1-8), like this first one, also features four kinds of horses.

Either the man on the red horse dismounted and stood in the ravine, or the horse itself stood there with the rider still on him. The Hebrew grammar would favor the former, as does verse 10. A more difficult problem is the location of the scene. Rather than "myrtle (trees)" the LXX presupposes "in the midst of the mountains" (הֶהָרִים, for the MT הַהֲדַסִּים), perhaps because of the problematic "ravine" that follows. Moreover, the sixth vision, a counterpart to this one, also refers to mountains (Zech. 6:1). The fact that these two visions share

---

3. H. G. May, "A Key to the Interpretation of Zechariah's Visions," *JBL* 57 (1938): 173-84.

much in common does not, however, demand that they resemble each other in every respect. The myrtle (*Myrtus communis*) is a particularly appropriate element of this vision. A fragrant, decorative shrub that sometimes reaches the size of a tree, it was used in connection with the Feast of Tabernacles and in postbiblical times in betrothal celebrations.[4] Its perpetual greenness and aromatic and other qualities provided a suitable setting for the inauguration of YHWH's dominion, which is everlasting and pleasant in every way. The specific and particular functions of the horses of vision eight (Zech. 6:1-8) may indeed assist in elucidating the meanings of their colors (see pp. 183-87), but it is fruitless to speculate about such meaning especially because the colors here and in vision eight do not coincide. As for the three horses that stood in the background, it is not certain whether they had riders, though presumably they did, as the plural pronouns of the speakers of v. 11 imply.

Additional Notes

1:8 The colors and other descriptions of the horses here and in chapter 6 have resulted in considerable variation in the ancient versions and in modern translations. All agree on the "red" and "white," so the issue is the שְׂרֻקִּים, rendered by KJV "speckled," by JPSV "sorrel," by JB "chestnut," by NASB "sorrel," and by NIV "brown." Though 1:8 and 6:2-7 share much in common, including four different colored horses, there is no reason to assume that the horses must match, an error on the part of many ancient and modern scholars. For now, then, only the passage at hand will receive attention in its own right. Comparisons will be made when chapter 6 comes up for consideration.

The LXX renders שְׂרֻקִּים with a double translation, καὶ ψαροὶ καὶ ποικίλοι, "dapple gray and spotted." The Peshitta and Vg have only "variegated," apparently an attempt to harmonize the LXX tradition. R. P. Gordon, on the basis of Gen. 30:32, 33, 35, 39; 31:8, suggests that the best Targumic reading here is קרוחין, "white-spotted," a translation in line with the other ancient versions (R. P. Gordon, "An Inner-Targum Corruption (Zech. I 8)," *VT* 25 [1975]: 216-21).

Because שְׂרֻקִּים clearly has the meaning "red, ruddy" in Hebrew (BDB, 977; KBL, 932-33) and the cognate languages (cf. Arab. *sharaqa*, Akk. *šarqu*), the versions derive their meaning, "variegated, speckled, spotted," from some other source. McHardy proposes that the reading in 1:8 should be שְׁחֹרִים (as in 6:2), meaning "black." This came about, he says, because of a system of abbreviations in which שׁ represented שְׁחֹרִים of 6:2. Because the four horses of each vision must

---

4. *Encyclopaedia Judaica* (Jerusalem: Keter, 1972), 12:717-28, s.v., "myrtle."

have the same colors (a dubious and unproved assumption), שׂ must have stood in 1:8 and was subsequently and erroneously read שְׂרֻקִּים (W. D. McHardy, "The Horses in Zechariah," *In Memoriam Paul Kahle*, eds. M. Black and G. Fohrer [Berlin: Verlag Alfred Topelmann, 1968], 174-79).

Gordon offers the suggestion ("An Inter-Targum Corruption [Zech. I 8]") that the versions may reflect another root שָׂרַק, meaning "comb, card" (BDB, 977). How this would yield "speckled" or the like is not clear. He also refers to a meaning "dappled," known to both Ibn Janāḥ and Kimchi (p. 218). Modern lexicons attest no such meaning, however, so it is likely that the medieval rabbis were themselves dependent on the LXX and other ancient versions, the source of whose dependence in turn can no longer be ascertained. Most likely they were trying to bring 1:8 in line with 6:2-7 and therefore rendered שְׂרֻקִּים as though it were equivalent to בְּרֻדִּים אֲמֻצִּים in 6:3—"dappled strong." This will be considered at greater length later.

In conclusion, שְׂרֻקִּים rests on unassailable textual evidence and undoubtedly means "ruddy, sorrel," or the like. The versions, like many modern scholars, appear to have fallen victim to a desire to harmonize 1:8 with 6:2-7, an unnecessary and improper endeavor.

C. INTERPRETATION OF THE VISION (1:9-15)

Translation

⁹Then I said, "What are these, sir?" The messenger who spoke to me said, "I will show you what these are." ¹⁰The man standing among the myrtle trees spoke up and said, "These (are the ones) whom YHWH has sent to walk about on the earth." ¹¹These then responded to the Angel of YHWH, the one standing among the myrtle trees, "We have been walking about on the earth, and now the whole earth is at rest and quiet." ¹²The Angel of YHWH then asked, "YHWH of hosts, how long will you not have compassion on Jerusalem and the cities of Judah with which you have been indignant for these seventy years?" ¹³YHWH then addressed the messenger speaking to me with good, comforting words. ¹⁴The messenger speaking to me said to me, "Cry out. Thus says YHWH of hosts, 'I am exceedingly jealous for Jerusalem and for Zion. ¹⁵But I am greatly displeased with the nations that take their ease, for I was a little displeased, but they enhanced the (resulting) harm.'"

Exegesis and Exposition

The meaning of the colors of the horses in the present vision (v. 8) may not be clear, but because the interpretation offers no explanation, it is clearly not important. The specific and particular functions of the horses of vision eight (Zech. 6:1-8) may indeed assist in elucidating the meanings of their colors (see pp. 183-87), but it is fruitless to speculate about such meaning here, especially because the here and in vision eight do not coincide. What is important is that the horses represent the irresistible dominion of YHWH over the whole earth. Once His wrath against the nations has run its course, He will turn to His own people with grace and forgiveness.

A major difficulty in the passage is to ascertain the number of figures involved and their identity.[5] First of all, it is apparent that a messenger of God is in close conversation with the prophet. Three times he is described as "the messenger who spoke to me" (vv. 9, 13, 14). The term for "messenger" (מַלְאָךְ, *mal'āk*) is frequently translated "angel" and may be here as well. A second clearly defined individual is the man among the myrtle trees (v. 10), already introduced in the vision itself (v. 8). A plain reading of the account suggests that he is the same as the "Angel of YHWH" (v. 11), who also is described as standing among the myrtles. This common point almost certainly makes them one and the same.

A third actor is YHWH (v. 13) or YHWH of hosts (v. 12). He cannot be the same as the Angel of YHWH, inasmuch as the two are in conversation (v. 12). This is a remarkable and important contribution to the theology of the Angel of YHWH, for, as is well known, the Angel of YHWH appears pervasively in the OT as the agent of YHWH and, indeed, almost as His incarnation (cf. Gen. 18:2, 13, 17, 22; Ex. 23:20-21; Josh. 5:13-15; Judg. 6:11-24; 13:2-20).[6] Whatever might be said elsewhere, in this vision YHWH and His Angel are separate persons.

It seems, then, that Zechariah stands with an interpreting messenger and that both of them hear the answer to Zechariah's question as given by the man among the myrtles, that is, the Angel of YHWH. His answer regarding the meaning of the horses is confirmed by the riders of the horses themselves (v. 11). Overwhelmed by his own response, the Angel of YHWH addresses YHWH and asks how long the 70 years of discipline will last (v. 12). YHWH answers but directs His response to the messenger-interpreter standing by Zechariah, for it is Zechariah who raised the first inquiries about the vision he had seen. That messenger in turn speaks to Zechariah, commanding him to deliver the Word of God to his people (v. 14).

---

5. Clark sees only two, identifying the Angel of YHWH with the angel in the midst of the trees. This appears to be a majority view. See David J. Clark, "The Case of the Vanishing Angel," *BT* 33 (1982): 214-15.
6. See Gerhard von Rad, *Old Testament Theology*, 2 vols. (Edinburgh: Oliver and Boyd, 1962), 1:285-89.

The mission of the four horses and their riders (or at least the rider of one of them, the red horse) was to walk about on the whole earth (v. 10). The verb form here, the hithpaʿel of הָלַךְ (*hālak*, "walk"), is extremely significant, for in that stem the verb frequently has the idea of dominion. To walk about on the earth is to assert sovereignty over it. A few examples must suffice. When Abram's allocation in Canaan was pointed out to him, he was told to "walk about" in it (Gen. 13:17). The king of Tyre, in his hubris, "walked up and down" in proclaiming his kingship (Ezek. 28:14). Satan, when questioned by God as to his whereabouts, said he had been "walking up and down" in the earth (Job 1:7), clearly asserting his lordship over it and all its inhabitants (Job 2:2-3). Here in vision one (and in vision eight as well [Zech. 6:7]) it is YHWH who, through the symbolism of four cavalry charges, is announcing that He is Lord of all.

The result of their traversing the earth is that it is now at rest and quiet (v. 11).[7] It is now a suitable time for YHWH to undo the judgment of the 70-year exile by displaying His compassion upon His elect people (v. 12), a hope that, in fact, is already being realized. Despite His discipline of Jerusalem and Judah, they are still the nation of the covenant for whom YHWH is uniquely concerned. His "jealousy" for Judah (v. 14) is, after all, an expression of His singular interest in her and His determination to restore her.[8] The reference to Zion focuses on the Davidic reign as a part of the messianic program of redemption.[9] The nations, on the other hand, have become the object of YHWH's judgment, for the relatively insignificant displeasure He felt toward Israel has been augmented by them as they helped bring about an even greater measure of retribution than He intended (v. 15).

The last clause of v. 15, וְהֵמָּה עָזְרוּ לְרָעָה, reads literally, "and they helped to evil." What is in view is that YHWH would have punished up to a certain point, but the wicked nations helped Him to make the judgment of Israel even more severe. Deissler draws attention to similar ideas concerning Assyria (Isa. 10:5 ff.) and Babylonia (Isa. 47:6 f.;

---

7. This speaks of the peace brought about by the Persian conquests, a peace, however, that ultimately was achieved by YHWH through Persia, His "four horsemen"; Samuel Amsler, *Aggée, Zacharie 1-8*, CAT (Neuchatel: Delachaux & Niestlé, 1981), 63.
8. Cf. G. Sauer, *Theologische Handwörterbuch zum Alten Testament*, ed. E. Jenni and C. Westermann, 2 vols. (München: Chr. Kaiser Verlag, 1976), 2:647-50, s.v. קִנְאָה.
9. J. J. M. Roberts, "The Davidic Origin of the Zion Tradition," *JBL* 92 (1973): 343-44.

Jer. 50:29; 51:24) in particular. He suggests, correctly, that there may be a warning here for Persia as well.[10]

The vision, though clearly with eschatological implications, relates to the historical circumstances of the late sixth century. The *Pax Persiaca*, brought about by Cyrus, had been strengthened and expanded under Darius. He had put down rebellions attendant to his accession to the throne in 522 b.c. and in 520-19, the very year of this vision, and brought Egypt to heel, thus reducing the whole Eastern world to his control.[11] What he could not know, of course, was that it was YHWH, God of Israel, who had brought universal peace. The horses of Darius were, in fact, the horses of the Lord.

The conditions were suitable, then, for the 70-year exile to be over. Jeremiah had first referred to the 70 years, dating their end with the demise of the Chaldean kingdom (Jer. 25:11-12), an event that took place in 539 b.c. with Cyrus's conquest of Babylon (cf. Ezra 1:1). The beginning of the 70 years was 605, the fourth year of Jehoiakim (Jer. 25:1). Technically this leaves a period of less than 70 years, actually about 66 (605-539). The same prophet referred to the 70 years commencing in the fourth year of Zedekiah (Jer. 28:1; cf. 29:10), c. 594.[12] This would require, if taken literally, a completion date of c. 524, close to but not exactly in the year of the rebuilding of the Temple under Zerubbabel in 520.

It was clearly understood, however, that the 70 years had flexible *termini ad quem* and *a quo*, for their termination also is connected to the completion of the second Temple.[13] This seems clear from our passage (cf. v. 16), for if the 70 years had expired with the fall of Babylon, the concern about its ending would never be raised here in 519 b.c. Zechariah 7:5, in the context of fasting and other cultic matters and dating from 518, also supports the idea of the 70 years ending with the completion of the Temple, that is, in 516. This would tie in nicely with the date of the destruction of the earlier Temple in 586, exactly 70 years before. It is in keen anticipation of the nearness of the end of that era that prophet and people alike ask their questions about that event and its meaning for them (cf. Hag. 1:2).

---

10. A. Deissler, *Zwölf Propheten III. Zefanja, Haggai, Sacharja, Maleachi* (Wurzburg: Echter Verlag, 1988), 273.
11. Eugene H. Merrill, *Kingdom of Priests: A History of Old Testament Israel* (Grand Rapids: Baker, 1987), 488-91.
12. J. A. Thompson, *The Book of Jeremiah*, NICOT (Grand Rapids: Eerdmans, 1980), 544.
13. C. F. Whitley, "The Term Seventy Years Captivity," *VT* 4 (1954): 72.

D. ORACLE OF RESPONSE (1:16-17)

Translation

16"Therefore, YHWH says, 'I have turned toward Jerusalem with compassion; My house will be rebuilt in it,' says YHWH of hosts, 'and a (measuring) line will be stretched out over Jerusalem. 17Proclaim again and say, Thus says YHWH of hosts, 'My cities will once more overflow with prosperity, and once more YHWH *will comfort Zion and choose Jerusalem.'"

Exegesis and Exposition

It was pointed out in the Introduction (p. 64) that many of Zechariah's visions, including this one, are accompanied by oracles, the primary purposes of which are (1) to confirm the message of the vision, (2) to provide further understanding of its meaning, and (3) to exhort the audience to implement whatever injunctions it might convey.

The vision report itself said that YHWH spoke "good, comforting words" (v. 13) to the interpreting messenger; now the explicit content of those words appears in the oracle.[14] Using the past tense to express a fait accompli, YHWH says He has turned (שוב, *šûb*) to Jerusalem with compassion (רַחֲמִים, *raḥămîm*).

There is some question as to the translation for the verb שוב here. First of all, is it past or future, and second, does it mean "turn" or "return"? The form is a qal perfect and usually is construed as past. If it is to be rendered "return," it should no doubt be construed as future, however, in line with the following imperfect "will be built." If taken as "turn," on the other hand, it is best to see it as past. The reason is that שוב, combined with רַחֲמִים, conveys a covenant idea. YHWH has "turned with compassion" and because of that the Temple will be rebuilt. That it has already happened is clear from careful attention to vv. 12-13. The Angel of YHWH has asked, "How long will you not have compassion (לֹא־תְרַחֵם)?" to which YHWH answers comforting words. These words are that He has already turned to them in compassion and that the Temple construction is nearly finished. It is likely that His turning in compassion occurred once the conditions for it had been met, namely, the relaying of the Temple foundations in 520 B.C. (cf. Hag. 1:8, 13; 2:4)[15].

---

14. David L. Petersen, *Haggai and Zechariah 1-8*, (London: SCM, 1985), 151.
15. William F. Holladay, *The Root Šûbh in the Old Testament* (Leiden: Brill, 1958), 28. Holladay does not include this verse as an example of שוב in a covenant sense, but he does draw attention to the original reading 'ἐπιβλέπω ("look with favor") in LXX^B for 'ἐπιστρέφω ("return to") in A and א. This suggests an ancient tradition at least for שוב as "turn to" in a covenant sense in Zech. 1:16.

The two technical terms *šûb* and *raḥămîm* are stock vocabulary in covenant contexts (Deut. 13:17; Pss. 71:29; 85:7; Jer. 12:15; Mic. 7:19-20; Zech. 8:15),[16] and here the expression makes clear that the terms have been met whereby YHWH and His people may once more enjoy covenant fellowship. In response to Haggai's appeal to rebuild the Temple (Hag. 1:8) the people had been obedient (1:12), thus making possible the guarantee that YHWH was with them (1:13; 2:4). Moreover, once the ceremony of laying the Temple foundation had taken place (Hag. 2:18), YHWH had said that He would bless from that time onward (2:19).

The work of Temple building had begun on September 21, 520 (Hag. 1:15), about five months before Zechariah received the night visions, but it was far from finished. In fact, it seems that as late as December 18 only the foundation had been laid. What had been started would now be brought to fruition (Zech. 1:16; cf. 4:9). Indeed, not only would the Temple be rebuilt but the surveyor's line (a synecdoche for reconstruction)[17] would stretch out over all Jerusalem and even the outlying cities (vv. 16b-17). They would become abundantly prosperous (lit., "spread out from goodness").

Then, in a closing couplet of synonymous parallelism and freighted with covenant overtones, YHWH said He would "comfort" and "choose." The former verb translates נָחַם (nāḥam), a term that frequently appears in covenant renewal passages (Isa. 49:13; 51:1-3; 52:9; 61:1-2).[18] It suggests the basis for YHWH's elective overtures—his pure grace. Likewise, and more explicitly stated, He said He will choose once more. The verb בָּחַר (bāḥar)[19] is a favorite term to describe God's sovereign, unconditional choice of a people to whom He will relate in salvation and service (Deut. 4:37; 7:6-7; 12:14; 14:2; 1 Kings 8:16; 11:34; 1 Chron. 28:4, 5, 6; 2 Chron. 6:6; Pss. 33:12; 78:67, 68, 70; Isa. 41:8; 43:10; 44:1, 2; Ezek. 20:5; Hag. 2:23; Zech. 2:12; 3:2).

Additional Notes

1:17 For the MT נָחַם the LXX has ἐλγήσει, presupposing רָחַם. This would be preferable in the context, since it provides a good follow-up to the cognate noun רַחֲמִים in v. 16. The more difficult MT should, however, be retained.

---

16. Ibid., 69.
17. That קָוָה (so to be pointed, or read קַו with Qere) means to build here is clear from the parallel בֵּיתִי רִבָּנֶה, "my house will be built." Cf. Isa. 44:13; Jer. 31:38-39. This is a sign of the restoration of Jerusalem and the Temple. See Baruch Halpern, "The Ritual Background of Zechariah's Temple Song," *CBQ* 40 (1978): 178 n. 31.
18. H. J. Stoebe, *THAT* 2:62-63, s.v. נחם.
19. H. Wildberger, *THAT* 1:294, s.v. בחר.

3
Vision Two: The Four Horns (1:18-21; HB 2:1-4)

A. CONTENT OF THE VISION (1:18, 20; HB 2:1, 3)

This brief vision account consists of two parts interwoven as the content (vv. 18, 20) and interpretation (vv. 19, 21). There is, in this instance, no accompanying oracle.[1] Moreover, just as visions one and eight complement each other by similar themes and perspective, so this vision and number seven (5:5-11) are a matched pair. They each have two parts and each is concerned with the nations, four unnamed in vision two and Shinar, or Babylon, in vision seven.

Translation

[18]I looked again and saw four horns. [19]So I said to the messenger who spoke with me, "What are These?" He replied, "These are the horns that have scattered Judah, Israel, and Jerusalem." [20]Next YHWH showed me four blacksmiths. [21]I said, "What have these come to do?" He answered, "These are the horns that have scattered Judah, so that no one could raise his head. But these (others) have come to

---

1. Petitjean, following A. Van Hoonacker and H. Junker, takes 2:3-13 (HB 2:7-17) to be "une sorte de commentaire des deux visions [1:18-21 and 2:1-2]." If he is correct, this vision does indeed have an accompanying oracle; Albert Petitjean, *Les Oracles du Proto-Zacharie*, (Paris: J. Gabalda, 1969), 89.

terrify them (and) to throw down the horns of the nations which raised (their) horn against the land of Judah in order to scatter it."

Exegesis and Exposition

The connections between this vision and the first are also striking. That there were four horses in vision one and four horns and four craftsmen in this one is significant.[2] The implied hostility of the nations in vision one (vv. 12, 15) is explicit in vision two (vv. 19, 21). Finally, just as the horses of the first vision were YHWH's instruments of dominion over all the earth (vv. 10, 11), so the four craftsmen reduce the nations to defeat (v. 21).

The use of the horn of an animal as a metaphor for political and military power is familiar not only in the OT but in ancient Near Eastern literature in general.[3] It suggests power, authority, prestige, and influence. In perhaps the earliest biblical usage, Hannah sings of her triumph over her foes in terms of the exaltation of her horn (1 Sam. 2:1). She concludes that song by declaring that YHWH will strengthen His coming king and exalt the horn of His anointed one (v. 10). Thus, to exalt the horn is synonymous with providing strength.

In the poetic literature the connection is even plainer. David describes YHWH as his rock, fortress, deliverer, shield, tower, and horn (Ps. 18:2; HB 18:3). Psalm 75:10 (HB 75:11) speaks of the defeat of the wicked in terms of the cutting off of their horns. The prophets employ the image similarly. Jeremiah refers to the defeat of Moab as the cutting off of his horn (Jer. 48:25), whereas Micah speaks of the iron horn of the daughter of Zion whereby she will shatter her enemies (Mic. 4:13). Daniel's descriptions of the various world kingdoms of his day include the metaphor of animals with horns (Dan. 7-8).

The immediate source of Zechariah's language might, in fact, be traced to Daniel.[4] He had identified the horned beasts of his visions and dreams with empires and nations such as Babylon, Media, Persia, and Greece, some of which (undoubtedly Babylon at least) are in Zechariah's purview as well.

---

2. For a view that sees 1:7–2:17 (EB 2:13) as a single literary unit, with 1:7–2:9 (EB 2:5) as a subdivision, see W. H. Joubert, "The Determination of the Contents of Zechariah 1:7–2:17 Through a Structural Analysis," *OTWSA* 20-21 (1977-83): 66-82.

3. B. Couroyer, "Corne et Arc," *RB* 73 (1965): 510-21. As the title suggests, this article proposes that "horn" is often symbolic of a war bow, a symbol appropriate to this vision.

4. Samuel Amsler, *Aggée, Zacharie 1-8, Zacharie 9-14*, CAT (Paris: Neuchatel, 1981), 68.

B. INTERPRETATION OF THE VISION (1:19, 21; HB 2:2, 4)

Exegesis and Exposition

Because the vision contains two elements—the four horns and the four blacksmiths—the interpretation also is divided into two parts. In response to the query regarding the horns, the angelic interpreter first merely asserts that they are scatterers of Judah, Israel, and Jerusalem. He goes on, under further interrogation, to associate the horns with the nations. Thus it is the nations that have used their horns, that is, their military might, to effect the dispersion of God's people.

As for the smiths, their task, the messenger says, is to bring down these nations, to nullify the effect of their great power. The ultimate result presumably would be to reverse the scattering so that the dispersed could return again to their land.

The מַלְאָךְ (*mal'āk*) here is the same messenger as the interpreter in the first vision.[5] Though he is mentioned only after the first part of this vision (v. 19), he obviously provides the answer to the question of v. 21 as well. The answer he offers to the question concerning the identity of the horns is clear enough insofar as their function is concerned, but the order in which he lists the objects of the horns' attack—Judah, Israel, Jerusalem—is not so clear. Nor is it clear why only Judah is mentioned as the victim in the second section of the vision.

Perhaps to alleviate this problem, some LXX witnesses omit Jerusalem, whereas others omit Israel. More commonly, but with no basis in the text, the name Israel is simply regarded as an unwarranted interpolation.[6] If, however, one views the names not as having chronological sequence, as is usually done, but in some other pattern, the difficulties disappear. Because Judah alone appears at the end of the pericope, she must be central. Israel, then, denotes the nation in its broadest sense, Jerusalem in its narrowest. The scattering was total, from the greatest extent to the most central and local extreme.[7]

Earlier exegetes tended to seek for four particular nations or

---

5. The phrase הַמַּלְאָךְ הַדֹּבֵר בִּי ("the messenger who spoke to me") becomes a stereotype for the *angelus interpres* and in all its occurrences (1:9, 13, 14, 19; 2:3; 4:1, 5; 5:5, 10; 6:4) refers to the same person. See David J. Clark, "The Case of the Vanishing Angel," *BT* 33 (1982): 214-15.

6. H. G. Mitchell, *A Commentary on Haggai and Zechariah*, ICC (Edinburgh: T. & T. Clark, 1912), 132.

7. So Joyce G. Baldwin, *Haggai, Zechariah, Malachi,* (London: Tyndale, 1972), 104.

events to account for the four oppressive horns.[8] The symbolism of four, however, makes that approach very unlikely. What is suggested here and elsewhere by that number is the universal character of the persecution of God's people by the nations. From the time of her settlement in Canaan until the fall of Jerusalem to the Babylonians, the story of Israel's struggle had been the same. It was only that that final destruction had been so climactic and irreversible that it stands out in the text at hand. The scattering here is most particularly the Babylonian diaspora that had just recently been at least partially overcome.[9]

The smiths likewise cannot be further identified, though the historical context of the vision might favor the universal dominion of Cyrus and the Persians. The noun חָרָשׁ (*ḥārāš*), used here as their designation, means any skilled artisan regardless of his medium. In two passages, however, the task of the *ḥārāš* takes on a meaning most appropriate to this message of Zechariah.[10] The first is Isa. 54:16 which, in the context of the restoration of Judah under the aegis of Cyrus, speaks of a *ḥārāš* who creates an instrument for his own use. The chiastic pattern of the verse suggests that this *ḥārāš* is also a *mašḥît* (מַשְׁחִית), a "destroyer," whose task it is to bring to ruin. A smith could thus be a devastator.

Ezek. 21:36 (EB 21:31) refers to חָרָשֵׁי מַשְׁחִית (*ḥārāšê mašḥît*), lit., "workers of destruction," who will destroy the people of YHWH. It is in this sense that Zechariah is referring to the four *ḥārāšîm*. They have come forth to throw down the arrogant nations that have scattered God's elect. The Persians, and most particularly Darius, again come to mind.[11] The Babylonian horn has been cut off by the instruments of Darius, artisan of YHWH. The promise of rebuilding in vision one (1:16-17) can now become possible.

---

8. So Theodore of Mopsuestia, for example. See Theophane Chary, *Aggée-Zacharie, Malachie*, (Paris: Librairie Lecoffre, 1969), 64.
9. Karl Elliger, *Die Propheten Nahum, Habakuk, Zephanja, Haggai, Sacharja, Maleachi*, ATD 25 (Göttingen: Vandenhoeck & Ruprecht, 1982), 109 n. 1.
10. Klaus Seybold, "Die Bildmotive in den Visionen des Propheten Sacharja," in *Studies on Prophecy*, VTSup. 26, ed. D. Lys et al. (Leiden: Brill, 1974), 104. For a rejection of this position, see Robert M. Good, "Zechariah's Second Night Vision (Zech 2, 1-4)," *Bib* 63 (1982): 58.
11. Kurt Galling, "Die Exilswende in der Sicht des Propheten Sacharja," *VT* 2 (1952): 20-21.

4

Vision Three: The Surveyor (2:1-13; HB 2:5-17)

A. CONTENT OF THE VISION (2:1-2; HB 2:5-6)

This third vision finds its counterpart in vision six, that concerning the flying scroll (5:1-4).[1] This is evident in that both have to do with measuring and/or dimensions, but particularly in that their focus has narrowed from cosmic or even international interest to Jerusalem itself. Vision three defines the locus and importance of Jerusalem, whereas vision six obliquely pertains to civil and religious law within the community.

Translation

¹I looked again, and there was a man with a measuring line in his hand. ²I asked, "Where are you going?" He replied, "To measure Jerusalem in order to determine its breadth and its length."

Exegesis and Exposition

The persona of vision three are only the prophet himself and a man, otherwise unidentified, to whom the prophet speaks directly. This is the first time in the visions proper that Zechariah has been an

---

1. Carol L. Meyers and Eric M. Meyers, *Haggai, Zechariah 1-8*, AB (Garden City, N.Y.: Doubleday, 1987), 158.

interlocutor.[2] He observes that the man has something in his hand, an object designated in Hebrew as חֶבֶל מִדָּה (*ḥebel middâ*, "measuring line"). *Ḥebel* alone is a generic term for any kind of cord or rope, but with *middâ* it refers to a surveyor's line (as here).[3] Without the qualifier *middâ* ("measure") it still has the nuance of measuring, as in 2 Sam. 8:2 where David lines the Moabites up for slaughter. Amos uses the word *ḥebel* with reference to the subdivision of Israel by the Assyrians following the conquest of Samaria (7:17). Here surveying is clearly in view as properties are measured out for redistribution.

What Zechariah sees is a remeasurement of Jerusalem in order to reestablish the ancient boundary lines preparatory to the city's full reoccupation. Jeremiah had anticipated such a day when he, prior to the fall of Jerusalem, had redeemed the property of his uncle against the day when the Babylonian exile would be over and land could be reclaimed (Jer. 32:6-15). With full confidence in the promises of YHWH, Jeremiah had avowed that "houses, fields, and vineyards will once more be bought in this land" (v. 15).

Ezekiel had seen a similar scene, but the surveyor in his vision measured out the land with a reed rather than a cord (Ezek. 40:3). His objective was the same, however: to designate the allocations of properties for both sacred and secular use. Specifically, in Zechariah's case, the task of the man is to measure Jerusalem by breadth and length. The reason breadth precedes length may be because of the orientation of the city. The focus of the ancient Palestinian was on the east, so he naturally would give east-west measurements before north-south. Jerusalem, of course, was on a north-south axis, so its length would be determined by those compass points, whereas its width would be narrower, on the east-west plane. Petersen points out that city sizes are not usually given in terms of length and breadth in the OT and that only here and in Ezekiel 40-48 are breadth and length employed in this manner. In Ezekiel the breadth (east-west) is much longer than the length (north-south) of each of the subdivisions of the land.[4]

B. INTERPRETATION OF THE VISION (2:3-5; HB 2:7-9)

Translation

³At this point the messenger who spoke to me went out, and another messenger came to meet him. ⁴This one said to him, "Hurry,

---

2. Baruch Halpern, "The Ritual Background of Zechariah's Temple Song," *CBQ* 40 (1978): 178 n. 48.
3. H.-J. Fabry, *TDOT*, 4:174-76, s.v. חבל.
4. David L. Petersen, *Haggai and Zechariah 1-8*, (London: SCM, 1985), 168-69.

speak to this young man as follows: 'Jerusalem will be a place of open land because of the multitude of people and animals there. ⁵"But I," YHWH says, "will be a wall of fire surrounding her and glory in her midst."'"

Exegesis and Exposition

The interpreting messenger (or angel) appears again for the third time, now to provide further information to the prophet than he had already obtained from the surveyor. To do this the messenger takes an unusual initiative in stepping forward to the scene of action. There he is met by still another messenger, who instructs him to disclose to Zechariah ("this young man") that the surveyor is in process of laying out allotments in and around Jerusalem in preparation for the burgeoning population that will live there. This is particularly necessary because the old boundary lines defined by the walls will need to be redrawn in light of the absence of those walls.

Many commentators understand the young man (נַעַר) to be the surveyor because the measuring he is undertaking will be useless inasmuch as Jerusalem will be a city without walls.[5] However, the point of the prophetic vision is not to instruct an inexperienced angel, but the prophet himself.[6] It is Zechariah who must understand that the city to come will spill out over its ancient walls and that YHWH will become the wall, the measurements of which the surveyor is taking.

The presence of a secondary messenger is unusual in the night visions, only vision one also attesting to his presence. There he appeared as the "man among the myrtle trees" (1:8), later identified as the Angel of YHWH (1:11). In a sense, he was an interpreter for the interpreter, a role he plays as well in vision three. It is impossible, however, to deduce that he is the Angel of YHWH here, the other parallels between the visions notwithstanding.[7]

The second messenger, with a sense of great urgency, commands the first to run to Zechariah with the meaning of the vision. This urgency is communicated by the double imperative in Hebrew, רֻץ דַּבֵּר (*rūṣ dabbēr*, "run, speak"). This can only mean that what is about

---

5. H. G. Mitchell, *A Commentary on Haggai and Zechariah*, ICC (Edinburgh: T. & T. Clark, 1912), 158.

6. Theophane Chary, *Aggée-Zacharie, Malachie*, (Paris: Librairie Lecoffre, 1969), 67.

7. As Unger points out, it is gratuitous to identify the second messenger as the Angel of YHWH, for "both his indefinite designation and his implied attendance on the surveyor put him in a subordinate position" (M. F. Unger, *Zechariah*, [Grand Rapids: Zondervan, 1963], 45).

to happen is imminent. Neither the messenger nor Zechariah can be slow to hear it and act upon it.

What is in view is the reoccupation of Jerusalem by such a vast population that the walls that once circumscribed it will become inadequate. The text reads literally, "Jerusalem will sit/dwell as open regions," the last phrase to be taken as an adverbial accusative. The next phrase ("without walls") in many translations can only be inferred from the passage, but, in line with reference to the wall in v. 5, it is a logical inference. The term פְּרָזוֹת, as a designation for unwalled settlements, occurs elsewhere in the OT only in Ezek. 38:11 and Est. 9:19. Jeremias draws attention to the distinction in the latter passage between the walled city of Susa and the undefended villages of the Persian countryside in which the Jewish exiles lived.[8] The peril of life in unwalled settlements was well known in ancient times.[9]

The problem, of course, is the historical referent. Does the vision have only eschatological significance, or can it relate to Zechariah's own circumstances? In my judgment it does both. The eschatological aspect is brought out clearly in v. 5, so only the historical will be addressed just now. The evidence must begin with a look at the situation in Jerusalem in the time of Nehemiah, in 445 B.C., some 75 years after the revelation of the night visions. The first crisis related in Nehemiah's memoirs is that of the ruinous state of Jerusalem, particularly the absence of walls (Neh. 1:3). It was, in fact, that crisis that prompted Nehemiah to journey to Jerusalem and, as governor of Judah, to supervise the rebuilding of the walls (Neh. 2:9–6:19).

One should not assume from this that there had been no walls around Jerusalem from 586 B.C., the date of the Babylonian conquest, to 445 when Nehemiah completed his work. In fact, Ezra attests that walls existed in the time of King Artaxeres I (464-424). They were built, it seems, before his reign, probably in that of his immediate predecessor, Xerxes (Ezra 4:12). Nehemiah's complaint, moreover, is that the walls of Jerusalem have been destroyed and need to be rebuilt. Because their destruction was news to him, the reference could not be to the walls of 586, for he surely was well aware that those walls had been leveled by Nebuchadnezzar's armies. These must be walls subsequently built and then destroyed once more.[10]

Preliminary work on walls may have begun as early as 520, Zechariah's own day, as Ezra 5:3, 9 expressly states. The resistance

---

8. Christian Jeremias, *Die Nachtgesichte des Sacharja* (Göttingen: Vandenhoeck & Ruprecht, 1977), 170 n. 30.
9. See Yigael Yadin, *The Art of Warfare in Biblical Lands* (London: Weidenfeld and Nicolson, 1963), 16-24.
10. H. G. M. Williamson, *Ezra, Nehemiah*, WBC (Waco, Tex.: Word, 1985), 172.

this project engendered appears to have left the walls unfinished, for all subsequent references to building in that period are limited to the Temple itself (Ezra 6:7-8, 14-15). If indeed walls were begun then, they were not sufficient to enclose the city and for all practical purposes left Jerusalem as an open space without protection. As suggested above, this condition must have continued at least until the reign of Xerxes (485-464). This means, then, that if vision three has anything to do with Zechariah's own times, there must have been a period either then or later when Jerusalem was populated sufficiently to expand beyond the perimeters of the earlier walls. This viewpoint may be surmised from several lines of evidence from within Ezra-Nehemiah.

First, the contingent of Jews that returned from exile under Sheshbazzar's leadership in 538 B.C. numbered 42,360 citizens in addition to 7,337 slaves and 200 singers, or a total of 49,897 (Ezra 2:64-65). It is interesting that they brought with them more than 8,000 animals (2:66-67). Admittedly, not all of those people settled in Jerusalem, but one gets the impression that many did (2:70; 4:4).

Since it appears that most of the Jewish exiles taken into Babylon originated in Jerusalem and not the towns and villages of Judah (2 Kings 24:12-16; 2 Chron. 36:19-20; Jer. 39:9-10), it follows that they and their descendants would have returned to Jerusalem as well. The priests, Levites, and other cultic personnel settled throughout the land in accordance with Mosaic requirement, but it is noteworthy that Ezra says that only "some of the people" settled outside the city (2:70). The total he gives, in fact, would be 8,540 (vv. 21-35), leaving about 41,357 for Jerusalem, less the aforementioned religious persons, about 5,022 in number (vv. 36-58), or 36,335 in all in Jerusalem. It is true that this must have included several contingents, but Ezra is careful to exclude his own later group from them (Ezra 2:1-2; cf. 8:1). It is very unlikely that preexilic Jerusalem ever contained as many as 40,000 persons, so the population in Zechariah's time and later would clearly have been unable to live within the preexilic walls. Broshi estimates that the city had 24,000 inhabitants in 700 B.C., a population that was so large it was forced to live in the unwalled suburbs to the north and west as well as within the city proper. Prior to that, he argues, the walled city contained only 6,000-8,000 inhabitants.[11]

Eighty years later Ezra himself led about 5,000 more individuals back to Judah (Ezra 8:1-14),[12] most of whom apparently settled in or about Jerusalem, thus swelling the already considerable population

---

11. M. Broshi, "The Expansion of Jerusalem in the Reigns of Hezekiah and Manasseh," *IEJ* 24 (1974): 23-24.
12. Williamson, *Ezra, Nehemiah*, 110.

(Ezra 8:31-32). When Nehemiah arrived 13 years after that, he found whatever walls had been built reduced to rubble and set about making repairs. The full course of his walls can no longer be determined, but they appear to have been less extensive than those of preexilic times.[13] With the ruin of the walls that preceded his coming, the population of the city had evidently evacuated, for Nehemiah notes that the city was "large and spacious but the people within it were few" (Neh. 7:4). Williamson takes this to mean a reduction of population, an unsuitable situation that Nehemiah sought to rectify later on (Neh. 11:1-2).[14]

In conclusion, it is impossible to know a great deal about the construction and configuration of walls about Jerusalem in the postexilic period, including the time of Nehemiah. What is clear is that for the greater period of time there were no walls or none sufficient, at least, to provide protection. Whether this was the result only of harassment from unfriendly neighbors or also because of a population that had outstripped the capacity of the earlier walls cannot be known. It likely was a combination of the two.

The eschatological import of the vision is much less debatable. The time will come, Zechariah learns, when there will be no need of walls to protect the great population of the city, for YHWH Himself will be a wall of fire and a source of glory (v. 5).[15] Such a vision of Jerusalem first appears in Ezekiel in an eschatological passage (38:10-13) that speaks of the nation's security despite the absence of material fortification. When the enemies of Israel advance upon them, YHWH will send fire against them (39:6) with the result that His holy name will be known in the midst of Israel (39:7). The juxtaposition of the themes of unwalled villages, fire, and YHWH's glorious presence is certainly striking and instructive.

Though the imagery is different, one can nevertheless hardly fail to connect the fire and glory of this vision with the language of the exodus and wandering narratives.[16] YHWH had led His people out

---

13. Kathleen Kenyon, *Digging Up Jerusalem* (London: Ernest Benn, 1974), 181-85.
14. Williamson, *Ezra, Nehemiah*, 270-71.
15. Petersen associates this "wall of fire" with the fire altars that surrounded the unwalled Persian city Pasargadae, altars that symbolized the cosmic god Ahura Mazda and his strength and protection (D. L. Petersen, *Haggai and Zechariah 1-8*, 171). Although there is no doubt that the Jewish exiles may have known of such a phenomenon, inner-biblical imagery itself is sufficient to account for Zechariah's language. For the use of the "wall of fire" motif in postbiblical literature, see Ira Chernus, "'A Wall of Fire Round About': The Development of a Theme in Rabbinic Midrash," *JJS* 30 (1979): 68-84.
16. L. G. Rignell, *Die Nachtgesichte des Sacharja* (Lund: CWK Gleerup, 1950), 77-78.

of Egypt by a guiding and protecting pillar of fire (Ex. 13:21; cf. 14:19-20, 24, 25; Pss. 78:14; 105:39), one associated with His glory (Ex. 33:9). Isaiah 4:5 is especially relevant, for it too looks forward to the day when YHWH will create over Zion and her people "a flaming fire at night, for over all the glory will be a canopy." That glory will, of course, be His own presence (vv. 10, 11; cf. Hag. 2:9).

C. THE ORACLE OF RESPONSE (2:6-13; HB 2:10-17)

1. WARNING TO BABYLON (2:6-9; HB 2:10-13)

Translation

⁶"Ho, there! Flee from the northland!" says YHWH, "for like the four winds of heaven I have scattered you," says YHWH. ⁷"Ho, Zion, escape, you who live with the daughter of Babylon." ⁸For thus says YHWH of hosts, "After glory has He sent Me to the nations plundering you, for he who touches you touches the *opening of My eye. ⁹I am about to shake My hand over them, so that they will be a spoil to their own slaves. Then you will know that YHWH of hosts has sent me.

Exegesis and Exposition

This oracle,[17] unlike that of 1:16-17, does not respond immediately or peculiarly to the preceding vision but serves more as a summation of the message of the first three visions as a whole, much like 6:9-15 provides an oracular conclusion to the last three visions. The points of commonality between these two pericopae will be explored at some length below. For now it is important to note that the oracle at hand has a twofold thrust: warning to Babylon (vv. 6-9) and promised blessing to Judah (vv. 10-13). In both cases the message is addressed directly to Judah, both as an exiled (vv. 6-7) and a restored (vv. 10-11) people.

There is no question as to the location of the "northland" (v. 6), for the next verse identifies it as Babylon. This fixes the setting, then, as the Babylonian exile, the occasion for God's people having been scattered to the four winds. But that is precisely the problem, for the exile, by Zechariah's time, had already come and gone. In what sense could YHWH be appealing for Zion to return from Babylonian bondage? The question might be answered partially in the recognition that the return to the homeland was not complete. Indeed, it appears likely that only a minority of the exiles ever returned. But this can

---

17. For a careful analysis of this oracle, see Albert Petitjean, *Les Oracles du Proto-Zacharie*, (Paris: J. Gabalda, 1969), 89-94.

hardly be in mind here, for Zion or the daughter of Zion (v. 10) is none other than the reconstituted community, the remnant that was the nucleus of the redeemed covenant people. They have already come home by 519 B.C.

It is more likely that the answer must be found once more in the eschatological realm. The prophets universally attest that the return from Babylon under Cyrus was by no means the only example of such a thing. Indeed, they knew of a dispersion far more serious and widespread than anything known in biblical times, a dispersion nonetheless couched in terms of a Babylonian exile (cf. Deut. 28:64; 30:1-4; Isa. 40–55; Ezek. 12:15-16; Mic. 4:10). It is that great scattering yet to come that is the subject here. But the emphasis is not on the judgment but on restoration.[18] YHWH will send His people into exile but will bring them triumphantly back again for one overriding reason— that they might know that YHWH of hosts has sent one to deliver them (v. 9).

That the aspect is primarily eschatological is put beyond question by the comparison of the scattering of Judah to the spreading of the four winds; it is universal in scope, not just a localized diaspora. "Four winds" is most likely a way of speaking of the four quarters of the earth, that is, the whole earth.[19] Jeremiah, referring to a scattering of the Elamites, says that YHWH will disperse them by the four winds from the four quarters of the heavens, so that "there will be no nation where the outcasts of Elam will not come" (Jer. 49:36). Daniel describes in the same terms the distribution of the divided Macedonian empire (Dan. 11:4).

There will be an escape for God's people from this worldwide dispersion. In fact, Zion is commanded to escape, as the imperative mode makes clear. The language once again is unmistakably eschatological, for in this kind of prophetic discourse Zion is the favorite term used to describe the eschatological kingdom.[20] "Daughter of Babylon" (v. 7) is simply a synonym for Babylon itself, but again one much at home in end-time speech (Isa. 47:1; Jer. 50:42; 51:33).[21]

After the double command of "flee" and "escape," directed to Zion, YHWH states the reason for His desire that His people should do so—for their good and His glory. Verses 8 and 9 are unusually difficult because of the confusion about the subject and the agent.

---

18. Meyers and Meyers, *Haggai, Zechariah 1-8*, 103.
19. D. Winton Thomas, "The Book of Zechariah, Chapters 1-8," *IB*, 6:1065.
20. Cf. Stolz, s.v. "Zion," *THAT*, 2:550-51.
21. Petersen observes that the phrase "daughter of Babylon," in collocation here with "daughter of Zion" (vv. 7, 10), suggests the diminution of the former and the exaltation of the latter (*Haggai and Zechariah 1-8*, 176).

YHWH speaks in v. 8, but the verb in the next clause, שְׁלָחַנִי (*šĕlāḥanî*, "sent me"), appears to suggest that some unknown subject has sent YHWH Himself "after glory." If indeed the pronominal suffix refers to YHWH, the subject also must be YHWH, because only God could so act in reference to deity. The meaning then would be, "After glory I have sent Myself." This is obviously a highly circuitous way to say something that could be said much more plainly.

The BHS note suggests that שְׁלָחַנִי be emended to שֹׁלֵחַ עֲנִי (*sōlēaḥ 'ănî*), to be rendered "I am sending." While this would provide a happy solution, it lacks any support in the text or the versions. Another way must be sought.

The best approach may be to construe the standard introductory phrase of v. 8 not as a direct quotation formula ("thus says YHWH") but as an introduction to the task of the prophet himself who, therefore, becomes the referent in the pronominal suffix ("He has sent me"). One could then translate something like, "YHWH of hosts has said the following, that after glory He has sent me. . . ." This may indeed have been the understanding of the scribes who recognized the difficulty in v. 8*b* of the first common singular suffix on "eye" (עֵינִי, *ʿênî*, "my eye") and through a *tiqqun sopherim* altered it to "his eye" (עֵינוֹ, *ʿênô*).[22] This allows the prophet to continue to be the speaker throughout the verse. If the first singular suffix is retained, YHWH must be the subject of the predicate שָׁלַח, (*šālaḥ*, "sent") and the original problem remains. For that reason we argue for the following rendering of v. 8: "YHWH of hosts has said the following, that after glory He has sent me to the nations plundering you, for he who touches you touches the opening of His eye." It is Zechariah who has been sent, clearly only in the sense of his being a herald from Jerusalem.

The phrase "after glory" is also problematic. Both BHK and BHS try to clarify it by proposing אֲשֶׁר כְּבֹדוֹ (*'ăšer kĕbōdô*) for אַחַר כָּבוֹד (*'ahar kābôd*). This alters the translation from "after glory" to "according to his glory," a reading that is both ingenious and reasonable. Again, however, no ancient witnesses support such a proposal, so it must be understood as it stands. The particle אַחַר by itself can function as either an adverb, a conjunction, or a preposition[23] but with the fol-

---

22. H. G. Mitchell, *A Commentary on Haggai and Zechariah*, 146. The reading עֵינוֹ (*ʿênô*) is now attested in the Qumran fragment 4 Q 12ᵉ, so far the oldest extant witness to Zech. 2:12 (EB, 2:8). Thus, it may not be a true *tiqqun* at all and may, in fact, represent the original as a euphemism. See Russell Fuller, "Early Emendations of the Scribes: The Tiqqun Sopherim in Zechariah 2:12," in *Of Scribes and Scrolls*, ed. Harold Attridge, John J. Collins, Thomas H. Tobin (Lanham, Md.: University Press of America, 1990), 26-27.

23. BDB, 29-30.

lowing noun כָּבוֹד is doubtless here a preposition of place or an adverbial conjunction of time or purpose. If the former, the idea is that the sending immediately followed in the wake of glory, a most difficult conception. If viewed temporally, the sending succeeded the glory, that is, sprang from it. Thus, perhaps, "After (the display of His) glory, He sent me."[24] This would not be unusual, for the self-disclosure of YHWH's glory was often the occasion of or motivation for the ministry of the prophets (cf. Isa. 6). It is obvious that the glory of YHWH had been most manifest to Zechariah in the night visions he was experiencing.

The third possibility, that אַחַר refers to purpose, seems most satisfactory.[25] The idea is that the prophet has been sent in order to restore and magnify the glory of YHWH. He has gone to the nations only in the sense of his proclamation of salvation and judgment (cf. Ezek. 39:21).

The recipients of Zechariah's message or ministry here are the nations who plunder Zion. The present participle שֹׁלְלִים (*šōlĕlîm*) implies not necessarily that the plundering is occurring at the moment but that it is characteristic of the nations that they are plunderers of God's elect people.[26] This is only one example of their "touching" them, a touching that is tantamount to laying injurious hand on YHWH Himself. The verb נָגַע (*nāgaʿ*, "touch"), especially with the preposition בְּ (*b*), usually denotes to touch harmfully,[27] and it clearly does here, as the plundering has already indicated.

With v. 9 the subject shifts once more as YHWH declares that He will shake His hand over these foes of Zion just described. The shaking of the hand is a use of the verb נוּף (*nûp*, "shake") in a hostile sense.[28] It is as though YHWH has an instrument of war that He is about to bring down upon Babylon and the nations. In a most ironic twist, these nations who plundered Zion will become a plunder of their erstwhile slaves.[29] Isaiah particularly supports this notion in his de-

---

24. This is the explanation of Petitjean, who provides an exhaustive history of interpretation as well as a full analysis of occurrences of אַחַר; *Les Oracles du Proto-Zacharie*, 109-19.
25. Carola J. L. Kloos, "Zech II 12: Really a Crux Interpretum?" *VT* 25 (1975): 729-36.
26. The Meyers see this as a note of caution concerning Persia, which, though up to this point had adopted a benign policy toward the Jews, could never fully be trusted (*Haggai, Zechariah 1-8*, 166).
27. BDB, 619.
28. Samuel Amsler, *Aggee, Zacharie 1-8, Zacharie 9-14*, CAT (Neuchatel: Delachaux & Niestlé, 1981), 75. Cf. Isa. 10:32; 11:15; 13:2; 19:1*b*; Job 31:21.
29. This, of course, has roots in the Exodus spoliation of Egypt by redeemed Israel (Ex. 12:36; cf. Ezek. 39:10; Obad. 17). See Chary, *Aggée-Zacharie, Malachie*, 69.

scription of the second exodus of God's people from the Babylonian bondage (Isa. 45:3, 14; 49:22-23; 60:5-6, 10, 16, 17; 65:13-16; cf. Hag. 2:7; Zech. 14:14). The lesson is clear. From the very beginning YHWH had said to Abraham in that great covenant affirmation of Gen. 12:3: "I will bless them that bless you, but him who curses you I will curse." That pledge was never abrogated and proved to be in force even with respect to the postexilic community of Judah.

Shifting the subject one more time, Zechariah establishes the credibility of his message and ministry by declaring that once YHWH's gracious act of restoration had occurred, it would be obvious to all the world that YHWH had sent him (v. 9b). Like Moses long before, and in a similar context of judgment and redemption, Zechariah's credentials would be validated by YHWH's faithfulness to the word He had proclaimed through His servants the prophets (Ex. 3:12; 4:1-5).[30]

Additional Notes

2:8 The famous "apple of his eye" derives from a *hapax legomenon* (בָּבָה, *babâ*), cognate to Aramaic בָּבָא (*bābā'*) or Akkadian *bābu*, both meaning "gate." It is thus the opening of the eye that is intended here or, perhaps with most modern scholars, the pupil.[31] In either case it represents one of the most important and vulnerable parts of the body. To strike a blow at Zion is to strike one at YHWH, wounding Him in a most sensitive area, to carry out the full import of this bold anthropomorphism.

2. BLESSING FOR JUDAH (2:10-12; HB 2:14-17)

10"Sing out and be happy, daughter of Zion, for look, I have come; I will settle in your midst," says YHWH. 11"Many nations will join themselves to YHWH in that day, and they will be *My people. Indeed, *I will settle in your midst." Then you will know that YHWH of hosts has sent me to you. 12YHWH will inherit Judah as His portion in the holy land and will choose Jerusalem again. 13Be silent, all flesh, in YHWH's presence, for He is roused in His holy dwelling place.

Exegesis and Exposition

From a word of warning to Babylon and the nations (vv. 6-9) the prophet turns to one of blessing for Judah. These two ideas are closely

---

30. For fulfillment of prophecy as attestation to a prophet's integrity and authenticity, see J. Lindblom, *Prophecy in Ancient Israel* (Oxford: Basil Blackwell, 1962), 213-15.
31. Unger, *Zechariah*, 50.

connected, for the blessing of God's own people can come ultimately only when all hostile powers have been put down. The two parts of the oracle also hang together literarily around the themes of the daughter of Babylon versus the daughter of Zion (vv. 7, 10) and the mighty acts of YHWH as empirical evidence of the integrity of Zechariah as a prophet (vv. 9, 11).

The expression "daughter of Zion," like "daughter of Babylon," is a personification that in this case suggests not only the corporateness of Judah's existence as one people of YHWH, but the tenderness that YHWH feels toward her as the Father. There is also the likelihood that the phrase is merely a circumlocution for Jerusalem, as several other references in the OT attest.[32] Thus David speaks of the gates of the daughter of Zion (Ps. 9:14), which contextually is Jerusalem. Song of Solomon, in parallel stanzas, equates the daughters of Jerusalem with the daughters of Zion (3:10-11). This last reference is of no relevance to the matter of Zion and Jerusalem as daughters, but it does show that Zion and Jerusalem are synonymous.

Isaiah commonly employs the phrase to denote Jerusalem. He remarks that the daughter of Zion has been left as a hut in the field (1:8), a "besieged city." Also, he speaks of the washing of the daughters of Zion parallel to the cleansing of Jerusalem (4:4). An even more remarkable parallel occurs in Isa. 37:22, in which the daughter of Zion and the daughter of Jerusalem are one and the same. More apropos of the use in Zechariah is the eschatological passage Isa. 62:11-12. There the daughter of Zion is told, "Your salvation is coming," the result of which is that she will be called "one sought out, an unforsaken city."

Jeremiah (6:1-2; Lam. 1:6, 7; 2:10), Micah (1:12-13; 4:8), Zephaniah (3:14), and Zechariah elsewhere (9:9) use the same figure. The fact that YHWH goes on to say in the present oracle that He will live in the midst of Zion puts the Zion=Jerusalem equation beyond doubt, for the Temple was in the Holy City. Even though He may inherit all of Judah as His allotment, YHWH pledges to choose Jerusalem above all (v. 12).

Zion's response to the redemption promised in vv. 6-9 is a ringing cry of joy. The verb expressing this (רָנַן, rānan) is a neutral one conveying the idea of a loud, piercing cry or shout. Coupled with שָׂמַח (śāmaḥ, "be happy"), as here, it means an expostulation of indescribable joy.[33] One could even translate the verbs as a hendiadys, "shout

---

32. Second Kings 19:21; Isa. 52:2; Lam. 2:13; cf. Ps. 76:3 [EB 76:2]; Isa. 10:32 (Q). See H. Haag, *TDOT*, 2:332-38, s.v. בַּת.
33. Chary points out that this combination of verbs is found nowhere else but that רָדַן, with synonyms of שָׂמַח, occurs frequently as an expression of thanks for deliverance from exile (e.g., Isa. 44:23; 49:13; 54:1; Jer. 31:7; Zeph. 3:14-18); T. Chary, *Aggée-Zacharie, Malachie*, 70-71.

joyfully." The reason for such unmitigated joy is that YHWH is coming and will live in Zion's midst.

One of the major tenets of ancient Israel's faith that distinguished her from the paganism of the ancient world was her concept of the immanence, the nearness, of her God as opposed to the aloofness of the gods of the nations. They had their altars and idols, to be sure, but these were only tangible means of having access to deities that were otherwise beyond human reach. YHWH also is utterly transcendent, as the OT consistently affirms. But—and this is the revolutionary contribution of Israel's theology—He also lives among His people, even if invisible. The covenant relationship between them calls for a place where He resides on earth and in which He can be approached.

This "theology of presence"[34] appears as early as Genesis, where it is emphasized that "God walked in the garden" with man (Gen. 2:8). It continues in the stories of the patriarchs, who time after time were conscious of the presence of YHWH among them (Gen. 17:22; 18:1, 22; 32:22-30). Moses most dramatically was aware of YHWH's presence (Ex. 3:1-5; 19:3, 20; 33:17-23), and it was he who articulated the truth that YHWH, the God who made covenant with Israel, desired to live among His people, particularly in Tabernacle and Temple. He told Moses, after the Book of the Covenant was delivered, "Make for me a dwelling-place that I may dwell among them" (Ex. 25:8). He then promised that His presence would go with them (Ex. 33:14). The Psalms (68:16, 18 [HB 68:17, 19]; 74:2) and prophets (Isa. 8:18; Joel 3:17, 21; Zech. 8:3, 8) also describe YHWH as the one who dwells in their midst. This is the message of the NT as well, for God according to John "became flesh and dwelled among us" (John 1:14). A major eschatological theme there is the eternal residence of God among His redeemed ones (Rev. 21:3). That theme, of course, is consonant with that of the OT, where the promise appears that "I will set My tabernacle among you" and "will walk among you and be your God" (Lev. 26:11-12). Ezekiel, in the same eschatological context, proclaims the promise of YHWH that "I will set My sanctuary in their midst forever . . . and the nations will know that I am YHWH who sanctifies Israel, when My sanctuary is in their midst forever" (Ezek. 37:26-28). Even the name of Jerusalem in that day will be יְהוָה שָׁמָּה (*YHWH šāmmâ*), "Yahweh is there" (Ezek. 48:35).[35]

---

34. This theme forms the center of the theology of Samuel Terrien (*The Elusive Presence*, San Francisco: Harper & Row, 1978). Terrien refers to Zech. 2:10 as an announcement of the "imminence of Yahweh's advent in a language reminiscent of the priestly description of the wilderness tabernacle" (p. 395).

35. For a helpful collocation of the relevant passages on this theme, see Richard D. Patterson, "Joel," in *EBC*, ed. Frank E. Gaebelein (Grand Rapids: Zondervan, 1985), 7:265-66.

Both Haggai (2:4, 9) and Zechariah share this theology of divine presence, a note that was especially meaningful in the days of the regathered community that was struggling to build a Temple worthy of God's dwelling-place. But Zechariah is particularly concerned to orient this theological truth to the age to come, when not just Israel or Judah, but all nations, would join themselves to YHWH and be His people (2:11). This, too, is a hope shared by the united voice of the prophets, for it has ever been the purpose of YHWH to redeem all the peoples of the earth to Himself in a mighty display of grace. Of these peoples (גּוֹיִם, *gôyim*) He will make a nation (עָם, *'ām*), the disparate becoming one in a common faith and mission.[36] It is these, all peoples, who will know YHWH, and it is they among whom He will live in that day.

A hint of this universal dominion appears already in the early psalms (e.g., Pss. 22:27-28 [HB 22:28-29]; 67:2-4 [HB 67:3-5]; 72:11, 17; 86:9), but the great eschatological sections of the prophets spell it out in glorious detail. Isaiah refers to the latter days (cf. "that day" in Zech. 2:11) in which all nations will make pilgrimage to the house of YHWH and will walk in His ways (Isa. 2:2-3). They will see His glory and will worship Him (66:18-20). Micah concurs (Mic. 4:1-2), adding the promise that the gathered nations will no longer go to war but will sit in peace under their vines and fig-trees (4:3-4). Zephaniah, too, speaks of an assembling of nations who, following their purification, will praise YHWH as one people (Zeph. 3:8-9).

Jeremiah says that Israel's repentance will make possible the blessing of the nations (4:1-2), but it is only after the exile that hope for the nations once more becomes a major concept. Haggai hints of it (2:7), but it is Zechariah who raises the issue to the forefront. In our present passage (2:11) he casts the verb "join" (לָוָה, *lāwâ*) in the niphal stem, suggesting that it is YHWH who joins the nations to Himself as an act of grace.[37] They also come as an act of their own will (Zech. 8:22-23), complementing the process of salvation initiated by YHWH. "In that day," Zechariah says finally, "YHWH shall be king over the whole earth" (Zech. 14:9; cf. vv. 16, 17). When that happens, those to whom the prophet is speaking will know that he has been a true

---

36. Petersen, *Haggai and Zechariah 1-8*, 182.
37. The niphal can be either reflexive ("join themselves") or passive ("be joined"), but a holistic biblical soteriology demands the latter, for it is always YHWH who takes the initiative in salvation. Meyers and Meyers point out that the phrase "they will be my people" is covenant language, such as is used in Jer. 31:33, and in 32:38 with reference to the new covenant between God and His people. His role in covenant making is that of sovereign, the one who brings people into covenant with Himself (*Haggai, Zechariah 1-8*, 169).

messenger of YHWH. He will have passed the acid test of prophetic credibility, the fulfillment of the prophetic word (v. 11; cf. 2:9; Deut. 18:20-22).

Zechariah continues his marvelous disclosure of end times by asserting that not only will the nations confess YHWH and become His people, but YHWH will take as His special allotment in all the created universe the land of Judah, the "holy land" (v. 12). This focus on Judah, and specifically on Jerusalem, is a well-established emphasis in the OT, as we have already noted. All the nations will be His, but the very heart of the nations will be Judah and the holy city.[38]

The word used to designate YHWH's relationship to Judah in the eschaton is the verb נָחַל (nāḥal, "inherit"), a term commonly used in legal texts to refer to inheritance or other means of acquisition of property or possessions.[39] Preparation for this eschatological dimension lies already in the historical record of the OT, where YHWH's ownership of territory and/or possessions is clearly spelled out as a function of His sovereignty. In the broadest sense, "the whole earth is mine," He says (Ex. 19:5), testifying thereby to His right to distribute it in turn to His elect people as a covenant grant (cf. Lev. 25:25-46). In a narrower sense, Canaan becomes His land, a נַחֲלָה (naḥălâ) or "inheritance" He provided for His ungrateful people. The same collocation of land and inheritance occurs in Jer. 16:18. Psalm 79:1 defines the inheritance of YHWH as the Temple and, by extension, Jerusalem. Finally, Zechariah also designates Jerusalem as YHWH's inheritance, and with it the land of Judah.

Of interest here is the increasingly narrow parameters of YHWH's inheritance, from the whole earth to the Jerusalem Temple. This narrowing of compass runs parallel, however, to an increasing broadness of His saving activity, for He becomes, in the end, not just the God of Abraham, Isaac, and Jacob but the God of the nations. The eschatological vision is that of the Sovereign One reigning from the Temple in Jerusalem over all His redeemed creation, a vision supported particularly in the exilic and postexilic prophetic literature (Ezek. 36:22-23; 37:21-28; 38:16, 23; 39:7; 47:21-23; Hag. 2:7-9; Zech. 8:3, 20-23; 9:9-10; 14:9-11, 16). This insistence by Haggai and Zechariah on the importance of the Temple as the earthly center of YHWH's universal dominion must have provided great impetus to their community to undertake Temple reconstruction as a necessary precondition to that eventuality.

The oracle closes with a solemn injunction to all humanity to be silent before YHWH (v. 13), an understandable reaction to the glori-

---

38. Kenneth L. Barker, "Zechariah," in EBC, 7:620.
39. E. Lipinski, TWAT, V:3/4:cols. 342-55, s.v. נָחַל.

ous revelation just disclosed. How can human lips speak in the presence of a holy God, one who has saved His people in mighty demonstrations of power in the past and who is now aroused once more to do the same.[40] The arousing (or awakening) of YHWH does not suggest He has been asleep, but the verb עוּר (*'ûr*) as used here means to "incite to activity."[41] He is in His holy dwelling place (מָעוֹן, *mā'ôn*), no doubt a reference here to the heavenly realm, from whence He will shortly come to make His abode among His people. The prophet's allusion in v. 12 to the "holy land" (אַדְמַת הַקֹּדֶשׁ, *'admat haqqōdeš*) as the earthly home of YHWH, who will come (v. 13) from His "holy dwelling-place" (מְעוֹן קָדְשׁוֹ, *mě'ôn qādšô*), is a most striking literary device.[42]

Additional Notes

2:11 To avoid the unexpected and unannounced reference by the prophet to himself at the end of v. 11, the LXX and Syr. read (or alter) the pronominal afformatives on לִי and שָׁכַנְתִּי to לוֹ and (presumably) שָׁכְנוּ respectively, resulting in, "many nations will join themselves to YHWH in that day and they will be His people. Indeed, they will settle in your midst." While this brings this verse into conformity with an otherwise third person account, such jarring interruptions of subject are not at all foreign to Hebrew syntax, especially when, as here and in v. 9, there is a formulaic phrase such as "you will know that YHWH of hosts has sent me (to you)." Mitchell (*A Commentary on Haggai and Zechariah*, 147) cites several other examples (Ezek. 11:10, 12; 13:9, 14).

---

40. Joyce G. Baldwin, *Haggai, Zechariah, Malachi*, (London: Tyndale, 1972), 112.
41. BDB, 755.
42. Petitjean, *Les Oracles du Proto-Zacharie*, 150.

5
Vision Four: The Priest (3:1-10)

A. CONTENT OF THE VISION (3:1-5)

As many scholars have noted, vision four, although certainly part of the series of eight in Zechariah, is quite different from the others.[1] First, only it and the next (4:1-4) deal with actual, identifiable human persons. Second, the usual vision introduction formula is lacking. Characteristically the prophet sees (1:8, 18; 2:1; 4:2; 5:1; 6:1) but here is shown (hiphil of רָאָה, *rā'â*; v. 1) by an unknown subject. Third, there is no interpreting messenger here, contrary to the other visions where an angel (1:9, 19; 2:3; 4:5; 5:5; 6:4) or YHWH Himself (1:21) serves that role. So much an aberration is this omission that some scholars find no interpretation section to this vision at all. Petersen, e.g., limits the vision to vv. 1-5, followed by two oracular responses (vv. 6-7, 9; and v. 8) and a final verse (v. 10) building upon one of the oracular responses. He argues that neither response belongs originally to the vision.[2] Finally, there appears to be an absence of standard formulaic

---

1. Carol L. Meyers and Eric M. Meyers, *Haggai, Zechariah 1-8*, AB (Garden City, N.Y.: Doubleday, 1987), lvii, 179.
2. David L. Petersen, *Haggai and Zechariah 1-8*, (London: SCM, 1985), 202. Quite clearly, however, the Angel of YHWH provides an interpretation of the vision in vv. 6-7, a section that gives every impression of being original to the vision proper, particularly inasmuch as the Angel of YHWH is mentioned otherwise in the vision (vv. 1-5).

language in the vision, such as "raising my eyes," "looked/saw," "again," "what/where/whither?" an angel asking "what?" and so forth.

Some of these observations may be significant, but not to the extent of doubting the originality of vision four to the series or to arguing on form-critical or other grounds that it fails to qualify as an apocalyptic message. With that in mind it is helpful to take an overview of the passage.

Joshua, the high priest with whom Zechariah was personally acquainted, appears in the prophet's vision in a state of ritual impurity, so much so that he is being condemned for it by Satan in the very presence of YHWH. YHWH, however, views Joshua as a chosen vessel and demands that he be considered as such and provided appropriate attire. This is done, and then Joshua is told that if he continues to be faithful to YHWH, he will have a place of ongoing prominence in the purposes of YHWH. The lesson to be learned, so the oracular section (vv. 8-10) points out, is that Joshua and his colleagues are a sign of what YHWH is about to do by means of His servant the Branch, who will be a foundation stone of redemption and restoration.

Translation

¹Next he showed me Joshua the high priest standing before the messenger of YHWH, and Satan was standing on his right to accuse him. ²*YHWH therefore said to Satan, "May YHWH rebuke you, O Satan; may YHWH, who has chosen Jerusalem, rebuke you. Is this one not a brand snatched from the fire?" ³Now Joshua was dressed in filthy clothing while standing before the messenger. ⁴The latter spoke up to those standing in His presence, "Take the filthy clothing from him." Then He said to him, "Look, I have absolved you of your iniquity and *will dress you in fine attire." ⁵*Then I spoke up, "Let a clean turban be put on his head." So they put a clean turban on his head and clothed him, the messenger of YHWH standing (nearby).

Exegesis and Exposition

As already noted, the vision commences abruptly without the usual formula. The anonymity of the subject draws immediate attention to Joshua, not to the prophet himself or someone else. This Joshua is the same as that mentioned by Haggai (Hag. 1:1), namely, the son of Jehozadak.[3] He appears one more time in Zechariah (6:11) and

---

3. For a discussion of Joshua and his Aaronic and Zadokite lineage, see the commentary on Haggai 1:1. See also Nigel Allan, "The Identity of the Jerusalem Priesthood During the Exile," *HeyJ* 23 (1982): 259-69; James C. VanderKam, "Joshua the High Priest and the Interpretation of Zechariah 3," *CBQ* 53 (1991): 553-70.

is well known in the books of Ezra (2:2; 3:2, 8; 4:3; 5:2; 10:18) and Nehemiah (7:7; 12:1, 7, 10, 26). Ezra mentions him as one of the early leaders of the returnees to Jerusalem in 538 B.C., listing him after Zerubbabel, with whom he is often mentioned and usually in that order. He was instrumental in getting an altar set up (3:2) and in organizing the work of rebuilding the Temple (3:8-9). He stood with Zerubbabel in resisting the overtures of the Jews' enemies, who wanted to participate in the project at first (4:3) but then tried to bring it to a halt.

Neither Ezra nor Nehemiah describes Joshua as "high priest." This is left to Haggai and Zechariah, though clearly the prominence of Joshua among the priests in even the accounts of Ezra and Nehemiah leaves no question that they also knew him as such (cf. especially Neh. 12:1, 7). He was a direct descendant of Aaron through Zadok, founder of the line of priests established by David and Solomon (1 Chron. 6:3, 8-15). His father Jehozadak had gone into Babylonian exile in 586, so it is likely that Joshua was already advanced in years when he returned to Jerusalem in 538, nearly 50 years later. Certainly by the year of Zechariah's night visions (519) Joshua was an old man.

On the other hand, he was apparently the grandfather of Eliashib, the high priest contemporary with Nehemiah c. 445 B.C. (Neh. 12:10; cf. 3:1). Williamson maintains the possibility (though why is not clear) that Joiakim, son of Joshua, may have filled the nearly 80-year period between 519 and 445, but he thinks it improbable.[4] Joshua, however, could easily have served until 500 or so, and Eliashib may have begun as early as 465, leaving Joiakim with only 35 years. Frank Cross arbitrarily dates Joshua's birth c. 570, making him only 50 in 520. Then, on the basis of what he calls papponymy, he considers Eliashib to be the great grandson of Joshua, dating his birth c. 495. This requires Joiakim to hold office for only 25 years rather than 35. Whether Cross's papponymy hypothesis is correct or not, the four generations of priests from Jehozadak through Eliashib (c. 445) could easily occupy the 150 years.[5] However that may be, there is no reason to question the role of Joshua and his genealogical and chronological linkages in either direction.

The setting of the vision is quite clear. Joshua is standing in a tribunal, where he is being accused of unfitness for the priestly ministry. The judge is the messenger (or angel) of YHWH. The implied definite article makes it virtually certain that this being is the same

---

4. H. G. M. Williamson, *Ezra, Nehemiah*, WBC (Waco, Tex.: Word, 1985), 363.
5. Frank M. Cross, "A Reconstruction of the Judean Restoration," *JBL* 94 (1975): 10, 17.

as the messenger of YHWH in 1:11, 12. There he was distinguished from YHWH Himself (v. 12), but here he is identified with Him (v. 2).[6] This appears even more likely inasmuch as Satan is accusing Joshua before the messenger, a notion that finds no support elsewhere in the Bible.[7] The adversary always argues his case before God, not a representative of God, as the very similar scene in the prologue of Job establishes beyond doubt.

There the heavenly court is assembled, and Satan comes before God to report on his activities (Job 1:6-7). He has asserted his dominion over the earth, he says, but God is quick to point out that Job has not capitulated (v. 8). Satan then begins his series of accusations against both Job and God, claiming that Job's ability to survive is because of the protective hedge of grace that God has placed about him (1:9-11; 2:4-5). Throughout the scene Satan is in dialogue with God, who sits as judge in the case. The same understanding exists in the NT, where the power and sovereignty of God and the authority of Christ finally go unchallenged because the "accuser of the brethren," who accused them before God continuously, has been cast down (Rev. 12:10).

A possible objection to the identification of the messenger with YHWH in our passage is that the messenger appears to quote YHWH in vv. 6-7, thus differentiating himself from YHWH. However, this is not a serious problem at all, for a careful reading of Angel of YHWH passages makes it clear that the messenger, though distinguished from YHWH, often speaks as YHWH (cf. Gen. 16:7-13; 21:17; 22:11-12, 15-16; 31:11-13; Judg. 6:11-24; 13:15-20). That is, the messenger of YHWH is YHWH as He discloses Himself to human beings.

The accuser in the scene is unnamed, being designated only as הַשָּׂטָן (*haśśāṭān*, "accuser or adversary"). As is clear from the Job story,

---

6. This is so obviously true, and problematic, that most modern scholars, following the Syriac (cf. Additional Notes), emend "YHWH" to "Angel of YHWH." See, e.g., H. G. Mitchell, *A Commentary on Haggai and Zechariah*, ICC (Edinburgh: T. & T. Clark, 1912), 153. Such special pleading is oblivious to the witness of the OT to the interchangeability of YHWH and the Angel of YHWH.

7. Day attempts (following Nils Johansson, *Parakletoi* [Lund: Gleerup, 1940], 35) to connect Zech. 3:1-7 to Job 16:20; 33:23 where a *mēlîṣ* ("intercessor," "mediator") and *mal'āk* ("angel") respectively appear as intermediaries (Peggy L. Day, *An Adversary in Heaven* [Atlanta: Scholars Press, 1988], 90-94, 101-2). This association is fallacious in that no case at all can be made for the celestial nature of the interpreter in Job 16:20 (cf. N. H. Tur-Sinai, *The Book of Job* [Jerusalem: Kiryath Sepher, 1967], 269-70). Moreover, in Job 33:23, as Tur-Sinai points out (pp. 471-73), the angelic spokesman is not addressing an interpreter, but he is one. He is speaking to God on behalf of man.

the adversary is a powerful angelic being who has direct access to the heavenly courts themselves. A comprehensive biblical theology deduces that he was incarnated in the serpent of the temptation account in Genesis 3.[8] How and why he became the adversary remains a mystery, but it is plain throughout the Scriptures that he is subservient to the sovereignty of God and that his pernicious conduct as the accuser is something permitted to him by an all-wise God. The commonly held position that primitive Israelite theology regarded Satan as at first an upright being employed by God for high and holy ends and that he was viewed as having departed from that role in historical times to become the adversary of God finds no support in the Bible.[9] In fact, the NT teaching is the very opposite: "The devil sins from the beginning" (1 John 3:8).[10]

Nonetheless, the doctrine of a personal devil or accuser, known by name as Satan, only gradually emerged in OT revelation. When it originated cannot be known because there is no agreement on the date of the prologue of Job,[11] where, as we noted, Satan is mentioned many times. Apart from Zechariah, the only other reference to him by name is in 1 Chron. 21:1. There the author attributes David's temptation to number Israel to Satan rather than to God, as the parallel narrative in 2 Samuel 24 implies. Besides revealing the theological development that took place by the time of the Chronicler, it is noteworthy that he omits the definite article and refers to the adversary not as "the Satan" but as "Satan." The function of the accuser thus was equivalent to his personal name.

Here (as in 1 Chron. 21:1) the accuser and the accused are standing, the former at the right side of the latter. The posture and language of the courtroom are self-evident.[12] The accusation is not stated but may be inferred from v. 3: Joshua is clothed with filthy garments. Satan therefore challenges his right to function in the cult

---

8. Walther Eichrodt, *Theology of the Old Testament* (London: SCM, 1967), 2:205-9.
9. For the history of the development of this view, see Day, *An Adversary in Heaven*, 5-15.
10. "Beginning" here refers to the beginning of human history when Satan was already a fallen being; cf. Geerhardus Vos, *Biblical Theology* (Grand Rapids: Eerdmans, 1954), 44-45. Before that time he had, indeed, existed as a perfect being until, because of hubris, he rebelled against God and was removed from his lofty position, as Isaiah 14 and Ezekiel 28 suggest. See J. Barton Payne, *The Theology of the Older Testament* (Grand Rapids: Zondervan, 1962), 291-95.
11. For the various views, see R. K. Harrison, *Introduction to the Old Testament* (Grand Rapids: Eerdmans, 1969), 1036-41.
12. N. L. A. Tidwell, *"Wā'ōmar* (Zech. 3:5) and the Genre of Zechariah's Fourth Vision," *JBL* 94 (1975): 347.

under those circumstances. YHWH the judge speaks up, perhaps even before Satan can open his mouth, and rebukes him to his face. The fact that it is YHWH who invokes YHWH to rebuke supports the thesis that the messenger of YHWH in this scene is indeed YHWH Himself.

The rationale for the rebuke is that Satan has overlooked the fact that YHWH, who has chosen Jerusalem, has declared Joshua to be a brand snatched from the fire (v. 2). The reference to YHWH as "He who has chosen" (הַבֹּחֵר, *habbōḥēr*) Jerusalem establishes the connection between this vision and the preceding oracle (and the first as well) where YHWH, speaking with reference to the eschaton, promises to choose Jerusalem again (2:12; cf. 1:17; 2 Chron. 6:6; Isa. 14:1 [Israel]). "He who has chosen Jerusalem" thus orients the vision to the end times, but it also draws attention to Jerusalem as the place of YHWH's habitation, particularly in the Temple.

The high priest of that Temple, at least in the early postexilic period, is Joshua, one compared here to a brand snatched from the fire. One should not look for too much hidden meaning in the metaphor.[13] All that YHWH is saying is that when it looked as though all was lost as far as the covenant community and its worship were concerned, YHWH graciously stepped in and rescued a remnant by means of which He would reconstitute a believing people.[14] The same figure of speech appears in Amos 4:11, where YHWH describes the survivors of His various judgments on Israel as a brand (אוּד, *'ûd*, as in Zech. 3:2) snatched from the burning. The concept of a remnant is most evident.[15] What Satan must understand is that man looks on the outward appearance, but God looks on the heart. Joshua, indeed, and with him the entire remnant nation,[16] may be impure, but the elective grace of God is still in effect. He has snatched Joshua from the fire and will do something wonderful for him.

The scene that meets the human eye is that of a high priest dressed in garments stained with excrement,[17] a sign of the vilest

---

13. As Stuhlmueller suggests, "brand from the burning" is proverbial speech used to describe a narrow escape (Carroll Stuhlmueller, *Haggai and Zechariah*, ITC [Grand Rapids: Eerdmans, 1988], 78).
14. Inasmuch as the OT high priest represented the whole covenant people generally (Ex. 28:12, 29, 39, etc.), it is certain that Joshua here symbolizes the remnant nation. See the case for this made by Kenneth L. Barker, "Zechariah," in *EBC*, ed. Frank E. Gaebelein (Grand Rapids: Zondervan, 1985), 7:623.
15. For Zechariah's contribution to "remnant theology," see Gerhard F. Hasel, *The Remnant* (Berrien Springs, Mich.: Andrews Univ., 1972), 260-63.
16. Siebeneck is correct in suggesting that Joshua here represents the nation as a whole; Robert T. Siebeneck, "The Messianism of Aggeus and Proto-Sacharias," *CBQ* 19 (1957): 319.
17. "Excrement" is the best rendering of צוֹאִים (BDB, 844; KBL, 789-90). Deut.

defilement. The same way of describing human sinfulness is found in Isa. 4:4 where, interestingly enough, the daughters of Zion will be cleansed from their filthiness in a purging associated with the coming of the "Branch," a messianic figure introduced in Zech. 3:8 in connection with our present vision. As distasteful and shocking as this may be in general terms, the appearance of the high priest so defiled was beyond comprehension. His dress was to be of the finest, purest linen, especially on the Day of Atonement (Lev. 16:4), so to see him this way was to see him in a state of absolute cultic and spiritual disqualification.

The laws of ritual purity are most explicit regarding a case like this. In Leviticus 22 YHWH instructs Moses to excommunicate any priest who tries to minister with his "uncleanness" upon him (22:3). The word used here is טֻמְאָה (*ṭum'â*), a generic term for uncleanness, but one that would include the specifics of this vision. The only remedy for a condition like this is the ritual bath that cleanses him and allows him once more to minister the priestly office (Lev. 22:6-7). A change of garments would obviously be necessary as well.[18]

Against this background, the accusation of Satan regarding Joshua is most cogent. Joshua indeed is unclean and unsuitable for service. But precisely at this point of his need YHWH speaks, commanding those attending Him to remove Joshua's filthy garments and to replace them with "fine attire" (v. 4) or, as BDB suggests (p. 323), "A robe of state taken off in ordinary life" (cf. Isa. 3:22). He passes from a condition of utmost defilement to one of unsurpassed glory. It is significant, however, that מַחֲלָצָה, the word used here to speak of the new garments, is not the normal one for the robes of the high priest (בִּגְדֵי־קֹדֶשׁ, "holy garments"; cf. Ex. 28:2). Rather, it describes the apparel of royalty or wealth. The point is that Joshua forms with Zerubbabel a dyarchic rule in which the high priest increasingly enjoyed political as well as cultic authority. The turban of v. 5 also supports this understanding.[19]

Not to be missed is the hint of interpretation in the middle of v. 4. In the course of the exchange of garments YHWH says to Joshua, "I have absolved you of your iniquity." The hiphil of עָבַר (*'ābar*, "absolve") stresses the fact that the removal of the sin is an act of grace; it is YHWH who causes it to happen. The issue is not so much one of

---

23:14 (EB 23:13) commands the Israelites in the wilderness to dispose properly of excrement (צֵאָה), for otherwise YHWH will not walk among them but, to the contrary, will turn away from them.

18. Halpern draws attention to the clothing of Aaron and his sons as part of their ordination and investiture; Baruch Halpern, "The Ritual Background of Zechariah's Temple Song," *CBQ* 40 (1978): 173; cf. Ezek. 44:18-19.
19. See D. L. Petersen, *Haggai and Zechariah 1-8*, 198.

mere ritual disqualification, as serious as that is, but of iniquity in general.

Once the rich, clean apparel has been placed on the priest, he gains also a new turban for his head (v. 5). This object (צָנִיף, *ṣānîp*) distinguished the high priest from his fellows (Ex. 28:39),[20] but the most striking thing about it was the inscription attached to its front, "Holy to YHWH" (Ex. 28:36). The defilement and unholiness of Joshua have been dealt with so radically that he now appears as the epitome of holiness.

In a remarkable twist to this whole episode, the messenger of YHWH, who has up till now issued the condemnation against the accuser and the commands to deal with Joshua's impurity, stands aside while Zechariah himself speaks up.[21] As a priest he was very much aware of all the implications of what he saw, and so it seems that when Joshua stood reclothed with all but the headdress, the prophet could no longer restrain himself. "Let them put a clean turban on his head," he cried out. Such interruption of a vision by the one receiving it is not common in other prophets (cf. Isa. 6:8), but it does occur frequently elsewhere in this very book (cf. 1:9, 19, 21; 2:2; 4:2, 4; etc.). What is unique here is the command of a mere man to bring about a purpose of God.

Additional Notes

3:2 An attempt to circumvent the problem of the messenger of YHWH and YHWH Himself as interchangeable figures appears to be at the root of the Syriac reading "messenger of YHWH" for the MT "YHWH." This, of course, is unnecessary.

3:4 The difficult inf. abs. הַלְבֵּשׁ for the expected imperfect l.c.s. אַלְבִּישׁ or (if the proposed transposition of BHS be accepted) 2 m.p. impv. הַלְבִּשׁוּ or pret. 3 m.p. וַיַּלְבִּישׁוּ is perfectly acceptable in light of the frequent use of infinitive absolute for a finite verb. Cf. GKC, 113z.

3:5 Zechariah's sudden interruption in the MT has prompted the Vg and other ancient witnesses to read "he said" for "I said," allowing

---

20. The usual word for the high priest's turban is מִצְנֶפֶת, cognate to צָנִיף but limited to priestly dress. Chary sees in the new dress of Joshua his messianic character, "in type du Christ, prêtre et roi" ("as a type of Christ, priest and king"). His suggestion that Zerubbabel was already in decline, and thus Joshua was taking his role as prince, has no basis in history or the text, however (Theophane Chary, *Aggée-Zacharie, Malachie* [Paris: Librairie Lecoffre, 1969], 77).

21. Tidwell, "*Wā'ōmar* (Zech. 3:5) and the Genre of Zechariah's Fourth Vision," 343-44, 354-55. Tidwell views 3:1-7 form-critically as a "council scene," a standard feature of which is a single intrusion or outburst that produces a final, conclusive word or deed from YHWH. Zechariah's "outburst" (v. 5) is therefore much to be expected.

YHWH to continue as the subject. The LXX tries to resolve the tension by omitting the verb וָאֹמַר ("then I said") and commencing the sentence with the jussive יָשִׂימוּ ("let them set") or imperative וְשִׂימוּ ("set"), thus again making YHWH the subject. Both of these alternatives, although possible and even helpful, are unnecessary once it is granted that the recipient of the vision may participate in his own revelation, a phenomenon that occurs many times within this book alone. (See the commentary on this verse.)

B. INTERPRETATION OF THE VISION (3:6-7)

Translation

⁶Then the messenger of YHWH charged Joshua, ⁷"Thus says YHWH of hosts, 'If you will walk in My ways and keep My requirements, then you will judge My house and keep My courts; and I will give you free access among these who stand by.'" (3:6-7)

Exegesis and Exposition

Having invested Joshua with pure, clean clothes and a spotless turban, thereby signifying the removal of his ritual impurity, YHWH reveals to him the meaning and purpose of what He has done. He has prepared him for a larger role in the covenant community, provided Joshua meets the conditions of obedience incumbent in that relationship.

There is more than mere suggestion or proposal here. The verb עוּד (*ʿûd*, "charged") in the hiphil carries the idea of bearing witness or testifying or, as in this case, delivering a solemn exhortation.[22] Joshua has not been cleansed for nothing. He must now respond to the act of grace by assuming the task to which his reinstatement has called him. There are, however, two conditions that must be met, one having to do with his way of life and the other with his specific vocation as priest.

First, Joshua must walk in the ways of YHWH. This way of describing a godly pattern of life is particularly native to covenant contexts, where "way" (דֶּרֶךְ, *derek*) is a metaphor for covenant fidelity.[23] It is not surprising that the idiom occurs many times in Deuteronomy and the "Deuteronomistic" literature, given the covenant basis of that literature. Deuteronomy 8:6 commands Israel to walk in the ways of YHWH, an exhortation coupled with that of fearing Him. In the famous covenant charge of Deut. 10:12-22, YHWH lists the

---

22. BDB, 730.
23. Alfons Deissler, *Zwölf Propheten III. Zefanja, Haggai, Sacharja, Maleachi* (Würzburg: Echter Verlag, 1988), 278-79.

requirements of the relationship: to fear Him, walk in His ways, love Him, serve Him, and keep His ordinances and statutes. The verb "keep" (שָׁמַר, *šāmar*) is the same as that in the second part of the charge to Joshua (Zech. 3:7). A third example must suffice, that in Deut. 28:9, where YHWH promises to make Israel a holy people (cf. Ex. 19:6) if they "keep the commandment" and "walk in his ways." The charge to Joshua the priest to walk in the ways of YHWH must clearly be seen in a covenant framework.

The second part of the admonition, to "keep my requirements," refers to the particular office to be filled by the one who has entered into covenant relationship with YHWH. The cognate accusative based on the verb meaning "to guard or watch," (שָׁמַר מִשְׁמֶרֶת, *šāmar mišmeret*) is, again, most at home in covenant passages (cf. Deut. 11:1; Gen. 26:5; 1 Kings 2:3). With particular application to the office of priest, which is the matter of concern in our passage, the same cognate accusative construction appears elsewhere.[24] The Aaronic priests must "keep the charge of YHWH" lest they die (Lev. 8:35: cf. 22:9). In Ezekiel's vision of the eschatological Temple, YHWH rebukes His people for having broken the covenant by not keeping the charge of His holy things (Ezek. 44:8). The new order of priests, the Zadokites, will, however, keep the charge entrusted to them (44:16; cf. 48:11). Nehemiah reports that as late as his own time the Jews rejoiced that the priests and Levites had kept the charge of God, particularly with respect to purification (Neh. 12:45).

There can be no question, then, that Joshua's commission pertains to a priestly function within the framework of a covenant relationship. The faithful disposition of the two prerequisites just described in reference to this will result in three clearly defined benefits. First, Joshua will judge the house of YHWH. This idiom occurs only here, but since "house of YHWH" or "house of God" refers primarily to the tabernacle or Temple, for Joshua to judge the Temple suggests a meaning for the verb דִּין (*dîn*) such as "rule" or "govern." This anticipates a quasi-political role of the high priest that gained increasing reality with the decline of postexilic secular authority.[25] By the beginning of the Ptolemaic era (c. 300 B.C.) both political and religious power became centered in one man, the high priest.[26] Joshua's governing seems, first of all, to speak of his domination of the Temple and all its functions.

---

24. T. Chary, *Aggee-Zacharie 1-8*, 76.
25. Rex Mason, "The Prophets of the Restoration," in *Israel's Prophetic Tradition*, ed. Richard Coggins, Anthony Phillips, and Michael Knibb (Cambridge: Cambridge Univ., 1982), 147.
26. Victor Tcherikover, *Hellenistic Civilization and the Jews* (Philadelphia: Jewish Publication Society, 1966), 58-59.

The second promised benefit is that Joshua will "keep the courts" of YHWH. The word translated "courts" (חָצֵר, *ḥāṣēr*) can mean any enclosed area or even a village or settlement, but the strong parallelism between the word here and "house" in line A makes it certain that the outlying precincts of the Temple are in view. Governing the Temple extends to keeping watch over its courts and enclosures.

The third promise is that Joshua will have free access among those who are standing by. This is a circumlocution for the literal "walkings" (מַהְלְכִים, *mahlĕkîm*), but the sense is clearly that Joshua as the dominant figure in the cultus—indeed, as its ruler—will come and go as he chooses among "these who stand by." Who these latter are is not at all fully spelled out in the passage. They are simply those who are "standing." Clues as to their identity must be found within the vision passage itself. It is worth noting that the participial form of the verb "to stand" (עָמַד, *ʿāmad*) occurs six times in the vision, four times in the singular (vv. 1 [bis], 3, 5), and twice in the plural (vv. 4, 7). Joshua, Satan, and the messenger of YHWH are all standing in the former singular uses, so the "standing ones" of v. 4 are beyond doubt to be understood as the "standing ones" of v. 7. Those in v. 4 appear to have been individuals attending upon YHWH, for a normal understanding of the syntax would suggest that the pronominal suffix on "presence" (לְפָנָיו, *lĕpānāyw*) has as its most immediate referent the subject of the clause, namely YHWH. Thus, YHWH commands these of the heavenly council standing before Joshua to remove his filthy garments. These same ones who assist Joshua in this process will constitute the "standing ones" among whom he will walk freely, that is, the angels of heaven.[27]

One might object that it is unlikely that even angelic attendants could either dress or disrobe the high priest, but where details of the dressing procedure are available they seem to support this very idea. At the initial establishment of the Aaronic priesthood, YHWH commanded Moses to clothe Aaron and his sons (Ex. 28:41; 28:8-9; Lev. 8:7-9; Num. 20:28). Whether this set a pattern for all time cannot be determined, but in the visionary form in which the robing of Joshua takes place one cannot argue out of hand that angelic agents were not employed to assist with the high priest's clothing.

---

27. K. L. Barker, "Zechariah," in *EBC*, 7:624-25. In the vision they clearly are angelic beings, but in Joshua's actual earthly ministry they must be human associates of the priest. See R. T. Siebeneck, "The Messianism of Aggeus and Proto-Zacharias," 320. For a comprehensive study of the nature and function of the heavenly council, see E. Theodore Mullen, Jr., *The Assembly of the Gods: The Divine Council in Canaanite and Early Hebrew Literature* (Chico, Calif.: Scholars Press, 1980).

C. ORACLE OF RESPONSE (3:8-10)

Translation

⁸"Hear now, Joshua the high priest, you and your companions who are sitting before you, *these men are a symbol: I am about to bring My servant, the Branch. ⁹As for the stone which I have set before Joshua, upon (the) one stone there are seven eyes. I am about to carve an inscription on it," says YHWH of hosts, "that I will *remove the iniquity of that land in one day. ¹⁰In that day," says YHWH of hosts, "everyone will invite his friend under the vine and under the fig-tree."

Exegesis and Exposition

The interpretation of the vision (vv. 6-7) did not completely clarify its message, a task now left to the oracle as well.[28] It is important that both vision and oracle be construed as two sides of the one revelation in order for the full import to be appreciated. Thus Joshua, who has been central to the vision, is addressed in the oracle. It is likely that his companions are those of the priestly and levitical offices who served with him. The fact that they are sitting means nothing more than that Joshua himself was likely sitting as Zechariah addressed him as God's spokesman.[29]

The visionary nature of the oracle finds further elaboration in the reference to the men as signs, to the branch, and to the engraved stone with eyes on it. Again, it is sound hermeneutics to interpret the vision by the oracle but also the oracle by the vision.

With a sharp command YHWH addresses both Joshua and his companions who sit before him. Their positioning is significant because they are לְפָנֶיךָ (*lĕpānêkā*, "before you") here, whereas in the vision the "standing ones" were לְפָנָיו (*lĕpānāyw*, "before him"), i.e., YHWH, and thus also in Joshua's presence. That is, they sustained the very same physical relationship in both cases, in a circle of comradeship as it were. Moreover, these men here are described as a "sign," a term in Hebrew (מוֹפֵת, *môpēt*) that connotes a phenomenon that is an act of God Himself designed to communicate some mysterious

---

28. The Meyers (*Haggai, Zechariah 1-8*, 222) describe this as a "supplementary oracle," a piece much at home in its canonical context. Van der Woude, however, sees it as part of an original literary unit (A. Van der Woude, "Zion As Primeval Stone in Zechariah 3 and 4," in *Text and Context: Old Testament and Semitic Studies for F. C. Fensham*, JSOTSup 48, ed. W. Claassen [Sheffield: Sheffield Academic Press, 1988], 243).
29. J. Baldwin, *Haggai, Zechariah, Malachi*, 116.

truth.[30] Their being symbolical men might relate to the role they played in the vision,[31] but more likely they have something to do with the coming of the Branch, a statement appearing in the next clause, probably as an epexegetical comment. That is, these men are a sign concerning the coming of the Branch and of revived and restored Israel as a priestly nation.[32]

The collocation of "servant" (עֶבֶד, *'ebed*) and "branch" or "sprout" (צֶמַח, *ṣemaḥ*) is highly allusive messianically.[33] Haggai had used the term "servant" to describe Zerubbabel (Hag. 2:23; cf. commentary on Haggai, pp. 56-57), and, of course, the prophet Isaiah employs it prolifically in reference to an individual Messiah as well as the nation Israel (41:8, 9; 42:1, 19; 43:10; 44:1, 2, 21; 45:4; 48:20; 49:3, 5, 6, 7; 52:13–53:12). "Branch" is not as common a messianic epithet but is more precise in its connection to the Davidic dynasty. Psalm 132:17 expresses this connection by the use of the cognate verb צָמַח (*ṣāmaḥ*, "sprout"): "There [Zion] I will cause the horn of David to sprout up." Jeremiah records the promise of YHWH: "I will raise up to David a righteous branch who will reign as king" (Jer. 23:5; cf. 33:15).

That a royal messianic figure is in view can hardly be disputed.[34] Moreover, Zechariah later goes on to aver that this Branch-servant will build the Temple of YHWH (6:12-13). This task was already committed to Zerubbabel, at least in early postexilic Judah (Hag. 1:1, 8, 12). It is tempting therefore to identify the Branch of Zechariah 3:8 with Zerubbabel, a possibility to be examined carefully later on. One must remember that Joshua, too, was charged with this responsibility (Hag. 1:1, 12, 14), and it is that fact that gives special cogency to the suggestion that it is he specifically who is in mind here, at least typologically. The difficulty in his being the Branch in the full messianic sense is, of course, his lack of descent from David. H. G. Mitchell sees Joshua in view here, but he bases his conclusion on the false notion that Zerubbabel could not be in view because he had not yet appeared on the political scene.[35] The crowning of Joshua in 6:11 and

---

30. S. Wagner, *TWAT IV*: 6/7, 1983, cols. 750-59, s.v. מוֹפֵת. Eichrodt draws attention to the connection between Joshua and his priestly colleagues as a sign on the one hand, and the Davidic branch of 6:9-15 on the other (Walther Eichrodt, "Von Symbol zum Typos," *TZ* 13 [1957]: 509-22).
31. Albert Petitjean, *Les Oracles du Proto-Zacharie*, (Paris: J. Gabalda, 1969), 169.
32. The priests now begin to serve a prophetic function inasmuch as they signal the coming of the Branch. Cf. Unger, *Zechariah*, 64.
33. For an exhaustive survey of usage, see Petitjean, *Les Oracles du Proto Zacharie*, 182-84, 194-206.
34. Halpern, "The Ritual Background of Zechariah's Temple Song," 169.
35. H. G. Mitchell, *A Commentary on Haggai and Zechariah*, 156.

his association (if not identification) with the Branch (6:12) also support the idea that Joshua, too, is a messianic figure.[36] Margaret Barker, appealing to Isa. 4:2 (though not to Jer. 23:5; 33:15, perhaps because they hurt her case), argues that "branch" is a priestly epithet in Zechariah both here in 3:8 and in 6:12. Thus Zerubbabel is nowhere in view in either passage. The prophet, she says, is cast as a messianic Temple builder in order to promote the Jerusalem priesthood over others, particularly over the priesthood in Samaria.[37]

This understanding of the matter gives good sense to the means whereby Joshua and his friends are a sign: they portend the coming of the Davidic ruler. As Joshua rules over the Temple and cult, so the Branch will come to exercise His dominion. This leads nicely into the stone set before Joshua, for in the context of the Branch as Temple builder the stone must be taken to be a foundation-stone for that structure.[38] Indeed, Zerubbabel and Joshua had already laid the foundation of the second Temple (Ezra 3:10; cf. Hag. 2:15, 18; Zech. 8:12), an act that prepared the way for God's cleansing and renewal of His sinful people (Hag. 2:14; cf. 2:19).

Stone as a messianic symbol is also well known throughout the Bible, for the foundation upon which God's future Temple of redemption and dominion must rest is none other than the messianic figure of whom this scene provides a foreshadowing. As Kenneth Barker points out, the Messiah was, in His first advent, a stumbling stone and rock of offense (Ps. 118:22-23; Isa. 8:13-15; Matt. 21:42; 1 Peter 2:7-8) but now is the chief cornerstone of the church (Eph. 2:19-22). In the eschaton He will be "the dependable rock of the trusting heart."[39] Thus, behind this vision hovers the unmistakable aura of messianic promise and fulfillment.

Remarkable about the stone of the present oracle is that it has seven eyes (Zech. 3:9). Seven in biblical numerology signifies fullness or completeness, so the seven eyes suggest omniscience or undimmed vision.[40] In vision five (Zech. 4:1-14) the seven eyes are identified as

36. Meyers and Meyers, *Haggai-Zechariah 1-8*, 203-4.
37. Margaret Barker, "The Two Figures in Zechariah," *HeyJ* 18 (1977): 41-42.
38. Albert Petitjean, *Les Oracles du Proto-Zacharie*, 179-82. Van der Woude takes the stone to be the temple mountain itself on the basis of the mythological notion of the "primeval stone," the אֶבֶן־אַחַת ("one stone") of v. 9 (A. S. Van der Woude, "Zion As Primeval Stone in Zechariah 3 and 4," 244-45). For other views, see E. Lipiński, "Recherches sur le Livre de Zacharie," *VT* 20 (1970): 25-30. Lipiński himself links the stone in Zechariah 3 with the stone of the wilderness from which Moses extracted water. The seven עֵינָיִם are "seven fountains" from which flow streams of forgiveness and cleansing (pp. 29-30). Thus Lipiński reads עַיִן II ("fountain spring") rather than עַיִן I ("eye").
39. K. L. Barker, "Zechariah," 626.
40. Meyers and Meyers, *Haggai, Zechariah 1-8*, 209. For other interpretations,

the eyes of YHWH that "run to and fro over the whole earth" (4:10). This universal attention by YHWH is an affirmation of His sovereign control, His unlimited dominion (cf. 1:10). Hanani the prophet had long before taught King Asa of Judah that "the eyes of YHWH run to and fro over the whole earth to show himself strong on behalf of those whose heart is upright toward him" (2 Chron. 16:9).

In addition to the eyes, however, there is about to be engraved on the stone an inscription reading, "I will remove the iniquity of that land in one day." This admittedly novel interpretation[41] of v. 9b rests on several factors. First, it seems evident that the stone in question is the cornerstone of a building, in this case most likely the Temple of YHWH.[42] Second, in the ancient Near Eastern world cornerstones invariably bore inscriptions attesting to the builder and the purpose for which the building was erected.[43] The eyes on the stone would be the divine signature identifying YHWH as the real architect and builder of the structure. The necessary statement of purpose is the rather oblique reference to the function of the Temple as a place of expiation of sin. When the Davidic branch comes and the Temple of YHWH is complete, the iniquity of all the land will be removed, all in one day.

This removal of iniquity calls to mind the taking away of the iniquity of Joshua in the vision (v. 4). It is most evident that the two ideas, and hence the two passages, are to be taken together. Joshua, "snatched from the fire" by divine grace, is a prototype of the whole nation, the "kingdom of priests" (Ex. 19:6), that will also finally achieve cleansing and forgiveness. When that comes to pass, YHWH pledges, everyone will invite his friends to sit in peace with him under the vine and the fig-tree (Zech. 3:10). This is a common image in the eschatological literature to describe the day of YHWH's universal dominion (Mic. 4:4; cf. 1 Kings 4:25).

In summary, vision four describes a day of redemption in which Joshua the high priest, typical or representative of Israel as a priestly people, will be cleansed of his impurities and reinstalled in his capacity as high priest. This presupposes a Temple in which this can take place, so Joshua will build such a structure. Again, this Temple is only

---

see Albert E. Rüthy, "'Sieben Augen auf einem Stein,'" *TZ* 13 (1957): 522-29. Rüthy emends to עֲוֹנִים ("sins") and says the stone contained seven sins. His association of this with the 12 stones of the priestly mitre is clearly a non sequitur.

41. See, however, Petitjean (*Les Oracles du Proto-Zacharie*, 185), who comes close to this view.
42. Samuel Amsler, *Aggee, Zacharie 1-8, Zacharie 9-14*, CAT (Neuchatel: Delachaux & Niestlé, 1981), 85.
43. Petitjean, *Les Oracles du Proto-Zacharie*, 184-85.

the model of one to come, one whose cornerstone is YHWH Himself. That cornerstone contains the glorious promise of the regeneration of the nation, a mighty salvific event that will be consummated in one day (Isa. 66:7-9).

Additional Notes

3:8 The MT has "they" (הֵמָּה) are "men of a sign," which appears to exclude Joshua himself. Syriac reads "you" (אַתֶּם), which includes Joshua. It is very likely that Joshua is a part of the sign and that "they," by a shift of object by the speaker, could include all of them. It is also possible that the independent personal pronoun is functioning as a copula and thus is not to be translated. See Bruce K. Waltke and M. O'Connor, *An Introduction to Biblical Hebrew Syntax* (Winona Lake, Ind.: Eisenbrauns, 1990), 16.3.3.

3:9 The troublesome מַשְׁתִּי (*maštî*) of the MT, rendered by the standard lexicons as "depart" in the qal (BDB, 559; KBL, 506), should be compared to Akkadian *mêšŭ*, "to forgive, disregard sins" (CAD/M II, p. 41).

6
Vision Five: The Menorah (4:1-14)

A. CONTENT OF THE VISION (4:1-3)

Vision five forms a matching pair with vision four, both in terms of its juxtaposition to it and its subject matter.[1] Both deal with cultic persons or objects (the high priest and the menorah respectively), both mention historical persons contemporary to the prophet (Joshua and Zerubbabel), both refer to temple building, and both reach their climax on a strong messianic note. For all these reasons it is to be expected that the two visions are mutually interpretive. In addition, because there is a clear process of theological development in the series of night visions, all that has gone before will need to be kept in mind as this fifth vision is unfolded.

Translation

¹The messenger who spoke with me then returned and awakened me as one is awakened from his sleep. ²He said to me, "What do you

---

1. The Meyers do not count our vision four (Zech. 3:1-5 [7]) as a numbered vision—describing it instead as the "prophetic vision"—so this is their fourth out of seven, the centerpoint of the series (Carol L. Meyers and Eric M. Meyers, *Haggai, Zechariah 1-8*, AB [Garden City, N.Y.: Doubleday, 1987], liii-lx). Nevertheless, there are points of similarity between 3:1-7 and 4:1-14 (and differences, of course), enough to make the case that their juxtaposition is deliberately arranged to form a matching pair. See Christian Jeremias, *Die Nachtgesichte des Sacharja*, (Göttingen: Vandenhoek & Ruprecht, 1977), 202.

see?" *I answered, "I have looked and seen a menorah of pure gold
with its *receptacle on top and seven lamps on it with seven and
seven pipes going to the lamps upon the top. ³(There are) also two
olive trees by it, one on the right of the receptacle and the other on its
left."

Exegesis and Exposition

The prophet here sees in vision five a menorah flanked by olive
trees, the whole of which symbolizes the Spirit of YHWH. That Spirit
will enable Zerubbabel to complete the temple project, which had
already begun. The conduits of the supply of the spirit that energizes
this work, that is, the olive trees, are two anointed ones who stand by
and serve the sovereign Lord of the earth. The task only hinted at in
vision four is spelled out clearly: the Temple is to be finished. And the
means, also only enigmatically suggested in the symbol of the branch
(3:8), is also clarified. It is through Zerubbabel, made powerful by
God's own Spirit. He, with Joshua, has been anointed for this holy
task, and the two of them represent the two great messianic offices,
priest and king, that are central to the sovereign rule of YHWH over
all things.

The "messenger who spoke" to Zechariah, a principal figure in
the previous visions except the last (cf. 1:9, 13, 14; 2:3), returns now
and awakens the prophet. Since he continues in a visionary state, the
awaking cannot be from the vision but from a state of lethargy within
the vision.[2] The verb עוּר (*ûr*, "awaken"), in fact, frequently means to
"stir up" or incite to some kind of action. It is the word used in Hag.
1:14 to speak of YHWH's stirring up the spirit of Zerubbabel and
Joshua to continue work on the Temple (cf. Jer. 51:11; Ezra 1:1).
Zechariah is not waking from sleep, then, but his sensibilities have
been so heightened as to be comparable to a man waking from a
slumber. Otherwise, there is no point to the repetition of the idea that
he was awakened "as one is awakened."

Once Zechariah is aroused, the "messenger who spoke" asks him
what he sees. His answer is that he has seen (perfect tense) a golden
menorah, an article that would be immediately recognizable by a
priest such as Zechariah. The menorah[3] was the lampstand of the

---

2. H. G. Mitchell, *A Commentary on Haggai and Zechariah*, ICC (Edinburgh:
T. & T. Clark, 1912), 161.
3. Menahem Haran, *Encyclopedia Judaica* (Jerusalem: Keter, 1972), 11: cols.
1355-63 s.v. "menorah." Critical scholars who date the tabernacle menorah
to the P sources of postexilic times generally reject the seven-branched
version of P as the model for Zechariah's vision. On archaeological grounds
they see it as a single stand with a lamp on top with several spouts. See,
e.g., David L. Petersen, *Haggai and Zechariah 1-8*, (London: SCM, 1985),
217-23.

tabernacle/Temple, located on the south side of the Holy Place. According to the detailed description of Ex. 25:31-37, it was made of pure gold. It consisted of a central lamp with three branches extending from each side, each of which held a lamp. There were thus seven separate lamps in all. The lamps themselves were in the form of a cup (גְּבִיעַ, gābîaʿ), which served as a receptacle for the oil. The purpose of the menorah obviously was to illuminate the interior of the Holy Place (Ex. 25:37), but it also spoke of the illumination of the presence of YHWH Himself.

The menorah of Zechariah's vision, although having much in common, also differs considerably with the menorah of Exodus.[4] First, it appears to have a general vessel for storing the oil located somewhere above the center of the menorah. Called a גֻּלָּה (gullâ), it cannot be the ordinary cup for oil at the top of the central stem and branches, for that is always known as a gābîaʿ, as already noted. It seems rather to have been a reservoir from which pipes distributed oil to the cups on the lamps. The word appears elsewhere to describe a water pool (Josh. 15:19), a bowl (Eccles. 12:6), or the bowl-like shape of the tops of the Temple pillars (1 Kings 7:41). This leads to a second difference, namely, the pipes (מוּצָקוֹת, mûṣāqôt), which are never mentioned in connection with the menorah of the tabernacle/Temple. The reason for them here is obvious. The oil is not poured into the lamps by the Levites but comes from the olive trees via the reservoir and from thence into the cups. There is no human hand or effort whatsoever. The third difference is the presence of the olive trees, something unthinkable within the confines of the sanctuary. That the trees directly yield their oil without benefit of plucking and crushing the olives is also suggestive of the visionary nature of this menorah, and hence its allowable differences from the historical object.

The number and distribution of the pipes is somewhat problematic. The MT reads literally, "seven and seven pipes to the lamps which are upon its top" (v. 2). The latter part of the statement locates the seven lamps upon the tops of the central stand and the six branches. "Seven and seven" may be a distributive use of numerals[5] to indicate that there were seven pipes on each side of the menorah so that each cup was replenished by two pipes. The reason for this is not clear unless the two olive trees each have seven pipes leading not only into the central reservoir but from it to the seven lamps. The LXX sidesteps the problem by omitting the first "seven" so that there are seven pipes for seven lamps.

---

4. For an excellent overview of the whole problem, see Robert North, "Zechariah's Seven-Spout Lampstand," *Bib* 51, (1970): 183-206.
5. GKC, 134q.

Another interpretation that enjoys considerable favor is that there are seven pipes going to each of the seven lamps, making forty-nine in all![6] This almost unimaginable spaghetti-like configuration not only seems overly complicated as a practical matter, but its meaning would also be extremely difficult to recover. Moreover, the notion that there are seven pipes into *each* of the cups rests on a reading into the passage of something that is not there. The phraseology is simply "seven and seven pipes to (or pertaining to) the lamps." Only an overly wooden interpretation can find a total of forty-nine such conduits.

Many scholars take מוּצָקוֹת (*mûṣāqôt*, rendered here "pipes") as referring to the spouts of the lamp basins, openings made in ceramic lamps by pinching the soft clay into a spout-like aperture.[7] This is in line with the configuration of lamps excavated all over Palestine whose oil "flowed" in the sense that it was transmitted by the wick from the lamp to the flame. This would generate a translation such as "seven spouts to the lamps which were upon its top." The difficulty inherent in such a translation has led these same scholars to visualize each cup as having seven spouts or, again, forty-nine in all. The typical rendering that results is, "there are seven lamps on it, each of the seven with seven spouts, for the lamps which are on top of it."[8] This is almost a necessary translation if *mûṣāqôt* is taken to be a spout, because it is self-evident that each lamp would have at least one spout.

However, the verb יָצַק, from which מוּצָקוֹת derives, clearly means "flow, pour, cast" (BDB, 427), so it is difficult to see how the "flowings" to the lamps from the top basin can be explained by spouts and wicks. Clearly a conduit such as a pipe is required. Difficulties this may raise in terms of cost, complexity, and the like are minimized because this was a vision.

On balance it seems that the best understanding is that there is one menorah with an oil reservoir suspended above it. This provides oil to the seven lamps of the menorah through seven pipes on each side, or fourteen in all. The reservoir itself is connected to two olive trees, one on each side of it. How this latter aspect functions is clarified in the vision interpretation to follow (v. 12).

The major source of lamp oil in ancient Palestine was the olive, so it is not surprising that two olive trees appear in the vision to provide that fuel. It is important to note that the trees are not to the left and

---

6. Merrill F. Unger, *Zechariah* (Grand Rapids: Zondervan, 1963), 71.
7. North, "Zechariah's Seven-Spout Lampstand," 185.
8. Meyers and Meyers, *Haggai, Zechariah 1-8*, 227.

right of the menorah, but that they flank the reservoir. The oil cannot go straight to the cups but must be mediated through the upper container that receives it directly from the trees.

Additional Notes

4:2 For the MT Kethib "he said" it is preferable to read with the Qere, many Cairo MSS, and most of the versions "I said."

The LXX, Syriac, and Targums eliminate the *mappiq* in וְגֻלָּהּ, in order to read the vocable as the feminine noun גֻּלָּה, "bowl." The Masoretic spelling appears to take the form as a 3 f.s. suffix on a noun גֹּל, otherwise unattested. A 3 f.s. suffix on גֻּלָּה, would, of course, result in גֻּלָּהּ. Perhaps, with most scholars, an emendation involving the dropping of the *mappiq* is in order (as in v. 3). See Kevin Cathcart and Robert P. Gordon, *The Targum of the Minor Prophets* (Wilmington: Michael Glazier, 1989), 193.

B. INTERPRETATION OF THE VISION (4:4-6, 11-14)

Translation

⁴Then I asked the "messenger who spoke to me," "What are these, sir?" ⁵The "messenger who spoke to me" replied, "Do you not know what these are?" So I responded, "No, sir." ⁶Therefore he told me, "This is the Word of YHWH to Zerubbabel, 'Not by strength and not by power but by my Spirit,' says YHWH of hosts."

· ·

¹¹Next I asked him, "What are these two olive trees on the right and left of the menorah?" ¹²And I asked again, "What are these two extensions of the olive trees, which by means of the two golden pipes are emptying out the golden (oil)?" ¹³He replied to me, "Do you not know what these are?" And I said, "No, sir." ¹⁴So he said, "These are the two anointed ones who stand by the Lord of the whole earth."

Exegesis and Exposition

Baffled by what he has seen, the prophet proceeds to ask several questions of the interpreting messenger. This time the interpretation is divided by the oracular response section (4:7-10) between the two interpretation sections (4:4-6, 11-14). Zechariah first inquires as to the menorah and all its appurtenances and then, following the oracle, asks about the two olive trees.

The reason for such an arrangement of the vision has been a matter of much speculation. Older scholarship generally proposed that the oracle was an unwieldy insertion into a unified vision pericope,[9] one consisting of 4:1-6*a*, 10*b*-14. There is no evidence for that at any possible redactionary stage and, in fact, there are good reasons for suggesting that the present order of the material is most deliberate, reflecting both structural and thematic patterns.[10]

First, it is clear that the whole section ends in a most climactic manner: "These are the two anointed ones who stand by the Lord of the whole earth." In light of the obvious coupling of visions four and five, it is interesting to note that vision four begins with Joshua the high priest standing before the messenger of YHWH (3:1). As we shall see, there is good reason to think that Joshua is one of the two olive trees, so that his appearance in both places forms an inclusio around the two visions.

Within the present vision there are also signs of bracketing. Verse 13 records a question by the interpreting messenger as to whether Zechariah understands what he has seen. His answer is negative. The identical question and response occur in v. 5. Immediately before each of these, attention is directed to the two olive trees (vv. 3, 11). The two sections dealing with olive trees and their meaning envelop the central oracular section, not so much, it seems, for clarifying the message as for providing an appropriate climactic conclusion and one that rounds off the vision of the priest that commences in Zechariah 3:1.

With this in mind, it is quite evident that the present structure of the passage intends Zechariah's question of v. 4 to include everything in his purview but the olive trees. His lack of comprehension is met by another question from the interpreting messenger: "Do you not know what these are?" (v. 5). The intent is not to verify that Zechariah is in ignorance, but to drive home the point that he cannot possibly understand what he has seen without supernatural insight. The two parts of the vision are equally mysterious and equally demand outside interpretation.

That interpretation follows. All that the prophet has seen, the messenger says, is the Word of YHWH to Zerubbabel (v. 6). This remarkable association of vision with word makes crystal clear the purpose of such media as visions. They are a means of communicat-

---

9. So, e.g., A. Van Hoonacker, *Les douze petits Prophètes* (Paris: Librairie Victor Lecoffre, 1908), 613-16; D. J. W. Rothstein, *Die Nachtgesichte des Sacharja*, (Leipzig: Hinrichs, 1910), 121-27; D. Ernst Sellin, *Das Zwölfprophetenbuch* (Leipzig: A. Deichert, 1922), 454-55; Karl Elliger, *Die Propheten Nahum, Habakuk, Zephanja, Haggai, Sacharja, Maleachi*, ATD (Göttingen: Vandenhoek & Ruprecht, 1982), 110-11, 126-27; Friedrich Horst, *Die Zwölf Kleinen Propheten, Nahum bis Maleachi*, HAT 14 (Tübingen: J. C. B. Mohr, 1964 [1936]), 232-33.
10. L. G. Rignell, *Die Nachtgesichte des Sacharja* (Lund: CWK Gleerup, 1950), 163-65.

ing the mind of God as surely as a word in propositional form could. Moreover, this is not primarily a word to the prophet but to Zerubbabel, who is mentioned here for the first time in the book (v. 6*a*). A further linkage between this first part of the interpretation and the oracle is established by this reference to Zerubbabel, for his name occurs only three more times in Zechariah, all in the immediately following oracle section. To have completed the interpretation section here by attaching vv. 11-14 would, of course, separate these references to Zerubbabel.

Those scholars who view vv. 6*b*-10*a* as a later insertion do, admittedly, include the name Zerubbabel in v. 6*a* with that insertion, thus designating the opening phrase as v. 6*a*β. Their view falters not so much here as at the end, in v. 10*a*, where the prophet says that "these seven will rejoice." Since there is no reference to seven things in the oracle, scholars such as Petersen[11] must resort to all kinds of manipulations of v. 10 to remove the "seven" from v. 10*a* and place it in v. 10*b*. Petersen's composite translation of v. 10 is:

> For whoever despised the day of small things
>   will rejoice when they see the tin tablet
>   in the hand of Zerubbabel (10*a*).
> These seven are the eyes of Yahweh;
>   they range about over all the earth (10*b*).

Apart from such idiosyncrasies as "tin tablet" for "plumb-line" (which may be a good suggestion), the proposed rendering does violence to the MT as it stands and can be sustained only in the interest of removing "seven" from v. 10*a* (where it belongs), a line belonging to the allegedly interpolated oracle. A literal translation of v . 10 is:

> For who has despised the day of small things?
>   These seven will rejoice when they see the
>   plumb-line (or tin tablet) in the hand of Zerubbabel (v. 10*a*).
> These are the eyes of YHWH,
>   they run about through all the earth (v. 10*b*).

It is clear that both "seven" and "Zerubbabel" belong in v. 10*a*, and that "seven" cannot be torn from the oracle in order to conform to a theory of source division. The subject of the first clause is מִי, the singular interrogative pronoun and not a plural indefinite pronoun as Petersen suggests. The predicate "despised" (בַּז) is also singular in agreement with the subject. "Rejoice" (שָׂמְחוּ) and "see" (רָאוּ) are both plural and need a plural subject. Petersen's "whoever" is, as noted, singular (מִי) and therefore cannot be the subject. [12] Only שִׁבְעָה־אֵלֶּה

---

11. D. L. Petersen, *Haggai and Zechariah 1-8*, 215, 238.
12. Cf. Rignell, *Die Nachtgesichte des Sacharja*, 160.

("these seven") can serve this function in the text as it exists. Petersen's "these seven" is an interpretation, not a translation, for the text actually reads, as suggested already, "these are the eyes," referring back to the "seven" mentioned in v. 10a.

In conclusion, it is unwarranted to assume a certain redactionary stance and then to buttress it by realigning the elements of the text in question. There can be no doubt that Zechariah composed the passage as is and that the "seven" of v. 10a is defined by him as the "eyes of YHWH" in v. 10b. Unfortunately many modern versions follow Petersen in taking "who" or "whoever" as the subject of "rejoice" and "see," rather than "these seven," as the text, as awkward as it stands, requires (thus NIV, JB, JPSV, NEB). Others, however, follow the sense of MT in its traditional rendering (RV, NASB, KJV, NKJV, RSV).

By the date of the night visions, February 15, 519 B.C. (1:7), work on the Temple had begun again in earnest, thanks to the encouragement of Haggai especially (Hag. 2:20-23). That prophet had revealed to the governor that YHWH was about to shake all creation and overthrow all kings and kingdoms by His mighty power. Their military forces particularly would disintegrate before YHWH of hosts. As for Zerubbabel, he would be elevated, becoming the very signet of YHWH—the expression of His sovereignty in the earth.

Against that background the menorah vision finds considerable elucidation. The focus cannot be on the menorah itself but on its source of illumination, the oil that provides its fuel. The reservoir—the lamps, the pipes—all have to do with this fundamental idea that the menorah is useless without the power that energizes it. Likewise the task of temple building and, indeed, of the establishment of the sovereignty of YHWH and His kingdom cannot be accomplished apart from divine enablement; hence the word of YHWH: "Not by strength and not by authority, but by my Spirit" (v. 6).

The pungent, precise style in which this affirmation is made adds to the sense of military flavor inherent in the terminology itself. The strength (חַיִל, *ḥayil*) in view here is almost always military in connotation.[13] In fact, it could as well be translated "army" here or at least "military strength." Similarly, the word for "power" (כֹּחַ, *kôaḥ*), though more generic, is frequently used to describe the prowess of armies in battle, especially in Chronicles and other late literature (cf. 2 Chron. 14:11; 20:12; 26:13; Dan. 8:22, 24; 11:25). What Zerubbabel must do as leader of his people cannot be done by normal human resources and means.[14] It must be done by the appropriation of supernatural power.

---

13. BDB, 298-99.
14. As Amsler suggests, all the resources of Persia were at Zerubbabel's dis-

That power is the power of the Spirit of YHWH of hosts. That epithet of YHWH, "of hosts" (צְבָאוֹת, *ṣĕbā'ôt*), is in itself descriptive of YHWH's role and function as the mighty warrior, the commander of heaven's armies.[15] The Spirit of YHWH is His awesome power, made available to human beings who serve Him at His command. OT theology is not clear concerning the person of the Holy Spirit, the third person of the Godhead who is so central to NT revelation. It prepares for the personal Spirit in many places, however, by suggesting that what the Holy Spirit does in the NT YHWH's Spirit has done in the Old.[16]

In the very beginning one sees the Spirit of God moving upon the primordial waters in creation (Gen. 1:2). The workers on the tabernacle are filled with his Spirit, enabling them to do their creative work (Ex. 28:3; 31:3). Moses' assistants were filled with the spirit of wisdom so they could help him judge the people (Num. 11:17-29). Many of Israel's judges accomplished their mighty works of deliverance because the Spirit of God was upon or even within them (Judg. 3:10; 6:34; 11:29; 13:25; 14:6, 19; 15:14, 19). The prophets prophesied truthfully and powerfully as the Spirit gave them utterance (2 Kings 2:9, 15, 16; Ezek. 2:2; 3:12, 14; 8:3; 11:1, 5).

Particularly relevant and instructive to our problem is the reference to the Spirit of YHWH in the commissioning oracle of Isa. 11:1-5, one recognized by all scholars to be messianic and eschatological. The similarity of language in that passage and in Zech. 3-6 is noteworthy and deserves somewhat detailed attention. Isaiah first speaks of a "sprout" (נֵצֶר, *nēṣer*) from the root of Jesse (11:1). Though the word here is different from the "branch" referred to in Zech. 3:8 (צֶמַח, *ṣemaḥ*; cf. 6:12; Jer. 23:5), the messianic allusion is exactly the same.[17] Isaiah reports that the Spirit of YHWH will rest on this individual, a Spirit granting him wisdom, understanding, counsel, might, knowledge, and the fear of YHWH (Isa. 11:2). With those capacities the messianic ruler will exercise justice for the righteous and administer judgment to the godless (11:3-5).

posal, but even these could not overcome the sense of discouragement felt by the struggling community; Samuel Amsler, *Aggée Zacharie 1-8, Zacharie 9-14*, CAT (Neuchatel: Delachaux & Niestlé, 1981), 93.
15. Patrick D. Miller, Jr., *The Divine Warrior in Early Israel* (Cambridge, Mass.: Harvard Univ., 1973), 145-55.
16. T. C. Vriezen, *An Outline of Old Testament Theology* (Oxford: Basil Blackwell, 1970), 211-17. For a full discussion of the latency of the Holy Spirit in the OT, see Eugene H. Merrill, "Is the Doctrine of the Trinity Implied in the Genesis Creation Account?" in *The Genesis Debate*, ed. Ronald F. Youngblood (Grand Rapids: Baker, 1990), 110-29.
17. S. Wagner, *TWAT* V:5/6, s.v. נֵצֶר.

Zerubbabel, the branch (Zech. 6:12), will also accomplish mighty works by the power of the Spirit (Zech. 4:6). This will include the completion of the Temple (4:7-8; 6:12-13), the assumption of rulership (6:13; Hag. 2:23), and the reduction of iniquity and iniquitous forces (3:9; Hag. 2:21-22).

His role is further clarified in the interpretation of the second half of the vision, Zech. 4:11-14. Once more at a loss to understand the vision he has seen, Zechariah asks about the identity of the two olive trees. This time the location of the trees is not as specifically defined. The vision had placed them on the right and left sides of the upper bowl or reservoir, whereas Zechariah, in the interpretation, points out that they are to the right and left of the menorah as a whole. The meaning, of course, is unchanged. The difference in perception may be explained by Zechariah's interest not in the menorah and its various parts but in the two trees. That, in fact, is his question: "What are these two olive trees?"

So curious and agitated is the prophet that he does not wait for an answer to this question before he asks another: "What are the two extensions of the olive trees, which by means of the two golden pipes are emptying out the golden (oil)?" What he sees here is not completely disclosed in the vision section and will require some comment. The word translated "extensions" (שִׁבֳּלִים, *šibbŏlîm*) means literally "ears," usually ears of grain (Gen. 41:5). Here the agricultural use is clearly precluded, except that whatever is in view appears to sustain the same relationship to an olive tree that an ear does to a stalk of grain. It may be the most outstretched branches or perhaps the olives themselves considered collectively.[18]

In any event there are two of these that are either adjoining two golden pipes or by means of these pipes are discharging their oil. This appears to complete the picture of the vision, for in it the only pipes were the seven on both sides of the menorah whose function apparently was to connect the seven lamps to the reservoir above (v. 2). There is no suggestion as to how the oil was conveyed from its ultimate source (the trees) to the reservoir, a deficiency that seems to be addressed by the two golden pipes. Whether אֲשֶׁר בְּיַד (*'ăšer bĕyad*) in v. 12 should be taken as an idiom of agency ("which by means of") or location ("which are beside")[19] makes little difference, for the total process seems quite clear. From points of issuance on the two trees, two golden pipes conduct their oil to some destination, presumably the reservoir from which the fourteen other pipes feed it to the lamps.

---

18. Meyers and Meyers, *Haggai, Zechariah 1-8*, 255-56; Amsler, *Aggée, Zacharie 1-8, Zacharie 9-14*, 89.
19. For both, see BDB, 391.

The term for the two golden pipes is different from that used to describe the fourteen. Here it is צַנְתְּרוֹת (ṣantĕrôt), evidently a plural of צִנּוֹר (ṣinnôr). The word is a *hapax legomenon*, however,[20] and its meaning can be determined only by the fact that these objects convey something from the extensions of the trees to another location. Either pipe, trough, sluice, or something of the kind is required. North chooses the option "funnel" on the basis of a supposed connection to צִנּוֹר of Ps. 42:8 (EB 42:7), a word he renders "bell" rather than "pipe" or "spout." Because of its funnel-like shape, he says, it was possible for a bell to be construed as a funnel. It is impossible, however, to derive צַנְתְּרוֹת from צִנּוֹר on the basis of present evidence, though something like "pipe" (צִנּוֹר) is clearly related.[21] The fact that they are gold only matches them with the golden menorah.

But what are they conveying? The Hebrew literally says only that they "were emptying from themselves (or from the trees) the gold." Since the trees are olive trees and the menorah lamps are burning olive oil, one can only deduce that the "gold" is referring to the color of the oil. This obviously is not an altogether inaccurate description of olive oil, but the fact that the color is designated would tend to support the view that its color is not what is significant, but its value.[22] The menorah and all its equipment are pure gold, and so is its oil. Precious indeed are all the elements of the vision.

Thus far, then, the prophet Zechariah has described what he has seen, but he cannot understand its significance. For a second time the interpreting messenger underlines the prophet's inability to comprehend by asking him if indeed he fails to discern these aspects of the vision, and again the prophet must say no (v. 13). At this point the messenger reaches the climax of the whole dialogue by declaring that the olive trees are "the two anointed ones who stand by the Lord of the whole earth" (v. 14).

The term "anointed ones" calls to mind a familiar messianic epithet. In fact, "Messiah" is merely a transliteration of מָשִׁיחַ (māšîaḥ), "anointed." The Hebrew word here in Zechariah is different, however. It is בְּנֵי־הַיִּצְהָר (bĕnê hayyiṣhār, lit., "sons of fresh oil"; BDB, 844). Ordinarily this word for oil denotes only a product, something to be bought and sold and without any particular cultic use or significance. The reason the normal noun *māšîaḥ* does not occur in our passage is, however, quite clear. The whole scene has focused on the menorah and, in particular, on the two olive trees on either side. It is

20. Frederick E. Greenspahn, *Hapax Legomena in Biblical Hebrew* (Chico, Calif.: Scholars Press, 1984), 185.
21. North, "Zechariah's Seven-Spout Lampstand," 187.
22. Unger, *Zechariah*, 79.

important, then, to connect these two anointed ones with the trees that symbolize them, that is, with olive trees.[23] They are not just anointed but are anointed with the oil of these trees.

Only two kinds of officials were anointed in OT Israel, the high priest and the king.[24] The act of anointing set the individual apart for special service and also symbolized his enduement with the gifts necessary to his carrying out the work for which he had been chosen. As in the Zechariah vision, the oil of anointing was associated with the Spirit of God. It spoke of both His presence and His enablement.

Anointing is especially prominent in reference to Aaron and his sons (Ex. 28:41; 29:7; 30:30; Lev. 4:3; 6:22; 7:36; 8:12) and to David and his dynasty (1 Sam. 16:3, 12-13; 2 Sam. 2:4; 12:7; 22:51; 23:1; Pss. 2:2; 18:50 [HB 18:51]; 84:9 [HB 84:10]; 89:20, 38, 51 [HB 89:21, 39, 52]). There can be little doubt that Zechariah, by referring to "the two anointed ones" with such specificity, has in mind these two anointed offices, priest and king. These are the two who "keep standing" (present participle of עָמַד, *ʿāmad*) by the Lord of all the earth, that is, who are constantly at the ready to serve Him.[25]

Kenneth Strand disputes this whole identification, insisting that "sons of oil" has nothing to do with anointing but is a description of the olive trees themselves. The weakness of his view is apparent in his inability to provide a satisfactory explanation for two trees rather than one (the two pillars of the Solomonic Temple?) and the lack of attention to the unity of Zech. 3 and 4, which demands that both Joshua and Zerubbabel be recognized as anointed leaders.[26]

More immediate to Zechariah's own time and perspective, the two anointed ones would likely refer to the latest generations or representatives of the respective offices, namely, Joshua and Zerubbabel. Both were direct descendants of the heads of their lines, Aaron and David. Both have already been singled out (Zech. 3; 4:6; cf. Hag. 1:1, 12, 14) as contemporaries of the prophet who have been greatly involved in the restoration of the postexilic community. Both, finally, have given evidence of having been chosen by God (Zech. 3:2; Hag. 2:23) to serve Him in significant capacities. More will be said about this identification in the next section and in the final oracle of 6:9-15.

23. A. S. Van der Woude, "Die Beiden Sohne des Öls (Sach. 4:14): Messianische Gestalten?" in *Travels in the World of the Old Testament*, ed. M. Heerma Van Voss (Assen: Van Gorcum, 1974), 265.
24. R. de Vaux, *Ancient Israel* (London: Darton, Longman & Todd, 1961), 103-6.
25. Joyce G. Baldwin, *Haggai, Zechariah, Malachi* (London: Tyndale, 1972), 124.
26. Kenneth A. Strand, "The Two Olive Trees of Zechariah 4 and Revelation 11," *AUSS* 20 (1982): 257-61.

The apostle John picked up on the menorah vision in his apocalyptic description of the Temple in remote eschatological times (Rev. 11:1-13). It is not possible or even necessary here to look at the entire pericope of which the two anointed ones are a part. What is important to note is that the two olive trees are accompanied by two menorahs, not one as in Zechariah (Rev. 11:4). This is sufficient to indicate that the Apocalypse is not intending to replicate or even comment precisely on the menorah vision of Zechariah, but only to use it as allusive material in support of an entirely different message.

The two visions do share some things in common, however, besides the trees and menorahs. They both focus on the Temple (Rev. 11:1-2; cf. Zech. 4:9-10; 2:1-5) and its measurements and rebuilding; they both at least obliquely refer to military confrontation (Rev. 11:3; Zech. 4:6); and, most significantly, in both the two olive trees are "standing before the Lord of the (whole) earth" (Rev. 11:4; Zech. 4:14). To John it is crystal clear that the menorah vision of Zechariah has fundamentally to do with the two olive trees as witnesses to the saving and reigning purposes of YHWH.[27] His understanding of who they were historically apparently was of little importance to him in his presentation of his apocalyptic message.

C. ORACLE OF RESPONSE (4:7-10)

Translation

[7]"Who are *you, O great mountain? Before Zerubbabel you will become a plain. And he will bring forth the capstone with shoutings of 'Grace! Grace!' because of it." [8]Moreover, the word of YHWH came to me as follows: [9]"The hands of Zerubbabel have laid the foundations of this house, and his hands will complete it." Then *you will know that YHWH of hosts has sent me to you. [10]For who has disregarded the day of small things? These seven will see with joy the *tin tablet in Zerubbabel's hand. These are the eyes of YHWH, those that run to and fro through all the earth.

Exegesis and Exposition

Though virtually all commentators agree that vision five is divided by the insertion of an oracle, they do not agree regarding the oracle's extent or to the manner or means by which it found its place in the current shape of the passage. Critical scholars generally argue that the oracle embraces 4:6b-10a so that the words "Then he spoke to me, saying (v. 6a), these are the eyes of YHWH . . . (v. 10b)" belong

---

27. Ibid., 259-60.

with the vision text.[28] The oracle thus would begin, "This is the word of YHWH to Zerubbabel" (v. 6*b*). Moreover, they postulate that the oracle circulated independently and was only later inserted here because of the need to provide, alongside Joshua, another individual to make up the two olive trees (v. 3) and two anointed ones (v. 14). Also, the strong emphasis on the high priesthood in Zechariah 3 called for an equally strong emphasis on the Davidic ruler, who with the priest was instrumental in the restoration of the community.[29]

Even though all of this makes good sense on the supposition that the oracle was not original to the vision, there are good reasons to believe that the passage was composed all at once and in its present form.[30] One should begin by noting that there is no manuscript or textual tradition to the contrary. This would at least minimize the possibility of a late redaction. In all fairness it should be said that most scholars who deny the original unity of the material believe it was placed in its present position shortly after the time of Zechariah or even by Zechariah himself. If, however, the oracle fits as uncomfortably into the vision as most of the same scholars allege, how can it be possible that Zechariah or anyone else with any literary sensitivity did not smooth out the transitions between vision to oracle and oracle to vision? In fact, if the notion of an insertion be abandoned altogether, there is no evidence of anything but a smooth transition.

If one accepts the view that the oracle commences in v. 6*b*, then the interpretation of the menorah (1-3), which begins in vv. 4-5, follows the oracle in v. 10*b*. The menorah, then, is interpreted as "the eyes of YHWH, running to and fro through the whole earth." Besides splitting up the vision and its interpretation, this explanation for the menorah is strange indeed. The reference to "seven" in v. 10*a*, when compared to 3:9, makes it very clear that "eyes of YHWH" in v. 10*b* is an explanation of "seven" in v. 10*a*. Verse 10 is, therefore, an indivisible whole. If this is so, the vision cannot resume at v. 10*b*. Nor can it do so at v. 11 if it ends before the oracle of v. 6*a*, for the introduction of v. 6*a*, "he answered and spoke to me saying," would then pick up with "Then I answered," etc. (v. 11).

The only way to preserve an interpretation for the menorah that is not separated from the vision itself is to assume that v. 6*b* is that

---

28. See note 11 above.
29. For a history of the problem and a survey of the various views, see especially Albert Petitjean, *Les Oracles du Proto-Zacharie* (Paris: J. Gabalda, 1969), 207-15.
30. See, e.g., A. Van der Woude, "Zion as Primeval Stone in Zechariah 3 and 4," in *Text and Context: Old Testament and Semitic Studies for F. C. Fensham*, ed. W. Claassen, JSOTSup 48 (Sheffield: Sheffield Academic Press, 1988), 238-40.

interpretation.[31] This not only retains a literary unit of content + interpretation but, as we have seen, makes good sense. The menorah with all its aspects, especially the oil, symbolizes the power of the divine spirit. This leaves the second part of the vision, the olive trees, as a separate interpretation beginning in v. 11.

If the oracle section then be limited to vv. 6*b*-10*a*, a problem remains as to the lack of a proper introductory formula. Ordinarily, as form-critical studies have shown, an oracle begins with a statement such as, "Therefore, thus says YHWH" (cf. 1:16).[32] This is provided if one takes v. 6*b* to be the commencement of the oracle: "This is the word of YHWH to Zerubbabel, saying."

Careful analysis of just the oracles of Zechariah will, however, show how inconsistently formulae of this kind are employed. It does occur in 1:16, as we have noted, but it is lacking in 2:6, in its regular form at least. Here the "says YHWH" follows the command to flee Babylon. In 3:8-10 there is no "says YHWH" until v. 9*b*. Looking again at 4:7-10 one should not be surprised that the phrase "The word of YHWH came to me" (v. 8), the equivalent of "says YHWH," comes later in the oracle. Its absence at the beginning is, in other words, nothing particularly strange.

A final consideration in favor of the original unity of v. 6 and of the commencement of the oracle with v. 7 is the fact that it is unlikely that an oracle mediated through Zechariah would begin with the introductory phrase, "This is the word of YHWH to Zerubbabel" (v. 6*a*). One would expect it to say (as it does in v. 8), "The word of YHWH came to me." In its canonical context the reference to Zerubbabel follows a proper oracular form: "Therefore, he told me, 'This is the word of YHWH to Zerubbabel,'" etc. Moreover, if one begins the inserted oracle with the message "'Not by strength and not by power but by my Spirit,' says YHWH of hosts," it is difficult to see to what this abrupt announcement refers. One would expect the problem or difficulty to be stated, or at least implied, before this resolution of it is offered. This is indeed the case if the menorah vision itself becomes the occasion for such an observation. The menorah with its flow of oil is indicative not of human strength but of divine power.

The reason for the insertion of the oracle at this point, is, as suggested above, the association of Zerubbabel in the interpretation of the first part of the vision (v. 6) with Zerubbabel in the oracle itself (vv. 7, 9, 10). Having noted that the menorah vision culminates in

---

31. Baldwin, *Haggai, Zechariah, Malachi*, 121; Unger, *Zechariah*, 74.
32. Claus Westermann, *Basic Forms of Prophetic Speech* (Philadelphia: Westminster, 1967), 149-53.

Zerubbabel and his work of temple building, the prophet immediately delivers his oracle in which Zerubbabel is the central feature.

If that work is to be done, it must be done through the energy of the Spirit of YHWH, for the task that lies ahead is like a veritable mountain in immensity and difficulty. The prophet is confident that this mountainous project can be completed with God's help and so, addressing the mountain of obstacles, asks rhetorically, "Who are you, O great mountain?" (v. 7). Mountain as metaphor for insuperable opposition or resistance is common in the OT, especially when it is overcome and reduced to a valley or plain (Isa. 40:4; 41:15; 42:15; 64:1, 3; Mic. 1:4; Nah. 1:5; Jer. 4:24; 51:25-26; Hab. 3:10; Zech. 14:4-5). Zerubbabel will be able to face this mountain, level it to a plain, and completely achieve the rebuilding committed to his charge.

Petitjean suggests, perhaps too literally, that the mountain is the massive heap of temple ruins that must be cleared before the new structure can be undertaken in its place. His references to Neo-Babylonian texts that describe such ruins in a similar way are quite persuasive.[33] Halpern, following Lipiński, takes the mountain to be the ruinous heap of the old Temple and the stone to be the one extracted from that ruin to serve as a foundation for the new building.[34] However, the text does not explicitly state that the stone is taken from the mountain. Moreover, this cannot represent the Temple because Zerubbabel is told that he will level the mountain, a task clearly impossible for him because that had happened 70 years before. Later Halpern must concede this.

That the process of building is actually in view in the metaphor of the leveled mountain is evident from the reference to the הָאֶבֶן־הָרֹאשָׁה (hā'eben hārō'šâ), literally "the top-stone" (v. 7). Continuing in the language of construction, the prophet speaks of the completion of the work in terms of the positioning of the capstone. David L. Petersen sees הָאֶבֶן־הָרֹאשָׁה as semantically equivalent to Akkadian *libittu maḫrītu*, "the first brick." This was involved in a ritual in which a brick was extracted from a ruined edifice and set to one side while offerings were made and a lament was sung over it. The purpose apparently was to bridge the gap between the old building and a new one.[35] Although this is a most interesting and plausible comparison,

---

33. Petitjean, *Les Oracles du Proto-Zacharie*, 257-58.
34. Halpern, "The Ritual Background of Zechariah's Temple Song," *CBQ* 40 (1978): 170.
35. Petersen, "Zerubbabel and Jerusalem Temple Reconstruction," *CBQ* 36 (1974): 368. See also Richard E. Averbeck, "Biblical Temple Building Accounts in Light of Ritual and Structure in the Gudea Cylinders" (Paper delivered at the annual meeting, Society of Biblical Literature, Kansas City, Mo., November 24, 1991), 1-15.

160

Zech. 4:9, with its attention to beginning and completing, seems to favor capstone as a sign of completion.[36] In brief compass, then, Zechariah describes the whole project from site preparation to finished structure. Historically, the former had been done (Ezra 3:10) over great opposition, but the building lay still unfinished as of 519 B.C., the date of the oracle.

Not only would the capstone signify the completion of the Temple, but shouts of acclamation as it was set in place would explain how it was done. "Grace! grace!" the crowds would declare, testifying to the faithfulness of YHWH in bringing it to pass.[37] This is in line with YHWH's own affirmation that what Zerubbabel would accomplish would be "not by might and not by power but by My Spirit." Haggai had also promised Zerubbabel that YHWH would be with him (Hag. 1:13; 2:4), overcoming whatever obstacles stood in his way (Hag. 2:21-23).

As though his message to Zerubbabel thus far were not clear enough, Zechariah goes on to be most explicit as to what overcoming mountains and raising capstones were all about. He calls to mind that Zerubbabel had already, nearly 20 years earlier, made preparation for the Temple foundation (v. 9; cf. Ezra 3:8-10; 5:16; Hag. 2:18). Now the hands that had begun the work would finish it, a promise repeated in 6:12-13 and fulfilled four years later, in 515 B.C. (Ezra 6:15). As a result, Zechariah says, the covenant community would know that YHWH had sent him as a prophet to them (v. 9). The acid test of the reliability of his message would be YHWH's endorsement in terms of fulfillment (cf. 2:11).

Coming back to the present, the prophet acknowledges that one can easily look down upon or be little impressed by small things, in this case the meagerness of the Temple (v. 10; cf. Hag. 2:3). The people in the natural course of events had every reason to believe that the project would amount to nothing, so sparse were their resources and so formidable the opposition. But this was not the natural course of events. "These seven," Zechariah says, "will rejoice" when they see the tin tablet in Zerubbabel's hand.

The number seven has already taken a prominent place in Zechariah (3:9; 4:2), signifying there, as in apocalyptic literature generally (Ezek. 40-48; Rev. *passim*), the idea of fullness or completeness. In the vision of the priest, Zechariah had seen a stone with seven eyes

---

36. For a much more fanciful discussion, see Edwin E. Le Bas, "Zechariah's Enigmatical Contribution to the Corner-Stone," *PEQ* 82 (1950): 102-22. Van de Woude favors the idea that it is the primeval stone of myth, Mount Zion as the "navel of the earth" (A. Van der Woude, "Zion As Primeval Stone in Zechariah 3 and 4," 241).

37. S. Amsler, *Aggée, Zacharie 1-8*, 94.

(3:9), a symbol representing omniscience. The matter is put beyond doubt here, for the prophet declares flatly that the "seven" that rejoice are the eyes of YHWH that "run to and fro through the whole earth" (v. 10).

This interpretation, again, depends on the unity of v. 10 and the deliberate integration of the oracle (vv. 7-10) into the surrounding vision and interpretation (see n. 11 above). If one grants that "seven" belongs with v. 10*a*, as the Masoretic verse structure requires, then the only reasonable antecedent is the "eyes" of 3:9. To think of inanimate objects, such as seven lamps or seven pipes (v. 2), rejoicing and seeing stretches the imagination even in vision literature. Van de Woude resolves the issue by seeing the seven lamps as symbols of YHWH's eyes and then associating the whole with the stone and eyes of 3:9.[38] The eyes of YHWH rejoice when human eyes cannot because He is omniscient, knowing the end from the beginning. Zerubbabel can rejoice in that the Temple foundations are laid, something he saw with his own eyes (Ezra 3:11). YHWH can rejoice because He, in omniscience, can see the completion of the work. There is no day of small things with Him, because the end is as firm and fixed as the beginning.

David Petersen, following Richard Ellis, has suggested that Zerubbabel's Temple, like those of Middle Babylonian and Achaemenid times, contained an inscription engraved on a tin plate as part of a dedicatory foundation deposit (v. 10).[39] This would speak of the glory of the Temple as comparable to that of any other in the pagan world and would also suggest a connection with the engraved stone of vision four, the foundation stone upon which is engraved the message of forgiveness and restoration of the remnant as a covenant people (3:9).

Another connection with an earlier vision appears at the end of v. 10, where the eyes of YHWH are said to "run to and fro through all the earth." This picture of His universal knowledge and dominion finds a parallel in vision one, where the four horses have been engaged in asserting that dominion by "walking to and fro through the earth" (1:10, 11). That also is in connection with temple building, for as a result of the conquest and resulting peace accomplished by the

---

38. A. S. Van der Woude, "Zion As Primeval Stone in Zechariah 3 and 4," 243-45.
39. D. L. Petersen, "Zerubbabel and Jerusalem Temple Reconstruction," 370-71. See also Halpern, "The Ritual Background of Zechariah's Temple Song," 171-73. Van der Woude, however, takes it as an apposition to "stone," i.e., a "*bĕdîl*-stone," a "separation" stone that describes the primeval mountain as separating chaos from the cosmos (A. Van der Woude, "Zion Primeval Stone in Zechariah 3 and 4," 243). Resort by the prophet to pagan myth in a case like this is hardly convincing. See Additional Notes.

heavenly horsemen the stage has been set for the Temple to be rebuilt (1:16). The verb here (שׁוּט) is different from that in 1:10, 11 (הָלַךְ), but they are synonymous as their use in parallel members in Job 1:7 and 2:2 makes clear. Both verbs, therefore, can denote dominion or conquest.

Additional Notes

4:7 MT אַתָּה הַר־הַגָּדוֹל poses some difficulty in that one would expect the article with הַר in this construction. Perhaps BHS is correct in proposing that the ה of אַתָּה should be assigned to הַר, giving אַתְּ הָהָר הַגָּדוֹל־. Those scholars who suggest that מִי־אַתָּה should be isolated from the following clause ("who are you" [You are] a great mountain, etc.) do so against the Masoretic tradition that places the conjunctive accent Darga between אַתָּה and הַר.

4:9 With some Cairo MSS the Syriac, Targums, and Vg read the plural verb form here rather than the singular. This, indeed, would be consistent with the 2 m.p. suffix on the preposition at the end of the line. However, when the community is addressed collectively, the singular "you" is most appropriate. The shift to the plural at the end is not at all inconsistent with Hebrew usage, particularly in the covenant texts in Deuteronomy (cf. GKC, 145b-g).

4:10 Part of the cause for rejoicing is the sight of Zerubbabel with הָאֶבֶן הַבְּדִיל (hā'eben habbědîl), the "stone of tin," in his hand. This difficult term is usually thought to refer to a plumb line, taking bědîl as a derivative of בָּדַל, (bādal, "to separate") and thus indicating a carpenter's tool.[40] The picture would be that of Zerubbabel holding a plumb line as part of the construction work on the Temple. Besides the inherent difficulty of associating bědîl with bādal semantically as plumb line, bědîl ordinarily refers to a metal alloy or tin itself (BDB, 95). In addition, the plumb line would hardly be used once the Temple was actually completed, a situation required by the order of events in the oracle.

---

40. Thus, H. G. Mitchell, *A Commentary on Haggai and Zechariah*, 191, and most scholars since.

7
Vision Six: The Flying Scroll (5:1-4)

A. CONTENT OF THE VISION (5:1-2)

In line with the structural pattern of the night visions, visions six and three are a matching pair.[1] In support of this the Meyers point first to such matters in common as the national focus of both, that is, the centrality of Judah in the restoration program. Second, a solitary individual in both visions is the immediate recipient of them, contrary to the other visions where multiple recipients appear, at least secondarily. Third, there is the measuring line in vision three with which the unidentified surveyor is about to measure the breadth and length of Jerusalem. Vision six features a scroll that also is measured, but this time in terms of length and breadth. Finally, the scroll is flying, just as the man of vision three is on the move to accomplish his task.

Translation
   ¹Then I turned and looked, and there was a flying scroll. ²Someone said to me, "What do you see?" And I replied, "I see a flying scroll twenty cubits long and ten cubits wide."

---

1. Carol L. Meyers and Eric M. Meyers, *Haggai, Zechariah 1-8*, AB (Garden City, N.Y.: Doubleday, 1987), 287-90. In line with their designation of the fourth vision as an unnumbered "prophetic vision," their fifth vision corresponds to our sixth.

Exegesis and Exposition

The correspondence in form and content just suggested for visions six and three ought to yield clues to mutual interpretation and, indeed, such is the case, as will become clear in the discussion. For now it is sufficient to identify what is seen and to make preliminary efforts to determine its significance. It is striking that this vision plays down any human activity. Zechariah sees merely a scroll moving, apparently without human aid. Even the interrogator is unnamed and undisclosed except by the third person pronominal form "he said" (v. 2), translated here "someone said." Presumably this is the "messenger who spoke," so common to the other visions (1:9; 4:5; 5:5; 6:4, 5).[2] The fact that he appears in the matching vision of the surveyor by that common epithet (2:3) makes it certain that the same figure is meant by the anonymous "he" or "someone" of this vision. Still, his lack of disclosure here is meaningful; it is likely that it is to draw full attention to the scroll itself.

The scroll,[3] of course, is the familiar leather or parchment "book" consisting of single sheets sewn end on end and rolled around wooden rollers at either end. The writing on the scroll would ordinarily be on the inside of the roll, with only the description of its contents or other brief notations written on the outside. Usually the length of the scroll would be many times its width, the width being the measurement of a single sheet from top to bottom. This seldom exceeded 8-12 inches, and the length would rarely be more than 25-30 feet.

The measurements here are so different from the norm, both in overall terms (except for the length) and in terms of proportion, that one must realize immediately that the dimensions are really not of the scroll itself but of something described within the scroll. Thus the 20 × 10 cubits (about 30 × 15 feet) either define an actual area or refer to something or some place whose length is twice its width.

Among biblical objects or places with these measurements are the Holy Place in the Tabernacle (Ex. 26), the "porch" of Solomon's Temple (1 Kings 6:3), and the great bronze altar of the Temple (20 cubits long and 10 high; 2 Chron. 4:2). All three of these have to do with the sanctuary, the place where YHWH meets with His people.[4]

---

2. Thus Wilhelm Rudolph, *Haggai-Sacharja 1-8–Sacharja 9-14–Maleachi*, KAT (Gütersloh: Verlaghaus Gerd Mohn, 1976), 115 ("Der Dolmetscherengel").
3. The term is בִּגְלָה, for which see W. S. LaSor, *ISBE*, 4:363-64 s.v. "scroll."
4. As Chary suggests, Zechariah's focus in chaps. 3 and 4 has been on the Temple, so it is natural to assume that it and its measurements would be in view here (Theophane Chary, *Aggée-Zacharie, Malachi* [Paris: Librairie Lecoffre, 1969], 99).

As the interpretation shows in vv. 3-4, the connection of the scroll with the dwelling-place of YHWH leads to the conclusion that the scroll contains the covenant document that binds YHWH and the nation together.

Though the entire Torah could doubtless be composed on a great "billboard" of 30 × 15 feet, it is unlikely that this is the configuration in view. More likely, Zechariah is describing a scroll 30 feet long and 15 feet thick. That is, when the scroll is rolled up, it is 15 feet in diameter.[5] Such an enormous scroll is obviously unrealistic, but its great size is a deliberate attempt to conform to the various tabernacle and Temple measurements noted above and, perhaps, to make it visible to the whole community as it passed by over their heads (cf. Hab. 2:2).

B. INTERPRETATION OF THE VISION (5:3-4)

Translation

³Then he said to me, "This is the curse going forth across the whole earth, for whoever steals, on the one hand, according to it will be purged out; and whoever swears, on the other hand, according to it will be purged." ⁴"I will send it forth," says YHWH of hosts, "and it will enter the house of the thief and that of the one who swears falsely in My name. It will lodge in the midst of his house and destroy it with its timber and stones."

Exegesis and Exposition

The interpretation of the vision is filled with covenant terminology and motifs that make it certain that the scroll either is the Torah or contains covenant texts of the Torah. The unidentified speaker of v. 3 immediately equates the scroll with the "curse" (הָאָלָה, *hā'ālâ*), a technical term referring to the sanctions of covenant documents.[6] As early as patriarchal times when Eliezer, servant of Abraham, was sent to Nahor to fetch a wife for Isaac, Abraham put him under oath to get a wife there and not from among the Canaanites. But he had told Eliezer that, if he made the effort and yet failed, he would be free from the אָלָה, (*'ālâ*), the sanction or curse of the oath (Gen. 24:41).

Deuteronomy is especially rich in covenant language and the occurrence of *'ālâ* there is especially instructive, particularly in the

---

5. For various suggestions, including this one, see Meyers and Meyers, *Haggai, Zechariah 1-8*, 279-83.
6. Baruch Halpern, "The Ritual Background of Zechariah's Temple Song," *CBQ* 40 (1978): 178-79.

great "concluding charge" of chapter 29.[7] There Moses, in a parallel
construction (v. 12), makes *'ālâ* synonymous with בְּרִית (*bĕrît*) or "covenant" itself (cf. v. 14). Then in more specific terms he warns any who
would seek to avoid the curse of covenant violation by renaming it a
blessing instead (v. 9). Such a one will find, to his dismay, that all the
sanctions of the covenant will be brought to bear against him, and he
will be purged from off the earth (vv. 20-21).

The flying scroll of Zechariah mentions only two of the covenant
stipulations, violation of which will invite the sanction of curse.
These two, however, represent the whole law, for the one has to do
with interpersonal, human relations and the other with man's responsibility before God.[8] The first, the one who steals (present participle of גָּנַב, *gānab*), violates the eighth commandment (Ex. 20:15), a
breach, therefore, of the whole "second half" of the law (cf. Lev. 19:18;
Deut. 4:5-6; Matt. 19:19). He who swears falsely in the name of
YHWH (v. 4), who uses his name "in vain" or for illegitimate purposes, violates the third commandment (Ex. 20:7), a statute that is
representative of the first part of the law. Whoever breaks either or
both parts has sinned grievously, for he has violated the covenant that
YHWH has made with him and to which he, as part of the chosen
nation, has sworn.

Verse 3 is elliptical and difficult, particularly in the second half.
The Hebrew says literally, "for anyone who steals from this according
to it has been purged out." The crux is "from this" (מִזֶּה, *mizzeh*), for
otherwise it is clear that a judgment comes upon the thief according
to the sanction written in the scroll. The past tense of the verb נָקָה
(*nāqâ*), "has been purged out," must be understood in terms of the
edict of the law, a fait accompli, but in this context the form should be
translated "will be poured out." As for *mizzeh*, its repetition with כָּמוֹהָ
(*kāmôhā*)), "according to it," at the end of the verse strongly suggests
some kind of correlative idea such as "thus . . . thus" or, as we are
proposing, "on the one hand . . . on the other hand." (cf. Ex. 17:12;
26:13; Ezek. 45:7; 47:7, 12; 48:21.) Chary draws attention to the
phrase מִזֶּה וּמִזֶּה הֵם כְּתֻבִים, "They were written on this side and that," in
Ex. 32:15, a particularly pertinent text in that it refers to the two
sides of the tablet on which the Mosaic Law was inscribed.[9]

Another problem with the predicate "has been purged out" (נָקָה,

7. Moshe Weinfeld, *Deuteronomy and the Deuteronomic School* (Oxford: Clarendon, 1972), 62-63, 67, 107.
8. Samuel Amsler, *Aggée, Zacharie 1-8, Zacharie 9-14*, CAT (Neuchatel: Dela-chaux & Niestlé, 1981), 97; Carroll Stuhlmueller, *Haggai & Zechariah*, ITC (Grand Rapids: Eerdmans, 1988), 92.
9. T. Chary, *Aggée-Zacharie, Malachi*, 100; cf. L. G. Rignell, *Die Nachtgesichte des Sacharja* (Lund: CWK Gleerup, 1950), 185.

niqqâ), in addition to its tense, is the fact that the niphal usually connotes "to be free from guilt" or "exempt from punishment."[10] This would yield a meaning exactly opposite from that proposed here, for it would be saying that the thief and he who swears will be freed from guilt (or has been freed from guilt). Petersen[11] offers the following rendition as a way of solving the problem of both the tense and the voice:

This is the curse which is going out
                    over all the earth;
for all who steal have remained up till
                    now unpunished,
and all who swear (falsely) have remained
                    up till now unpunished.

While this is agreeable to the grammar and syntax, it seems unnecessary for two reasons. First, the whole thrust of the interpretation section (vv. 3-4) is present and future, not past. Also, how true could it be to say that up till now thieves and blasphemers have gone unpunished? Second, the niphal of nāqâ can and does have the meaning of "be cleaned out" or "purged."[12] The clearest example is in Isa. 3:26, where YHWH says of Zion that "her gates will mourn and she will be emptied out, sitting on the ground." Nearly always where the idea of being free or exempt from blame or punishment is in view, the verb is followed by the preposition מִן (min, "from") (cf. Gen. 24:8, 41; Num. 5:19; 5:31; Judg. 15:3; Ps. 19:14 [EB 19:13]), something lacking here.

What this purging is all about is explained in v. 4. The scroll, YHWH says, is something He has sent out. He is its author in terms of both its content and its intended purpose. It is a message but also a weapon by which He will judge His recalcitrant people. It is His powerful word that accomplishes the objective for which it is sent, whether that be salvation or condemnation (Isa. 55:11). Wielded by YHWH, the scroll will enter the house of the thief and of him who swears falsely in YHWH's name. And the visit will not be only momentary. Using a verb normally found in situations of hospitality (לוּן, lûn), the prophet relates that the scroll will "spend the night," that is, will stay until its intended mission is accomplished.[13]

---

10. C. Van Leeuwen, THAT 2: cols. 101-6, s.v. גקה.
11. David L. Petersen, Haggai and Zechariah 1-8 (London: SCM, 1985), 245.
12. Merrill F. Unger, Zechariah (Grand Rapids: Zondervan, 1963), 88; D. Winton Thomas, The Book of Zechariah, IB (New York: Abingdon, 1956), 6:1075. Though this is a rare meaning in Hebrew, the cognate languages attest it in abundance. Thus Akk. naqû in the G means "to pour out" (CAD/N1, 336) and in the N "to pour out as a libation" (340).
13. W. Rudolph, Haggai-Sacharja 1-8–Sacharja 9-14–Maleachi, 117.

That mission is transparently clear—the scroll will demolish the house to the last timber and stone. Although this should be taken literally to some extent as referring to material structures, the use of "house" as a metaphor for one's family and life is more likely. The scroll as the covenant Word of God contains the message that judges and brings to ruin all human efforts at salvation and success. The covenant breaker will find that his sins against God and against men will lead inexorably to utter devastation.

In concluding comment on this vision, another instructive but contrastive parallel should be drawn to vision three. There the surveyor was about the business of building, the result of which was a city with no wall of protection but YHWH Himself, the "wall of fire" (2:5). Here the scroll does not build but, to the contrary, destroys, leaving neither wall nor roof nor foundation. In the first case, the remnant people who trust confidently in YHWH will find adequate shelter in His presence among them. In the present case, the thief and blasphemer will know nothing of this protective grace but only the wrath of a holy God whose covenant mercies have been spurned (cf. Hab. 2:9-11).

8
Vision Seven: The Ephah (5:5-11)

A. CONTENT OF THE VISION (5:5-7)

This is one of the most perplexing of the night visions of Zechariah because of both grammatical and syntactical conundrums and the rather bizarre nature of what is being presented. Before an effort is made to dissect the vision itself, it might be well to compare and contrast it with vision two, its literary counterpart.[1]

In both, the "messenger who spoke to me" is essential to the introduction to and interpretation of the vision (1:19, 21; cf. 5:5, 8, 10, 11). In both, the prophet confesses his ignorance of what he sees and asks for an explanation (1:19; cf. 5:6). In the vision of the horns they are pushing in all directions, scattering "Judah, Israel, and Jerusalem," clearly a reference to the Babylonian dispersion. In the ephah vision, contrariwise, it is personified wickedness that is going into exile, borne along by flying women who finally deposit her in Shinar, that is, Babylon. Finally, both visions share a common interest in the international scene, particularly Persia in Zechariah's own day.

Translation

⁵Then the "messenger who spoke to me" went out and said to me, "Look and see what this is that is going out." ⁶I answered, "What is it?" And he replied, "This is the ephah that goes forth." Moreover, he

---

1. Carol L. Meyers and Eric M. Meyers, *Haggai, Zechariah 1-8*, AB (Garden City, N.Y.: Doubleday, 1987), 311-12.

said, "This is their 'eye' in all the earth." [7]Then there was a lead disk raised up; (in connection with) this (there was) one woman sitting in the midst of the ephah.

Exegesis and Exposition

In this vision, as in vision five, it is the interpreting messenger who takes the initiative to introduce the scene (v. 5; cf. 4:1). He commands the prophet to take note of "this" (feminine gender) that is going forth. The "going forth" (יָצָא, *yāṣā'*) of both the messenger and the still-unnamed object heightens the sense of movement and brings an air of excitement to what follows. The reason for the feminine demonstrative pronoun becomes evident first when the messenger, responding to Zechariah's query, tells him that what he sees is an ephah (a noun in feminine gender). The ephah is the familiar unit of solid or liquid measure approximately equivalent to five gallons. Sustaining the movement of the scene, the interpreting messenger repeats that the ephah is "going forth" (v. 6). And, amazingly enough, it is going airborne.

The grammatical feminine gender now takes on new meaning, for there is a woman (feminine) in the ephah, one who personifies wickedness (v. 8). This line of thought has other implications that will now be explored.

First, it is necessary to deal with the very much debated "their eye" in v. 6*b*. Many versions translate "their appearance,"[2] a clearly attested rendering for Hebrew עַיִן (*'ayin*) (Lev. 13:5; Num. 11:7). That may, indeed, be the preferred translation, but that does not solve the difficulties. The LXX and Syriac read "their iniquity," based on a reading עֲוֹנָם, (*'ăwōnām*) for the MT עֵינָם, (*'ênām*).[3] This would solve the problem of meaning nicely, especially in light of "wickedness" in v. 8, but the text-critical principle of *lectio difficilior* would tend to rule that out.

The answer lies, we submit, in letting Zechariah supply his own fund of language and imagery. He has used the phrase בְּכָל־הָאָרֶץ (*běkol hā'āreṣ*), "in (or through) all the earth," three times previously in the book (1:10, 11; 4:10) and does so once again later (6:7). Without exception it occurs in contexts having to do with dominion, especially YHWH's universal rule. In one of those instances "eyes" is part of the formula, namely, in 4:10. There YHWH identifies the "seven" of v. 10*a* as "the eyes of YHWH which run to and fro through the whole earth."

2. NASB, NKJV, KJV.
3. See also NIV, RSV, NEB, JB. Margaret Barker, on the basis of the Qere of 1 Sam. 18:9, suggests that עֵינָם be read as an inf. cst. plus suffix, עֵינָם, "their hostile eye (that is, attitude) toward the whole land"; Margaret Barker, "The Evil in Zechariah," *HeyJ* 19 (1978): 22.

As argued at that passage, this refers to YHWH's omniscience by which He knows the end from the beginning.

This is likely the import of "their eye" in 5:6. Without repeating the whole cliché, "their eye which runs to and fro through the whole earth," the interpreting messenger compresses it to simply "their eye . . . through the whole earth." What he has in mind, if this view be correct, is that the forces of evil, like YHWH Himself, assert dominion over all the earth, though in their case it is woefully nonomniscient and pitifully inadequate. Yet, like Satan in the prologue of Job (Job 1:7; 2:2), they make the effort oblivious to the sovereignty of YHWH, who will someday call their hand and hold them to account. The ephah and its contents, then, represent the antitheocratic powers of this world with their pseudo-dominion of all the earth. This interpretation has in its favor an inner-hermeneutical method without resort to textual emendation.

In continuation of the vision the prophet sees, in a literal rendering, "a round (thing) of lead" (v. 7). In the context this can only mean a cover for the ephah (v. 8). The fact that it is lead suggests its very heavy weight.[4] Then, in another syntactically problematic statement, the interpreting messenger says of the raised lid and the ephah, "and this one woman sitting in the midst of the ephah." "This" (זֹאת, *zō't*) probably does not refer to the woman because one would expect a reverse word order if that were the case, namely, הָאִשָּׁה הַזֹּאת (*hā'iššâ hazz'ōt*), and a definite article on *'iššâ* to conform to the definite pronoun.[5] The best solution, it seems, is to view the pronoun *zō't* as a nominative absolute to be rendered "as for this," meaning "as for this whole vision thus far."[6] Then the sentence can go on as the translation above has proposed.

The messenger goes on to point out that there was "one woman" sitting in the ephah. The point, of course, is that there is one here as opposed to two others, mentioned later (v. 9), who transport her to her destination.[7] It is when the cover is raised up that the woman therein becomes visible to the prophet. That a woman could be contained in a five-gallon vessel is, in actual life, impossible. But in a vision such things are not only possible but frequently insisted upon

---

4. Samuel Amsler, *Aggee, Zacharie 1-8, Zacharie 9-14*, CAT (Paris: Neuchatel, 1981), 100.
5. GKC, 34e. It is true that GKC, takes Zech. 5:7 as an example of apposition in which אִשָּׁה אַחַת is apposite to זֹאת (GKC, 136d n. 1), but this is certainly not required and, in context, seems unlikely.
6. Rudolph takes זֹאת as a deictic particle in the sense of "see!" LXX reflects this with the translation ἰδού; Wilhelm Rudolph, *Haggai-Sacharja 1-8–Sacharja 9-14–Maleachi*, KAT (Gutersloh: Verlaghaus Gerd Mohn, 1976), 118. The translation then could be, "Look, one woman sitting," etc.
7. Meyers and Meyers, *Haggai, Zechariah 1-8*, 302.

in order to draw attention to the surreality of the experience and its divine origination.

B. INTERPRETATION OF THE VISION (5:8-11)

Translation

8He then said, "This is wickedness," and he thrust her down into the midst of the ephah and placed the lead weight upon its top. 9Then again I looked and saw two women going forth with wind in their wings (now they had wings like those of a stork), and they lifted up the ephah between earth and heaven. 10I asked the "messenger who spoke to me," "Where are they taking the ephah?" 11He answered me, "To build her a house in the land of Shinar. When it has been prepared, *she will be set down there in her own resting-place."

Exegesis and Exposition

At last the woman is identified—she is "wickedness." This identification also explains the use of the feminine gender up to and including the occupant of the ephah, for רִשְׁעָה (*rišʿâ*), translated "wickedness," is an abstract noun in Hebrew and thus grammatically feminine. It is appropriate therefore that a woman represent this moral condition, but it seems that one should make no more of it than that, at least for now. Nor can one more narrowly define wickedness here since it is a rather general term encompassing all kinds of civil, religious, and cultic misbehavior.[8] Despite this, many scholars suggest that the woman here represents idolatry but, as Chary points out, זוֹנָה or some such term would be used rather than רִשְׁעָה. The few uses of רִשְׁעָה in the OT (about a dozen) show it to be the opposite of צְדָקָה or, as Chary translates it, "méchanceté" or "perversité" (cf. Deut. 9:4; Prov. 11:5; Ezek. 18:20; 33:12, 19).[9] Margaret Barker suggests that the evil here is very specific—"commercial malpractice," an interpretation based on the ephah in the vision. She goes on to say that this was only representative of a general condition of lawlessness (hence LXX νομία) in Jerusalem.[10]

That the woman is dangerous is most apparent, for no sooner has the interpreting messenger pronounced her name than he slams the heavy cover down upon the ephah to be certain that she cannot escape. The urgency is magnified in the double use of the verb שָׁלַךְ (*šālak*) in v. 8. The messenger "threw" the woman into the ephah and

---

8. C. Van Leeuwen, *TWAT* 2: cols. 813-18, s.v. רשע.
9. Theophane Chary, *Aggee-Zacharie, Malachie* (Paris: Librairie Lecoffre, 1969), 102-3.
10. M. Barker, "The Evil in Zechariah," 23-24.

"threw" the lead weight upon its top. The reason for lead is also now clarified, for the ephah has become not only a means of conveyance but a cage, as it were, in which wickedness is to be carried off against her will. Such a cage needs a door that cannot be opened by its occupant. The peculiar expression in Hebrew אֶבֶן הָעֹפֶרֶת ('eben hā'ōp-eret), "stone of lead," simply means that the cover of an ephah vessel would normally be stone. Lead is used here in place of stone, hence a "lead-stone."[11]

Once this is done the ephah takes wings as it were and begins its flight. But the wings are actually those of two women and are described as "stork-like" wings (v. 9). The stork (חֲסִידָה, ḥăsîdâ) was one of the unclean birds of Leviticus 11, one that could not be eaten because it was an "abomination" (Lev. 11:13, 19). Yet, as its name suggests (from חָסִיד, ḥāsîd, "loving, faithful, constant"), it was noted from ancient times as a bird that took affectionate care of its young.[12] There is thus the paradoxical picture of an unclean bird, appropriate considering its mission and cargo, providing the tenderest care for its charge as it fulfilled the mandate of YHWH.[13]

That the bearers of the ephah are also women is consistent with the feminine flavor of the entire vision. Moreover, the motherly attention accorded the task demands the sensitivity that women can best supply. But what they do is made possible by resources outside their natural abilities, for they had "wind in their wings." Since that would be a normal expectation in flight, its mention here is significant. Doubtless there is a *double entendre* here, for רוּחַ (rûaḥ) means spirit as well as wind. The same Spirit of God that empowered Zerubbabel in temple building (4:6) was now at work transporting wickedness to her destination.[14]

Almost always where heaven and earth are mentioned together, it is in that order as a frozen form or stock expression. Here, however, the ephah is lifted up "between the earth and the heavens," that is,

---

11. The identification of the אֶבֶן הָעֹפֶרֶת (v. 8b) with the כִּכַּר עֹפֶרֶת (v. 7a) shows that the cover is not stone at all but lead. The former, "the stone of lead," is the same as the latter, "a cover of lead." Thus, the cover is a stone ordinarily, but here it is a slab (or circle) of lead. See Meyers and Meyers, *Haggai, Zechariah 1-8*, 299-300.
12. R. K. Harrison, *ISBE*, 4:631, s.v. "stork."
13. Joyce G. Baldwin, *Haggai, Zechariah, Malachi* (London: Tyndale, 1972), 124. Rudolph draws attention to the reference to the stork in Jer. 8:7, where the prophet speaks in complimentary terms of its sensitivity to its appointed times and tasks (W. Rudolph, *Haggai-Sacharja 1-8—Sacharja 9-14—Maleachi*, 120).
14. As Halpern puts it, "the iniquity of the land is dispatched to Mesopotamia" (Baruch Halpern, "The Ritual Background of Zechariah's Temple Song," *CBQ* 40 [1978]: 180).

the upper sky (v. 9). The reason for that most likely is that this is the trajectory of the flight from the viewpoint of the earthbound observer. Those standing on the ground see the ephah departing from the earth toward the heavens. A parallel case in which "earth" precedes "heaven" and in which the Spirit is the agent of levitation occurs in Ezekiel 8. There the prophet describes his experience of being lifted up "between earth and heaven" (v. 3) by the Spirit. Interestingly enough, this time the journey is exactly opposite: Ezekiel is not moving from Jerusalem to Babylon but from Babylon to Jerusalem (v. 3), where he sees every kind of wickedness in the very Temple of YHWH (vv. 5-17). It is this wickedness that must be purged and its practitioners who must be removed from the land.

At a loss to understand the destination of the flying ephah, Zechariah asks about it and learns from the interpreting messenger that it is Shinar. There the stork-like women will build wickedness a house, and when it is finished they will settle her there. Shinar is an ancient name for Sumer and Akkad, the district in which the earliest of cities such as Babel, Erech, Accad, and Calneh were located (Gen. 10:10).[15] Babel, of course, is the same as Babylon, "the gate of the gods" (Akk. *bābu* + *ilāni*, or *bābilāni*). Erech is the Sumerian city Uruk (modern Warka), near the Persian Gulf. Accad (or Akkad) is Agade, the capital of the Old Akkadian empire of Sargon. Calneh (if not Calah) cannot be identified with certainty, for it can hardly be the same as the city by that name just north of Aleppo in Syria.

Reference to Shinar is tantamount to reference to Babylon, for that city becomes the very epitome of humanistic independence of and resistance to God and His sovereignty. It was at Babylon, in the land of Shinar, that the rebel human race erected a great ziggurat, the purpose of which was to frustrate God's mandate to "be fruitful, multiply, and fill the earth" (Gen. 1:28; 9:1). The men of Babylon had said, "Let us make a name for ourselves, lest we be scattered abroad upon the surface of the whole earth" (Gen. 11:4). From that time Babylon became synonymous with arrogant human independence, the very fountainhead of antitheocratic social, political, and religious ideology.

The leader of the campaign of eastern kings against Canaan and Abraham was "Amraphel king of Shinar" (Gen. 14:1). This was the first act of aggression against the people of YHWH by a hostile power. But not until the rise of the Neo-Babylonian Empire under Nabopolassar in 627 B.C. was it evident that the ancient archenemy of YHWH in days of old would rear his ugly head in history and in

---

15. Claus Westermann, *Genesis 1-11: A Commentary* (London: SPCK, 1984), 517.

eschatological time to come in a mighty effort to challenge the salvific purposes of God on earth through His elect people. Even before that revival of Shinar had actually come about, the prophets anticipated this challenge and were fully aware of its historical and theological significance. Isaiah, writing a century before Nabopolassar, composed a collection of oracles in which he set forth the role and destiny of Babylon (chaps. 13-14). Her coming judgment, he said, was nothing less than an expression of the fearful day of YHWH (13:6), a day of cruel war and cosmic dislocation. Proud Babylon would be overthrown as Sodom and Gomorrah were in days gone by (13:19). YHWH would then have compassion on His own people (14:1) and through the Medes and Persians (13:17) would deliver them from captivity (14:2) and reduce Babylon to the depths of Sheol (14:3-20). It is Isaiah who describes the king of Babylon as the "daystar" who said, "I will exalt my throne above the stars of God" (14:12-13), a clear reminiscence of human arrogance in the Tower of Babel story.

Babylon as the center of Jewish dispersion is very much a theme in Isaiah's prophecies concerning the restoration. In a remarkable personification, YHWH commands the "virgin daughter of Babylon" to come off her throne and become a shameless, naked slave (Isa. 47:1-3). She will no longer be called the "mistress of kingdoms" (v. 5), the one who boasts "I am and there is no one else besides me" (v. 5). Instead, she will experience sudden and calamitous judgment, all her enchantments and religious apotropaic devices notwithstanding (47:11-15). The epithets "virgin daughter" and "mistress" are particularly striking in light of the feminine tone of Zechariah's vision of the ephah. One may certainly concede that Babylon is addressed in female terms because such Hebrew abstract noun forms as "kingdom" (מַמְלָכָה, *mamlākâ*) are feminine (i.e., "[kingdom of] Babylon"), but her association with the feminine noun "wickedness," as in Zechariah 5:8, is also significant.

Jeremiah also focuses much attention on Babylon and, as a contemporary with the rise of the Neo-Babylonian kingdom, he was in a particularly strategic position to assess her meaning to his own day and to the ages to come. In a long oracle section devoted to Babylon (chaps. 50-51) the prophet predicts her collapse at the hands of a northern power (50:2-3), a fall that will free God's covenant people to return to their own land (vv. 4-10).

Throughout this series of oracles Jeremiah continues, with Isaiah, the feminine description of Babylon. She is like a wanton heifer (50:11) who has striven against YHWH (50:24), a clearly antitheocratic stance. She has exhibited pride against Him (v. 29) as well, but "the proud one will fall" (v. 32). When the northern foe begins to descend on Babylon, her king will suffer convulsions "like a woman in travail" (v. 43), her mighty men will cower and "become as women" (51:30). The "daughter of Babylon" will become like a threshing-floor at the time of the treading of grain (v. 33). Though she should try to ascend to the heavens in her pride, she will be dragged down (v. 53) and utterly overthrown (v. 58).

Throughout these lengthy passages in Isaiah and Jeremiah there are both historical and eschatological perspectives. Frequently it is difficult to separate them, but that is not necessary, for Babylon— whether in the past, present, or future—is the paradigm of wickedness and of hostility to all the gracious purposes of God.[16] To Zechariah, however, Babylon's (or Shinar's) role must be exclusively future, for by 520 B.C. she had fallen and had been swallowed up by the irrepressible and well-nigh universal Persian Empire. This no doubt is one reason he does not use the name Babylon in the ephah vision (but see 2:7; 6:10), preferring Shinar instead. Shinar, besides taking the theme of Babylon as antagonist back to the very beginning (Gen. 10:10), creating thereby a kind of "historical inclusio," lends a more trans-historical sense to the message.

Before this long discussion of Shinar and Babylon can be concluded, it is important to see how NT apocalyptic treats the theme. In vision John saw Babylon fall, "she who made all nations drink of the wine of the wrath of her fornication" (Rev. 14:8). She is the "great harlot," the "mother of the harlots and of the abominations of the earth" (17:1, 5). More significantly, she is "the great city that reigns over the kings of the earth" (17:18). She will be destroyed in one day, however (18:8, 10, 19)—a destruction so irremedial that it is compared to the casting of a huge millstone into the sea, from which it can never be retrieved (18:21).

Zechariah, then, takes his place in a long, full tradition regarding Shinar, or Babylon, as the seat of iniquitous rebellion against God. For wickedness in the ephah vision to be transported to Shinar is for it to return to where it belongs. It had come from Babylon, as it were, and had dogged the steps of God's people, leading at last to their destruction and captivity at her hands. But in the day of restoration, YHWH will remove wickedness from His land and force it to return whence it came.[17] In that day of triumph she (wickedness) will submit meekly to the Lord of all the earth and will settle in the "house"[18]

16. Chary, *Aggée-Zacharie, Malachie*, 104.
17. Meyers and Meyers, *Haggai, Zechariah 1-8*, 308.
18. As most commentators agree, בַּיִת ("house") here means Temple. The ephah will be set up on its "base" (מְכֻנָה), i.e., the foundation upon which such cult objects were placed in Mesopotamian temples. For such stands in OT temples, see 1 Kings 7:27; 2 Kings 23:13, 16; Jer. 27:19; Ezra 3:3; David L. Petersen, *Haggai, and Zechariah 1-8* (London: SCM, 1985), 261-62.

built especially for her until the day of her final disposition, something Zechariah does not explicitly address.

Additional Notes

5:11 The MT verb form וְהֻנִּיחָה is somewhat problematic. As pointed it appears to be hophal of נוּחַ, but if so, it is the only example. Perhaps with the LXX (καὶ θήσουσιν υτό, "and they will set it") it should be repointed to hiphil וְהִנִּיחָה, "they will set it."

9
Vision Eight: The Chariots (6:1-8)

A. CONTENT OF THE VISION (6:1-4)

If ever a case could be made for matching complementary visions throughout the unfolding of the night visions structure in Zechariah, it can be made here. This last of the eight shares so much in common with the first that the two, at least, must be viewed as book ends enveloping the whole series.[1] These points of commonality should be addressed first, then the present vision can better yield its meaning.

First, the two visions concern four principal objects each. Vision one describes four horses (and presumably horsemen), whereas vision eight speaks of four chariots, each of which has horses attached to it. There is apparently some difference in the color of the horses in the respective visions, for in number one they are red (two of them), sorrel, and white, but in number eight they are red, black, white, and variegated.[2] Second, the horses in the one vision and the chariots in the other are servants of YHWH who go forth at His bidding to "walk to and fro through the earth" (1:10; cf. 6:7). In other words, both visions speak of YHWH's universal hegemony. In the third place, the "messenger who spoke to me," the interpreting messenger, is important both in disclosing the vision and in elucidating its meaning (1:9;

---

1. Carol L. Meyers and Eric M. Meyers, *Haggai, Zechariah 1-8*, AB (Garden City, N.Y.: Doubleday, 1987), 332.
2. See discussion on this below.

cf. 6:4). Fourth, the horses of vision one stand among myrtle trees in a valley or ravine; the chariots of vision eight come out from between two mountains, evidently also through a valley. Finally, both visions share a cosmic, universalistic interest. Vision one mentions "through the earth" twice (1:10, 11) and notes that "all the earth is at rest and is quiet" (v. 11*b*). Then, as the visions progressed, there was an increasingly narrow focus on the international scene (vision two), Judah and the land (vision three), and the Temple and priesthood (vision four). At this point the trend reverses, beginning with Temple rebuilding and Zerubbabel's role (vision five), Judah and the land (vision six), the international scene (Babylon; vision seven), and finally "through the earth" repeated three times in vision eight.

Unlike vision one, number eight does not have its own oracle of response, though, as will be argued later, the oracle that follows it (6:9-15) may serve it as such as well as bringing the whole series to an end.

Translation

¹Once more I looked and saw four chariots going forth from between two mountains, mountains of bronze. ²With the first chariot there were red horses, with the second black horses, ³with the third white horses, and with the fourth spotted, all strong horses. ⁴Then I asked the messenger who spoke to me, "What are these, sir?"

Exegesis and Exposition

Turning now to the details of the vision, one is struck by the occurrence at once of a verb that has dominated Zechariah's visions, the verb "come forth" or "go forth" (v. 1). In its various forms יָצָא (*yāṣā'*) appears 15 times in 77 verses, including the introduction and oracles. More striking, however, is the accelerating rate at which the word appears. It occurs not once in visions one and two, once in vision three, not at all in vision four, once in the oracle of vision five, twice in vision six, four times is vision seven, and seven times in vision eight. While this trend must not be given undue importance, it does appear to suggest an intensely heightened sense of activity, one that reaches a dramatic climax in the interpretation of oracle eight, where, with an ironic twist, the last verse ends, "they who go out toward the north country have given My spirit rest in the north country" (v. 8). The flourish of activity of the visions, occasioned by YHWH's work of renewal and redemption, at last comes to a peaceful end when His sovereignty is established.

What Zechariah sees "going forth" in this vision are four chariots emerging from between two mountains. Of particular note is the fact that these mountains are bronze. The chariot (מֶרְכָּבָה, *merkābâ*) in the

OT is primarily a war machine, not just a mode of transportation (cf. Ex. 14:25; Josh. 11:6; Judg. 4:15; 1 Sam. 8:11; 1 Kings 12:18; 22:35), and in apocalyptic literature represents YHWH Himself (cf. the chariot wheels of Ezek. 1:15-21 as theophany) or His conveyance (Isa. 66:15; cf. Ps. 68:4, 17 [HB 68:5, 18]; Hab. 3:8).[3] There are four of them in the vision, a number symbolizing the worldwide extent of the travels of the chariots (cf. 1:8).

Mountains frequently symbolize kingdoms in the OT, again particularly in eschatological texts (cf. Isa. 41:15; Jer. 51:25; Dan. 2:35 ["great rock"]), but it is not likely that that is in mind here for at least two reasons. First, there is nothing in the interpretation section (vv. 5-8) that would support such a view and, second, there is within Zechariah itself a much better option, namely, the mountain that was split in two, leaving a valley in between (14:4). Coupled with this is the mountain of vision five (Zech. 4:7), that which before Zerubbabel would become a level place.

In the latter passage the mountain was seen to be an obstacle standing in the way of Zerubbabel to prevent him from discharging the task of temple-building and administering the affairs of the revived Davidic state. Because of its impenetrability, its sheer hardness, "mountain of bronze" would be an apt description. A problem remains in that only one mountain appears in vision five, whereas there are two here in vision eight. This may be where Zechariah 14:1-8 fits into the equation.[4] In the day of YHWH, Zechariah says, YHWH will stand on the Mount of Olives, which will split asunder beneath His feet, in effect creating two mountains, one to the north and one to the south. A great valley will lie between, providing a way of escape for the besieged of Jerusalem and also a conduit through which living waters can flow from Jerusalem to the eastern (Dead) sea (v. 8; cf. Ezek. 47:1-12).

Though the scenes are quite different in all three passages, the common imagery and symbolism cause one to suspect that the author is using stock literary devices in an integrative way to communicate one overall, consistent message. The four chariots are sent forth to reclaim all the earth for the suzerainty of YHWH, a result that also follows the splitting of the mountain in the day of YHWH (Zech. 14:9). Once this is brought to pass, there will be peace in Jerusalem (14:11) and in the whole earth (6:7-8).

To each (not "in each" as some translations read) chariot there are

---

3. Christian Jeremias, *Die Nachtgesichte des Sacharja* (Göttingen: Vandenhoeck & Ruprecht, 1977), 123-25.
4. Merrill F. Unger, *Zechariah* (Grand Rapids: Zondervan, 1963), 102.

attached draught horses, various in color.[5] The first has red horses, the same color as the first horse in vision one (אָדֹם, *'ādōm*; 1:8). The second has black (שָׁחֹר, *šāḥōr*), whereas the second horse in vision one was also red. The third chariot is drawn by white horses (לָבָן, *lābān*), but the third horse of vision one was sorrel (שָׂרֹק, *śārōq*) or "reddish brown." The horses of the fourth chariot are, according to the prevailing view, "spotted strong" (בְּרֻדִּים אֲמֻצִּים, *bĕruddîm 'ămuṣṣîm*), and the fourth of the first vision was white. Thus, only the first and fourth horses of the chariot vision were of the same hue as the horses in vision one.

The Apocalypse also describes four horses, whose riders have the assignment of going throughout the earth to administer plague and death (Rev. 6:1-8). There can be no doubt that the seer here is dependent on Zechariah for his basic imagery, but the work of the horsemen is spelled out in much greater and more specific detail. The colors are white, red, black, and pale or "yellowish green" (χλωρός, *chlōros*).[6] The three visions have only the white and red horses in common. The black horses are in Revelation and Zechariah's vision eight. The pale one is unique to Revelation, the sorrel to vision one, and the "spotted strong" one to vision eight. As a result of this seeming lack of pattern, many scholars conclude that the colors of the horses either are not significant or have significance only in their own contexts.[7] What that significance may be is very difficult to determine, at least in the Zechariah visions. The Apocalypse is a little more helpful in this respect because the effect of the various horses and horsemen is spelled out.[8] Thus, the white horse is mounted by a rider with a royal crown, who goes forth to conquer (Rev. 6:2; cf. 19:11). One might reasonably conclude that "whiteness" symbolizes conquest in war. This would be very much in line with the visions of the horsemen (Zech. 1:8, 11) and chariots (Zech. 6:3, 6).

The red horse of the Apocalypse carries its rider on an errand of slaughter, resulting in the removal of peace from the earth (Rev. 6:4). The sword he carries is a graphic symbol of bloodshed, a symbol clearly communicated by the color. Again, both Zechariah visions feature the red horse on a mission of at least implicit slaughter. The

---

5. For a helpful comparison of the colors of the horses in vision eight according to the MT and the principal versions, see L. G. Rignell, *Die Nachtgesichte des Sacharja* (Lund: CWK Gleerup, 1950), 200-201.
6. William F. Arndt and F. Wilbur Gingrich, *A Greek-English Lexicon of the New Testament and Other Early Christian Literature* (Cambridge: At the University Press, 1957), 890-91.
7. See the helpful excursus by Joyce G. Baldwin, *Haggai, Zechariah, Malachi* (London: Tyndale, 1972), 138-40.
8. Unger, *Zechariah*, 102-3.

black horse is associated with famine brought about by severe shortages of food staples (Rev. 6:5-6). Only the chariot vision refers to black
horses, and they ride off to the north (Zech. 6:6). If they suggest
famine, their role in subduing YHWH's foes is to do so by creating
loss of crops. Interestingly, the white horses follow the black in this
case, indicating, perhaps, that conquest follows famine. Finally, the
fourth horse of John's vision is pale. This obviously has to do with the
pallor of death, since the rider of the horse is named Death (Rev. 6:8).
The death he brings is the final result of the marauding of the previous horsemen, for Death, with Hades, kills with sword and famine.

As noted already, this last horse is unique to the Apocalypse,
unless it is the same as either a red or the sorrel horse of Zechariah's
first vision or the "spotted strong" one of his eighth vision. This matter must now be considered, even though it necessitates some attention to the interpretation section of vision eight (Zech. 6:5-8).

A major problem lies in the apparent description of the fourth
horses as "spotted strong" (v. 3). The problem is exacerbated by vv. 6
and 7, where the "spotted" horses appear to be distinguished from the
"strong." Are these two different horses? If so, does this mean that the
fourth chariot was drawn by a team of mixed colors (v. 3)? Why are
the red horses not mentioned again with reference to their particular
mission?

Some of the ancient versions such as the Syriac and Aquila have
attempted to resolve the dilemma by reading the אֲמֻצִּים ('amuṣṣîm,
"strong (ones)," of v. 7a as אֲדֻמִּים ('ădummîm), "red (ones)." This would,
of course, allow the red horses a role and would not force "spotted"
and "strong" to refer to separate horses. However, the Hebrew text
tradition is unanimous in supporting the Masoretic reading.

The answer lies, perhaps, in noting that the chariots are dispersed
in only two directions, north and south (6:6). Most modern scholars,
under the assumption that the vision *must* require a fourfold destination to all the compass points, resort to all kinds of emendations and
additions to the text in order to meet that requirement and also to
find an assignment for the red horse.[9] There is nothing inherent in the
scene to demand four directions, and the passage makes perfectly
good sense without the resorts frequently undertaken to bring that
about.

The vision shows the black horses going to the north with the
white ones following.[10] Then the spotted horses turn to the south and

9. H. G. Mitchell, *A Commentary on Haggai and Zechariah*, ICC (Edinburgh: T.
& T. Clark, 1912), 179-80.
10. Kenneth Barker observes that a slight change in the Hebrew text (from
אַחֲרֵי הֶם, "after them," to אַחֲרֵי הַיָּם, "after the sea") yields the meaning

appear to be followed by the strong ones. All but the red are accounted for. When one recalls that vision one had two red horses, one of which was mounted by none other than "the messenger (or Angel) of YHWH" (1:8), then it is tempting to assign to that red horse, at least, a position of pre-eminence. It is the horse of the commander, perhaps. May it not be that the red horses of vision eight also draw the chariot of the commander, the messenger of YHWH? In vision one it is the other three horses—the red, sorrel, and white—that are identified as those who go out to walk to and fro through the earth, not the one on which the messenger of YHWH rides.[11] Likewise, the absence of the red horses in the execution of dominion in vision eight may be accounted for on the supposition that they are, as the commander's horses, exempt from the actual task of securing the sovereign's kingdom. The fact that in both instances the horses are red tends to give increased credibility to this view.

This still leaves the matter of the "spotted strong" horses of the fourth chariot. In light of the distinction that many interpreters draw in the interpretation section (vv. 6-7) between the spotted on the one hand and the strong on the other,[12] it seems necessary at first glance to distinguish between them in v. 3. However, that results in the assumption that there were at least four horses to each chariot and that in the case of this one two were "spotted" and two were "strong." The assumption must extend to the later separation of these horses, so that the spotted pull one chariot and the strong still another. But the record is silent about where an extra chariot might be found to accommodate the team that was separated out from its original chariot. Clearly this multiplication of hypotheses has little to commend it.

What is needed is a fresh reading of the account without resorting either to preconceived ideas about how many horses and chariots are needed or to wholesale patching up of a text that enjoys close to universal manuscript and versional support. First, the adjective "strong" (אֲמֻצִים, *'ămuṣṣîm*) at the end of v. 3 should be understood as in apposition not only to "spotted" (בְּרֻדִּים, *běruddîm*) but to "white" (לְבָנִים, *lĕbānîm*), "black" (שְׁחֹרִים, *šĕḥōrîm*), and "red" (אֲדֻמִּים, *'adummîm*) as well. That is, all four horses are "strong."[13] For the translation with this interpretation, see the beginning of this section.

"toward the west." He also suggests that the MT as it stands could mean the same on the basis of similar phrases in Isa. 9:12 (11 MT) and Job 18:20 (Kenneth L. Barker, "Zechariah," in *EBC*, ed. Frank E. Gaebelein [Grand Rapids: Zondervan, 1985], 7:638).

11. Meyers and Meyers, *Haggai, Zechariah 1-8*, 112.
12. Noted but not accepted by Theophane Chary, *Aggée-Zacharie, Malachie* (Paris: Librairie Lecoffre, 1969), 106-7.
13. Rignell, *Die Nachtgesichte des Sacharja*, 201-2; Meyers and Meyers, *Haggai, Zechariah 1-8*, 322.

If we turn to the interpretation section (vv. 5-8) with this in mind, the scene appears to be this: the black and white horses go north while the spotted one goes south. Then the speaker says, "Thus the strong (ones) went forth," etc. There are only three chariots that go, then, not four, just as there were only three horses that rode off through all the earth in vision one. In this important respect, as well as in others already noted, the two visions coincide.

B. INTERPRETATION OF THE VISION (6:5-8)

Translation

5The messenger replied to me, "These are the four spirits of heaven that are going forth from having presented themselves before the Lord of all the earth.6*The (chariot) that (has) with it the black horses is going to the north country and the white ones are going after them, but the spotted ones are going to the south country. 7Thus *the strong ones are going forth, having sought (permission) to go (in order) to walk about upon the earth." He had said, "Go! Walk about upon the earth!" So they did so. 8Then he cried out to me and spoke as follows: "Look! The ones going forth to the northland have brought rest to *my spirit concerning the northland."

Exegesis and Exposition

In response to Zechariah's question as to the identification and meaning of the horses and chariots (v. 4), the interpreting messenger said they were heavenly spirits, four in all. "Spirits" is preferred to "winds" here for רוּחַ (*rûaḥ*), both because of the superhuman, militaristic work the spirits must perform (cf. 4:6) and because they have just come from the presence of the Lord of the earth.[14] The four must include the red horses, even though they do not go on from this point to serve the Lord abroad. What Zechariah has seen are the four coming between two mountains (6:1), having come there from heaven itself. This, of course, would include the red ones since they also must hear the commissioning charge.

The heavenly scene from which these spirits have come is that of the sovereign אָדוֹן, (*'ădôn*) of all the earth, who is surrounded by His council and issues them orders concerning matters of the cosmic realm.[15] Such a scene is fairly common in the OT (cf. 1 Kings 22:19-23; Job 1:6; 2:1; Ps. 82:1; Isa. 6:1) as an anthropomorphic device to depict

---

14. K. Barker, "*Zechariah,*" 637. Baldwin suggests "winds" inasmuch as the steeds, like winds, travel over the whole earth (Baldwin, *Haggai, Zechariah, Malachi*, 131).
15. E. Theodore Mullen, *The Assembly of the Gods* (Chico, Calif.: Scholars Press, 1980), 275.

YHWH's dominion over all creation. The scene is similar to one in which human monarchs surround themselves with their courtiers. Four of these chariots or spirits have presented themselves before Him to attend to His bidding. What they actually are, whether angels or human instruments, cannot be determined, nor is it important. What is important is that they are expressions of the will of YHWH Himself. That there are four denotes, of course, that the divine purpose will find universal fulfillment (cf. 1:18-21).

Spirits often appear in the OT as ministers of YHWH. The term cannot yet bear the full-blown theological idea of the Holy Spirit, but is likely interchangeable with angels or to be taken as an extension of YHWH. David encourages the angels of YHWH to bless Him, describing them as those "mighty in strength, that fulfill His Word" and "do His pleasure" (Ps. 103:20-21; cf. Heb. 1:14). The author of the very next psalm extols YHWH "who makes spirits [or winds] His messengers (and) flames of fire His servants" (Ps. 104:4).

The black horses and chariot, having passed the portals of heaven (the two mountains?), make their way to the northland followed by the white horses. The geography of Palestine being what it is, one must go north even to go to the northwest and northeast. Thus none of the horses goes directly east or west. Indicative of this are the references to Assyria and Babylonia being north of Palestine when in fact they were to the northeast and east (cf. Jer. 1:14-15; 4:6; 6:1; 25:9; 46:10). Even Persia is considered to be in the north (Isa. 41:25; Jer. 50:3; 51:48). Therefore, any nation that must be reached by going north from Palestine can be in view.[16] If black and white have the same symbolic meaning here as in the Apocalypse, the vision may be suggesting that famine will break out in the north followed by conquest. Because the southbound horses have a color unlike any in the Apocalypse, however, it is unlikely that the symbolism of the colors, if any, can be pressed.[17]

The spotted horses and their chariot went the only other direction possible—to the south. Again, this would include all the nations of earth approachable from that direction, including Africa and Arabia. This perspective allows all four compass directions to be covered without the need to emend the text to include east and west, and thus demand the addition of another chariot and team of horses.

Once the chariots have departed, the interpreting messenger, describing all their horses as "the strong ones" (v. 7),[18] says they are about to go to and fro through the earth, having received permission

---

16. Unger, *Zechariah*, 106.
17. David L. Petersen, *Haggai and Zechariah 1-8* (London: SCM, 1985), 270-71.
18. Chary, *Aggée-Zacharie, Malachie*, 106-7.

from the Lord of the earth to do so. This rendering of the tenses and of the whole sequence of events seems to make most sense of the passage, particularly because it delivers the interpreting messenger from the responsibility of giving the chariots permission to go about their work. The fact that the chariots had stood in attendance before the Lord of the earth (v. 5) would strongly suggest that it was He who authorized their mission (v. 7). The whole turns on וַיְבַקְשׁוּ (*wayĕba-qĕšû*), "they sought (permission)," in v. 7. Following the rather strong disjunctive accent *Rebia*ʿ, this verb would likely not form a compound idea with the preceding verb "went forth" ("went forth and sought") but would rather introduce a parenthetical idea, such as "now they had sought (permission) to go," etc.

As noted previously (1:10-11), the idiom "walk to and fro through the earth" is an expression of dominion. The Lord of the whole earth is in process of bringing His domain under His sovereign sway, an assignment He entrusts to the chariots and horses. In terms of the historical and political milieu of Zechariah, this very likely refers to the conquest of Babylonia and other antitheocratic powers by the Persians, beginning with Cyrus and continuing on to the reign of Zechariah's contemporary, Darius Hystaspes. If so, the chariots could be symbolic of the Persians who, unknown to them, were used by YHWH to bring peace to the earth and salvation to His people. In fact, the summary of the vision states that "the ones going forth to the northland have brought rest to my spirit concerning the northland." The objective of subduing the northern (Babylonian?) powers has been achieved.

Isaiah first announced the use of Persia by YHWH to bring the intractable and cruel Babylonian oppressor to heel. YHWH described Cyrus, the founder of the Persian Empire, as "My shepherd," the one who "does all My pleasure" (Isa. 44:28). Even more remarkable, Cyrus was His "anointed one" whose hand He strengthened to subdue nations (45:1). Of great interest in light of the bronze mountains of Zechariah's vision is the statement concerning Cyrus that YHWH would go before Him and "shatter the gates of bronze" (45:2). Earlier, Isaiah had more obliquely referred to Cyrus as the "one from the east" to whom YHWH gave nations and "made him rule over kings" who would be but dust and stubble before him (Cyrus; 41:2).

The Chronicler (2 Chron. 36:22-23) and Ezra (1:1-4) record the edict of Cyrus, whom YHWH stirred up to deliver His people. He proclaims that YHWH had given him all the kingdoms of the earth and had commissioned him to build the house of YHWH in Jerusalem. Ezra (6:6-12, 22; 7:6, 11-26; 9:9) and Nehemiah (2:8; 11:23) consistently attest to the favor of the Persian kings, who time after time overrode the machinations of the Jews' enemies.

There can be little doubt that Zechariah's vision pertains to his own times, but its eschatological, apocalyptic character means it cannot be limited to that era. The picture here, as throughout the apocalyptic literature, is one of final and universal dominion by YHWH over His creation. How that will take place is a major part of the message of the oracles of Zechariah in chapters 7-14.

Additional Notes

6:6-7 The attempt by BHS to provide four chariots and to include the red horses results in a proposal to add whole clauses to the text without any MSS or ancient version attestation. This subjective method that refuses to accept difficult texts as they are, especially when a reasonable way can be found to explain them, is methodologically unsound.

6:6 אֲשֶׁר־בָּהּ is certainly an elliptical way to refer to the chariot with black horses. The reference back to אֵלֶּה (v. 5) makes it clear, however, that a chariot is in mind.

6:8 The rather abrupt personal pronominal suffix "my" has caused some scholars to suggest that רוּחִי, "my spirit," originally read רוּחַ י(הוה), "spirit of YHWH," with the *Tetragrammaton* having been first abbreviated to י (Yodh) and the י then having become attached to רוּח. This would eliminate the shift of subject from the interpreting angel or Angel of YHWH ("he cried," v. 8*a*) to YHWH Himself; but, with most scholars, I see no reason to object to the sudden appearance of YHWH as subject in v. 8. Cf. Chary, *Aggée-Zacharie, Malachie*, 107-8. Baldwin's view that the angel here reveals his identity as the Lord of the whole earth is untenable because elsewhere the "angel who spoke to me" (v. 4) is distinguished from YHWH or the Angel of YHWH (Baldwin, *Haggai, Zechariah, Malachi*, 132). For a correct assessment, see H. G. Mitchell, *A Commentary on Haggai and Zechariah*, 181.

THE VISIONS OF ZECHARIAH

Number	Text	Symbol(s)	Interpretation
1	1:7-17	Four Horsemen	Yahweh's Sovereignty in Israel's Restoration
2	1:18-21	Four Horns	The Persecution and Dispersion of God's People
3	2:1-13	The Surveyor	Preparation for Restoration
4	3:1-10	The Priest	Renewal of Israel's Priestly Ministry
5	4:1-14	The Menorah	Messiah as Priest and King

6	5:1-4	The Flying Scroll	Judgment for Covenant Disobedience
7	5:5-11	The Ephah	The Return of Evil to Babylon, Its Place of Origin
8	6:1-8	The Chariots	Yahweh's Final and Universal Dominion

10
Concluding Oracle (6:9-15)

A. THE SELECTION OF THE PRIEST (6:9-12a)

That this section is cast in the literary genre of oracle is accepted by scholarship in general, but how it relates to its larger literary context is a matter of some debate. The subject matter is so different from vision eight (6:1-8), which it immediately follows, that it cannot be an oracular response to that vision specifically. Yet the peace and sovereignty achieved by the chariots of that vision are quite compatible with the conditions necessary for Joshua and the Branch to wear the crowns that presuppose those circumstances. The building of the Temple particularly demands cessation of opposition and hostility for its successful conclusion.

On the other hand, this oracle is not a part of the series that commences with chapter seven, for that collection is dated more than a year later (7:1). Moreover, its subject matter is closer to that of the preceding visions and oracles than to what follows. References to Joshua and the Branch alone make that clear.

The case to be argued here is that this oracle serves as a comment on and climax to the night visions as a whole.[1] As the passage receives

---

1. For arguments to this effect—particularly stressing the connection between 6:9-15 and chaps. 3 and 4—see A. Van Hoonacker, *Les Douze Petits Prophetes* (Paris: Librairie Victor Lecoffre, 1908), 628-29. Cf. A. Petitjean, *Les Oracles du Proto-Zacharie* (Paris: J. Gabalda, 1969), 268-70; Carol L.

detailed treatment, this thesis will find increasing support. YHWH has revealed in a neat chiastic pattern His subjugation of the nations and deliverance of His covenant people, an act of redemption and restoration that focuses in visions four and five on the elevation of Joshua and Zerubbabel to positions of honor and influence. Not surprisingly, then, these same two persons are the central concern of this final, summarizing oracle. With this connection in mind the oracle will help to synthesize what has preceded it, but the visions also can and must inform the meaning of the text before us.

Translation

⁹The word of YHWH came to me as follows: ¹⁰*"Take from among the dispersion, namely, Heldai, Tobijah, and Jedaiah, all of whom have come from Babylon, and come in that same day and go to the house of Josiah son of Zephaniah. ¹¹Then take silver and gold and make crowns, setting (them) upon the head of *Joshua son of Jehozadak, the high priest. ¹²ᵃThen speak to him, 'Thus says YHWH of hosts,

Exegesis and Exposition

In typical oracular formula (cf. 1:1, 7; 7:1, 8; 8:1, 18; etc.) Zechariah declares that YHWH's Word, a word of commission, came to him (6:9). His task is to select from among the Diaspora who had returned from Babylon three men who are to accompany him to the house of a fourth man, Josiah son of Zephaniah. He, with them, is to make crowns for Joshua the high priest and, apparently, for the Branch. Once this is done, it will be clear to the community that YHWH has sanctioned the Temple construction and endorsed the word of the prophet. They will then come even from distant places to finish the work.

The identity of all these men, except Joshua, is not at all clear. The name Heldai (v. 10) belongs to only one other figure in the OT, one of David's mighty men (1 Chron. 27:15). Related to it is the name Huldah, one of the prophetesses in the days of Josiah (2 Kings 22:14). The name Tobijah, on the other hand, is much more common. It is possible, but by no means certain, that the Tobijah of the oracle is the same as the exile who returned from Babylon with Zerubbabel and Joshua (Ezra 2:60).[2] The problem with this is that he was one of the individuals whose genealogical roots could not be ascertained

---

Meyers and Eric M. Meyers, *Haggai, Zechariah 1-8*, AB (Garden City, N.Y.: Doubleday, 1987), 366-67.

2. The Meyers raise and reject this possibility for part of the reasons we suggest (Meyers and Meyers, *Haggai, Zechariah 1-8*, 341).

(2:59) and who therefore could not function in the priesthood (2:62). Jedaiah's name occurs also in Ezra's list of priests (2:36), and he may indeed be the Jedaiah of Zechariah. In fact, Ezra notes that he was of the house of Joshua, very likely Joshua the high priest (cf. 1 Chron. 9:10; Ezra 2:2).[3] Josiah son of Zephaniah is otherwise unknown. There was a priest named Zephaniah who was second to the high priest at the time of the fall of Jerusalem (2 Kings 25:18), but there is no way of knowing if Josiah was his descendant.[4]

There is at least some chance that, in terms of their names, the men listed in Zechariah 6:10 were priests, and it is most likely they were given their assignment here.[5] That was to take silver and gold on the very day they were assembled at Josiah's house to fashion a crown (or crowns) for Joshua the high priest. The word for crown (עֲטָרָה, *'ăṭārâ*) here is the normal one for a royal crown (2 Sam. 12:30; Ps. 21:3 [HB 21:4]; Song 3:11; Jer. 13:18), though נֵזֶר (*nēzer*) is also so used.[6] However, *'ăṭārâ* is never used in the OT to speak of the head-dress of a priest; the term then is either *nēzer*, *miṣnepet* (מִצְנֶפֶת), "turban" or "mitre," or *ṣānîp* (צָנִיף), "mitre" or "diadem" (cf. Zech. 3:5). This is most significant because the crowning of the priest here must have regal implications.

A slight problem exists at this point as to the number of crowns involved. The MT reads the plural עֲטָרוֹת (*'ăṭārôt*), whereas several LXX MSS, the Syriac, and Targums read the singular עֲטֶרֶת (*'ăṭeret*).[7] There is nothing inherently improbable about there being two crowns, especially in a vision, so the MT should be accepted. It is possible that the use of two precious metals, silver and gold, suggests that one crown was silver and the other gold. Whenever the metal of crowns is known in the OT, however, it is always gold, so both crowns here are probably manufactured of both metals.[8]

---

3. Meyers and Meyers, *Haggai, Zechariah 1-8*, 341.
4. Samuel Amsler, *Aggée, Zacharie 1-8, Zacharie 9-14*, CAT (Neuchatel: Delachaux, & Niestlé, 1981), 107, tentatively identifies Josiah as son of the priest Zephaniah and suggests also that the "Hen" of v. 14 was an epithet given him because of his hospitality. For other ideas concerning Hen, see below.
5. D. Ernest Sellin, *Das Zwölfprophetenbuch* (Leipzig: A. Deichert, 1922), 469-70.
6. Petitjean, *Les Oracles du Proto-Zacharie*, 283.
7. For a complete discussion of the versional evidence and the views of major commentators, see L. G. Rignell, *Die Nachtgesichte des Sacharja* (Lund: CWK Gleerup, 1950), 223-25.
8. The Meyers prefer the view that two crowns, one silver and the other gold, are intended, the former being intended for Joshua and the latter, the monarchic crown, to be placed in the Temple (v. 14) (Meyers and Meyers, *Haggai, Zechariah 1-8*, 349-55). Unger, though offering the interpretation that only one crown appears here, makes the apt connection between it

The crowning of the high priest was an important part of his investiture, though, as just remarked, the crown was not that of royalty. When Aaron and his sons were set apart, Moses placed on Aaron's head a mitre (מִצְנֶפֶת *miṣnepet*). On the front of it there was a golden plaque (צִיץ זָהָב, *ṣîṣ zāhāb*) bearing the inscription, "Holy to YHWH" (Ex. 28:36-38). The mitre itself was made of linen (v. 39), so it was quite different from a silver or golden crown. The symbolism of the mitre and plate was to communicate to the people that the high priest had the responsibility of making atonement for them in matters of cultic participation, that is, in matters pertaining to holy things (Ex. 28:38).[9] The clean turban placed on Joshua's head in vision four communicates this same idea (Zech. 3:4-5). Some of this intercessory or substitutionary element of the high priest's ministry may be in view in the present oracle, but the crowning with a royal and not priestly diadem makes it certain that that is not the primary emphasis.

Additional Notes

6:10 For the MT מֵאֵת some scholars (so Sellin, 468) suggest מַשְׂאֵת ("contributions of"), yielding "Take contributions of the dispersion." This then leads to the specification, silver and gold (v. 11). However, the text as it stands indicates that the men named are a select group from the dispersion, a notion that makes excellent sense here. Others regard לָקוֹחַ as an elliptical or pregnant construction, yielding "Take [silver and gold] from the exiles, Heldai, Tobijah, and Jedaiah, . . . " (cf. A. B. Davidson, *Hebrew Syntax* [Edinburgh: T. & T. Clark, 1901], §88 Rem. 2)

6:11 Because of the problems of crowning the high priest, the reference to the Branch (v. 12), and the work of temple-building, many interpreters (cf. Elliger, 128) read "Zerubbabel son of Shealtiel" in place of "Joshua son of Jehozadak, the high priest." This highly arbitrary procedure has no ancient text-critical support and is purely in the interest of a hypothesis about the discrediting of Zerubbabel and coincident elevation of Joshua. Theories ought not to dictate

---

and the multiple crown of the returning Messiah in Rev. 19:12 (Merrill F. Unger, *Zechariah* [Grand Rapids: Zondervan, 1963], 112). Lipiński proposes that the afformative in both places (vv. 11, 14) reflects an archaic fem. sing. ending as in Phoenician and certain Hebrew divine and place names (E. Lipiński, "Recherches sur le Livre de Zacharie," *VT* 20 [1970]: 34-35). Barker suggests that the plural is used as a "plural of extension," an "ornate crown with many diadems" (Kenneth L. Barker, "Zechariah," in *EBC*, ed. Frank E. Gaebelein [Grand Rapids: Zondervan, 1985], 7:639).

9. U. Cassuto, *A Commentary on the Book of Exodus* (Jerusalem: Magnes, 1967), 384-85.

texts, however; instead, texts should underlie and justify theories. See commentary on v. 12.

B. THE SIGNIFICANCE OF THE PRIEST (6:12*b*-15)

Translation

¹²*ᵇ*"Look—the man whose name is Branch, who will sprout up from his place and build the Temple of YHWH. ¹³Indeed, he will build the Temple of YHWH and will be covered with splendor, sitting and ruling upon his throne. Moreover, *there will be a priest upon his throne and wholesome counsel will be between the two of them. ¹⁴The *crowns will belong to *Helem, Tobijah, Jedaiah, and *Hen son of Zephaniah as a memorial in the Temple of YHWH. ¹⁵Then those who are distant will come and build the Temple of YHWH (that you might know that YHWH of hosts has sent me to you). This will all come to pass if you completely obey the voice of YHWH your God."' "

Exegesis and Exposition

The Word of YHWH through Zechariah is now directed specifically to Joshua (v. 12*a*), thus distinguishing him from the man named Branch (12*b*). It is Branch (צֶמַח, *Ṣemaḥ*) who will sprout up (יִצְמַח, *yiṣmaḥ*) from his place and build the Temple of YHWH. There is no doubt as to who Branch is, for he has already appeared in vision four as the servant of YHWH (3:8), a messianic offspring of David (Isa. 11:1; 53:2; Jer. 33:15; cf. Hag. 2:23). His connection with the "stone" (Zech. 3:9) finds explication in Zech. 4:7-10, where Zerubbabel is named as Temple builder. Thus, converging lines of identification within Zechariah and elsewhere make it certain that Zerubbabel is in view in the present oracle. As a direct offspring of the line of David he is well-qualified to sit on the royal throne of Judah, something clearly stated in v. 13.

For Zerubbabel to sit on the throne as king, whether in reality or as a prototype of the future, eschatological ruler, necessitates a coronation. The reason for two crowns now becomes apparent—Joshua wears one as priest and Zerubbabel another as king. To return briefly to v. 11, it is important to note that YHWH instructs Zechariah and his colleagues to make *crowns* of silver and gold and place them on Joshua's head. As already noted, many scholars render "crown" (singular), but only by relying on the versions. Others, in the interest of maintaining a certain ideological point of view that sees the rise of a hierocracy at the expense of secular government, explain the appar-

197

ent difficulty as a badly botched attempt by redactionary circles to expunge Zerubbabel from the record.[10]

But the text before us makes perfectly good sense with the double personality and double crown perspective it presents. What the narrative is saying is that crowns are made, only one of which is to be worn by Joshua. One could even translate the relevant passage, "Take silver and gold and make crowns, placing one on the head of Joshua the high priest" (v. 11).[11] This admittedly presupposes an elliptical expression of something like "make crowns (and of these one is Joshua's) and place it," etc. Such ellipsis is a common feature of biblical Hebrew.[12]

As for Zerubbabel, he will "sprout up" from his place and build the Temple. "His place" (תַּחְתָּיו, *taḥtāyw*) implies a lowly station, one hardly likely to develop into anything as grand as the rule of the Davidic kingdom. This need not suggest that Zerubbabel himself was considered insignificant or lacking in necessary qualifications, for his connection to the Davidic dynasty was unimpeachable. What is in view here is the perceived unlikelihood of any revival of that dynasty at all in postexilic Judah.[13] It is this pessimistic assessment of things that sets the tone for the discouragement and lethargy so clearly evident in Haggai (1:2, 9; 2:3-4, 14). Humanly, there was no hope of ever recovering the glory days of the ancient kings. The ground was dry and infertile, and the rains of blessing had long since ceased.

But a sprout will spring up out of dry ground, Isaiah had predicted (Isa. 53:2), and Zechariah is here to say that Zerubbabel, in some sense at least, is that new growth. From the lowliness of hopelessness he will be elevated to the throne itself, thus restoring glory to Israel and confidence in her God. A sign of divine favor upon him and the nation is the completion of the Temple, an accomplishment made sure by the repetition of the promise (vv. 12b-13a).[14]

The latter part of v. 13 has engendered a great deal of discussion inasmuch as it seems to suggest that the Branch, just enthroned and

---

10. Friedrich Horst, *Die Zwölf Kleinen Propheten. Nahum bis Maleachi*, HAT 14 (Tübingen: J. C. B. Mohr, 1964 [1936]), 238; Adam S. Van der Woude, "Serubbabel und die messianischen Erwartungen des Propheten Sacharja," *ZAW* 100 (1988): 138-56, esp. 147-53.

11. So David L. Petersen, *Haggai and Zechariah 1-8* (London: SCM, 1985), 272.

12. E. W. Bullinger, *Figures of Speech Used in the Bible* (London: Eyre & Spottiswoode, 1898), 1-130.

13. Petitjean, *Les Oracles du Proto-Zacharie*, 286. M. Barker takes "from his place" to mean that it is Joshua who will take the place of Zerubbabel as Temple builder. This is in line with her view that Zechariah is promoting the Jerusalem priesthood above all others (Margaret Barker, "The Two Figures in Zechariah," *HeyJ*. 18 (1977): 43).

14. K. Barker, "Zechariah," 640.

ruling, will also be a priest. The result of this understanding of things is either that Joshua is the Branch, an impossibility in light of v. 12, or that Zerubbabel usurps the office of priest from Joshua, also impossible because of Zerubbabel's non-Aaronic lineage and historical evidence to the contrary. The solution lies in the chiastic pattern of vv. 11-13 in which Joshua is identified as priest, the Branch as builder, the Branch rules, and the priest rules. It might be structured as follows:

A   Joshua the priest is crowned (11*b*)
  B   The Branch sprouts up (12*a*)
    C   The Temple is built (12*b*)
    C'   The Temple is built (13*a*)
  B'   The Branch is enthroned (13*b*)
A'   The priest is enthroned (13*c*)

The priest and his role provide an inclusio bracketing the Branch and his role.

The two come together in v. 13*d*: "wholesome counsel will be between the two of them." Whatever this means, it appears here to identify two separate persons, giving support to the view that Joshua and the Branch (Zerubbabel) are both the center of attention. Both are crowned and enthroned, charged with administering, under YHWH, the affairs of their respective civil and religious realms.

The phrase "wholesome counsel" or, literally, "counsel of peace" is difficult. The most likely meaning is that the two function in a mutually beneficial and positive way, that is, they complement each other.[15] This relationship is a reestablishment of the theocratic community going as far back as Moses in which the headship of the nation was dyarchic, shared by prince and priest. The quality of office here has already been anticipated in vision five where Zerubbabel and Joshua appeared as olive trees, anointed ones who "stand by the Lord of all the earth" (Zech. 4:11, 14).[16]

---

15. This need not at all suggest that there had been party strife between the royal and priestly factions as Wellhausen, Haller, and Sellin proposed, for in the words of Van Hoonacker, "les partis de Josue et de Zorobabel n'ont sans doute jamais existé que dans l'imagination trop féconde des historiens qui les out inventés" ("the parties of Joshua and Zerubbabel have, without doubt, never existed except in the too fertile imagination of those who invented them") (Van Hoonacker, *Le Sacerdoce lévitique*, cited by Petitjean, *Les Oracles du Proto-Zacharie*, 293 n. 2).

16. M. Barker identifies the two parties here (and in the menorah vision, 4:11-14) as two priestly branches that Zechariah was attempting to reconcile (Margaret Barker, "The Two Figures in Zechariah," 45-46). Her evidence is extremely circular, however.

There is no evidence in history that these two rulers, especially Zerubbabel, actually wore their royal crowns. To the contrary, Zechariah seems to say that the crowns were committed to Helem, Tobijah, Jedaiah, and Hen who placed them in the Temple of YHWH as a memorial (v. 14).[17] They were more ceremonial than anything else and, like symbols or trophies of the faithfulness of YHWH, were placed on exhibition. Almost like a magnet they would attract the far-flung exiles to Jerusalem to participate in temple-building and kingdom restoration. Subsequent returns such as those under Ezra and Nehemiah must have been encouraged by the renewal of hope initiated by Joshua and Zerubbabel, who so marvelously cooperated in achieving YHWH's new redemption.

Then, perhaps in a parenthetical observation, the prophet declares that the return to the land brought about by the events of this oracle will put beyond any doubt that he is a true spokesman of YHWH (v. 15). The whole community would have to confess that fact, implying no doubt that Zechariah, like all prophets, was continually challenged as to his authority and authenticity. But the fulfillment was not automatic; implicit obedience to YHWH's Word was essential. In the strongest way of expressing the kind of obedience required, the infinitive absolute before an imperfect (שָׁמוֹעַ תִּשְׁמְעוּן, *šāmôaʿ tismeʿûn*),[18] YHWH makes clear that there is a part that His people must play if they are to realize the fullness of His grace.

What is ultimately at stake here is not just the crowning of two persons in 519 B.C., no matter how important these two might be in terms of their own circumstances or even in terms of what they symbolize. Joshua and Zerubbabel are signs (Zech. 3:8), anointed ones (4:14) whose messianic significance is unmistakable (Hag. 2:23; Zech. 3:2-5; 6:11-13). That is, they point toward something far more remarkable and transcendent than even they themselves could have anticipated. The historical here is merely a portent of the eschatological to follow.

As already intimated the dual roles of priest and king are central themes of OT history and theology.[19] Man was created to have dominion over all things (Gen. 1:26-28) and, like a priest, to stand between God and His creation (Ps. 8:5-8 [HB 8:6-9]). When Israel was elected by YHWH and redeemed from Egyptian bondage, she entered into covenant with Him as "a holy nation, a kingdom of priests" (Ex.

---

17. Joyce G. Baldwin, *Haggai, Zechariah, Malachi* (London: Tyndale, 1972), 137.
18. *GKC*, 113l-n.
19. For the latter period in particular, see W. J. Dumbrell, "Kingship and Temple in the Post-Exilic Period," *RTR* 37 (1978): 33-42.

19:4-6). Orders of priests and lines of kings emerged in the course of redemptive history, always independent of each other yet complementing one another.

Beginning with David, however, there was the undeniable fact that royal and priestly rule would someday merge in one individual, the scion of David. This anointed one of YHWH would be His son who would reign from Zion and be heir of all the nations (Ps. 2:2, 6-8). Moreover, he, as universal ruler, would also be a priest after the line of Melchizedek (Ps. 110:2, 4). Christian theology identifies this offspring of David as Jesus Christ, a point elaborated in great detail by the author of the epistle to the Hebrews (Heb. 5:1-10; 7:1-25). Postbiblical Judaism, though recognizing the messianic role of both priest and king in the eschaton, failed to bring them together into one; hence the dual messiahship of the Qumran sect and other communities.[20]

Apart from Psalm 110 there is no OT passage that comes as close as this one in Zechariah to uniting the royal and priestly offices.[21] With this in mind, the "wholesome counsel between the two of them" takes on a greatly enhanced meaning. Joshua and Zerubbabel are messianic forerunners whose persons and functions prototypically portray that One to come who died as servant, intercedes as priest, and will return as king, even Christ Jesus.

Additional Notes

6:13 In line with the view that Zerubbabel is the subject of the entire verse (except the last clause), LXX reads "and the priest will be on his right hand." There is every reason to believe that this is a gloss to explain the admittedly awkward "There will be a priest on his throne" when the antecedent appears still to be Zerubbabel, the Branch. Mastin suggests that it might have appeared to the LXX translators inappropriate for a priest also to sit on a throne (Heb. כִּסֵּא), for which there is evidence as well in the LXX of 1 Sam. 1:9; 4:13, 18, where it translates not by θρόνος but by δίφρος. Thus he concludes, "The reading of the LXX is to be understood as exegesis of the Masoretic Text" (B. A. Mastin, "Short Notes: A Note on Zechariah VI 13," *VT* 26 [1976]: 113-16).

6:14 Again some MSS of the LXX, Syriac render singular "crown"

---

20. Helmer Ringgren, *The Faith of Qumran* (Philadelphia: Fortress, 1963), 171-73; J. R. Villalón, "Sources Vétéro-Testamentaires de la Doctrine Qumranienne des Deux Messies," *RevQ* 8 (1972): 53-63. Villalón maintains that the name Joshua is not original to the passage, having been worked in later by sacerdotal interests (56-57).
21. L. G. Rignell, *Die Nachtgesichte des Sacharja* (Lund: CWK Gleerup, 1950), 229.

for the same reason as in v. 11 (cf. comment on v. 11). Tg. Ps.-J. omits reference to a crown altogether. For possible reasons, see Cathcart and Gordon, *The Targum of the Minor Prophets*, 199.

With "Helem" compare "Heldai" in v. 10. Most scholars take "Helem" to be a corruption of "Heldai" (חלם←חלדי), but it is difficult to see how this could have gone unchallenged in the Masoretic tradition and most versions, especially in the self-same passage. Probably Helem and Heldai were different persons. Baldwin, however, citing Heled in 1 Chron. 11:30, known otherwise as Heleb (2 Sam. 23:29) and Heldai (1 Chron. 27:15), proposes that Helem was interchangeable with Heldai (Baldwin, *Haggai, Zechariah, Malachi*, 137).

"Hen son of Zephaniah" is more difficult because v. 10 identifies the son of Zephaniah as Josiah. The Syriac simply emends חֵן to יֹאשִׁיָּה (*yō'šiyyâ*) in line with v. 10, but that hardly explains the existing text. BHS suggests a transposition of "son of Zephaniah" and "Hen," thus making them separate persons. It might be best to understand it, then, as a construct with "son of Zephaniah" and render the line something like, "the crowns will be (given over) to Helem, Tobijah, and Jedaiah, to the kindness (חֵן) of the son of Zephaniah, as a memorial," etc. Unger, however, offers the plausible suggestion that Hen was a nickname for Josiah to describe his hospitality and liberality (Unger, *Zechariah*, 117). Close to this is Demsky's identification of חֵן plus the preposition לְ with Akkadian *laḫḫinu*, the title of an official in Assyria responsible for the collection of garments and silver. The term occurs also in the Elephantine papryi as *lĕḥēn* of YHWH. Demsky identifies Josiah as this *lĕḥēn* and translates, "for the *lḥn* son of Zephaniah." This suggestion, apart from a needed לְ to precede לְחֵן, is most attractive (Aaron Demsky, "The Temple Steward Josiah ben Zephaniah," *IEJ* 31 [1981]: 100-102).

PART 2
Oracles Concerning Hypocritical Fasting (7:1–8:23)

1
Hypocrisy of False Fasting (7:1-14)

Chapters 7 and 8 of Zechariah lie between the night visions of chapters 1-6 and the self-designated oracles of chapters 9-14 (cf. מַשָּׂה, *maś-śâ*, in 9:1; 12:1). The two chapters are bound by the common theme of fasting, a theme elaborated in both its negative (chap. 7) and positive (chap. 8) expressions by a series of pericopes form-critically defined as oracles, though not designated as such by the prophet himself.[1] For a discussion of the form-critical character of chapters 7 and 8 and the relationship of this section to chapters 1-6 and chapters 9-14, see the Introduction to Zechariah, pp. 68-74.

A. INTRODUCTION AND CONCERN (7:1-3)

Translation

¹In the fourth year of Darius the king, on the fourth (day) of the ninth month, Kislev, the Word of YHWH came to Zechariah. ²Now (the people of) Bethel had sent Sharezer and *Regem-Melech and their men to entreat the favor of YHWH ³by asking the priests of the house of YHWH of hosts and the prophets, "Should I weep on the fifth month, separating myself as I have done over the years?"

---

1. For an excellent case for the literary unity of chaps. 7-8, see David J. Clark, "Discourse Structure in Zechariah 7:1–8:23," *BT* 36 (1985): 328-35.

Exegesis and Exposition

A most evident indication of the break between chapter 7 and what precedes it is the dating formula of v. 1. The previous visions had occurred in one night, the 24th of the eleventh month of the second year of Darius, that is, February 15, 519 B.C. (1:7). The date of this revelation is the fourth day of the ninth month in year four of Darius, or December 7, 518 B.C., about 22 months later.

It is fruitless to speculate about the impact of Zechariah's visions, particularly his crowning and enthronement of Zerubbabel and Joshua, which he presumably carried out in response to his charge of. 6:9-15. The biblical record unfortunately is silent about such matters and, indeed, apart from the tantalizingly brief historical references here there is little that can be known about the period at all. Neither Zerubbabel nor Joshua is mentioned again in Zechariah (though, of course, that does not mean that they had become inactive or even had died), even though Zechariah had been told that Zerubbabel would complete the Temple (6:12-13), a task accomplished on March 13, 514 B.C. (Ezra 6:16).[2] Ezra says (3:14) that the Jews "went on successfully with the building under the prophesying of Haggai the prophet and Zechariah the son of Iddo, and they completed the building." Although, as Williamson points out, this cannot prove anything about the tenure of these two prophets,[3] it does provide some insight into the period from August 29, 520, until March 13, 515. Thereafter the record is completely silent until the coming of Ezra.[4]

That progress was well underway on the Temple by the date of this oracle is evident from the delegation that came to Jerusalem to inquire of the Lord through the priests and prophets, the former being associated with the house of YHWH (v. 3). This presupposes that the cult was being carried out there with some degree of formality and legitimacy, a fact that further implies a rather complete Temple complex. That it was not totally finished is also quite clear (cf. 8:9, 13). Where the travelers came from and even who they were is a matter of some disagreement. The Hebrew reads literally, "He sent Bethel, Sharezer, and Regem-melech, and his men. . . ." This could mean that Bethel (that is, the community at Bethel) sent the others, thereby designating Bethel as the place of origin, or Bethel may be joined with Sharezer to create one name, Bethel-Sharezer. One should then translate, "Bethel-Sharezer sent both Regem-melech and his men. . . ."

---

2. Richard A. Parker and Waldo H. Dubberstein, *Babylonian Chronology 626 B.C.–A.D. 75* (Providence, R.I.: Brown Univ., 1956), 30.
3. H. G. M. Williamson, *Ezra, Nehemiah*, WBC (Waco, Tex.: Word, 1985), 16 83.
4. P. R. Ackroyd, *Israel Under Babylon and Persia* (Oxford: Oxford Univ., 1970), 173.

Francis North understands the passage in a totally different way. He argues that the LXX and Tg. place the destination (not the origin) of the journey at Bethel. Thus he says the focus of the cult shifted to Bethel after the destruction of the Jerusalem temple. The priests of Bethel were Aaronic, whereas those of the restoration were Zadokite. The latter soon replaced the Aaronic priests and even claimed to be descendants of Aaron. Thus the Bethel shrine became extinct, a point underscored by the Masoretic tradition that has a delegation coming *from* Bethel and not going *to* Bethel. Besides its dependence on a hypothetical view of the origin of the Zadokite priesthood, North's position depends on a tiny minority of Hebrew and LXX texts, too few to overthrow the traditional view.[5] E. Lipiński takes the subject of the verb "sent" to be Darius and argues that "Bethel" is an "accusatif de determination locale" ("accusative of place") even though it lacks the normal *hē locale* (other examples are 2 Kings 2:4; Jer. 26:22; 29:28). Thus, he agrees with North that ""Bethel"" is the destination, but he takes בֵּית־אֵל (Bethel) not as referring to a place name but as "the house of God," i.e., the Jerusalem Temple. Darius, he says, has sent a delegation to Jerusalem to show his interest in the work of the Temple, especially in light of the fact that the predicted 70 years until its reconstruction were nearly fulfilled.[6] Why a pagan king should declare that he had wept and fasted over the ruined Temple (v. 3) is a serious problem to Lipiński's hypothesis, so serious that he has to assume that the words were "posée au nom du roi" ("asked in the king's name") and that the shift of subject to Zechariah in vv. 4ff. is redactional (p. 41). Obviously, the redactional adjustments that have to be made to make the narrative support his view weaken its credibility. Not to be overlooked in the whole matter of destination is why the Jerusalem cult, already so well established since the Exile, should seek information from a "fringe" religious center like Bethel.[7]

While names compounded with Bethel are otherwise attested at Elephantine and in Neo-Babylonian texts,[8] it seems best here to take Bethel as the city name and subject of the predicate.[9] This allows the conjunction (which otherwise is awkward) to remain on Regem-

---

5. Fancis S. North, "Aaron's Rise in Prestige," *ZAW* 66 (1954): 191-99.
6. E. Lipiński, "Recherches sur le Livre de Zacharie," *VT* 20 (1970): 35-42.
7. See Nigel Allan, "The Identity of the Jerusalem Priesthood During the Exile." *HeyJ* 23 (1982): 264.
8. Hyatt gives many examples and even goes so far as to suggest that a certain *shirku* (a type of temple servant) named Bīt-ili-shar-uṣur may be the Bethel-Sharezer of Zech. 7:2 (J. Philip Hyatt, "A Neo-Babylonian Parallel to *Bethel-Sar-Eṣer*, Zech. 7:2," *JBL* 56 [1937]: 387-94). It is difficult to believe, however, that an officiant at a pagan Babylonian temple would become a staff person in a Jewish cult (so Hyatt, 394).
9. Wilhelm Rudolph, *Haggai-Sacharia 1-8–Sacharia 9-14–Maleachi*, KAT (Gütersloh: Verlaghaus Gerd Mohn, 1976), 136-38.

melech, since the series would now begin with Sharezer, and also comports better with the Masoretic accent tradition that places a rather strong disjunction (Zaqeph) between "Bethel" and "Sharezer." Finally, there was a lively postexilic community at Bethel of more than 200 men (Ezra 2:28; but cf. Neh. 7:32).[10] Coming as they did from a place long associated with apostate worship (1 Kings 12:29-33; 2 Kings 10:29; Jer. 48:13; Amos 3:14; 4:4; 7:13), these men would be particularly concerned to determine orthodox praxis on behalf of those who sent them.

The practice in mind is that of weeping and fasting in the fifth month, something the people of that community had done for a number of years. "Fasting" is implied by the niphal infinitive of נָזַר (*nāzar*, "separating myself"), a verb used here to denote a consecratory withholding of oneself (from food),[11] and is made certain by YHWH's response in v. 5 where the normal term for fasting (צוּם, *ṣûm*) occurs. The lamentable occasion that had given rise to this observance was the destruction of Solomon's Temple, a disaster that had occurred almost exactly 70 years earlier, on August 14, 586 B.C. (2 Kings 25:8).[12] This was on the seventh day of the fifth month, so the next anniversary was just a few months away, about August 2, 517.

A particular problem with the observance was that it had no sanction in Israel's ancient religious traditions as did other holy days. Was it appropriate, then, to create holy days to observe occasions that had arisen in the post-Mosaic period? It obviously was being done de facto, but until the ecclesiastical authority structures were back in place in Jerusalem it was impossible to get an official ruling, hence the delegation.

Additional Notes

7:2 Syriac Syrohexapla, Ethiopic presuppose וְרַב־מָג, the title of a high official, meaning here "chief officer of the king"; Winton Thomas, *IB*, 1082. LXX has Αρβεσεερ ὁ Βασιλεύς, perhaps reflecting "*rabsaris*, the king." A *Rabsaris* was a kind of an Assyrian official (cf. 2 Kings 18:17). See H. G. Mitchell, *Haggai and Zechariah*, 198.

---

10. Commenting on the postexilic occupation of Gibeah, Gibeon, Bethel, and Shechem, Lapp observed that "especially noted is the apparent prosperity of these towns in the late 6th century in marked contrast with evidence from sites excavated to the south of Jerusalem" (Paul W. Lapp, "Tell el-Fûl," *BA* 28 [1965]: 6).
11. J. Kühlewein, *TWAT*, II:50, s.v. נזיר. Kühlewein points out that נזר as a verb in the niphal occurs four times (Lev. 22:2; Ezek. 14:7; Hos. 9:10; Zech. 7:3) in the sense of separation from unclean things, from YHWH Himself, or from food.
12. Parker and Dubberstein, *Babylonian Chronology 626 B.C.–A.D. 75*, 28; A. Malamat, "The Last Kings of Judah and the Fall of Jerusalem" *IEJ* 18 (1968): 154-55.

B. CRITICISM OF FASTING (7:4-7)

Translation

⁴The Word of YHWH of hosts then came to me, ⁵"Speak to all the people of the land and to the priests as follows: 'When you fasted and lamented in the fifth and seventh (months) throughout these seventy years, did you indeed fast to me, to me, indeed? ⁶And when you eat and drink, are you not eating and drinking for yourselves?'" ⁷Should (you) not (have obeyed) the words that YHWH cried out through the former prophets when Jerusalem was inhabited and at rest and her surrounding cities, the Negev, and the shephelah were also inhabited?

Exegesis and Exposition

What may have appeared to be an innocent question about the propriety of fasting was instead a question fraught with hypocrisy, as YHWH's response puts beyond any doubt. It therefore appears that the query to Zechariah by the Bethelites may not have been so much a matter of piety as it was of posturing. May it not be that the delegation was trying more to impress the prophet than to gain instruction from him?

Be that as it may, the reply by YHWH was in fact a sharp rebuke. Their fasting and mourning, not only on the fifth but the seventh month and for 70 long years, was an empty exercise designed to enhance not YHWH but those who engaged in it in such a hypocritical manner. In other words, their religion had become one of outward show with no inner content. Evidence for that appears in the next section, vv. 8-14.

The seventh month (v. 5) evidently refers to the murder of Gedaliah, the Jewish governor appointed by Nebuchadnezzar after the fall of Jerusalem (Jer. 40:5). He was a grandson of Shaphan, quite likely the scribe who first read the Temple scroll and brought it to King Josiah for his perusal (2 Kings 22:5, 8-11). His father Ahikam (2 Kings 22:12) later interceded on Jeremiah's behalf to deliver him from a plot against his life (Jer. 26:24).[13] Gedaliah thus came from an honored family, one that enjoyed the confidence of good King Josiah. Josiah was strongly pro-Babylonian (2 Kings 23:28-29), so there is every reason to think that Gedaliah's appointment to high office by Nebuchadnezzar was a way of rewarding one of Josiah's own close confidants.

However it happened, some anti-Babylonian survivors of Jerusalem's destruction and exile, led especially by Ishmael of the royal

---

13. For arguments supporting these relationships, see J. A. Thompson, *The Book of Jeremiah* (Grand Rapids: Eerdmans, 1980), 653.

house of David (Jer. 41:1), formed a conspiracy with Baalis, king of Ammon, to assassinate Gedaliah (Jer. 40:13-14). This they managed to do on the seventh month of a certain year (Jer. 41:1), perhaps as late as 581 B.C. This date arises from the fact that the Babylonians undertook a campaign against Jerusalem in that year (Jer. 52:30), one that may have come about, according to some scholars, in retaliation for the murder of Gedaliah.[14]

The death of Gedaliah was an extremely traumatic event for the community already crushed nearly to annihilation by the loss of the Temple, the ruin of the Holy City, and the deportation of most of its leadership. The wrath of Babylonia that must have followed this subordination to its sovereignty would in itself give cause for the remnant to lament its further suffering. For nearly 70 years these twin events of such sad recollection—the ruin of the Temple and violent death of the first exilic leader—had been commemorated.

The form that YHWH's question takes in regard to the genuineness of the fasting and grief betrays in itself their lack of sincerity. The Hebrew, by use of the infinitive absolute and independent pronoun, can hardly be captured in English. Literally YHWH asks (v. 5), "Fasting, did you fast to me, me?" Our translation above tries to bring out this nuance, which is both emphatic and skeptical.[15] The rhetorical question posed by YHWH requires no answer by the people, but YHWH Himself responds in a most ironic way. Just as they ate and drank for their own benefit and to their own satisfaction, so, he implies, did they fast (v. 6). Their religious activity was self-centered and self-fulfilling. It failed to satisfy the demands of a holy and loving God.

Verse 7 commences so elliptically that many scholars[16] (following the LXX and other witnesses) emend the sign of the accusative אֵת (*'et*) to the demonstrative pronoun אֵלֶּה (*'ēlleh*), "these," to read "Are not these the words," etc., and then proceed to eliminate vv. 8-9a (so BHS). The "words" referred to in v. 7 thereby become the words, "Execute true judgment," etc., in v. 9b. Such an approach seems almost essential unless one either takes "words" as the object of "cried out" or postulates a missing verb of which "words" is the object.[17] The former option is precluded by the fact that "cried out" is not in the

14. P. R. Ackroyd, *Israel Under Babylon and Persia*, 36-37.
15. Merrill F. Unger, *Zechariah* (Grand Rapids: Zondervan, 1963), 124.
16. So, e.g., Friedrich Horst, *Die Zwölf Kleinen Propheten. Nahum bis Malachi*, HAT 14 (1936; reprint, Tübingen: J. C. B. Mohr, 1964), 238-40.
17. The אֵת could also mark the subject of a verbless major clause; see Bruce K. Waltke and M. O'Connor. *An Introduction to Biblical Hebrew Syntax* (Winona Lake, Ind.: Eisenbrauns, 1990), 183.

independent clause with "words." The second, therefore, must be entertained. Because the appeal by the prophet here is to attend to the words of the former prophets (any prior to himself), something earlier generations did not do, a verb such as "hear" or "obey" would be in order. Thus, we propose, "should (you) not (have obeyed) the words," etc.

This seems preferable to the NIV and other versions that must supply "these" and then refer the message of vv. 5b-6 to the former prophets. That is, "these words" suggests in this view an appeal by the prophet Zechariah to the conditions of a previous generation with little or no direct relevance to his own hearers. Zechariah is not asking whether such and such were the words of early prophets, but his concern is whether his own contemporaries will obey those words. As for the ellipsis, it is even possible that Zechariah, having referred to eating and drinking in v. 6, is intending to use those verbs metaphorically in his question in v. 7. Thus, "Should (you) not (have eaten and drunk) the words which YHWH cried out by the former prophets?"[18]

The past to which Zechariah alludes is the preexilic past, a time when Jerusalem, its suburbs, and even more distant parts of Judah were occupied and at rest (v. 7). The message he is proclaiming, then, is not a new message. It is an old one, but that was spurned, leading to a depopulation of the land and upheaval and chaos in place of tranquillity.

The Negev was in the south of Judah and consisted largely of desert. For the Negev to be populated, one must envision times of unusually suitable climatic conditions and freedom from hostility. This is even more true of the Shephelah, the "lowlands" between Judah and the western plains. Its towns were historically in constant danger from the Philistines and other marauders who could easily penetrate their relatively weak and vulnerable defenses. Only when Israel and Judah were unusually strong could the conditions Zechariah describes prevail. His point is very apparent: If mighty and prosperous Jerusalem and Judah were overthrown for failing to heed the words of warning of earlier prophets, how much more important was it for his own audience to pay strict attention to those words in a day when their community was struggling for its very survival. This is no time for hypocritical self-indulgence.

---

18. A position akin to this is held by Hoftijzer, who joins v. 7 to v. 6, taking הֲלוֹא to be "a strengthening particle that can be used also in the midst of the sentence, and not only at its beginning" (J. Hoftijzer, "The Particle *'t* in Classical Hebrew," *OTS* 14 [1965]: 76).

C. INSTRUCTION CONCERNING FASTING (7:8-14)

1. Basis for Genuine Fasting (7:8-10)

Translation

⁸Again the Word of YHWH came to Zechariah and said, ⁹"Thus said YHWH of hosts, 'Exercise true judgment and show brotherhood and compassion to each other. ¹⁰You ought not to oppress the widow, orphan, stranger, and poor, nor should anyone secretly plot evil against his brother.'"

Exegesis and Exposition

In the previous verses YHWH drew attention to the former prophets and the words they had spoken concerning fasting and hypocrisy. Zechariah then urges his own contemporaries to give heed to those words from the past and to apply them to their own situation. Now YHWH more specifically lays down the basis for true worship, including fasting, by appealing to earlier canonical principles that provide its moral and spiritual framework. That YHWH is referring to the past is not determined by the speech formula itself in vv. 8-9, for the form here is standard prophetic introduction.[19] Rather, the preterites beginning in v.11 clearly demand the past tense in v. 9: "Thus said YHWH of hosts."

Typically in biblical citation of earlier material, it is not always possible to determine precisely the source of the allusion. This is the case here, for though YHWH in a sense is "quoting scripture," as vv. 11-12 make clear, His text could have come from any number of places.[20] Micah 6:8 comes to mind with its insistence that what is good is for God's people to "execute justice, love brotherhood, and walk humbly with your God." Isaiah had exhorted the people to "attend to justice and do righteousness" (Isa. 56:1). Ezekiel describes the

---

19. So Samuel Amsler, *Aggée, Zacharie 1-8, Zacharie 9-14* CAT (Neuchatel: Delachaux & Niestlé, 1981), 116, 117.
20. Petitjean helpfully points to other passages where מִשְׁפָּט and אֱמֶת (v. 9a) occur, including Zech. 8:16 (cf. Pss. 19:10 [EB 19:9]; 25:9-10; 89:15 [EB 89:14]; 111:7; 119:160; Isa. 16:5; 42:3; 59:14-15; Jer. 4:2; Ezek. 18:8). Likewise, the combination מִשְׁפָּט and חֶסֶד (v. 9a, b) is elsewhere attested (Pss. 25:9-10; 33:5; 89:15 [EB 89:14]; 101:1-2; Jer. 9:23; Hos. 2:21; 12:7; Mic. 6:8). Finally, Petitjean cites relevant passages that provide a background for v. 10 (Pss. 94:6; 146:9; Ex. 22:20-23; Jer. 7:6; 22:3; Ezek. 22:7; Mal. 3:5) (A. Petitjean, *Les Oracles du Proto-Zacharie* [Paris: J. Gabalda, 1969] 324, 328, 330-31). As Donald Gowan points out more succinctly, "Zechariah's summary reflects the ethos of the rest of the Old Testament" (Donald E. Gowan, "Wealth and Poverty in the Old Testament," *Int* 41 [1987]: 341).

righteous man as one who executes "true justice between one man and another" (Ezek. 18:8). The same prophet commanded, "Take away violence and spoil and execute justice and righteousness" (45:9).

As for the injunctions of Zechariah 7:10, again there are abundant possibilities for precedent texts, especially in the writings of Moses. In the Book of the Covenant YHWH warns, "You shall not oppress any widow or orphan" (Ex. 22:22 [HB 22:21]; cf. Deut. 24:17-18).[21] Micah, always concerned with the ethical dimensions of true religion, predicts woe on those who "devise iniquity and work out evil" at night so that when the morning comes they can implement their wicked schemes against their fellow man (Mic. 2:1; cf. Nah. 1:11).

Fasting or any other religious practice that is not founded on a true covenant faith toward God and relationship to one's fellow in the covenant community is of little value and, in fact, is to be avoided at all cost. The language of YHWH's exhortation here is sprinkled with covenant terminology, so much so that it is quite apparent that He is measuring the efficacy of religious observances against the requirements of the vertical and horizontal dimensions of the covenant relationship (cf. 5:1-4). One need only note such words as מִשְׁפָּט (*mišpāṭ*, "justice," v. 9*b*); אֱמֶת (*'emet*, "truth," v. 9*b*); חֶסֶד (*ḥesed*, "brotherhood" or "loyalty," v. 9*b*); רַחֲמִים (*raḥămîm*, "compassion," v. 9*b*); and אָח (*'āḥ*, "brother," vv. 9*b*, 10*b*) to see how deeply immersed in covenant thought the whole passage is.[22]

What has happened in the distant past as well as the more recent history of God's people is that they have abandoned the principles of covenant obligation and behavior and yet have kept up with its cultic trappings. The real mission of the delegation from Bethel thus becomes all the more clear. Having jettisoned true covenant faith, the community they represent has tried to erect in its place a facade of religious activity, particularly commemorating the disasters of destruction and exile, and then has sought endorsement of their hypocrisy from the priestly and prophetic leadership of Jerusalem. This cannot be given, the passage declares, until the very heart of covenant commitment be rediscovered and reaffirmed.

---

21. The widow and orphan were particularly vulnerable and dependent, inasmuch as the only "welfare" system that existed was within the family with a husband and father. See F. C. Fensham, "Widow, Orphan and the Poor in Ancient Near Eastern Legal and Wisdom Literature," *JNES* 21 (1962): 129-39.
22. For most of these, see Paul Kalluveettil, "Declaration and Covenant," *An Bib* 88 (Rome: Biblical Institute, 1982), 20-91. Cf. also the insightful discussion of Kenneth L. Barker, "Zechariah," *EBC*, ed. Frank E. Gaebelein (Grand Rapids: Zondervan, 1985), 7:646-47.

2. Rebellion against YHWH's Word (7:11-12)

Translation

[11]But they refused to give attention, turning (instead) a stubborn shoulder and stopping their ears so they could not hear. [12]Indeed, they made their heart (like a) *diamond, so that they could not obey the Torah and the words which YHWH of hosts sent by His Spirit through the former prophets. Therefore, there came great wrath from YHWH of hosts.

Exegesis and Exposition

The response of earlier generations to YHWH's covenant appeal was consistently and inflexibly negative. Rather than open-mindedly receiving the word of witness from the prophets, the people had, literally, "given a shoulder of stubbornness" (v. 11). The same idiom occurs in the important covenant résumé section of Nehemiah where the author, reviewing YHWH's past dealings with His people, says that they "gave a shoulder of stubbornness" to Him and would not listen to His commandments (מִצְוֹת, *miṣwôt*); instead, they sinned against His ordinances (מִשְׁפָּטִים, *mišpāṭîm*). All the time YHWH had been seeking to bring them back again to His law (תּוֹרָה, *tôrâ*) (Neh. 9:29). All of these are technical terms in covenant texts (cf. Ex. 24:3, 12), so the opinion that Zechariah 9 should be viewed from that perspective finds even further support here.[23]

Another idiom in v. 11 worth noting is "stopping the ears." Literally, the phrase says that the people "made their ears heavy." This construction occurs in only one other place in the OT, namely, Isa. 6:10. There, however, YHWH commands the prophet to proclaim the message of salvation and judgment until its very hearing, without result, will cause the people's ears to become heavy, that is, insensitive to response. The doleful effect will be the removal of the stubborn resisters to God's overtures of grace until only a tiny remnant remains.

These two expressions would certainly have pricked the minds and hearts of Zechariah's hearers, reminding them of the wayward-ness of their fathers. But their fathers learned nothing from the prophets who had confronted them. Besides turning the shoulder and stopping the ears they had set their hearts like a diamond, an impenetrable and impervious shield against truth. Both the Torah of Moses and the inspired words of the prophets failed to make an impression (v. 12). The result was predictable: YHWH of hosts sent great wrath against them.

---

23. F. Charles Fensham, *The Books of Ezra and Nehemiah*, NICOT (Grand Rapids: Eerdmans), 1982, 229-30, 232-41.

So much was this the pattern of the long history of Israel and Judah that it was not necessary for Zechariah to cite specific instances of defection. The people themselves were well aware of their sordid past and could have supplied their own register of particulars. They might well have recalled the words of 2 Kings 17:7-23, which provided in summary form what YHWH was referring to in Zechariah. It was because of Israel's sin that she fell to Assyria (v. 7). Every prophet and seer had pleaded with God's people to "turn from your evil ways and observe My commandments and statutes, according to all the Torah which I commanded your fathers" (v. 13). Here again the collocation of covenant terms (מִצְוָה [miṣwâ], "commandment"; חֹק [ḥōq], "statute"; תּוֹרָה [tôrâ], "law") is striking, giving evidence once more that the sin of Israel and Judah was fundamentally the sin of covenant violation. It is in line with this tradition of disobedience that YHWH speaks through Zechariah to the postexilic generation as well.

Additional Notes

7:12 The Hebrew word used here (שָׁמִיר) occurs elsewhere in a simile for hardness only in Ezek. 3:9, where it is frequently translated "diamond." In that passage it is described as something harder than flint, so diamond is a reasonable suggestion. On the other hand, it is questionable as to whether the diamond was known to ancient Israel so that what is in view is more likely an adamantine such as corundum. LXX translates שָׁמִיר in Zech. 7:12 as ἀπειθῆ, "disobedient," thus indicating lack of understanding of the Hebrew word. The Vg. renders it *adamas*, "hard, impervious." See Merrill F. Unger, *Unger's Bible Dictionary* (Chicago: Moody, 1957), 736-37.

3. JUDGMENT BECAUSE OF REBELLION (7:13-14)

Translation

13It then came about that, just as He cried out but they would not obey, so "they will cry out but I will not listen," said YHWH of hosts. 14"Rather, I will blow them away in a *storm among all the nations with which they are unfamiliar." Thus the land became desolate because of them, no one crossing through or returning, for they had made the desirable land a waste.

Exegesis and Exposition

The changing tenses in this passage pose a problem until the various speakers are sorted out. Beginning with v. 11 Zechariah is clearly the speaker, reporting the reaction of earlier generations to the covenant requirements of YHWH. This continues on into v. 13 as the preterite וַיְהִי (*wayĕhî*) shows, but following the major accent *ath-nah* after שָׁמְעוּ (*šāmēʿû*), "they (would not) obey," there is a series of imperfects and YHWH speaks (v. 13*b*). It is apparent that Zechariah is quoting YHWH's response to the refractoriness of the rebels, a response that naturally would be in the imperfect (that is, present or future time) in that past context.[24] The YHWH speech continues on to v. 14 and ends with "unfamiliar." Zechariah then speaks, bringing the oracle to a close.

In a pungent chiastic thought pattern (v. 13)[25] the prophet recounts the reaction of YHWH to the spurning of His overtures in the past:

A   He cried out
    B   They did not listen
    B'   They will cry out
A'   He (I) will not listen.

He had warned them through the prophets about the disaster that would surely attend their present course of action, but they had given no heed. Now they would do the crying out, pleading for mercy and forbearance, but His ears would be stopped up.

Instead of deliverance, the people of old had experienced the whirlwind of God's wrath, a storm of fury that had driven them to lands they had never even heard of before. Second Kings 17:6 lists some of these, and others are mentioned in other places as a result of both the Assyrian (1 Chron. 5:26) and Babylonian (Ezra 2:59; Est. 8:11; 9:2; Jer. 44:1; Ezek. 3:15) deportations. Hosea had used the same verb, סָעַר (*sāʿar*, "to storm") to describe the same judgment of YHWH. Israel, he said, would be like "chaff driven with the storm out of the threshing-floor" (Hos. 13:3).

All had come to pass as YHWH had prophesied, a fact that Zechariah's audience knew all too well, for it was they who were now trying to recover from the awful effects of the sins of their fathers and the wrath of God it provoked. The land had become desolate as a result, so much so that it appeared to be virtually uninhabited (cf. Ezek. 36:32-36). Hardly a soul could be found criss-crossing it, for there was no one there with whom to do business. What had once been a place "flowing with milk and honey," a veritable paradise (חֶמְדָּה [*ḥemdâ*], "desirable land"), would become a place of unutterable wasteness (v. 14). Jeremiah used the word *ḥemdâ* in a similar way when he described Canaan as a "delightful land," a worthy heritage

---

24. A. Petitjean, *Les Oracles du Proto-Zacharie*, 353-54.
25. This is seen also but not developed by Carol L. Myers and Eric M. Meyers in *Haggai, Zechariah 1-8*, AB (Garden City, N.Y.: Doubleday, 1987), 404.

for YHWH's people Israel (Jer 3:19). Its contrast, שַׁמָּה (*šammâ*, "waste"), is a favorite term of the prophets to describe the aftermath of YHWH's devastation of the land. Like paradise lost it became a desert devoid of life and pleasure (Hos. 5:9; Isa. 5:9; 13:9; 24:12; Jer. 2:15; 4:7; 18:16).

This part of the oracle section ends rather abruptly with no explicit statement as to what those who engage in hypocritical religious practice, particularly fasting, can expect. But what is not explicitly stated may be inferred without mistake. Unless members of Zechariah's audience, in this case the Bethel delegation, but by extension all persons of the postexilic community, understand the abhorrence with which YHWH views religious observance that is only superficial and self-serving, they can expect the same calamitous results as those experienced by their forefathers. This is precisely the burden of Zechariah's prophetic colleague Haggai as well (Hag. 1:4-6), and Haggai pointed out that the dire results of such behavior had already begun to manifest themselves (1:9-11; 2:16-17).

Additional Notes

7:14 The verb form here (אְסָעֲרֵם) is a piel, to be construed as a factitive, thus "act like a storm." My translation is an attempt to smooth this out and therefore is rather expansive. For the anomalous pointing under the first radical, cf. GKC, 52n.

217

2
Blessing of True Fasting (8:1-23)

This continuation of the long oracle on fasting commences with a reversal of the tragic circumstances with which the previous section ended.[1] There YHWH had described the scattering of the preexilic covenant people to the four winds and the empty desolation of the land that ensued (7:14). This had been done because of the hypocritical infidelity of the nation down through the years (7:9-12). Zechariah's own contemporaries were guilty of the same perfidy, especially with regard to a falsely pious and self-interested practice of commemorating the collapse of Jerusalem and the Temple by a ritual of fasting. They were therefore in danger of suffering the same consequences.

But this is not what YHWH plans or desires for His people. Rather, He is "zealous" for them, so much so that He will display His great wrath on their behalf. Throughout this passage there are the overtones of YHWH's guardian protection of Judah. A dominant motif reflecting this concern and his capacity to achieve it is the self-ascription "YHWH of hosts." As noted previously, this epithet, which is a favorite of the postexilic prophets speaks of YHWH's omnipotent and universal sovereignty. In an age when tiny Judah had nearly been swallowed up by the mighty empires of the day and when even after

---

1. For a poetic analysis of this pericope demonstrating, among other things, its unity, see Siegfried Mittmann, "Die Einheit von Sacharja 8, 1-8," in *Text and Context: Old Testament and Semitic Studies for F. C. Fensham*, JSOTSup 48 (Sheffield: Sheffield Academic, 1988), 269-82.

her restoration from Babylonia she had found life to be tenuous at best, it was important that her prophets assure her that YHWH, her God, was the commander of the empire of heaven. The leader of hosts was sufficient for the times.

Of a total of 36 occurrences of "YHWH of hosts" in Zechariah, 15 are in this one oracle, the highest concentration of the phrase in the OT with the possible exception of Malachi. Even more remarkable, it occurs six times in the present passage alone, a passage that focuses narrowly on eschatological restoration. So humanly impossible will that be, it can come to pass only by the resources of the Almighty One.

A. RESTORATION OF JERUSALEM (8:1-8)

Translation

¹Then the Word of YHWH of hosts came to me as follows: ²"Thus says YHWH of hosts, 'I am very greatly zealous for Zion; indeed, I am zealous for her with rage.' ³Thus says YHWH, 'I have returned to Zion and will live in the midst of Jerusalem. Now Jerusalem will be called "truthful city," "mountain of YHWH of hosts," "holy mountain."' ⁴Thus says YHWH of hosts, 'Old men and women will once more live in the plazas of Jerusalem, each one with his staff in his hand because of advanced age. ⁵And the streets of the city will be full of boys and girls playing there.' ⁶Thus says YHWH of hosts, 'Though it be difficult in the sight of the remnant of this people in those days, will it also be difficult in my sight?' says YHWH of hosts. ⁷Thus says YHWH of hosts, 'I am about to save My people from the east country and from the west. ⁸And I will bring them to settle in the midst of Jerusalem. They will be My people, and I will be their God, in truth and righteousness.'"

Exegesis and Exposition

It is YHWH of hosts who testifies to His zeal for His people (v. 1). The cognate accusative form ("zealous with zeal") in which this is expressed conveys the intensity of God's feelings.² As is well known, "zeal" and "jealousy" are both translations of the Hebrew noun קִנְאָה (*qin'â*) and semantically are interlocked. Thus YHWH is a "jealous God" (Ex. 20:5), one who tolerates no rivals real or imaginary and who is zealous to protect His uniqueness and maintain the allegiance of His people to Himself alone. He is also jealous for His people, that is, He is protective of them against all who would challenge them or

---

2. Merrill F. Unger, *Zechariah* (Grand Rapids: Zondervan, 1963), 134.

claim to be elect alongside them. Therefore, He is zealous to safe-guard their interests and come to their defense. This is the way the clause "I am zealous for her with rage" (v. 2b) should be taken.[3] Those who would presume to interdict YHWH's purposes for Judah may expect to incur His awful wrath.

Reference to Zion in prophetic literature is by far most often found in eschatological contexts. Thus already in Zechariah and in a passage very similar to this (1:14-17), the Lord speaks of His zeal for Jerusalem, i.e., Zion, and promises a glorious restoration in both historical and eschatological times. The same promise, again featuring Zion, occurs in Zech. 2:7-13. The eschatological springs from the historical and cannot be separated from it. This is one reason that the two frequently seem to merge and why a "dual fulfillment" is not only possible but necessary. Here, by way of example, YHWH says He "*has* returned to Zion"[4] and *will* settle in the midst of Jerusalem" (v. 3a). His return was a historical event attendant to the return of the remnant from exile (cf. Ezra 6:12; 7:15; Hag. 1:13; 2:4; Zech. 1:16; 2:10). In one sense He already had settled in Jerusalem, but now He says He will live there. The verb here is שָׁכַן (*šākan*), which connotes a permanent residence as opposed to a temporary one. Though יָשַׁב (*yāšab*) is synonymous with *šākan* and even used in parallel constructions with it (cf. Isa. 18:3; Jer. 49:31), *šākan* is more commonly used in eschatological descriptions of YHWH's residence on earth.[5]

When YHWH makes His abode in Jerusalem, the city will be radically transformed. It will now be "truth city, mountain of YHWH of hosts, holy hill" (v. 3b). Isaiah had described Zion as a place where truth had fallen in the street and was absent altogether (Isa. 59:14-15). But truth will be revived and come to live there once more.

---

3. Though the parallelism חֵמָה/קִנְאָה may suggest a translation of "ardor" (so Joyce G. Baldwin, *Haggai, Zechariah, Malachi* [London: Tyndale, 1972], 149) or something similar, חֵמָה never has that meaning elsewhere (cf. BDB, 404; KBL, 309). In spite of this, Petitjean makes the use here an exception and says that חֵמָה "exprime l'ardeur avec laquelle Jahvé intervient en faveur d'Israël" ("expresses the ardor with which YHWH intervenes in Israel's favor") (A. Petitjean, *Les Oracles du Proto-Zacharie* [Paris: J. Gabalda, 1969], 368). Schunck does not attest one example of the vocable with this meaning (K.-D. Schunck, *TDOT*, 4:462-65, s.v. חֵמָה).

4. Though שַׁבְתִּי can be rendered as a narrative perfect ("I am returned") or *perfectum propheticum* ("I will return"), the assurance given to members of the postexilic community, especially since they have begun the restoration of the Temple and thus have met the prerequisites for His coming, is that He is already among them (Hag. 1:8, 13; 2:4-5, 19). He has returned and now will live among them. See Carol L. Meyers and Eric M. Meyers, *Haggai, Zechariah 1-8*, AB (Garden City, N.Y.: Doubleday, 1987), 408.

5. Victor P. Hamilton, *TWOT* 2:925, s.v. שָׁכַן. Cf. Petitjean, *Les Oracles du Proto-Zacharie*, 133-35.

The psalmist identified Zion as the "holy hill" on which the messianic king would reign (Ps. 2:6), and as "the joy of the whole earth," the "holy hill," "the city of the Great King" (48:1-2, [HB 48:2-3]). To renewed Jerusalem, both Isaiah (2:2-3) and Micah (4:1-3) attest, the nations will come, for the city will be elevated above all the mountains (cf. Zech. 14:10).

The transformation will include a full repopulation of the city. Through use of a merism the prophet looks to the day when the oldest and the youngest (i.e., the citizenry as a whole) will inhabit the city (vv. 4-5). In his own day that was not a reality, for the refugees who returned home under Sheshbazzar and Zerubbabel were relatively few in number. Even in Nehemiah's day, 80 years later, he had to conscript enough residents from the countryside to give the capital an adequate population (Neh. 7:4; 11:1-2).

The fact that the old men and women lean on walking-sticks does not detract from the joy and renewal of this millennial scene but merely emphasizes the great age of some of the populace (cf. Isa. 65:20). At the other extreme, the streets will teem with children at play (cf. Jer. 31:12-13). The entire scene is one of security and happiness.

For the city of Zechariah's day to undergo such astounding transformation as just described would be nothing short of miraculous. Indeed, in anticipation of the skepticism that this message would surely elicit, YHWH goes on to say that just because the whole prospect is difficult for human perception it is not difficult for Him, for He is "YHWH of hosts" (v. 6, twice). Within a chiastic form[6] He makes the point very firmly:

A   Thus says YHWH of hosts
  B   It will be difficult
    C   in the sight of the remnant
        but
    C' in my sight
  B' (will) it be difficult?
A' says YHWH of hosts

One reason this transformation would seem so absurd is that only a "remnant of the people" (שְׁאֵרִית הָעָם, *šĕʾērît hāʿām*) were there to hear the promise. How could this tiny band be sufficient for so glorious a prospect? The answer lies in a gathering of others, "My people" YHWH calls them (v. 7), whom He will deliver from the whole earth. Again, as "YHWH of hosts" He is about to save (the *futurum instans*

---

6. Noted also by Mittmann, "Die Einheit von Sacharja 8, 1-8," 276.

use of the hiphil participle of יָשַׁע [yāšaʿ], "to save")[7] them, that is, to restore them to covenant fellowship and deliver them from exile, bondage, and dispersion. This calls to mind the message of Hosea where sinful Israel, the "not My people" (Hos. 1:9), will be transformed into "My people," the "sons of the living God" (1:10; 2:1; cf. Isa. 11:11-12; 43:1-7; Jer. 30:7-11; 31:7).

The specific points of origin of these regathered people of YHWH are the east and the west (v. 7). The terms for the directions here are much more cosmic in scope than the usual ones, referring respectively to the rising and setting of the sun. This suggests that the immigrants will come not only from the immediately surrounding areas but from the very ends of the earth.[8] This is also the import of limiting the scope to the two directions, for the sun relates to the earth only in terms of east and west, not north and south.

It is true, of course, that the prophets usually describe the restoration of Judah as a movement from north and south as well as east and west. Isaiah does so in the order east, west, north, and south (43:5-6) or even just north, west, and "the land of Sinim" (49:12). Jeremiah locates the source as north (3:18; 16:15: 23:8; 31:8) especially, no doubt, because he so often connects the dispersion with Babylonia. Zechariah's formula is unique to him though the use of מִזְרָח (*mizrāḥ*) for east and מְבוֹא הַשֶּׁמֶשׁ (*mĕbôʾ haššemeš*, lit. "going in of the sun") is common (see, respectively, Josh. 23:4; Pss. 103:12; 107:3; Isa. 46:11; Dan. 8:9). Zechariah seems intent on magnifying the extent of the Diaspora and the supernatural power of YHWH in regathering His people from one end of the earth to the other in order to fill up the holy city.

YHWH had said He would dwell in the midst of Jerusalem (v. 3). Now He says He will bring His people back so that they might do the same (v. 8a). When that has come to pass, they will become His people. He in turn will become their God. This is not to say that a covenant relationship will then and there be forged for the first time, for they had been His people from the day of their election in the patriarchs (Gen. 12:2; 17:5-6) and redemption from Egypt (Ex. 2:7; 4:22-23). Their sin, however, had driven a wedge between them and YHWH so that, as Hosea so poignantly put it, they became "not My people" in terms of their functional position. By a mighty act of grace YHWH "will bring them back" (8a). This verb, in the hiphil stem, places all the initiative in God's hands. He is about to save them (v. 7),

---

7. GKC, 116p.
8. Wilhelm Rudolph, *Haggai-Sacharja 1-8–Sacharja 9-14–Maleachi*, KAT (Gütersloh: Verlaghaus Gerd Mohn, 1976), 148.

and He will bring them back. The result of this gracious work is that once more Israel, in function as well as in promise, will be His people.

That the covenant is the framework in which all this takes place is most apparent in the last phrase of v. 8: "in truth and righteousness." It is in that sphere that the redemptive grace of God finds a basis, for He had made covenant with His people and had placed Himself in obligation to keep it, their unfaithfulness notwithstanding.[9] The truth (אֱמֶת, *'ĕmet*) and righteousness (צְדָקָה, *ṣĕdāqâ*) here are hallmarks of integrity that attest to the sincerity of the mutual commitments. The same phrase occurs in Isaiah, who says of the wayward Israelites that they "swear by the name of YHWH and invoke the name of the God of Israel, but not in truth (*'ĕmet*) or in righteousness" (*ṣĕdāqâ*) (Isa. 48:1). Thus their profession of allegiance was hollow because it was not undergirded with genuine commitment to covenant principle.

B. PROSPERITY OF JERUSALEM (8:9-13)

Translation

9"Thus says YHWH of hosts, 'Let your hands be strong, you who hear these words in these days from the mouth of the prophets who were there at the founding of the house of YHWH of hosts, that the Temple might be built. 10Before that time there was no wage payment for man or beast, nor was there any rest from adversity to those who came and went, because I had pitted everybody, each one, against his neighbor. 11But now I will not be to the remnant of this people as I was in former days,' says YHWH of hosts, 12'for there will be a *peaceful sowing time, the vine will produce its fruit and the ground its yield, and the heavens will drop down dew. Then I will allow the remnant of this people to possess all these things. 13Then it will be that just as you were a curse to the nations—both the house of Judah and that of Israel—so I will save you and you will be a blessing. Do not be afraid! Let your hands be strong!'"

Exegesis and Exposition

This section is neatly bracketed within the exhortations "Let your hands be strong" (vv. 9, 13), a refrain that is singularly appropriate to it. YHWH has promised that Jerusalem will be restored, repopulated, and reconfirmed as the center of His covenant interests (vv. 1-8). Now it is important for the remnant people there to shoulder the responsibilities requisite to the fulfillment of the promise. Their deliverance

---

9. Baldwin, *Haggai, Zechariah, Malachi*, 150.

and return may depend wholly on God's grace (vv. 7-8), but prosperity in the land, both now and in the eschaton, is directly related to obedience and hard work.

YHWH's message thus turns from the future to the present, to those who are hearing (present participle) in the days of the oracle itself. The messengers to whom they are listening are the prophets who were in attendance at the day the foundations of the Temple were laid, some two years earlier. Who beyond Haggai and Zechariah they may have been must remain unknown, but these two were on the scene from the very beginning.[10] That the reference here is to the rebuilding that commenced in the second year of Darius and not to the initial attempts at construction in 536 B.C. (cf. Ezra 3:8) is clear from the following verses (10-12).[11] The verb describing the founding of the Temple (יֻסַּד [*yussad*], "founding," v. 9), appears in the same form in Hag. 2:18 where, as is clear from the context, Haggai also is referring to the work that got underway in 520 B.C.[12] (see Commentary on Haggai, *loc. cit.*).

Also like Haggai, Zechariah alludes to the days of social and economic distress that characterized life in Judah before the people rearranged their priorities and got about the business of putting YHWH and the Temple at the center of their community life. Before those days, Zechariah says, there was severe unemployment for both man and animal. Neither one's services were in demand, so there was no payment of wages (v. 10*a*). Haggai had said that even when wages were earned they had little value in the inflated economy. In fact, it was as though they put their earnings into purses with holes (Hag. 1:6).

Moreover, there had been social unrest in those days as well. No one dared to come and go because of crime and violence. Literally the text says either "There was no peace from the adversary" or "There was no peace from the distress" (v. 10*b*). The words for "adversary" and "distress" are homonyms (צָר, *sar*), and either one fits reasonably well here. The latter may be less tautological and therefore better stylistically.[13] The reason for this state of affairs is that YHWH had

---

10. For a review of the possibilities, see Petitjean, *Les Oracle du Proto-Zacharie*, 386-87.
11. David L. Petersen, *Haggai and Zechariah 1-8* (London: SCM, 1985), 305.
12. Meyers and Meyers, *Haggai, Zechariah 1-8*, 421.
13. For strong (but unconvincing) arguments that "enemy" or "adversary" is to be preferred, see Petitjean, *Les Oracles du Proto-Zacharie*, 392-94. The structure of v. 10*c-d* favors "adversity" or "distress" because Zechariah is saying that there was no peace to any who went out or came in (10*c*), *for* YHWH had set every man against his brother (10*d*). That is, it was fraternal strife, not external, that caused the trouble. See, for this view, Meyers and Meyers, *Haggai, Zechariah 1-8*, 421-22.

set man against man. This antagonistic spirit caused distress to the whole community and made life unsafe and unhappy.

The social disintegration described here does not likely refer to the problems the Jews had at the hands of the Samaritans and other hostile neighbors. They did indeed suffer in this respect, as Ezra and Nehemiah make abundantly clear, but the whole thrust of the message here, especially in light of its obvious similarities to that of Haggai, is that the present problems were internal and of their own making (cf. Hag. 1:4, 9-12; 2:14). The struggle of a man against his neighbor here is an internecine conflict, the most sorrowful and damaging of all.

It is YHWH, however, who brought this expression of animosity about (v. 10*b*). He had "sent out" everybody with a pugnacious desire to harm his neighbor. The verb used to express this act of YHWH (שָׁלַח, *šālaḥ*, preterite form here) is highly idiomatic in this passage. Ordinarily it is to be rendered as "sent," but here it must be nuanced to "pitted" or "set in opposition."[14] Such a usage may be found also in 2 Kings 24:2; Ezek. 28:23; Amos 4:10. Besides the lexical or semantic difficulty there is also that of theodicy. How could YHWH stir up strife and conflict among brothers? The answer no doubt lies in the widely attested biblical idea of the removal of moral restraint by YHWH from evil men, who then are free to pursue a course of violence and evil (cf. Isa. 19:2; Amos 3:6; 9:4).

Whatever YHWH had done to wicked Judah before the Temple project resumed with full force, He would not repeat in the present because the preaching of the prophets had been effective (v. 11). As Haggai had said in response to their reordering of priorities, "From today I will bless you" (Hag. 2:19). Because the conditions had been met for blessing, it would be forthcoming without delay in everyday life. In an elliptical statement of promise—"for the seed of peace" (v. 12)—YHWH guarantees that planting time from then on would not be interrupted by the turmoil that characterized the earlier period. Furthermore, the erstwhile barren vineyards and fields would produce crops, contrary to recent experience (cf. Hag. 1:6; 2:16-17), and the heavens would grant nourishing moisture to ensure continuation of these bounties. This, too, would be a reversal of the drought (Hag. 1:10-11) and harmful weather conditions (Hag. 2:17) that had made it nearly impossible to survive before.

In summary, YHWH says He will allow the remnant of the nation, those who made up the community to which this very message was directed, to possess all the things about which He had just spoken.

---

14. Cf. M. Delcor/E. Jenni, *THAT* 2:915, s.v. שׁלח. They render the verb here "loslässt Menschen gegeneinander."

This token of blessing would signify that Israel and Judah together, that is, the whole covenant nation, would themselves be a blessing to the nations and no longer a curse. This juxtaposition of blessing and curse recalls the ancient patriarchal covenant pledges of YHWH in which He had said, "I will bless those who bless you, but him who curses you I will curse; and in you all the clans of the earth will be blessed" (Gen. 12:3).[15] In fact, Abraham was commissioned to "be a blessing" (Gen. 12:2).

Through most of her history Israel had been a curse to the nations in the sense that she had failed to winsomely attract the nations to the one true God. As a "kingdom of priests" (Ex. 19:6) she was derelict in not mediating His saving grace to them so that they, too, could become part of the community of faith. But now, YHWH says, "you will be a blessing." That this has eschatological ramifications cannot be denied, but one need look no further than to the Jewish Messiah, Jesus Christ, to see what untold blessing Israel has been to the world. With that glorious prospect in view, YHWH again encouraged the people to cease being afraid and to strengthen themselves for the work. This task was by no means limited to the sheer physical work of building the Temple and reestablishing the foundations of a postexilic nation. It was a work of the spirit as well, one designed to enthrone YHWH as sovereign over them and to bring to perfection the ministry of servanthood to which He had elected and redeemed them.

Additional Notes

8:12 For the apparently incomplete phrase "for the seed of peace" (כִּי־זֶרַע הַשָּׁלוֹם) the LXX reads "I will sow peace" (אֶזְרְעָה שָׁלוֹם). This destroys the parallelism in the verse with the next lines, however. Other versions (Syr Tg. Neb.) attest "her seed (will be) peace" (זַרְעָהּ שָׁלוֹם), but again the parallelism suffers. It is best to see this as an example of ellipsis, with the verb in the following clauses understood here as well.

C. EXPECTATIONS FOR JERUSALEM (8:14-17)

Translation

    [14]"For thus says YHWH of hosts, 'As I had *planned to harm you when your fathers incited Me to wrath,' says YHWH of hosts, 'and I was not sorry, [15]So, to the contrary, I have planned in these days to do

---

15. Samuel Amsler, *Aggée, Zacharie 1-8*, CAT (Neuchatel: Delachaux & Niestlé, 1981), 123.

good to Jerusalem and the family of Judah—do not fear! ¹⁶These are the things you should do: Speak truth, each of you, to one another. Judge in truth and wholesome judgment in your gates. ¹⁷Do not plot evil in your hearts against one another. Do not favor a false path—these are all things that I hate,' says YHWH."

Exegesis and Exposition

This section could easily be treated with the preceding (vv. 9-13), for its themes and emphases are essentially the same. However, the introduction is standard for oracle pericopes (cf. 8:1, 9, 19), and there is an advancement in thought in terms of the parenthesis at the end of the passage (vv. 16-17).¹⁶ Its central message is that in view of the restoration and promised prosperity of Judah, YHWH has certain expectations from her. She must, as covenant people, observe the stipulations of covenant and live life commensurate with her renewed status.

Once more YHWH reaches back to the past, to the time when the preexilic and even pre-second Temple generations had shamefully refused to honor the commitments they had made to center their national life and destiny on the principles of the covenant. As a result, He had found it necessary to apply discipline, a judgment based not only on the principle of correction but one brought to bear by the wrath their obstinate behavior elicited.

The theodicic problem here (v. 14) is the same as that in v. 10*b*. Usually the verb זָמַם (*zāmam*) has a negative connotation, that is, to plan or devise something harmful. The only exception with God as subject, in fact, appears to be in v. 15 where YHWH also plans to do good (BDB, 273).¹⁷ But the "evil" He does is not moral in content but disciplinary, as its opposite "good" in v. 15 makes clear. It takes the form of something hurtful or harmful that seeks to produce consciousness of sin and a desire for repentance.¹⁸

The confusing reference to both "you" (that is, the audience being addressed) and "your fathers" (the former generation) should be explained by the corporate and timeless nature of the people of Israel. When YHWH addressed their fathers in the past, He addressed them as well. One could as well translate, "As I had planned to harm you, Israel (or Judah), when your fathers," etc. This passage is important in its assertion of the fundamental unity of the people of God through the ages.

---

16. For an analysis that sees the section as promise (vv. 14-15) and exhortation (vv. 16-17), see Petitjean, *Les Oracles du Proto-Zacharie*, 407.
17. S. Steingrimsson, *TDOT* 4:88, s.v. זמם.
18. A. van Hoonacker, *Les Douze Petits Prophètes* (Paris: Librairie Victor Lecoffre, 1908), 646.

The harm YHWH brought to the fathers may have been administered with reluctance, but it was not with remorse or second thought.
It was a punishment that had to be inflicted to achieve the higher
goal of bringing them into conformity with His purposes for them as
a servant nation. Jeremiah uses the same verb translated here as
"sorry" (v. 14b) (נִחַם, niḥam) to express YHWH's lack of regret for
having destroyed the cities of the plain (Jer. 20:16). It was something
that had to be done to safeguard His own holiness.

But what He had done with respect to the fathers is the exact
opposite of what He will do now. Now He plans (also זָמַם) to bring
benefit and blessing, not harm, to Jerusalem and Judah (v. 15). This is
possible because the warnings from their own prophets (v. 9) have
been heeded and the prerequisites for providential favor have been
met. The strongest contrast in action is conveyed between vv. 14 and
15. YHWH had planned harm (רַע, ra') before but now plans good (טוֹב,
ṭôb; here in infinitive construct הֵיטִיב, hêṭîb). Then He had shown no
compassion (לֹא נִחָמְתִּי, lō' niḥāmtî), but now He once more (שַׁבְתִּי, šabtî)
has reversed His course of action entirely. Then their fathers had
caused YHWH to be filled with wrath (הַקְצִיף, haqṣîp), but now He says
to them, "do not fear" (אַל תִּירָאוּ, 'al tîrā'û). All this is in line with the
restoration and prosperity promised in vv. 1-13.

The evidence for their restored religious and spiritual life follows
in vv. 16 and 17, which, with 7:8-10, form an inclusio around this
section of the oracle concerning fasting.[19] It is a unit that speaks, first
of all, of the scattering of the nation for violation of the basic tenets of
covenant behavior (7:11-14) and then of their regathering as an act of
God's grace (8:1-15). The fathers had been commanded to "exercise
true judgment and show brotherhood and compassion to each other"
(7:9). Now YHWH says the present generation must "judge in truth
and wholesome judgment" (8:16). The heart of covenant faith on the
social plane is that one must love his neighbor as himself.

Those of old also learned that they must not oppress the disadvantaged among them or hatch up evil against one another (7:10).
Zechariah's audience hears similar words of exhortation: "Do not plot
evil in your hearts against one another" (8:17).[20] They must also not
"love a false oath," something that was in direct contradiction of the
Torah itself (Ex. 20:16). All these things He hates, says YHWH.

---

19. Petitjean, *Les Oracles du Proto-Zacharie*, 412-13.
20. Greenfield draws attention to the idiom חָשַׁב בַּלֵּב ("to think in the heart";
    i.e., "to plot") and its Aramaic equivalent 'št blbb in Sfire II B 5 (cf. also
    Zech. 7:10); Jonas C. Greenfield, "Idiomatic Ancient Aramaic," in *To
    Touch the Text. Biblical and Related Studies in Honor of Joseph A. Fitzmyer,
    S.J.*, ed. Maurya P. Horgan and Paul J. Kobelski (New York: Crossroad,
    1989), 50.

Additional Notes

8:14 Despite the position of the accent *Gereš* over זְמַמְתִּי, the verb should be translated as perfect, exactly as in v. 15.

D. PILGRIMAGE TO JERUSALEM (8:18-23)

Translation

[18]**The word of YHWH of hosts came to me as follows,** [19]**"Thus says YHWH of hosts, 'The fast of the fourth month and that of the fifth, seventh, and tenth will become for the house of Judah joyful and happy, pleasant feasts; so love truth and well-being.'** [20]**Thus says YHWH of hosts, *'It will yet be that people will come, residents of many cities.** [21]**The inhabitants of one will go to another and say, "Let's go up at once to beseech the favor of YHWH , to seek YHWH of hosts. Indeed, I will go also."'** [22]**Many people and strong nations will come to seek YHWH of hosts in Jerusalem and to beseech the favor of YHWH.** [23]**Thus says YHWH of hosts, 'In those days it will happen that ten men from all the languages of the nations will seize, indeed, latch onto, the garment of a Jew and will say, "Let us go with you, for we have heard that God is with you."'"**

Exegesis and Exposition

This final section of the oracle of Zechariah 7-8 comes full circle to the theme with which the oracle began, the concern for fasting.[21] At the beginning a delegation of Bethelites had come to Jerusalem to ask about the propriety of (or to seek commendation for) their observance by fasting because of the destruction of the Temple and the assassination of Gedaliah, the first Babylonian political appointee from among the survivors (7:1-7). Here is one more example of the careful craftsmanship with which Zechariah arranged his material, for 7:1-7 is clearly a bracketing device with 8:18-23.[22] Other clues are the pilgrimage to Jerusalem by both the Bethelites (7:2-3) and the peoples of the nations (8:20-21) "to beseech the favor of YHWH" (לְחַלּוֹת אֶת־פְּנֵי יְהוָה, [*lĕ ḥallôt 'et pĕnê YHWH*], 7:2; 8:21). Also in common, if by contrast, is the fact that at the beginning only one city sent its representatives (7:2), but at the end "all the languages of the nations" will be represented (8:23). Finally, fasting in sorrow will be turned into feasting for joy (7:3; cf. 8:19).

The men of Bethel had mentioned only two occasions for fasting,

---

21. Petersen, *Haggai and Zechariah 1-8*, 312.
22. S. Amsler, *Aggée, Zacharie 1-8*, 124.

but here at the end of the oracle there are four. Those on the fifth and seventh months have already been considered (7:5), so now attention must be directed to those on the fourth and tenth months. The fourth month without much doubt marked the event of the breach of Jerusalem's walls by the Babylonians in the eleventh year of King Zedekiah (Jer. 39:2). The date, the ninth day of the fourth month, was on or about July 18, 586 B.C.[23] This access to the city marked the end of its resistance, so the king and his royal guard attempted to escape, unsuccessfully as it turned out (Jer. 39:3-5). The Temple remained standing for four more weeks, falling at last on August 14 (cf. 7:3; 2 Kings 25:8).

The fast of the fourth month was to commemorate the siege of Jerusalem that commenced on the tenth day of that month in 588 B.C. (2 Kings 25:1; Jer. 52:4). This was approximately on January 15 in the modern calendar.[24] The city therefore was able to hold out for about two and one half years until its walls were penetrated and the siege lifted. At least four times a year the survivors of those disasters and their descendants remembered the events and mourned with fasting and other observances. Not until the return under Cyrus, the initial attempts at rebuilding, and the laying of the foundations of the Temple under Joshua and Zerubbabel was their hope even partially realized that the tragedies might be undone.

It was, of course, the preaching of Haggai and Zechariah that generated the most confidence that YHWH was about to restore the people's fortunes. Haggai urged the building of the Temple, an act that would result in YHWH's pleasure and presence (1:7, 13). Its completion would also bring about the upheaval of nations who would fill it with their tribute (2:6-7). Despite all the setbacks of the past, Haggai said, from that day of renewed commitment onward YHWH would bless them (2:19). Zechariah joined his colleague and in vision and oracle held forth the promise that YHWH was about to do something more glorious than they had ever before witnessed. He would restore the nation (1:16-17; 2:10; 3:9; 4:9; 8:3-8, 11-13), appoint his messianic leaders (3:5, 7-8; 4:7-8, 14; 6:12-13), and rule as sovereign over the nation and over all other nations (1:10-11; 2:5, 10-11; 6:7-8; 8:8).

In most succinct terms in the present unit this change from the tragedies of yesterday to the triumphs of tomorrow will be a change from fasting to feasting (v. 19). No longer when the fourth, fifth,

---

23. Richard A. Parker and Waldo H. Dubberstein, *Babylonian Chronology 626 B.C.–A.D. 75* (Providence, R.I.: Brown Univ., 1956), 28; A. Malamat, "The Last Kings of Judah and the Fall of Jerusalem," *IEJ* 18 (1968): 154-55.
24. Malamat, "The Last Kings of Judah and the Fall of Jerusalem," 150-51.

seventh, and tenth months roll around will there be mourning; instead, there will be joyful and happy festivity. Literally the Hebrew reads: "Fasting . . . will become for the house of Judah rejoicing and gladness, and appointed times of good things." It may be better to take the substantives "rejoicing" and "gladness" as adjectival here (even though this is impossible grammatically because of the difference in number), for the purpose appears to be to characterize the nature of the feasts—they will not be sad but happy. As for טוֹבִים (ṭôbîm), "good," the idea again is the contrast between the mournful fastings and joyful feastings. Thus, "pleasant" is the better rendering. Together, then, a freer rendering could be: "Fasting . . . will become . . . joyful, happy, and pleasant times of feasting."[25]

The last clause in v. 19 is rhetorically awkward. Following His description of the transformation of fasts to festivals YHWH says, in imperative terms, "Love the truth and the peace." So out of place does this appear that BHS suggests it may be a later addition to the text. The problem remains, however, as to why anyone would want to add it.

The most satisfying solution may be to take this clause (more accurately rendered, "Love truth and well-being") as the resumption of a condition that must be met by Judah before the mourning can be turned to joy. In effect what YHWH is saying is, "If you want the above-mentioned transformation to occur, love truth and well-being." These terms appear just above in v. 16 ("truth and wholesome [i.e., peaceful] judgment") as the essence of covenant law on the horizontal or interpersonal dimension. Furthermore, in v. 17 YHWH had said that the people must not love (אָהֵב, 'āhēb, the same as the verb in v. 19) a false oath. The collocation of these three words—"truth," "well-being," and "love"—in two nearly adjoining verses supports the thesis that the condition for covenant renewal and blessing is mentioned, even if interruptively, to make clear the human element in achieving YHWH's purposes for His people.[26]

The point having been made that the time for lamentation about the past is about to be transformed into a time of celebration, specific causes of or accompaniments to that change follow (vv. 20-23). First of all, there will be a mass pilgrimage of the peoples of the earth to seek YHWH at Jerusalem. At some time yet (עֹד, 'ōd) to come people from

---

25. Karl Elliger, e.g., translates it "schönen Festen"; Karl Elliger, *Die Propheten Nahum, Habakuk, Zephania, Haggai, Sacharja, Maleachi*, ATD (Göttingen: Vandenhock & Ruprecht, 1982), 133.
26. Rudolph makes the cogent point that this clause is the direct answer to the Bethelite delegation's question in 7:3; Wilhelm Rudolph, *Haggai-Sacharja 1-8–Sacharja 9-14–Maleachi*, KAT (Gütersloh: Verlaghaus Gerd Mohn, 1976), 151.

many cities (not "people and the residents of many cities") will come, those from one place encouraging others from other places to join them without delay in paying homage to Him.

The idea of the nations coming in pilgrimage to the Temple of YHWH at Jerusalem is a major eschatological theme.[27] Haggai hinted at this when he described the stirring of the nations and their presentation of their wealth to the Temple coffers (Hag. 2:7). Zechariah himself had already affirmed this explicitly in the oracle of vision three (2:11). "Many nations," he said, "will join themselves to YHWH in that day and will become My people." Isaiah long before prophesied that "in the latter days" (Isa. 2:2) all nations would flow into Jerusalem and multitudes would say "Let us go up to the mountain of YHWH, to the house of the God of Jacob, and He will teach us of His ways and we will walk in His paths" (2:3).

The same prophet, in an apostrophe to Zion, proclaimed that "foreigners will build your walls and their kings will serve you" (Isa. 60:10) and they will call her "the city of YHWH, the Zion of the Holy One of Israel" (60:14). More than that, the time will come when the nations will come to witness God's glory (66:18) and all humankind will worship before Him (66:23). Jeremiah, too, is aware of this momentous day, for he says that "at that time [Israel and Judah] will call Jerusalem the throne of YHWH, and all nations will be gathered to it, to the name of YHWH, to Jerusalem" (Jer. 3:17).

No prophet excels Zechariah himself in his presentation of the universal pilgrimage of nations and their confession of YHWH's kingship. Besides our passage at hand, he expostulates at length on that theme in chapter 14. Further comment must await discussion of that passage, but for now it is sufficient to note that the prophet sees a day when "YHWH will be king over all the earth" and then the nations "will go up every year to worship the King, YHWH of hosts, and keep the feast of Tabernacles" (14:9, 16). The language in those verses is clearly that of pilgrimage and is in that respect consonant with the language of 8:20-23.

The purpose of the pilgrimage as stated here is "to beseech the favor of YHWH" (v. 21). This idiom (לְחַלּוֹת אֶת־פְּנֵי, *lĕḥallôt 'et pĕnê*) always connotes the idea of appeasement, of entreaty to a powerful person to show leniency of mercy when he might be inclined otherwise.[28] A famous example of its use is in the story of the golden calf, where YHWH had resolved to destroy wicked Israel because of their

---

27. E. H. Merrill, "Pilgrimage and Procession: Motifs of Israel's Return," in *Israel's Apostasy and Restoration: Essays in Honor of Roland K. Harrison*, ed. Avraham Gileadi (Grand Rapids: Baker, 1988), 261-72.
28. K. Seybold, *TDOT*, 4:408-9, s.v. חָלָה.

apostasy while Moses was on the mountain (Ex. 32:1-10). True to his mediatorial role Moses "beseeched the favor of YHWH His God," reminding Him of His covenant promises (vv. 11-13). It is because the nations realize that they have historically sinned grievously against the one true God that they will come on the day of repentance and solicit His grace.

It is impossible to know what prompts this desire but it is urgent, as the terse wording here makes clear. "Let us go at once" (נֵלְכָה הָלוֹךְ, *nēlĕkâ hālôk*), they say, expressing by the infinite absolute form the most intense kind of resolve. None will be satisfied only to encourage others to go. Each will say, "I will go, indeed, I (will)" (21c). It is more than a matter of mere curiosity; rather, it is a shared sense of individual responsibility.

Building on the statements of the pagan peoples themselves, Zechariah enlarges the picture by describing the pilgrims as "many peoples" and "strong nations" (v. 22). This will be a movement on a universal scale, not one limited to a scattering of cities or to nations that participate out of weakness and inability to remain independent. The mightiest will be there, knowing full well that YHWH is sovereign even over them. Again one recalls Isaiah's appeal for YHWH, "Look to me and be delivered, all the ends of the earth, for I am God and there is no other" (Isa. 45:23). So indelibly will this great truth be pressed upon the hearts of the nations that "every knee will bend and every tongue swear" to Him (v. 23).

Continuing in the speech of eschatological discourse, Zechariah says that "in those days," that is, the end days of history, 10 men from "all the languages of the nations" will seize upon a Jew and agree to go with him to Jerusalem and the Temple, for it will be manifest to them that God is with the Jew in a unique way.[29]

This is the only place Zechariah refers to the eschaton in this particular phrase בַּיָּמִים הָהֵמָּה (*bayyāmîm hāhēmmâ*), "in those days," but this is a favorite way of designating the end of time in prophetic literature.[30] Joel spoke of the outpouring of God's Spirit upon all His people "in those days" (Joel 2:29 [HB 3:2]). Also, he said, when Judah

29. Lipiński argues that the translation "Jew" for יְהוּדִי in v. 23 is anachronistic and should read "Judean." Therefore, the passage does not speak of Gentile conversion but of Jewish pilgrimage, the "ten men" referring to the customary *minyan*. It speaks of a return of the Diaspora and not an eschatological universalism (E. Lipiński, "Recherches sur le Livre de Zacharie," *VT* 20 [1970]: 42-46). It is wholly arbitrary to conclude that "Jew" was a post-Zechariah ethnic term. For examples of even preexilic usage of the term in this way, see Jer. 32:12; 38:19; 40:11, 12; 52:28, 30. Carroll translates it this way in all these passages (Robert P. Carroll, *Jeremiah*, OTL [London: SCM, 1985]).
30. Petitjean, *Les Oracles du Proto-Sacharie*, 434-35.

is restored "in those days," YHWH will gather all nations to judge them in the "valley of Jehoshaphat" for the ill treatment they showed His people (3:1 [HB 4:1]). The phrase is also common to Jeremiah. He announces that "in those days" the ark will recede in significance, for YHWH Himself will be enthroned in Jerusalem and all the nations will be gathered there (Jer. 3:16-17). Also "in those days" the righteous Branch will sprout up, Judah and Jerusalem will be delivered and protected, and the royal and priestly messiah(s) will assume their eternal offices (33:15-17).

Zechariah's use of the phrase is optimistic and positive. "Those days" will be a time when the nations of earth will realize that "salvation is of Israel" and that Israel's God is to be found especially in His Temple in Jerusalem. At a ten to one ratio, then, they will outnumber the Jews who return to seek the face of YHWH. The number "ten" is not to be pressed literally but is symbolic in the Bible of totality or comprehensiveness (cf. Gen. 31:7; Ex. 34:28; Lev. 26:26; 1 Sam. 1:8; Job 19:3; Dan. 1:12, 20; Amos 6:9). The universal thrust here is seen also in the fact that these "ten men" come from "all the languages" of the nations. This is a way of describing the far-flung dimensions of this regathering. It will not be from just the surrounding Hamito-Semitic world but from nations so distant that their very languages are exotic and incomprehensible (cf. Acts 2:5-11).

So urgent will be the desire of the nations to learn of YHWH that they will "seize" (חָזַק, *ḥāzaq*) the "wing" (כָּנָף, *kānāp*) of a man, that is, whatever flies out from him, most likely a flapping garment.[31] The verb *ḥāzaq* in the hiphil often denotes almost a violent grabbing of something with the intention of not letting go (BDB, 305). Isaiah reflects something of this intensity of desire when he speaks of various nations whose people will fall down before Israel and beg, confessing that "God is in your midst" and "There is no other God" (Isa. 45:14). "Even to him," the prophet says, "will men come" (45:24). Jerusalem will someday be known to them as "the city of YHWH, the Zion of the Holy One of Israel" (60:14).

It is particularly interesting that the reason the nations will want

---

31. Petersen offers the suggestion that the כָּנָף was some readily identifiable element of a Jewish garment, perhaps tassels affixed to its corners (D. L. Petersen, *Haggai and Zechariah 1-8*, 319). Bertman, though he fails to associate כָּנָף with a tassel, provides an interesting account of garments with such appendages (Stephen Bertman, "Tasseled Garments in the Ancient East Mediterranean," *BA* 24 [1961]: 119-28). For suggestions that the seizing of the garment here has messianic overtones (i.e., the hem of Jesus' robe), see J. T. Cummings, "The Tassel of His Cloak: Mark, Luke, Matthew—and Zechariah," in *Studia Biblica* II, ed. A. Livingstone, Sixth International Congress on Biblical Studies, 1978, JSOTSup 2 (Sheffield: Sheffield Academic Press, 1980), 47-61, esp. 52.

to join themselves to the Jew is that they will have heard that God is with them. The usual divine name YHWH does not occur here because the field of interest is much broader than Israel, with which the name YHWH as a covenant name is especially related. Rather, the generic Elohim (אֱלֹהִים) is used, for it suddenly is obvious to all the nations that their "god" is Israel's "God."[32] What they have been seeking through the millennia of human history has at last been found. Thus, the role of Israel as a kingdom of priests mediating the saving grace of God to a fallen world will have come to pass. The age of the gospel and the church marks the beginning of that process, for in and through the Jew the salvific message and event have already come to pass in Christ. But the fullness of redemption awaits the eschaton, the time when "every knee will bend and every mouth will confess that Jesus Christ is Lord to the glory of God the Father" (Phil. 2:11; cf. Isa. 45:23).

Additional Notes

8:20 The phrase עֹד אֲשֶׁר, lit., "yet that," requires expansion such as that suggested here. The context allows something like "it will yet come to pass that," etc.

---

32. Baldwin, *Haggai, Zechariah, Malachi*, 156.

PART 3
Oracle Concerning YHWH's Sovereignty
(9:1–11:17)

1
Coming of the True King (9:1-17)

Zechariah 9-14 makes up the third main division of the book, the others being the night visions of chaps. 1-6 and the oracles on fasting in chapters 7-8. This final division itself consists of two parts, the oracle concerning the nations (chaps. 9-11) and that concerning Israel (chaps. 12-14). As we explained in the Introduction to Zechariah, though most scholars accept the unity of this part of the book, very few nonconservatives view chapters 9-14 as originating with Zechariah the prophet. Usually they attribute it to a "Zecharianic school" or argue that it, along with Malachi, was a late addition to the minor prophets corpus, having no original connection to Zechariah. "Evidence" for this is the phrase "oracle of the Word of YHWH," which occurs at Zech. 9:1; 12:1; Mal. 1:1. Because most critics also assume that Malachi was written by an anonymous author, "Malachi" (meaning only "my messenger"), these last two oracle sections of Zechariah make up, with Malachi, a trio of anonymous prophetic compositions that were joined because of the common formula and alleged common anonymity.[1]

One must admit that once he begins a careful study of chapters 9-14 he is immediately made aware of the change of mood, outlook, style, and composition of this part of the book compared to the first eight chapters. The grammar, syntax, and lexicography are much

---

1. Otto Eissfeldt, *The Old Testament: An Introduction* (Oxford: Basil Blackwell, 1965), 440.

more complex, and the text-critical nature of the material itself suggests that Zech. 9-14 has raised its own special difficulties since the
earliest times.

One need only continue his analysis of the material at hand to
realize, however, that the prophet in this section has entered another
realm of thought and perspective, much as did Isaiah in the latter
part (chaps. 40-66) of his work. To fail to see this (or to ignore its
implications) and then to argue, on the basis of the differences, that
the same author could not write the whole is to beg the question.[2]
Moreover, to deny that a single author could change his composition-
al techniques to accommodate different genres or tasks is to place
restraints on ancient writers that modern critics would not tolerate if
placed on themselves by others. The perspective of Zech. 9-14 *is* different from the first part of the book. It is primarily eschatological, it
lacks any indisputable connection to contemporary persons or
events, and it is dominated by cryptic allusions to cosmic, redemptive, and messianic themes that have no accompanying interpretation, contrary to the case in Zech. 1-8. In short, the prophet has
broken free of the mold in which he cast the material of the first part
and has created a new form in which to express the grand and glorious ideas that permeate his thinking in the second part. One of these
key ideas is the coming of the true king (9:1-17), proper preparation
for which is of utmost importance (9:1-8).

A. HISTORICAL AND ESCHATOLOGICAL PREPARATION
FOR HIS COMING (9:1-8)

Translation

**¹Oracle (of) the Word of YHWH concerning the land of Hadrach,
Damascus being its focus: *The eyes of men, especially of the tribes
of Israel, are toward YHWH, ²(as are those of) Hamath also, which
adjoins it (and) Tyre and Sidon, though (they are) very wise. ³Tyre
built herself a fortification and piled up silver like dust and gold like
the mud of the streets. ⁴Nevertheless the Lord will dispossess her and
cast her strength into the sea—she will be consumed by fire. ⁵Ash-
kelon will see and be afraid, Gaza will be in great anguish, as will
Ekron, for her *hope has been *dried up; the king will be lost to
Gaza, and Ashkelon will no longer be inhabited. ⁶A mongrel (people)
will dwell in Ashdod, for I will cut off the pride of the Philistines. ⁷I
will remove their blood from their mouth and their abominable**

---

2. R. K. Harrison, *Introduction to the Old Testament* (London: Tyndale, 1970),
   952, 954-55.

things from their teeth; then they will become a remnant for our God,
like a clan in Judah, and Ekron will be like Jebusites. **⁸Then I will
encamp about My house (to protect) as a *guard from anyone crossing to and fro; so no one will cross over against them anymore (as an)
oppressor, for now I Myself have seen it.**

Exegesis and Exposition

The Masoretic tradition begins this second section (and indeed
the whole division, chaps. 9-11) with the single word מַשָּׂא (*maśśā'*),
best translated "oracle." This technical term in prophetism derives
from the verb נָשָׂא (*nāśā'*), "to lift, carry." Hence, some versions translate *maśśā'*, "burden." Though this may be helpful in suggesting that
the Word of YHWH entrusted to the man of God becomes a responsibility or load he must bear or risk divine displeasure, or it conveys a
message burdensome to his audience, the etymological nuance does
not adequately communicate the sense of joy and privilege that also
attended prophetic proclamation. It is better, therefore, to employ a
more neutral term, such as oracle or speech, to convey the full sense
of the term.[3]

It is also worth noting that in addition to its reference to foreign
nations, *maśśā'* occurs in eschatological contexts, particularly in Isaiah (13:1; 14:28; 15:1; 17:1; 19:1; 21:1, 11, 13; 22:1; 23:1). Nahum and
Habakkuk introduce their entire books with this term, books that
have eschatological elements. The piling up of eschatological language and themes in Zech. 9-14 makes it beyond doubt that *maśśā'* as
used by Zechariah is within that prophetic framework.

Though *maśśā'* serves as an introduction, perhaps even as a heading, to Zech. 9, it most likely should be taken as a noun in construct to
the next phrase, that is, "the oracle of the word of YHWH concerning
the land of Hadrach." The Masoretic accent appears to support this,
and the syntax favors it as well.[4] For the first time in the book the
prophet directs a message to or about or against pagan nations, vision seven (5:5-11) being a possible exception. But he does so to provide a backdrop to the coming of the messianic king who will take his
royal throne as a result of conquest. The Word of YHWH concerns
Hadrach because Hadrach is the first place in the line of march. It is
most likely that this place name (חַדְרָךְ, *ḥadrāk*) refers to the well-
known Hatarikka, cited in the annals of Tiglath-Pileser III (745-727

---

3. P. A. H. de Boer, "An Inquiry into the Meaning of the Term מַשָּׂא," *OTS* 5
   (1948): 197-214, esp. 203-4, 214; H.-P. Muller, *TWAT*, V 1/2:23, s.v. מַשָּׂא;
   Magne Saebø, *Sacharja 9–14. Untersuchungen von Text und Form* (Neukirchen-
   Vluyn: Neukirchener Verlag, 1969), 137-40.
4. Paul Hanson, *The Dawn of Apocalyptic* (Philadephia: Fortress, 1975), 296.

B.C.) of Assyria.[5] This was a province or district located to the south of
Aleppo, reaching perhaps as far as Damascus. If so, Zechariah may be
saying that Damascus was the "seat" or capital of the Hadrach region.
Thus the word מְנֻחָה, (*měnuḥâ*, "resting-place") could be rendered
"seat." Comparison with Ugaritic texts and with 1 Chron. 28:2; Ps.
132:7; and Isa. 66:1 shows that it can mean "throne dais," however, so
that Damascus may be the throne-center of the Hadrach region.[6]
What makes this interpretation problematic is the masculine pronominal suffix on *měnuḥâ*, whereas its antecedent, "land" (or even
Hadrach), is feminine. Both "YHWH" and "Word" are masculine, and
either could be the referent. In the former case one would then translate "Damascus is his throne-dais."[7] In the latter, the rendering would
be, "Damascus is its resting-place" in the sense of its focus, a meaning
given in the translation above. The oracle, then, is addressed to Hadrach in general but specifically or beyond that to Damascus.[8]

However Hadrach and Damascus are otherwise related, Damascus is clearly to the south. The beginning of an itinerary can be
perceived, a march moving from north to south, ending at last at
Jerusalem (v. 8). The march has no sooner begun when it commands
the attention of all the surrounding peoples, including Israel. This at
least appears to be the meaning of the rather confusing "for to YHWH
is the eye of man and all the tribes of Israel" (1*b*). Efforts to emend
"eye of man" to "Aram has committed iniquity" (BHS) are unsuccessful because this necessitates that Israel also be included as perpetra-
tors of sin that causes YHWH to move south in judgment. If anything
is clear, it is that He has not come to judge but to save His people (v.
8). Furthermore, removal of "man" (better, "mankind") here softens
the tone of universalism that is so dominant throughout the oracle.
What is in view is that the triumphant procession of YHWH has
captured the attention of the whole world.[9] To refer to God's people as
the "tribes of Israel" in this postexilic period points to the es-

---

5. James B. Pritchard, ed., *Ancient Near Eastern Texts Relating to the Old Testament* (Princeton, N.J.: Princeton Univ., 1969), 282-83. Cf. Benedikt Otzen,
   Studien über Deuterosacharja, ATD 6 (Copenhagen: Prostant Apud Munksgaard, 1964), 66-67.
6. Hanson, *The Dawn of Apocalyptic*, 296-97.
7. Ibid., 297.
8. Theophane Chary, *Aggée-Zacharie, Malachie* (Paris: Librairie Lecoffre,
   1969), 152. D. R. Jones argues that Hadrach and Damascus do not come in
   for judgment because מְנֻחָה never bears the sense of hostility elsewhere. The
   conquest, then, begins in v. 3 with the cities of Phoenicia and Philistia; D.
   R. Jones, "A Fresh Interpretation of Zechariah IX–XI," *VT* 12 (1962):
   242-46.
9. Kenneth L. Barker, "Zechariah," in *EBC*, ed. Frank E. Gaebelein (Grand
   Rapids: Zondervan, 1985), 7:657-58.

chatological milieu of the passage, a time when the scattered tribes will be reassembled.

Particularly concerned about YHWH's activities, in addition to Israel, are Hamath, bordering on Damascus (v. 2), and Tyre and Sidon. If Damascus is coming in for God's wrath, can these other places be far behind? Jeremiah, in an oracle against Damascus, had spoken also of the consternation of Hamath because of Damascus's problems (Jer. 49:23). Tyre (Isa. 23:1-17; Jer. 25:22; 47:4; Ezek. 26–28; Amos 1:9-10) and Sidon (Isa. 23:3, 4, 12; Jer. 25:22; Ezek. 27:8; 28:21) receive a great deal of attention in judgment oracles, and despite their self-ascribed wisdom (v. 2b, cf. Ezek. 28:3-5, 12) once more stand in threat of divine punishment.

Hamath was a territory to the west and north of Damascus, occasionally cited as on the northern border of Israel, roughly the territory of modern-day Lebanon (Num. 13:21; Josh. 13:5; Amos 6:14). Tyre and Sidon lay west and northwest of Damascus on the Mediterranean coast and were celebrated for their merchandising and for their strategic locations and invulnerability. Their names often are symbolic of human pride (Ezek. 28:2, 6, 9, 17). Zechariah notes that Tyre had built up fortifications behind which she amassed and hoarded her great revenues of silver and gold (v. 3), precious metals in such abundance as to be compared to the very dust and mud of the city streets (Ezek. 27:33; 28:4, 5).

All this will come to nought, however, for YHWH will strip away all her resources and cast her "power" into the sea, burning what is left (v. 4). For the first time Zechariah uses the divine epithet Adonai (אֲדֹנָי, "the Lord") rather than YHWH. Ordinarily YHWH is pointed with the Hebrew vowels of Adonai and read Adonai by the Masoretes and pious modern Jews. The name means "lord" or "sovereign" and is used here most appropriately in describing YHWH's procession in war against his foes (cf. Deut. 3:23; 9:26; Pss. 37:13; 55:9 [HB 55:10]; 59:11 [59:12]; 110:5; Isa. 10:16, 23; 22:5, 12; 28:2, 22; 40:10; 65:15; Ezek. 9:8; Amos 8:9, 11; Zeph. 1:7; Zech. 9:14).[10]

Commentators are divided as to what is being cast (lit., "destroyed") into the sea in v. 4.[11] The Hebrew word חַיִל (ḥayil) with a

---

10. Lacocque suggests also that it was because the god of Tyre was named Adon. Thus the passage is heightened in its polemic (André Lacocque, *Zacharie 9-14*, CAT [Neuchatel: Delachaux & Niestlé, 1981], 149).
11. Thus Wilhelm Rudolph, *Haggai-Sacharja 1-8–Sacharja 9-14–Maleachi*, KAT (Gütersloh: Verlaghaus Gerd Mohn, 1976): "Ringmauer" (p. 167); Joyce G. Baldwin, *Haggai, Zechariah, Malachi* (London: Tyndale, 1972): "wealth" (p. 160); Alfons Deissler, *Zwölf Propheten III. Zefania, Haggai, Sacharja, Maleachi* (Würzburg: Echterverlag, 1988): "Streitmacht" (p. 294); K. Elliger, *Die Propheten Nahum, Habakuk, Zephanja, Haggai, Sa-*

pronominal suffix looks exactly like חֵל (*ḥēl*) with certain suffixes. *Ḥayil* means "strength, wealth, army" (BDB, 298), whereas *ḥēl* means "fortress, rampart" (ibid.). The apparent chiasm of the passage can perhaps resolve the issue. Tyre had built a fortification (A) and accumulated wealth (B). Now she will lose her wealth, that is, be dispossessed (B′), and her fortifications will be cast into the sea (A′). Thus v. 3*a* and v. 4*b* are a matching pair as are 3*b* and 4*a*.[12] In this manner, literary construction may provide a clue to meaning.

The list of those places, filled with consternation at YHWH's coming, continues with Ashkelon, Gaza, and Ekron, all Philistine city-states (v. 5). When Ashkelon sees what has happened to her northern neighbors, she will be afraid, Gaza even more so, and Ekron most of all. Gaza will lose its king and Ashkelon its entire population. A chiastic pattern is observable once again with Ekron in the midst of the city list: Ashkelon–Gaza–Ekron–Gaza–Ashkelon.[13] A fourth city, Ashdod, will be occupied by a mongrel people (v. 6). When all is said and done, proud Philistia will be shamed and embarrassed.

Philistia, like the nations and cities already mentioned, comes in for strong rebuke in the oracles of other prophets as well. Amos spoke of the destruction of Gaza by fire (Amos 1:7), a disaster that would burn its palaces to the ground (cf. Zech. 9:5). He predicted that Ashdod would be depopulated (1:8), Ashkelon would lose her ruler (1:8), and Ekron would be struck by the hand of YHWH (1:9). Zephaniah, in similar language, describes the abandonment of Gaza, the desolation of Ashkelon, the evacuation of Ashdod, and the uprooting of Ekron (Zeph. 2:4).

In summation, Zechariah declares that the blood of the Philistines will be removed from their mouth and their "abominable things" from their teeth. Thoroughly chastened and purified, Phi-

---

charja, Maleachi, ATD (Göttingen: Vandenhoeck & Ruprecht, 1982): "Bollwerk" (p. 144); Otzen, *Studien über Deuterosacharja*: "Festungswerk" (p. 238); Lacocque, *Zacharie 9-14*: "richesse" (p. 149); P. Lamarche, *Zacharie IX-XIV. Structure Litteraire et Messianisme* (Paris: Librairie Lecoffre, 1961): "puissance" (p. 37); T. Chary, *Aggée-Zacharie, Malachie*: "rempart" (p. 154); Merrill F. Unger, *Zechariah* (Grand Rapids: Zondervan, 1963): "military power" (p. 155).

12. It is somewhat surprising that Lamarche, whose purpose is to describe such literary phenomena in "Deutero-Zechariah," fails to see this small chiasm in his larger chiastic structure of 9:1-8 (Lamarche, *Zacharie IX-XIV*, 42).

13. Chary notes this but concludes (incorrectly in my opinion) that the centrality of Ekron is to draw attention to the fact that she receives the most glorious promise of all—to be like a Jebusite (v. 7). To the contrary, at this point these are not promises of blessing but words of impending judgment (T. Chary, *Aggée-Zacharie, Malachie*, 158, 160-61). The shift to blessing does not occur until v. 7*b*.

listia will become a remnant for God, like a clan in Judah. Ekron, one of her city-states, will be like the Jebusites who, by Zechariah's time, had been totally assimilated into Judah. Ekron, the center of the chiasm suggested above, may, by synecdoche, represent all the Philistine cities and thus speak of a more general redemption of a Philistine remnant.[14]

The blood and abominable things refer, also by synecdoche, to the religious perversions of the Philistines. This no doubt included the slaughter of animals that were considered by Israelites as being unclean and the eating of animal flesh that had not been properly drained of its blood in line with ritual requirement.[15] Unfortunately too little is known of the Philistine cult to be able to understand precisely what these practices might have been.[16] It is also possible to consider another figure here, that of hyperbole. The Philistines were a particularly cruel and violent people who showed little mercy for their victims (Judg. 16:21; 1 Sam. 31:8-10). One could say in modern idiom that they were "bloodthirsty," the exact idea that may be in mind here.

The "abominable things," however, seem to point to the former idea, that of despicable religious activity. The Hebrew word here (שִׁקֻּץ, šiqquṣ) suggests acts and objects associated with paganism.[17] Deuteronomy describes the idolatry of Egypt and the wilderness nations with this term (Deut. 29:17), while Hosea uses it to speak of Israel's apostate behavior at Baal-Peor (Hos. 9:10). Nahum prophesies that Nineveh someday will be covered by šiqquṣ because of her idolatry and witchcraft (Nah. 3:6). Jeremiah equates such abomination with adultery and whoredom (Jer. 13:27). But it is Ezekiel who uses the word the most, a fact that is important in light of Ezekiel's priestly, cultic interest. He says that Israel had defiled the Temple with her abominations (5:11). Also, he points out that Israel's abominable behavior was in direct contrast to the covenant requirements that bound them to YHWH (11:21). The time will come, however, when she will put such detestable things behind her, including her addiction to idolatry (37:23).

The removal of these things, as well as suggesting the conversion of the Philistines, should be taken in the sense of bringing these evils to an end. As an expression of his dominion, YHWH will terminate the degrading and offensive practices of the pagan world. This is certainly the intent of the passage, for the whole thrust is that of the

---

14. K. Barker, "Zechariah," *EBC*, 7:659.
15. Ernest Sellin, *Des Zwölfprophetenbuch* (Leipzig: A. Deichert, 1922), 498.
16. For archaeological evidence, see Trude Dothan, *The Philistines and Their Material Culture* (New Haven, Conn.: Yale Univ., 1982), 219-51.
17. H. J. Austel, *TWOT*, 2:955, s.v. שִׁקֻּץ.

campaign of YHWH toward the holy city, one in which He brings all hostile forces under His control. This being the case, one must take Philistia's description as a clan and Ekron's as a Jebusite (v. 7*b*) in a contrastive way. These heathen people will be included within the covenant of God, but only in the small numbers of a remnant. The point of vv. 5-7*a* is the awesome wrath of YHWH against the Philistines (and by extension the preceding nations as well), a judgment that leads to the reversal in v. 7*b*.

The word אַלֻּף (*'allup*), sometimes rendered "chief" or something similar, also means "clan" or "family." Thus, in the famous passage in Micah, the prophet addresses Bethlehem and says, "You who are too small to be among the clans of Judah, from you will come forth one who is to be ruler in Israel" (5:2). This hyperbole, among other things, shows that an *'allup* is a small jurisdiction indeed. The Philistine remnant, then, will be so reduced in size as to be like a Judean *'allup*. Similarly, Ekron will be like the Jebusites who, at their historical greatest (cf. 2 Sam. 5:6-10), were an insignificant people. After David's conquest of their city, Jerusalem, they must have been assimilated by the Israelites until there were virtually none at all left.

When the itinerary is complete, YHWH says that He will have arrived at His house, that is, the Temple, and will surround it with His own presence so that no hostile force can ever again oppress His people. The guarantee of this is that YHWH has already seen it (v. 8). This anthropomorphic assertion is a way of describing the foreordination and immutability of YHWH's purposes. What He sees in advance must surely come to pass.[18]

The march that commenced in the north will overwhelm successively Hadrach, Damascus, Hamath, Tyre, and Sidon, and four of the Philistine cities. It will end at Jerusalem with YHWH, triumphant in His procession, standing guard over His house and His people. In the tradition of holy war He has come against the foe, defeated him in battle, and established Himself as ruler in His royal palace. This is precisely the pattern seen elsewhere in such holy war passages as Ex. 15:1-18, many of the Psalms (e.g., 2, 9, 24, 29, 46, 47, 48, 65, 68, 76, 77:17-21 [EB 77:16-20], 89b, 97, 98, 104, 106:9-13, 110), Isaiah (11:1-9, 42:10-16, 43:16-21, 51:9-11, 52:7-12), and Hab. 3:1-19.[19]

This leads then to the question of the historicity of or, better, the historical reality that lies behind Zech. 9:1-8 (and, indeed, much of chaps. 9-14). Scholars have been so hopelessly divided on this matter that the pericope, and with it sometimes all of Zech. 9-14, has been

---

18. Baldwin, *Haggai, Zechariah, Malachi*, 162.
19. P. Hanson, *The Dawn of Apocalyptic*, 299-320; also Hanson, "Zechariah 9 and the Recapitulation of an Ancient Ritual Pattern," *JBL* 92 (1973): 37-59.

dated all the way from the time of Tiglath-Pileser III[20] (745-727 B.C.) of Assyria to the time of the Maccabees in the second century B.C.[21] This range of possibilities has arrived from efforts to pinpoint the scenes of conquest depicted here and relate them to known historical campaigns. The fact that scholarship as a whole has never even approached consensus on the matter ought long ago to have rendered this kind of subjective method obsolete.[22] Unfortunately that is not the case, as even recent studies show.[23]

What has traditionally been overlooked is that this is eschatological literature which, though being grounded in the present time of the prophet (hence, well-known place names), views the future in very stylized and conventional patterns. The point here is that YHWH, like many conquerors before Him in human history, will manifest Himself in the last days as a vanquishing hero. Because most conquests of Palestine originated in the north, He will come from the north as well, smashing all hostile powers before Him until He comes to Zion, the city where He is pleased to live among men. One should not, therefore, look to precise historical events of which this is an account, nor should one even anticipate a future scenario in which

20. See, e.g., Friedrich Horst, *Die Zwölf kleinen Propheten. Nahum bis Maleachi*, HAT 14 (Tübingen: J. C. B. Mohr, 1964), 246-47. Malamat places the prophecies about Gaza and Ashdod (vv. 5-7) in the time of Sargon II (722-705). The reference to Tyre (vv. 3-4) he associates with the sieges of that city by Shalmaneser V and by Sargon (720-719 B.C.). Therefore, he argues, the events of vv. 1-2 must also have occurred about that time (A. Malamat, "The Historical Setting of Two Biblical Prophecies on the Nations," *IEJ* 1 [1950-51]: 149-54). Lipiński also locates the setting of 9:1-8 in the time of Tiglath-Pileser, going so far as to suggest that Damascus was under Israelite control then and that the ark may actually have been in Damascus ("son bivouac," v. 1) (E. Lipiński, "Recherches sur le Livre de Zacharie," *VT* 20 [1970]: 46-50).
21. A strenuous attempt by Delcor to date the passage at ca. 312 B.C. on the basis of alleged references to Alexander the Great is a case in point. See M. Delcor, "Les Allusions à Alexandre le Grand dans Zach IX 1-8," *VT* 1 (1951): 110-24.
22. For a history of interpretation, see Otzen, *Studien über Deuterosacharja*, 11-34.
23. So, e.g., A. Deissler, *Zwölfpropheten* IV. *Zefanja, Haggai, Sacharja, Maleachi* (1988), 294-95 (Alexander's campaigns); J. Alberto Soggin, *Introduction to the Old Testament*, 3d ed. (London: SCM, 1989), 406-7. The most commonly held view, one accepted by the majority of conservative scholars, is that Zechariah predicts the conquest of Syria-Palestine by Alexander the Great; see, e.g., Unger, *Zechariah*, 152-59. However, even Leupold, who espouses this interpretation on the whole, sees the prophecy as one "so designed by divine providence as to cover the victorious progress of Alexander the Great" but yet as not being strictly fulfilled in Alexander because of the lack of correspondence of certain parts, especially v. 7, with historical reality (H. C. Leupold, *Exposition of Zechariah* [Grand Rapids: Baker, 1971], 165-66, 170).

God will literally march from Hadrach to Jerusalem, establishing his dominion over all opposition. What is at hand is a formulaic way of asserting an unquestionably literal establishment of YHWH's kingship in the end times, a suzerainty to be achieved in the pattern well known to Zechariah and his fellow countrymen on the human level. The next section (vv. 9-10) will put this beyond doubt.

Additional Notes

9:1 Various expedients have been pursued to make this phrase more intelligible. Some scholars emend אָדָם to אֲרָם and עֵין to עָרֵי and render, "the cities of Aram." Others read עֵין אֲרָמָה, "surface of the earth," which Dahood supports even without the final ה (M. Dahood, "Zachariah 9:1: "'EN 'ĀDĀM," CBQ 25 [1963]: 123-24). P. van Zijl, citing Akkadian and Ugaritic parallels, sees the "eye of YHWH" as His sovereignty and providence. By taking the preposition ל as the asseverative, he translates, "Behold, Yahweh is the eye of man, as well as all the tribes of Israel." The meaning, he says, is that if people know that YHWH is the all-seeing eye they will beware of Him (P. J. van Zijl, "A Possible Interpretation of Zech. 9:1 and the Function of 'the Eye' ['Ayin] in Zechariah," *JNSL* 1 [1971]: 59-67). That the superstition of the "evil eye" of the ancient Near Eastern world (as of van Zijl) would be linked to divine providence and power in the OT is extremely doubtful. For the views of the medieval rabbis Rashi, Ibn Ezra, and Qimhi, and of many modern scholars, see E. Zolli, "'Eyn Adam (Zach. IX 1)," *VT* 5 (1955): 90-92. Zolli himself proposes that 'Eyn Adam is a city, one mentioned in Josh. 3:16 as Adam and known today as Ed-Damieh. Adam was located in the Jordan Valley and because of its association with spring flooding was called "'Eyn 'Adam," taking עֵין as "fountain" or "spring" rather than "eye." Zechariah, Zolli says, is harking back to the days of conquest under Joshua as a sign of YHWH's ongoing victories. This is admittedly ingenious, but it seems difficult to believe that only here was the saga of Adam celebrated as a paradigm of past glory.

9:5 The difficult מֶבְטָה, as presently pointed, requires a noun מַבָּט (BDB, 613), "expectation," plus 3 f.s. suffix. However, there is a better attested noun מִבְטָח, "confidence" (BDB, 105), though the sense would demand a מִן prefixed preposition as well as the pronominal suffix, or מִמִּבְטָחָה. Another possibility is (so Tg. Ps.-J.) the noun בֶּטַח, "security" (BDB, 105), thus מִבְטָחָה. The LXX reads "from her hope," apparently a reflection of the first option, the one accepted here as well.

הֹבִישׁ: "Dried up"—rather than the common translation "confounded" (NASB) or "shamed," taken to be the hiphil participle of בּוֹשׁ—is preferred here. This is based on the hiphil perfect of the stative verb יָבֵשׁ, "be dry" (BDB, 386), a meaning that suits the use with "hope" better. This does require an agent, most likely Adonai of v. 4. Cf. A. Deissler, *Zwölfpropheten III. Zefanja, Haggai, Sacharja, Maleachi*, 294.

9:8 For מִצָּבָה, "guard, watch?" (BDB, 663), which is a *hapax legomenon* (from נָצַב, "take a stand"), Mitchell (p. 272) suggests that the LXX presupposes מַצֵּבָה, "pillar." This is possible, but in addition to rejecting the more difficult reading, it is hard to see what a cult object of this kind (or even a memorial post) is doing in this context. One would have to suppose something like, "I will encamp about My house like a (protective) pillar from anyone," etc. The translation "guard" seems feasible in every way. It is likely, moreover, that the LXX presupposes מַצָּבָה ("fortification") for its ἀνάστημα. See T. Jansma, *Inquiry into the Hebrew Text and the Ancient Versions of Zechariah IX-XIV* (Leiden: Brill, 1949), 69 n. 24. KBL (p. 554) reads our form מַצָּבָה rather than מִצָּבָה as in BDB and the MT. Perhaps, as a few MSS attest, it is to be understood as מִצָּבָא, i.e., "from" or "against the army," with מִצָּבָה as an aural error for מִצָּבָא. For a good discussion, see Saebø, *Sacharja 9-14*, 49-51.

B. HISTORICAL AND ESCHATOLOGICAL EVENT OF HIS COMING (9:9-10)

Translation

⁹Rejoice greatly, daughter of Zion;
  Shout, daughter of Jerusalem.
  Look! Your king is coming to you;
  He is legitimate and victorious,
  Humble and riding upon an ass,
  Upon a young ass, foal of a she-ass.
¹⁰I will *cut off the chariot from Ephraim
  And the horse from Jerusalem;
  And the battle-bow will be cut off.
  Then He will speak peace to the nations.
  His dominion will be from sea to sea
  And from the river to the ends of the earth.

Exegesis and Exposition

This text is one of the most messianically significant passages of all the Bible, in both the Jewish and Christian traditions. Judaism sees in it a basis for a royal messianic expectation,[24] whereas the NT

---

24. Joseph Klausner, *The Messianic Idea in Israel* (London: Allen and Unwin, 1956), 203-40.

and Christianity see a prophecy of the triumphal entry of Jesus Christ into Jerusalem on the Sunday before His crucifixion (Matt. 25:5; John 12:15). Thus, though the fulfillment may be in dispute, there is unanimous conviction that a descendant of David is depicted here, one who, though humble, rides as a victor into his capital city Jerusalem. The way will have been prepared by the imposition of universal peace, following which the king will exercise dominion over the whole world.

It is obvious that the Christian interpretation as presented in the NT does not square exactly with the full dimensions of the prophecy, for Jesus, though described as having entered Jerusalem in precisely the manner envisioned by Zechariah, died within days of the event, never having been accepted as king or having made any active claim to the throne of David. The response to this dilemma within the Christian tradition has been to see the Triumphal Entry as a historical prototype of an eschatological event that must yet take place.[25] His entry into Jerusalem was as much for the purpose of demonstrating that the time for dominion had indeed not come as it was for displaying at least some measure of the glory that would attend His coming when everything was ready at the end. The servant who would someday be exalted as king must first of all suffer and die on behalf of those who would make up His kingdom in the ages to come.

It is important to make this distinction, one inherent already in the Zechariah passage but certainly not clearly spelled out. One clue to the anticipation of a twofold event—a Palm Sunday as well as eschatological procession—lies in the clear difference in tone or emphasis between v. 9 and v. 10. In v. 9 the coming one, designated king to be sure, nevertheless is described as "humble" or "lowly," a most inappropriate way to speak of one whose triumph is complete in every respect. Only in v. 10 is that triumph translated into universal dominion. The lowly one of v. 9, though victorious in some sense, does not achieve the fruits of that victory until v. 10.[26]

Admittedly, exegesis of the passage apart from NT considerations would never uncover the distinction just suggested between the verses.[27] There is every appearance here of a single message, an-

---

25. R. T. France, *Jesus and the Old Testament* (London: Tyndale, 1971), 103-6; John W. Wenham, *Christ and the Bible* (Leicester: InterVarsity, 1972), 60; F. F. Bruce, *This Is That. The New Testament Development of Some Old Testament Themes* (Exeter: Paternoster, 1968), 106-7; Lamarche, *Zacharie IX-XIV*, 120-23.

26. Unger, *Zechariah*, 165.

27. Thus the blending of the two messianic roles in Qumranic and other pre-Christian Jewish exegesis. See Klausner, *The Messianic Idea in Israel*, 392, 394; E.-M. Laperrousaz, *L'Attente du Messie en Palestine à la Veille et au*

nouncing the arrival of a just and lowly king who will triumph over his foes, establish worldwide peace, and reign over a universal kingdom. His elevation from humility to sovereignty appears to occur almost simultaneously with his arrival in Jerusalem.

But this is precisely why the Christian exegete must do his work against the backdrop of the entire revelation of God, OT and NT alike. All judgments about the OT text must be suspended until the fullness of the biblical witness is brought to bear. Then and only then can one be said to be doing biblical exegesis in the proper sense of the term, for exegetical method must embrace a hermeneutic of the whole and must recognize the indispensable contribution of a synthetic, comprehensive biblical theology.[28] The passage in question (and any other in fact) must seek its fullest meaning in subsequent revelation, particularly when that revelation takes pains (as in this case) to cite an antecedent passage and offer its own interpretation.

This does not relieve the exegete of the task of viewing the passage in its own historical, cultural, and literary context, however. It is already apparent that these verses belong to the larger pericope concerning the coming of the true king (9:1-17) and that they have been introduced by the account of YHWH's triumphant march from Hadrach to Jerusalem (9:1-8).[29] The question of the relationship between the southward procession and the entry of the king into the holy city must now be addressed.

The matter is complicated by the ambiguity of subject throughout. It seems clear from v. 4 that Zechariah is tracing the course of Adonai's movements against the various lands of vv. 1-7. Presumably the speaker in v. 7 is YHWH, even though Zechariah refers to "our God." YHWH clearly is the subject of v. 8, for He encamps around His house, almost certainly a reference to the Temple. Since YHWH is speaker in 7*a* and 8, it must be He who also says "our God" in 7*b*.[30] This is at first difficult to comprehend, but one must remember that

Début l'Ère Chrétienne (Paris: Picard, 1982), 94-320; Pierre Grelot, "Le Messie dans les Apocryphes de l'Ancien Testament. État la Question," in *La Venue du Messie. Messianisme et Eschatologie*, ed. É. Massaux (Louvain: Desclée de Brouwer, 1962), 19-50, esp. 22-32.

28. Walter C. Kaiser, Jr., *Toward an Exegetical Theology* (Grand Rapids: Baker, 1981), 131-47.

29. Hanson describes the subject of vv. 9-10 in terms of "the victorious return of the Divine Warrior to his Temple." This, of course, is in line with his analysis of 9:1-17 as a whole as a divine warrior hymn drawing on the ritual pattern of the conflict myth (P. Hanson, *The Dawn of Apocalyptic*, 320-21). Thus, vv. 9-10 are an integral part of the whole piece.

30. H. G. Mitchell, *A Commentary on Haggai and Zechariah*, ICC (Edinburgh: T. & T. Clark, 1912), 268, suggests a sudden shift of speaker back to the prophet himself, but this is unnecessary.

such self-references on the part of God are not at all unusual (see in Zechariah alone 1:12; 6:12-13, 15; 8:9; 10:12; 12:7-9; 14:1-3).

The speaker of vv. 9-10 must also be YHWH, as the cutting off of the instruments of war in v. 10 suggests. Therefore, the king in view cannot be YHWH, though His regal procession is the culmination of that undertaken by YHWH in vv. 1-8. YHWH, in an apostrophe to Zion, refers to the coming king as a separate individual, one who cannot be YHWH Himself because of his lowly estate (v. 9*e*). The "he" of v. 10*d* most naturally refers to the king, as does "his" dominion in v. 10*e*.

What emerges from this interweaving of subjects and persons is a distinction between YHWH and the king on one hand and a merging of the two on the other.[31] The merging occurs inasmuch as the king comes into Jerusalem (v. 9*c*), just as YHWH had done in the less direct allusion in v. 8. A reasonable conclusion is that YHWH, in the person of the king, had undertaken the march from Hadrach south, culminating in His triumphal entry into Jerusalem. "Behold, your king comes!"[32]

A glance at our translation of the passage reveals a rather tightly constructed poem of 12 lines arranged essentially in six couplets of virtually synonymous parallel members (9*a*, *b*; 10*e*, *f*), a modified terraced structure (9*e*, *f*; 10*a*, *b*), and members related in a logical fashion (9*c*, *d*; 10*c*, *d*). The formal symmetry is complemented by a symmetry of content, both by comparison and by contrast.[33] Thus, lines 1 and 2 speak of the center of the king's dominion as being Zion or Jerusalem. Lines 11 and 12 describe its perimeters as the whole extent of the earth itself. The two bicola could thus form a merismic inclusio embracing the totality of the king's sphere of sovereignty.

31. C. Stuhlmueller, *Haggai and Zechariah*, ITC (Grand Rapids: Eerdmans, 1988), 121-25.
32. Ringgren, in a study of the phrase "behold, your king comes," concludes that it "is used to proclaim the immediate coming of a king, or of Yahweh as king, in order to conquer his enemies and/or to save his people." Examples elsewhere of the concept he cites are Deut. 33:2; Pss. 96:11-13; 98:7-9; Isa. 30:27; 35:4; 40:9-10; 60:1; 62:13; Hab. 3:3 (Helmer Ringgren, "Behold Your King Comes," *VT* 24 [1974]: 207-11).
33. Lamarche outlines it as follows:
    a) Jérusalem (9*a-b*)
    b) roi victorieux (victorious king) (9*c*-4)
    c) âne (donkey) (9*e-f*)
    c') chevaux (horses) (10*a-b*)
    b') paix (peace) (10*c-d*)
    a') toute la terre (the whole earth) (10*e-f*)
(P. Lamarche, *Zacharie IX-XIV*, 45-46). Butterworth accepts this analysis with some modification (G. Michael Butterworth, "The Structure of the Book of Zechariah." Dissertation for King's College, London, 1989, 180-81).

The central thrust of lines 3 and 4 is that the king is triumphant and just, a notion supported by lines 9 and 10, which form a counterpart. Finally, lines 5 and 6 depict the king riding in humility upon a lowly ass, a young one at that. Lines 7 and 8, on the contrary, speak of the destruction of the horse-drawn chariots and the steeds of the cavalry, proud animals on which rode even prouder warriors. There can be no doubt that this magnificent poem is a self-contained literary piece that nonetheless depends on its setting for its full meaning.

Once YHWH has secured Jerusalem against hostile intruders (v. 8), her king is able to enter. This should elicit spontaneous outbursts of joyful acclamation, for the king is coming to her, legitimate in his role and victorious in his accomplishments. The tenderness of YHWH's address to the city may be seen in the expressions "daughter of Zion" and "daughter of Jerusalem." He has chosen her for Himself (1:14, 17) and in the person of the king has come to live in her midst (8:2-3).[34]

The coming of a king to Israel in the last days, and in particular the offspring of David, is a promise and hope that permeate the OT. David himself understood that YHWH would settle His people in a permanent dwelling (2 Sam. 7:10) and would make of his lineage an everlasting dynasty (2 Sam. 7:11-13). Many of the psalms echo this promise. Psalm 2 proclaims God's affirmation that He has set His king upon His holy hill Zion (v. 6) and that He will bequeath to Him, as His son, all the nations as an inheritance (vv. 7-8). In even more striking terms the author of Psalm 45 refers to the king as *'ĕlōhîm*, describing His throne as everlasting (v. 6 [HB v. 7]). Psalm 89 promises that David's seed will be established forever and His throne set through all generations (v. 4 [HB v. 5]).

The prophets, too, anticipate the coming messianic king. Isaiah speaks of the "son" on whose shoulder the responsibility of government will be laid. Following a list of His exalted and glorious epithets, the prophet goes on to say that there will be no end to the growth of His kingdom and that from the throne of David He will rule with justice and righteousness (Isa. 9:6-7). The same prophet anticipates a throne established on *ḥesed*, the fundamental principle of

---

34. For these and other nuances, see Saebø, *Sacharja 9-14*, 76-79. The rendering of צַדִּיק by "legitimate" rests on the well-known equation with Akk. *kīnātu/kittu*, a term referring to the legitimacy of a king's rule as well as its just quality. Cf. *CAD/K*, 383-84, 468-70. Such a usage also finds support in the OT itself where, especially in Isa. 40-55, Yahweh's righteousness and right to rule are described in various forms of the *ṣdq* root (cf. Isa. 41:10; 42:5-6; 45:19); J. J. Scullion, "*Ṣedeq-Ṣedaqah* in Isaiah cc. 40-66," *UF* 3 (1971): 341; R. A. Rosenberg, "Yahweh Becomes King," *JBL* 85 (1966):301; C. F. Whitley, "Deutero-Isaiah's Interpretation of *Ṣedeq*, *VT* 22 (1972): 473.

covenant relationships, and on this throne will sit one from the line of David "judging, seeking justice, and quick do to righteousness" (16:5). Amos prophesies the raising up of the fallen "hut" of David, the clearing away of its ruins, and the rebuilding of its palaces as in days long ago (9:11).

Zechariah, then, stands in a long tradition of hope in a rejuvenated Davidic kingship. Like the prophets just cited and others, he sees the king of the Triumphant Entry as righteous and "legitimate" or "vindicated" (צַדִּיק, *ṣaddîq*), that is, as wholly suitable and declared to be such in His exercise of sovereignty.[35] Moreover, He is victorious if, indeed, this is the correct understanding of נוֹשָׁע (*nôšā'*) in v. 9d. This niphal form of the verb יָשַׁע means literally "delivered" or "saved," so as He comes the king is "legitimate" and "delivered." In the context of v. 8 this is a reasonable interpretation, for there YHWH is said to have encamped about His house, thereby protecting it from enemy attackers. Nevertheless, it seems better to take the word as meaning victorious, that is, He is delivered, having overcome His foes.[36] Many of the versions render the participle as active, yielding the translation "saving (one)" or "savior."[37] This may presuppose a different Hebrew *Vorlage*,[38] or understand the niphal as reflexive, "showing himself a Savior, Deliverer."[39] In either case, this shifts the attention from the king to the objects of His salvation, a view that seems out of line with the overall impression of the passage, namely, that of a triumphal or victorious entry.

No sooner has the poet exalted the king by describing His victo-

---

35. Otzen, *Studien über Deuterosacharja*, 136-37. Cf. 1 Sam. 23:3; Isa. 9:5-6; 11:4; 16:5; Jer. 22:1-5, 1-17; 23:5-6.
36. Chary sees the active "just" and passive "saved" as a deliberate juxtaposition designed to reveal "la personnalité nouvelle du messie, tout entier sous la mouvance de Dieu 'juste et sauvé' par grâce" ("the new personality of the Messiah, completely under the moving of God, 'just and saved' by grace") (T. Chary, *Aggée-Zacharie, Malachie*, 166). It is better, with Mitchell, to understand it as "victorious" in the sense that the royal figure has been delivered "by the grace, and in the might, of the God of Israel" (H. G. Mitchell, *A Commentary on Haggai and Zechariah*, 273). For other passages referring to the Messiah or the king as "saved," see Ps. 18:4 [EB 18:3]; Isa. 49:4-5; 50:7-9; 53:11. Chary points out also (p. 165) that Zechariah appears to have depended on Zeph. 3:14-18 for his language in 9:9, but uses the niphal rather than Zephaniah's hiphil.
37. Thus the LXX σῴζων. Cf. NIV ("having salvation"), KJV ("having salvation"), NASB ("endowed with salvation"), NKJV ("having salvation"). The NEB "his victory gained" is an excellent rendition, combining both the passive and active aspects.
38. It suggests hiphil מוֹשִׁיחַ as in Isa. 43:3; 49:26; 60:16; Jer. 30:10; 46:27. Sellin reads the hiphil, in fact, rather than the MT niphal (E. Sellin, *Das Zwölfprophetenbuch*, 499-500).
39. K. Barker, "Zechariah," in *EBC*, 7:662.

rious entrance than he abruptly turns to His mode of transportation, one that seems most unbecoming to a great monarch. He is "lowly," riding on an ass. By itself the reference to the ass is not a sign of a humble station, for kings are known to have ridden even mules, Solomon himself being a case in point (1 Kings 1:33).[40] But here the king is described as lowly, a term (עָנִי, 'ānî) commonly employed with reference to the most impoverished and despised elements of Israelite society,[41] and He rides not just on an ass (חֲמוֹר, ḥămôr) but on a young ass (עַיִר, 'ayir), offspring of a she-ass (אָתוֹן, 'ātôn).[42] This is hardly expressive of a conquering hero riding at the head of victorious armies, but speaks of peace and humility.[43]

Within our context, again, the lowliness of the king is set in startling juxtaposition to His victorious arrival (v. 9a-d) and the destruction of YHWH's enemies (v. 10a-d), precisely to magnify the fact that whatever success the king achieves must be attributed to the enabling power of YHWH. David's response to the promise to him that his (David's) dynasty would endure forever reflects this same amazing juxtaposition. "Who am I," he asked, "and what is my family that you brought me to this point?" (2 Sam. 7:18). It is most evident to David that his promotion to king from the shepherd fields of Bethlehem was a rise from lowly humility to lofty eminence.

Isaiah speaks of the servant of YHWH in a similar vein. The servant "will be highly exalted and lifted up," he said (Isa. 52:13). From such a degraded position that He was hardly recognizable as a man He would startle and put to silence the nations of the earth and their rulers (vv. 14-15). From the unpromising beginning of a tender plant and root from dry soil (53:2) He would ultimately share equally with the rich and great (53:9, 12). Though Isaiah here does not identify the servant as a king, in another servant passage he declares that the

---

40. The donkey was, of course, commonly used in Middle Bronze Mari as a royal steed; E. Lipiński, "Recherches sur le livre de Zacharie," *VT* 20 (1970): 51-52.

41. By a slight revocalization (עֲנִי to עָנִי) Köhler takes the word to be a ptcp. of עָנָה and translates "triumphierend," citing Ps. 18:35c [HB 18:36c]; B. Köhler, "Sacharja IX 9. Ein Neuer Übersetzungsvorschlag," *VT* 21 (1971): 370; thus also E. Lipiński, "Recherches sur le Livre de Zacharie," 50-53. Unfortunately, neither the ancient texts nor the NT support this reading.

42. For the various terms and the use of the ass in the ancient Near Eastern world, see W. S. McCullough, *IDB*, 1-260-61, s.v. "ass."

43. Harrelson points out that עַיִר בֶּן־אֲתוֹנוֹת finds an exact equivalent in the Mari texts in *ḥayarum TUR atānim*, the ass slain in covenant-making. The only other OT occurrence is in Gen. 49:11 where the messianic ruler is associated with a pure-blooded ass. The king of Zech. 9:9-10 comes, then, in peace and to fulfill the covenant (Walter Harrelson, "Nonroyal Motifs in the Royal Eschatology," in *Israel's Prophetic Heritage*, eds. B. W. Anderson and Walter Harrelson [New York: Harper, 1962], 159-63).

chosen servant will establish justice in the earth (42:4). This is much in line with the sentiment of Zechariah 9:9*d* and 10*d*.

The NT use of our passage is most interesting.[44] Both Matthew and John clearly understand Jesus to be the triumphant king, but neither quotes more than v. 9. Matthew says, "Look! Your king is coming to you, meek and riding on an ass, and on a colt, foal of an ass" (Matt. 21:5)[45]. He quotes Zechariah 9:9*c, e-f* only, omitting "He is legitimate and victorious" (9*d*). Matthew is fully aware that it is not appropriate to view the whole passage as predictive of the triumphal entry of Jesus in the gospel era, for He was not indeed riding in triumph.[46] Lines *a, b*, and *d* of v. 9 and all of v. 10 await a future eschatological fulfillment (cf. Rev. 19:11-16).

John's citation is even more brief: "Look! Your king comes, sitting on an ass's colt" (12:15). Whereas Matthew sees Jesus as the king, but a king in humble and peaceful circumstances, John emphasizes the peaceful element alone.[47] Thus only the portion of Zechariah's announcement that is appropriate to that stage of Jesus' ministry is adduced by the evangelists.

Zechariah, addressing the strictly eschatological aspect of the king's coming, sees a day when YHWH will deliver Ephraim (that is, Israel) and Jerusalem (that is, Judah) from the encroachments of the enemy nations (9:10*a-c*). The passage as a whole requires this interpretation as opposed to one that sees Ephraim and Jerusalem themselves being disarmed by YHWH.[48] Verse 8 has already made it clear that it is the enemy without that requires Him to encamp around His Temple. Moreover, v. 10*d* suggests that once the instruments of war are broken off there will be peace among the nations. They will no longer have either the means or the will to continue their bellicose ways. This peace will accompany or issue from the universal rule of the king, for YHWH now refers in the third person to Him (10*c-e*).

---

44. See Herman Patsch, "Der Einzug Jesu in Jerusalem," *ZTK* 68 (1971): 1-26; Roman Bartnicki, "Das Zitat von Zach ix, 9-10 und die Tiere im Bericht von Matthäus über dem Einzug Jesu in Jerusalem (Matt. XXI, 1-11),'' *NovT* 18 (1976): 161-66.

45. The fact that Matthew (as opposed to Mark and Luke) speaks of two animals has led some scholars to accuse Matthew of having misread the poetic parallelism of Zech. 9:9 in such a way as to see two animals rather than one; cf. W. F. Albright and C. S. Mann, *Matthew*, AB 26 (Garden City, N.Y.: Doubleday, 1971), 252. This need not be the case at all, as has been shown by S. Lewis Johnson, "The Triumphal Entry of Christ," *BSac* 124 (1967): 222.

46. Robert H. Gundry, *Matthew. A Commentary on His Literary and Theological Art* (Grand Rapids: Eerdmans, 1982), 408-9.

47. Edwin D. Freed, "The Entry into Jerusalem in the Gospel of John," *JBL* 80 (1961): 337-38.

48. So, e.g., Lacocque, *Zacharie 9-14*, 155, and most scholars.

From "sea to sea" can mean from the Gulf of Aqaba to the Mediterranean, and from "the river to the ends of the earth" is a way of describing everything from the Euphrates to Arabia and Africa. Here, however, the scope is much broader, for the prophet's view is the cosmic one typical of eschatological prophecy.[49]

Additional Notes

9:10 The unexpected first person subject here has induced the LXX and other witnesses to read הִכְרִית (hiph. pf. 3 m.s.) for הִכְרַתִּי (hiph. pf. 1 c.s.). The resulting translation would be, "He will cut off the chariot from Ephraim," etc. Although this provides good continuity with the use of the third person pronoun in vv. 9*d* and 10*d, e*, the *lectio difficilior* should favor the MT. Besides, YHWH has already promised to defend His people in v. 8, so there is no surprise in His resumption of that promise here.

C. DELIVERANCE AND CONQUEST OF HIS PEOPLE (9:11-17)

Translation

[11]Moreover, as for you, because of the blood of your covenant, I will release your prisoners from the pit where there is no water. [12]Return to the stronghold, you prisoners, with hope; today I am declaring that I will return double to you. [13]I will bend Judah (as) My (bow), I will fill the bow with Ephraim, I will stir up your sons, O Zion, against yours, O Greece, and I will make you like a warrior's sword. [14]Then YHWH will appear over them, and His arrow will go forth like lightning; the Lord God will blow the trumpet and will sally forth on the southern storm-winds. [15]YHWH of hosts will guard them, and they will devour, and will subdue with sling-stones. Then they will drink, and will become clamorous as with wine, full like the (sacrificial) basin, like the corners of the altar. [16]In that day YHWH of hosts will deliver them as the flock of His people, for (they are) the precious stones of a crown sparkling over His land. *[17]How precious and fair! Grain will make the young men flourish and new wine the young women.

Exegesis and Exposition

This pericope flows naturally from the preceding one and, therefore, the addressee here, as in v. 9, must be Zion or Jerusalem. The connection is established by the particle גַּם (*gam*), "moreover," which indicates that the one who has been promised such wonderful bless-

---

49. Magne Saebø, "Vom Grossreich zum Weltreich," *VT* (1978): 83-91.

ings as the coming king will provide has even more to anticipate.[50]
The introduction of v. 11 by the independent personal pronoun אַתְּ (*'at*,
"you") draws attention to that pronoun, as our nominative absolute
translation suggests. It is you, Zion, who are the special object of
YHWH's saving purpose.

Using the metaphor of imprisonment, YHWH says He will release
Zion's prisoners from the waterless pit. This is a backward reference
to the release and restoration of the Babylonian exiles as a historical
type, though nowhere else is the word "pit" (בּוֹר, *bôr*) used to describe
that experience.[51] Pits, however, were common places of confinement
in the ancient world. Joseph was thrown into a pit—one, it should be
noted, without water (Gen. 37:24). Jeremiah, too, was incarcerated in
a pit without water (Jer. 38:6). The significance of this is that pits
frequently were dug precisely to contain water, so that one without it
was unusual. Moreover, a waterless pit would guarantee quick death
by thirst unless one were supplied with drinking water.[52]

Isaiah, referring most likely to Cyrus, says that YHWH had called
him to "bring the prisoners from the prison and those who dwell in
darkness from the place of confinement" (Isa. 42:7). These prisoners,
as the context puts beyond doubt (cf. 42:16, 18, 19; 43:8), are the
Jewish exiles. They had been, as it were, in a waterless pit of captivity. Isaiah also speaks of the condition of the people in exile as one of
thirst and dryness (41:17; 43:20; 44:3; 55:1), a metaphor for their
spiritual craving for the familiar places and practices of the homeland.[53]

If, indeed, there is reference here to a historical deliverance, the
prophet still has an eschatological one primarily in mind as the entire context attests. God's people had been in the "pit" of Babylonian
exile, but they would find themselves in a worse predicament in the
end of the age. From that pit God would again retrieve them according to His faithfulness to His covenant promises. What He has done in
the past provides encouragement for those who face an uncertain and
even hopeless future.

The basis for the release of the prisoners from the pit, Zechariah
says, is "the blood of your covenant." This remarkable statement is
most likely a synecdoche in which the blood, the sign of the covenant,
stands for the covenant itself.[54] The offering of sacrifices was an indis-

---

50. GKC, 153. Cf. Saebø, *Sacharja 9-14*, 188.
51. W. R. Harris, *ISBE* (1986) 3: 874-75, s.v. "pit."
52. Baldwin, *Haggai, Zechariah, Malachi*, 168.
53. Rex Mason, *The Books of Haggai, Zechariah, and Malachi*, CBC (Cam-
    bridge: Cambridge Univ., 1977), 92.
54. More particularly it is a genitive of attribute in which the purpose of the
    blood is stated: to make covenant; GKC, 128q.

pensable element of covenant making in the ancient Near East. The death of the animal involved, represented by the spilling of its blood, was part of a covenant sanction and suggested not only the binding together of the partners in covenant but the punishment that could be expected were one of the parties to violate its terms. One example of many that could be given is particularly apropos of the covenant here in Zechariah, and that is the sealing of the Sinaitic covenant with blood (Ex. 24:1-8).[55] Once the general and specific stipulations had been disclosed and Israel had sworn to enter covenant with YHWH, an altar and 12 pillars were erected at the foot of the mountain. Peace-offerings then followed, the blood of which was dashed against both the altar, symbolizing YHWH, and the pillars, symbolizing the 12 tribes. Moses then said, "Look, the blood of the covenant" (v. 8), the very terminology used by Zechariah.[56] Clearly, then, YHWH has released the prisoners from Babylonian exile because of the covenant He had made with His people long ago. This is what He had promised to do in the great blessings sections of the covenant texts of Leviticus (26:40-45) and Deuteronomy (30:1-10).

Now that the release from bondage has been effected, YHWH exhorts the prisoners to return to the stronghold (v. 12a). The hapax legomenon form here (בִּצָּרוֹן, biṣṣārôn) is a biform of the regular noun meaning "fortification" (מִבְצָר, mibṣār). In the present passage it is a metaphor to describe the very opposite of pit or prison, that is, a place of deliverance and security. This cannot mean Judah or Jerusalem, however, for they have already returned to these places.[57] What is in view is YHWH as a stronghold, an idea that is common in the OT (Pss. 18:2 [HB 18:3]; 31:3 [HB 31:4]; 71:3; 91:2; 144:2; Jer. 16:19; Nah. 1:7).[58] That this is the intent is clear from the second line of the verse: "I will return double to you." Thus the whole is bound together by the same verb, שׁוּב (šûb). "Return (שׁוּבוּ, šûbû) to the stronghold . . . and I will return (אָשִׁיב, 'āšîb) double to you." The full blessing of YHWH awaits those who take refuge in Him as their stronghold. Those who remain outside, distant from Him, remain without the benefits of His promises.

---

55. E. Kutsch understands this to be a reference to the covenant with Abraham involving circumcision ("Beschneidungsblut"), not the Mosaic Covenant (Ernst Kutsch, "Das Sog. 'Bundesblut' in Ex. XXIV 8 und Sach IX 11," *VT* 23 [1973]: 29-30). This view is not compelling because it overlooks the Exodus parallels here that clearly relate to the Sinaitic covenant.

56. T. Chary, *Aggée-Zacharie, Malachie*, 171.

57. Many scholars emend the rare לְבִצָּרוֹן to לד צִיּוֹן (Marti, Sellin, Horst), צִיּוֹן לבת (Duhm, Nowack) or the like, thus connecting it to Zion. But see Otzen, *Studien über Deuterosacharja*, 241; Saebø, *Sacharja 9-14*, 55-56.

58. Unger, *Zechariah*, 166.

To return "double" (מִשְׁנֶה, *mišneh*) suggests a double portion of
blessing. The same noun occurs in Job 42:10 to describe Job's latter
state. Interestingly, the language of Job's restoration is much the
same as that of our Zechariah text.[59] YHWH turned (שָׁב, *sab*) the
captivity (שְׁבִית! read with Qere שְׁבוּת, *šĕbût*) of Job when he prayed for
his friends, and YHWH gave Job twice (*mišneh*) as much as he had
before. Even more pertinent because of its eschatological orientation
is Isa. 61:7: "Instead of your shame (you will have) double (*mišneh*),
and instead of dishonor they will rejoice in their portion (חֵלֶק, *ḥēleq*);
therefore, in their land they will possess double (*mišneh*)—
everlasting joy will be theirs." Here the parallelism links "double"
with "portion," putting beyond doubt the legal and covenant nature
of the passage (cf. Isa. 40:2; 61:8-9).[60]

A specific manifestation of that blessing, one much in line with
the stronghold motif and the militaristic theme of the whole oracle,[61]
is the use YHWH will make of Judah, Ephraim (i.e., Israel), and Zion
(v. 13). He will "bend" (דָּרַךְ, *dārak*, lit. "tread") Judah as one bends a
bow (cf. Pss. 7:13 [EB 7:12]; 11:2; 37:14; Jer. 50:14, 29; 51:3; etc.),
filling her (the bow) with Ephraim as an arrow. Zion will be stirred
up against Yawan (i.e., Greece) and will become like a sword in
YHWH's hand.

The intense use of metaphor and simile here is clear in its intent,
but the historical allusions, if any, have caused great differences of
opinion. It is quite apparent that YHWH will use His people as weapons against another nation, namely, Greece. But how is this to be
taken? For the same reason that some scholars date Zech. 9:1-8 to a
preexilic period because of alleged historical allusions to Tiglath-
Pileser or some other Neo-Assyrian ruler, so others wish to date
9:11-17 to the third century or so because of the reference to Greece,
something, they say, that would not be likely before the rise and fall of
Alexander the Great.[62]

---

59. Lacocque, *Zacharie 9-14*, 158.
60. P.-E. Bonnard, *Le Second Isaïe* (Paris: Librairie Lecoffre, 1972), 420.
61. For a good review of the military terminology here, see Saebø, *Sacharja 9-14*, 194.
62. So S. R. Driver, *An Introduction to the Literature of the Old Testament* (Edinburgh: T. & T. Clark, 1913), 349; Eissfeldt, *The Old Testament. An Introduction*, 437; Otto Kaiser, *Introduction to the Old Testament* (Oxford: Basil Blackwell, 1975), 288; Georg Fohrer, *Introduction to the Old Testament* (London: SPCK, 1970), 466-67. Others posit עַל־בָּנַיִךְ יָוָן (13*b*) to be a gloss but still date the passage late. So Horst, *Nahum bis Maleachi*, 279-80. Hanson, *The Dawn of Apocalyptic*, 298, regards the disputed phrase as a gloss but dates the passage early. He argues that it upsets the meter, but it also clearly upsets an early date unless one can concede some measure of prediction.

As pointed out earlier, once it is understood that vv. 1-8 are the conventional language of holy war conquest, there no longer remains any need to isolate a specific historical background against which the oracle should be interpreted. The same applies here. By the late sixth century it was most evident that the next major world power would arise in the west in the form of the Aegean peoples.[63] The Persians had already encountered the Greeks and would do so increasingly under the successors of Darius, Xerxes, and Artaxerxes. It did not even require divine revelation to see that this was imminent. But one should not conclude from this that a literal confrontation of a military sort between Greece and Israel was in view. This, again, is the language of eschatology,[64] and all that is being said is that whatever hostile power should ever arise against the covenant people can expect to meet resounding defeat at the hands of their God, who wields them as potent weapons en route to the establishment of His universal sovereignty.

This is the thrust of v. 14. YHWH will appear over them, that is, as a banner or standard[65] guaranteeing the victory of His people. As in days of old when he defeated Pharaoh and delivered Israel, He will shoot His arrows like lightning (Pss. 18:13-14 [HB 18:14-15]; 144:5; Hab. 3:4-5), He will blow the trumpet for advance and will ride forth on the chariot of the windstorms of the south (Pss. 18:10 [HB 18:11]; 68:4, 33 [HB 68:5, 34]; 104:3; Isa. 19:1). As is well known, this is the imagery of holy war, a medium especially expressive of YHWH's conflicts and conquests in eschatological times. To look for historical connections in such passages is fruitless except where references are made to past events, such as the Exodus, as illustrations of what YHWH can do as divine warrior.

The holy war theme continues in v. 15 with the epithet "YHWH of hosts" and further expansion of His anticipated conquests. Defended by YHWH, His chosen ones will "devour" (אָכַל, 'ākal) and "subdue" (כָּבַשׁ, kābaš, lit. "tread underfoot") the "sling-stones" (קֶלַע, qelaʿ). This is a very difficult line if one takes קֶלַע as direct object in that one does not easily conceive of these verbs with this object. *Kābaš* is a word frequently used to express the establishment or exercise of dominion

63. Edwin Yamauchi, *Greece and Babylon. Early Contacts Between the Aegean and the Near East* (Grand Rapids: Baker, 1967), 61-84.
64. Baldwin, *Haggai, Zechariah, Malachi*, 168-69.
65. The word נֵס (nēs), or some other term for banner or pennant, does not occur here, but this is clearly the intent of the niphal יֵרָאֶה, "will be seen (over them)." See George E. Mendenhall, *The Tenth Generation* (Baltimore: Johns Hopkins, 1973), 56-66; Thomas W. Mann, *Divine Presence and Guidance in Israelite Traditions: The Typology of Exaltation* (Baltimore: Johns Hopkins, 1977), 252-58.

(Gen. 1:28; Num. 32:22, 29; Josh. 18:1, Mic. 7:19),[66] so, admittedly it is not entirely out of the semantic field of overcoming a weapon such as sling-stones. In fact, the literal meaning of "walking about on" these stones would graphically illustrate mastery over them. To "devour" them, however, is another matter. The LXX accordingly presupposes a reading יָכְלוּ (*yākĕlû*), "they will prevail," a verb much more fitting, particularly with *kābaš*. Less acceptable is the proposal of *BHS* to emend אַבְנֵי־קֶלַע (*'abnê-qelaʿ*), "sling-stones," to בְּנֵי־קֹבַע (*bĕnê-qōbaʿ*), "deceivers," or even בְּנֵי־קֶלַע (*bĕnê-qelaʿ*), "slingers." There is simply no textual warrant for either of these.[67]

The best solution is to understand "sling-stones" as an adverbial accusative and to postulate an object such as the "flesh" of the enemy (Deut. 32:42; 2 Sam. 2:26; 11:25; 18:8; Jer. 2:30; Hos. 11:6). This matches the next line nicely, "they will drink, and will become clamorous," etc. What they drink, of course, is the blood of their enemies, a figure also common elsewhere (Num. 23:24; Ezek. 39:17-20). The LXX again proposes an alternative, דָּם (*dām*), "blood," or דָּמָם (*dāmām*), "their blood," for הָמוּ (*hāmû*), "they will become clamorous." The whole line would then read, "they will drink blood like wine."[68] The problem with this, again, is that it requires emendation of the MT or at least resort to another *vorlage* of the LXX, something totally unnecessary. It is better to see both "eat" and "drink" as having unexpressed but clear objects ("flesh" and "blood" respectively). The verb *kābaš*, "subdue," would then have "sling-stones" as adverbial accusative, and *hāmû*, "become clamorous," would have "as with wine" also as an adverbial accusative. A free rendering might be:

> "They will devour (human flesh);
> they will subdue with sling-stones.
> They will drink (human blood);
> they will become clamorous as with wine."

This finds excellent support in v. 15*d*: "They will be full like the (sacrificial) basin, like the corners of the altar." Having satiated

---

66. Wagner, *TWAT*, IV 1/2: cols. 54-60, s.v. כָּבַשׁ.
67. Many scholars take אַבְנֵי־קֶלַע to be the subject of the clause: "the sling-stones will devour and conquer," or, as Chary renders it, "dévoreront victorieusement" ("devouring victoriously") (T. Chary, *Aggée-Zacharie, Malachie*, 172). Cf. A. Van Hoonacker, *Les Douze Petits Prophètes* (Paris: Librairie Victor Lecoffre, 1908), 667; Horst, *Nahum bis Maleachi*, 174; Elliger, *Die Propheten Nahum, Habakuk, Zephanja, Haggai, Sacharja, Maleachi*, 151. Elliger (and many others) emends כָּבַשׁ to בָּשָׂר so as to read, "the sling-stones will devour flesh," etc.
68. So H. G. Mitchell, *A Commentary on Haggai and Zechariah*, 280, 284; cf. Saebø, *Sacharja 9-14*, 198-200.

themselves with the flesh and blood of their fallen enemies, YHWH's armies will be like the vessels of the sanctuary filled with the flesh and blood of sacrifice. This bold figure suggests that the death of YHWH's foes is in some sense an offering to Him.[69] The sanctuary basin was a bowl used at the altar to hold the blood to be dashed upon it and other objects as part of the ritual (Ex. 27:3; 38:3; Num. 4:14; 1 Kings 7:50; 2 Kings 12:13). The word "corners" (זָוִית, *zāwît*) is rare in Hebrew, being no doubt a loan word from Aramaic,[70] and in the context certainly refers to the corners of the great bronze altar, that is, to the "horns" of the altar (cf. Ex. 27:2).[71] To these corners the sacrificial blood was liberally applied (Ex. 29:12; 30:10; Lev. 4:7, 18; 8:15). This description of the use of flesh and blood in sacrifice is particularly significant, coming as it does from the priest-prophet Zechariah.

The eschatological character of the oracle is underlined again in v. 16 by the use of the classic phrase "in that day" (cf. 2:11; 3:10; 12:3, 4, 6, 7, 9, 11, etc.). Thus, the references to Hadrach, Damascus, and even Greece must be viewed as having end-time significance especially. Having used His people as weapons of destruction and death, YHWH will, as their God, deliver them in an ongoing way as a shepherd preserves his flock. Then, in an abrupt change of figure,[72] He refers to His own as precious stones bedecking a crown, stones that will shine brilliantly over all His land.[73] The crown (נֵזֶר, *nēzer*) represents the sovereignty of YHWH over all His realm, but the brightest, most spectacular aspect of that reign will be His own precious redeemed ones. It is they who will emblazon forth His glory.

A major obstacle with this view is the most uncertain מִתְנוֹסְסוֹת (*mitnôsĕsôt*), translated here "shining." The verbal root נָסַס (*nāsas*), since it is cognate to the noun נֵס (*nēs*), "ensign, banner," is sometimes

69. Elliger, *Die Propheten Nahum, Habakuk, Zephanja, Haggai, Sacharja, Maleachi*, 152.
70. Marcus Jastrow, *A Dictionary of the Targumim, the Talmud Babli and Yerushalmi, and the Midrashic Literature* (New York: Pardes, 1950), 1:386. Cf. C. F. Jean and Jacob Hoftijzer, *Dictionnaire des Inscriptions semitiques de L'Ouest* (Leiden: Brill, 1965), 73.
71. For full discussion, see Taeke Jansma, *Inquiry into the Hebrew Text and the Ancient Versions of Zechariah IX-XIV* (Leiden: Brill, 1949), 70-78; Saebø, *Sacharja 9-14*, 60-61. Otzen takes מִזְרָק to be a gloss on זָוִיּוֹת, but this is uncalled for in light of the well-known Aramaic usage (Otzen, *Studien über Deuterosacharja*, 245).
72. So abrupt is the shift here that Bewer suggests כַּצֹּאן, "like a flock," be emended to יָצִיץ, "will shine" (Julius A. Bewer,"Two Suggestions on Proverbs 30:31 and Zechariah 9:16," *JBL* 67 [1948]: 62). This arbitrary adjustment of the text has absolutely no basis.
73. Baldwin, *Haggai, Zechariah, Malachi*, 170.

translated "be high or conspicuous" (BDB, 651). The verb, however, is likely a denominative of *nēs* and so would express the idea of functioning as a standard or banner, that is, to attract attention. "Shining" is therefore appropriate either way, for if the precious stones of the crown are raised up, they will in any case draw attention to the crown and to him who wears it.[74]

At the end of this section of his oracle the prophet bursts out in an expostulation of praise (v. 17). But whom or what he is praising is not entirely clear because of the ambiguous nature of the text. Literally the first line reads, "For what His good and what His fair." The pronominal suffix in this case is referring to YHWH, so the line should be rendered, "How good and fair He is!"[75] The following line seems not to support this, however, nor does the preceding context. Having just referred in v. 16*b* to the jewels of the crown, it is natural to assume they are still in mind in v. 17. Thus, "How precious (טוֹב, *ṭôb*) and fair it (that is, all of this description) is!"[76] Then, as though to explain the preciousness and fairness of these jewels, which after all are YHWH's people, Zechariah says that they have become so by the nurturing of YHWH who has given His young men grain and His young women new wine. One may recall the appearance of Daniel and his friends when they refused the king's dainties and feasted upon the fare accorded them by their own traditions: "At the end of ten days their appearance was better (טוֹב, *ṭôb*) and they were fatter than all the youths who had eaten of the king's delicacies" (Dan. 1:15).

Additional Notes

9:17 Many scholars place v. 17 (or even 16*b*) after 10:1. Thus van Hoonacker arranges the text as 9:16*a*; 10:1; 9:17; 9:16*b*; van Hoonacker, *Les Douze Petits Prophètes*, 668-69. This does make a smoother transition, but there is no textual warrant for the rearrangement. Mitchell described v. 17 as "superfluous," arguing that it is different from all that precedes it in both form and context (H. G. Mitchell!, *A Commentary on Haggai and Zechariah*, 281-82). He is correct that v. 17 is interruptive but fails to account for it as a spontaneous outburst of praise. Otzen connects v. 17 with 10:1 as part of a "positives

---

74. Chary draws attention to similar ideas in Ex. 24:10; Ezek. 1:26; Rev. 22:18-22; T. Chary, *Aggée-Zacharie, Malachie*, 175-76.
75. Thus Lacocque, *Zacharie 9-14*, 160.
76. Chary, *Aggée-Zacharie, Malachie*, 176; Otzen, *Studien über Deuterosacharja*, 246. It is also possible to take the singular pronoun as referring to the delivered remnant as a collective entity; thus K. Barker, "Zechariah," in *EBC*, 7:667.

Fruchtbarkeitsmotiv" ("positive fertility motifs"), imbedding it within the following structure:

9:16–10:3a {
- 9:16: Positives Hirtenbild (positive shepherd images)
  - 9:17–10:1: positives Fruchtbarkeitsmotiv (positive fertility motifs)
  - 10:2a: negatives Fruchtbarkeitsmotiv (negative fertility motifs)
- 10:2b-3a: negatives Hirtenbild (negative shepherd images)

(Benedikt Otzen, *Studien Über Deuterosacharja*, 218). This seems most reasonable and in any case allows v. 17 to stay where it is.

2
Restoration of the True People (10:1-12)

The first part of this oracle concerning the nations focused on the coming of the true King to take His place of sovereignty over them (chap. 9). The focus now shifts to the elect people of the King who will, in a second exodus, come from all the nations to the promised land where they will share His dominion with Him. This part, like the first, has its roots in history but its larger perspective in the eschaton. The oracle deals with issues and problems immediately germane to the prophet Zechariah's own situation in life. It transmutes its solutions to those matters that will arise at the end of history as well. In a sense, therefore, the present is a prototype of the future, though the future will bring a triumphant culmination for YHWH's kingdom program and His purposes for His people.

A. REJECTION OF JUDAH'S WICKED LEADERSHIP (10:1-3a)

Translation

¹Ask rain of YHWH in the time of the latter-rain, even of YHWH who makes thunder-storms, and He will give everyone rain-showers and green growth in the field. ²For the teraphim have spoken wickedness, the augurers have seen a lie, and as for the dreamers, they have disclosed emptiness and console in vain; therefore they set out like

**sheep (and) are afflicted because they have no shepherd. ³ªI am en-
raged because of the shepherds and will punish the he-goats.**

Exegesis and Exposition

Zechariah turns first of all to the problem of evil leadership in the
historical community of Israel, dividing his attention between the
spiritual and political aspects. Things have been bleak, indeed, as
the whole history of Israel and Judah could attest, but there was hope
now in light of the restoration from exile and particularly in light of
God's gracious promises concerning the age to come. All His people
need do is ask for rain, that is, the showers of His blessing (v. 1), and it
is certain to come. The "latter-rain" (מַלְקוֹשׁ, *malqôš*) refers, in the
context of the agricultural cycles of Palestine, to the renewal of sustained rains in the spring of the year, commencing usually about
March or April.[1] The "former rains" were those of the autumn, following the harvest-time.

"Latter rain" is also a term with eschatological significance, referring to the pouring out of divine blessing in the coming age. Hosea,
speaking of YHWH's reviving of His people at the end time, puts it in
terms of YHWH's coming "as the rain, as the latter rain that waters
the earth" (Hos. 6:3). Joel associates it with a time of abundant harvest, the wheat, vineyards, and olive trees having soaked up its
nourishment so as to yield their fruit. All this is to make up for the
years devastated by the ravages of pest and insect (Joel 2:21-25). This
is a reference to Israel's historical experience, one to be succeeded by
a time of blessing in the latter day.

Jeremiah points out to his preexilic contemporaries that despite
the withholding of the former and latter rains, Judah had remained
adamantly in rebellion against YHWH (3:3). His blessings upon her
in the past when He had poured out those rains upon her, had met
with no response except more disobedience and recalcitrance (5:24).
The result had been the exile, a time of drought and despair, of a "pit
without water" (Zech. 9:11). Zechariah therefore offers hope that the
latter rain of prosperity will come once more.

Such blessing is possible, he says, because it is YHWH "who makes
thunderstorms." The word translated "thunderstorms" here is חֲזִיז
(*ḥăzîz*), frequently rendered "lightning flash," "thunderbolt" (BDB,
304), or "storm cloud" (KBL, 286). It occurs otherwise only in Job
(28:26; 38:25) where it also ought to be understood as violent rain
because in the first place it is parallel to "rain" (מָטָר, *māṭār*) and in the
second passage to "flood" (שֶׁטֶף, *šeṭep*). Here in Zechariah it also is
poetically synonymous with *māṭār*, "rain." The outpouring of these

---

1. Denis Baly, *The Geography of the Bible* (London: Lutterworth, 1957), 47-52.

refreshing waters will result in green growth in the fields, a sight familiar to anyone who has been in Palestine following the latter rains.

This end-time vision is in sharp contrast to the conditions addressed by the prophet in his own day. Judah had suffered a devastating crisis of leadership in both her spiritual and political life, one no doubt partially redressed, at least, by the exile and by the postexilic leaders such as Zerubbabel, Joshua, and perhaps even Zechariah and his prophet-colleague, Haggai. Throughout the history of Israel and Judah resort had been made to illicit religious channels such as teraphim, augurers, and dreamers (v. 2), all of whom delivered nothing but falsehood and emptiness.

Teraphim[2] were small household images thought to represent supernatural powers and to be a means of eliciting information from the spirit world (cf. Gen. 31:19, 34-35; 1 Sam. 19:13, 16; Hos. 3:4). When the king of Babylon was marching south to campaign against Palestine and the Transjordan, he came to a fork in the highway. Not knowing whether to go on to Jerusalem or to Rabbah first, he "consulted the teraphim" and "looked in the liver" (Ezek. 21:21). What he was doing, Ezekiel says, was using "divination." The word for "divination" (קֶסֶם, *qesem*) here occurs also in another form in our passage, translated "augurers" (קוֹסְמִים, *qôsĕmîm*). As Ezekiel indicates, inspection of animal livers was one of the techniques of divination. Other means were the "shaking of arrows" (Ezek. 21:21) and "consulting the teraphim." The first practice is well documented in ancient Near Eastern divination,[3] but the last two are not, at least by this name.

Another means of receiving supernatural disclosure was the dream, a well-known medium both within and outside the OT.[4] When the dream was inspired by God it was, of course, a perfectly appropriate means of determining YHWH's purposes. When, however, it was brought into the service of illicit revelation, it was soundly condemned (Deut. 13:2-6; Jer. 23:27-32; 27:9; 29:8). Zechariah condemns it here as he does the other means of divination. The teraphim have spoken wickedness (אָוֶן, *'āwen*), the augurers have seen a lie, and the dreamers (literally, "the dreams") have unveiled emptiness (שָׁוְא, *šāw'*).[5] The comfort all have proffered has been in vain.

2. Anne E. Draffkorn, "Ilāni/Elohim," *JBL* 75 (1957): 216-24, esp. 222-23.
3. Technically, this was known in Mesopotamia as hepatoscopy, a sub-discipline of extispicy, the inspection of internal organs in general. See A. L. Oppenheim, *Ancient Mesopotamia* (Chicago: Univ. of Chicago, 1964), 213-15.
4. A. Leo Oppenheim, *The Interpretation of Dreams in the Ancient Near East*, TAPS (Philadelphia: American Philosophical Society, 1956).
5. Many interpreters take חֲלֹמוֹת as a direct object of יְדַבֵּרוּ and render, "The

The result of this abysmal search for spiritual illumination and guidance has been the aimless wandering of the people of Israel like sheep. Unwilling to attend to the Word of God revealed through the legitimate voice of His prophets, they have lost their moorings and have set out, like so many nomads, without chart or compass.

The allusion to sheep affords the prophet a shift from consideration of spiritual leadership, such as that provided by the prophets, to that of the kings in the political realm.[6] In the ancient Near East, as well as in Israel, kings were commonly described as shepherds.[7] They had the task of leading, protecting, and nurturing the human "flocks" under their control. Jeremiah is particularly rich in "shepherd-sheep" imagery. He excoriates the priests for failing to seek YHWH, the prophets for prophesying by Baal, and the shepherds (i.e., kings) for transgressing against the Lord (2:8). But he also holds out hope that YHWH will give shepherds someday who will "feed" the people with knowledge and understanding (3:15).

In a passage remarkably close in sentiment to this one, Jeremiah complains that the shepherds have become insensitive, "not inquiring of YHWH" (10:21). As a result the flocks have become scattered. Thus, the connection between divination and lack of sound political leadership is well established in both prophets (cf. also Jer. 23:1-2; 50:6). The "shepherd oracle" of Ezekiel 34 is equally enlightening. The prophet asks if it is not the task of the shepherd to feed the sheep (v. 2). Indeed it is, but the shepherds (kings) of Israel have only eaten the sheep and clothed themselves with their wool (v. 3). The sheep thus

---

augurers see (or, have seen) a lie and speak empty dreams." So Paul D. Hanson, *The Dawn of Apocalyptic* (Philadelphia: Fortress, 1975), 324. Against this is the use of the verb "speak" with dreams. One would expect that they dream empty dreams. Moreover, the parallelism is better if חֲלֹמוֹת is taken as a figure (metonymy) for dreamers and made a subject. The verse would then take the form:

a   teraphim   have spoken   wickedness
b   augurers   have seen   a lie
c   dreamers   have spoken   emptiness

The last line, then, becomes a summary of the disappointment caused by all three practitioners:

d   they (all)   comfort   in vain

For arguments supporting חֲלֹמוֹת as a subject, see W. Nowack, *Die kleinen Propheten*, HAT (Göttingen: Vandenhoeck und Ruprecht, 1903), 295-96.
6. Note the connection between the "flock" of 9:16 and the "sheep" of 10:2*b*, a connection picked up in the analysis of Benedikt Otzen, *Studien über Deuterosacharja*, ATD 6 (Copenhagen: Prostant Apud Munksgaard, 1964), 218-19.
7. J. de Fraine, *L'Aspect Religieux de la Royauté Israélite* (Roma: Pontificio Istituto Biblico, 1954), 352-54, 137-38 (Israel).

became scattered (v. 5), wandering over the whole earth (v. 6). YHWH therefore was against His shepherds (v. 10). He will now regather His dispersed flock (v. 12) and bring them back to the fold, so that He can be their shepherd (v. 15). In the day of His salvation He will feed them through His shepherd David (v. 23). YHWH, in fact, will be their God and David, the shepherd, will be their ruler (v. 24). No wonder Jesus the Messiah could refer to Himself as both the Son of David (Matt. 9:27; 15:22; 20:30; 21:9; Mark 12:35; Luke 20:41) and the "good shepherd" (John 10:11-16).

The OT record is replete with references to the kings of Israel, beginning with Saul (1 Sam. 28:3-7), who sought after illicit channels of revelation and ended up leading the people to ruin and dispersion. One thinks of Ahab (1 Kings 16:31; 22:6-12), Ahaziah (2 Kings 1:2), Ahaz (2 Kings 16:15), and Manasseh (2 Kings 21:6) of whom such things are explicitly affirmed.

Because of this history of wicked leadership, especially on the part of the kings, YHWH was angry and would punish those responsible (v. 3a). This had already come to pass with the destruction of Jerusalem and deportation of the last Davidic king, but the threat still stands against contemporary rulers or any who might arise in the future (2 Sam. 7:12-14). Changing the imagery slightly, Zechariah describes the leaders as "he-goats," not shepherds. This animal customarily led the flocks and as a metaphor for leadership frequently appears as a substitute for the shepherd. Thus Isaiah places "he-goats" (עַתּוּדִים, 'attûdîm) in parallel with "kings" (14:9).[8] Zechariah employs the word as a synonym of "shepherd" only to create a good poetic couplet:

> "Because of the *shepherds* I am angry,
> And because of the *he-goats* I will punish."

B. SELECTION OF JUDAH'S RIGHTEOUS LEADERSHIP (10:3b-7)

Translation

3bFor YHWH of hosts has visited His flock, the house of Judah, and will make them as His majestic war horse. 4From Him will come forth the cornerstone, the peg, the battle bow, and every ruler. 5And they will be like warriors trampling the mud of the streets in battle. They will fight, for YHWH will be with them, and will put to shame the mounted men. 6I will strengthen the house of Judah and deliver

---

8. Patrick D. Miller, Jr., "Animal Names as Designations in Ugaritic and Hebrew," *UF* 2 (1970): 184.

the house of Joseph and *will bring them back because of My compassion for them. They will be as though I had never rejected them, for I am YHWH their God and therefore will hear them. ⁷Ephraim will be like a warrior and will rejoice as with wine. Their children will see and rejoice; their heart will exult in YHWH.

Exegesis and Exposition

The focus of this part of the oracle shifts in the middle of v. 3 from the past and present to the future and from a negative assessment of Judah's leadership to a positive one. Up to and through the Babylonian exile God's people, like sheep, had wandered aimlessly in the absence of sound spiritual and political direction. Now things already were beginning to improve under the postexilic leadership (cf. Hag. 2:20-23; Zech. 4:6-9; 6:12-13). But the present was only a dim harbinger of things far more glorious to come. The establishment of God's kingdom in the eschaton would bring with it new human leadership as well. The best was yet ahead.

In an effective double entendre, YHWH had said in v. 3*a* that He would visit (פָּקַד, *pāqad*) the "he-goats," the wicked kings, with judgment. Now in 3*b* He says He will visit (same verb) His flock with blessing.⁹ To remove all uncertainty concerning the identity of the flock, He spells it out—it is the house of Judah. Far from being the meek and easily bullied sheep of the past, they will become a mighty charger on which YHWH can ride to battle. This is reminiscent of the martial language of 9:13, where Judah was described as a bow, Ephraim as an arrow, and Zion as a sword of battle.

Continuing in the same imagery but with a strong mixture of messianic language, YHWH foresees Judah as the source of four elements: the cornerstone, the peg, the bow, and the ruler. These should be interpreted in the context of holy war that prevails here and not in that of architecture or construction or something else.¹⁰ "Cornerstone" or "corner tower" (פִּנָּה, *pinnâ*) occurs as a metaphor for a leader, such as a king or governor (Judg. 20:2; 1 Sam. 14:38; Isa. 19:13). With that in mind it seems quite clear that Zechariah is alluding to a future human figure who will provide the very foundation for a revived kingdom structure.¹¹ Paul understood this one to be Christ, "the chief cornerstone" (Eph. 2:20). As for the peg (יָתֵד, *yātēd*), the

9. Rex Mason, *The Books of Haggai, Zechariah, and Malachi*, CBC (Cambridge: Cambridge Univ., 1977), 99.
10. Hanson, *The Dawn of Apocalyptic*, 330-31.
11. Chary points out that this epithet is used consistently to refer to "les chefs" ("the rulers") who are "ceux du tout-Israël réuni" ("those of a re-unified Israel"). It is thus an eschatological term here (Theophane Chary, *Aggée-Zacharie, Malachie* [Paris: Librairie Lecoffre, 1969], 180).

word can refer to a tent peg or, as is likely here, to a peg in the wall from which items could be suspended.[12] It must be sturdy, for, as Ezekiel notes (15:3), one would hardly use wood from a vine in its manufacture.

Eliakim ben Hilkiah is described as such a peg in Isa. 22:15-25. With the predicted removal of Shebna from office the weight of the Davidic government would rest upon the major-domo Eliakim, servant of King Hezekiah (Isa. 36:3). But he would not be capable of supporting such a load and so would be torn from the wall (22:25). This no doubt was to signify the impending doom of the royal house itself.

In his famous prayer of confession Ezra rejoiced that God had shown the postexilic community grace in preserving a remnant and in providing a "peg" in the holy place. The collocation of remnant and peg here (Ezra 9:8) suggests that they share much in common, just as they do in Zechariah. In the latter it is the eschatological remnant that will give rise to the peg, the stout hook on which all of Judah's hopes for the future can be suspended.

"Battle bow" as a personal epithet is otherwise unknown in the OT, though Babylonia is called "battle mace" by Jeremiah (Jer. 51:20).[13] Zechariah himself uses the term with reference to the conquest by the messianic king who will break the battle bow of the enemy (9:10). A more helpful reference, however, is that of 9:13 where YHWH says He will "bend" Judah as a warrior bends a bow. Since Judah is in view in 10:3-5 as the source of the bow, it cannot be Judah as a whole but someone who comes from Judah. This idea is, of course, consistent with OT messianic theology (cf. Gen. 49:10).

Finally, that "every ruler" shall come from Judah (v. 4c) is not a matter of surprise, for that too is a major OT theme. David and all his descendants were, after all, sons of Judah. Zechariah uses a rather strange word for ruler here, however, the participle form of נֹגֵשׂ (nāgaś), "to oppress." Normally one would expect "king" (מֶלֶךְ, melek), "prince" (נָשִׂיא, nāśî'), or the like, but here occurs a term usually reserved for oppressive, tyrannical rule (Ex. 3:7; 5:6, 10; Isa. 3:12; 9:3; 14:2, 4; Dan. 11:20). Zechariah already used the same participle to describe cruel, despotic rulers (9:8). The reason for its use here appears to be the harsh tone of the language of conquest throughout the pericope. When YHWH achieves His final hegemony He will, through

---

12. H. G. Mitchell, *A Commentary on Haggai and Zechariah*, ICC (Edinburgh: T. & T. Clark, 1912), 289.
13. Mason draws attention to its use to designate kings of the ancient Near East, especially in Egyptian texts (Mason, *The Books of Haggai, Zechariah, and Malachi*, 100).

His appointed Davidic rulers, ruthlessly put down all opposition.[14] To His foes His total, violent domination of them will cast Him as an oppressor, a dictator to whom they must submit against their will.

This impression gains support in v. 5 where the aforementioned rulers (and perhaps the cornerstone, peg, and battle bow as well) will be like warriors treading down in the mud of the streets. Though the object of their treading is not disclosed, the use of the verb בּוּס (*bûs*) elsewhere makes it clear that enemies are in view (Pss. 60:12 [HB 60:14]; 108:13 [HB 108:14]; Isa. 14:25; 63:6).[15] They will prevail over these foes, for YHWH will be with them, a classic expression of holy war. Even the proud horsemen will be chagrined and embarrassed at the success of YHWH's armies. With their great speed they might ordinarily escape (Amos 2:15), but in the day of YHWH there will be no way to avoid His terrible wrath (cf. Hag. 2:22).

By way of recapitulation and emphasis YHWH again, and plainly, speaks of the strengthening of Judah and deliverance of Joseph (i.e., Israel). The verb גָּבַר (*gābar*) has strongly militaristic overtones, especially in the piel (cf. 10:12). It speaks here of strengthening in battle, as the previous context would surely support.[16] Likewise, Joseph is "delivered" (יָשַׁע, *yāšaʿ*), a word commonly employed in the sense of preservation in battle (Deut. 20:4; Judg. 3:9; 6:36-37; 7:7; 1 Sam. 14:23; Isa. 49:25; Hos. 1:7). They will be brought back to YHWH in the sense of full restoration as His people. That this meaning is intended, and not a restoration from exile or bondage, is clear from the clarifying statement, "they will be as though I had never rejected them" (v. 6*d*). The basis for their reacceptance is the great compassion YHWH feels for them and the fact that He will hearken to their cries and respond in covenant commitment (cf. 13:9).

Reference to Israel as Joseph, though not unique here (v. 6), is not common (2 Sam. 19:20; Pss. 78:67; 80:1 [HB 80:2]; 81:5 [HB 81:6]; Ezek. 37:16; Amos 5:6, 15; 6:6). Very likely its occurrence here anticipates the exodus motif of vv. 8-12, for it was Joseph who arranged for his family to join him in Egypt, it was he who urged his descendants to move his remains to the promised land (Gen. 50:25), and it was because of a pharaoh "who knew not Joseph" (Ex. 1:8) that oppression of the Israelites commenced in Egypt—an oppression that eventually led to the Exodus of God's people a few decades later.

The description of God's people as warriors (v. 5) recurs here at

---

14. Chary, *Aggée-Zacharie, Malachie*, 180-81.
15. Otzen, *Studien über Deuterosacharja*, 249; Wilhelm Rudolph, *Haggai-Sacharja 1-8–Sacharja 9-14–Maleachi*, KAT (Gütersloh: Verlaghaus Gerd Mohn, 1976), 195.
16. H. Kosmala, *TDOT*, 2:368, s.v. גָּבַר.

the end of this unit, with Ephraim so designated (v. 7a). Ephraim, or Israel, had previously appeared in metaphor as an arrow (9:13) projected by YHWH from Judah, the bow in YHWH's climactic victory over evil. There the victory was followed by a lavish banquet of celebration in which the rollicking merrymaking sounded as though it had been induced by wine when, in fact, the victors had figuratively eaten the flesh and drunk the blood of the vanquished (9:15). Here again Ephraim's heart will rejoice as with wine, as will that of his offspring. Together they will exult in YHWH, celebrating His glorious triumph over all opposition. The merriment associated with wine is a well-known biblical image (Ps. 104:15; Eccl. 9:7; 10:19; Isa. 5:11-12; 24:9), though, of course, literal drunkenness is universally condemned (Prov. 20:1; 21:17; 23:30; Isa. 5:22; 28:7; Hos. 4:11; Joel 1:5; Eph. 5:18; 1 Tim. 3:8).

Additional Notes

10:6 The MT וְזוֹשַׁבוֹתִים is extremely problematic (see Jansma, 86-87). The form is anomalous for any verb and probably should read וַהֲשִׁבוֹתִים, as in v. 10 and in Jer. 12:15, the hiphil pf. csc. of שׁוּב. The MT appears to base the form on יָשַׁב, "cause to settle" in the hiphil (cf. GKC, 72x). The Syriac, Tg. Neb., and Vg follow the former suggestion, and the LXX follows the latter. שׁוּב appears to make better sense here, though יָשַׁב certainly would fit (cf. Saebø, *Sacharja 9-14*, 66-67).

C. JUDAH AND THE SECOND EXODUS (10:8-12)

Translation

8I will whistle for them and gather them, for I have redeemed them; then they will multiply as they did before. 9Though I sow them among the nations, they will remember in far-off places—they and their children will come alive and return. 10I will bring them back from the land of Egypt and gather them from Assyria. I will bring them to the land of Gilead and to Lebanon, for not enough room will be found for them. 11He will cross the sea of distress and smite the turbulent sea. All the depths of the Nile will dry up, the pride of Assyria will be humbled, and the scepter of Egypt will depart. 12Thus *I will strengthen them in YHWH, and *they will walk up and down in His name, says YHWH.

Exegesis and Exposition

The Exodus of Israel from Egypt under Moses was not only the great saving event that made Israel a nation and brought her into fellowship with YHWH—it also became the paradigm of all God's redemptive work on behalf of all individuals and peoples who placed their confidence in Him. Thus, for example, the restoration of the exilic community is defined by Isaiah as a second exodus (Isa. 40:3-5; 43:1-7, 14-21; 48:20-22; 51:9-11).[17]

Haggai also spoke to the restored people in this vein, declaring that YHWH was with them just as He had been with their fathers in the day of the Exodus and wilderness (Hag. 2:4-5). Zechariah, then, shared a well-established tradition when he looked at the eschatological deliverance of Israel in terms of exodus.

Just as redemption, that is, election, theologically preceded the actual exodus escape from Egypt (Ex. 2:24; 3:7-8; 4:22-23; 6:2-8), so it is on the basis of an already effected redemption that YHWH's people will enter into the eschatological land of promise. Isaiah makes precisely the same point when he, also looking to the end of the age, proclaims that "the ransomed (פְּדוּיִם, *pĕdûyim*, the same verb as here in Zech. 10:8) of YHWH will return and come with singing to Zion" (Isa. 35:10). In words very similar to these in Zechariah, Jeremiah speaks of the ultimate gathering of Israel as follows: "He who scattered Israel will gather him and keep him as a shepherd does his flock. For YHWH has ransomed (again, פָּדָה, *pādâ*) Jacob and redeemed (גָּאַל, *gāʾal*) him from one stronger than he" (Jer. 31:10-11). Once more, it should be noted, the restoration is predicated on an already existing redemption.[18]

The process of regathering will begin when YHWH "whistles" for His people, whose ears are tuned to Him, to return (v. 8). Though there is some doubt as to whether שָׁרַק (*šāraq*) should be rendered "whistle,"[19] it clearly denotes an audible signal of some kind. Isaiah says that in the day of YHWH He will raise high a battle flag and will sound a signal for His people to return from the ends of the earth (5:26). The two acts represent both visual and audible communication. Once the people have been gathered they will multiply as they did in ancient days under Moses (Ex. 1:7, 12; Deut. 1:10). The pitiful postexilic remnant will once more become the mighty and innumerable host of God (Zech. 2:4; 8:4-5).

This restoration, says YHWH, will come to pass even though Israel, like so much seed, should be sowed among the nations (v. 9a). Seed may exist in a rather cohesive form in the bag of the farmer but when he sows it, it becomes scattered and separated, so much so that it

---

17. Bernhard W. Anderson, "Exodus Typology in Second Isaiah," in *Israel's Prophetic Heritage*, ed. Bernhard W. Anderson and Walter Harrelson (London: SCM, 1962), 177-95.
18. Merrill F. Unger, *Zechariah* (Grand Rapids: Zondervan, 1963), 182.
19. Thus, e.g., Sellin, "herbeizischen" ("to hiss"); D. Ernest Sellin, *Das Zwölfprophetenbuch* (Leipzig: A. Deichert, 1922), 506.

would be humanly impossible to gather it all together again. But the seed of Abraham is rational, sensitive seed, and once it is quickened and stimulated by the call of God, it will pick itself up from wherever it has fallen and will gather with its fellows back in the care of God who first planted it in His judgment.

It is difficult to know whether וְחָיוּ (wĕḥāyû) in v. 9b should be rendered "they will live," "they will still be alive," or "they will come alive."[20] All are possible according to the semantic range of the verb and its grammatical and syntactical usage. If the farming allegory be pressed, the last option would appear to be eliminated, whereas either of the first two could be appropriate, because technically a seed is alive when it is planted and all through its period of germination. But biblical language elsewhere views exiled and scattered Israel as dead (cf. Ezek. 37). Only divine revivification can make her God's people again and make possible her restoration to covenant service.[21]

Nowhere is this more clear than in the "valley of dead bones" vision of Ezekiel 37. The prophet saw extremely dry bones scattered everywhere and dubiously asked whether such bones could ever live again. Indeed they could, said YHWH, and commanded the man of God to prophesy over them (v. 4). Once he did, sinews, flesh, and skin began to come together and at last the spirit entered the newly formed corpses "and they lived" (וַיִּחְיוּ, wayyiḥyû; v. 10). YHWH then interpreted this remarkable phenomenon, identifying the bones as the whole house of Israel whose hope had dried up and died (v. 11). Israel was dead, then, because her hope was dead. She could be made alive by a renewal of her hope.

The apostle Paul used an agricultural analogy in a similar way to teach the truth of bodily resurrection. He told the Corinthians that a seed cannot produce a plant unless that seed first die (1 Cor. 15:36). Therefore, human death is a prerequisite to resurrection of the body (vv. 42-44). Jesus made an even bolder declaration when referring to the need for the disciple of the Lord to die to himself so that he can live for Christ and for his fellowman: "Unless a wheat grain falls into the ground and dies, it remains alone; however, if it dies it produces much harvest" (John 12:24). Neither Paul nor Jesus (nor our

---

20. These are the usual renderings of the verb in the qal. Some scholars emend וְחָיוּ to חִיּוּ (piel), "give life to," and take אֶת as *nota accusativi*; thus, "They will give life to their children and will return." So, e.g., Chary, *Aggée-Zacharie, Malachie*, 180, who translates the verb as "rear up." This is not in keeping with the total biblical idea that it is YHWH who takes the initiative in redemption and regeneration, nor can Chary's translation stand in light of the regular meanings of חָיָה. His rendition is based on the LXX ἐκθρέψουσιν. Cf. Taeke Jansma, *Inquiry into the Hebrew Text and the Ancient Versions of Zechariah IX-XIV* (Leiden: Brill, 1949), 91.
21. Unger, *Zechariah*, 183.

Zechariah passage) is offering botanical instruction. What they are saying is that from a phenomenological standpoint a seed appears to die when it is sowed. When it germinates and produces a plant, however, it appears to have come alive from the dead.

Alive once more, the people of Israel will return to the Lord and to the land (9*b*), not by unaided power, but by the supernatural hand of YHWH who will bring them (10*a*). Their point of origin, in line with the exodus motif that informs the whole pericope, will be Egypt. But that a literal repetition of the exodus event of the past is not in view is clear from the further statement that they will come also from Assyria.

Reference to Assyria here (and cf. v. 11) has caused many scholars to date this part of the oracle at least to a preexilic period when Assyria was the preeminent world power and only an Assyrian deportation had actually taken place.[22] Such a view, however, is insensitive to the particular lexicography of eschatological prophecy. The presence of Assyria here can no more assist in the date of this passage than could the list of place-names in 9:1-17 contribute to a chronological orientation of that unit. What must be done is to recognize that Egypt and Assyria here represent the universal distribution of the exiles of all ages. The combination or juxtaposition of Egypt and Assyria had become a cliché long before Zechariah's time. By far Israel's most persistent and hostile foes, these two nations epitomized bondage and exile throughout the OT tradition.[23]

A particularly instructive passage in this respect appears in Isaiah who speaks of a highway linking Egypt and Assyria in the last days (19:23). More remarkable, Egypt will worship with Assyria, and the two of them will join with Israel to create a source of blessing to the whole earth (v. 24). In that day Egypt will be called the people of YHWH, Assyria the work of His hands, and Israel His inheritance (v. 25). This obviously speaks of the universal dominion of YHWH when even Israel's erstwhile enemies will recognize and submit to His sovereignty.

Elsewhere Isaiah centers the eschatological dispersion of Israel in Egypt and Assyria, exactly as Zechariah does. At the blowing of the trumpet (cf. the "whistling," Zech. 10:8), he says, those about to perish in Assyria and the outcasts in Egypt will return to the Holy Land

---

22. Though this was generally the position of earlier critics, some today, notably B. Otzen, continue to advocate a preexilic (in Otzen's case, a Josianic) date for 10:10-11; Otzen, *Studien über Deuterosacharja*, 42-45, passim.
23. André Lacocque, *Zacharie 9-14*, CAT (Neuchatel: Delachaux & Niestlé, 1981), 168.

and worship YHWH in Jerusalem (27:13). They will travel a highway from Assyria like that one they took from Egypt, a way prepared by YHWH (11:16). As they went to Egypt and were there oppressed, so they have known the animosity of the Assyrians (52:4). Hosea prophesies that Israel will return to those places. "Ephraim," he says, "will not dwell in YHWH's land but will return to Egypt and eat unclean things in Assyria" (Hos. 9:3). But in the last days "they will come trembling like a bird out of Egypt and a dove out of the land of Assyria" (11:10).

Zechariah goes on (v. 10b) to locate Israel's destination from the future diaspora in, of all places, Gilead and Lebanon. Gilead was situated east of the upper Jordan Valley, and Lebanon was directly north and northwest of Canaan. Neither was within the confines of the promised land as laid out in eschatological texts (cf. Gen. 15:18-21; Num. 34:2-12: Ezek. 47:15-20). The clue to correct interpretation lies in v. 10b which, unfortunately, is quite elliptical. Literally, the clause in question says, "and there will not be found for them." The context, as most versions agree, requires that land be the scarce commodity. One could therefore translate "I will bring them to the land of Gilead and to Lebanon *until* no room can be found for them," or, as we have done, "for not enough room," and so forth. However, as we have shown, Gilead and Lebanon are never designated as falling within the land of promise; they must serve the function here of accommodating the overflow.[24] So full will the land of Palestine be that not all the refugees will find a place of residence there.

The Exodus under Moses was often described, particularly in poetry, in mythological terms as though the Red Sea and Pharaoh's armies were monsters over whom YHWH, the warrior, prevailed.[25] Behind this imagery it is quite likely that creation myths should be understood, though clearly the biblical authors had demythologized the pagan accounts and held fast to a creation and Exodus as events of genuine history. Their use of such imagery can be explained both as a polemical device by which YHWH, not the heroes of the myths, is truly creator and conqueror, and as a literary vehicle that more

---

24. So Joyce G. Baldwin, *Haggai, Zechariah, Malachi* (London: Tyndale, 1972), 176.
25. For important studies, see F. M. Cross, *Canaanite Myth and Hebrew Epic* (Cambridge, Mass.: Harvard Univ., 1973), 121-44; P. D. Miller, Jr., *The Divine Warrior in Early Israel* (Cambridge, Mass.: Harvard Univ., 1973), 113-17; David Noel Freedman, *Pottery, Poetry, and Prophecy* (Winona Lake, Ind.: Eisenbrauns, 1980), 179-86; Millard C. Lind, *Yahweh Is a Warrior* (Scottdale, Pa.: Herald, 1980), 46-60.

graphically could narrate the profound theology of YHWH in conflict with evil.[26]

Following the prose narrative of the Exodus story (Ex. 14:21-31) is a poetic account (Ex. 15:1-18) in which YHWH, "the man of war" (v. 3), casts Pharaoh and his armies into the depths of the sea (v. 4). By the blast of His nostrils the waters piled up, and the floods stood at attention (v. 8). Earth, at YHWH's command, swallowed up the pursuing Egyptians (v. 12). When all was finished YHWH, as a sign of His conquest, established His palace from which He will reign forever (vv. 17-18).

Isaiah especially takes up this literary use of myth. He identifies Egypt as Rahab, a name unknown outside the Bible but symbolizing evil resistance to YHWH's purposes (30:7; cf. Job 9:13; 28:12; Ps. 89:10 [HB 89:11]). Then, in a lament passage of extraordinary impact because of its mythic allusions (51:9-11),[27] he urges YHWH to awaken and arouse Himself for battle as He did in ancient times. It is YHWH, he says, who cut Rahab to pieces, piercing the monster. It is He, moreover, who dried up the sea (cf. Ex. 14:22, 29; Zech. 10:11), the waters of the deep (תְּהוֹם, *tĕhôm*; cf. Gen. 1:2; Ex. 15:5, 8; Isa. 63:13), so that His redeemed ones could pass over.

Zechariah describes the passage as one through the "sea of distress" (v. 11), a metonymy meaning the sea, the crossing of which produces a feeling of distress, a most understandable reaction. Efforts to emend the MT בַּיָּם צָרָה (*bayyām ṣārâ*), "through the sea, distress," to בְּיַם מִצְרַיִם (*bĕyam miṣrayim*), "through the sea of Egypt (BHS),"[28] not only have no textual warrant but seem totally unnecessary. In fact, "sea of Egypt" is never used elsewhere to describe the Red Sea.

As YHWH passes through the sea, He stretches out His arm and

---

26. See Peter C. Craigie, "The Poetry of Ugarit and Israel," *Tyn Bul* 22 (1971): 19-26, 28-31; Craigie, "Deborah and Anat: A Study of Poetic Imagery," *ZAW* 19 (1978): 381.

27. Roy F. Melugin, *The Formation of Isaiah 40-55* (Berlin: Walter de Gruyter, 1976), 160; James D. Smart, *History and Theology in Second Isaiah* (London: Epworth, 1965), 182-83.

28. Thus, e.g., K. Elliger, *Die Propheten Nahum, Habakuk, Zephanja, Haggai, Sacharja, Maleachi*, ATD (Göttingen: Vandenhoeck & Ruprecht, 1982), 155, 157; F. J. Botha, "Zechariah X. 11a," *ExpTim* 66 (1955): 177, suggests בְּיוֹם, "in a day (of affliction)." He takes the *daghesh forte* of the MT to reflect an original *waw*. When the copyist read *yodh* instead, he inserted the *daghesh* to indicate doubling. This is attractive in that "sea of affliction" occurs nowhere else, whereas "day of affliction" does (Ps. 20:2 [EB 20:1]; 50:15; Prov. 24:10; 25:19; Jer. 16:19; Obad. 12, 14; Nah. 1:7). However, "sea of affliction" makes sense here and requires no emendation. For other objections, see D. Winton Thomas, "Zechariah x.11a," *ExpTim* 66 (1955): 272-73.

smashes its waves as a warrior smites the heads of his enemies or as Marduk or Baal smote Ti"'amat and Yamm respectively.[29] Isaiah again is helpful (Isa. 27:1) as he speaks of YHWH's eschatological victory against the monster Leviathan, another denizen of the deep. YHWH will visit him with the sword and will slay Tannin who inhabits the sea. This calls to mind Psalm 74:12-14[30] where the poet celebrates God's kingship by reflecting on His division of Yamm (the sea) and the breaking of the heads of Tannin and Leviathan. Yamm was a persistent foe of Baal in the Ugaritic epics, one who finally was overcome by him. Leviathan reflects another ancient Canaanite monster of the epics, Lotan, whereas Tannin, as well as being attested at Ugarit, appears to be an inner-biblical epithet describing a dragon (Jer. 51:34) or sea monster (Gen. 1:21), perhaps, in light of Isa. 51:9, another term for Rahab. Jeremiah compares Nebuchadnezzar to Tannin, a monster who has swallowed up Zion (51:34). Because of this cruelty, Babylonia's sea and source of water will be dried up (v. 36). The collocation of Tannin and sea (*yam*) in this passage is certainly in line with Zechariah's observation that, after YHWH has smitten the turbulent sea, He will dry up the depths of the Nile. The death of the sea is followed by its disappearance, its drying up.

Nile here is not another name for the Red Sea, obviously, but as the chiasm makes clear is a name for Egypt. Thus the Nile (= Egypt) dries up, Assyria's pride is humbled, and Egypt loses its scepter. Verse 11 as a whole should therefore be analyzed formally as a synonymously parallel bicolon followed by a synonymously parallel tricolon in chiastic order:[31]

He will cross the sea of distress,
And (he will) smite the sea of turbulence.

All the depths of the Nile will dry up (A),
(All) the pride of Assyria will be humbled (B),
The scepter of Egypt will depart (A').

This last line puts beyond any question the termination of Egypt's (and Assyria's) royal authority. YHWH, having defeated both mighty

---

29. See respectively, James B. Pritchard, ed. *Ancient Near Eastern Texts Relating to the Old Testament* (Princeton, N.J.: Princeton Univ., 1955), 67, 131.
30. Mitchell Dahood, *Psalms 51-100*, AB (Garden City, N.Y.: Doubleday, 1968), 205-6.
31. Though Lamarche does not suggest this chiasm in v. 11, he does note one in vv. 10-11, namely, Egypt, Assyria . . . Assyria, Egypt. The Nile could, therefore, be the centerpoint of this structure, and for this reason becomes a synonym for Egypt, thus avoiding repetition of the name Egypt itself (P. Lamarche, *Zacharie IX-XIV. Structure Littéraire et Messianisme* [Paris: Librairie Lecoffre, 1961], 60, 62-63).

powers, representative of all earthly dominion, will then take up His own sovereignty.

The exercise of that sovereignty will be through God's redeemed people whom, YHWH says, He will strengthen for the task. The verb here, the same as in v. 6, is גָּבַר (*gābar*, "strengthen"), a word whose field of meaning is associative of military prowess. The world has become, as it were, occupied territory and until evil has been completely eradicated, it must be suppressed by force. The last clause of v. 12 is most conducive to this whole notion of dominion, for God's people, says YHWH, "will walk up and down in His name."

The hithpael stem of the verb "walk" (הִתְהַלֵּךְ, *hithallēk*), as was pointed out in reference to Zech. 1:10-11, has become a technical term to denote dominion. To walk up and down or to and fro on the earth is to assert lordship over it. The planting of the feet presumably represents the head of the victor on the back of the vanquished. This is a favorite term of Zechariah, for of about a dozen uses of the verb with this meaning, six are in this prophecy (1:10, 11; 6:7 [3t.]; 10:12). This is much in keeping with the emphasis throughout the book on the ultimate triumph of YHWH and His restored people. His feet will someday stand on the Mount of Olives (14:4), testifying that He has come to inaugurate that rule.

Additional Notes

10:12 Because it appears awkward for YHWH to say "I will strengthen them in YHWH," BHK and BHS suggest emending גִּבַּרְתִּים ("I will strengthen them") to גְּבֻרְתָם ("their strength [will be in YHWH])." This is unsupported in the ancient versions and is an unnecessary resort, as our discussion of a similar case in Zech. 2:11 makes clear.

The LXX, followed by the Syriac, suggests יִתְהַלָּלוּ ("they will glory in [his name]") for יִתְהַלָּכוּ ("they will walk about"). This is a needless (and probably baseless) option because "walking to and fro" or the like is a common idiom in Zechariah to express dominion, and the entire pericope that this concludes has to do with YHWH's establishment of His reign. To walk "in His name" is simply to do so in His authority. For versional variations, see Jansma, *Inquiry into the Hebrew Text and the Ancient Versions of Zechariah IX-XIV*, 92.

3
History and Future of Judah's Wicked Kings (11:1-17)

This final section of the long oracle concerning the nations begins, as did the previous section (10:1-3a), with a scalding denunciation of the spiritual and political leaders of Israel in the past. As in the previous unit, YHWH describes these rulers as shepherds (11:4-17).[1] There are otherwise great contrasts between the two passages, for in the former one the resolution of the problem of evil shepherds is the raising up of a good one who will lead his people to triumph over their enemies (vv. 3b-7), having brought them back to their land from the ends of the earth (vv. 8-12). The present unit, however, views the prophet himself as a good shepherd, one who enacts God's role in response to the people's rejection of divine leadership despite the care and love He had lavished upon them (vv. 4-14). As a result of the spurning of the good shepherd, an evil, uncaring one will rise up. He, too, will ultimately be judged and punished for his abandonment of the flock (vv. 15-17).

Chapter 11 is clearly one of the most difficult in all the book. The protagonists are not always easily identified, the role of the prophet *vis à vis* YHWH and the people is confusing, and the whole temporal orientation uncertain. Some clue as to the latter may exist in v. 8—"I

---

1. For a survey of views that take Zech. 11:4-17 as an allegory of the good and bad shepherd, see A. S. van der Woude, "Die Hirtenallegorie von Sacharja XI," *JNSL* 12 (1984): 139-49.

cut off three shepherds in one month"—but whether one should seek a historical, an allegorical, or even just a symbolical meaning here is itself debatable. As always, it is crucial that the passage not be studied independent of its immediate and larger context, for whether or not it circulated in that form at one time, it is now solidly enmeshed within a canonical setting and must be understood in those terms. Allusions within the passage to imagery and symbolism employed elsewhere should and can contribute to the meaning of the overall piece.

A. SUMMATION OF THEIR JUDGMENT (11:1-3)

Translation

¹**Open your gates, Lebanon,**
   So that the fire may devour your cedars.
²**Howl, fir tree,**
   Because the cedar has fallen, the majestic ones have been
   destroyed.
 Howl, oaks of Bashan,
   Because the inaccessible forest has fallen.
³**Listen to the howling of shepherds,**
   Because their magnificence has been destroyed;
 Listen to the roaring of young lions,
   Because the pride of the Jordan has been devastated.

Exegesis and Exposition

The unit opens with a poem consisting of a stanza of a 2:3 pattern and one that is 2:2:2.[2] The two strophes themselves are linked by the repetition of "howl" (יְלֵל, *yālal*) at the beginning of the last line of the first stanza and the first line of the second stanza. It is obvious immediately that the poem is filled with symbolism, for Lebanon, the fir tree, and the oaks of Bashan are all addressed by the speaker who clearly is YHWH as the opening of the next section (v. 4) declares. What is not so obvious within the poem itself is the meaning of these symbols as well as the cedars, the forest, the young rams, and the "pride of the Jordan."

---

2. P. Lamarche, *Zacharie IX-XIV. Structure Littéraire et Messianisme* (Paris: Librairie Lecoffre, 1961), 63. For a different approach leading to similar results, see Paul Hanson, *The Dawn of Apocalyptic* (Philadelphia: Fortress, 1975), 335. Hanson, in addition to determining structure and meter, advances the following scheme of prosodic units:
   v. 1   1:1
   v. 2   1:1::1:1
   v. 3   1:1::1:1
This is in line with my own analysis.

Attention to the following verses makes it rather apparent that the objects mentioned under the guise of trees and animals are the same as the shepherds.[3] As already noted "shepherd" is a common way of referring to kings in the ancient Near East and the OT, an epithet particularly favored by Zechariah (10:2, 3; 11:3, 5, 8, 15, 16, 17; 13:7). The lament of the poem, then, introduces the occasion for the lament, namely, the destruction of the evil shepherds (11:8, 17).

Perhaps next in prominence to shepherd as metaphor for king is that of a plant, especially a tree.[4] One thinks of the parable of Jotham, a son of Gideon who tried to warn his countrymen of the danger in allowing his brother Abimelech to become king over them after Gideon's death (Judg. 9:7-15). He said that the trees sought one who could lead them, and they first asked the olive tree to do so. He refused, so the trees next asked the fig tree, who also declined. The vine similarly refused the invitation, but at length the bramble agreed to serve if they would meet his harsh terms. To Jotham, Abimelech was the bramble.

Isaiah, referring to YHWH's judgment on the Assyrians, declared that he would prune off the boughs, hew down the high tree, cut down the thickets, and fell mighty Lebanon (10:33-34), all alluding to the king.[5] Ezekiel, in a lengthy passage (31:3-18),[6] calls the Assyrian (any one of a number of Assyrian rulers) "a cedar of Lebanon" (v. 3). It became so lofty and strong that all the birds of the sky made their nest in its branches (v. 6). Even the cedars of the "garden of God" were no match for it (v. 8). Its pride, however, brought it low, for YHWH delivered it over to one who cut it down (v. 12). Thus will Pharaoh, who also is a great tree (v. 18), come crashing to the ground.

Nebuchadnezzar saw himself in a dream as a tree whose top reached into the heavens (Dan. 4:10). It was large and beautiful, but it was cut down leaving only a stump in the earth. So Nebuchadnezzar, Daniel interpreted, would be cut down but not entirely destroyed, for the "stump" of his reign would be left from which new growth would eventually issue (4:23).

To return to the poem of Zechariah 11:1-3, it is evident from the poetic parallelism that Lebanon does not refer to the nation in any sense but to the source of the mighty cedar tree. Thus, Lebanon and

---

3. See Magne Saebø, *Sacharja 9-14. Untersuchungen von Text und Form* (Neukirchen-Vluyn: Neukirchener Verlag, 1969), 231-33.

4. Benedikt Otzen, *Studien über Deuterosacharja*, ATD 6 (Copenhagen: Prostant Apud Munksgaard, 1964), 163-64.

5. John N. Oswalt, *The Book of Isaiah Chapters 1-39*, NICOT (Grand Rapids: Eerdmans, 1986), 275-76; Edmond Jacob, *Esaïe 1-12*, CAT VIIIa (Genève: Labor et Fides, 1987), 157-58.

6. Walther Zimmerli, *Ezekiel 2*, Hermeneia (Philadelphia: Fortress, 1983), 145-53.

cedar tree are equivalent terms. The cedar[7] (אֶרֶז, *'erez*), celebrated for its size and shapeliness, occurs elsewhere as a metaphor for a king in addition to Judges 9, cited above (cf. 2 Kings 14:9; Isa. 14:8; Ezek. 17:3; Amos 2:9). The fir[8] (בְּרוֹשׁ, *bĕrôš*) likewise represents powerful rulers, usually but not always in parallel construction with cedar (Ezek. 31:8). The oaks[9] (אַלּוֹן, *'allôn*) of Bashan, native to the high plateaus east of the upper Jordan, were justly praised for their deep-rooted strength. Amos refers to the Amorite (no doubt King Sihon) as one who was as high as the cedar and as powerful as the oak (2:9).

The message of the first strophe (vv. 1-2) is that it is fruitless for Lebanon to resist, for the cedar (i.e., a king) is going to be devoured in God's fiery judgment. When this happens, the fir tree (another king) will burst out in lament over the demise of the cedar, "the majestic one."[10] The oaks will next commence to wail because of the falling of the forest that seemed so invulnerable. The parallelism makes it clear that "forest" (יַעַר, *ya'ar*) is synonymous with "cedar."[11] Both the fir and the oak bemoan the passing of the cedar, for it is apparent that they too stand in jeopardy. The fact that there are three trees in the couplet leads one to suspect that the three shepherds of v. 8 are relevant to the total interpretation.

The second strophe shifts the imagery from trees to shepherds but, as suggested earlier, there is a strong link between them. There is also a howling or wailing by the shepherds because their magnificence has been defaced. The word translated "magnificence" (אַדֶּרֶת, *'adderet*) occurs as a description of the cedar trees in v. 2 in the adjectival form אַדִּרִים (*'addirîm*, "majestic ones"), providing yet another bridge between the tree and the shepherd images. The poetic form also demands that "young lions" (כְּפִירִים, *kĕpîrîm*) be a synonym for shepherds or kings. Indeed, such a description of rulers occurs elsewhere (Nah. 2:12; Ezek. 19:5-6); to find it so used here is not surprising.[12] Like the trees mentioned above, once a shepherd is removed, others will roar in frustration and fear, to mingle several metaphors. Specifically, the poem informs us, the lions will roar because the "pride of the Jordan" has been devastated.

This idiom refers to the lush vegetation that once grew in the

---

7. J. C. Trever, *IDB*,1:545-46, s.v. "cedar."
8. J. C. Trever, *IDB*, 2:268, s.v. "fir."
9. J. C. Trever, *IDB*, 3:575, s.v. "oak."
10. So André Lacocque, *Zacharie 9-14*, CAT (Neuchatel: Delachaux & Niestlé, 1981), 171. He draws attention to a parallel in Ezek. 17:13.
11. H. G. Mitchell, *A Commentary on Haggai and Zechariah*, ICC (Edinburgh: T. & T. Clark, 1912), 297.
12. Theophane Chary, *Aggée-Zacharie, Malachie* (Paris: Librairie Lecoffre, 1968), 183.

Jordan Valley, so luxuriant that by contrast the flora of the remainder of the land looked scrubby. In OT times lions and other now nonextant animals found cover there.[13] Jeremiah speaks of a conquest of Edom that will be like a lion coming from the "pride of the Jordan" (Jer. 49:19; cf. 50:44). Zechariah is saying, therefore, that when the foliage of the Jordan Valley has been uprooted and destroyed, the young lions will be exposed, no longer having a place to hide. The poem then comes fully around to the felling of trees, the note on which it began.

B. THE PROPHET AS A SHEPHERD (11:4-14)

1. HIS CHARGE BECAUSE OF JUDAH'S WICKED KINGS (11:4-6)

Translation

⁴Thus said YHWH my God, "Shepherd the flock destined to slaughter. ⁵Those who buy them slaughter them and are not held guilty; those who sell them *say, 'Blessed be YHWH, for I am rich.' Their own shepherds do not have compassion for them. ⁶Indeed, I will no longer have compassion for the inhabitants of the land," says YHWH, "but instead I will turn every last man over to the power of his neighbor and to his king; they will devastate the land, and I will not deliver (it) from them."

Exegesis and Exposition

In a most unusual development YHWH addresses Zechariah and commands him to undertake a series of actions, doing so in the place of YHWH Himself. Thus the prophet is to play a role. In many respects this is not at all unique to Zechariah. Many of the other prophets did the same thing.[14] Hosea married Gomer, "a wife of harlotry," in order to dramatize the unfaithfulness of Israel to YHWH and to show that just as he could forgive his wayward wife, YHWH, too, would forgive the covenant infidelity of Israel and restore her to Himself (Hos. 1-3). Isaiah went about dressed as a prisoner of war as a sign of YHWH's judgment on Egypt and Ethiopia through Assyria (Isa. 20:2-4). Jeremiah smashed pottery vessels in the Valley of Hinnom to illustrate the smashing of Judah by the Babylonians (Jer. 19:1-15), and he wore prisoners' shackles around his neck to predict the bondage to be suffered by his nation at the hands of those same Babylo-

---

13. Nelson Glueck, *The River Jordan* (London: Lutterworth, 1946), 63, 120.
14. Robert C. Dentan, "The Book of Zechariah, Chapters 9-14," *IB*, 1102-3. For many examples, see J. Lindblom, *Prophecy in Ancient Israel* (Philadelphia: Fortress, 1965), 165-73.

nians (Jer. 27:2-11). Ezekiel, more than all other prophets, acted out before his countrymen the plans and purposes that YHWH had for them. He drew a picture of the city of Jerusalem under siege (Ezek. 4:1-3), he dug a hole through the wall of his house as a sign of the breaching of the city walls and the need for escape (12:1-16), and he cut and scattered his hair to demonstrate the forms that the impending destruction and scattering of God's people would take (5:1-12).

There is no reason to deny that most if not all of these dramatizations actually occurred. This can hardly be the case with Zechariah's commission, however, as vv. 7-14 will make clear. The things he is said to have done there simply could not have been done by his own hand.[15] It is most likely that he did them internally, in his own mind, and that he then communicated to his hearers what he had done.[16] Actually what he said he did is what YHWH had done in the past, before the Exile.[17] Zechariah enters into the experience of YHWH and shares the emotion and heart of YHWH, so that man, as much as possible, might understand what motivated Him to act as He did in judgment.

Zechariah's commission, first of all, is to shepherd the flock of slaughter (v. 4). The phrase "flock of slaughter" is the literal rendering of a Hebrew genitive that means "flock destined to slaughter," or the like.[18] The reason this is necessary is that the flock has been bought and sold by strangers and left unattended or unprotected by their own shepherds. Those who buy (or bought, in light of the true historical setting in the past)[19] then slaughter them with impunity, and those who sell them profit from their sale and have the gall to attribute their successful profiteering to YHWH.

The buyers and sellers appear to be foreign kings as their opposition to the flock's "(own) shepherds" suggests.[20] It is impossible and

15. Lester V. Meyer, "An Allegory Concerning the Monarchy: Zech. 11:4-7; 13:7-9," in *Scripture in History and Theology*, ed. A. L. Merrill and T. W. Overholt (Pittsburgh: Pickwick, 1977), 226.
16. For this reason, as noted above, most scholars describe vv. 4-17 as an allegory. See Joyce G. Baldwin, *Haggai, Zechariah, Malachi* (London: Tyndale, 1972), 179.
17. Meyer, "An Allegory Concerning the Monarchy: Zech. 11:4-17; 13:7-9," 232-33.
18. Feigin makes the point that "flock of slaughter" is a technical term used to refer to flocks sold in a profane manner for the meat market. They could therefore be slaughtered for that purpose with impunity (Samuel Feigin, "Some Notes on Zechariah 11 4-17," *JBL* 44 [1925]: 204).
19. That vv. 4-6 speak of a fait accompli, a current situation brought about by past failures, is implied by Paul Hanson, *The Dawn of Apocalyptic*, 342-43, 346. Furthermore, since the epithet "shepherd" invariably refers to kings in the OT, except for the messianic ruler to come, its use here must pertain to the period of the monarchy, that is, the preexilic era.
20. Denton, "The Book of Zechariah," 1103.

unnecessary to try to identify them, for they can be any of a number of such rulers and nations that exploited Israel over the years. The language is figurative, describing the various episodes in history when the nation suffered defeat and loss and when she became a bargaining chip among the great nations who squabbled over her. The very language of merchandising is used commonly in the book of Judges to refer to YHWH's deliverance of Israel to hostile powers. Over and over the narrative says He "sold" (מָכַר, *mākar*, as here in Zech. 11:5) them to different foes (2:14; 3:8; 4:2, 9; 10:7). Though Zechariah is not attributing the selling to YHWH, the same notion of Israel being sold is nonetheless in view in the Judges passages and elsewhere (1 Sam. 12:9; Ps. 44:12 [HB 44:13]; Isa. 50:1; Joel 3:7-8 [HB 4:7-8]).

Worse than the treatment Israel received from the Egyptians, Amalekites, Edomites, Amorites, Philistines, Assyrians, Babylonians, and others was the neglect of her own kings. Far from defending the nation from the maraudings of these hostile powers, the kings of Israel and Judah turned a deaf ear and showed no compassion. But YHWH goes on to say that even He withdrew His compassion (v. 6).[21] The particle כִּי (*kî*) that introduces v. 6 is usually taken as an adverbial conjunction ("therefore," "so," and the like). The context would favor the so-called asserverative, however, thus something like "indeed" (GKC, 160ee). This provides a climax to the story of Israel's woes, for not only had her enemies bought and sold her and her shepherd-kings neglected her, but YHWH Himself had run out of patience. This may seem to be an incredibly harsh statement, one inconsistent with YHWH's covenant love for His people, but similar language occurs elsewhere. Jeremiah, using the same verb for compassion as does Zechariah (חָמַל, *ḥāmal*), records YHWH's displeasure with Judah by saying, "I will not pity (חָמַל) nor spare nor have compassion (רָחַם, *rāḥam*, a synonym of חָמַל), in order that I might destroy them" (Jer. 13:14). He expresses the same sentiment in Lam. 2:2, 17, and 21. Ezekiel prophesies that YHWH will destroy Jerusalem with no pity (חָמַל) (5:11; 7:4, 9; 8:18). A precedent for YHWH's compassionless discipline of His people is not difficult to come by.

The fact that YHWH completes the chastisement begun by foreign oppressors and even by Israel's own kings does not exonerate those oppressors from responsibility for their evil ways. YHWH acts out of a spirit of correction, but they out of one of spiteful selfishness and depravity. Therefore, He can condemn the foreign oppressors for

---

21. My rendering of the action as past is in line with the view, expressed already, that vv. 4-6 reflect a résumé of God's dealings with His people in preexilic times, a history about to be enacted by Zechariah himself (vv. 7-14).

their hostility toward His people, even though He may have allowed them, as part of a greater purpose, to undertake their pernicious ways.

The judgment announced here by YHWH, whether effected by wicked men or by Himself directly, consists of a wholesale subjugation of the covenant people to neighboring powers and their kings. They devastated the land, and YHWH did nothing to interfere. This seems to be the preferred interpretation of the difficult clause rendered literally, "I am causing each man to be found by the hand of his neighbor and by the hand of his king" (v. 6*b*).[22] "Hand," of course, symbolizes power, so what happened is that everyone in the land came under the power of their neighbor and "his king." "Neighbor" (רֵעַ, *rēaʿ*) frequently occurs in a reciprocal relationship with "man" (אִישׁ, *ʾîš*) to mean "one another," but that does not seem to fit well here. First, the singular suffix on "king" would have an unclear antecedent in "one another," but an obvious one in "neighbor." Second, the plural subject of "devastate" makes much more sense with reference to "neighbor" (viewed collectively) than with the idea that the people of Israel are devastating their own land. Verse 5 has already intimated that destruction came from without, from the nations neighboring Israel. Third, if the devastators are the "one another" of Israel, in what sense would YHWH say He will not deliver the land from them, if, indeed, "land" is to be supplied in our translation at all? If it is "them" that should be supplied, as most versions suggest, then the problem is exacerbated, for the people of Israel would have to be delivered from themselves, a strange idea, indeed.

The major objection to our translation "neighbor" is that *rēaʿ* seldom has that meaning concerning an outsider.[23] Usually it refers to a fellow-citizen or a friend or acquaintance. One might expect גֵּר (*gēr*, "sojourner") or נָכְרִי (*nokrî*, "alien") instead. One clear example of *rēaʿ* with the meaning "neighbor" is attested in Prov. 6:1 where it occurs in parallelism with זָר (*zār*, "stranger"). Others are Ex. 11:2; 1 Sam. 28:17. So few examples may seem to be weak evidence on which to build a case, but it at least raises the possibility. Another suggestion is that רֵעֵהוּ (*rēʿēhû*, "his neighbor") be repointed to רֹעֵהוּ (*rōʿēhû*, "his shepherd").[24] The sentence then would read, "I will turn every last man over to the power of his shepherd, namely, his king; they will devastate the land," etc. In addition to the strong Masoretic tradi-

---

22. Unger, though being overly precise in my opinion, correctly identifies "neighbor" as an outside power (to him Babylon) (Merrill F. Unger, *Zechariah* [Grand Rapids: Zondervan, 1963], 193).

23. J. Kühlewein, *TWAT* 2; cols. 786-91, s.v. רֵעַ.

24. Thus BHS. Cf., e.g., Friedrich Horst, *Die Zwölf kleinen Propheten. Nahum bis Maleachi*, HAT 14 (Tübingen: J. C. B. Mohr, 1964), 252.

tion,[25] however, there is the problem of the plural subject with "devastate" if "shepherd" is the antecedent.

On balance, it appears best to understand this passage (v. 6) to mean that YHWH will withhold His compassion for His people Israel, delivering them instead to neighboring peoples and their kings who will beat down the land of Israel with no interference from YHWH. This, of course, is precisely what took place in the last decades of Israel's and Judah's history leading up to their respective captivities by the Assyrians and Babylonians, and on into the future as well.

Additional Notes

11:5 The verb "say" is actually singular here, "says" (יֹאמַר). As Barker points out, this (and יַחְמוֹל, "spare," in v. 5) "general plural" is used to suggest an individualizing or distribution over every individual (K. Barker, "Zechariah," in *EBC*, 7:678).

2. HIS ENACTMENT OF YHWH's REJECTION OF THE WICKED KINGS (11:7-11)

Translation

7So I shepherded the flock destined for slaughter, *therefore the most afflicted of the flock; then I took two staffs, calling one "pleasantness" and the other "binders," and I shepherded the flock. 8Next I eradicated the three shepherds in one month, for I ran out of patience with them and, indeed, they loathed me as well. 9I then said, "I will not shepherd you; that which dies, let it die, and that which is to be eradicated, let it be eradicated. As for those who survive, let them eat each other's flesh." 10Then I took my staff "pleasantness" and cut it in two to annul *my covenant that I had made with all the peoples. 11So it was annulled that very day, and thus the most afflicted of the flock who kept (trust) with me knew that that was the word of YHWH.

Exegesis and Exposition

Responding to the commission YHWH had given him, Zechariah says he shepherded the flock destined for slaughter, the very ones who had been bought and sold by the nations, left defenseless and unpitied by their own kings, and even delivered over by YHWH to those who did them harm (vv. 4-6). This torn and tattered remnant he describes as "the most afflicted of the flock" (עֲנִיֵּי הַצֹּאן, *'ăniyyê hāṣ-*

---

25. In fact, there is no variation suggested in any of the ancient versions. See Taeke Jansma, *Inquiry into the Hebrew Text and the Ancient Versions of Zechariah IX-XIV* (Leiden: Brill, 1949), 98-100.

ṣō'n)[26] both because they had been destined for slaughter and because they had suffered so terribly at the hands of their persecutors.

In line with my argument above, I believe here as well that Zechariah shepherds the flock only as he enters YHWH's own experience in preexilic historical times. That is, Zechariah is reliving YHWH's dealings with His people in allegory (if only in his own mind) and is reporting in a fresh way what Israel's history was really all about. Israel had so grievously sinned against her God that there was only a pitiful little flock left of those who kept covenant with Him, and that little flock itself was victimized by oppressors both without and within the nation. They were even caught up in the judgment that YHWH brought upon the nation as a whole. All of this is documented in the history of the nation in preexilic times, and by the time the Assyrian and Babylonian deportations had come about there was nothing left but the most afflicted of all, a point that Jeremiah, particularly, makes time and again (40:11-15; 42:1-6; 44:11-14). It was only by God's grace that these survived at all, for He preserved a remnant in line with His immutable covenant commitment (Lev. 26:40-45; Deut. 30:1-10).

Zechariah says he shepherded the flock that, because it was destined for slaughter, was the most afflicted of the flock (v. 7). In this way he distinguishes between Israel as a whole and the oppressed remnant within Israel that had maintained its covenant faith. An indispensable instrument in shepherding was the shepherd's staff, so Zechariah says he took two of them, one named "pleasantness" and the other "binders." With these, he says, he shepherded the flock (v. 7). The former name speaks of the relationship between YHWH and His people (v. 10) and the latter of that between Israel and Judah (v. 14).

This use of staffs or wooden poles to represent people or signify relationships was not new to Zechariah. When Aaron's authority as priest was challenged, Moses ordered that his name be engraved on a staff representing the tribe of Levi and that the leaders of the other tribes do likewise on their respective staffs (Num. 17:1-11). Through a test of their ability to sprout growth Aaron was vindicated.

Closer to Zechariah's experience was that of Ezekiel who also took two wooden poles, one standing for Judah and the other for Israel (Ezek. 37:15-23). Ezekiel took the two poles and joined them together as one signifying that in the time of eschatological restoration there

---

26. Though most scholars, with the LXX, read לִכְנַעֲנֵיֵ ("to the Canaanites of") for לָכֵן עֲנִיֵּי ("therefore, the poor of"), this is unnecessary and probably incorrect. P. R. Davies shows that the same phrase as in the MT occurs in the Damascus Document to describe the faithful remnant of the community that produced this important postbiblical text (P. R. Davies, *The Damascus Document* [Sheffield: JSOT, 1982], 150-51).

will no longer be division between Israel and Judah, for they will be one people with one king and one God. In a sense what Ezekiel did in his dramatization was to effect a reversal of what Zechariah is about to do.

First, however, Zechariah says he "eradicated" (כָּחַד, *kāḥad*) the three shepherds in one month because he had lost patience with them and they loathed him (v. 8). This removes any doubt as to whether Zechariah was doing anything more than carrying out a demonstration for all to see. Clearly he was reliving YHWH's own experience in Israel's history by symbolically ridding the land of three kings. This approach to the matter precludes the diversity of opinions characteristic of many who view this passage as strictly prophetic. It is not necessary (or valid) to look for a time when three Ptolemies or Seleucidae or Romans lost their lives in one month,[27] for YHWH here is rehearsing the past as the pericope as a whole makes clear.

This does not solve all the problems, of course, for one must now look for three kings of Israel and/or Judah who perished in one month or at least were dethroned in that period of time. One thinks, for example, of Elah, Zimri, Tibni, and Omri of Israel (1 Kings 16:8-20). Elah was assassinated by Zimri who occupied the throne for only seven days when he committed suicide. Tibni succeeded him, with some following at least, but was soon disposed of by Omri. Thus three kings (or pretenders) died within one month. It is difficult to see what significance this series of events has to Zechariah's message and times, however.

Another possibility is the era of Zechariah, Shallum, and Menahem,[28] particularly striking in that Shallum is credited with a reign of one month (2 Kings 15:8-16). Shallum assassinated Zechariah, reigned one month, and then fell in death to Menahem. The problem with this identification is obvious. Only two kings are cut off, not three, and again the relevance of the episode to the prophet Zechariah is not easy to establish.

The best solution may be to take the period "one month" as a code word for a short time.[29] If this is allowed, then the relatively rapid succession of kings at the end of Judah's preexilic history may be in view.[30] Jehoiakim died in 597 B.C., his son Jehoiachin was deported

---

27. For a host of opinions, see Theophane Chary, *Aggée-Zacharie, Malachie* (Paris: Librairie Lecoffre, 1969), 181-83.
28. Maurer, Hitzig, and Ewald, cited by Mitchell, *A Commentary on Haggai and Zechariah*, 307.
29. Thus Lacocque, *Zacharie IX-XIV*, 177, who cites Hos. 5:7 as comparable.
30. A. Van Hoonacker, *Les Douze Petits Prophètes* (Paris: Librairie Victor Lecoffre, 1908), 675.

three months later, and his brother Zedekiah was captured and blinded eleven years after that (2 Kings 24:1–25:7). Although eleven years is not one month, it is a brief period of time compared to Israel's long history and, from Zechariah's viewpoint, may have appeared to be a short time indeed. What favors this view, despite its problems, is that the end of the kingdom of Judah did indeed mark the end of YHWH's patience, and it is clear also that these last three kings despised YHWH and spurned His overtures toward them (v. 8; cf. 2 Kings 23:37; 24:9, 19-20).

Once the shepherds had been eradicated, YHWH (through Zechariah) turned to another audience and said He would no longer shepherd them, and whatever among them was destined to die of itself or be eradicated, let it go ahead and do so. The survivors of all these, He said, could resort to cannibalism (v. 9).[31] The audience in question is somewhat problematic. It cannot be the just-mentioned shepherds because of the use of the feminine gender of the pronouns and verbs in v. 9. What is probably in view is the people in general ("I will not shepherd you" [masc.]) and the sheep "destined for slaughter" (v. 4) whose owners "slaughter them" (fem.) and whose sellers, having "sold them" (fem.) say, Blessed be YHWH (v. 5).[32]

It is these most afflicted ones, on whom YHWH Himself had said He would no longer have compassion (v. 6), who will die, be eradicated, and resort to cannibalism (v. 9). This last gruesome judgment, particularly, was predicted by Jeremiah as he anticipated the siege and fall of Jerusalem (19:9). He then reflected on its fulfillment in the Lamentations. "Shall women eat their fruit?" he asks (Lam. 2:20), and then answers his own question: "The hands of the pitiful women have boiled their own children, they were their food in the destruction of the daughter of my people" (Lam. 4:10). This again appears to support the conclusion that the three stricken shepherds of v. 8 are the last three kings of Judah who saw with their own eyes these horrible things that came upon their people.

To dramatize the fact that the fall of Jerusalem and exile of Judah

---

31. These survivors are called הַנִּשְׁאָרוֹת, the fem. plur. niphal ptc. of the verb שָׁאַר from which שְׁאֵרִית, "remnant," derives. Thus it is likely that remnant theology is in view, as was suggested in vv. 4, 7. Cf. 2 Chron. 34:21; Isa. 4:3; H. Wildberger, *TWAT* 2:854, s.v. שׁאר. For cannibalism as treaty curse, see Delbert R. Hillers, *Treaty-Curses and the Old Testament Prophets* (Rome: Pontifical Biblical Institute, 1964), 62-63.

32. The word for flock, צֹאן, is feminine and is the antecedent to the pronoun "them" in the last two references. The masculine cannot, therefore, refer to the flock, so perhaps implies some masculine subject such as עַם, "people." This appears to be borne out by the breaking of the covenant with the "peoples" of v. 10.

was tantamount to the breaking of YHWH's covenant, Zechariah took the staff named "pleasantness" and broke it in two (v. 10). This, he says, was to mark the rupture of the relationship between YHWH and "all the peoples." Ordinarily this phrase (כָּל־הָעַמִּים, kol-hā'ammîm) refers to the pagan nations, but here it must refer to the chosen people in their divided entities of Israel and Judah.[33] That this is likely is apparent from the context where a divided (v. 14) and scattered (vv. 5-6) people seem very much in mind. Moreover, the notion of a covenant with all the nations is otherwise unattested in the OT. The closest to such an idea is Isa. 42:6 (cf. 49:8) where YHWH says of His servant that He will make him to be a "covenant of the people" (עָם, 'ām), a "light of the nations" (גּוֹיִם, gôyim). This is not to say, however, that YHWH has made a covenant with the nations, in the sense of a formal treaty document, but that the Servant will be the very essence of the relationship brought by such a covenant.[34] He will *be* the covenant. This, of course, was brought to pass in the atoning death and reconciling resurrection of Jesus Christ (Heb. 12:24; cf. Matt. 26:28; 1 Cor. 11:25).

For YHWH to break His covenant with His people is not to suggest an irreparable breach, for the OT witness pervasively attests to the inviolability of that fundamental relationship (Ps. 89:34 [HB 89:35]; Isa. 54:9-10; Jer. 31:35-37; 33:19-26). What is meant is that the benefits of that covenant—in this case, the benefit of protection from conquest and deportation—have been withheld. In that sense, YHWH has exercised His right as Suzerain to bring to bear the curses of the covenant upon His disobedient vassal Israel, something He had threatened to do at the onset of the covenant arrangement (Lev. 26:14-33; Deut. 28:15-68).[35] He broke His covenant by allowing His people to break it and thus to invite the suspension of its privileges.

When it came to pass, "the afflicted of the flock," that is, "the flock destined to slaughter" (vv. 4, 7) who "kept trust with" YHWH, knew

---

33. So Otzen, *Studien über Deuterosacharja*, 154; cf. Van Hoonacker, *Les Douze Petits Prophètes*, 672. Baldwin takes the expression to mean the Jewish colonies scattered among the nations as in 1 Kings 22:28 and Joel 2:6 (Baldwin, *Haggai, Zechariah, Malachi*, 184). Caquot, however, understands it to refer to the nations of Solomon's time whom God had raised up to chastise Solomon (1 Kings 11:14-25), in this sense having made a covenant with them (A. Caquot, "Breves Remarques sur L'Allegorie des Pasteurs en Zacharie ll," in *Mélanges Bibliques et Orientaux*, ed. A. Caquot, S. Legasse, et M. Tardieu [Neukirchen-Vluyn: Kevelaer, 1985], 52-53).
34. E. J. Young, *The Book of Isaiah* (Grand Rapids: Eerdmans, 1972), 3:119-21.
35. For the breaking of a scepter to symbolize treaty curse in the ancient Near East, see D. Hillers, *Treaty-Curses and the Old Testament Prophets*, 61. Hillers cites parallels in the Code of Hammurabi rev. xxvi 45-51 and in Ugaritic in *UT* 127, 17-18; 49 vi 28-29.

that what had come to pass was according to the Word of YHWH that He had proclaimed through His prophets from the beginning (cf. Lev. 26 and Deut. 28). Those who "kept trust" were clearly those who had maintained their covenant faith, for the verb translated here "kept trust" is שָׁמַר (*šāmar*), a verb much at home in covenant technical language (Ex. 19:5; 20:6; Lev. 18:4; 26:3; Deut. 4:2, 40; 5:10; 6:2, 17; 11:1, 8; Josh. 23:6; Ps. 89:31 [HB 89:32]; Ezek. 11:20; 17:14; Amos 2:4).[36] It was only those who had eyes to see and ears to hear who could interpret the catastrophic events of the overthrow of Jerusalem and the Temple as the fulfillment of the prophetic word. And yet even they who were obedient to the end could not escape the judgment occasioned by the apostate flock of YHWH and its evil shepherd-kings (vv. 6, 9).

Additional Notes

11:7 For לָכֵן עֲנִיֵּי, the LXX reads לִכְנַעֲנֵיֵי, "to the merchants of" (the flock), a reading repeated in v. 11. The line would thus be rendered, "So I shepherded the flock destined to be slaughtered for the sheep merchants." This helps to resolve the difficult לָכֵן with its peculiar following subordination, but it is not necessary to good sense and appears to have been an attempt by the LXX to introduce clarity. See the commentary.

11:10 The omission of the pronominal suffix on בְּרִית in the Syr. and Tg. Neb. is clearly to remove Zechariah as the agent of covenant. This also explains the change from "that I had made" to "that he had made," the latter referring to YHWH. However, when it is understood that Zechariah is not only enacting the role of YHWH in the breaking of the covenant but is representing YHWH, "my covenant" is as much suitable to the prophet as to YHWH.

3. HIS FEE FOR SERVING AS THE SHEPHERD (11:12-14)

Translation

¹²Then I said to them, "If it seems good to you, give me my wage, but if not, refrain from it"; so they weighed out my wage—thirty pieces of silver. ¹³YHWH thus said to me, "Throw to the potter that exorbitant price at which I am appraised by them." So I took the thirty pieces of silver and threw them to the potter at the house of YHWH. ¹⁴Then I cut the second staff in two, that is, "binders," in order to annul the (covenant of) brotherhood between Judah and Israel.

---

36. Paul Kalluveettil, *Declaration and Covenant*, AnBib 88 (Rome: Biblical Institute, 1982), 48, 126.

Exegesis and Exposition

Zechariah, standing in for YHWH, had, contrary to the evil shepherds, been a good shepherd to the flock of Israel and Judah. He had shepherded the flock "destined for slaughter" (v. 7) when their own shepherd-kings had shown them no compassion (v. 5) and, worse still, had shown him nothing but contempt (v. 8). For this service Zechariah inquired about wages. What did such loving, solicitous care deserve? The answer was, thirty pieces of silver.

The historical context of this unit is, again, difficult to establish. It is entirely possible in the nature of the case that the prophet ally performed the actions attributed to him here, although the reference to the Temple (v. 13) might be a little premature for Zechariah's own time, inasmuch as it was not completed until three years after the last recorded date of the book (7:1).[37] On the whole it is preferable to locate the entire scene in the late preexilic period as was done with the whole section 11:1-11. What is involved here in this view is the utter rejection of the worth of YHWH and His sacrificial love throughout covenant history and particularly in the closing years of the Southern Kingdom.

Thirty (pieces) of silver (probably 30 shekels, the shekel being the basic unit of silver), not an insignificant amount in literal terms (cf. Neh. 5:15),[38] was the amount of compensation to be paid a slave owner were his slave to be gored to death (Ex. 21:32). It was also the sum required for a woman who vowed herself to YHWH in special dedication (Lev. 27:4). Jesus was betrayed by Judas for 30 silver shekels (Matt. 26:15), an amount clearly in antitypical fulfillment of that here in Zechariah.

---

37. Some scholars propose that all or parts of Zech. 9-14 were written as late as 480 B.C., long after the Temple was rebuilt. See Kenneth L. Barker, "Zechariah," in *EBC*, ed. Frank E. Gaebelein (Grand Rapids: Zondervan, 1985), 7:598.
38. The shekel weighed about 0.41 ounces, so at five dollars per ounce U.S., 30 shekels would be worth $61.50. The Code of Hammurabi prescribes a monthly wage for a laborer of one shekel, a unit weighing about 0.30 ounces. If this were the case in Israel, 30 shekels would be the wages for 2½ years; R. de Vaux, *Ancient Israel*, 76, 204-5. For other examples of "thirty shekels" as a conventional payment, see K. Luke, "The Thirty Pieces of Silver (Zech. 11:12f.)," *IndTS* 19 (1982): 26-30. Luke, on the basis of Sumerian analogues, suggests that "thirty" came to be a term meaning anything of little or no value (p. 30). In this he follows Erica Reiner, "Thirty Pieces of Silver," in *Essays in Memory of E. A. Speiser*, AOS 53, ed. William W. Hallo (New Haven, Conn.: American Oriental Society, 1968), 186-90. Though the 30 shekels elsewhere in the OT may well be taken literally, the context of Zech. 11:12 may indeed support Reiner and Luke in seeing it as a pittance here. So also E. Lipiński, "Recherches sur le Livre de Zacharie," *VT* 20 (1970): 53-55.

The significance of the wage is its connection to the value of a slave. In a monstrous irony and perversion of priority, the shepherding of the sovereign, a service of untold value, is appraised at only the comparative pittance of the lifetime service of a mere human slave. In assessing the worth of a slave, in fact, it was not his intrinsic value that was at stake, but the estimated value of his service to the master over a normal lifetime. It is not the preciousness of Zechariah or even YHWH that is being evaluated here but the worth of their services as shepherd.[39]

That it is YHWH who is being appraised and not Zechariah is made certain in v. 13 by YHWH's ironic and indignant description of this pittance by the phrase "exorbitant price"[40] and by His command to the prophet to cast the shekels by which *He*, YHWH, was valued to the potter. C. C. Torrey, following the LXX, Aquila, Symmachus, understands הַיּוֹצֵר (*hayyôṣēr*) to refer not to a potter but to a "founder," that is, a shaper of metal objects. From this he deduces that there must have been a foundry attached to or associated with the Temple. This would be necessary, he says, to melt down gifts of assorted shapes and sizes and to recast them into standard forms.[41]

This is an attractive interpretation except for the fact that the shekels are "thrown" into the יוֹצֵר (*yôṣēr*), not merely presented there for remolding. If the idea of a foundry is correct, however, Delcor's view that Zechariah (i.e., YHWH) threw the shekels there in order for them to be cast into an idol is most appealing. In other words, the people have chosen idolatry.[42] On the whole, it seems best to understand the destination of the shekels as the potter, rather than the founder. The potters' shops were usually located near refuse pits where the shards and other unusable or broken materials could be cast (Jer. 18:2; 19:1-2). The place of the potter, then, was not only a place of creation and beauty but one of rejection and ruin. It became a metaphor for a scrap heap.[43]

---

39. As Chary points out, the problem here is that "c'est un blasphème que de réduire Dieu à une valeur marchande"; ("it is blasphemous to reduce God to the role of a merchant") (T. Chary, *Aggée-Zacharie, Malachie*, 190).
40. G. W. Ahlstrom connects אֶדֶר, "exorbitant," to Akkadian *adaru*, "a vessel of metal," and by repointing יוֹצֵר to יוֹצֵר (a *qutl*-form), in line with the Peshiṭta, suggests the latter to be some kind of vessel. Thus אֶדֶר הַיְקָר would be in apposition to יוֹצֵר and the phrase rendered something like, "cast it into the vessel, the splendid container" (G. W. Ahlstrom, "אֶדֶר," *VT* 17 [1967]: 1-7). Even though this accords with the MT (except for vocalization), it goes against all ancient versions except the Peshiṭta.
41. C. C. Torrey, "The Foundry of the Second Temple at Jerusalem," *JBL* 55 (1936): 247-60.
42. M. Delcor, "Deux Passages Difficiles: Zach VII 11 et XI 13," *VT* 3 (1953): 76-77.
43. James L. Kelso, *The Ceramic Vocabulary of the Old Testament*, BASOR

The 30 shekels are, to YHWH, like so much refuse because of the insulting attitude they represent. By casting them, a symbol of the value of YHWH's service, on the rubbish heap, Zechariah is, through the use of a figure called metonymy of adjunct, representing YHWH's own rejection by the people who have offered so little appreciation. But the imagery is even more suggestive than all that, for the potter here is evidently located in or near the house of YHWH (v. 13).

Because there is no direct biblical or archaeological evidence that the Temple precincts accommodated a potter's shop, many scholars accept the Syriac reading הָאוֹצָר (hā'ôṣār, "treasury") for the MT's הַיּוֹצֵר (hayyôṣēr, "potter").[44] Matthew appears to support this when he reports that Judas, convicted of the wrong he did, returned the 30 pieces of silver to the Temple (Matt. 27:5). The priests and elders refused to accept it, however, for it was "blood money" and therefore not fit for the Temple treasury (v. 6). The word for "treasury" here (κορβανᾶς, korbanas) is a Greek transliteration of the Aramaic term for the Temple treasury (קָרְבָּנָא, qorbānā'). It occurs only here in the NT.[45] It is, therefore, possible that Matthew reflects the reading of the Syriac Peshitta (or that source common to them).

Against this is the fact that yôṣēr appears in the Zechariah passage (v. 13) as a place of rejection, not acceptance. It is in disgust that the shekels are cast there, a mood that is not likely to be true of the donation of the silver to the Temple treasury. Moreover, Matthew does not explicitly say that Judas cast the silver into the treasury. In fact, he points out that it was returned to the Temple (ναός, naos) and cast down there. The priests then took the money and, quite to the contrary of depositing it in the treasury, used it to purchase a "potter's field," a place for strangers to be buried in (Matt. 27:7-10). It is important to note Matthew's allusion to a potter here, suggesting that he was familiar with the Masoretic reading relative to the silver shekels and the potter's shop. There is clearly no contradiction between Zechariah's act of casting the shekels into the Temple and Matthew's narrative of Judas doing the same. What Zechariah adds is that there is a potter in or about the Temple, whereas Matthew speaks of the money eventually being spent on a potter's field.[46]

Supp. 5-6 (New Haven, Conn.: American Schools of Oriental Research, 1948), 7-11.

44. Thus, e.g., D. Ernest Sellin, *Das Zwölfprophetenbuch* (Leipzig: A. Deichert, 1922), 509, 515-16. For a defense of the MT, see Wilhelm Rudolph, *Haggai-Sacharja 1-8–Sacharja 9-14–Maleachi*, KAT (Gütersloh: Verlaghaus Gerd Mohn, 1976), 202-3. Cf. Jansma, *Inquiry into the Hebrew Text and the Ancient Versions of Zechariah IX-XIV*, 105-6.

45. D. A. Carson, "Matthew," in *EBC*, ed. Frank E. Gaebelein (Grand Rapids: Zondervan, 1984), 8:561-62.

46. Ibid., 8:564.

Because the Temple service must have required an enormous amount of clay vessels, if only for the use of the clergy, there is every reason to think that there must have been a "Temple potter" nearby, perhaps even in the Temple grounds.[47] This would be a suitable place for Zechariah to cast the insulting wages as a sign of Judah's rejection of her God. It follows that Judah's fee, though not necessarily thrown into the potter's shop, would meet the typological requirements of purchasing a field of burial for the outcasts of society, a field near the refuse heaps of the potters of Jerusalem.

Zechariah, having accomplished this part of his commission, then took the second staff, the one named "binders," and cut it in two (v. 14). The name denotes the joining of the two nations Israel and Judah into one people of God. The cutting of the staff, then, means the unbinding of the binders, the rupture of the brotherhood of the two kingdoms.[48] This had been a fait accompli since the time of the division of the kingdom under Jeroboam and Rehoboam,[49] and the exile of Israel and then that of Judah brought about a historically irrevocable breach that awaits the eschatological day for its healing (Ezek. 37:15-23). From the time of the Babylonian deportation until the present century the people of the Lord were not Israel, but Judah, not the Israelite, but the Jew. The breaking of the brotherhood has been a fact for more than 2,000 years and only with the establishment of the state of Israel has that restoration of brotherhood begun to take shape.

The messianic and christological implications of Zechariah 11:12-14 are well known but fraught with even more difficulties than have already been suggested above. It is my view that these verses are part of the imaginative reenactment by Zechariah of YHWH's dealings with His people in historical, preexilic times. Yet, both Jewish and Christian traditions recognize that the meaning is not exhausted by the historical dimension. There is a future as well as past orientation.

---

47. Baldwin cites the need for the work of the potter in Temple worship (Lev. 6:28) and suggests that Jeremiah must have been close to the potter's shop as he preached his "potter's sermon" (18:6) and bought an earthenware bottle near the Temple (19:1); Baldwin, *Haggai, Zechariah, Malachi*, 185.

48. Otzen, *Studien über Deuterosacharja*, 165. For arguments that Israel here in fact means Samaria and that it is the Samaritan-Jewish rupture that is in view, see M. Delcor, "Hinweise auf das Samaritanische Schisma im Alten Testament," *ZAW* 74 (1962): 281-91, esp. 285-91; K. Elliger, *Die Propheten Naham, Habakuk, Zephanja, Haggai, Sacharja, Maleachi*, ATD (Göttingen: Vandenhoeck & Ruprecht, 1982), 164.

49. A. Caquot, "Breves Remarques sur L'Allegorie des Pasteurs en Zacharie 11," 51.

Both Matthew (Matt. 26:15; 27:9) and Luke (Acts 1:18-19) allude to or quote from the Zechariah passage in support of their accounts of the rejection and betrayal of Jesus by Judas and of Judas's final outcome. Only Matthew, however, professes to cite an OT text as prophetic of these events (27:9). Strangely enough, he attributes the citation to Jeremiah rather than Zechariah, a fact that has caused great consternation to all schools of scholarship as the Introduction has already pointed out.

In addition to what has been said there, one should note before drawing conclusions about Matthew's accuracy one way or the other that a NT "quotation" of the OT does not necessarily conform to the norms of modern documentation.[50] Rather, it follows conventions commonly practiced and well understood within rabbinic as well as early Christian circles. It could take the form of "testimonia," in which lists of messianic passages, or passages of other common interest, were compiled without regard for context or even chronological order. It could depend on versions other than the Hebrew Masoretic tradition such as the LXX, the favorite "Bible" of the primitive church. Finally, quotations could be of a topical type in which OT passages, connected by some sort of linkage of key words, would be associated with an author whose writings particularly focused on them.

This last option best explains Matthew's use of the OT, for no OT prophet says more about the potter than does Jeremiah.[51] It is quite likely, then, that references to the potter, such as in Zechariah 11:13, were subsumed under Jeremiah in light of the latter's inordinate interest in such matters. Matthew, then, is "quoting" Jeremiah in the sense that he is alluding to the subject matter of the potter, something especially associated with Jeremiah.

As for its being messianic prophecy, our passage surely is such in terms of its use by Matthew, who says that the OT is being fulfilled in the selling of Jesus by Judas. Just as YHWH was priced at only 30 silver shekels as far as His service to Israel was concerned, so Jesus was viewed by Judas and his generation as having no more value than a slave. The rejection of YHWH is a type of the rejection of Jesus. In this sense, then, Zechariah 11:13 is a prophecy fulfilled in Matt. 27:9.[52]

---

50. Walter C. Kaiser, Jr., *The Uses of the Old Testament in the New* (Chicago: Moody, 1985), 1-14.

51. For an excellent discussion of the whole matter of the "double fulfillment" in Matthew of the passages in Zechariah and Jeremiah, see Robert H. Gundry, *The Use of the Old Testament in St. Matthew's Gospel*, NovTSup 18 (Leiden: Brill, 1967), 122-27.

52. Carson, "Matthew," in *EBC*, 8:528, 560-66.

C. THE EVIL SHEPHERD(-KING) TO COME (11:15-17)

Translation

[15]YHWH said to me, "Once more take up the equipment of an unwise shepherd. [16]Indeed, I am about to raise up a shepherd in the land who will not oversee the ones headed to eradication, will not seek the *scattered, and will not heal the broken. Moreover, he will not nourish the one that is well but will eat the flesh of the fat ones and tear off their hoofs.

[17]Woe to the *worthless shepherd
    Who leaves the flock;
May a sword fall upon his arm and his right eye.
May his arm totally wither away,
    His right eye become completely blind."

Exegesis and Exposition

This climax to the long oracle beginning with chapter 9 ends the oracle on a pessimistic note indeed. Throughout chapter 11 the theme has been that of the sheep and the shepherds. The sheep are God's chosen people, Israel and Judah, and the shepherds the evil kings who abandoned their subjects in their times of greatest need, particularly just prior to the Babylonian conquest and deportation. Zechariah, playing the role of and speaking for YHWH, has done all he can as the good shepherd to minister to the flock but to no avail. They have spurned him utterly, counting his service to them as of no more value than the service of a slave. He therefore broke his covenant with them in terms of their appropriation of its benefits and also broke off the brotherhood between Israel and Judah. The only hope now is for a shepherd who will come and in tender love and omnipotent power effect a reunion and restoration. Such a one will come, as Zechariah 9:9-10 makes clear, but not until the sinful rebellion of God's people runs its course. Before they can accept that Good Shepherd to come, they must have one last fling with a ruler who will utterly disappoint them. This is the shepherd on whom the prophecy now focuses.

Once more YHWH commands Zechariah to dramatize His message. He is to take up the implements of an unwise, a foolish, shepherd. The term used to describe him (אֱוִלִי, *'ĕwilî*) is commonly employed in the wisdom literature to designate the man without God.[53] Thus the sage says, "The fear of YHWH is the chief part of knowledge, but the foolish despises wisdom and instruction" (Prov. 1:7). He also despises his father's correction (15:5; cf. 16:22), engages in needless

---

53. H. Cazelles, *TDOT*, 1:137-40, s.v. אֱוִיל.

controversy (20:3), and is absolutely insensitive to change (27:22). In short, the foolish is the antithesis to the wise and godly man in every way.

Jeremiah uses the same adjective to describe YHWH's people (4:22). "They are foolish," he says, "they do not know me." Thus, to be foolish is to be ignorant of God. It is not surprising that a foolish people would submit to a foolish shepherd.

Up till now I have argued that the shepherd imagery pertained to events of the past, that Zechariah in fact was reliving the history of his own people. That history indeed provided a prototype of future events occasionally (as in vv. 12-13) but essentially was antecedent to the prophet's own time (i.e., was preexilic). Now, however, there can be no doubt that the orientation is exclusively future in both historical and eschatological terms. This is apparent because Zechariah does not actually act out his role as foolish shepherd (apart from taking up the equipment of a shepherd), nor is there any place for such a figure in Israel's past if, indeed, our view that Zechariah 11:1-14 finds its setting in the past is at all correct.

It is fruitless, then, to try to identify the foolish shepherd as someone anterior to the prophet. This means that some figure after Zechariah must be sought, but that very search is encumbered with a host of problems. Candidates from Pekah to Ptolemy IV have been proposed,[54] but in the nature of the case with little persuasive evidence. It is best perhaps to see in the shepherd the whole collective leadership of Israel from Zechariah's time forward, culminating at last in that epitome of godless despotism, the individual identified in the NT as the Antichrist (1 John 2:18, 22; 4:3; 2 John 7; cf. Matt. 24:5, 24; 2 Thess. 2:3-4).[55] It is only when that leadership is seen to be what it truly is—foolish and antithetical to God—that it will be discarded by the people and destroyed by YHWH who Himself will then assume the reins of government (Rev. 13:1-18; 14:9-12; 19:19-21; cf. Dan. 11:36-45).[56]

The "shepherd in the land" (v. 16), then, is the structure of anti-God leadership that commenced as early as the postexilic days of Zechariah. This seems conclusive in light of the incipient action of the participle מֵקִים (*mēqîm*), in הִנֵּה־אָנֹכִי מֵקִים ("I am about to raise up," v. 16).[57] "In the land" locates the rule of the shepherd as being in Israel, the holy land. The shepherd will be the king of Israel, but one

---

54. For the latter, see Mitchell, *A Commentary on Haggai, Zechariah, and Malachi*, 315, and for a list of other candidates see Otzen, *Studien über Deuterosacharja*, 149, esp. nn. 13-14.
55. Chary, *Aggée-Zacharie, Malachie*, 193.
56. K. Barker, "Zechariah," in *EBC*, 7:680.
57. GKC, 116p.

who fails in all his regal responsibilities toward the flock. He will not oversee the ones headed to eradication nor seek the scattered nor heal the broken.

The word translated "headed to eradication" (נִכְחָדוֹת, *nikḥādôt*) is a niphal participle of the verb כָּחַד (*kāḥad*), and it occurs only here and in v. 9 in that form. There is clearly, then, a connection between the poor defenseless sheep of v. 9 who are left to their tormentors and those of v. 16 who will have no oversight from the foolish shepherd. The feminine gender in both places might even suggest that these are the ewes, the sheep least able to fend for themselves. The import of their being "headed for eradication" (thus the nuance of the participle) is that unless they get such oversight there is no hope of their survival. The term "oversight" (פָּקַד, *pāqad*) speaks here of shepherdly care.[58] It is the same verb that occurs in 10:3 where YHWH, angry with the evil shepherds, says that He will oversee His flock instead and will change them from weak and persecuted sheep into mighty warhorses (cf. Jer. 23:2).

Fundamental to the work of a shepherd was his concern for any sheep that might have separated from the flock and gone its own way (Isa. 53:6; Matt. 18:12-14). Yet the foolish shepherd will not seek the scattered one who goes astray. Nor will he heal the broken ones. By contrast one thinks of the good shepherd of this passage (above) and of Psalm 23 who leads, restores, guides, comforts, feeds, and administers healing oils (v. 5).

Even the sheep who is healthy and sound[59] has much to fear, for the foolish shepherd will stop nourishing it. Indeed, he will take advantage of its fatness by slaughtering it for meat to satisfy his own appetite. So thorough and cruel will be his disposition of these defenseless ones that he will rip their very hoofs from them. This is probably a hyperbole to suggest that by the time the wicked shepherd is through with his flock there is nothing left but the unusable feet. A similar figure occurs in Amos 3:12 where YHWH says that just as a

---

58. Victor P. Hamilton, *TWOT*, 2:731-32, s.v. פָּקַד.
59. The form here is נִצָּבָה, the niph. ptc. of נָצַב, "to take one's stand" (BDB, 662). The meaning, therefore, is "one who stands firm" or the like. Lacocque translates "celle qui est ferme sur ses pattes" ("the one stable on its feet"), which makes excellent sense; Lacocque, *Zacharie IX-XIV*, 179. Others emend in some way or other. Horst, e.g., reads הָרְעֵבָה ("was hungrig ist"), from רָעֵב "be hungry" (BDB, 944); Friedrich Horst, *Die Zwölf kleinen Propheten. Nahum bis Maleachi*, HAT 14 (Tübingen: J. C. B. Mohr, 1964), 252. Nowack takes it to be הַנַּחְלָה ("kranke?" "sick"); W. Nowack, *Die kleinen Propheten*, HAT (Göttingen: Vandenhoeck und Ruprecht, 1903), p. 405. Such proposals lack any kind of significant support in the ancient witnesses. Cf. Jansma, *Inquiry into the Hebrew Text and the Ancient Versions of Zechariah IX-XVI*, 107-8.

shepherd might find in the lion's mouth only two legs or the piece of an ear, so He will rescue the remnant of Israel in the day of judgment.[60]

YHWH is not oblivious to the shepherd who so abuses and exploits His people, however. As testimony to His concern He pronounces a woe in a poetic quatrain that completes the oracle (v. 17).[61] Shifting the adjective slightly (אֱלִיל, ['ĕlîl], "worthless," for אֱוִלִי, ['ĕwilî], "unwise"[62]), YHWH now describes the foolish shepherd as a worthless one,[63] worthless because he leaves the flock. The woe-judgment that will come upon him will be a sword that wounds his arm and his right eye.[64] Without the arm to retrieve and carry the sheep (cf. Luke 15:5) and the eye with which to search and find (cf. Matt. 18:12), the shepherd truly is worthless, now not only in a moral sense but in a practical, functional sense as well.

So serious will the wounding be that the arm will completely wither away and the eye will become sightless.[65] Why the shepherd is not killed is unclear, but he is so severely incapacitated that he can no longer continue as a shepherd. Thus for all practical purposes he ceases to be a problem for the sheep of God's pasture. The point is that those who rule over the people of YHWH and who abuse that privilege can expect the awesome judgment of God that results in their deposition and replacement by shepherds who more lovingly and faithfully discharge their responsibilities.

The oracle ends on a pessimistic note, but the message as a whole has not ended. In the final oracle of the book (chaps. 12-14) there is the glorious hope of a shepherd to come who, though smitten (13:7),

---

60. S. Feigin, "Some Notes on Zechariah 11:4-17," *JBL* 44 (1925): 203-13, cited by Lacocque, *Zacharie IX-XIV*, 180.
61. Lamarche takes the poem as a tristich in line with the BHS alignment (Lamarche, *Zacharie IX-XIV*, 71). Hanson's analysis of the piece, one he calls a "woe oracle" for obvious reasons, appears to reflect a four-line construction, which is like my own analysis (P. Hanson, *The Dawn of Apocalyptic*, 339).
62. For comment on this *Wortspiel*, see Saebø, *Sacharja 9-14*, 249. He sees it as an element binding v. 17 to the rest of the pericope. Cf. also Meyer, "An Allegory Concerning the Monarchy: Zech. 11:4-17; 13:7-9," 233.
63. Because אֱלִיל occurs in the singular only here and in Isa. 10:10, H. D. Preuss questions it in both places, proposing that it be read אֱוִילִי in Zech. 11:17 as in 11:15; Preuss, *TDOT*, 1:285, s.v. אֱלִיל. This not only destroys the word-play, but more to the point it has little support from the versions (Tg. Neb. and Syr. being the exceptions). See text note on v. 17.
64. It is because of the blinding of the shepherd's eye that van Hoonacker (and other scholars) identify him with Zedekiah, Judah's last king (2 Kings 25:7) (A. Van Hoonacker, *Les Douze Petits Prophètes*, 679).
65. The Hebrew here—כָּהֹה תִכְהֶה—is a particularly emphatic construction, the infinitive absolute. It leaves no question that the shepherd will become completely sightless. Cf. K. Barker, "Zechariah," in *EBC*, 7:680.

will recover and stand triumphant at last in the day of YHWH (14:9, 16).

Additional Notes

11:16 If in fact הַנַּעַר means "scattered," this is the only example of the word in the OT with this meaning. A homonym occurs with the meaning "youth" or "lad," but it never applies elsewhere to anything but a human being. It is likely, as the versions all attest, that "scattered" is correct, being a derivative of the verb נָעַר, "to shake." The נַעַר, then, is something "shaken off" or scattered.

11:17 Many scholars, with the Syr. and Tg. Neb., read אֱוִילִי, "foolish one," for אֱלִיל, "worthless one," to bring it in line with v. 15. There is clearly a correction process at work in the Syr. and Tg. Neb. to accomplish this very purpose, so the original and correct reading is without doubt that of the MT.

PART 4
Oracle Concerning Israel (12:1–14:21)

1
Repentance of Judah (12:1-14)

The final great oracle of Zechariah, embracing all of chapters 12-14, stands in sharp contrast with what has immediately preceded in chapter 11. There the prophet has reviewed the dismal history of the chosen nation Israel throughout monarchial times, emphasizing over and over again the failure of her kings, the shepherds, to discharge their responsibilities as undershepherds of YHWH Himself. Even more tragic is that wicked and foolish leadership had not come to an end with the Exile. It will continue on into Judah's future, finally reaching its climax in an evil shepherd par excellence who will violently persecute and destroy the flock only to be incapacitated himself by the wrathful intervention of YHWH.

The oracle of chapters 12-14, on the other hand, picks up the eschatological themes of chapters 9-10.[1] The triumph of Jerusalem over her foes in 12:1-9 has a counterpart in 9:11-17. The rejection of the false prophets and their idolatrous ways in 13:1-6 is an echo of the same thing in 10:1-3. YHWH as the good shepherd who gathers His remnant flock in 13:7-9 finds precedent in 10:4-7. The triumphant advent and conquest of YHWH in 14:1-8 is the subject of 9:1-8 as well. The manifestation of YHWH as king in 14:9-11 is addressed in 9:9-10.

---

1. The following analysis agrees with that of Lamarche in a general way, though in details, such as the delimitation of the relevant passages, there is some difference. See P. Lamarche, *Zacharie IX-XIV. Structure Littéraire et Messianisme* (Paris: Librairie Lecoffre, 1961), 112-13; see also the Introduction to this commentary, pp. 82ff.

Finally, the restoration of the people of YHWH in the manner of a second exodus and their dominion with YHWH over all creation is the theme of both 14:12-21 and 10:8-12. The major difference between the two oracles (chap. 11 excepted) is that 12-14 expands greatly on the themes of 9-10 and introduces a cosmic, universalistic motif that is not as clearly perceived in the latter.[2] Moreover, 12-14 focuses on the messianic aspect of the eschatological redemption, going so far as to identify YHWH Himself as the messianic figure (12:10-14; 13:7-9). Nothing in 9-10, with the possible exception of 9:9-10, comes close to this idea.

Few writings of the OT are so consistently and persistently rooted in the eschaton as this. That classic eschatological formula "in that day" or the like occurs 19 times in just 45 verses, or once in every 2½ verses. All the hallmarks of eschatological language, style, and motif are here and will be pointed out in the course of the exposition. No more fitting conclusion could be found for the writings of a prophet who lived and ministered among the tiny, disappointed, frustrated, and pessimistic community of postexilic Judah. With his friend Haggai he is saying, in effect, that the small beginnings of restoration they see in the undertaking of the Zerubbabel temple will be eclipsed beyond comprehension by the glory that someday will fill that place (Hag. 2:7) and, indeed, the whole earth (Zech. 14:9).

A. SECURITY OF GOD'S PEOPLE (12:1-9)

Translation

¹The oracle of the Word of YHWH concerning Israel: Says YHWH, He who stretches out the heavens and lays the foundations of the earth, who forms the spirit of man within him, ²"I am about to make Jerusalem a cup that causes reeling to all the surrounding nations; indeed, Judah *will also be included when Jerusalem is besieged. ³Also in that day I will make Jerusalem a heavy burden for all the nations, and all who carry it will be heavily scarred; yet all the

---

2. I cannot accept Hanson's view that the reverse is the case—that chapters 12-14 "are written from a perspective which has narrowed from the very broad international scope of the earlier Divine Warrior Hymns to a myopic concern with Judah and Jerusalem" (Paul Hanson, *The Dawn of Apocalyptic* [Philadelphia: Fortress, 1975], 355). He belies his own position by subsequent reference to the universalism of this section, especially in chapter 14 (cf. pp. 374, 376-77, 378, 379, 381, 383, 386). What Hanson fails to see is that, though Judah and Jerusalem become the focus of chapters 12-14, they do so only because it is in relationship to His own people that YHWH will at last bring about his universal dominion.

peoples of the earth will be gathered against it. ⁴In that day," says
YHWH, "I will strike every horse with confusion and its rider with
madness. I will open My eyes on behalf of the house of Judah, but I
will strike every horse of the nations with blindness. ⁵Then the leaders of Judah will say to themselves, 'The inhabitants of Jerusalem are
a *strength to *me in YHWH of hosts, their God. ⁶In that day I will
make the leaders of Judah like a firepot among sticks and a burning
torch among sheaves, and they will devour all the surrounding nations right and left. Then (the people of) Jerusalem will settle once
more in their place, Jerusalem. ⁷YHWH also will deliver the tents of
Judah first, so that the splendor of the house of David and that of the
inhabitants of Jerusalem may not exceed that of Judah. ⁸In that day
YHWH Himself will defend the *inhabitants of Jerusalem, so that in
that day the stumbler among them will be like David and the house of
David (will be) like God, like the Angel of YHWH before them. ⁹Thus
it will be in that day that I will seek to destroy all the peoples that
come against Jerusalem."

Exegesis and Exposition

The oracle is introduced by the technical term מַשָּׂא (*maśśā'*) as
was the previous one (9:1). But this oracle concerns Israel primarily,
in contrast to chapters 9-11, which mainly are concerned with the
other nations. It is, of course, an oversimplification to say that the
headings of the respective oracles denote their exclusive content, for
both deal with the nations and Israel. However, the emphasis of each
is clearly suggested by their opening statements.

One of the clues that the thrust of the oracle is eschatological is
the fact that it concerns "Israel" as opposed to Judah. Israel, from
Zechariah's standpoint, was a thing of the past, for the northern tribes
had gone into exile two centuries before his time, never to return as an
entity. But he, as well as other prophets, understand a day when all the
exiled and scattered people of YHWH will be regathered and become
Israel once again (9:1; 12:1; cf. Jer. 13:11; 31:10-12, 31; Ezek. 40-48
[*passim*]; Joel 2:27; 3:2; Zeph. 3:14-15; Mal. 1:5). This initial reference
to Israel thus sets an eschatological tone for the entire oracle.[3]

That tone is reinforced by the set of epithets in participial form
that describe YHWH—they are of a cosmic, creative nature. He is the
"one who stretches out" (נֹטֶה, *nōṭeh*) the heavens, the "one who lays the
foundations" (יֹסֵד, *yōsēd*) of the earth, and the "one who forms" (יֹצֵר,
yōṣēr) the spirit of man (v. 1). Isaiah is particularly rich in such use of

---

3. Rex Mason, *The Books of Haggai, Zechariah, and Malachi*, CBC (Cambridge:
Cambridge Univ., 1977), 114-15.

divine self-predication.[4] In a veiled polemic against Babylonian deities, YHWH refers to Himself as the creator who "stretched out" the heavens (42:5; cf. 40:22). Then, in defense of His role as redeemer, He again calls Himself "the stretcher forth" (נֹטֶה, *nōṭeh*) of the heavens (44:24), using in both places the same verb as Zechariah's. It is a word at home in the field of architecture and building, referring either to the measuring line (Isa. 34:11; Lam. 2:8) or to the erection of a tent (Jer. 10:12).

Isaiah describes YHWH also as the "founder" (יֹסֵד, *yōsēd*) of the earth (51:13), exactly as Zechariah does. This creation language is common in contexts where YHWH's skill and power are being noted and/or praised (Job 38:4; Pss. 24:2; 104:5). The stretching out of the heavens speaks of superstructure, whereas the laying of foundations obviously speaks of the basis upon which things rest. It is a merismus, describing the totality of YHWH's creation.

As for YHWH's being the "former" of man's spirit, Isaiah once more provides parallels. The verb (יָצַר [*yāṣar*], "form") is indigenous to craftsmen who work in clay and other malleable materials. As such a craftsman, YHWH refers to Himself as the "former" of Israel (43:1; cf. vv. 7, 21) and the "former" of the servant (49:5). He also formed the earth (45:18), thus again attesting to His power as Creator. Though Zechariah uniquely describes YHWH as the former of man's spirit, the psalmist is close when he speaks of YHWH as the one who forms the hearts of people (Ps. 33:15).

The theological purpose for these epithets in Zechariah, as well as in Isaiah 40-55, is to underline the creative and redemptive role of YHWH.[5] He redeems because He is the omnipotent creator, and He creates new things in order to redeem. Here at the brink of a new age it is important to know that the same God who brought everything into existence in the first place is well able to usher in the new creation of a restored people in a renewed and universal kingdom.

That renewal will take place through and find expression in YHWH's chosen people Judah, and in that order. YHWH will use them as an instrument by which He does battle with the nations and brings them under His dominion. First, He says, he will make Jerusa-

---

4. Eugene H. Merrill, "Literary Genres in Isaiah 40-55," *BSac* 144 (1987): 144-56.

5. André Lacocque, *Zechariah 9-14*, CAT (Neuchatel: Delachaux & Niestlé, 1981), 185-86. Lamarche points out that the creation theme at the beginning of this final oracle "nous prépare à l'ébranlement cosmique du c.14 d'où naissant de nouveaux cieux (14, 7) et une nouvelle terre (14, 8-10)" ("prepares us for the cosmic convulsion of chapter 14 in which are brought to birth the new heavens and a new earth"). Thus, new creation must find its roots in the original creation (Lamarche, *Zacharie IX-XIV*, 75).

lem a "cup of reeling," that is, a cup, which, when drunk by the nations, will cause them to stagger and stumble as a drunken man (v. 2).[6] The same metaphor (with a different word for "cup") occurs in Isa. 51:17, 22. There it is explained as a manifestation of divine wrath. Jeremiah is commanded to serve the nations a "cup of the wine of wrath" that will cause them to "reel to and fro and be mad" because of the sword YHWH will send upon them (Jer. 25:15-16).

That is the effect of the cup in Zechariah's oracle. All the surrounding nations will "drink" of Jerusalem, that is, will partake of her in hostility and conquest, but they will end up inebriated. Judah, too, will cause the same reaction by extension. This seems to be the best understanding of the second half of v. 2 in light of the parallel construction.[7] The participial form of the verb שׂים (*śîm*, "set/make") suggests that what YHWH is going to do is imminent: "I am about to make Jerusalem a cup." Thus the ultimate act of YHWH in the eschaton has its roots and initial stages in the present, in history.

Changing the metaphor, YHWH says that "in that day" he will make Jerusalem "a stone of a burden" or a heavy, rough burden. Here the chosen people are likened to pillage being carried off by the victors. But they will be heavier than the looters bargained for, so heavy and jagged that they will scrape and lacerate the shoulders of those who try to spirit them away (v. 3). This is similar to Ezekiel's description of the armies of Nebuchadnezzar that had become "bald of head and worn of shoulder" in their unsuccessful siege of Tyre (Ezek. 29:18). This appears to refer to their carrying of material for siege-works, but the imagery is the same.[8] In spite of these grievous results,

---

6. Joyce G. Baldwin, *Haggai, Zechariah, Malachi*, (London: Tyndale, 1972), 188-89. The word translated "cup," סַף, has a homonym meaning "threshold," and this is the rendering in some versions, e.g., NEB: "I am making the steep approaches (lit. threshold) to Jerusalem slippery for all the nations pressing round her." Though this has some LXX support (cf. Jansma, *Inquiry into the Hebrew Text and the Ancient Versions of Zechariah IX-XIV*, 111-12), the context clearly favors the idea of a cup, particularly because this is a well-known idiom. By a series of text relocations Driver also makes a case for סַף as threshold: Jerusalem will become "a slippery glacis for all the nations (gathered) round against Judah, and it (sc. Judah) will be (involved) in the siege (directed) against Jerusalem" (G. R. Driver, "Old Problems Re-examined," *ZAW* 80 [1968]: 178-79). Such handling of the text is less than persuasive.
7. The text here is very obtuse. It reads literally (v. 2b), "moreover, upon Judah will it be in the siege against Jerusalem." It might be best, as NIV apparently does, to construe v. 2b with v. 3 and render it, "Judah will be besieged as well as Jerusalem. (3) On that day," etc. Cf. Kenneth L. Barker, "Zechariah," in *EBC*, ed. Frank E. Gaebelein (Grand Rapids: Zondervan, 1985), 7:680-81; R. Tournay, "Zacharie XII-XIV et L'Histoire d'Israël," *RB* 81 (1974): 358.
8. Lacocque refers to Isa. 8:14-15 and 28:16 for parallels. In the former God is

all the nations will nonetheless be gathered about Jerusalem with evil intent.

Drunken and scarred already, the nations come in for further judgment. Their horses and their cavalrymen will become confused. This latter expression (שִׁגָּעוֹן [*šiggā'ôn*], "madness") occurs in 2 Kings 9:11 to refer to the prophet whom Elisha had sent to Jehu to inform him that he was to be king. The young man had run so hard and long that he was out of breath and appeared to be beside himself. In other words, he acted like a madman. The pagan ecstatic prophets, having worked themselves up into a frenzy, also were considered mad (Jer. 29:26; Hos. 9:7).[9] To add to their incapacitation YHWH will blind the horses of the enemy. He, however, will open His own eyes on behalf of the house of Judah.

When all this comes to pass, the leaders of Judah will realize that the people of Jerusalem have been their greatest strength, for in their being used by YHWH of hosts as a discomfit to their enemies these people have guaranteed that the nation also would survive (v. 5).[10] This is in sharp contrast to the attitude of the evil kings of Israel in the past who had no compassion for the people (11:5) and that foolish shepherd to come who neither oversees, seeks out, nor heals those committed to him (11:16).

The rulers, thus encouraged, will themselves be a source of divine judgment on the nations (v. 6). YHWH compares them to a "firepot among sticks" and a "burning torch among sheaves." This is an un-

---

a "stone of stumbling," and in the latter Zion is a cornerstone; Lacocque, *Sacharie 9-14*, 186. Sellin draws attention to references in 2 Mac. 4:12-15 where presumably heavy stones were lifted as part of gymnastic competitions (D. Ernest Sellin, *Das Zwölfprophetenbuch*, [Leipzig: A. Deichert, 1922], 521). This is more an inference than anything else. The stone, in fact, is usually taken to be the discus. Cf. G. R. Driver, "Old Problems Re-examined," 180. He cites and rejects the view of scholars who follow Jerome in making comparison with athletic contests in Jerome's own day, c. A.D. 400.

9. Abraham J. Heschel, *The Prophets* (New York: Harper & Row, 1962), 395-405. As Heschel points out, the prophets of YHWH were not indeed mad as their pagan counterparts were, but at times they were accused of being so in the intensity of their inspiration and utterance.

10. Though Chary is correct in suggesting that v. 5 introduces the elevation of the Davidic royal house that finds its culmination in v. 8, he appears to overlook the fact that it is the *people* of Jerusalem (not the king) who inspire the national leaders, something emphasized in vv. 2-3 (Theophane Chary, *Aggée-Zacharie, Malachie* [Paris: Librairie Lecoffre, 1969], 199). Tournay proposes that the final *yodh* on יֹשְׁבֵי is a dittograph so that the line should read, "La force pour moi, o habitants de Jérusalem, est en Yahvé Sabaot leur Dieu" ("My strength, O inhabitants of Jerusalem, is in Yahweh of Hosts, their God") (Tournay, "Zacharie XII-XIV et L'Histoire d'Israël," 360-61). This is an attractive proposal but lacks support in the versions.

usual use of this word for pot (כִּיּוֹר, *kîyyôr*). Normally it designates a cooking vessel (1 Sam. 2:14) or a basin for water, such as the laver of the tabernacle (Ex. 30:18) or Temple (1 Kings 7:30).[11] Here, in an ironic twist, the bowls for water will become receptacles of fiery coals that will burn up all the surrounding woods that threaten Israel. One must think of the poem introducing chapter 11, where the prophet refers to the leaders of the nations as trees and speaks of their destruction in terms of a fiery conflagration (11:1-3).

The nations on both left and right will be consumed. Because the inhabitants of Palestine oriented themselves to the east, the left side would be the north and the right side the south. These are the directions in which the chariot horses of Zechariah's eighth vision rode in undertaking their conquest of the whole earth (6:6). Once this conquest has been achieved, the people of Jerusalem can once more settle down in their rightful place (12:6*b*). The repetition of "Jerusalem" in the last clause of v. 6 prompted certain LXX traditions to delete the second occurrence.[12] Other scholars suggest בְּשָׁלֹם (*bĕšālôm*), "in peace," for בִּירוּשָׁלָם (*bîrûšālāim*), "in Jerusalem."[13] This insensitivity to poetic device undercuts the impact that is intended. "Jerusalem shall again settle in its own place, Jerusalem." There can be no doubt where Jerusalem belongs.

The eschatological favor will not be limited to Jerusalem, however. In fact, Jerusalem will not even enjoy pride of place among all of God's people, for there will be even-handed distribution of God's blessing. This is clear from His promise to begin the saving and restoring process with the "tents of Judah" first (v. 7). This is logically understandable in that Jerusalem's security cannot be assured until all the surrounding territory is brought under YHWH's protection. Theologically it is important to remember that the whole nation of David, the tribe of Judah, is included in the plan of ultimate redemption (cf. Jer. 30:18).[14]

---

11. James L. Kelso, *The Ceramic Vocabulary of the Old Testament* (New Haven, Conn.: ASOR, 1948), 20. As Kelso argues, the *kiyyôr* of Zech. 12:6 must be a pottery bowl because it contains burning charcoal with which to start a fire. Otherwise it is always made of copper. R. P. Gordon cites Targumic לכוש (now attested also in 11 Q tg Job, col. 36, line 6) for כיור, but offers no translation. Possibly it means "like a reed" or "like straw" (R. P. Gordon, "The Targum to the Minor Prophets and the Dead Sea Texts: Textual and Exegetical Notes," *RQum* 8 [1974]: 428-29).
12. Taeke Jansma, *Inquiry into the Hebrew Text and the Ancient Versions of Zechariah IX-XIV* (Leiden: Brill, 1949), 115.
13. See, e.g., Friedrich Horst, *Die Zwölf Kleinen Propheten,* HAT (Tübingen: J. C. B. Mohr, 1964), 254. For a contrary view see Benedikt Otzen, *Studien über Deuterosacharja,* ATD 6 (Copenhagen: Prostant Apud Munksgaard, 1964), 263.
14. Tournay cites such texts as Gen. 49:8-10; Num. 24; 1 Chron. 28:4; Pss.

"Tent," of course, should not be taken literally here, for it is synonymous with a dwelling-place in general. But the habitations of the villagers outside Jerusalem must have suffered by comparison to the grander, more substantial abodes of the upper classes of the city. Hence, says YHWH, in that day of blessing to come He will deliver the outlying villages first so that their comparative inferiority to the splendor of the city, and particularly the splendor of the royal palace, might enjoy some compensation (v. 7b). "Splendor" (תִּפְאָרָה, *tip'ārâ*) is a term not so much of aesthetic significance as of quality. The democratization of the eschatological kingdom will ensure that all its elements are of equal standing before YHWH.[15]

An even more remarkable comparison follows in v. 8. "In that day," YHWH says, He will defend the residents of Jerusalem in such a powerful way that the weakest among them will be like David. This is a reference to David the warrior who, the maidens sang, had "slain his ten thousands" (1 Sam. 18:7). The weak here are literally the "stumblers" (נִכְשָׁל, *nikšāl*) or "feeble ones." Hannah in her prayer sang of these when she said, "The bows of heroes are broken, but the stumblers are girded with strength" (1 Sam. 2:4). Isaiah said with reference to the restoration of the exiles, "The young men will faint and tire and the youths will stumble indeed, but those who wait for YHWH will renew their strength" (40:30-31).

It is such weak ones that YHWH promises to make like mighty David. But in an even more startling hyperbole He says He will make the house (i.e., dynasty) of David like God. Then, as though this were an overstatement, He qualifies His comparison by saying that David's house will resemble the Angel of YHWH,[16] that manifestation of God who was before them, that is, who led the people of Israel in bygone days (cf. Ex. 14:19; 33:2; cf. 1 Sam. 29:9; 2 Sam. 14:17, 20; 19:27). The comparison to God (אֱלֹהִים, *'ĕlōhîm*) is not, however, without precedent. When Moses was reluctant to return to Egypt to lead his people to freedom, YHWH said that He would make Aaron Moses' mouth and that Moses would "be to him [Aaron] as God" (Ex. 4:16). Admittedly, the comparison is between functions and not ontologies, but the comparison is nonetheless striking.

(One must not, in any case, allow literary device such as hyperbole to determine one's understanding of theological content

---

18:51 [EB 18:50]; 78:68; and 89:4, 21, 50 [EB 89:3, 20, 49]; Isa. 55:3; Tournay, "Zacharie XII-XIV et L'Histoire d'Israël," 362.

15. Merrill F. Unger, *Zechariah* (Grand Rapids: Zondervan, 1963), 212.

16. Chary suggests that this is not a concession but that the prophet is equating the Angel with God (clearly a possibility given the apposition) and perhaps as a messianic figure such as that of Mal. 3:1 (T. Chary, *Aggée-Zacharie, Malachie*, 200).

in a passage such as this. All that is being done is the erection of an argument a posteriori to magnify YHWH's glorious redemption of His people. The weak become strong and the strong become stronger, as powerful as God Himself if the syllogism requires it to be so.)

Granting this extravagant language and the truth it conveys, it is no wonder that YHWH rounds off this message about the security of God's people as He does (v. 9). Once more employing the eschatological cliché "in that day," He summarizes His intentions by saying that in the ways just described in vv. 1-8 He will bring about the destruction of the people who come against Jerusalem. This done, He will effect a change within His people, one encouraged no doubt by the marvelous display of His grace and power just described.

Additional Notes

12:2 The difficult phrase וְגַם עַל־יְהוּדָה יִהְיֶה בַמָּצוֹר עַל־יְרוּשָׁלָ͏ִם, translated here "indeed, Judah will also be included when Jerusalem is besieged," reads literally, "also against Judah will be in the siege against Jerusalem." The LXX suggests: "and against Judah will be a siege" with "against Jerusalem" evidently to be taken as an appositional gloss. BHS proposes that the present text reflects a mixed reading consisting originally of "and also against Judah there will be a siege" and "and also Judah will be in a siege," presumably against Jerusalem. The passage certainly is obtuse, but our rendering must reflect at least the thrust of the message. Its difficulty alone does not justify the arguments raised for the suggested alternatives.

12:5 The *hapax* אַמְצָה, "strength," is rendered by the LXX as though from מָצָא, "to find," thus, אֶמְצָא לִי; "May I find the inhabitants of Jerusalem (to be) in YHWH of hosts, their God." This kind of aural similarity could easily occur, but the meaning, if anything, is less clear than before.

The reference to the plural "leaders" seems to require that לִי, "to me," be לָנוּ, "to us," or something else agreeable. The Tg. Neb. seeks to resolve the disharmony by presupposing לְיֹשְׁבֵי for לִי יֹשְׁבֵי. Thus one would translate not "to me the inhabitants of" but "to the inhabitants of." The full line might be rendered, "(There will be) strength to the inhabitants of Jerusalem in YHWH of hosts, their God." While this is ingenious and may be correct, the more difficult reading is likely to have remained unaltered from the original.

12:8 The MT has singular יוֹשֵׁב for expected יֹשְׁבֵי (LXX). There is no need for emendation, however, because the singular clearly is intended to be taken collectively, and the following singular participle נִכְשָׁל may also have influenced the use of the singular accusative substantive.

B. MOURNING OF GOD'S PEOPLE (12:10-14)

Translation

¹⁰"I will pour out upon the house of David and the inhabitants of Jerusalem a spirit of grace and supplication so that they will look to Me, the one they have pierced through. They will lament for Him as one laments for his only son, and (there will be) a bitter cry for Him as the bitter cry for the first-born. ¹¹In that day the lamentation in Jerusalem will be as great as the lamentation of Hadad-Rimmon in the plain of Megiddo. ¹²The land will lament, each clan by itself—the clan of the house of David by itself and their wives by themselves; the clan of the house of Nathan by itself and their wives by themselves; ¹³the clan of the house of Levi by itself and their wives by themselves; and the clan of the Shimeites by itself and their wives by themselves—¹⁴all the clans that remain, each one by itself and their wives by themselves."

Exegesis and Exposition

Once YHWH has accomplished His work of judgment on the nations through Judah and Jerusalem and has secured His people against further danger from them, He will begin to work a work of grace among the redeemed. Whether or not there is a cause-and-effect relationship here—the act of judgment elicits a response of mournful repentance—is not clear. There can be no doubt, however, that the one follows the other, nor can there be any question as to the ultimate means whereby the contrition of this passage comes to pass. It is YHWH who pours out a spirit of grace and supplications.[17]

It would be theologically premature to identify the spirit here with the third person of the Godhead. The term רוּחַ (*rûaḥ*) in this case should be understood as a persuasion or conviction from YHWH that prompts a course of action. But it is a spirit of grace and supplications. This means that there is divine motivation to repentance, that it is not something worked up by the people themselves. Grace (חֵן, *ḥēn*) essentially has to do with a favorable disposition or act in the OT.[18] When God or even men show grace, they act without reciprocat-

---

17. Baldwin, *Haggai, Zechariah, Malachi*, 190.
18. Mason's translation "pity" for חֵן seems much too weak in that the entire subsequent context speaks of repentance (vv. 10b-14), something that is prompted by more than mere pity (Mason, *The Books of Haggai, Zechariah, and Malachi*, 118). Even the translation "compassion" of D. N. Freedman and J. R. Lundbom (*TDOT*, 5:35, s.v. חָנַן) seems wide of the mark. It is after the spirit of grace is poured out that the people look to the pierced one and commence to mourn. Hanson sees the sequence correctly but insists on translating "pity" (P. Hanson, *The Dawn of Apocalyptic*, 356). Van Hoonacker has caught the intent, I believe, with his observation that

ing for a previous gesture of kindness. As in the language of Christian theology, it is an expression of unmerited favor.

The spirit of grace, then, is the spirit that YHWH pours out upon His people though they little deserve it. It is the spirit of conviction that what they have done in violation of YHWH's will has been wrong, and it is the spirit of desire to seek forgiveness and restoration. Thus there is also the spirit of supplications (תַּחֲנוּנִים, taḥănûnîm). This Hebrew word, cognate to חֵן, (ḥēn, "grace") conveys the idea of seeking for favor and so is the other side of the coin of grace.[19] In short, YHWH has extended His grace to enable His people to seek it in the first place. Without that spirit having moved them so, they would never have sought the face of YHWH in repentance.

Grace, however, is an abstraction. There must be some occasion in or from which it takes shape, some act or object that produces an awareness of one's need for the divine favor. This, YHWH says, comes about in the eschaton when His people, who have rejected Him for the most part through the aeons of history, look on Him, the one they have pierced (v. 10b). This is an extremely difficult text within the confines of its OT setting, not least because of differing text traditions. It is important that the text first be established; then its meaning can be considered.

In this disputed section the majority of the Hebrew MSS read וְהִבִּיטוּ אֵלַי אֵת אֲשֶׁר־דָּקָרוּ (wĕhibbîṭû 'ēlay ēt ăšer-dāqārû), "they will look to Me, the one they have pierced through." A few, however, read אֵלֵי אֵת אֲשֶׁר ('ĕlēy ēt 'ăšer), "to the one whom," etc., employing the poetic form of the preposition אֶל.[20] Other Hebrew MSS, however, reflect a *vorlage* that requires a rendering, "they will look on Me in place of him whom they pierced."[21] The end result is that it is not YHWH who is pierced but someone else. Clearly the notion of YHWH being subjected to such a highly anthropomorphic conception was more than some devout

---

"c'est Jahvé qui répand sur les habitants de Jerusalem l'esprit de grâce et de prière; c est vers lui, comme conséquence de l'opération de cet esprit, que le peuple élève ses regards" ("it is Yahweh who pours out on the inhabitants of Jerusalem the spirit of grace and prayer; it is toward Him, as a result of the work of this spirit, that the people lift up their eyes") (A. Van Hoonacker, *Les Douze Petits Prophètes* [Paris: Librairie Victor Lecoffre, 1908], 683).

19. Ap-Thomas takes it as epexegetical to חֵן and renders, "a spirit of favour, or rather, of supplications for favour." This hardly affects the sense as a whole and, in fact, explains well the use of these cognate terms (D. R. Ap-Thomas, "Some Aspects of the Root *ḤNN* in the Old Testament," *JSS* 2 [1957]: 138).

20. Jansma, *Inquiry into the Hebrew Text and the Ancient Versions of Zechariah IX-XIV*, 118 n. 56.

21. Jansma, 118, cites 38 MSS of Kennicott's edition, and 13 MSS, of de Rossi's.

scribes could countenance. The Hebrew evidence overwhelmingly favors the traditional reading of the MT.

There is no textual reason, then, for rejecting the reading, "they will look to Me, the one they have pierced through." The difficulty lies, therefore, in the hermeneutical and theological aspects of the question. As to the former, the passage clearly teaches that YHWH (the speaker throughout in the absence of clues to the contrary), having poured out the spirit of grace leading to the people's supplications, will be seen by them as having been pierced by them. This will cause the people to break out in lament for Him, the one over whom they will grieve as they would over the death of a first-born son.

It is immediately apparent that the shift in pronoun from "they will look to *Me*" to "they will lament for *him*" is at the crux of the matter. If YHWH has been pierced through, who is the "him" who is being lamented? Or, to put it another way, why should the lament not be for YHWH, the one who has been pierced through? It is questions like these, of course, that gave rise to the textual options adduced above.

The most satisfying resolution, it seems, is to admit of a change in pronoun as a grammatical, stylistic feature without a change of the subject. That is, it is YHWH throughout who is describing the situation, and it is He who is the subject at every point. It is He who has been pierced and He whom His people, having come to their senses as to what they have done, mourn in repentance. From YHWH's viewpoint it is "Me" that is the focus; from the standpoint of the people it is "Him." Such a transition from one person to another is not at all uncommon in Hebrew composition, especially in poetic and prophetic language (GKC, 144p).

The theological question is even more profound, particularly in a strict OT confinement.[22] At the outset it must be affirmed that the OT witness knows nothing of a "mortal God," one who can be fatally wounded as in this passage. Even at its most anthropomorphic extreme there is nothing approaching what occurs here in a literal reading of the text. The great fourth servant song of Isaiah 52:13–53:12 is no exception, for the servant there, in terms of the OT understanding alone, is totally distinct from God.

This leads one to conclude that the piercing here in Zechariah 12:10 is figurative or substitutionary. The first of these will be considered and then the other. First, YHWH has been pierced by His people in the sense that they have wounded His holiness and violated His

---

22. For an excellent presentation of the major views, see Baldwin, *Haggai, Zechariah, Malachi*, 190-92.

righteousness.[23] The verb "to pierce" (דָּקַר, *dāqar*) occurs only 11 times in the OT, twice in Zechariah. Besides here in 12:10 it appears in the very next pericope, in 13:3. A comparison of the two passages is most striking and enlightening. The main thesis of 13:1-6 is that idolatry and false prophecy will be removed from the land in the day of YHWH. If a false prophet arises and continues his deceitful ways, his father and mother will "pierce him through" (*dāqar*) in accordance with the law of Moses at this point (Deut. 13:6-11).

The use of this uncommon verb (*dāqar*) in both passages, coupled with the idea of the parents of the false prophet putting him to death, on the one hand, and the "death" of YHWH who will be mourned as a son, on the other hand, compels one to view the two units as reflecting the same basic theme. The false prophet must, according to the law, be slain for his perfidy. The true "prophet," however, has been slain for his righteousness and integrity, something not unheard of in the annals of Israelite religious history. Zechariah 12:10-14 stands, then, in radical juxtaposition and contrast to 13:1-6, the one focusing on the true prophet and the other on the false.

A second possibility is that YHWH was pierced in the sense that someone who represented Him was pierced.[24] This allows the text to stand as is and to direct the focus on the persons represented by both the "Me" and the "him." YHWH is pierced, only indirectly of course, so the eyes of those who wounded Him are directed to the person who directly received the mortal blow. The problem with this interpretation is that it is impossible to identify this second party short of concluding that it is a messianic figure—to the Christian, Jesus Christ.[25] While the NT witness, to be discussed below, makes this not only possible but necessary in the fullest sense, ordinary hermeneutics would insist that the figure have some relevance, if only typological, to the time and audience of the prophet himself.[26] It seems best,

---

23. M. Delcor, "Un Problème de Critique Textuelle et d'Exégèse," *RB* 58 (1951): 193-95. Winandy draws attention to a parallel in Luke 2:34-35 where the piercing clearly must be taken metaphorically (J. Winandy, "La Prophétie de Syméon," *RB* 72 [1965]: 341-44). Winandy does not understand Zech. 12:10 this way, however.
24. This is held by the majority of scholars. See, e.g, Lamarche, *Zacharie IX-XIV*, 83; Chary, *Aggée-Zacharie, Malachie*, 202; C. von Orelli, *The Twelve Minor Prophets* (Edinburgh: T. & T. Clark, 1893), 366-67; A. F. Kirkpatrick, *The Doctrine of the Prophets* (London: Macmillan, 1901), 473.
25. Jewish tradition links Zech. 12:10 with the well-known messianic figure, the "son of Ephraim," mentioned in 2 Esd. 7:28-31; Apoc. Baruch 29, 30, 40; Enoch 90:38; C. C. Torrey, "The Messiah Son of Ephraim," *JBL* 66 (1947): 253-77.
26. R. T. France, *Jesus and the Old Testament* (London: Tyndale, 1971), 83-86, 153, 154.

then, to adopt the interpretation that it is YHWH who has been pierced, if only in a figurative way.

As far as the messianic character of 12:10 is concerned, there can be no question of its being taken that way in early Jewish tradition, to say nothing of NT Christology.[27] The gospel of John reports: "Another scripture says, 'They will look on him whom they pierced'" (John 19:37). Though John appears to follow a non-Masoretic reading[28] here, he is "quoting" Zech. 12:10 in support of the prediction of Jesus' crucifixion. The same author, in the Apocalypse, refers to the second advent of Christ with the words: "Every eye will see Him, even they who pierced Him" (Rev. 1:7). This allusion to Zechariah goes beyond that of the gospel to include the idea of looking as well as piercing.[29]

The description of the reaction to the pierced one is also suggestive of messianic language. When the people see what they have done in their spiritual blindness, they will lament as one laments for his "only son" (הַיָּחִיד, *hayyāḥîd*), his "first-born" (הַבְּכוֹר, *habbĕkôr*). יָחִיד (from יָחַד, *yāḥad*, "be united") conveys the idea of a one and only.[30] It is the term YHWH chose when speaking to Abraham about Isaac whom he was about to slay on Moriah: "Take your son, your only son (יְחִידְךָ, *yĕḥîdĕkā*), whom you love" (Gen. 22:2). The LXX renders the Hebrew word *yāḥîd* as ἀγαπητος (*agapētos*, "beloved"), the same word the NT writers use to describe Jesus, "the beloved Son" of God (e.g., Matt. 3:17; 17:5; Luke 9:35). The NT dependence here is obvious.

The word בְּכוֹר (*bekor*) also is a messianic term as far as the NT is concerned. The LXX usually renders this by πρωτότοκος (*prōtotokos*, "firstborn"), a term used several times with reference to Jesus in the NT.[31] Paul describes God's Son as "the firstborn of all creation" (Col. 1:15), certainly not in the sense of a chronological priority but as the Son par excellence. He is also the "beginning, the firstborn from

---

27. For a host of rabbinic and medieval Jewish scholars who take Zech. 12:10 messianically, see Lacocque, *Zacharie 9-14*, 191; France, *Jesus and the Old Testament*, 190-92. Cf. M.-J. Lagrange, *Le Messianisme chez les Juifs* (Paris: Librairie Victor LeCoffre, 1909), 251-56; R. Schnackenburg, "Das Schriftzitat in Joh 19, 37," *Wort, Lied und Gottesspruch*, FS für Joseph Ziegler, ed. Josef Schreiner (Würzburg: Echter Verlag, 1972), 2:239-47.
28. That is, he reads "on him" rather than "on me" with MT. See Raymond E. Brown, *The Gospel According to John (xiii-xxi)*, AB (Garden City, N.Y.: Doubleday, 1970), 938.
29. As France indicates, John 19:37 concentrates on the past fact of piercing and Rev. 1:7 on its future effect. The latter passage also connects the pierced one with the parousia of the Son of Man predicted in Dan. 7:13 (R. T. France, *Jesus and the Old Testament*, 207).
30. Paul R. Gilchrist, *TWOT*, 1:372-73, s.v. יָחַד.
31. Michaelis points out that πρωτότοκος occurs 130 times in the LXX, translating בְּכוֹר 111 times (W. Michaelis, s.v. πρωτότοκος, *TDNT*, ed. G. W. Bromiley [Grand Rapids: Eerdmans, 1968], 6:871-82).

among the dead" (Col. 1:18), the apostle goes on to say. Again, it is most evident that the NT depends on the idea of the firstborn in the OT (cf. Ex. 4:22; Num. 3:13; Ps. 89:27 [HB 89:28]; Jer. 31:9) for its technical language as well as its theological concept.

In summary, v. 10 anticipates the day when the royal house of David and all Jerusalem will receive from YHWH a spirit of grace, enabling those people to seek His forgiveness for millennia of waywardness. Once this is granted, or simultaneous with it, they will look to YHWH, the one they have mortally wounded by their heartbreaking behavior, a look that produces in them a sense of great sorrow. The only sorrow comparable is that of the loss of a first-born son in death. Such sorrow is a sign of genuine repentance, as the following verses on into chapter 13 make clear.

The only apt comparison to the grief that Jerusalem will display is that expressed with reference to Hadad-Rimmon in the plain of Megiddo (v. 11). Many scholars take this to be the weeping that attended the violent and premature death of King Josiah at Megiddo when he foolishly interposed his tiny army between the Egyptians under Pharaoh Necho and the Assyrians under Ashurbanipal (2 Kings 23:28-30).[32] The chronicler reports that Jeremiah composed a lament (Jer. 22:10?) over Josiah, and to the very day of the chronicler singers commemorated the tragic event. In fact, it became a statute (חֹק, *ḥōq*) that the observance be recited from that time on (2 Chron. 35:25).

The major difficulty with this is the reference to Hadad-Rimmon. The grammar of the passage seems to demand that Hadad-Rimmon be either a subjective or objective genitive with "lamentation." That is, it can be the lamentation that is voiced by Hadad-Rimmon or the lamentation caused by Hadad-Rimmon. The name itself is a compound of two Amorite or Canaanite divine names, that of the god of storm and that of the god of thunder.[33] Both phenomena are appropriate to a single function, that of the rain or fertility god.

In the case of a subjective genitive, Hadad-Rimmon would have

---

32. R. Tournay, "Zacharie XII-XIV et L'Histoire d'Israël," 369; Raphael Giveon, " 'In the Valley of Megiddon' (Zech. xii: ii[sic]," *JJS* 8 (1957): 160; C. F. Keil, *The Twelve Minor Prophets* (Edinburgh: T. & T. Clark, 1871), 2:390. This interpretation is based largely on the Tg. Neb., which reads (in the English of Jansma): "Like the mourning for Ahab the son of Omri whom killed Hadadrimmon the son of Thabrimmon and like the mourning for Josiah the son of Aaron whom killed Pharaoh Ḥagira (the lame)" (Jansma, *Inquiry into the Hebrew Text and the Ancient Versions of Zechariah IX-XIV*, 118).

33. M. Delcor, "Deux Passages Difficiles: Zach XII 11 et XI 13," *VT* 3 (1953): 68-69; Flemming F. Hvidbverg, *Weeping and Laughter in the Old Testament* (Leiden: Brill, 1962), 117-20; Jonas C. Greenfield, "The Aramean God Ramman/Rimmon," *IEJ* 26 (1976): 195-98.

to be a place name, it seems, for it is unlikely that the lamentation of a pagan deity would be an apt point of comparison to an act of repentance by God's people for being idolatrous in the first place. There is, however, no place of this name known in either the OT or in other prosopography. The objective genitive view—that there was lamentation in Megiddo because of Hadad-Rimmon—is much more plausible but not without its difficulties. There is no known shrine in Megiddo associated with Hadad-Rimmon,[34] nor is there any extant myth describing his death or similar calamity that would occasion such lament. The "weeping for Tammuz" in Ezek. 8:14 comes to mind, as does the Baal epic from Ugarit in which there is great lamentation over Baal upon his death at the hands of Mot.[35] Baal, of course, is just another way of describing Hadad.

Again, the major objection to this is the lack of any evidence for a Hadad-Rimmon shrine at Megiddo where such lamentation might have taken place at such an exaggerated level as to make it a point of comparison. Moreover, the fact that deep sorrow for sin in Judah should be compared to the lament of pagans over a catastrophe that had befallen one of their mystic deities seems most unlikely.[36] It might be best in the final analysis to assume that there was a place by this name at or near Megiddo, one perhaps marking the spot where Josiah fell, and that it was there that the periodic lamentations for the godly king took place.

To return to the present passage, it is noteworthy how the lamentation over the pierced one will be manifest. Each clan (so מִשְׁפָּחָה, *mišpāḥâ*, is best rendered) of Judah will lament by itself (v. 12*a*). This suggests that a community or corporate repentance will not be suffi-

---

34. Greenfield notes that Rammān had a shrine in Damascus and that King Ben-Hadad's father, who ruled in Damascus, was named Tabrimmon. Damascus is close to Megiddo but hardly close enough to qualify as "in" the Valley of Megiddo (Greenfield, "The Aramean God Ramman/Rimmon," 187). Tournay connects the place of lamentation with Carmel and its foothills, an area famous for the worship of Baal-Hadad (Tournay, "Zacharie XII-XIV et L'Histoire d'Israël," 368-69).
35. Hvidberg, *Weeping and Laughter in the Old Testament*, 118.
36. Indeed, Delcor finds such a comparison "bien répugner à la notion de transcendance du Dieu d'Israel" ("most repugnant to the idea of the transcendence of the God of Israel") (M. Delcor, "Deux Passages Difficiles: Zach XII 11 et XI 13," 70). He argues, therefore, that the Tg. Neb. and Syr. readings that speak of a "Son of Amon" underlie the MT and should be retained. Thus הֲדַד־רִמּוֹן by slight emendation becomes יְד(י)ד (cf. יָחִיד, v. 10) or (more drastic) בֶּן־אָמוֹן, "son of Amon." Josiah was, of course, a son of Amon (Delcor, 72). In response, it is far more likely that the MT is correct and that Tg. Neb. and Syr. have tried to make sense of an obtuse text and at the same time avoid reference to places or persons connected with paganism.

cient, for each member and entity of that community is individually culpable and must individually give account before God. Even wives cannot depend upon the repentance of their husbands, for, as Ezekiel said in respect to personal responsibility, the old proverb to the effect that the fathers have eaten sour grapes and their children's teeth are set on edge will be annulled. From now on the principle will apply that "the person who sins, that one will die" (Ezek. 18:4).

The particularizing of the mourning begins at the top of the socio-political-economic ladder, the royal house. The clan of David is not exempt from repentance, for with few exceptions the dynasty of David, which ruled over Judah, failed to discharge its responsibility as shepherd over the flock. That it is the succession of Davidic kings and not literally David is made clear by the reference to the clan of Nathan that follows (v. 12*b*).

Nathan was the third son of David born in Jerusalem, apparently an elder brother of Solomon by a different wife (2 Sam. 5:14; 1 Chron. 3:5). Though the kings of Judah from Solomon to the tribe of the Exile were descendants of Solomon (1 Chron. 3:10-16), it is quite apparent that a change occurred at that point and that royal descent began to be traced through Nathan.[37] This is hinted at in the OT genealogical and dynastic records and made explicit in the NT. Zerubbabel, as we have noted already (see pp. 146ff.) was of royal blood but was not of the line of Solomon. Though in one list he is called the son of Pedaiah (1 Chron. 3:17-19), he is usually considered to be the son of Shealtiel (Ezra 3:2, 8; 5:2; Neh. 12:1; Hag. 1:12, 14; Matt. 1:12; Luke 3:27). Probably he was, in fact, the grandson of Shealtiel. Jehoiachin, however, left no male heir (Jer. 22:3) and yet had "sons" (1 Chron. 3:17). These sons may have been offspring of a daughter who, according to Luke's genealogy, married Neri, a descendant of David in a parallel line through Nathan (Luke 3:27). Luke also records that Zerubbabel was of the Nathan lineage, as was Jesus Himself (Luke 3:23-31). Because the prophet Zechariah was a contemporary of Zerubbabel, he would naturally refer to the Davidic house of his own time as the "clan of Nathan," for by then the line of descent had already shifted from Solomon to Nathan.[38]

The "clan of Levi" (v. 13) refers to the whole priestly or religious side of Israel's life, just as "clan of David" spoke of the political. The Shimeites, then, were the descendants of Levi who presumably dominated the Levitical classes in the postexilic era. Shimei was, according to the genealogies, the grandson of Levi through Gershom (Ex.

---

37. Chary, *Aggée-Zacharie, Malachie*, 205.
38. Alfred Plummer, *A Critical and Exegetical Commentary on the Gospel According to S. Luke*, ICC (Edinburgh: T. & T. Clark, 1905), 104.

6:16-17; cf. Num. 3:17-18). He was not a priest inasmuch as the priests traced their lineage back to Gershom's brother Kohath (1 Chron. 6:1-3), so he represents specifically the Levites.[39] Yet the priests and their wives would also be included under the general Levitical umbrella, for the purpose here is to suggest a general repentance embracing the totality of political and religious life.

This is clear from the last verse (v. 14), which summarizes by including all the rest, that is, those not included before. Thus, the entire society of Judah will, in the day of YHWH's coming, repent of their sins as they face up to His inexpressible salvation opened up to them by the pouring out of His grace.

---

39. R. Tournay, "Zacharie XII-XIV et L'Histoire d'Israël," 369-70.

2
Refinement of Judah (13:1-9)

A. CLEANSING OF GOD'S PEOPLE (13:1-6)

Translation

[1]"In that day there will be a fountain opened up for the house of David and the inhabitants of Jerusalem for sin and for impurity. [2]And it will also be in that day," says YHWH of hosts, "that I will cut off the names of the idols from the land, and they will never again be remembered. Moreover, I will remove the prophets and unclean spirit from the land. [3]Then if anyone prophesies still, his father and mother who gave him life will say to him, 'You cannot live, for you lie in the name of YHWH.' Then his father and mother who gave him life will pierce him through when he prophesies. [4]So it will be in that day that each prophet will be ashamed of his vision when he prophesies and will no longer wear the hairy cloak to deceive. [5]Instead he will say, 'I am no prophet—indeed, I am a farmer, for a man has *made me his bondsman from my youth.' [6]Then someone will ask him, 'What are these wounds on your chest?' and he will answer, 'Some which I suffered in the house of my friends.'

Exegesis and Exposition

The lamentation of repentance that results when Judah sees the one whom they have pierced by their apostate disobedience will in turn result in their forgiveness, an act described in the present unit as

327

a purification or cleansing.[1] As is always the case with genuine conversion there are both negative and positive aspects. The positive consists of the restoration to fellowship that takes place when sin has been forgiven (v. 1). The negative involves the removal of those habits and attitudes that occasioned the interruption of fellowship between God and His people in the first place (vv. 2-6).

This is true of all times and circumstances, but the present oracle continues to be rooted firmly in the eschaton as "in that day" of v. 2 makes most clear (cf. vv. 2, 4). Therefore, the cleansing here has to do with a final work of YHWH, one that the context specifically links to His elect people Israel. It is described in the metaphor of a fountain, an artesian well (מָקוֹר, *māqôr*), that gushes forth to provide cleansing for the house of David and inhabitants of Jerusalem. In particular it will remove "sin" (חַטָּאת, *ḥaṭṭā't*) and "impurity" (נִדָּה, *niddâ*), the former having to do with lack of conformity to the divine will and the latter with the condition or state of defilement brought about by any breach of the principles of holiness.[2] One is more an active expression of sin and the other a passive result. Here in the passage both have to do with the matter of idolatry and false prophets. The sin was the rejection of YHWH and violation of His covenant. The impurity is the condition of the people because of their sin of repudiating YHWH and turning instead to idols and false prophets. Thus the two are the obverse and reverse of the same coin.

The cleansing fountain is opened specifically to the house of David and inhabitants of Jerusalem, for they are the two entities singled out in 12:10, the ones upon whom YHWH will pour out the spirit of grace and supplication. They, however, are only representative of the whole redeemed people, as 12:12-14 puts beyond doubt. What is important to note here is that the cleansing fountain of 13:1 is presupposed by the divine initiative of grace in 12:10. It is only when the people of YHWH face up to Him as the one whom they have wounded and then repent sincerely of their wickedness that the fountain of cleansing is opened up to them. This is not in any way contrary to the Christian gospel message (Rom. 10:9-10; cf. Tit. 3:5).

---

1. Many scholars connect 13:1 with chapter 12 and commence the next pericope with 13:2. Otzen, e.g., joins 13:1 to 12:12-14 because of a common "kultischen charakter"; Benedikt Ozten, *Studien über Deuterosacharja*, ATD 6 (Copenhagen: Prostant Apud Munksgaard, 1964), 179. It seems more likely, however, that 13:1 represents the positive side of Israel's conversion and 13:2-6 the negative so that the two must go together.
2. See, respectively, K. Koch, *TDOT*, 4:310, s.v. חָטָא ("religious disqualification of specific human acts and modes of conduct"); J. Milgrom and G. E. Wright, *TWAT*, V 1/2: cols. 251-52, s.v. נִדָּה ("Unreinheit"); Milgrom and Wright suggest that נִדָּה in Zech. 13:1 is a synonym of חַטָּאת.

As part and parcel of the cleansing—indeed, as its manifestation —is the cutting off of the very names of the idols that Israel and Judah had embraced so frequently in the course of their history. The verb "to cut off" (כָּרַת, *kārat*) is particularly poignant here because it is the technical term used to describe the making of a covenant (בְּרִית כָּרַת, *kārat běrît*), that is, "to cut a covenant." Israel had broken the covenant time and time again, particularly in the worship of other gods in idolatry. Now YHWH has restored the covenant relationship and will "cut off" the names of the idols. This means not only to do away with them by some destructive act such as that of Elijah on Mount Carmel (1 Kings 18:38-40), but to remove their very remembrance from the minds and hearts of the people (v. 2; cf. Hos. 2:19).

The main focus of the passage is not on the idols, however, but on the false prophets who either speak falsely in the name of YHWH or as spokesmen of the false gods represented by the prophets. In either case they are not motivated by the spirit of YHWH but by an "unclean spirit," unclean both because of its inherent nature as demonic and because it inspires the prophets to proclaim lies and other misleading and unclean speech.[3] A classic illustration of this combination of a false prophet and an unclean spirit occurs in the heavenly scene described by the prophet Micaiah (1 Kings 22:19-23) who tells Ahab and Jehoshaphat that he saw YHWH surrounded by His royal court and seeking their counsel as to how to confound Ahab. Finally a "lying spirit" (רוּחַ שֶׁקֶר, *rûaḥ šeqer*) volunteers to inspire Ahab's prophets to advise him to go to battle and to assure him of victory.

According to Judges 9:23 God sent an "evil spirit" (רוּחַ רָעָה, *rûaḥ rā'â*) between Abimelech and the Shechemites. Its task was to cause the Shechemites to become traitorous toward Abimelech and turn on him. An "evil spirit" (also *rā'â*) *from* YHWH also came upon Saul once the spirit *of* YHWH had left him (1 Sam. 16:14). This spirit terrified him and could be controlled only when David played soothing music

---

3. Otzen points out that the phrase רוּחַ הַטֻּמְאָה is a *hapax legomenon* and refers here to cultic uncleanness because that is the regular meaning of טֻמְאָה (cf. 6:10; Jer. 2:23; Ezek. 22:3; 23:7; Hos. 5:3); Otzen, *Studien über Deuterosacharja*, 195. In that case, the false prophets in view here are instrumental in leading the people into ritual defilement, an idea that finds support in the נִדָּה of v. 1. In other words, they would appear to be "cult prophets" rather than "ordinary" false prophets. On the other hand, the context suggests that "unclean" cannot be taken too technically, for the prophets are described as "speaking lies" (v. 3) and wearing the "hairy garment" (v. 4), one associated not exclusively with cultic prophets. It might be better to follow Mitchell who says that the spirit of uncleanness "must be the disposition to neglect the precepts of Yahweh, or even worship the abominations of other peoples" (H. G. Mitchell, *A Commentary on Haggai and Zechariah*, ICC [Edinburgh: T. & T. Clark, 1912], 337).

on his harp (16:23). Though not involving prophesying in these cases, the notion of harmful, evil spirits is very much at home in the OT.

It is in light of the ultimate sovereignty of YHWH over all creation, including the spirit world, that these instances must be understood. Though not the source of the wickedness that these unclean spirits purvey, YHWH could and did release them to accomplish His own mysterious purposes of judgment and discipline. Even Satan, the epitome of the evil spirits, could become a servant of YHWH, testing and evaluating the character of godly Job (Job 1:6-12; cf. 1 Chron. 21:1).

It is evident, then, that the unclean spirit of our passage is a spirit inspiring the false prophets who prophesy lies in the name of YHWH. He allows them to carry out their pernicious ministry, but when the time of repentance and renewal comes, He banishes them from the land (v. 2). If any persists in prophesying (clearly as a false prophet, as v. 3 shows), the ancient Mosaic penalty must be brought to bear: his father and mother must put him to death (Deut. 13:6-11; cf. 18:20-22). Though the penalty of Deuteronomy is in immediate connection with false prophets who urge the people to follow other gods (Deut. 13:1-5), those who speak lies in YHWH's name are subject to the same judgment (Deut. 18:20).

As noted with reference to Zech. 12:10, the false prophet, though a beloved son of his parents, must be slain by them by being pierced through (דָּקַר, *dāqār*), presumably with a spear or lance. The same verb occurs not only in 12:10 but in Num. 25:8 where an Israelite man and Midianite woman, engaged in a pagan act of sexual intercourse designed to facilitate the worship of Baal at Peor (Num. 25:1-3), were slain by being thrust through with a spear. The conceptual connections between that incident and the idolatry and false prophetism of Zech. 13:1-6 are quite apparent.

The result of such exposure and subsequent application of the death penalty will be an attempt on the part of the charlatan prophets to deny their involvement in false prophesying. They will be ashamed of their visions and will cast aside the clothing customarily worn by prophets to indicate their profession (v. 4). "Ashamed" is a literal translation of בּוֹשׁ (*bôš*), the verb used here, but it is shame in the sense of a refusal to divulge what one knows or has seen. This is certainly a rare nuance of the verb, but its essential correctness is sustained by consideration of the parallel structure. Leaving aside the introductory formula, "in that day," the verse reads as follows:

> Each prophet will *be ashamed* of his vision when he prophesies,
> and they will no longer *wear* the hairy cloak to deceive.

Besides the assonance of the underlined verbs (יֵבֹשׁוּ, *yēbōšû*, and יִלְבְּשׁוּ,

yilbĕšû), "wear to deceive" clearly corresponds to "be ashamed." Thus, just as the removal of the hairy cloak is for the purpose of hiding the true identity of the false prophet, so his being ashamed of his vision also accomplishes that objective.

The "hairy garment" (אַדֶּרֶת שֵׂעָר, *'adderet śē'ār*) was the distinctive attire of many of the OT prophets, notably Elijah. He wrapped his face in such an apparel when confronted by the living God at Horeb (1 Kings 19:13) and, on transferring his office to Elisha, did so by casting the hairy cloak upon him (19:19). He used it also to part the Jordan River (2 Kings 2:8), a feat Elisha was able to duplicate using the same cloak (2:14). John the Baptist, a NT prophet in the tradition of Elijah, was recognized as such by his clothing of camel's hair (Matt. 3:4).

Though this no doubt communicated something of a rustic, casual nature, the word *'adderet* itself connotes a garment of glory or magnificence. The office of prophet, after all, was one of exalted privilege, for the prophet was none other than the herald of the Great King. His very apparel should be a token of the lofty position he held. The word (without "hairy") appears in Josh. 7:21 to describe the beautiful Babylonian garment found by Achan in the ruins of Jericho.[4] So highly prized was it that he took it for himself rather than give it over to YHWH, as the *ḥērem* on Jericho required.

The false prophets of the age to come will not only deny that they have had visions, then, but they will also remove the visible sign of their glory—their hairy garments. These they had worn, not as the regular attire of false prophets, but to simulate true prophets and thus to deceive those who heard them. Now they will even seek to conceal that they were prophets at all, for the risk of exposure was too great. Their true nature will be found out after all, and they will face the penalty the law demanded of pagan prophets.

Beyond this denial of vision and change of apparel, the false prophet in that day will verbally affirm that he is no prophet (v. 5). Like Amos (who was telling the truth, unlike these), he will assert that he is a farmer (Amos 7:14). The repetition of the first person independent personal pronoun אָנֹכִי (*'ānōkî*), "I," suggests the vigor of his protestations.[5] Literally, he will say, "Not a prophet am I; a worker of the soil am I!" That farming is not a recent occupation, he says, is evident from the fact that he has been a bondman from the days of his youth.

Those who have known him know better, however, and one will

---

4. Woudstra notes the connection between the garment of Josh. 7:21 and the mantle of Elijah and says of the latter that "though made of hair it may have been a beautiful article of clothing" (Marten H. Woudstra, *The Book of Joshua*, NICOT [Grand Rapids: Eerdmans, 1981], 129 n. 48).

ask, "If you are no prophet, how do you explain these wounds on your chest?" (v. 6) His answer is a feeble lie, "I got them in the house of friends."[6] Even without the hairy cloak, then, the false prophet can be identified—by the wounds on his chest. Such translations for this last phrase as "between the arms" or the like are much too literal. Comparative Semitic evidence has been helpful in clarifying the idiom.[7] The OT itself makes clear that it is the thorax that is intended, for in 2 Kings 9:24 the arrow Jehu shoots at King Joram of Israel strikes him "between the arms," piercing his heart.

Incisions on the body were characteristic of many of the religious practitioners of the ancient Near East, particularly among the Canaanites. The OT, in response to this sign of paganism, warns the priest and prophets of Israel (and, indeed, the people at large) to forgo such things in the interests of maintaining pure faith toward YHWH (Lev. 19:28; Deut. 14:1). The purpose of these self-lacerations is not entirely clear, but they apparently had something to do with sympathetic rituals undertaken to induce certain action by the gods. A biblical case no doubt is that of the contest between Elijah and the Baal prophets at Carmel. After those prophets had prayed and pleaded for Baal to ignite their sacrifices, with abysmal lack of success, they became frenzied and began to cut themselves until the blood poured from their veins and arteries (1 Kings 18:28).[8] The objective was to

---

5. So also the word order. Cf. Merrill F. Unger, *Zechariah* (Grand Rapids: Zondervan, 1963), 227.
6. H. L. Ginsberg suggests that אָדָם הִקְנַנִי ("a man indentured me") be emended to אָדֹם הִשְׁקוּנִי ("I was plied with the red stuff"). His point is that this prophet has become hallucinatory because of his wild drinking, a condition that even results in physical wounds (cf. Prov. 23:29-35). The "tiller of the soil," he says, is reminiscent of Noah (Gen. 9:20 ff.) who became drunk on his wine (H. L. Ginsberg, "The Oldest Record of Hysteria with Physical Stigmata, Zech. 13:2-6," in *Studies in the Bible and the Ancient Near East*, ed. Y. Avishur and J. Blau [Jerusalem: E. Rubinstein, 1978], 23-27). Although ingenious and to be applauded for its polemic against the commonly held view that postexilic prophetism was becoming anathema, Ginsberg's approach is highly fanciful and based on arbitrary emendation.
7. The Ugaritic Ba'al Epic offers an example:

    ylm ktp zbl ym
    bn ydm ṯpṭ nhr (CTA 2, iv:16)
    It struck the shoulders of prince Yam,
    Between the arms of Judge Nahar.

    Here the parallel to shoulders (*ktp*) makes it clear that "between the arms" (lit. "hands"), *bn ydm*, refers to the chest. See J. C. L. Gibson, *Canaanite Myths and Legends* (Edinburgh: T. & T. Clark, 1977), 44.
8. John Gray, *I & II Kings* (London: SCM, 1970), 399; H. H. Rowley, "Elijah on Mount Carmel," *BJRL* 43 (1960-61): 208-9; D. R. Ap-Thomas, "Elijah on Mount Carmel," *PEQ* (1960), 146-55.

impress the deity with their act of wholesale devotion and self-denial so much that Baal would have no recourse but to be moved to send the fire from heaven for which he was so famous.

It is not possible to know whether that was a common feature of Canaanite or pagan Israelite practice and particularly whether such self-induced wounds were *ad hoc* in response to particular crises or were a regular part of the markings of a prophet. Our passage in Zechariah would suggest the correctness of the latter view, for the marks the prophet bears are so typical of those of the prophets that they betray him as one. His excuse that they came from a brawl in the house of friends convinces no one. The Hebrew translated here "friends" usually means "lovers" and could mean that here as well.[9] Because "lovers" in the OT is a term regularly applied to illicit relationships, particularly in the cultic realm where the gods were the "lovers," the prophet's plight in such a case would be all the more damning, because he may be confessing that he was the victim of self-inflicted wounds in a pagan temple. In any event, his charade is unconvincing, for in the day of YHWH such pretense will be exposed for what it is.

Additional Notes

13:5 הִקְנַנִי ("indentured me"): The Hebrew of the MT says literally, "a man made me his bondsman from my youth." This unexpected addition to the statement that he is a farmer has led some scholars to suggest that אָדָם הִקְנַנִי, "a man acquired me," be read אֲדָמָה קִנְיָנִי, "the land is mine" (cf. אֲדָמָה in the previous phrase); so Alfons Deissler, *Zwölf Propheten III. Zefanja, Haggai, Sacharja, Maleachi* (Würzburg: Echter Verlag, 1988), 309. Wellhausen had first proposed such an emendation in 1898 in his *Die Kleinen Propheten*, 201. R. P. Gordon has now adduced a Targum witness to this reading, giving Wellhausen unexpected support (R. P. Gordon, "Targum Variant Agrees with Wellhausen," *ZAW* 87 [1975]: 218-19). This hardly yields better sense and, in fact, is not nearly as persuasive an argument as to say that he is a farmer and has been one for years.

---

9. The word מְאַהֲבָי (pi. ptc. of אָהֵב, "to love") means lit., "my lovers" or "those who love me." The gender indicates male lovers, so many scholars suggest that the prophet here is professing to have been in the pagan temple associating with fellow practitioners of the rites carried on there (cf. Jer. 22:20; Ezek. 16:33; Hos. 2:5). So Rex Mason, *The Books of Haggai, Zechariah, Malachi*, CBC (Cambridge: Cambridge Univ., 1977), 122. It makes more sense to take the word in a normal social sense as "friend," however, for if the man is trying to deny his association with prophetism, why would he admit to having been in the company of false prophets whose ritual frequently involved bodily laceration?

B. PRESERVATION OF GOD'S PEOPLE (13:7-9)

Translation

⁷Awake, sword, against My shepherd,
  against the man (who is) My associate,
  says YHWH of hosts.
  *Strike the shepherd that the flock may be scattered;
  I will turn My hand against the insignificant ones.
⁸It will happen in all the land, says YHWH,
  that two there will be cut off and die,
  but the third will be left there.
⁹Then I will bring the third into the fire,
  and I will refine them like silver is refined
  and will try them as gold is tried.
  They will call on My name and I will answer,
  I will say, 'It is My people,' and they will say, 'YHWH is my
  God.'" (13:7-9)

Exegesis and Exposition

Because of the many affinities between this poem and the shepherd themes of chapter 11, many scholars connect the two, viewing the poem as a climax to the entire shepherd metaphor that commences in chapter 11 (or even in 10:2-3) and continues, though in more hidden form, through chapters 12 and 13.[10] Some even go so far as to argue that the poem is misplaced, having originally followed 11:15-17.[11] Although there clearly are especially close links between the poem and chapter 11, there is no need to conclude that the poem is not at home in its present place. In fact, there are good reasons for its appearance precisely where it is as a continuation of and response to the diatribe against idolatry and false prophets that immediately precedes it (13:1-6).

By using such terms as "fountain," "sin," "uncleanness," idols," and "unclean spirit" (13:1-2a), the prophet has obliquely at least addressed the matter of corrupt cult and priesthood. Then, turning to the prophets who preach lies and practice pagan divination, he has obviously brought wicked prophetism within his purview (13:2b-6). The third element of Israel's institutional life, the monarchy, yet re-

---

10. For a summary of such views, see Otzen, *Studien über Deuterosacharja*, 192-93. Van Hoonacker takes the extreme position of arranging the "allégorie du prophète pasteur" as follows: 11:4-17 + 13:7-9 + 10:3c-12 (A. Van Hoonacker, *Les Douze Petits Prophètes*, 671-80).
11. So, e.g., Wilhelm Rudolph, *Haggai-Sacharja 1-8–Sacharja 9-14–Maleachi*, KAT (Gütersloh: Verlaghaus Gerd Mohn, 1976), 227-28; Van Hoonacker, previous note.

mains to be censured and judged; that is the burden of the present poem.

As noted repeatedly, Zechariah's favorite way of referring to Israel's kings is as shepherd. There can be no doubt that he has the kings in view here as well but in an exclusively eschatological setting as the whole context of chapter 13 makes plain. Thus the connection is not so much with previous shepherd sections, as with its own canonical setting. For example, the false prophet suffers death at the hands of his own parents by being pierced through (v. 3). In the poem the shepherd becomes the victim of a sword, invoked to come and slay him (v. 7). Bearing self-inflicted wounds (מַכּוֹת, *makkôt*), which he says were the result of blows inflicted (הֻכֵּיתִי, *hukkîtî*) by friends, the false prophet stands condemned (13:6). In the poem the call goes out to strike (הַךְ, *hak*) the shepherd for his faithlessness in carrying out his regal responsibilities (v. 7). In all three places where "wound" or "strike" occurs the same verb, a form of נָכָה (*nākâ*) is used. The connection between 13:4-6 and 13:7-9 could hardly be stronger.[12]

The poem (if, indeed, it is that) consists of three stanzas, the first of which (v. 7) concerns the shepherd-king, the second (v. 8) the decimation of the flock, and the third (v. 9) the purification and restoration of the remnant of the flock. In a loose way this third section harks back to v. 1, the idea of purification forming an inclusio around the whole chapter.[13]

By means of apostrophe YHWH summons the sword against "My

---

12. Lamarche shows the indispensability of 13:7-9 in its present place in his analysis of the unity of 12:10–13:9:

Quelqu'un est transpercé;	Pasteur frappé par
(Someone is pierced through)	(The shepherd struck by)
deuil, purification et retour	l'épée; purification et
(mourning, purification	(the sword; purification and)
and return)	
à Dieu (12:10–13:1)	retour à Dieu (13:7-9).
(to God)	(return to God)

Idoles et faux prophètes
(Idols and false prophets)
supprimés (13:2-6)
(suppressed)

Thus 13:7-9 serves as a counterpoint to 12:10–13:1, the whole revolving around the idea of the rejection of idolatry (P. Lamarche, *Zacharie IX-XIV. Structure Littéraire et Messianisme* [Paris: Librairie Lecoffre, 1961], 108). So also R. Tournay, "Zacharie XII-XIV et L'Histoire d'Israel," *RB* 81 (1974): 372.

13. Lamarche divides the poem into two strophes, vv. 7-8 and v. 9. The first, he says, describes the chastisement that falls on the shepherd and the flock. The second describes the purification and return to God (Lamarche, *Zacharie IX-XIV*, 92).

shepherd." The use of the possessive pronoun suggests a closeness of relationship in which the king functions alongside and on behalf of YHWH. This is a notion thoroughly grounded in the OT (Deut. 17:14-17; Pss. 2:6-9; 45:1-2 [HB 45:2-3]; 72:1-4). A remarkable confirmation of this ideology follows in the description of the shepherd as "My fellow," or "associate." This noun (עָמִית, *'āmît*) occurs otherwise only in Leviticus where it appears in parallel to YHWH (6:2) and God (25:17) but usually as a general term for fellow-man (19:11, 15, 17; 25:14, 15). In the two parallel constructions the parallelism is not poetic, but the juxtaposition is such as to afford an unusually close connection between *'āmît* and the divine name. Thus, 6:2 reads in part, "If anyone commits a trespass against YHWH and deals falsely with his fellowman," etc. The other, 25:17, says, "You shall not wrong one another (that is, your fellow), but you shall fear your God."

This language of association pales in comparison to the bold assertion by YHWH that the shepherd-king, in effect, is his "fellowman."[14] All the more poignant, then, is the command to the sword to strike this one so that the flock may become scattered. In this act not only will the leaders of the community suffer the blow of YHWH's righteous indignation, but so will the flock, "the insignificant ones" as they are described. This command is akin to the determination of YHWH, expressed earlier, to deliver the inhabitants of the land, the "poor of the flock," into the hands of their persecutors (11:5, 6, 9). He will, in the last day, turn His hand against these least ones, for they too stand condemned with their rulers.

Some scholars understand the second line of the verse to mean "strike the shepherd *and* the flock will scatter" rather than "*that* the flock may be scattered."[15] This is often the result of assuming that the flock is innocent, and it is only because of judgment on the shepherd that the sheep also suffer. Others see an exclusively messianic motif here in which the shepherd himself is innocent, being condemned and put to death unjustly.[16] This view no doubt is greatly influenced by the piercing of YHWH, the messianic prototype, in 12:10. The two

---

14. Lacocque, quoting S. B. Frost (*OT Apocalyptic*), renders the term "my peer" (André Lacocque, *Zacharie 9-14*, CAT [Neuchatel: Delachaux & Niestlé, 1981], 197). He goes on to suggest (incorrectly, in our view) that this "fellow" is the high priest. This goes against the overwhelming OT evidence that "shepherd" is a royal epithet.
15. Thus Unger, *Zechariah*, 233. Unger (and most evangelicals), however, views the shepherd as the Messiah only, so the smiting of the shepherd is not punishment for wrong but his deliverance over to a vicarious death for sinners. The whole context of 13:1-9 can hardly sustain such a limited view.
16. R. C. Dentan, "The Book of Zechariah," *IB* (Nashville: Abingdon, 1956), 6:1109-10.

passages, however, have very little in common otherwise. Moreover, the innocence of the shepherd is refuted by the fact that it is YHWH's command, not permission, that he be slain. Any appeal to Isaiah 53:10—[17] "it pleased YHWH to bruise him"—seems wide of the mark if for no other reason than that Zech. 13:7-9 is solidly imbedded in a context (13:1-6) that insists on the whole as being an indictment of Israel's leadership—priestly, prophetic, and royal. To this one should add the observation that to "turn the hand upon" almost always connotes an act of judgment (cf. especially Ps. 81:14 [HB 81:15]; Isa. 1:25; Amos 1:8).[18]

In addition to all this, the scattering of the sheep, far from being an accidental consequence of the striking of the shepherd, is, in fact, for the purpose of ridding the flock of the elements that must be purged. This consists of two-thirds of the sheep, a figure that most likely means the majority as opposed to the remnant, the one-third (v. 8). The remnant who survive the purging will pass through a refining process designed to equip them to have minds and hearts that are open and responsive to the sovereign claims of YHWH (v. 9).

The fractions here call to mind a passage in Ezekiel that sheds considerable light on the problem of the scattered sheep in Zechariah and how their affliction is to be understood.[19] YHWH had commanded Ezekiel to cut his hair and then to burn a third of it at the conclusion of the Babylonian siege of Jerusalem (5:2). A second third must then be struck (תַכֶּה, *takkeh*, from נָכָה [*nākâ*], "smite") with the sword and the third scattered to the wind. These last, the dispersed ones, will provide the matrix from which a remnant will issue, a select number of "hairs" that will pass through the refining fires (5:3-4).[20] Ezekiel goes on to define the fire of v. 2 more narrowly as pestilence, the sword as slaughter in war, and the scattering as exile

---

17. So Joyce G. Baldwin, *Haggai, Zechariah, Malachi* (London: Tyndale, 1972), 198.

18. Mason, *The Books of Haggai, Zechariah, and Malachi*, 111. Tournay, citing Isa. 56:11; Jer. 10:21; 12:10; 23:1-3; and Ezek. 34 says the text is speaking of "un mauvais pasteur qui doit payer de sa vie ses négligences et ses fautes"; ("an evil shepherd who must pay with his own life for his negligence and shortcomings") (Tournay, "Zacharie XII-XIV et L'Histoire d'Israel," 372).

19. Saebø, *Sacharja 9-14. Untersuchungen von Text und Form* (Neukirchen-Vluyn: Neukirchen Verlag, 1969), 279; Otzen, *Studien über Deuterosacharja*, 193. It is important to remember, of course, that Ezekiel's vision related primarily to the historical event of Babylonian exile, whereas Zechariah's oracle is exclusively eschatological. One could say, however, that Ezekiel provides a typological model of a future judgment described by Zechariah.

20. Charles L. Feinberg, *The Prophecy of Ezekiel* (Chicago: Moody, 1969), 36-37.

(v. 12; cf. 6:8). The "hairs" that remain of the deportation he identifies as the remnant who, in captivity, will remember YHWH and come to know that he indeed is YHWH (6:8-10).

There appears to be some contradiction in Zechariah's description in terms of the destiny of the third one-third. He agrees with Ezekiel that two-thirds die, but implies that the rest remain in the land. However, there is no contradiction at all. What Zechariah says conforms to the historical fact, reflected in Ezekiel, that after the population of Judah and Jerusalem died of hunger and sword, only the survivors (those remaining alive) obviously were left in the land. But they too went "into the fire" (v. 9), that is, the fire of exile as Ezekiel described it (Ezek. 5:4; cf. 5:12). It is in exile that they were refined like silver and tried or assayed like gold. It was there, in the crucible of purification, that they called upon the name of YHWH and that He answered them. It is there, finally, that they became again the true people of YHWH and that they said of Him, "YHWH is my God" (cf. Hos. 2:23).

In an eschatological repetition of exile, then, the shepherd-kings of Israel will suffer the wrath of God (cf. 11:8), the flock-people will endure pestilence and sword (cf. 11:6, 9), and the surviving community will be scattered (cf. 11:16). But from the dispersed population will emerge a purified remnant that knows and confesses YHWH, one that will experience the incomparable joy of being known as His people. These are the ones in view at the beginning of chapter 13, those of the house of David, and of the inhabitants of Jerusalem to whom the fountains of cleansing will be opened up. They are the redeemed who will remember YHWH while in exile and who, in a mighty second exodus, will return to the land to exercise dominion in His name (10:8-12).

The forgoing understanding of the identity of the shepherd and sheep must, however, be balanced by careful attention to the NT use of the passage, especially of v. 7. Both Matthew and Mark cite the verse as a quotation of Jesus who, anticipating His forthcoming suffering and death, said, "all of you will be offended in me tonight, for it is written, 'I will strike the shepherd, and the sheep of the flock will be scattered abroad'" (Matt. 26:31; Mark 14:27 is not significantly different). Clearly both evangelists regard the Zechariah text as a messianic testimonial as, indeed, must Jesus Himself have done.[21] How, then, can this use of the text be squared with the view of a king

---

21. For matters such as Matthew's use of the LXX and his citation of the Zechariah text otherwise, see Donald A. Carson, "Matthew," in *EBC*, ed. Frank E. Gaebelein (Grand Rapids: Zondervan, 1984), 8:540-41.

(or monarchy itself) who is condemned and punished by God and a dispersed Israel?

The answer (as in the case with 12:10) must be either that Jesus and the authors of the gospels see in Zech. 13:7 a prefiguring or prototype of a suffering Messiah, a kind of exegesis well known in first-century rabbinic circles;[22] or they merely use the language in a proverb-like way to express what happens when a shepherd becomes incapacitated or removed altogether. One could say that it is a maxim that when shepherds are struck down sheep inevitably scatter.[23] Such an interpretation has in its favor the fact that the sub-pericope 13:7-9 has strong linkage to 13:1-6, and the whole together appears to speak of divine judgment in the eschaton against priests, prophets, and kings.[24] In addition, it can be argued that neither Matthew nor Mark has Jesus' comment saying that He is fulfilling prophecy. He seems to be simply affirming the aphorism of the cause and effect established by the removal of a shepherd from his flock.

The history of Christian exegesis insists on more than this, however, almost univocally understanding Zechariah 13:7 as a messianic prophecy pure and simple.[25] Such a long standing and persistent tradition cannot be ignored for surely it is based on the correct assumption that Jesus and the evangelists saw in the shepherd and sheep more than did Zechariah in his own time and context. That is, Jesus viewed the verse as transcending the narrow confines of its historical and literary environment and as having allusion to Himself and His disciples as well. As has been noted, this kind of exegesis was commonly employed by the rabbis and by Jesus and the early church.[26] Although it might appear to be incompatible with the

---

22. See Michael Fishbane, *Biblical Interpretation in Ancient Israel* (Oxford: Clarendon, 1985), 350-79, 501-3.
23. Lane appears to take the reference in Mark 14:27 to reflect a proverbial saying: "Even as sheep are scattered in panic when their shepherd falls, so the death of Jesus will cause the disciples to desert him" (William L. Lane, *The Gospel According to Mark*, NICNT [Grand Rapids: Eerdmans, 1974], 511).
24. F. F. Bruce shows that the Zadokite document (the "Damascus Document"), which cites Zech. 13:7, suggests that the shepherd is evil (F. F. Bruce, *Biblical Exegesis in the Qumran Texts* [London: Tyndale, 1960], 38-39). This, of course, cannot prove that Jesus, too, interpreted Zech. 13:7 that way, but it does show that there was some such exegetical tradition. France proposes that the shepherd in view was identified by the Qumran community as the Teacher of Righteousness who was neither a messianic figure nor evil (R. T. France, *Jesus and the Old Testament* [London: Tyndale, 1971], 177).
25. See, e.g., Kenneth L. Barker, "Zechariah," in *EBC*, ed. Frank E. Gaebelein (Grand Rapids: Zondervan, 1985), 7:686-87.
26. James D. Smart, *The Interpretation of Scripture* (London: SCM, 1961), esp. 104-15.

view that insists that an OT text (or any other) be understood exclusively within its own context, such a method, when used or sanctioned by Jesus Christ and the authoritative apostles, must be accepted as a legitimate prophecy in every sense of the term. This does not invalidate the meaning of Zech. 13:7-9 as developed above, but it raises it to another dimension in which messianic truth can be communicated by a text that may never have been so intended by the original prophet-author.

Additional Notes

13:7 For the masc. sg. imperative הַךְ, "strike," some LXX recensions presuppose an infinitive absolute construction הַכֵּה אַכֶּה, "I will surely strike." The same tradition is followed in Matthew who renders the verb as πατάξω. Matthew's use of the LXX has no bearing, however, on the correctness of the MT here, a reading that should be retained precisely because of its comparative difficulty.

3

Sovereignty of YHWH (14:1-21)

The second great oracle and the entire prophecy of Zechariah end on the grand and glorious note of the sovereignty of YHWH and the establishment of His universal and eternal kingdom. The cosmic, eschatological sweep of this last portion, nine times punctuated by the phrase "in that day" or the like, is almost without compare in the prophetic literature of the OT for the richness of its imagery, the authority of its pronouncements, and the majestic exaltation of the God of Israel who will be worshiped as the God of all the earth.

Again, however, it is the people of YHWH who are central to the revelation. The pivotal concern of the passage is to show that YHWH comes on their behalf in order to complete at long last all the purposes for which He had elected, redeemed, and preserved them. It is, in fact, as YHWH proves true to His covenant word to Israel that He most effectively and dramatically evinces His glory. When Israel has finally fulfilled her covenant mandate as a kingdom of priests, drawing the nations of earth redemptively to YHWH her God, then, and only then, will her mission and the course of human history simultaneously come to an end. Then and only then will YHWH be all in all. This is the organizing principle of Zechariah's climactic word, the summation of all that has gone before.

A. DELIVERANCE OF HIS PEOPLE (14:1-8)

1. THEIR TRIBULATION (14:1-2)

Translation

¹A day of YHWH is about to come when your spoil will be divided in your midst. ²For I will gather all the nations against Jerusalem to do battle; the city will be taken, its houses plundered, and *the women violated. Then half of the city will go into exile, but the remainder of the people will not be cut off from the city.

Exegesis and Exposition

It is indigenous to the purposes of God in the face of the Fall that triumph comes through tribulation. Sacred history from beginning to end testifies to this, for the inflexible law that a grain of wheat, unless it falls into the earth and dies, remains alone is applicable to the very creation itself. It "groans and travails in pain with us until now . . . waiting for the redemption" (Rom. 8:22-23).

It is not surprising therefore that the prophet here speaks of the day of YHWH in the context of struggle and conflict (vv. 1-2). Hanson describes the whole of Zech. 14 as a composition whose structure "is derived from the ancient ritual pattern of the conflict myth, as that pattern was mediated on Israelite soil by the Jerusalem royal cult." The first two verses, he says, embody the motif of the "attack of the nations" in a salvation-judgment oracle.[1] The restoration and dominion cannot come until all the forces of evil that seek to subvert it are put down once and for all. Specifically, the redemption of Israel will be accomplished on the ruins of her own suffering and those of the malevolent powers of this world that, in the last day, will consolidate themselves against her and seek to interdict forever any possibility of her success. The nations of the whole earth will come against Jerusalem, and, having defeated her, will divide up their spoils of war in her very midst.

It is important to note that it is YHWH who gathers the nations, for His design is not only to purify His people in tribulation (cf. 13:8-9) but to provide an occasion for the destruction of their enemies. Joel speaks of that day as a time when YHWH will bring His people back into the land but will also gather the nations in the

---

1. Paul D. Hanson, *The Dawn of Apocalyptic* (Philadelphia: Fortress, 1975), 371-72. While one may quibble over the presuppositions that inform his language, his assessment of the material as conflict language is appropriate.

Valley of Jehoshaphat (that is, "YHWH judges") so that He might judge them there for the mistreatment of His people (Joel 3:1-3). Micah also describes the assembling of the nations against Zion and says that they little realize why they are there, namely, to be sheaves on the threshing-floor of YHWH's judgment (Mic. 4:11-13). But it is Ezekiel who provides the fullest account (chaps. 38-39).[2] The nations, he says, will come to war against Israel, a land living in peace and prosperity (38:11). But they come, again unawares, so that they might know YHWH in His mighty power (38:16). When it looks as though all is lost, YHWH will intervene and reduce the invading hordes to ignominious defeat (39:4-6).

There is, however, something unique to the account of Jerusalem's siege in Zech. 14:1-2, and that is the clear statement that the city falls to the enemy and suffers subsequent spoliation, rape, and deportation. It seems, then, that Zechariah cannot be referring to the same invasion as that recounted by Joel, Micah, and Ezekiel, for their narratives explicitly or implicitly affirm that the city goes unscathed, having been delivered by YHWH peremptorily. In fact, Zechariah himself has already described a scene in which Jerusalem, though attacked, has suffered no loss and, indeed, is able to administer her enemies a lethal blow (12:1-9). Zechariah also distinguishes between a battle in which Jerusalem is overrun and one in which she escapes through divine intervention.[3]

This distinction is carefully drawn elsewhere in the OT prophets but even more so in the NT. It is necessary, then, to give at least brief attention to some details of eschatological chronology, lest it appear that all end-time events are simultaneous. Our analysis of Zech. 9:9-10, an eschatological message divided between the two advents of the Messiah, is enough to show that the day of YHWH may and, indeed, does have multiple aspects, the difference among which may not be apparent apart from the NT witness.

The discussion should begin in our present context, with Zech. 14:3-8. Here it is clear that the deliverance of Jerusalem will be coincident with the triumphant coming of YHWH, an epiphany so marvelous that it changes the very topography of the holy land. There is

---

2. M. Nobile draws several parallels between Zech. 14 and Ezekiel, especially Ezek. 36-48. His objective is to clarify some of the imagery of Ezek. 37:1-14 in terms of its relevance to a New Year festival. Of interest to us is his evidence for Zechariah's verbal and conceptual dependence on Ezekiel; Marco Nobile, "Ez 37, 1-14 come costitutivo di uno schema cultuale," *Bib* 65 (1984): 481-89.
3. Unger makes these distinctions in detail. See Merrill F. Unger, *Zechariah* (Grand Rapids: Zondervan, 1963), 238-71 *passim*, esp. 254-55.

no reason to take this in any but a literal way, unless one is prepared to deny a literal coming of YHWH as well. The effect of His coming is not only victory for His people (v. 3) but the establishment of His earthly kingdom (vv. 9-11). This cannot be the everlasting kingdom, however, for rebellion continues (vv. 13-15) and national distinctions remain in place (v. 16). Those nations that refuse His sovereignty and fail to do him obeisance will suffer plague (vv. 17-19). This, too, falls short of an eternal kingdom in which YHWH's rule is over a redeemed, obedient people. But it is not the kingdom of this age and world either, as the reference to the holiness of all things in it makes clear (vv. 20-21).

Zechariah thus distinguishes between the kingdom of YHWH's universal, unchallenged dominion and a preliminary one in which His lordship prevails and His own people are secure only as He exercises direct and forcible hegemony. And even this preliminary reign is contingent on His coming among His people, a coming that does not take place until Jerusalem has been savagely attacked, defeated, despoiled, and exiled (vv. 1-2).[4]

To return to the passage immediately at hand (vv. 1-2), it best fits those prophetic texts that refer to a great tribulation of God's people that precedes His cataclysmic intervention and deliverance. Amos is aware of this complex of events when he prophesies of the destruction of all but a remnant of God's people "in that day," followed by the raising up of the fallen tent of David, that is, the revival of the Davidic kingdom (Amos 9:8-15). Joel also knows of a day of destruction (1:15–2:11) to be followed by divine deliverance (2:18-20; 3:9-21 [HB 4:9-21]). Isaiah, too, predicts the purging of Zion (1:24-31) and her subsequent exaltation among the kingdoms who will, in the latter days," confess YHWH's sovereignty (2:2-4; cf. 4:2-6; 26:16–27:6; 33:13-24; 59:1–60:22; 65:13-25). Micah promises that YHWH will gather the people He has afflicted and that from them He will make the nucleus of a universal kingdom (Mic. 4:6-8).

---

4. It is impossible here to do more than outline a biblical eschatology of the kingdoms. For more complete treatments, particularly (but not exclusively) from the premillennial persuasion accepted here, see J. Dwight Pentecost, *Things to Come* (Grand Rapids: Zondervan, 1958); Charles C. Ryrie, *Dispensationalism Today* (Chicago: Moody, 1965); John F. Walvoord, *The Millennial Kingdom* (Findlay, Ohio: Dunham, 1959); Robert H. Gundry, *The Church and the Tribulation* (Grand Rapids: Zondervan, 1973); George E. Ladd, *Crucial Questions About the Kingdom of God* (Grand Rapids: Eerdmans, 1957); various essays in Carl E. Armerding and W. Ward Gasque, eds., *Dreams, Visions and Oracles* (Grand Rapids: Baker, 1977); Stanley D. Toussaint, "A Biblical Defense of Dispensationalism," in *Walvoord: A Tribute*, ed. Donald K. Campbell (Chicago: Moody, 1982), 81-91; Anthony A. Hoekema, *The Bible and the Future* (Grand Rapids: Eerdmans, 1979).

Jeremiah refers to the time of Judah's future judgment as the "time of Jacob's trouble" (Jer. 30:7), a day of unimaginable suffering that will be alleviated only by YHWH's coming and the reestablishment of the kingdom of David (vv. 8-11). He also envisions the day when YHWH, having given His people over to destruction and exile, will gather them out of all nations, make a new covenant with them, and bless them with unprecedented prosperity (32:36-44; cf. 33:10-18). Ezekiel adds to this his word of witness when he foresees the purifying wrath of God upon Israel succeeded by their restoration as His servant people in His holy mountain, that is, His kingdom to come (20:33-44).

It is Daniel, however, who provides the language of tribulation picked up by the NT in its revelation of eschatological detail painted only on broad strokes in the OT prophets. Referring to the end times ("at that time"; cf. 11:40), Daniel says that "there will be a time of trouble" unparalleled in world history and that "at that time your people will be delivered, everyone who is found written in the book" (Dan. 12:1). The word for "trouble" here (צָרָה, *sārā*) is the same as in Jer. 30:7, which speaks of the time of Jacob's trouble.

The usual rendering of *ṣārâ* in the LXX is θλῖψις (*thlipsis*), the very word used by Jesus in describing the Great Tribulation to come at the end of the age (Matt. 24:21, 29; cf. Mark 13:24). When asked by His disciples about His coming and the end of the age (v. 3), He said it must be preceded by wars and cosmic dislocations (vv. 4-8) and by personal suffering or tribulation (*thlipsis*) by his disciples (vv. 9-14). This is all preparatory for a "great tribulation" (θλῖψις μεγάλη, *thlipsis megalē*) in which His own elect people would be totally annihilated were He not to intervene (vv. 15-23). That intervention will come about with His sudden and dramatic return (vv. 27-28). Then, our Lord goes on to say, after the Tribulation will the Son of Man come on the clouds of heaven with power and great glory to regather His people (vv. 29-31). He will then sit on His glorious throne and gather all the nations before Him for judgment (Matt. 25:31-46).

The triumphant coming described in Jesus' Olivet discourse (esp. Matt. 24:30-31; 25:31) is the subject also of Revelation 19. The apostle John there sees the "King of kings and Lord of lords" descending from heaven and riding a white war horse. He wears a royal crown, and once He puts down His foes in battle, He will "rule them with a rod of iron" (Rev. 19:11-16). This rule will last for a thousand years and will involve the people of the Lord in positions of royal priesthood (20:1-6). After that period the wicked elements of the world will assemble for one last confrontation with the King, but they will be totally and eternally defeated and destroyed (20:7-15). Then at last the everlasting kingdom of God, on a recreated earth, will come to pass, and He and His redeemed ones will enjoy unbroken and un-breakable fellowship forever (chaps. 21-22).

The fully developed scenario of the Olivet discourse and the Apoc-alypse clarifies and considerably amplifies the less fully elaborated presentation of the prophets, particularly Zechariah. What they do is to make it clear that the day of YHWH comes not as a single climactic event, but that it arrives in stages. That is to say, it is a process and not an act, a process that commenced with every intervention of YHWH in salvation and judgment from the time of the prophets onward, and that will find its culmination, its ultimate and climactic expression, in the final judgment against the nations and the eternal salvation of the redeemed of all time.

To return once more to Zech. 14:1-2, the prophet's telescoped vision in which all of YHWH's actions seem simultaneous must be reexamined in the light of the full canonical witness. The day of YHWH will indeed include the defeat and pillaging of Jerusalem and the deportation of half her people. But this tragic circumstance is not the end of the story, for shortly thereafter YHWH will regather and restore them (cf. Zech. 8:1-8; 9:1-10; 10:8-12) and will make them an instrument of His own judgment against the nations who tormented them (12:1-9).

Additional Notes

14:2 There is an interesting example of Masoretic sensitivity to explicit sexual language in the Qere reading תִּשָּׁכַבְנָה, "be lain with," for Kethib תִּשָּׁגַלְנָה, "be raped" or "violated." Apart from its insight into early Jewish personal and social mores, this euphemistic substi-tution has little to commend it.

2. THEIR SALVATION (14:3-8)

Translation

3Then YHWH will go forth and fight against those nations just as He fought in the day of battle. 4His feet will stand, in that day, on the Mount of Olives which lies before Jerusalem on the east; and the Mount of Olives will be split in half from east to west, (leaving) a great valley. Half the mountain will move northward and the other half southward. 5Then *you will flee (by) *my mountain valley, for the valley mountains will extend to *Azel; indeed, you will flee as you fled from the earthquake in the days of Uzziah king of Judah. And YHWH my God will come and all the holy ones with you. 6It will also come about in that day that there will be no light—the splendid (things) *will congeal. 7It will happen in one day, one known to YHWH; not day or night, but at evening-time there will be light.

8Moreover, in that day living waters will issue from Jerusalem, half of them to the eastern sea and half of them to the western; it will happen in summer and in winter.

Exegesis and Exposition

The day of tribulation described in vv. 1-2 will be followed by the triumphant "going forth" of YHWH to do battle. This is the language of holy war as the last clause of v. 3 makes clear—"just as he fought in the day of battle."[5] The Hebrew construction, namely, the use of the infinitive construct of נִלְחַם (*nilḥam*, "to fight"), suggests here a traditional or customary *modus operandi*. One could render the verse as follows: "Then YHWH will go forth and fight (נִלְחַם, *nilḥam*) against those nations like his (usual) fighting (הִלָּחֲמוֹ, *hillāḥămô*), in the day of battle."[6] That is, YHWH will employ the same tactics and strategy and be driven by the same motivations as in the days of old when He entered into conflict with the nations on behalf of His people. The classic example is the defeat of Egypt in the Red Sea at the time of the Exodus, the most graphic account being the poem of celebration of YHWH's triumph, Ex. 15:1-18 (cf. 14:14; Deut. 1:30; 3:22; 20:4; Judg. 5:1-5; Ps. 68; Hab. 3:1-19).[7] Zechariah himself has already vividly described YHWH in this role of warrior (9:1-17; 10:4-5; 12:1-9).

The coming of YHWH to do battle will bring about cataclysmic changes in the terrain itself, as well as in the patterns of light and darkness and in the seasons (vv. 4-8).[8] Such cosmic phenomena are a regular part of the biblical descriptions of the establishment of YHWH's rule in the ages to come (Isa. 13:6-16; Joel 2:1-2, 10-11, 30-31 [HB 3:3-4]; Amos 5:18-20; Zeph. 1:14-18; Matt. 24:29-31; Mark 13:8; 2 Pet. 3:16). They attest to His power as Creator and to the new creation that will be founded upon the ashes of the old. The shaking of the heavens and earth, as Haggai points out (2:6-7), will accompany the shaking of the nations as YHWH comes to assert His dominion over them.

---

5. So Hanson, *The Dawn of Apocalyptic*, 374; cf. Carroll Stuhlmueller, *Haggai & Zechariah*, ITC (Grand Rapids: Eerdmans, 1988), 155-56.
6. Hanson takes the verb to mean "go forth" toward Zion, not from it. This is in line with the procession of holy war in which the warrior makes triumphal entry into the holy precincts (Hanson, *The Dawn of Apocalyptic*, 374-75). However, the new Exodus imagery is even more compelling, requiring YHWH to lead His people out of Zion and not in. There is, of course, a later triumphant return (v. 5*b*).
7. Theophane Chary, *Aggée-Zacharie, Malachie* (Paris: Librairie Lecoffre, 1969), 211; cf. Richard D. Patterson, "The Psalm of Habakkuk," *GTJ* 8 (1987): 163-94.
8. P. D. Miller, *The Divine Warrior in Early Israel* (Cambridge, Mass.: Harvard Univ., 1973), 140-41.

He apparently proceeds from Jerusalem, leading His people across the Kidron Valley to the Mount of Olives (vv. 3-4).⁹ This was the route followed by David when he was forced into exile by his son Absalom (2 Sam. 15:16, 30), and it is the direction that the departing glory of YHWH went as a sign of YHWH's personal "exile" and that of the nation that would shortly follow (Ezek. 11:22-25). In fact, King Zedekiah of Judah, in an effort to elude capture by the Babylonians, slipped out of the city and went "by the way of the Arabah" (2 Kings 25:4), that is, the lower Kidron Valley. He must have gone over or around the Mount of Olives, for he was eventually seized by the Babylonians at Jericho (Jer. 39:5). These examples demonstrate the significance of YHWH's leadership of His people as they escape the city preparatory to its eventual recovery through YHWH's victory.

One cannot help but compare Joel's account of these events with Zechariah's.¹⁰ Joel exhorts the nations to gather in the Valley of Jehoshaphat (יְהוֹשָׁפָט, *yĕhôšāpāṭ*), for there YHWH will judge (שָׁפַט, *šāpāṭ*) them (3:12 [HB 4:12]). The sun, moon, and stars will be darkened, the heavens and earth will quake, but YHWH will provide a place of refuge for His people (3:15-16 [HB 4:15-16]). Jerusalem, having been delivered and purified of the contamination of the nations, will be holy to YHWH, reserved from then on for the redeemed ones alone (3:17 [HB 4:17]).

The "valley of Jehoshaphat" is the same as the Valley of Kidron, the steep ravine between Jerusalem and the Mount of Olives to the east. The scene in Zech. 14 is that of invading armies that surround Jerusalem, pouring into the valley from north and south, thus preventing any escape in that direction. When all is lost, YHWH leads His people forth, and, like Moses at the Red Sea, parts the mountain by the very act of treading upon it (v. 4). Evidence of an exodus motif continues in the choice of verb to describe the division of the mountain, for it (בָּקַע [*bāqaʿ*], "split") is the same as that used to speak of the division of the waters (Ex. 14:16, 21; Neh. 9:11; Ps. 78:13; Isa. 65:12).

The splitting of the mountain creates a new valley, one that is on an east-west axis. This is clear from the compass points of the narrative that suggests that the cleft goes from east to west, exactly as the waters of the Red Sea were separated (Ex. 14:21-22). Zechariah ex-

---

9. This movement provides a typological setting for Jesus' Olivet discourse (Matt. 24:1–25:46), a sermon by our Lord that in many points is an exposition of Zech. 14. See Donald A. Carson, "Matthew," in *EBC*, ed. Frank E. Gaebelein (Grand Rapids: Zondervan, 1984), 8:496-523, for a host of allusions. As Carson says, the Mount of Olives is "an appropriate site for a discourse dealing with the Parousia" (496).
10. See Magne Saebø, *Sacharja 9-14. Untersuchungen von Text und Form* (Neukirchen-vluyn: Neukirchener Verlag, 1969), 292, 294-95.

plains the mechanics of it for them by pointing out that half the mountain moves northward and half southward. The "great valley" that emerges from this becomes a route of escape for Jerusalem's population so that the enemy forces alone are left in the valley of judgment.

The valley is called by YHWH "My mountain valley" (v. 5),[11] for it is He who created it for the occasion. His people, He says, will flee through it and run as far as Azel (see Additional Notes). This place is otherwise not mentioned but obviously lay at some distance east of Jerusalem. The plural "mountain valleys" that follows may suggest that a whole range of hills east of Jerusalem had to be breached to provide access all the way to Azel. The need for such means of egress is clear—there is no time to waste. Indeed, Zechariah compares the urgency of the flight to that which attended the escape from the earthquake in the days of King Uzziah. This is the same quake as the one by which Amos the prophet dated his initial visions—"in the days of Uzziah king of Judah . . . two years before the earthquake" (Amos 1:1). Recent research at Hazor gives evidence of such a seismic event in 760 B.C., one that must have been so significant as to provide a point of reference 250 years later.[12] The analogy is most apropos, for anyone who has ever experienced an earth tremor knows how important it is to remove himself from collapsing structures.

This is no mere earthquake in Zechariah, however, but a shaking of the whole universe as YHWH comes in judgment. Zechariah's account of what transpires beginning with v. 5 is somewhat convoluted because of the radical shifting of subjects but the overall thrust of the message is clear. YHWH is speaking and refers to "My" mountain valley, but then Zechariah appears to be the interlocutor with the words "YHWH my God." This is not sustained, however, for the speaker goes on to say that all the holy ones will come with "you" (rather than the expected "him").

The ancient versions were very much aware of the problems generated by this awkward syntax and offered their solutions.[13] The LXX, for "you will flee" (נַסְתֶּם, *nastem*), presupposes נִסְתַּם (*nistam*),

---

11. It is literally "valley of my mountains," that is, a valley between mountains. This most likely refers to the two mountains created by the splitting of the Mount of Olives. Cf. Joyce G. Baldwin, *Haggai, Zechariah, Malachi* (London: Tyndale, 1972), 202.
12. E. H. Merrill, *Kingdom of Priests: A History of Old Testament Israel* (Grand Rapids: Baker, 1987), 383.
13. See Taeke Jansma, *Inquiry into the Hebrew Text and the Ancient Versions of Zechariah IX-XIV* (Leiden: Brill, 1949), 131-32; cf. Benedikt Otzen, *Studien über Deutero-Sacharja*, ATD 6 (Copenhagen: Prostant Apud Munksgaard, 1964), 267-68.

"will be stopped up." Thus, "My valley-mountain will be stopped up." Then, a few Hebrew MSS read אֱלֹהִים (*'ĕlōhîm*), "God," for אֱלֹהַי (*'ĕlōhay*), "my God." This permits a rendering "and YHWH God will come," thereby eliminating the troublesome first person suffix. Finally, there is some evidence for the reading in עִמּוֹ (*'immô*), "with him," for MT עִמָּךְ (*'immāk*), "with you"—"all the holy ones with him." The only difficulty left after all this is done is YHWH's own self-reference as "YHWH God," which, of course, is not unusual anyway.

The reasons for the versional and MSS variations are most understandable, for it is clear that the ancients were bothered by the shifting subjects and made textual adjustments to bring some harmony to the material. It is best, however, to leave the text as it is and to try to understand it on its own terms. This calls for one to recognize the well-attested (and frequently mentioned) fact that biblical authors, especially in poetry, often are inconsistent in subject in passages where there is great movement and excitement. With this in mind I suggest that YHWH is the speaker in v. 5*a* (up through "king of Judah") and that Zechariah then interjects his own statement about "YHWH my God." This still leaves the difficult "holy ones with you," but Zechariah can still be the subject if he is addressing first the people and then YHWH. In any case, the singular suffix "you" at the end of the verse requires that the addressee be an individual, thus disqualifying the "people," who have hitherto been addressed.

The statement that "YHWH will come" rounds off the passage that begins in v. 3 with "YHWH will go forth." Just as His going forth was in the terminology of holy war, so His coming is, as the reference to the "holy ones" suggests. This phrase (קְדֹשִׁים, *qĕdōšîm*) occurs in the famous hymn (Ps. 89) extolling YHWH as warrior, to describe the heavenly assembly (vv. 5, 7 [HB 6, 8]).[14] He is YHWH of hosts, the one to be feared because of His exploits (vv. 7, 10 [HB 8, 11]). In fact, the "hosts" (צְבָאוֹת, *şĕbā'ôt*) themselves are the "holy ones," His celestial army. It is YHWH with His armies, then, that Zechariah sees. They are coming, now that Jerusalem is evacuated and her people safe, to destroy the hostile nations.

Far more problematic, but for different reasons, is Zech. 14:6-7. The prophet declares that there will be no light in the day of YHWH and then elaborates—"the splendid will congeal." The Greek, supported by other ancient versions, reads "and cold and ice," suggesting וְקָרוּת וְקִפָּאוֹן (*wĕqārût wĕqippā'ôn*) for the MT יְקָרוֹת יְקִפָּאוֹן (*yĕqārôt yĕqippā'ôn*).[15] Cold and ice are not the necessary consequence of no

14. E. Theodore Mullen, Jr., *The Assembly of the Gods* (Chico, Calif.: Scholars Press, 1980), 189-94.
15. Jansma, *Inquiry into the Hebrew Text and the Ancient Versions of Zechariah IX-XIV*, 132-33.

light, however, so this is hardly convincing. The meaning is that the loss of light is explained by the congealing of the heavenly bodies, their "thickening" as it were to the point that they cannot shine. Again, the Song of the Sea in Exodus 15 is helpful, for the same verb, "congeal," is used to speak of the thickening (or, perhaps, hardening) of the depths of the sea so that they could stand like walls on either side (v. 8).[16] Job speaks of his own formation in the womb as a "curdling" like that of cheese as it thickens (Job 10:10). The only other use of the verb, in Zeph. 1:12, also uses the language of a congealing of substance such as wine as a metaphor for insensitive self-confidence. Thus, the luminaries of heaven will become clouded over, thickened or congealed, so that their light will not shine forth.

This phenomenon will occur on a day known only to YHWH (v. 7; cf. Matt. 24:36; Acts 1:7), one unlike any other in that it will have no day or night. That is, it will not be divided up into the usual cycles of light and darkness. Instead, everything will be reversed so that in the evening, when darkness is expected, there will be daylight. The imagery here is strikingly reminiscent of that of the Genesis creation account. There is the phrase "one day" (יוֹם אֶחָד, *yôm 'eḥād*) common to both, in Genesis referring to the first day of creation (Gen 1:5).[17] But it was precisely at the beginning of that day that there was "no light," but only chaos. The establishment of order demanded the creation of light, so on that first day, a period of no daytime or nighttime, YHWH created light (v. 3). As a result there was now an evening (עֶרֶב, *'ereb*) and a morning (בֹּקֶר, *bōqer*), together making up (and in that order) "one day."

The similar motifs in the two passages must not conceal the fundamental difference, however, and that is that, whereas Genesis is describing creation out of chaos, Zechariah speaks of chaos out of creation.[18] The "one day" of Genesis was unique because light shone out of darkness in the morning. The "one day" of Zechariah is unique because darkness will obscure the light until, in a reversal of the

---

16. This was noted already by C. F. Keil, *Biblical Commentary on the Old Testament. The Twelve Minor Prophets* (Edinburgh: T. & T. Clark, 1871), 2:405. By rendering קִפָּאוֹן (with Q) as a noun, "frost," rather than the verb קָפָא, "congeal, thicken," Hanson has missed an opportunity to connect Ex. 15 with the "conflict myth" that he rightly sees elsewhere in Zech. 14 (Hanson, *The Dawn of Apocalyptic*, 371).
17. It is also possible to take יוֹם אֶחָד as "unique day," that is, one of a kind, one known only to God and never in human experience. See A. Van Hoonacker, *Les Douzes Petits Prophètes* (Paris: Librairie Victor Lecoffre, 1908), 689. Chary suggests that "known only to God" means that the day is predetermined by God and so known only to Him (cf. Matt. 24:36) (T. Chary, *Aggée-Zacharie, Malachie*, 215).
18. Hanson has caught the binary nature of the *Urzeit* and *Endzeit* nicely in his discussion of vv. 6-9 as recreation (Hanson, *The Dawn of Apocalyptic*, 376-79).

normal course of nature, the light will shine out of darkness in the evening. The eschatological day of YHWH is a de-creation in its judgment, but one that gives way to an even more glorious re-creation (cf. Isa. 13:10; 34:4; Jer. 4:23; Joel 2:2, 10, 31 [HB 3:4]; 3:15 [4:15]; Zeph. 1:2, 3; contrast Rev. 21:1, 5, 23-24; 22:5).

A token of that recreation is the issuance of living waters from Jerusalem, half of which flow to the eastern (that is, the Dead) sea and half to the western (Mediterranean) sea (v. 8). Contrary to the normal climatic pattern of Palestine, where the wadis and streams dry up in the summer, this river will flow with its refreshing waters the year round.

The Hebrew construction here requires "living" (חַיִּים, *ḥayyîm*) to function as an adjective and not a genitive noun, so that the idea is not waters that give life but waters that are "alive." This is a way of describing fast-flowing, sparkling streams that by their constant movement and shifting course appear to be living things. Frequently the term "living water" is translated "running water" (Lev. 14:5, 6, 50, 51, 52; 15:13; Num. 19:17), but in the prophetic literature it is used as a metaphor for YHWH's blessing (as in our passage) or even for YHWH Himself (Jer. 2:13; 17:13).[19]

Most instructive in understanding both the temporal setting and the function of these living waters is Ezek. 47, for though Ezekiel does not describe the waters there as "living" there can be no doubt that he has the same phenomenon in mind. Virtually all scholars, whatever their particular eschatological position, agree that Ezek. 40-48 is millennial. That is, it is a vision of a glorious day yet to come whether ideal or literal and actual.[20] Consistent hermeneutics favors the latter, so it seems that Ezekiel (and Zechariah) is anticipating the millennial reign of YHWH on earth and the building of a new Temple in which He will dwell among His people (cf. Ezek. 48:35).

Ezekiel, like Zechariah, sees waters flowing from Jerusalem, but he specifies that they originate in the Temple (v. 1). The stream that comes forth and runs toward the east increases in depth and width until it becomes a mighty river, impossible to cross (v. 5). It makes its

---

19. William L. Holladay, *Jeremiah 1*, Hermeneia (Philadelphia: Fortress, 1986), 92.
20. Charles L. Feinberg, *The Prophecy of Ezekiel* (Chicago: Moody, 1969), 233-39; John B. Taylor, *Ezekiel*, TOTC (London: Tyndale, 1969), 253-54; Walther Eichrodt, *Ezekiel: A Commentary* (London: SCM, 1970), 530-31; John W. Wevers, *Ezekiel: The Century Bible* (London: Nelson, 1969), 295-96; G. A. Cooke, *A Critical and Exegetical Commentary on the Book of Ezekiel*, ICC (Edinburgh: T. & T. Clark, 1936), 425-27; Keith W. Carley, *The Book of the Prophet Ezekiel*, CBC (London: Cambridge, 1974), 267; R. G. Hamerton-Kelly, "The Temple and the Origins of Jewish Apocalyptic," *VT* 20 (1970): 5.

way down into the Arabah and thence into the sea, obviously the Dead Sea because the result of the inflow of the river is that the sea is "healed" and begins to teem with life (vv. 8-9). Alongside the river are trees whose leaves never fade and whose fruit never fails, all because of the fructifying qualities of the waters (v. 12).

Though the scene in Zechariah differs in that he envisions streams flowing both east and west and fails to mention the details about the enlarging of the river and its energizing of the trees, the overall similarity is compelling.[21] Both prophets are looking at the imagery of millennial refreshment that attends the presence and power of YHWH as He comes to establish His sovereignty and to restore His people. John's Apocalypse describes the same glorious vision (Rev. 22:1-5).[22] He sees a river flowing from the throne of God, a stream lined with the tree of life. Most interesting and significant is that John, like Zechariah, connects this living stream with the reigning of YHWH through His redeemed ones (v. 5; cf. Zech. 14:9-11).

Additional Notes

14:5 As noted in the comments, some MSS and versions read וְנִסְתַּם for וְנַסְתֶּם. The rationale for this is the unexpected introduction of an audience not previously mentioned ("you") and the possibility of a *vorlage* that indeed did contain the verb סָתַם, "stop up," rather than נוּס, "flee." However, נִסְתַּם does occur in the next line in an apparently emphatic repetition of this one. Moreover, if the remainder of the text is left as is, it is strange to think that "my mountain valley" will be stopped up when it has just been opened for the purpose of providing an escape route.

Many scholars suggest an emendation גֵּיא הִנֹּם, "valley of Hinnom," for גֵּיא הָרַי, "the valley of my mountain" or "my mountain valley." This is most unsuitable geographically since Hinnom lies to the west of Jerusalem, not to the east as Zechariah's vision requires. Furthermore, the ancient textual witnesses reveal no such option.

Inasmuch as a place named Azel is otherwise unattested, some scholars propose אֶצְלוֹ, "near it." The relevant lines would then be rendered, with the alterations previously suggested, "My mountain valley will be stopped up, for the valley mountains will be near it." This would provide the idea that the Kidron will be blocked up at its northern and southern ends so that the people of Jerusalem can go straight through the defile created by the splitting of the Mount of Olives without interference from the enemy on either side. Though

---

21. Feinberg, *The Prophecy of Ezekiel*, 271; Walther Zimmerli, *Ezekiel 2*, Hermeneia (Philadelphia: Fortress, 1983), 513, 515.
22. Zimmerli, *Ezekiel 2*, 515.

ingenious, this approach is gratuitous, lacking any support in ancient texts. (Cf. Jansma, *Inquiry into the Hebrew Text and the Ancient Versions of Zechariah IX-XIV*, 131-32.)

14:6 The problem with the Hebrew here is primarily one of gender disagreement, for the word for "the splendid (things)" is feminine while the predicate is masculine. For this reason the Qere has קִפָּאוֹן (*qippā'ôn*), a noun (rather than the verb of Kethib) meaning "congelation" (BDB, 891). This yields the extremely elliptical "the splendid (things will come to a state of) congelation," or the like.

Because gender agreement is by no means consistent in Hebrew, it is best to take יְקָרוֹת (*yĕqārôt*) as the substantized adjective יָקָר (*yāqār*) in the feminine plural meaning "splendid" or "precious," with some feminine noun or nouns such as שֶׁמֶשׁ (*šemeš*), "sun," understood. Lacocque, e.g., supplies the missing words as follows: "Il arrivera en ce jour-là qu'il n'y aura plus de lumière (naturelle): (elle viendra) des choses précieuses en condensation" (André Lacocque, *Zacharie 9-14*, CAT [Neuchatel: Delachaux & Niestlé, 1981], 208). The predicate is likely the imperfect qal of קָפָא (*qāpā'*), "congeal," with an irregular long *ḥolem* (וֹ) that should be repointed to *šureq* (וּ) and with a reversal of the first two vowels, thus וְיִקְפָּאוּן or, as Horst and other scholars suggest, יִקְפָּאוּן, niph. impf. 3 m. p.; Friedrich Horst, *Die Zwölf kleinen Propheten. Nahum bis Maleachi*, HAT 14 (Tübingen: J. C. B. Mohr, 1964), 258. Cf. Saebø, *Sacharja 9-14*, 115. The various remedies that are needed to bring the form into conformity with standard Hebrew orthography show how intractable the problem is.

B. EXALTATION OF HIS PEOPLE (14:9-21)

1. THEIR SECURITY (14:9-11)

Translation

⁹YHWH will then be king over all the earth. In that day YHWH will be one and His name one. ¹⁰All the land will change (and be) like the Arabah from Geba to Rimmon, south of Jerusalem; and *she will be raised up and will dwell in her place from the gate of Benjamin to the place of the first gate to the corner gate, and from the *tower of Hananel to the royal winepress. ¹¹And people will dwell there, and there will no longer be a ban—Jerusalem will dwell in security.

Exegesis and Exposition

The victory of YHWH over the nations and the deliverance of Jerusalem from their malice will make possible the kingship of YHWH. This was the inevitable result of the pursuit of holy war, a point made already in Zechariah (1:11; 6:7; 9:1-10; 10:12). But in the eschaton He is king not merely in Jerusalem but from Jerusalem and over all the earth (cf. Isa. 2:2-4; Mic. 4:1-3). He has established His claims as sovereign by conquest and by re-creation (Isa. 65:17-19; 66:18-21).

With unmistakable reference to the Shema, the very heart of Israel's covenant faith and confession (Deut. 6:4-5), Zechariah proclaims that "in that day YHWH will be one (יְהוָה אֶחָד, *YHWH 'eḥād*) and His name one (שְׁמוֹ אֶחָד, *šĕmô 'eḥād*). The Shema declares, "Hear, O Israel, as for YHWH our God, YHWH is one (*YHWH 'eḥād*)." It is generally held by scholars of all persuasions that this is a confession not only of YHWH's self-consistency but of His uniqueness, His exclusivity.[23] In terms of comparative religion, it is a statement of monotheism. It was as the climax to the basic principles of the Deuteronomic Covenant that the Shema was first articulated (Deut. 5:1–6:3). In that more limited context it was an encapsulation of Israel's faith alone ("our God"), so that any nuance about His oneness in terms of exclusivity must be understood accordingly.

Zechariah, however, breaks out of that restricted viewpoint and speaks of the oneness of YHWH on a universal scale.[24] There is no reference to "our God," for YHWH will be the one and only God of all the nations. There will be only one name, the name of YHWH, upon the lips of the whole world of worshipers. This is precisely the point Isaiah makes when he speaks the word of YHWH: "There is no God but Me . . . none besides Me. Look to Me and be saved, all the extent of the earth, for I am God and there is no other. I have sworn by Myself that . . . every knee will bend and every tongue swear [that in Him is] righteousness and strength" (Isa. 45:21-24; cf. Phil. 2:10).

This does not cancel out the centrality of Israel to YHWH's salvific purposes, however. Jerusalem will continue to be the center from which will radiate the grace of God to all the earth. To express this centrality the prophet visualizes the leveling of the remainder of the Holy Land and the elevation of Jerusalem so that the city stands

23. So G. Braulik, *Deuteronomium 1-16, 17*, KAT (Wurzburg: Echter Verlag, 1986), 55-56; P. C. Craigie, *The Book of Deuteronomy*, NICOT (Grand Rapids: Eerdmans, 1976), 168-69; G. von Rad, *Deuteronomy: A Commentary*, OTL (London: SCM, 1966), 63; J. A. Thompson, *Deuteronomy*, TOTC (London: Tyndale, 1974), 121-22. Gordon now cites evidence from Ebla attesting to the otherwise well-known notion of describing the chief deity as "number one" (Cyrus H. Gordon, "Eblaitica," in *Eblaitica: Essays on the Ebla Archives and Eblaite Language*, ed. Cyrus H. Gordon, Cary A. Rendsburg, Nathan H. Winter [Winona Lake, Ind.: Eisenbrauns, 1987], 25).
24. Hanson expresses the emphasis on YHWH's oneness in v. 9 as "the resolution of the pairs of opposites" of vv. 6-8. That is, the old order, having been vanquished and redeemed by YHWH, will merge with the new in a harmonious whole (Hanson, *The Dawn of Apocalyptic*, 379).

high above, overlooking the surrounding terrain from a position of eminence and security (v. 10). It is likely that this is to be understood as a figurative flattening and exaltation (cf. Isa. 2:2; 40:9-10; 56:7; 65:11),[25] but regardless of that, the distinction between the dwelling-place of YHWH and the rest of the land is clearly drawn.

Geba, in one passage at least (2 Kings 23:8), represents the northernmost extent of Judah (cf. 1 Sam. 13:3, 16; 14:5; Isa. 10:29).[26] The name in Hebrew (גֶּבַע, *Geba‛*) is related to the word for "hill" (גִּבְעָה, *gib‛â*), so there is every likelihood that Zechariah is also using paronomasia to his advantage when he speaks of making every hill flat like the Arabah. Rimmon was in the far south of Judah (Job 15:32; 19:7) and thus marked her farthest extent in that direction.[27] The name may be related to that of the Semitic storm-god Rimmon, but its similarity to Hebrew רָמָה (*rāmâ*), "height," could easily lend itself to a further play on words. The whole land, from northern hill to southern height, will become level as the Arabah.

The Arabah is the southern extension of the Great Rift depression, which in Palestine runs from Lake Huleh in the north to the Gulf of Eilat in the south.[28] Specifically it refers to the region of the Dead Sea southward, an area unexcelled in all the land for flatness, particularly in the basin south of the Dead Sea. All the land will be as level as the Arabah while Jerusalem towers over it.

The boundaries of the city are hinted at (v. 10) but with too little data to be able to retrace them. Benjamin's Gate (cf. Jer. 37:13; 38:7), clearly on the north side of the city and opening toward the tribal area of Benjamin, was evidently where the king held court to pass on legal matters. The First Gate must also have existed on the north wall, for the next one named, the Corner Gate, is on a line with the Ephraim Gate, which is on the north (2 Kings 14:13).[29] The Tower of Hananel, Jeremiah says, is at the opposite extremity of the city from

---

25. Unger takes it in both senses, the physical elevation of Jerusalem suggesting its spiritual eminence (Unger, *Zechariah*, 260).
26. Aharoni argues that even though Geba (now Jeba‛) was somewhat south of the border of Judah in Josiah's time, as an administrative center it marked the major northern extent of the kingdom (Yohanan Aharoni, *The Land of the Bible* [London: Burns & Oates, 1966], 350-51).
27. Kallai identifies Rimmon (or En-Rimmon) as or near H. 'Umm-'er-Ramāmīm, c. 10 km. south of Tell Beit Mirsim; Zecharia Kallai, *Historical Geography of the Bible* (Jerusalem: Magnes, 1986), 357.
28. For an excellent overview, see Denis Baly, *The Geography of the Bible* (London: Lutterworth, 1957), 191-209, esp. 206-9.
29. J. Simons argues plausibly that the "First Gate" is identical to the "Ephraim Gate," between the Gate of Benjamin on the east and the Corner Gate on the West (J. Simons, *Jerusalem in the Old Testament* [Leiden: Brill, 1952], 277-78).

the Corner Gate (Jer. 31:38; cf. Neh. 3:1). The wall from the Tower of Hananel ends at the royal winepresses.[30]

To reconstruct the outline of the gates and walls, one must begin with the known and deduce the rest. The royal winepresses were at the extreme south of the city, near the Royal Pool and Royal Gardens (Neh. 2:14; 3:15). The Tower of Hananel was on the extreme north, so a line between the two would mark the greatest length of the city. This means the Corner Gate must, in fact, be on the northwest corner. The so-called First Gate, then, must be somewhere else, possibly, as Simons suggests, to be identified with the Ephraim Gate.[31] Since Jerusalem in the postexilic period occupied an area roughly in the shape of an isosceles triangle, with its base to the north, the two corners then would be the Corner Gate and the Benjamin Gate, west and east respectively, and the third corner would be the apex in the south near the royal winepresses. The Hananel Gate would be somewhere along the northern wall, probably at the northwest corner of the Temple area.[32]

The purpose of this description is not so much to give the precise delineations of the eschatological city but to enable Zechariah's own generation (and any other) to understand that the idealism of the future is rooted and grounded in the present, in actual history and geography. The God who led His people through spatial, temporal history will recreate the cosmos in those same categories.[33] This is why a literal hermeneutic is essential in the absence of compelling evidence otherwise.

Within the confines just elaborated, people once more will occupy Jerusalem (v. 11). No longer will there be fear of the "ban," for Jerusalem will from then on live in peace and safety. Reference to the "ban" (חֵרֶם, *ḥērem*) may appear strange here, for God's people were never subject to this radical expression of His wrath in which all living things were slain and all material things destroyed or confiscated. The prophet therefore must be harking back to the days of conquest when Jerusalem, a Jebusite city, was condemned to *ḥērem*

---

30. Simons emends יִקְבֵי הַמֶּלֶךְ, "royal winepresses," to קִבְרֵי הַמֶּלֶךְ, "royal sepulchers," on no other grounds than that the royal winepresses are mentioned only here in the OT. That does not seem convincing, especially in light of the univocal textual support for "winepresses" (Simons, *Jerusalem in the Old Testament*, 208 n. 2).
31. See n. 29.
32. Simons, *Jerusalem in the Old Testament*, 231.
33. Lacocque correctly draws attention to the covenant promises involved here (cf. v. 11) when he takes note of the delineations of the walls and towers as an expression of "la nouvelle assurance du caractère inexpugnable de la Ville" ("a fresh assurance of the impregnable nature of the city") (Lacocque, *Zacharie 9-14*, 210).

(cf. Deut. 7:2; 20:17; Judg. 1:21).[34] Unlike the Jebusites, God's people, living securely in Jerusalem, need never fear His wrath or that of the nations.

Additional Notes

14:10 The unusual verb form וְרָאֲמָה is a variation of the normal וְרָמָה, "she will be raised up." It is noteworthy that this word also involves a wordplay with the place name רִמּוֹן. The latter will be leveled, but Jerusalem will be exalted. The Syr. and Vg are certainly correct in suggesting מִמִּנְדָּל. The preposition evidently was lost by haplography.

2. THEIR VICTORY OVER ENEMIES (14:12-15)

Translation

12But this will be the plague with which YHWH will strike all the nations that have made war against Jerusalem: Their flesh will decay while they stand on their feet, their eyes will rot away in their sockets, and their tongue will melt away in their mouth. 13And there will be in that day a great confusion from YHWH among them; they will seize each other's hands and will lay hold upon one another. 14Moreover, Judah will fight at Jerusalem, and the wealth of all the surrounding nations will be gathered—gold, silver, and clothing in great abundance. 15Thus will be the plague upon horse, mule, camel, ass, and every animal in those camps—like that plague.

Exegesis and Exposition

In sharp contrast to the absence of *ḥērem* upon God's people is the infliction of plague upon all the peoples who have persecuted and tormented them. What YHWH administers is literally a "blow" or "strike" (מַגֵּפָה, *maggēpâ*, from נָגַף, *nāgap*, "to smite"), but in its qualifying context a horrible plague or pestilence of some kind.[35] The same word occurs with reference to the debilitation of the Philistines in the ark narrative (1 Sam. 6:4) and in the choices YHWH gave David when he sinned in taking the census of his armies (2 Sam. 24:21, 25). It refers also to a disease in which the "bowels fall out" because of it (2 Chron. 21:14-15), implying some kind of extreme dysentery.

Here in Zechariah it attacks both man (v. 12) and animal (v. 15), completely disabling them. Its effects are described by the same verb (מָקַק, *māqaq*) in three different forms. The flesh will decay (הָמֵק, *hāmēq*) while the warriors are on their feet, so sudden will the onset be.

34. Baldwin, *Haggai, Zechariah, Malachi*, 204-5.
35. H. Preuss, *TWAT*, V, 1/2: cols. 229-30, s.v. נָגַף.

The eyes will rot away (תִּמַּקְנָה, *timmaqnâ*) in their very sockets, and the tongue will melt (תִּמַּק, *timmaq*) in the mouth. The rapidity with which this occurs may suggest hyperbole, but certainly YHWH's judgment, whether in spiritual or physical ways, is instantaneous in its administration and can be instantaneous in its effects as well.

As though that were not incapacitating enough, YHWH will send confusion (מְהוּמָה, *mĕhûmâ*) among the warring nations (v. 13). The result will be a mutual decimation, for they will, in their madness, lash out at one another and thus destroy each other. Again, the ark narrative comes to mind, for after the Philistines of Gath had received the ark of the covenant from Ashdod, they experienced the plague and were thrown into confusion or discomfiture (1 Sam. 5:9).

A clearer parallel in terms of the results of the confusion—smiting one another in ignorance—is in the narrative of the battle between Saul and Jonathan, on the one hand, and the Philistines, on the other, near Beth-aven (1 Sam. 14:16-23). The historian relates that there was an uproar in the Philistine camp, so much so that they took up sword against each other in their confusion (*mĕhûmâ*).

The setting of this conflict, the prophet says, is Jerusalem (v. 14).[36] The battle narrative here, then, is a continuation of the one already described in connection with the escape of God's people through the valley opened up to them (vv. 4-8). Having thoroughly discomfited the enemy nations, YHWH will lead His people back to the battlefield where they will complete the defeat YHWH has already begun. Once this is done, the enormous wealth of the nations will be gathered up as the spoils of war.

The order of events thus far appears to be as follows: (1) YHWH allows the nations to attack, despoil, and deport His people in Jerusalem (vv. 1-2); (2) He comes to their defense in a triumphant march that brings with it cosmic and terrestrial transformation (vv. 3-8); (3) He defeats the hostile nations and takes their treasures as booty (vv. 12-15); (4) Jerusalem is elevated and becomes the center of

---

36. The phrase בִּירוּשָׁלָם, "in Jerusalem," should normally be translated "against Jerusalem," in connection with the verb נִלְחַם ("made war"). However, the context here makes it clear that Judah is joined with Jerusalem in battle, probably in or near the city. Chary reviews the problem and concludes that the preposition בּ should be taken in the "sens local." He does, however, reject the reference to Judah as part of the original text (Chary, *Aggée-Zacharie, Malachie*, 218-19). The Targums suggest that the surrounding peoples compel Judah to attack Jerusalem, the same understanding they have of 12:2; Jansma, *Inquiry into the Hebrew Text and the Ancient Versions of Zechariah IX-XIV*, 138. Cf. G. R. Driver, "Old Problems Re-examined," *ZAW* 80 (1968): 182. Driver thinks the preposition is ambiguous (as opposed to עַל, for example) because Judah, though intent on fighting the enemy, might by accident attack fellow Jews.

YHWH's universal reign (vv. 9-11). Thus, vv. 12-15 logically and thematically follow vv. 3-8. Lamarche suggests that the present structure reflects a chiasm, one that alone is sufficient to account for the order of events.[37] His approach (somewhat abbreviated here) is as follows:

- a) "A day is coming" (1-2a)
    - b) Jerusalem attacked and insecure (2a-b)
        - c) "in that day" (3-5)
            - d) "and it will come to pass in that day" (6)
                - e) "there will be a unique day" (7a)
            - d') "and it will come to pass in that day" (7b-8)
        - c') "in that day" (9-10a)
    - b') Jerusalem protected and secure (10b-11)
- a') "it will come to pass in that day" (12-15)

The same battle is addressed by Ezekiel who refers to the nations as Magog, Meshech, and Tubal (38:2; 39:1).[38] They will come against Jerusalem but will fall upon the mountains of Israel in ignominious defeat (39:4-5). Then Judah will "plunder those who plundered them and rob those who robbed them" (v. 10). Thus the spoil of Judah that had been divided among the nations (Zech. 14:1) will be returned to them.

The "wealth of all the surrounding nations" (v. 14) calls to mind the "precious things of all nations" of Hag. 2:7, including silver and gold in both instances. The words used to designate these "precious things" are different in each case (חֶמְדָּה, *ḥemdâ*, and חַיִל, *ḥêl*, respectively in Haggai and Zechariah), but the silver and gold of Hag. 2:8 suggests that they are indeed the same as the spoils in Zechariah. Haggai says that these will come in the day when YHWH "shakes all nations" (2:7), a shaking accomplished in part at least by war as YHWH comes to deliver His people (cf. Joel 3:9, 12, 16 [HB 4:9. 12, 16]). It is war also that yields the "wealth of all the nations" to Jerusalem in the eschatological triumph described by Zechariah. The precious things that come in the last days come not so much as voluntary offerings but as the tribute of the defeated nations to YHWH, whom they must confess as king (v. 9).[39]

---

37. P. Lamarche, *Zacharie IX-XIV. Structure Littéraire et Messianisme* (Paris: Librairie Lecoffre, 1961), 11.
38. C. Feinberg, *The Prophecy of Ezekiel*, 218-19; Taylor, *Ezekiel*, 243. Chary notes the common use by Zechariah (14:12, 13) and Ezekiel (38:21-22) of the terms מַגֵּפָה ("plague") and מְהוּמָה ("panic") and says that their use by Ezekiel "a inspiré notre auteur" ("has inspired our author"), i.e., Zechariah (Chary, *Aggée-Zacharie, Malachie*, 218).
39. That the offerings are involuntary is intimated at least by the verb form

This brief pericope (vv. 12-15) ends as it began, with a reference to the plague that YHWH will bring upon the enemy nations. The armies will disintegrate under its impact (v. 12), and so will the animals upon which ancient armies depended (v. 15). The passage is rounded off chiastically to bring the whole section about eschatological war to an end.

3. THEIR PLACE AS A CENTER OF PILGRIMAGE (14:16-21)

Translation

16It will come to be that all who are left of all the nations that came against Jerusalem will go up annually to worship the King, YHWH of hosts, and to observe the Feast of Tabernacles. 17But as for the one from all the clans of earth who does not go up to Jerusalem to worship the King, YHWH of hosts, upon him there will be no rain. 18If the clan of Egypt will not go up and come, *it will not (fall) upon them; there will be the plague with which YHWH smites the nations that do not go up to celebrate the Feast of Tabernacles. 19This will be the punishment of Egypt and of all nations that do not go up to celebrate the Feast of Tabernacles. 20In that day there will be on the bells of the horses "Holy to YHWH." The pots in the house of YHWH will be like the bowls before the altar. 21Every pot in Jerusalem and Judah will be holy to YHWH of hosts, and all who sacrifice will come and take some of them to boil in them. There will no longer be a Canaanite in the house of YHWH of hosts in that day.

Exegesis and Exposition

Once the great conflagration that marks the beginning of YHWH's millennial reign is over, the survivors among the nations, having of necessity come to acknowledge Him as king (v. 9), will come to Him regularly to offer Him homage. This is not to suggest that they have undergone conversion in the religious sense, for there is abundant evidence in this passage that such is not the case at all (vv. 17-19).[40] Rather, the pilgrimage that is made is akin to that required

---

אָסַף, "gathered." This is the pu. of אָסַף, a term that elsewhere refers to forced gatherings (cf. Isa. 24:22; 33:4; Ezek. 38:12; Hos. 10:10). Elliger draws attention to a similar pillaging in Ezek. 39:10, a passage, as we noted, that describes the same eschatological battle (K. Elliger, *Die Propheten Nahum, Habakuk, Zephania, Haggai, Sacharja, Maleachi*, ATD [Göttingen: Vandenhoeck & Ruprecht, 1982], 184).

40. Unger takes הַנּוֹתָר מִכָּל־הַגּוֹיִם ("everyone left of all the nations") in v. 16 to refer to the converted, whereas the disobedient of vv. 17-19 are the unconverted. He offers no evidence for this use of נוֹתָר except the fact that they worship YHWH (Unger, *Zechariah*, 265).

of all vassals in the ancient Near Eastern world who must, on stated occasions, proffer their allegiance to the overlord and seal it with tangible tribute of taxation and other material offerings.[41]

This is not contradicted by the use of the verb "worship" in v. 16, for that verb (הִשְׁתַּחֲוָה, *hištaḥăwâ*), in noncultic contexts, frequently means only to bow down or do obeisance (Gen. 43:28; Ruth 2:10; 1 Sam. 24:9; 2 Sam. 14:4; 1 Kings 1:31; 2 Kings 4:37).[42] Here in Zechariah, those who come are those who were "left over "(הַנּוֹתָר, *han-nôtār*) from the conflict of vv. 12-15. They have been reduced to vassalage by YHWH and must now come to bow before Him and to render the signs of their submission. This is precisely the picture in Isa. 60:4-14. "The wealth of the nations will come," Isaiah declares (v. 5), and they will bring tribute to the altar of YHWH (v. 7). Kings will serve Him (v. 10), bowing down before Him and calling Jerusalem "the city of YHWH, the Zion of the holy one of Israel" (v. 14).[43]

The particular occasion of pilgrimage is the Feast of Tabernacles. This was one of the three stated times in Israel's calendar when YHWH's people were obligated to appear before Him at the central sanctuary (cf. Lev. 23:34-44). Its purpose was both commemorative and agricultural in intent.[44] It was to celebrate YHWH's provision for them in the wilderness journey and also to mark the end of the annual harvests. Later its significance extended beyond the observance of these events to include the Day of Atonement on the tenth day of the seventh month and the first day of the month, that is, Rosh ha-Shanah, or New Year's Day. Thus, from the first through the twenty-second day of Tishri, the seventh month, Israel gathered in solemn assembly at Jerusalem, the whole complex of holy times being designated by the one celebration, the Feast of Tabernacles.

Though one should not go to the extremes of some scholars who view the Feast of Tabernacles as especially a time marking the enthronement of Israel's kings,[45] there is evidence that this was an occasion for some kind of recognition of the king as YHWH's son and

---

41. Paul Kalluveettil, *Declaration and Covenant*, AnBib 88 (Rome: Biblical Institute, 1982), 27; Dennis J. McCarthy, *Treaty and Covenant*, AnBib. 21 A (Rome: Biblical Institute, 1978), 104, 126, 132, 150, 287-88. Cf. *ANET*, 203.
42. H. Preuss, *TDOT*, 4:248-56, s.v. חוה.
43. Westermann correctly sees that this passage has nothing to do with the salvation of the nations. Rather, he says, "The aliens will rebuild the walls of Zion and their kings be obliged to serve Israel" (Claus Westermann, *Isaiah 40-66: A Commentary* [London: SCM, 1969], 360).
44. Roland de Vaux, *Ancient Israel* (New York: McGraw-Hill, 1965), 2:495-502.
45. So especially Sigmund Mowinckel, *The Psalms in Israel's Worship* (Oxford: Basil Blackwell, 1962), 1:118-22.

representative.[46] It is likely that in the person of the king, YHWH would sit enthroned and receive through His earthly representative the offerings brought in tribute by the people. For the nations to observe the Feast of Tabernacles was for them to come in submission before the King of all the earth and render to Him their expressions of subservience.

One of the features of the Feast of Tabernacles was the public reading of the Torah, that is, the covenant text that bound YHWH and Israel together (Deut. 31:9-13). It is quite possible that this reading involved the king, for he was to read from it all the days of his life (Deut. 17:18-20) in order that he might remain true to its demands upon him and the nation.[47] Ezra, the postexilic theocratic mediator, read the Torah publicly on the first day of the seventh month, that is, on New Year's Day (Neh. 8:2). He then led the people in reading about the Feast of Tabernacles and officiated in its observance (Neh. 8:13-18).

Immediately following the celebration of the Feast of Tabernacles, the Levites led the assembly in a great ceremony of covenant renewal (Neh. 9:1-38) culminating in a solemn commitment by the people to reaffirm their covenant allegiance to YHWH (9:38; cf. 10:29). Thus the Feast of Tabernacles, by this time at least (c. 440 B.C.), was firmly connected to covenant remembrance and renewal at which the community leadership played a central role.[48]

That the Zechariah passage should also be viewed against a covenant background is evident from v. 17 where it is stated that all who fail to go up to Jerusalem to acknowledge the sovereignty of YHWH will suffer the absence of rain.[49] This was a very specific covenant curse in the great covenant texts of the OT (cf. Lev. 26:4; Deut. 28:12, 24) and no doubt stands for a *pars pro toto* here. Because the Feast of Tabernacles was a celebration of the last great harvest, a time also associated with the "former rains," the withholding of rain would be

---

46. J. de Fraine, *L'Aspect Religieux de la Royauté Israélite*, AnBib 3 (Roma: Pontificio Instituto Biblico, 1954), 132-36.
47. For ancient Near Eastern parallels, see J. A. Thompson, *Deuteronomy*, 206.
48. Harrelson emphasizes this point and sees Zech. 14:16-21 as an expression of covenant observance, albeit involuntarily, on the part of the unconverted nations (Walter Harrelson, "The Celebration of the Feast of Booths According to Zech. XIV 16-21," in *Religions in Antiquity*, ed. J. Neusner [Leiden: Brill, 1968], 88-96).
49. Though one may reject his general "myth and ritual" approach, Aubrey Johnson properly connects the withholding of rain in v. 17 with failure to observe the Feast of Tabernacles (Aubrey R. Johnson, *Sacral Kingship in Ancient Israel* [Cardiff: Univ. of Wales, 1955], 49-52).

a particularly appropriate reminder of covenant violation.[50] The vassal who withholds his tribute may expect the Great King to withhold the means of its production.

Egypt in the Bible is frequently a type of the world at large (Isa. 27:13; Rev. 11:8). Here it is not distinguished, therefore, from the nations just mentioned but appears as a synonym for them. Furthermore, Egypt was not dependent on rain for its nourishment, so it is mentioned here to ensure that no nation escapes judgment.[51] Whether sustained by the showers or the Nile, the peoples who fail to submit to YHWH's kingship will suffer the consequences. Perhaps in an ironic twist of the Exodus itself, YHWH says that if Egypt does not "go up" (עָלָה, *ʿālâ*) and "come" (בֹּא, *bōʾ*), it will not enjoy the refreshing floods but rather will be inflicted with "plague" (מַגֵּפָה, *maggēpâ*), the same word that occurs in v. 12. A related term (נֶגֶף, *negep*) is used in the narratives of the Exodus plagues against Egypt, specifically of that which struck the people with death (Ex. 12:13). There will be both "natural" disasters and direct divine judgment on those who refuse to fulfill their roles as subject peoples.

In light of both *negep* as referring to the death of Egypt's firstborn in the Exodus and the use of the cognate *maggēpâ* in Zech. 14:12, one must conclude that the idea in 14:18 is that of punishment by death. Not only Egypt, but all the nations who do not go up to celebrate the Feast of Tabernacles, will experience the severest repercussions. The prophet views this extreme measure not as a whimsical or arbitrary act of God but as a "punishment" (v. 19). The word here is literally "sin" (חַטָּאת, *ḥaṭṭāʾt*), but by use of the metonymy of effect he speaks of the result in place of the cause.[52] That is, the plague is the aftermath of sin in the sense that it is its punishment. The sin is of the most egregious kind, for in the covenant context of the passage it is nothing short of rebellion and repudiation of YHWH's dominion.

The final unit of the chapter is enveloped by the recurring eschatological cliché "in that day" (בַּיּוֹם הַהוּא, *bayyôm hahûʾ*) (vv. 20*a*, 21*b*), a fitting finale to this book, which has such a profound eschatological interest. One may see, in addition to this enveloping, a chiastic arrangement centering in the phrase "Every pot in Jerusalem and Judah will be holy to YHWH of hosts" (v. 21*a*). The following schema may be helpful in seeing how the structure contributes to the

---

50. Kenneth L. Barker, "Zechariah," in *EBC*, ed. Frank E. Gaebelein (Grand Rapids: Zondervan, 1985), 7:696.

51. So Wilhelm Rudolph, *Haggai–Sacharja 1-8–Sacharja 9-14–Maleachi*, KAT (Gütersloh: Verlaghaus Gerd Mohn, 1976), 239.

52. K. Koch, *TDOT*, 4:309-19, s.v. חָטָא. As Koch puts it, "*chaṭṭāʾth* means not only the evil deed, but also the associated consequences" (p. 312).

focus on this idea of the lowliest and most profane becoming the holiest of all.

A In that day
  B There will be on the bells of the horses "Holy to YHWH"
    C The pots in the house of YHWH will be like bowls before the altar
      D Every pot in Jerusalem and Judah will be holy to YHWH of hosts
    C' All who sacrifice will come and take some of them to boil in them
  B' There will no longer be a Canaanite in the house of YHWH
A' In that day

The holy bells contrast with the unholy Canaanites; the common pots, transformed into sacred basins, will be used in Temple worship, and the despised vessels of profane use will become holy in the hands of YHWH.

The horse, though important in Israel, especially in a military capacity, was an unclean animal according to the ritual criteria (cf. Lev. 11:1-8).[53] In the day of YHWH, however, they not only will be free of that onus but will wear tinkling bells or plates bearing the inscription "Holy to YHWH." This, of course, was the inscription on the plate affixed to the miter of the high priest (Ex. 28:36-38). In the OT era he epitomized the principle of holiness, but in the age to come even the unclean animal will be radically transformed into something considered to be holy by YHWH. This is something the apostle Peter had to learn with regard to the acceptance of unclean Gentiles into the saving purpose of the Lord (Acts 10:9-16).

The pots (סִירוֹת, *sîrôt*)[54] were the lowliest vessels of all in the inventory of the tabernacle and Temple. They were used as receptacles for ashes (Ex. 27:3), and presumably, for other mundane purposes (Ps. 60:10 [EB 60:8]; Eccl. 7:6). In the Temple of the Millennium they will enjoy a much more exalted function, that of the bowls (מִזְרָקִים, *mizrāqîm*) before the altar. Their connection with the altar attests to their exalted and holy purpose, but the day will come when they will

---

53. Lacocque, *Zacharie 9-14*, 215. Lacocque draws attention to the same theme in Isa. 66:20.
54. James L. Kelso, *The Ceramic Vocabulary of the Old Testament*, BASOR Supp. 5-6 (New Haven, Conn.: American Schools of Oriental Research, 1948), 27. Kelso notes in reference to our passage that "*sîr* is the generic term used for all the ceramic cooking-pots of Jerusalem in contrast to *mizrāq*, the generic term for the metal bowls used at the altar:—the secular vs. the sacred."

be joined by their less honored fellows as holy instruments of worship.

Even more astounding, the pots of profane use, those of every household, will be transformed into holy containers for sacrifice (v. 21). Ordinarily used for household cooking (Ex. 16:3; 2 Kings 4:38), and even as a symbol for wicked Jerusalem (Ezek. 11:3; 24:3, 6), these domestic vessels, unclean by virtue of their very lack of consecration to sacred use, will be purified and made serviceable to the worship of YHWH.

Finally, Zechariah makes what appears to be a most negative conclusion to the whole matter of the secular becoming sacred when he foresees the day when there will no longer be a Canaanite in the house of YHWH (v. 21*b*). The Canaanite, of course, symbolized what was most reprehensible to YHWH, a lifestyle and worship completely antithetical to all He intended His people to embrace. They were a cursed people (Gen. 9:25), a nation to be annihilated by the conquest of Israel (Josh. 3:10). To think of their participation in the worship of YHWH at all was scandalous, and to envision their doing so within the holy precincts of the Temple was incomprehensible. In the day of YHWH, however, all are welcome. There is, in that sense, no longer a Canaanite, for all alike will be the people of YHWH.[55]

It is impossible to improve on Paul's own assessment of the transformation that will characterize that glorious day, for already in his own age, the age of the gospel that prepares the way for and makes possible the ultimate redemption of the world, he was able to say: "There can be neither Jew nor pagan, there can be neither slave nor freeman, there can be no male and female, for you all are one in Christ Jesus" (Gal. 3:28).

Additional Notes

14:18 The LXX and Syr. omit the וְלֹא and read "if the clan of Egypt does not go up and come among them, there will be a plague," etc. This alternative is attractive in that it removes the problem of the absence of rain from Egypt as a curse when, in fact, Egypt does not depend on rain for its survival in the first place. However, it seems that Egypt here stands for all the nations so that the lack of rain is

---

55. The view of many scholars that "Canaanite" should be rendered "merchant" or "trader" here (so, e.g., Mason, *The Books of Haggai, Zechariah, and Malachi*, 133), though possible semantically, is deficient in that it is unlikely that a merchant would be singled out from among all trades and professions as disqualified to worship. The point is that no one is disqualified, hence there will no longer be such a person as a "Canaanite." Lacocque understands this as a possibility, though apparently does not favor it (Lacocque, *Zacharie 9-14*, 215).

significant. Moreover, the *lectio difficilior* of the MT is presumptively in its favor. Van der Woude emends וְלֹא בָאָה וְ to וְלָאַב אָחוּ, "the pasture will remain arid" (A. S. Van der Woude, "Sacharja 14, 18," *ZAW* 97 [1985]: 254-55). Were there support from ancient witnesses, this would be a most attractive resolution of the bothersome extra לֹא.

Malachi

Introduction to Malachi

HISTORICAL CONTEXT

Haggai and Zechariah, as we have seen, are noteworthy for the chronological precision with which they related their lives and ministries to their historical milieu. This is not the case at all with Malachi. In fact, one of the major problems in a study of this book is that of locating it within a narrow enough chronological framework to provide a *Sitz im Leben* sufficient to account for its peculiar themes and emphases. It is this problem that must first be addressed before matters of authorship, unity, purpose, and the like can be undertaken.

Estimates of the date of Malachi have ranged between the extremes of the early exilic period[1] and a mid-second-century Maccabean provenence.[2] Arguments for and against these suggestions will be offered presently, but for now it is sufficient to note that the vast majority of scholars maintain a middle position—sometime in the fifth century B.C. It will not be necessary therefore to deal with the historical background beyond 400 B.C. Because the introductions to Haggai and Zechariah surveyed the scene down to 520, the beginning of the reign of the Persian King Darius I Hystaspes, the present ac-

---

1. Bruce Dahlberg, "Studies in the Book of Malachi" (Ph.D. Diss., Columbia Univ., 1963), 180-222. I owe this reference to my colleague, Mark Rooker.
2. Hans H. Spoer, "Some New Considerations Towards the Dating of the Book of Malachi," *JQR* 30 (1908): 167-86.

count of the larger international scene will begin there, to be followed by a brief overview of the life and times of fifth-century Judah.

Darius, whose fiercely contested accession to the Persian throne took place in 522, reigned until 486.[3] Once the early turbulence had settled down and he had brought the satrapies of Egypt and Abar Nahara (that is, everything west of the Euphrates, including Palestine, and known to the Assyrians as *eber nāri*, "across the river") under his own control once more, Darius launched a campaign of empire building. By 516 he had annexed parts of India to his domains and then set his sights on the north and west. After he failed to dislodge the Scythians in the Black Sea region he focused on the independent states of the Aegean islands. Before he could accomplish his objective of bringing them under control, he had to deal with the Ionian provinces which, though under Persian hegemony, decided to assist their island kinfolk. Having at last prevailed, Darius determined to press on to the west and conquer mainland Greece as well. Athens and her fellow city-states organized a united front, however, and in the battle of Marathon in 490 B.C. defeated the Persians and forced their withdrawal.

Shortly thereafter Darius died and was succeeded by his son Xerxes (486-465), the Ahasuerus of the Bible (Ezra 4:6; Esther 1:1).[4] Xerxes was well prepared for his new role, having served as vice-regent of the Babylonian satrapy for a number of years. Of a more domestic and cultural bent than his father, the new king turned first to the completion of palaces and public works that Darius had begun at Susa and Persepolis. But he could not preoccupy himself with these projects for long, for upon the death of his father various components of the empire began to assert their independence. After he first resecured Egypt, Xerxes raised an enormous military force and struck out for Greece in 481. Though he achieved initial success, he soon lost most of his navy at Salamis. Thereupon he returned to

---

3. For overall surveys of the history of Persia from the reign of Darius through that of Artaxerxes I, see A. T. Olmstead, *History of the Persian Empire* (Chicago: Univ. of Chicago, 1948), 107-354; G. B. Gray and M. Cary, "The Reign of Darius," *CAH*, 4:173-228; J. A. R. Munro, "Xerxes' Invasion of Greece," *CAH*, 4:268-316, and "The Deliverance of Greece," *CAH*, 4:317-46; Ephraim Stern, "The Persian Empire and the Political and Social History of Palestine in the Persian Period," in *The Cambridge History of Judaism. Introduction: The Persian Period*, ed. W. D. Davies and Louis Finkelstein (Cambridge: Cambridge Univ., 1984), 70-87; Peter R. Ackroyd, *Israel Under Babylon and Persia* (Oxford: Oxford Univ.,1970); Edwin M. Yamauchi, *Persia and the Bible* (Grand Rapids: Baker, 1990), 129-278.
4. This identification was put beyond doubt many years ago by Robert D. Wilson, *A Scientific Investigation of the Old Testament* (London: Marshall Brothers, 1926), 79-80.

Persia, leaving affairs in the hands of his commander Mardonius. This accomplished little, for within two years the Persians were defeated decisively at Platea and Mycale and were forced to withdraw to Anatolia.

This setback so discouraged and deflated Xerxes that he spent the last decade of his life in wanton self-indulgence and dissipation, a condition no doubt reflected in the book of Esther. At last he was assassinated by a courtier and replaced by Artaxerxes I (465-424), brother of the heir apparent Darius whom he had arranged to be murdered. Artaxerxes tried to suppress unrest in his empire by tax reforms and satrapal reorganization but to little avail. Egypt refused tribute payment by 460 B.C., and the Aegean states, under Athenian leadership, broke away once more. From 450 to 431 Persia and Athens struggled over the disputed territories until at last Athens became engaged in the Peloponnesian Wars and had to desist from engagement with Persia. This allowed Artaxerxes to pay attention to matters closer to home, including those in Yehud (Judea) about which the biblical narratives concern themselves. His death in 424 postdates any recorded biblical event and therefore can mark the end of this brief survey of Persian history.

It is against this broad background that the setting of Malachi must be understood. To define it further requires some attention to the affairs of the Jewish restoration community of which Malachi was a part and whose problems he addressed.[5] The biblical record unfortunately is silent about matters in Palestine between the sixth year of Darius (515 B.C.; cf. Ezra 6:15) and the seventh year of Artaxerxes (458; cf. Ezra 7:7) except for a passing reference to Xerxes (Ezra 4:6) and one to Artaxerxes just prior to the journey of Ezra to Jerusalem (c. 460; cf. Ezra 4:7-23). After that the account is comparatively complete until the end of the governorship of Nehemiah (c. 430 B.C.?; cf. Neh 13:6-7), thanks primarily to the treatise of Ezra-Nehemiah.

The "passing reference" to Xerxes concerns a letter of accusation written to him by certain antagonists of the Jews who wished to stifle the Jewish work of reconstruction and renewal. Ezra says this took place at the beginning of Xerxes's reign (4:6), that is, c. 486. Many scholars associate this effort with the Egyptian rebellion that accompanied Xerxes's accession to the throne, a reasonable but wholly unprovable suggestion.[6] This interpretation turns on the supposition that the suppression of Egyptian religion, especially the priesthood,

---

5. For this, see Peter R. Ackroyd, "The Jewish Community in Palestine in the Persian Period," in *The Cambridge History of Judaism*, 130-61.
6. Stern, "The Persian Empire and the Political and Social History of Palestine in the Persian Period," 73.

that resulted from the abortive rebellion, may have caused the Jews'
enemies to feel that Xerxes's policy toward Egyptian religion might
be applicable to that of the Jews as well. Thus, they felt free to interfere with the continuation of Jewish efforts to restore their community.[7]

In any event, nothing more is known until the second recorded
attempt at scuttling the rebuilding, which occurred "in the days of
Artaxerxes" (Ezra 4:7). This apparently preceded the return of Ezra in
458, for it was clearly the decree of Artaxerxes to forbid further work
on the walls of Jerusalem (4:21) that prompted Ezra to persuade the
king to issue an overriding decree (7:6, 11-26) and to allow him to
return to Jerusalem to bring it to pass. It is helpful to view this series
of events against the larger political scene already outlined. Egypt
had rebelled against Persia in 460-450 B.C., a rebellion put down after
five years by Megabyzus the satrap of Abar Nahara (Eber nāri). It is
entirely likely that Bishlam, Mithredath, Tabeel, and their allies took
advantage of this unrest to appeal to Artaxerxes to put an end to
Jewish rebuilding, especially in light of their allegation that the Jews
had tendencies to independence, a set of problems Artaxerxes did not
need at that particular moment (Ezra 4:7, 12, 15-16). Ezra, in that
case, had to convince the king that the Jews were loyal citizens, something he evidently succeeded in doing.[8]

Apart from these fragmentary episodes, nothing else can be
learned from the period from Zechariah to the return of Ezra, particularly in terms of community and religious life.[9] The Temple had
been completed by 515, as we noted, and one must assume that the
cultus was carried out according to Mosaic prescription and that the
state as a whole functioned in an orderly manner, at least for a few
years. With the arrival of Ezra in 458,[10] however, it becomes possible
to see that all was not well and that reformatory measures were
already necessary. Politically, there was unrest because of the rebel-

---

7. Julian Morgenstern postulates a Jewish rebellion in 485 led by a king
   Menahem and suggests that the Ezra 4:6 reference is in regard to the
   putting down of this rebellion with the collaboration of the Edomites,
   Moabites, Ammonites, and Philistines. See his series of studies entitled
   "Jerusalem—485 B.C." in *HUCA* 27 (1956): 101-79; *HUCA* 28 (1957): 15-47;
   HUCA 31 (1960): 1-29; and "Further Light from the Book of Isaiah upon
   the Catastrophe of 485 B.C.," *HUCA* 37 (1966): 1-28, esp. 3-4.
8. Anson Rainey, "The Satrapy 'Beyond the River,'" *AJBA* 1 (1969): 58, 62-63.
9. For archaeological and inscriptional information, see Morton Smith,
   "Jewish Religious Life in the Persian Period," in *The Cambridge History of
   Judaism,* esp. 233-50.
10. If, as I argue below, Malachi dates from 470 or so, then the problems
    adduced in Ezra were already flagrant many years earlier. See B.
    Dahlberg, "Studies in the Book of Malachi," 202.

lion of the western satrapies and one can, with good reason as we have already noted, conclude that Artaxerxes allowed Ezra to return to do what he could to stabilize things. At least the king's letter conveyed by Ezra gives that impression in places (Ezra 7:21, 23-26).

In other respects things were hardly more promising. Upon his return Ezra was made aware most dramatically of the spiritual and moral malaise that had begun to paralyze the life of the restoration community. This was epitomized in the matter of mixed marriage, a clear violation of the Mosaic laws of separation and purification (Ezra 9:1-4). Though serious in and of itself, this breach of covenant appears to have been but symptomatic of a more widespread spirit of compromise (9:1, 14).

The situation did not improve between the year of Ezra's reformation (9:5–10:44) in 458 and the beginning of Nehemiah's governorship 13 years later. To make matters worse, Megabyzus declared his jurisdiction independent of Persia in 449 B.C.. Though he came back into the fold two years later, the situation in Palestine had become so destabilized that one can well understand why Artaxerxes allowed his beloved cupbearer Nehemiah to go to Jerusalem in 445. The king must have been convinced that Nehemiah could straighten things out politically as well as accomplish the social and spiritual objectives for whose undertaking he had sought permission.

When Nehemiah arrived, he found the Jewish state in even worse shambles than he had anticipated. The walls of Jerusalem lay in ruins, the perennial foes of his people continued their unremitting harassment, and the spiritual and moral condition of the people was lamentable. After some religious and political appointments (Neh. 7:1-2) Nehemiah turned to the pressing economic concerns. Food and other staples had become scarce, inflation was rampant, and the rich were exploiting the poor by demanding exorbitant prices for goods (Neh. 5:1-5). In order to address these and other problems, Nehemiah assembled the people for a great ceremony of covenant renewal (7:73–9:38). In his prayer of public confession he alludes to the sins of the people that were sapping the spiritual vitality of the community (9:36-37). These are more clearly spelled out in the response of the people (10:28-39) who pledged to avoid intermarriage with pagans, to observe the sabbaths, to pay Temple taxes, to follow the regulations concerning tithing and the offering of the firstborn, and to be faithful to the ministry of the Temple.

Upon his return to Susa some 12 years later, things began to unravel once more, and when Nehemiah came back to Jerusalem (in 433 B.C.) after a brief stay in Susa, he had to face the same issues all over again. Tobiah the Ammonite, his adamant foe, had been granted living quarters in the sacred Temple and that by the high priest

Eliashib (13:4-5). The son of Joiada, another priest, had married a daughter of Sanballat, the current satrap of Abar Nahara (13:28). Moreover, Nehemiah found that the Levites were being neglected, the Sabbath was violated routinely, and illegal intermarriage was once more commonplace. By force of personal leadership and clearly recognized authority, Nehemiah responded to these issues and put the house of Judah in order. Though not demanding divorce as Ezra before him had done (Ezra 10:1-4), Nehemiah showed his intense displeasure over the matter and threatened dire consequences if such marriages should be contracted in the future (Neh. 13:23-27). The biblical account ends at this point, but there is no reason to doubt that Nehemiah's reforms remained intact for some time to come.

With this résumé of Persian and biblical history of the fifth century in view, it is appropriate now to consider the setting of Malachi. As suggested above, this is one of the major problems in the study of the book. The author nowhere identifies himself except by name, and apart from one or two oblique references, never links his work to a precise historical situation. Therefore, one must look to a whole milieu or climate against which the teachings and topics of the book can be highlighted, a most subjective procedure to say the least.

A single historical datum, Malachi's reference to the overthrow of Edom, has provided a benchmark for many scholars (Mal. 1:2-5). Bruce Dahlberg argued that the conquest in mind must be that under the Babylonians in connection with the assassination of Gedaliah, the Jewish governor appointed by Nebuchadnezzar. In reprisal, the Babylonians attacked the responsible parties and presumably included their Edomite allies in the process (Jer. 41:1-18).[11] Dahlberg is correct in asserting that Edom was antagonistic to both Judah and Babylon in Judah's last years (cf. Jer. 25:21; 27:1-11) and that she would fall to Babylon (cf. 9:25-26). However, it is gratuitous to assume that the destruction of Edom in Malachi 1:2-5 is the one in view in Jeremiah and, even if it is, to conclude that Malachi must be describing it as a contemporary event. Even Dahlberg's argument that Edom suffered two Babylonian campaigns—one in 587 and the other in 582-581—cannot help his case. Even though Dahlberg takes the former as having happened and the latter as still to come to pass (thus requiring a date of composition between the two dates), he cannot prove that the anticipated overthrow of Edom is precisely that of 582. All that is known is that it is still future to Malachi. The fact that the Edomites are not included in Jeremiah's account of the Babylonian second conquest of 582 (Jer. 52:30) certainly does not help Dahlberg's hypothesis.

---

11. B. Dahlberg, "Studies in the Book of Malachi," 202.

Inasmuch as a future destruction of Edom is anticipated in Mal. 1:4, when did it occur? The only time known in the extant historical literature is that of the Nabataean expulsion of the Edomites in 312 B.C., which resulted in their replacement by the Nabataeans and the subsequent development of a mixed people called Idumaeans.[12] Even if this is the case, all that it reveals is that the collapse of Edom is somewhere in Malachi's future. One could, of course, argue on dogmatic grounds that the "prediction" of Edom's fall was a *vaticinium ex eventu*, in which case the book (or at least 1:4) would have to be dated after 312 if that is the fall in question. Dogma has no place in determining historical reality, however.

A similar but more extreme position held by earlier scholars such as Spoer is that the predicted downfall must have occurred under Judas Maccabeus who administered a crushing defeat to the Idumaeans between 165 and 161 B.C.[13] Again, this is possible inasmuch as the event was future to Malachi, but if it be argued that the prophet is describing a past occurrence, Spoer's position suffers great difficulty, for Malachi is attested as early as the early second century in the apocryphal literature.[14] It must have been written some decades before that to be accorded any kind of status as Scripture by then.

A position more in line with the evidence of Malachi itself requires the book to have originated sometime in the fifth century, more likely in the first half. The prophet refers to the cultus as though it were in regular operation (1:6-14; 2:7-9, 13; 3:7-10), thus presupposing the rebuilding of the Temple and the re-establishment of its services. One might object that this could refer to a time prior to the destruction of Solomon's Temple, but Malachi's reference to Judah's "governor" (פֶּחָה, *peḥâ*) in 1:8 does not favor this. The term *peḥâ* does indeed occur before the Exile but always in reference to foreign officials (Isa. 36:9; Jer. 51:23) or as a nontechnical term for an Israelite overseer (1 Kings 10:15).[15] One should note that Gedaliah himself is never designated by this term but simply by the locution "the one appointed over" (הִפְקִיד, *hipqîd*). It is only in postexilic times that *peḥâ* becomes a technical term to refer to a Judean official such as gover-

---

12. Philip C. Hammond, *The Nabataeans—Their History, Culture and Archaeology*, SMA 37 (Gothenburg: Paul Åströms, 1973), 13.
13. Spoer, "Some New Considerations Towards the Dating of the Book of Malachi," 182-83.
14. Cf. Ben Sirach 48:10, which quotes Malachi 3:23-24. Ben Sirach was thought to have been written c. 180 B.C. Patrick W. Skehan, *The Wisdom of Ben Sira*, AB 39 (New York: Doubleday, 1987), 10, 534.
15. Ackroyd, "The Jewish Community in Palestine in the Persian Period," 155-58.

nor (cf. Neh. 2:9; Hag. 1:1, 14; 2:2, 21; *et passim*). Malachi's use is clearly at home in a postexilic context.

How early in that context is the matter now in question. Because the cultus is well established in the Temple, a date earlier than 500 B.C. seems unrealistic. Moreover, the issues that concern Malachi— religious irregularities, priestly corruption, hypocrisy, and divorce— are not at all raised in Haggai and Zechariah, a fact that tends to place Malachi considerably later in order for these aberrations to have arisen and to have become characteristic.

On the other hand, Ezra, who arrived in Jerusalem in 458 B.C., addresses none of these problems specifically, and except for inter- marriage, which is the focus of Mal. 2:11, seems unconcerned about such matters. In other words, Malachi's concerns are not Ezra's. One can only conclude that Malachi was later than Ezra, or that his min- istry of rebuke and correction had been effective. The latter seems preferable, for in order for Malachi to postdate Ezra his ministry would have had to coincide with the governorship of Nehemiah or even to have come later. This dating, in fact, is widely accepted.[16] Against this is the fact that Ezra and Nehemiah were contemporaries, and that both were concerned with the same issues, particularly in- termarriage with pagans.[17] Moreover, their reforms appear to have been successful, at least by the end of Nehemiah's tenure in 430 B.C. It is inconceivable that Malachi's message could reflect conditions in the latter part of that period (458-430) or, indeed, for many years thereafter.

But could not Malachi have composed his work early in the days of Ezra, before the Ezra-Nehemiah reforms took effect, and could not his preaching have provoked the reforms in the first place or at least have encouraged them?[18] This is possible, but once more it must be pointed out that Malachi's concerns are much different from those of either Ezra or Nehemiah, for he was almost wholly transfixed by concerns about the cult. It is much more likely that he spoke to and remedied conditions that prevailed before Ezra ever came on the scene, conditions that in fact Ezra faced (if at all) in a totally different form (Ezra 7:1-10). In short, a date between 500 and 460 seems best, 480-470 being a reasonable guess.[19]

---

16. So, for example, Otto Kaiser, *Introduction to the Old Testament* (Oxford: Basil Blackwell, 1975), 285-86.
17. For a brilliant study arguing for an even longer overlap and closer con- nection between Ezra and Nehemiah, see Leslie McFall, "Was Nehemiah Contemporary with Ezra in 458 B.C.?" *WTJ* 53 (1991): 263-93.
18. W. J. Dumbrell makes a strong case for Malachi's role as a stimulus for the reforms of Ezra and Nehemiah in "Malachi and the Ezra-Nehemiah Re- forms," *RTR* 35 (1976): 42-52.
19. For linguistic evidence leading to this conclusion, see Andrew E. Hill,

LITERARY CONTEXT

According to every canonical tradition, Malachi is the last of the prophets in the "scroll of the Twelve," that is, the 12 minor prophets. This suggests, among other things, that his book also was written last and provided a fitting climax to the whole prophetic collection by its collocation of the old and the new—the prophet Moses with the law and the prophet Elijah with the promise. Its location at the very end of the Christian canon enhances this climactic element all the more.[20]

The literary context of the book cannot be fully elaborated without some understanding of its authorship, date, and other matters. The date has just been reviewed, and the matter of authorship will be examined in the exposition of Malachi 1:1. Clearly, as the previous discussion has pointed out, Malachi is later than Haggai and Zechariah and, as the commentary will show, is dependent on them and on the rest of the antecedent revelation of the OT for its inspiration and major themes.[21] But the relationship is organic and self-conscious and cannot be the result of the attachment of an originally anonymous work to the composition of Proto-Zechariah simply because, as some scholars argue, it, like Zechariah 9:1 and 12:1, commences with the word מַשָּׂא (*maśśā'*), "burden" or "oracle."[22]

As Childs has demonstrated, no case can be made for the attachment of Zechariah 9-11 and 12-14 to Zechariah 1-8 on the basis of the term *maśśā'*—to say nothing of seeing Malachi as a third addition because it shares that heading with them.[23] In fact, the resemblances are quite ambiguous and superficial. In Malachi *maśśā'* appears to be in the absolute form and should be simply rendered "Oracle," not "oracle of." In Zechariah 9:1, however, it seems not to be a true heading at all but part of a poetic oracle that continues through v. 8. As for Zechariah 12:1, the entire first half of the verse functions as a superscription. Both 9:1 and 12:1 should be taken as constructs, "the oracle (burden) of," etc. Thus, Malachi is a case by itself and cannot have been

---

"Dating the Book of Malachi: A Linguistic Re-examination," in *The Word of the Lord Shall Go Forth*, ed. Carol L. Meyers and M. O'Connor (Winona Lake, Ind.: Eisenbrauns, 1983), 77-89.

20. For a helpful statement concerning the strategic canonical location of Malachi, see J. D. W. Watts, "Introduction to the Book of Malachi," *Rev Ex* 84 (1987): 373-74.

21. Ronald W. Pierce has drawn attention to the literary and thematic linkages between Haggai-Zechariah, on the one hand, and Malachi, on the other, thus supporting the canonical shape as a deliberate strategy ("Literary Connectors and a Haggai/Zechariah/Malachi Corpus," *JETS* 27 [1984]: 277-89).

22. Thus Otto Eissfeldt, *The Old Testament, An Introduction* (Oxford: Basil Blackwell, 1965), 440-41.

23. Brevard S. Childs, *Introduction to the Old Testament As Scripture* (London: SCM, 1979), 491-92.

placed where it is canonically only because of its being perceived as a homeless orphan in need of parental attachment. It appears where it does for clearly perceivable literary and theological reasons.

Language and Style

Scholarship is divided as to whether Malachi was composed as poetry or as prose. This is reflected in the two major modern editions of the Hebrew text in that *BHK* apparently sees little or no poetry at all in Malachi whereas *BHS* understands at least 1:6-8*a* to be such. If, as Alden suggests, parallelism is the *sine qua non* of Hebrew poetry, there indeed appears to be little poetry in the book.[24] Yet, it does not lack poetical quality, as the many examples of rhythmical pattern (1:11; 3:1; 3:6; 3:7), figures of speech (1:6, 9; 2:3, 6, 7; 3:2; 3:19-20) [EB 4:1-2]), and chiasmus (1:2-3; 2:7*a-b*; 2:17 *a-b*; 3:1*c-d*; 3:11; 3:24*a* [EB 4:6*a*]) make clear.[25] In addition there are such devices as antithesis 1:6-11), emphatic utterances (47 occurrences of YHWH in the first person out of 55 verses in all), graphic diction (2:3), verbal shifts (3:9; 4:4), and closure (1:6).[26]

Most characteristic of Malachi's style, however, is the rhetorical question, the essential element in what Wendland calls a "dialectic style which serves a didactic-admonitory purpose."[27] Though Malachi did not introduce this technique to the biblical literature (cf. Deut 29:23-24; 1 Kings 9:8-9; Isa. 49:11; 50:1-2; Jer. 12:12-13; 15:1-2; 22:8-9; Ezek. 11:2-3; 18:19; Amos 5:18; Hag. 1:9-10; 2:10-11), it occurs nowhere else with such frequency and as a fundamental part of the patterning of the material. At least seven times the prophet attributes the rhetorical question to his audience (1:2, 6, 7; 2:17; 3:7, 8, 13) and in turn asks such questions of them (1:6, 8, 9; 2:10, 15; 3:2).[28] How these questions provide organization and cohesion to the overall composition will be described in the following section.

In conclusion, careful analysis of specific literary devices and consideration of the overall form and structure of the work make it clear that Malachi, far from being, in the words of J. M. P. Smith, a work in which "the element of beauty is almost wholly lacking, there being but slight attempt at ornamentation of any kind,"[29] is rather

---

24. Robert L. Alden, "Malachi," in *EBC*, ed. Frank E. Gaebelein (Grand Rapids: Zondervan, 1985), 7:704-5.
25. Pieter A. Verhoef, *The Books of Haggai and Malachi*, NICOT (Grand Rapids: Eerdmans, 1987), 166-68.
26. Ernst Wendland, "Linear and Concentric Patterns in Malachi," *BT* 36 (1985): 108-21; S. D. Snyman, "Antitheses in the Book of Malachi," *JNSL* 16 (1990): 173-78.
27. Wendland, "Linear and Concentric Patterns in Malachi," 112.
28. Alden, "Malachi," 7:704.
29. John M. P. Smith, *A Critical and Exegetical Commentary on the Book of Malachi*, ICC (Edinburgh: T. & T. Clark, 1912), 4.

one of exquisite artistry. The fact that it is not as a whole to be described as poetry does not mean that it lacks a poetic impact in its craftsmanship as well as in its message.

Literary Integrity

The dialogic pattern of the book of Malachi has been recognized by scholars from earliest times as a self-evident indication of its unity. The major exceptions adduced by critical scholars are 2:11-12 (or 2:11*b*-13*a*) and 4:4-6, both of which are construed as later interpolations.[30] Some also assert that 1:11-14; 2:2, 7; and 3:16 may not be original.[31] These latter examples rest on extremely slender evidence of a most subjective nature, as the exposition later will show. As for 2:11-12, the passage dealing with mixed marriage and idolatry, one objection is that it "fits badly from a structural point of view . . . in the context of ii, 10-16 [so] it is probable that we have here a later addition."[32] The second major "addition," 4:4-6 (HB 3:22-24), is said to consist of an appendix (4:4) equating the message of Malachi with the Mosaic Law and a clarification of the identity of the anonymous messenger (4:5-6) referred to earlier (3:1).[33]

The charge that 2:11-12 does not fit the context betrays a lack of understanding of how the offending passage is integral to not only its immediate context but also the patterning of the book as a whole. This will become clear presently. The argument that the "appendix" (4:4) is an addition depends on the assumption that neither D nor P, which the appendix presupposes, was likely available at the time of the original composition of the book.[34] This approach obviously rests on a prior commitment to the existence and dating of only hypothetical sources and cannot therefore be taken seriously. Finally, to insist that 4:5-6 is a clarification of 3:1, and to offer no hard evidence to support such a claim, is clearly a flagrant example of begging the question. There is not the slightest reason that Malachi himself could not have penned these words of admonition (4:4) and hope (4:5-6), forming, as they do, a most appropriate epilogue to the entire OT prophetic witness.

In recent years form-critical research has identified the "catechetical format"[35] of Malachi as employing speech known as *Disputa-*

---

30. Georg Fohrer, *Introduction to the Old Testament* (London: SPCK, 1970), 470.
31. Friedrich Horst, *Die Zwölf kleinen Propheten, Nahum bis Maleachi,* HAT 14 (Tübingen: J. C. B. Mohr, 1964,) 261.
32. Eissfeldt, *The Old Testament, An Introduction,* 442.
33. Fohrer, *Introduction to the Old Testament,* 470.
34. Smith, *A Commentary on Malachi,* 81.
35. Roddy Braun thus speaks of Malachi's approach as "the catechetical device of the question and answer format" ("Malachi—A Catechism for Times of Disappointment," *CurTM* 4 [1977]: 299).

tionsworte, Streitgesprache, "casuistic-dialectic," and the like.[36] Regardless of the terminology used, it is clear that the book is organized around a series of six interrogations and responses, usually delimited as follows: 1:2-5; 1:6–2:9; 2:10-16; 2:17–3:5; 3:6-12; 3:13–4:3.[37] Malachi 1:1 is the introduction and 4:4-6 the conclusion. Thus, the entire corpus falls within this structure. It is impossible (and unnecessary) here to review all the approaches that proceed from this fundamental form-critical analysis, so only two will be adduced as representative.

In 1972, James A. Fischer[38] proposed to define the units in terms of "questionings," the first four of which embrace all of Malachi 1:2–3:5, *viz.,* 1:2-5; 1:6-2:9; 2:10-16; and 2:17-3:5. The first three questionings consist of one set of questions and answers, whereas the fourth has two sets. The fifth and sixth questionings have two and one sets of questions and answers respectively. But Fischer is not so much concerned with form as with the teaching underscored by the form, teaching embodied in the introductory statements in which each questioning is proposed to YHWH. To Fischer these statements are as follows: (1) YHWH loves Jacob (1:2*a*), (2) He is Israel's father (1:6*a*), (3) He is father of all the Israelites (2:10*a*), (4) He wants honesty, not words (2:17*a*), (5) He is faithful to His Word (3:6), and (6) a repetition of His desire for honesty, not mere words (3:13*a*). The responses to the questions reveal the following: (1) I loved Jacob, (2) I want honest worship, (3) I want real faithfulness, (4) I want you to believe that I am just, (5) I want real worship, and (6) I want honesty. Thus, the essential message of Malachi, according to Fischer, may be found in the statements that prompt the questions and their corresponding answers.

A more disciplined and consistent case for patternism is that of

---

36. For a brief overview of form-critical analyses of Malachi, see Hans Jochen Boecker," Bemerkungen zur formgeschichtlichen Terminologie des Buches Maleachi," *ZAW* 78 (1966): 78-79; see also Beth Glazier-McDonald, *Malachi, The Divine Messenger,* SBL Diss. Series 98 (Atlanta: Scholars Press, 1987), 19; Gerhard Wallis, "Wesen und Structur der Botschaft Maleachis," in *Das Ferne und nahe Wort,* ed. F. Maass (Berlin: A. Töpelmann, 1967), 229-37. Watts analyzes the book according to some sixteen units that he calls "speech acts." In line with modern "reader-centered" criticism he suggests that these "speech acts" contain gapping designed to draw the reader into the act by making him part of the process of achieving meaning. The subjectivity of such a method makes it risky, but Watts does provide some stimulating reaction to the text ("Introduction to the Book of Malachi," 376-79). Van Selms (arbitrarily he admits) divides the book into eight units, *viz.,* 1:1-5, 6-14; 2:1-9, 10-16; 2:17–3:5, 6-12, 13-18, 19-24 ("The Inner Cohesion of the Book of Malachi," *Ou-Testamentiese Werkgemeenskap van Suid-Afrika* 13-14 [1970-71]: 29).
37. Wendland, "Linear and Concentric Patterns in Malachi," 113.
38. James A. Fischer, "Notes on the Literary Form and Message of Malachi," *CBQ* 34 (1972): 315-20.

Ernst Wendland in his 1985 article, "Linear and Concentric Patterns in Malachi."[39] By "linear" Wendland means diachronic, a plan that divides Malachi up into the six traditional units that he calls "disputes." Each of these has three elements—assertion, objection, and response—the first two of which define the problem while the third provides the divine instruction. The linear pattern is thus A-O-R, though there may be subdivisions in the pattern of the different disputes. By way of example of both a simple linear versus a complex linear pattern, one can look at 1:2-5 and 3:6-12. The former has A (2*a*), O (2*b*), R (2*c*-5) whereas the latter is A (6-7*a*), O (7*b*), R (8*a*-12) subdivided into a further A (8*a*), O (8*b*), R (8*c*-12). The resulting message by this approach is, "The merciful yet Mighty Lord of Hosts calls his faithless people to repentance" (p. 114). Wendland summarizes this part of his discussion by affirming that "the criticism that there is no order in the presentation of the prophecy's thematic idea is quite unfounded," a statement that he has ably defended.

As for concentric patterning, Wendland sees not only a diachronic scheme in each of the literary units but a cohesion among them that is clearly manifested in chiasm or ring patterns, either A-B-A', A-B-C-B'-A' or some other variation. Again, only two examples can be given, and since 1:2-5 and 3:6-12 were used before to illustrate the linear approach, it will be interesting to see how they yield to this other. It will be best to set them out approximately as Wendland does. First, Dispute One (1:2-5):

A   YHWH refers to Jacob in blessing (2)
  B   YHWH's judgment upon Esau (3)
    C   Edom's lack of repentance (4*a*)
  B' YHWH's judgment upon Esau (4*b*)
A' YHWH refers to Jacob in blessing (5)

Dispute Five (3:6-12):

A   Introduction: a divine premise (6)
  B   Appeal—repent (7)
    C   Indictment: "you have robbed me" (8)
      D   Verdict: curse (9*a*)
    C' Indictment: "you are robbing me" (9*b*)
  B' Promise—blessings on those who repent (10-11)
A' Conclusion: a Messianic vision (12)

Wendland strengthens his case by pointing out such devices as parallelism, rhyme, alliteration, anaphora, and the like, all of which tie the individual pericopes together and each with the others. Al-

---

39. See n. 26.

though one must use utmost discretion in contending for such kinds of patternism, lest it result in imposition of a structure upon a text and not description of such structure within the text, Wendland's work on Malachi most assuredly is sober in its method and persuasive in its conclusions. The result is an appreciation for the composition as it stands: a piece demonstrating great creative unity as well as profound theological instruction. The task of those who maintain that certain portions of the book, such as 2:11-12 and the others already mentioned, were late interpolations has undeniably been made more daunting by this fresh, wholistic approach.

Literary Structure

In dealing with matters of the integrity of the book of Malachi, it has been necessary already to treat its structure as a response to certain prevailing critical positions that advocated either the likelihood of redactionary additions to or rearrangement of the original composition. There is no need to repeat that here or to elaborate. What follows then is an outline of the book that recognizes its literary structure on the one hand and yet provides a practical way of proceeding in the exposition on the other.

Introduction (1:1)
  I. God's Election of Israel (1:2-5)
  II. The Sacrilege of the Priests (1:6–2:9)
    A. The Sacrilege of Priestly Service (1:6-14)
      1. The Inferior Sacrifices (1:6-10)
      2. Their Insolent Spirit (1:11-14)
    B. The Sacrilege of the Priestly Message (2:1-9)
      1. The Corrupted Vocation of the Priests (2:1-7)
      2. The Covenant Violation of the Priests (2:8-9)
  III. The Rebellion of the People (2:10-16)
    A. The Disruption of the Covenant (2:10-13)
    B. The Illustration of the Covenant (2:14-16)
  IV. Resistance to YHWH (2:17–3:21 [EB 4:3])
    A. Resistance through Self-deceit (2:17–3:5)
      1. The Problem (2:17)
      2. The Promise (3:1-5)
    B. Resistance through Selfishness (3:6-12)
      1. The Problem (3:6-9)
      2. The Promise (3:10-12)
    C. Resistance through Self-sufficiency (3:13-21 [EB 4:3])
      1. The Problem (3:13-15)
      2. The Promise (3:16-21 [4:3])
  V. Restoration through YHWH (3:22-24 [EB 4:4-6])

Distinctive Teaching[40]

Malachi appeared on the scene at a time when the euphoria of the postexilic Jewish community following the rebuilding of the Temple and the restoration of social and political life was beginning to give way to cynicism in both the sacred and secular arenas. The priests had begun to become corrupt in their official capacities as well as in their private lives; the people had mingled themselves with the pagans around them by undertaking illicit marriages and pandering to false religious systems; and the nation as a whole had lost the ardor of messianic, eschatological hope, focusing its attention on the mundane necessities and pleasures of the here and now.

Malachi's message, as the prophetic word of YHWH, was one of rebuke and indictment of each of these ills and across the social spectrum, a message that ended, however, with a note of ultimate hope. In a series of disputations the man of God called to account all the guilty, challenging them to face up to and confess their sins to the Lord of the covenant before whom, in fact, they stood in arraignment. His word is strong, impassioned, and unrelenting, for he lived in critical times. Unless he could get his message across, there was real and imminent danger that all the gains of postexilic renewal would be irretrievably lost. As the last of Israel's kerygmatic heralds, Malachi reached back to the beginning of her covenant election and forward to the promise of covenant fulfillment, bridging the two with his urgent insistence that the theocratic people be worthy of their calling, for the King of all the earth was at hand.

TRANSMISSION OF THE TEXT

A glance at the critical apparatus of both *BHK* and *BHS* reveals that the majority of comment pertains to suggested improvement on difficult or anomalous Hebrew forms and phrases and not to variations preserved in the ancient non-Masoretic MSS or major versions. This is not surprising given the generally well-transmitted and perspicuous nature of the present received text. Those divergences from the MT by the LXX, Syr., Targum, Vg, and other witnesses that are attested to are generally not of a substantial nature but are the kind inherent in any attempt to translate one language into another. An exception appears to be that of the LXX arrangement of 3:22-24 (EB

---

40. For an excellent analysis of the theology of Malachi, see Ralph L. Smith, "The Shape of Theology in the Book of Malachi," *SoJT* 30 (1987): 22-27. Smith suggests four major themes: (1) concern about covenant; (2) concern about the cult; (3) concern about ethical conduct; and (4) concern about the future.

4:4-6). The Greek has 23, 24, 22, the change due no doubt, as Verhoef suggests,[41] to the desire for the book to end on a less threatening note and not because of a different *vorlage*.

Despite Ralph L. Smith's judgment that "there are some serious textual problems in the book of Malachi,"[42] his own examples show anything but (1:3, "jackals" or "pastures"?; 1:11, two hophal participles; 1:12, the problematic נִיבוֹ [*nîbô*, "fruit"]; 2:4, the uncertain לִהְיוֹת [*lhyt*]; 2:12, the difficult עֵר וְעֹנֶה [*'r w'nh*]; 2:15, "one" as either the subject or object of "make"). The exposition will deal with these and others (e.g., 1:5; 2:10, 17*a*) and will show that Verhoef's assessment that "the Hebrew text (MT) makes good sense and appears to be well preserved" (168) is no exaggeration.

---

41. Verhoef, *The Books of Haggai and Malachi*, 169.
42. Ralph L. Smith, *Micah-Malachi*, WBC (Waco, Tex.: Word, 1984), 300.

1

Introduction and God's Election of Israel (1:1-5)

A. INTRODUCTION (1:1)

Translation

¹Oracle: The word of YHWH to Israel through *Malachi.

Exegesis and Exposition

The book of Malachi, like Zech. 9-11 and 12-14, is introduced by the word מַשָּׂא (*maśśāʾ*), "oracle." Its meaning as a technical prophetic term has already been addressed (see pp. 66ff.). As noted in the Introduction, many scholars view Malachi as an anonymous work that freely floated at one time until, like the equally anonymous Zech. 9-11 and 12-14, it was joined to Proto-Zechariah (chaps. 1-8), thus finding its present place in the canon. Besides its common anonymity with the "Deutero-Zechariah" materials, it shared with them the *maśśāʾ* heading.

We observed, however, that the word *maśśāʾ* in Zechariah need not be a heading at all because it may well be in the construct-genitive form in both cases, introducing in typical oracular style an entire pericope. Here in Malachi, on the other hand, it seems clear that the word is in the absolute state, that is, it stands independently as a heading. Evidence for this, despite the similarity of wording in the initial clauses of both Zech. 9:1 and 12:1, on the one hand, and

Mal. 1:1, on the other, lies in the remainder of the formula of Mal. 1:1, which militates against viewing *maśśā'* as anything but absolute.[1] The stylized "the word of YHWH unto (אֶל, *'el*) X through (בְּיַד, *bĕyad*) Y" occurs elsewhere without *maśśā'* and (as here) without a verb (e.g., 2 Chron. 35:6). Also, the addressee is preceded by *'el* (not עַל [*'al*] as, for example, in Jer. 14:1; 46:1; Zech. 12:1), and the word is said to come literally "by the hand of" (בְּיַד, *bĕyad*), an idiom missing in Zech. 9:1 and 12:1 (but attested in Jer. 50:1; Hag. 1:1, 3; 2:1; cf. 1 Chron. 11:3; 2 Chron. 29:25; 35:6). Though only two other passages (Prov. 30:1; 31:1) suggest an absolute usage for *maśśā'*, its function here in Malachi 1:1 as such seems beyond question. In short, the oracular formula embracing אֶל . . . בְּיַד (*bĕyad . . . 'el*) and without the *maśśā'*, attested elsewhere; the redundancy inherent in taking *maśśā'* as construct; and the existence of absolute *maśśā'* elsewhere as a heading distance Malachi's use of the term from Zechariah's and favor its grammatical independence here.

Syntactically, the oracle is defined as "the word of YHWH to Israel through Malachi." That it is to Israel and not Judah, given the postexilic setting of the message, must be explained as reflecting at least a tinge of eschatological hope, for in the day of YHWH there will be only one people, Israel, as the eschatological promise elsewhere makes clear (Joel 2:27; 3:2, 16; Amos 9:9, 14; Zech. 9:1; 12:1). It also bears witness to the unity of all the covenant people.[2] More in line with the immediate context, however, is the likelihood that Israel is another term for Jacob, whose election is described in vv. 2-5. There is thus a reflection back on YHWH's covenant dealings with the nation, going back as far as the selection of Jacob over Esau. That nation was, of course, Israel, not just Judah, in those pristine days at Sinai.

The word to Israel is mediated through (בְּיַד, *bĕyad*, "by the hand of"; cf. Hag. 1:1) Malachi. Even though Malachi is not further identified by an adjective or apposition such as "the prophet" or by a statement of kinship or other introductory device as is usually the case (cf. Isa. 1:1; Ezek. 1:3; Hos. 1:1; Joel 1:1; etc.), one would not ordinarily question the appellation as a personal name (cf. Obad. 1). However,

---

1. Brevard S. Childs, *Introduction to the Old Testament As Scripture* (London: SCM, 1979), 491-92.
2. Richard R. Deutsch, *Calling God's People to Obedience. A Commentary on the Book of Malachi*, ITC (Grand Rapids: Eerdmans, 1987), 75-76. Dumbrell notes that Deuteronomy, like Malachi, is addressed to Israel and thus the prophet betrays his Deuteronomic orientation. He also sees "Israel" as a term of "prophetic ideal" to underline the oneness of the people of God; W. J. Dumbrell, "Malachi and the Ezra-Nehemiah Reforms," *RTR* 35 (1976): 44-45.

this is not the case at all as the vast literature on the matter clearly shows.

The principal objection to taking the appellation as the name of the author is that the same word appears in 3:1 where it must mean "my messenger." It is then assumed that there was no name in the original heading and to fill that void "my messenger" of 3:1 became the "Malachi" of 1:1.[3] If one were to object that there is no analogy to this lack of original citation of author in any of the canonical prophetic works, the response typically is that Zech. 9:1 and 12:1 provide such analogies, for Zech. 9-11 and 12-14, like Malachi, allegedly were originally anonymous.[4] The *petitio princeps* here is obvious. The critic assumes Zech. 9-11 and 12-14 to be independent of Zechariah, leaving the two compositions without attribution, and then concludes that they are anonymous. If this is the case, the anonymity of Malachi has its requisite analogies.

A secondary objection to Malachi as a personal name meaning "my messenger" is that it appears to be only hypocoristic of an anonymous epithet from *mal'ākîyāhû* or the like.[5] This is buttressed by the observation that the appellation is otherwise unknown as a personal name.[6] By way of reply to the last point, the uniqueness of a personal name is no hindrance to its authenticity, for there are many biblical examples (cf. Abraham, Moses, and David out of scores that could be cited) whose authenticity cannot be challenged and which, incidentally, are neither theophoric nor clearly hypocoristic.

As for the first point—the lack of normal naming elements—some scholars suggest, as indicated above, that Malachi is a shortened form of Malachijah, "YHWH is my messenger" or the like. Parallels are found in such names as Abi/Abijah (2 Kings 18:2; 2 Chron. 29:1) and Uri/Urijah (1 Kings 4:19; 1 Chron. 11:41).[7] But even lacking such evidence, names of the form Malachi occur, such as Ethni (1 Chron. 6:41) and Beeri (Gen. 26:34).[8] Appeals to orthographic ir-

3. Georg Fohrer, *Introduction to the Old Testament* (London: SPCK, 1970), 469.
4. Otto Eissfeldt, *The Old Testament, An Introduction* (Oxford: Basil Blackwell, 1965), 441.
5. Dumbrell, "Malachi and the Ezra-Nehemiah Reforms," 43; cf. John M. P. Smith, *A Critical and Exegetical Commentary on the Book of Malachi*, ICC (Edinburgh: T. & T. Clark, 1912), 9: "As the name stands, it can only mean 'my messenger.' This is a very unlikely appellation for a parent to bestow upon a child."
6. René Vuilleumier, *Malachie*, CAT (Neuchatel: Delachaux & Niestlé, 1981), 224 n. 7.
7. Wilhelm Rudolph, *Haggai–Sacharja 1-8–Sacharja 9-14–Maleachi*, KAT (Gütersloh: Gütersloher Verlagshaus Gerd Mohn, 1976), 247.
8. Theophane Chary, *Aggée-Zacharie-Malachie* (Paris: Librairie Lecoffre, 1969), 233.

regularity carry little weight, therefore, in determining whether Malachi is a name.

Finally, the fact that מַלְאָכִי (*mal'ākî*) occurs in 3:1 may be turned on its head to show that the prophet Malachi, far from deriving his name from that passage, is making a play on his own name to get across a point. Thus the man of God, "my messenger," looks to the day when YHWH, in His own words, says, "I send 'My messenger.'" This is no less possible than the constant use of the word group יְשׁוּעָה/יָשַׁע (*yāša'/yĕšûâ*), "he saves/salvation," by Isaiah (25:9; 33:2, 22; 35:4; 43:12; 49:25; 52:7, 10; 59:11; 60:18; 63:9) whose name means "salvation (is) of YHWH" or "YHWH saves." The objection that a parent would be unlikely to name a son "(YHWH is) my messenger"[9] is gratuitous in light of such bold names as Isaiah, Hosea (הוֹשֵׁעַ [*hôšēa'*], "salvation"), and Joshua (יְהוֹשׁוּעַ [*yĕhôšûa'*], "YHWH saves"). Besides, it is possible that the *yodh* afformative is not the first-person pronominal suffix "my" but a *yodh compaginis*, the original genitive ending (GKC, 90k), resulting in "messenger of (YHWH)" and not "(YHWH is) my messenger."[10] This relieves the problem of an overly-bold concept of YHWH serving as messenger to a prophet rather than vice-versa.

B. GOD'S ELECTION OF ISRAEL (1:2-5)

Translation

2"I have loved you," says YHWH, but you say, "How have You loved us?" "Was Esau not Jacob's brother," says YHWH, "yet I loved Jacob. 3As for Esau, I hated him; I made his mountains desolate and gave his inheritance over to the *jackals of the desert." 4Yet Edom said, "We are devastated, but we will once again build the ruined places." Thus says YHWH of hosts, "They indeed may build, but I will overthrow. They will be known as the wicked territory, the people against whom YHWH has eternal indignation. 5Your eyes will see (it), and then you will say, 'May YHWH be magnified *beyond the border of Israel!'"

Exegesis and Exposition

The covenant relationship initiated by YHWH with Israel, hinted at in v. 1, is fully developed in this introductory section of the book. This is clear from the election motif implied in the Jacob-Esau antithesis and in the technical language of covenant in vv. 2-3 especially.

---

9. Thus J. M. P. Smith, *A Commentary on Malachi*, 9.
10. Rudolph, *Haggai–Sacharja 1-8–Sacharja 9-14–Maleachi*, 247-48.

The scene shifts back to the patriarchal era when YHWH first made promise to Abraham of a seed and land through and in which he would bring blessing to all the earth (Gen. 12:1-3; 15:1-5, 18-21; 17:1-8). This was subsequently reaffirmed to Isaac (Gen. 26:1-4) and, most emphatically, to Jacob (Gen. 27:27-29; 28:13-15; 35:9-15; 46:2-4).

Of particular importance is the narrative of Gen. 27. There, by ruse and deceit, Jacob, though the younger son of Isaac, received both the birthright of the major share of the inheritance and the blessing to be transmitted forward in association with the seed and land promises. Members of Malachi's own generation of Jews were in direct succession to Jacob and were the recipients of the covenant blessing, as the equation of the "you" in the first clause of v. 2 with the "Jacob" in the last clause makes clear. YHWH loved them because He had first loved their patronymic ancestor Jacob.

Modern studies of covenant language have shown that the word "love" (אָהֵב, 'āhēb, or any of its forms) is a technical term in both the biblical and ancient Near Eastern treaty and covenant texts to speak of choice or election to covenant relationship, especially in the so-called suzerainty documents.[11] There may well be emotional overtones to the term, but fundamentally it is one of a legal or social nature. What YHWH is saying here, then, is that in ancient times He chose Jacob to be the special recipient of His grace, the channel through whom He would mediate His salvific purposes.

In answer to the question of Malachi's audience—"How have you loved us?"—the answer was plain. He loved them by choosing their father, a choice that was never annulled and whose benefits extended to them.[12] Evidence of that love was the fact that Israel survived through the ages up to the time of Malachi and his audience. Even Babylonian destruction of state and Temple and the exile of the flower of the community had not canceled the promise, for here they were, a century after the deportation, still alive and flourishing in their restored nation and renewed religious and social life.

Esau, on the other hand, had not only been "hated" (that is, rejected, as שָׂנֵא [śānē'] means in covenant terms)[13] in the original story, but his nation Edom had known nothing but YHWH's disfavor ever since. In fact, v. 3 seems to suggest that disfavor had finally found

---

11. William L. Moran, "The Ancient Near Eastern Background of the Love of God in Deuteronomy," *CBQ* 25 (1963): 77-87.
12. For the connection between covenant love and election or "choice" (בָּחַר, *bāḥar*), see Pieter A. Verhoef, *The Books of Haggai and Malachi*, NICOT (Grand Rapids: Eerdmans, 1987), 196-97.
13. E. Jenni, *THAT*, 2:835, s.v. שׂנא; Joyce G. Baldwin, *Haggai, Zechariah, Malachi*, TOTC (London: Tyndale, 1972), 223.

recent expression in a devastation of Edom that left her desolate and abandoned.

As noted in the Introduction scholars have suggested many occasions to which the passage may be alluding. The history of Edom is so sparsely documented that it is impossible to be certain, but most likely the circumstance in mind is the series of Babylonian incursions into Palestine and the Transjordan from 605-540 B.C.[14] The justification for this view is that the sparing of Judah from annihilation and her subsequent return and restoration are a mark of YHWH's love that would be particularly apparent to a postexilic audience. The contrast to that—the decimation and virtual non-recovery of Esau/Edom, the "hated"—would most likely be associated with the same event. Jacob survived despite the Babylonian conquest whereas Esau did not.

It is true that Edom at least partially recovered, a fact that v. 4 makes clear, but not for long, for by the end of the fourth century what was left of the nation was overrun by the Nabataeans, who went on to bring indigenous Edomite existence to an end by either physical annihilation or intermarriage. In the end there was (and is) no Edom, but Israel continued (and continues) on. In no clearer terms could YHWH communicate to His people what it meant for Him to love them.

So decisive would Edom's destruction be that it would be known thenceforth as "wicked territory" (גְּבוּל רִשְׁעָה, *gĕbûl rišʿâ*). When God's own people see it come to pass, they will say, "May YHWH be magnified beyond the border (*gĕbûl*) of Israel" (v. 5). This primary meaning of the word makes an interesting repetitive device in connection with the secondary meaning in v. 4.

The severity of YHWH's judgment on Edom is not only because of Edom's own specific national sinfulness (cf., e.g., Num. 20:14-21; Deut. 2:8; Jer. 49:7-22; Ezek. 25:12-14; Amos 1:11-12; Obad. 10-12) but more particularly because Edom is almost a paradigm in the OT of antitheocratic sentiment, a feeling especially to be condemned because Edom was a "brother people."[15] Just as Esau had despised his birthright (Gen. 25:34), so the Edomites typify those who despise the overtures of divine grace. The overthrow of Edom, then, both past

14. This would include the campaigns of Nebuchadnezzar (605-562 B.C.) and his successors, especially Nabonidus, who is thought to have ravaged Edom from time to time from his Arabian base at Teima; J. R. Bartlett, "The Moabites and Edomites," in *Peoples of Old Testament Times*, ed. D. J. Wiseman (Oxford: Clarendon, 1973), 243-44. Cf. John Bright, *A History of Israel*, 3d ed. (Philadelphia: Westminster, 1981), 377-78.
15. Rex Mason, *The Books of Haggai, Zechariah, and Malachi*, CBC (Cambridge: Cambridge Univ., 1977), 141.

and future, speaks of the judgment of all wicked nations that arrogantly rise up against YHWH and His elect people.

The result of Edom's downfall is the exaltation of YHWH "beyond the border of Israel" (v. 5). The reason for this recognition of YHWH by the nations surrounding Israel and even afar off is quite evident: YHWH has shown Himself faithful to the covenant. He had promised to the patriarchs that He would bless those who blessed them, but those who cursed them (like Edom) would be cursed. This marked the course of OT history and has never been abrogated. Thus there is an eschatological note here as well, for the exaltation of YHWH is a hallmark of the end times (Mic. 5:4).

The subject of the exclamation of v. 5 is somewhat ambiguous, perhaps deliberately. The oracle as a whole is addressed to Israel (v. 1), but v. 4 consists of a response to arrogant Edom. The eyes that see this humiliation of Edom may be those of Israel or of Edom or both.[16] In any event, YHWH is exalted when He demonstrates His sovereignty, an exaltation in which all men ultimately will share.

Additional Notes

1:1 For מַלְאָכִי, lit. "my messenger," the LXX has ἀγγέλου αὐτοῦ, "his messenger," possibly suggesting already an early tradition about the anonymous authorship of the book. On the other hand, this reading may reflect a deliberate glossing by the LXX to soften the impact of the prophet's being named "(YHWH is) my messenger." The result would be, perhaps, "(he is) his (i.e., YHWH's) messenger." The Targum offers: "By Malachi whose name is called Ezra the scribe." Hence the notion that Malachi is not a personal name receives support from that quarter as well. As a whole, however, the reasons favoring it as a proper name outweigh the objections.

1:3 *BHS* suggests נָתַתִּי, "I gave over" or the like, for לְתַנּוֹת, "to the jackals." This would provide a better parallelism to וָאָשִׂים of the previous colon, but it suffers from lack of major versional support.

1:5 With *BHK* and *BHS* it appears advisable to read לִגְבוּל as a dittograph and so to drop the prefixed לְ.

---

16. For the former (Israel), see, e.g., Vuilleumier, *Malachie*, 226. Most scholars attribute the doxology here to Israel.

2

The Sacrilege of the Priests (1:6–2:9)

The insensitive response by His people to YHWH's assertion that He loved them—"How have You loved us?" (v. 2)—begins to take on meaning in this section. Here the cold-hearted indifference of the priests in their service (1:6-14) and in their teaching (2:1-9) becomes most apparent, and it is this lack of love (that is, covenant commitment) on their part that prompts YHWH to remind them of His own faithfulness. How could the priests, who ought to epitomize the spirit of grateful compliance to the will of YHWH, reciprocate by being so professional and routine? So jaded had they become that they could no longer recognize the elective grace of their God even when it stared them in the face.

A. THE SACRILEGE OF PRIESTLY SERVICE (1:6-14)

1. THE INFERIOR SACRIFICES (1:6-10)

Translation

⁶" 'A son honors his father and a slave his master; if then I am a father, where is My honor, and if a master, where is My respect? asks YHWH of hosts of you, O priests who despise My name. But you say, 'How have we despised Your name?' ⁷You are offering defiled food upon My altar, yet you say, 'How have we defiled You?' By saying (that) the table of YHWH is despised. ⁸For when you offer the blind as a sacrifice, is that not evil? And when you offer the lame and sick,

is that not evil (as well)? Indeed, offer it to your governor. Will he be pleased with *you or receive you with favor?" asks YHWH of hosts. ⁹"But now petition God's favor that He might be gracious to us. With this kind of thing in your hands, how can He receive you with favor?" asks YHWH of hosts. ¹⁰"Would that one of you might close the doors, so that you no longer would kindle useless fires on My altar. I am not pleased with you," says YHWH of hosts, "and I will no longer accept an offering from you."

Exegesis and Exposition

By a series of comparisons and *a fortiori* arguments YHWH draws attention to the present backslidden condition of the cultus. In the everyday world, He points out, children honor their parents and slaves respect their masters. How can the priests of God, who give at least nominal assent to His sovereignty, treat Him with such utter disdain? Again, the language here is the stock vocabulary of covenant. Both "son" and "slave" are terms characteristic of suzerainty treaties, suggestive of subordination and yet mutual affection.[1]

Evidence of their disdain is the fact that the priests despise the name of YHWH. The verb used (בּוּז, *bûz*) here fundamentally means "to hold in contempt," that is, to view as unimportant. How unimportant may be seen in the application of the same verb to the "table" of YHWH (v. 7). The word here (שֻׁלְחָן, *šulḥan*) refers, in fact, to the altar, as the parallelism to מִזְבֵּחַ (*mizbēaḥ*), "altar," makes plain. The reason for referring to the altar here as a table is, first, to continue the human analogies already begun. The implied reference to the governor's table in v. 8 supports this. Moreover, covenant relationships also presuppose the use of tables, inasmuch as these transactions were usually cemented in ceremonies involving common meals shared by the king and his vassals with whom he had entered into covenant fellowship.[2] To despise the table of YHWH is to write off the importance of the covenant and to insult the sovereign who initiated it in His grace.

Further indication of the metaphor employed to describe the relationship between YHWH and the priests (and, by extension, the people) is the use of the word "food" (לְחֶם, *leḥem*, lit. "bread") in v. 7, rather than "sacrifice," "offering," or some other technical term. The

---

1. Theophane Chary, *Aggée-Zacharie-Malachie* (Paris: Librairie Lecoffre, 1969), 238. Cf. Paul Kalluveettil, *Declaration and Covenant*, AnBib 88 (Rome: Pontifical Biblical Institute, 1982), 133; Steven L. McKenzie and Howard N. Wallace, "Covenant Themes in Malachi," *CBQ* 45 (1983): 557-58.
2. Kalluveettil, *Declaration and Covenant*, 10-15, 120-21; Dennis J. McCarthy, *Treaty and Covenant*, AnBib 21 (Rome: Pontifical Biblical Institute, 1963), 163-64.

point is not that the sacrifices offered to YHWH were construed as food for Him to consume, a conception at home in ancient Near Eastern religions,[3] but only that the prophet is again anticipating the gifts made to the governor, gifts that consisted of food supplies for his table.

Having charged the priests with despising His altar, YHWH specifies how they have done so in response to their hypocritical query about it (v. 7). It is by presenting blind, lame, and sick sacrificial victims, animals that were ritually excluded according to the clear dictates of Torah law (Deut. 15:21). The reason for the law in the first place and for its rigid application here is most obvious. YHWH required offerings from one's labor and resources and as sovereign desired and deserved the best. It would be easy to part with livestock that was already of little value to the owner and sanctimoniously offer it up to YHWH as a pretense of devotion. As David said of the free offer of Araunah's threshing-floor and oxen, however, "I will not offer to YHWH my God burnt offerings which cost me nothing" (2 Sam. 24:24).

This was the spirit of sacrifice lacking in the priests of Malachi's day. Going through the *pro forma* of religious activity, they missed the real point: YHWH deserves the best. In fact, He says, would even a human governor accept such miserable fare? Surely not! And if that is the case, how presumptuous to think that the God of heaven and earth can suffer such indignity. Who the particular governor may have been cannot be known because the date of the utterance is uncertain, but for the point to be made it matters not at all.

The only remedy for this lamentable state of affairs is for the guilty priests to seek the face of YHWH in repentance. Only then can His favor extend once more to them and to all the community whom they represent (v. 9). But it seems unlikely that such repentance is forthcoming. The text is difficult here, reading literally "from your hands was this" (v. 9b).[4] The idea seems to be that as long as the hands of the priests continue to offer such inappropriate gifts, all overtures toward repentance will be hollow and meaningless. True repentance

---

3. DeVaux shows that there is no connection between sacrifice as "food" for YHWH in the OT and prevailing understanding in the ancient Near East (*Ancient Israel, Its Life and Institutions* [London: Darton, Longman & Todd, 1961], 433-35).
4. Glazier-McDonald suggests the phrase means, "since all this was your doing," that is, "from your hands" is tracing the fault to the wicked priests (*Malachi: The Divine Messenger*, SBL Series 98 [Atlanta: Scholars Press, 1987], 54). The line seems better understood, however, as a protasis to an asyndetic apodosis: "Since you have made such offerings, how can He receive you with favor?" So Joyce G. Baldwin, *Haggai, Zechariah, Malachi*, TOTC (London: Tyndale, 1972), 226.

must be accompanied by a radically different behavior. The forgiveness of YHWH may not require the offering of proper sacrifice as a prerequisite, but it certainly demands it as a consequence.

Until and unless that comes to pass, the priests might as well desist from the charade and close the Temple doors altogether (v. 10).[5] If that were done, at least the hypocritical service of the priests—an exercise worse than nothing at all—would come to an end. Altar fires that burn spurious sacrifices are not worth kindling. The smoke and ashes they produce are an offense to a holy God, a stench in His nostrils rather than a sweet savor (Isa. 65:1-5).

The rebuke here is reminiscent of that of earlier prophets who castigated their hypocritical contemporaries for confusing ritual with true worship. In a classic statement Micah asked, "How shall I come before YHWH and worship before the high God?" He then answered by a series of rhetorical questions. "Shall I come before him with burnt-offerings, with yearling calves? Will YHWH be pleased with thousands of rams or ten thousand rivers of oil? Shall I give my first-born for my transgression, the fruit of my body for the sin of my soul?" The answer is NO. "He has showed you, O man, what is good. What does YHWH demand of you but to do justly, to love kindness, and to walk humbly with your God?" (Mic. 6:6-8; cf. Ps. 40:6-8 [HB 40:7-9]).

This is precisely the message of Malachi to the postexilic priests who had perverted their calling to such an extent that they no longer practiced biblical religion and no longer could distinguish between a sterile, hypocritical professionalism and a sense of genuine servanthood before God and on behalf of the community.

Additional Notes

1:8 The LXX, Vg suggest a reading based, perhaps, on הֲיִרְצֵהוּ rather than the MT הֲיִרְצְךָ. This makes the referent to the suffix the offering rather than the offerer, thus: "will he be pleased with it?" The more difficult the MT is clearly original here. Moreover, it sustains the parallel with פָּנֶיךָ.

2. THEIR INSOLENT SPIRIT (1:11-14)

Translation

11"For from the rising of the sun to its setting My name will be great among the nations, and *incense will be offered in My name as

---

5. At Qumran, in fact, a "door-closer" came to be viewed as a pious worshiper who refused to offer vain sacrifice. So Jerome Murphy-O'Connor, "The Translation of Damascus Document VI, 11-14." *RevQ* 7 (1971): 553-56.

well as a pure offering everywhere; for My name will be great among the nations," says YHWH of hosts. 12"But you are profaning it by saying that the table of the Lord is polluted and its *fruit, that is, its food, is despicable. 13"You also say, 'How tiresome (it is).' You sniff at it," says YHWH of hosts, "and instead bring what is stolen, lame, or sick—these you bring for an offering. Should I accept this from you?" asks YHWH? 14"Cursed be the hypocrite who has a male in his flock but vows and sacrifices something blemished to the Lord, for I am a great king," says YHWH of hosts, "and My name is awesome among the nations."

Exegesis and Exposition

The reason for the sacrilegious behavior of the priests of YHWH, described so graphically in vv. 6-10, becomes clear in this section—their spirit itself is sacrilegious. They betray most lucidly the principle that good works must originate in pure hearts. It is no wonder then that these priests, by their works of hypocrisy and self-centeredness, reveal an attitude commensurate with their deeds, an attitude that at best can be described as haughty and contemptuous. This is all the more deplorable in that these priests and people belong to YHWH by covenant election. They of all nations on earth ought to manifest a spirit of true piety and obedience. To the contrary, they, by comparison to the worship of God by the nations to come, give every evidence of paganism.

The reference to the worship of the nations (v. 11) is one of the most difficult concepts in the prophecy. Taken without reference to general canonical context and a cohesive biblical theology, the verse appears to teach that in the prophet's own time there was universal recognition of YHWH or at least some high God by the nations and a corresponding purity of the worship they offered him.[6] The matter is not clarified, to say the least, by the fact that there are no finite verbs in the passage to lend some kind of chronological orientation. Does the prophet indeed speak of his own generation, or is he looking to an age to come?

From all that is known in terms of salvation history and the actual facts of ancient comparative religion, there were no large elements of people outside the Jewish community who even knew of YHWH, to say nothing of worshiping Him in the manner described by

---

6. This view, in fact, was held by many older scholars. See, e.g., W. Nowack, *Die kleinen Propheten*, HAT III/4 (Göttingen: Vandenhoeck und Ruprecht, 1903), 430; Karl Marti, *Das Dodekapropheton*, KHAT XIII (Tübingen: J. C. B. Mohr, 1904), 464. For a modern expression of that opinion, see Robert C. Dentan, "The Book of Malachi," *IB* 6 (New York: Abingdon, 1956), 1128-29.

Malachi.[7] Even were one to maintain that proselytes from Egyptian, Mosaic times onward had joined themselves to Israel and to covenant faith, the language of our text far surpasses, both in numbers and extent, the aggregate of any such conversions. And to say that pagan nations could or did come to YHWH apart from the mediation of Israel is to say something flatly contradicting the express purpose for Israel's very election, namely, to be a conduit through which saving grace could be transmitted and in identification with which the nations would become reconciled with God. As for the notion of some scholars that the passage teaches the possibility of true worship without reference to biblical revelation,[8] nothing could be more inimical to the full witness of biblical soteriology.

This means, therefore, that the prophecy is looking to a future day when the God of Israel will be the God of the nations.[9] Once more Malachi, whose overall message is grounded in the problems of his own times, moves forward to an eschatological day of salvation and, in league with his prophetic forebears (cf. Isa. 66:18-21; Jer. 3:17; 4:2; 12:14-17; and esp. Zech. 14:16-21), envisions a time of universal worship of YHWH. In a sense, then, this verse is interruptive of the flow of the passage inasmuch as the prophet is fundamentally concerned with matters immediately at hand.[10] But what more arresting and motivating resort could he employ than to contrast the pagan behavior of the covenant people of the present with the devout behavior of the covenant people of the future? In another *a fortiori* syllogism Malachi asks, in effect, "If the pagan nations in ages to come will magnify the name of YHWH (cf. v. 5) and worship with offerings of

---

7. So John M. P. Smith, *A Critical and Exegetical Commentary on the Book of Malachi*, ICC (Edinburgh: T. & T. Clark, 1912), 30. James Swetnam, in fact, holds that Malachi is referring to the Jewish diaspora community whose prayers and other expressions of worship were tantamount to sacrifice ("Malachi 1. 11: An Interpretation," *CBQ* [1969]: 206-7). The phrase "among the nations" seems to preclude this, however.

8. Friedrich Horst, *Die Zwölf kleinen Propheten. Nahum bis Maleachi*, HAT 14 (Tübingen: J. C. B. Mohr, 1964), 267.

9. Th. C. Vriezen, "How to Understand Malachi 1:11," in *Grace Upon Grace*, ed. James I. Cook (Grand Rapids: Eerdmans, 1975), 132; Th. Chary, *Aggée-Zacharie, Malachie*, 245. Baldwin points to a number of future, indeed, eschatological terms such as "from the rising of the sun to its setting" ("Malachi 1:11 and the Worship of the Nations in the Old Testament," *TynBul* 23 [1972]: 122-23).

10. Indeed, this very fact has led many scholars to see v. 11 as a poorly joined interpolation. See, e.g., Elliger, who views 1:11 (as well as 1:13-14; 2:2, 7) as secondary (*Die Propheten Nahum, Habakuk, Zephanja, Haggai, Sacharja, Maleachi*, ATD 25 [Göttingen: Vandenhoeck & Ruprecht, 1982], 195, 198).

incense and oblations, how can His own priests and people, the immediate beneficiaries of all His covenant grace, fail to do so?"[11]

Their failure is real, however, and in stark contrast to the ideal anticipated in the future. The nations one day will magnify and make offerings to His "name," that is, to YHWH Himself.[12] The word "name" (שֵׁם, *šēm*) occurs three times in v. 11. Its triple use here links the passage with the double use in v. 6, suggesting a parallelism between vv. 6-8 and 11-14, with vv. 9-10 serving as a fulcrum of hope (v. 9) and frustrated hope (v. 10). As in v. 6, therefore, the people of YHWH despise and profane that name (v. 12) and declare the "table" of YHWH to be polluted (cf. v. 7). They offer up ritually disqualified animals (v. 13; cf. v. 8*a*), an affront to YHWH the Great King (v. 14) for, as already stated in the parallel text, they would not dare do such a thing to a mere human governor (v. 8*b*).[13]

The reference to the "name" of YHWH, though common enough as a substitute for the person of YHWH in earlier times (cf. Ex. 23:21; Deut. 12:5, 11, 21; 16:2, 6; etc.), became a virtual epithet for YHWH (הַשֵּׁם, *haššēm*) by the end of the biblical period and increasingly so later on.[14] Malachi appears to give evidence of this trend, at least in these passages and in 3:16 and 4:2 [HB 3:20]. It is a trend toward a developing emphasis on the divine transcendence, one reflected also in the avoidance by the LXX of the common anthropomorphisms of the Hebrew text.

The name of YHWH is profaned, says the Lord, by the disdain shown His table (i.e., the altar) and its "fruit" (v. 12). That is, one cannot claim to revere God while at the same time fail to worship Him in a proper manner. The cultus is not the means of achieving a saving relationship with Him, but one cannot maintain that relationship and at the same time count the cultus as of no importance. That is clearly the import of this entire oracle.

The translation "fruit" for נִיב (*nîb*) is problematic, inasmuch as the vocable occurs only here and in the Qere of Isa. 57:19 in this form. The verb נוּב (*nûb*), "to bear fruit," is attested to in Pss. 62:11 [EB

---

11. Vriezen, "How to Understand Malachi 1:11," 134-35.
12. Dumbrell draws attention to the Deuteronomic concept of the divine name as an indication of ownership and sovereignty and to Malachi's use of this "name theology" ("Malachi and the Ezra-Nehemiah Reforms," *RTR* 35 [1976]: 45-46).
13. For another analysis suggesting parallels along other lines, see E. Ray Clendenen, "The Structure of Malachi: A Textlinguistic Study," *CTR* 2 (1987): 8-9.
14. Walther Eichrodt, *Theology of the Old Testament* (London: SCM, 1967), 2:40-45.

62:10] and 92:15 [EB 92:14] as well as in Proverbs 10:31; Zech. 9:17. The noun נוֹב (*nôb*) occurs in the Kethib of Isa. 57:19 where it refers to the "fruit of the lips," that is, to praise.

In our passage it must be understood as a synonym of אֹכֶל (*'ōkel*), "food," for it appears that *'ōkel*, is an explanatory gloss of נִיב to render the rare word intelligible.[15] The "food" is a reference to the sacrificial offerings, just as לֶחֶם (*leḥem*), "bread," was in v. 7. Very likely, therefore, *nîb* is fruit in the sense of "produce," the fruits of one's labor as it were. In this usage it would be comparable to the common word פְּרִי (*pĕrî*), which often has this nuance (cf. Gen. 4:3); Num. 13:20, 26,27; Deut. 7:13). All that YHWH is saying is that the wicked priests regard His altar and everything on it as of no account, as despicable.

Their utter contempt is most picturesquely portrayed by their dismissal of the whole thing—altars, incense, sacrifices, and all—as so much needless bother (v. 13). In their own words they say, "What weariness!"[16] The joy has left their worship, and it has become an onerous burden. The loss of a true understanding of worship leads easily to a total disregard or even repudiation of its requirements, and so these calloused ministers of the Temple sniff at their responsibilities, considering them as beneath their dignity, and go about establishing the cult on their own terms. This is summarized by their willingness to receive and to offer in sacrifice stolen, lame, and sick animals (cf. v. 8), a gesture that elicits the strongest abhorrence from YHWH who says (literally), "Can I be pleased with it from your hands?" The same verb רָצָה (*rāṣâ*) occurs in v. 8 where YHWH asks whether the governor would be pleased with an insulting gift. The argument is clear. If a mere human authority can be offended by a gift and an attitude that betrays indifference or even hostility, how can one expect the King of kings to feel other than the most abject revulsion?

Continuing with another example of ritual impropriety, YHWH singles out the individual who pretends that he will offer the male of his flock but presents instead a blemished animal (v. 14). The "male" (זָכָר, *zākār*) refers to the choicest animal, physically whole and well and in its prime (Ex. 12:5; 34:19; Lev. 1:3, 10; 4:23; 22:19). The hypocrite (lit., "deceiver," ptc. of נָכַל, *nākal*, "to be crafty") goes so far as to select such an animal from his flock, to make a public vow to offer it to YHWH, and then secretly to substitute for it an inferior animal. But what he does secretly among men is wide open before God. Such

---

15. A. Van Hoonacker, *Les Douze Petits Prophètes* (Paris: Librairie Victor Lecoffre, 1908), 714.
16. For the rare form מַתְּלָאָה, cf. GKC, 37c.

blasphemous duplicity brings down upon its perpetrator the divine curse, for YHWH is a Great King.

This reference to "curse" (אָרַר, *'ārar*) in juxtaposition to the epithet "Great King," carries strong overtones of covenant language.[17] In ancient Near Eastern treaties, especially in Hittite exemplars, the sovereign who imposed the treaty was called the "Great King." Failure on the part of the vassal partner to live up to its stipulations inevitably brought the possibility of punishment, of a curse. Such a concept is pervasive in Malachi; indeed, no other prophet proportionately refers more to covenant curse (cf. 2:2; 3:9; 4:6 [HB 3:24]). To offer a blemished sacrifice is to manifest egregious insubordination to the Great King and to invite the harshest punitive stipulations of the covenant agreement.

As the completion of an inclusio to vv. 11-14,[18] YHWH says that the evidence that He is a Great King lies in the fact that He is feared among the nations of the earth. This need not (as v. 11 does) suggest that the nations know Him redemptively, but only that His name or reputation has become known by His mighty deeds on behalf of His people. Examples of this are abundant in the later literature, especially in Ezekiel (25:5, 11, 14, 17; 26:6; 28:22), Daniel (2:47; 3:28-29; 4:37), and Ezra (1:1-4; 6:9-12; 7:12-16). Surely a God whose name is revered by the pagans deserves and has a right to demand that His servant people render Him appropriate homage.

Additional Notes

1:11 The presence of asyndetic *hophal* participles מֻקְטָר and מֻגָּשׁ has led most critical scholars to question the text at this point and to emend it in various ways. This is unnecessary, however, since מֻקְטָר can be taken as a substantive, just as the *hophal* ptc. מָשְׁחָת is in v. 14. Therefore, the verb קָטַר, "to make sacrifices smoke" (BDB, 882), has, in the *hophal*, the idea "that which is made to smoke," namely, incense (Lev. 6:15; 1 Chron. 6:34). As for מֻגָּשׁ, it functions here as a finite verb, "to be offered." Cf. James Swetnam, "Malachi 1:11: An Interpretation," *CBQ* 31 (1969): 200-201. Swetnam takes מֻקְטָר in a broader sense, however, as "an oblation." For "incense" as a correct translation, see Baldwin, "Malachi 1:11 and the Worship of the Nations in the Old Testament," 123.

1:12 The LXX and perhaps Tg. Neb. take נִיבוֹ as a dittograph for נִבְזֶה and so eliminate it. This results in "and its food is despicable," bringing it more in line with the parallel "the table of the Lord is

---

17. Klaus Baltzer, *The Covenant Formulary* (Oxford: Basil Blackwell, 1971), 66-68.
18. Clendenen, "The Structure of Malachi: A Textlinguistic Study," 9.

polluted." The very difficulty of MT is, however, presumptively in its favor.

B. THE SACRILEGE OF THE PRIESTLY MESSAGE (2:1-9)

1. THE CORRUPTED VOCATION OF THE PRIESTS (2:1-7)

Translation

¹"Now, O priests, is this commandment for you. ²If you do not listen and take it to heart to give glory to My name," says YHWH of hosts, "I will send the curse and will curse your blessings; indeed, I have already done so because you are not taking it to heart. ³I am about to rebuke your offspring and will spread offal upon your faces, the (very) offal of your festivals, and *you will be taken away with it. ⁴Then you will know that I have sent this commandment to you, (that) my covenant (might continue) to be with Levi," says YHWH of hosts. ⁵"My covenant with him was one of life and wholeness. I gave them to him to fill him with awe, and he indeed revered Me and stood in awe before My name. ⁶True teaching was in his mouth, unrighteousness was not to be found on his lips. He walked with Me in wholeness and uprightness and turned many from iniquity. ⁷For the lips of a priest should preserve knowledge and men should seek instruction from his mouth; for he is the messenger of YHWH of hosts.

Exegesis and Exposition

Though much of 1:6-14 is repeated here in 2:1-9 (2:2, cf. 1:6, 14; 2:5, cf. 1:14; 2:9, cf. 1:12),[19] the emphasis is completely different in that, whereas the former passage concerns the cultic activity of the priests, 2:1-9 pertains to their message or teaching ministry.[20] This twofold responsibility of the priest existed from the very beginning (Lev 10:11; Deut 31:9-13; 33:10), but with the gradual demise of OT prophetism the role of the priest as teacher became more and more prominent (cf. Hag. 2:11; Zech. 7:3). Ezra, of course, is the example *par excellence* (Ezra 7:10, 25; Neh. 8:9). Eventually, however, the priest as teacher became eclipsed by professional scribes and scholars who undertook this work.[21]

---

19. Ernst Wendland, "Linear and Concentric Patterns in Malachi," *BT* 36 (1985): 117.
20. Steven L. McKenzie and Howard N. Wallace separate 1:6-14 from 2:1-9 entirely, taking 2:1 as a new heading. The latter unit itself they divide between 2:1-4, a command threatening the priests with a curse for disobedience, and 2:5-9, YHWH's covenant with Levi. They take v. 4 as the hinge, one that allows vv. 5-9 to be the grounds for vv. 1-3. See their "Covenant Themes in Malachi," *CBQ* 45 (1983): 550.
21. R. de Vaux, *Ancient Israel*, 353-55.

But in Malachi's day the priests became indifferent to and indeed scornful of not only their duties as officiants in the cultus; they also became slack in teaching and preaching the Word of God. The prophet therefore addresses this side of their vocation as well as the other. The commandment (מִצְוָה, miṣwâ) of which he speaks (2:1) must be the adumbration of all that follows in this section, namely, instruction about the teaching ministry of the priests. This is especially for them, because the adjurations of the previous section (1:6-14) included some comments applicable not only to the priests but also to the general population (vv. 8, 13, 14).[22]

The term מִצְוָה, (miṣwâ, "commandment") is another technical covenant word, most appropriate here, as the explicit references to the priestly covenant that follow make clear (vv. 4, 5, 8).[23] Therefore, its violation in terms of not being seriously considered and of consequently denying YHWH the glory that comes in perfect obedience must elicit appropriate covenant sanction. Thus another technical term—"curse" (מְאֵרָה, mĕ'ērâ)—is introduced. The inevitable result of covenant unfaithfulness was the imposition of the curses that were always spelled out in covenant texts (cf. Lev. 26:14-39; Deut. 27:11-26; 28:15-57).[24] Disobedience of the priestly covenant is no different. That, too, will be met by a curse, one so severe that it will in effect cancel out any potential blessings. The language could not be stronger: "I will curse your blessings" (v. 2b). In fact, YHWH says, He has already done so, because it is a forgone conclusion that the priests will not take to heart His miṣwâ.[25]

The curse takes specific form in two ways:[26] YHWH will rebuke the priestly offspring and (using a most bold and graphic metaphor) will spread offal on the priests' faces. Just as such refuse would ordi-

---

22. One cannot overlook the close connection between 2:2 and 1:6, however, for both speak of honoring the name of YHWH, the latter passage with reference to the fifth commandment. Thus the מִצְוָה of 2:1 may be explicit to that extent. See George W. Harrison, "Covenant Unfaithfulness in Malachi 2:1-16," *CTR* 2 (1987): 65-66.
23. As Verhoef says, "God's 'command' for the priests is synonymous with his covenant with Levi, his institution of the priestly office"; (*The Books of Haggai and Malachi*, NICOT [Grand Rapids: Eerdmans, 1987], 238). This is why מִצְוָה should be translated in its technical sense and not as "decree," "announcement," and the like.
24. Delbert R. Hillers, *Treaty-Curses and the Old Testament Prophets*, Bib Or 16 (Rome: Pontifical Biblical Institute, 1964).
25. As Chary points out, the use of the verb שָׁלַח in the piel ("I will send") and the irreversible nature of the pronouncement of blessings and curses guarantee the effect. It is as good as done (T. Chary, *Aggée-Zacharie, Malachie*, 249).
26. Herbert C. Brichto, *The Problem of "Curse" in the Hebrew Bible*, JBL Mon. Series 13 (Philadelphia: Society of Biblical Literature, 1963), 133.

narily be carried away for disposal, so the priests will be carried away and, as it were, cast on the rubbish heap (v. 5).

The first of these judgments depends for its meaning on the determination of two disputed words, that translated "offspring" and that rendered "rebuke."[27] In place of "offspring" (זֶרַע, *zera'*, lit. "seed") some ancient versions, including the LXX and Vg, suggest "arm," which reflects the Hebrew זְרוֹעַ (*zĕrôa'*). Admittedly this provides good balance to "face" in the next line, but hardly makes sense with "rebuke." This leads to a further expedient of reading גֹּדֵעַ (*gōdēa'*), "cutting off," for the MT גֹּעֵר (*gō'ēr*), "rebuking." One could then understand the line as follows: "I am about to cut off your arm and will spread offal on your faces." Even if "offspring" be retained, the verb "cut off" would make excellent sense here.

Not a single ancient MSS or version attests *gōdēa'* here, however. This *ipso facto* virtually rules it out of consideration. The LXX has ἀφορίζω (*aphorizō*), "take away," perhaps reflecting a *vorlage* גָּרַע (*gāra'*). This verb, however, is inappropriate for either arm or seed, for the normal idiom is "cut off" in either case. As for "arm," the LXX has τον ὦμον (*ton ōmon*), "shoulder," which, though not a normal translation of *zĕrôa'* ("arm"), may be close enough.

The solution is to let the context determine the matter. The previous verse (v. 2) had said that YHWH would "send the curse" and "curse the blessings." This double threat most likely finds its double fulfillment in v. 3, so that the sending (i.e., uttering) of the curse is tantamount to the word of rebuke and the cursing of the blessings is expressed in the offal upon the faces.

A perusal of the curse sections of biblical covenant texts provides plenty of examples of the curse finding expression in the judgment of the offspring of covenant violators (Deut. 28:18, 32, 41, 53, 55, 57). It is not doing violence to these passages to suggest that the rebuke of offspring is an appropriate way to describe this kind of curse and its effects.[28] They are rebuked even though they may be innocent of collaboration with the infidelity of their parents, a point made in the Decalogue itself (Ex. 20:5).

The "cursing of the blessings" as "covering the face with offal" is not to be found in biblical curse texts because the setting here in Malachi is the cult and ministry in the cult by the priests. The principle of blessing being supplanted by curse is well established in such passages apart from specific references to priests (Deut. 28:12-15, 63). The blessing of the priest was the sheer privilege of handling the holy

---

27. For a good discussion of the text here, see Glazier-McDonald, *Malachi: The Divine Messenger*, 65-68.

28. A. A. Macintosh, "A Consideration of Hebrew גער," *VT* 19 (1969): 476-77.

things as the mediator between God and His people. The curse, then, would be disqualification from these ministries. In the coarsest language possible YHWH, clearly in metaphorical imagery, epitomizes the state of disqualification as the smearing of the priests' faces with offal. The matter described here (פֶּרֶשׁ, *pereš*) is the undigested contents of the stomach and intestines, something so loathsome and impure it must be carried outside the camp to be burned (Ex. 29:14; Lev. 4:11-12; 8:17; Num. 19:5). For this to be spread over the face of the priest rather than to be carried away from the holy precincts and consumed by fire was to constitute the most serious breach of ritual purity imaginable.[29] The blessing of offering sacrifice would thereby be turned into an indescribable curse.

One thinks of Joshua the high priest who, in a night vision of Zechariah, appeared in "filthy" garments, that is, garments covered with excrement (Zech. 3:3-4). Though the word there (צֹאָה, *ṣōʾâ*) is different from the one in Malachi, the imagery is exactly the same. Joshua was ritually defiled and needed to have his garments changed before he could continue his priestly ministry. The priests to whom Malachi is speaking will also need to be purified. Otherwise they, like the refuse, will be taken away and disposed of "outside the camp"(v. 3).

Appealing once more to the "commandment" (v. 4; cf. v. 1), YHWH informs the priests that the curse they can expect for its violation will testify that YHWH Himself has brought about its dire consequences, but that He has done so for a redemptive purpose— that the priestly covenant may continue. That covenant he describes as the covenant with Levi. Though the expression "covenant with Levi" occurs nowhere else in the Bible, Jeremiah refers to a covenant with the Levites (Jer. 33:21-22), and there is a reference in Num. 25:10-13 to a "covenant of peace" and the "covenant of an everlasting priesthood" made with Phinehas, grandson of Aaron and eventual high priest of Israel. Because Aaron and all his descent were offspring of Levi (Ex. 6:16-20), it is not inappropriate that the covenant with Phinehas could also be called the covenant with Levi.[30]

---

29. Verhoef, *The Books of Haggai, Malachi*, 242.
30. Many scholars maintain that because Malachi makes no distinction between priests and Levites, he must be dependent on Deuteronomic rather than Priestly (P) sources, for the latter argue for a superiority of the (Zadokite) priests over the Levites who are "a subordinate order who merely assisted the priests"; so Roddy Braun, "Malachi—A Catechism for Times of Disappointment," *CurTM* 4 (1977): 298. Besides permitting a dating of Malachi between Dtr (c. 550) and P (c. 450), this interpretation of the prophet seems to put him on the side of the "visionary idealists" (to use Hanson's terms) against the "hierocratic realists." The former champion the ancient Aaronic priesthood, whereas the latter endorse the later

In addition, of course, Levi was set apart from the beginning to serve as a priestly tribe. This is clear from the blessing of Moses on the tribe (Deut. 33:8-11) in which Moses refers to Levi's exploits in the wilderness on behalf of YHWH's honor. The first of these followed the apostasy of the golden calf (Ex. 32:25-29). When Moses asked who was any longer on the side of YHWH, the Levites stepped forward, wielded their swords of divine vengeance against their rebel brothers, and proved their fidelity. Another example is that alluded to above when Phinehas the priest slew a man of Israel who was engaged in sexual and spiritual immorality with a woman of Midian at Peor. "He was zealous for His God," says Moses, "and made atonement for the children of Israel" (Num. 25:13).

It seems evident that Mal. 2:4-6 is referring to these incidents, especially the latter, when it speaks of the covenant with Levi. That it includes the priests and is not, therefore, limited to the Levites as a sub-priestly class, is clear from vv. 7-8 where the priests are explicitly included within that covenant. In order, therefore, to understand the full thrust of the message here in Malachi, it is necessary to look at least briefly at the account in Numbers.

When Phinehas became aware of the pagan festivities into which some of the people had entered, he intervened in the manner described with the result that the plague that YHWH had already launched against the people was suspended (Num. 25:9). For this bold initiative, YHWH commended the priest, attributing to him the interdiction of divine wrath and, consequently, the salvation of the nation. For this, YHWH said, he would make with Phinehas a "covenant of peace" (v. 12; cf. Isa. 54:10; Ezek. 34:25; 37:2*b*), that is, "the covenant of an everlasting priesthood" (v. 13).

It is the word "peace" (שָׁלוֹם, *šālôm*) that links the narrative in Numbers directly with our Malachi text (Mal. 2:5). Phinehas, representative of all the Levites, became the recipient of YHWH's life and peace because of his zeal for YHWH's name. But there was the expectation of reciprocation, not only on the part of Phinehas but by his priestly descendants after him. That would take form in the fear and awe of the priests who stood before YHWH in service. This is precisely what the priests whom Malachi addressed were lacking (cf. 1:6;

(originally non-Levitical) Zadokite priesthood. This is very wide of the mark, however, for as Hanson admits, the biblical traditions themselves link Zadok with Phinehas and, hence, with Aaron (*The Dawn of Apocalyptic* [Philadelphia: Fortress, 1976], 220-28). Malachi is not taking sides in some hypothetical struggle among priestly contenders but is roundly condemning both priests and Levites for their perfidy. For a good review of the issue, see Glazier-McDonald, *Malachi: The Divine Messenger*, 73-80.

2:2), and its absence explained the curse that had already begun to fall upon them.

Evidence of Phinehas's loyal compliance to the covenant was the fact that "true teaching was in his mouth, unrighteousness was not to be found on his lips," and "he walked with [YHWH] in wholeness and uprightness and turned many from iniquity" (v. 7). Though little is known of Phinehas after the Baal of Peor incident (cf. Num. 31:6; Josh. 22:13-34), he is celebrated in the epic poetry of Israel as the one who "stood up and executed judgment; and so the plague was stayed. And that was reckoned to him for righteousness, to all generations forever" (Ps. 106:30-31).

Phinehas thus provided a paradigm of priestly character and behavior. He demonstrated in his own life a model of what it meant to be a faithful man of God. From such a sterling example a standard for all priests has been set and, in almost proverbial language, YHWH outlines His expectation for all those successors of Levi and Phinehas who serve Him with such exalted privilege. They should guard knowledge and impart the instruction of YHWH, for the priest is nothing less than the very messenger (מַלְאָךְ, *mal'āk*; cf. the name of Malachi) of YHWH (v. 7).[31] This is the ideal, indeed, the expectation that accompanies the covenant with Levi. Unfortunately Malachi's own priestly contemporaries had fallen very much short of the ideal and therefore were subject to the curse that inevitably follows any kind of covenant disloyalty.

Additional Notes

2:3 The MT reads lit. "he will carry you unto it," referring no doubt to the pile of refuse outside the camp that would be destroyed by fire. The LXX and Syr. appear to favor a reading "I will carry you away from beside me." This may clarify the elliptical MT but at the expense of robbing it of the strong impact that is clearly intended.

2. THE COVENANT VIOLATION OF THE PRIESTS (2:8-9)

Translation

8"You, however, have turned from the way. You have caused many to stumble in the law; you have corrupted the covenant with Levi,"
says YHWH of hosts. 9"Therefore, I have made you despised and abased before all people to the degree that you are not keeping My ways and are showing partiality in (your) instruction."

---

31. Baldwin points out that this is the first reference to a priest as a messenger of God. Perhaps the epithet derives from a play on the prophet's own name because of his preoccupation with the messenger concept (cf. 3:1) (*Haggai, Zechariah, Malachi*, 236).

Exegesis and Exposition

Having outlined the characteristics of righteous and faithful priests by recounting the exploits of the Levites and Phinehas, YHWH contrasts them with the present generation of priests. They have turned aside from the way, that is, the path to which the priest must adhere by virtue of his holy vocation. Moreover, far from imparting true instruction (cf. v. 6), indeed, from serving as a resource to whom men could appeal for such instruction (v. 7), these priests, by their teachings, erected roadblocks in the way of those seeking truth.

The definite article on תּוֹרָה (*tôrâ*), "instruction," suggests that here it is not just any teaching in general but indeed *the* instruction, namely, the Torah, the law of Moses. The defection of the priests is all the more serious, then, for they are actually creating obstacles to the people's access to the Word of God itself. To cause the people to "stumble in the Torah" is to so mislead them in its meaning that they fail to understand and keep its requirements. There can be no more serious indictment against the man of God. By this act of dereliction (and, no doubt, others unnamed) the priests have corrupted the Levitical covenant. This being the case, they must be prepared to accept the consequences, the imposition of the sanctions of the covenant. This, in fact, had already begun to transpire as vv. 2-3 make clear. But even these attitudes and acts of impiety and gross miscarriage of priestly responsibility had not annulled the priestly covenant itself. Guilty individuals in the office of priest might drift so far as to be disqualified and even put to death (Lev. 10:1-3), but the institution of priesthood itself would stand, because God had established it as an everlasting ministry. This has already been seen in the promise to Phinehas (Num. 25:13), and Jeremiah affirms the same when he says, "David will never lack for a man to sit upon the throne of the house of Israel, nor shall the priests the Levites lack for a man before Me to offer burnt-offerings, to burn grain-offerings, and to make sacrifice continually" (Jer. 33:17-18).[32]

Ezekiel, who preceded Malachi by a century or more, confronted a disobedient priesthood in his own day, and though he intimates that such evil ministers may expect divine discipline (Ezek. 44:10), they nevertheless will continue to have a role in the Temple cultus of the millennial kingdom (v. 11). In language that may have inspired Malachi, Ezekiel says that these priests "became a stumbling-block of iniquity" and so must bear their iniquity, that is, its penalty (v. 12).

---

32. As Verhoef puts it, "In its essence and according to its intent, the covenant relationship is unbreakable. But when one party does not live up to his obligations, the other party may take disciplinary steps" (*The Books of Haggai and Malachi*, 253).

Furthermore, they would play a subservient role to the Zadokite priests who had proved through the years their steadfastness and godliness (vv. 13-15).[33] The point to be stressed here, however, is that the Levitical covenant still stood, for it is one that God Himself inaugurated and to which He committed Himself.

To support the word of Ezekiel about the coming judgment of the faithless priests, Malachi says that already YHWH has made them to be despised and abased before the people. In a measure-to-measure application of justice he says that the priests have suffered these humiliations in proportion to the extent to which they strayed from the pathway and according to how much they created impediments to the people who sought instruction at their mouths (v. 9). The office of priest or Levite was a high and holy calling, one that should have instilled a feeling of awe and respect on the part of the people who enjoyed its intercessory benefits. For the holders of those offices, then, to disgrace themselves to the degree that they were depreciated in the eyes of the community was scandalous, for with the disgrace of the man there was an inevitable disdain for the office as well. There is little wonder that Malachi was sent to the priests with such a harsh word of condemnation.

---

33. Again, there is no real evidence for the view that Ezekiel was promoting a Zadokite priesthood as opposed to the Levites. He is simply judging between righteous and unrighteous ministers no matter their linkage to Levi and Aaron. The fact that Ezekiel calls the Zadokites "the priests the Levites" (44:15) makes this clear. De Vaux is no doubt correct when he takes the Levites of Ezek. 44:10 to be those of local shrines who had collaborated in syncretistic worship, whereas those of 44:15 were the clergy of Jerusalem who had by and large remained faithful to YHWH. He also notes that both groups of Levites are called priests in Ezek. 40:45-46; so the priest-Levite dichotomy simply does not exist in Ezekiel in the antithetical manner advocated by many scholars. See R. de Vaux, *Ancient Israel*, 364-65; so also Nigel Allan, "The Identity of the Jerusalem Priesthood During the Exile," *HeyJ* 23 (1982): 260-61.

3

The Rebellion of the People (2:10-16)

Having dealt with the issue of a corrupt priesthood, Malachi turns next to the general population. Even though their spiritual leaders may have failed them, the people must shoulder the responsibility for their own sinfulness as a nation and as individuals.

A. THE DISRUPTION OF THE COVENANT (2:10-13)

Translation

¹⁰Do we not all have one father? Did not one God create us? Why do we act treacherously to one another, thus profaning the covenant of our fathers? ¹¹Judah has acted treacherously, and abomination has been committed in Israel and Jerusalem. For Judah has profaned the holy (thing) of YHWH that He loves and has married the daughter of a foreign god. ¹²May YHWH cut off to the (last) man anyone who does this, him who is *awake and him who answers, from the tents of Jacob, as well as him who presents an offering to YHWH of hosts. ¹³For this again you do: You cover the altar of YHWH with tears, with weeping and groaning, because He no longer pays heed to the offering nor accepts it favorably from your hands.

Exegesis and Exposition

In strong covenant terms, Malachi urges the people to recognize their oneness, their solidarity as a chosen nation. This is evident, first of all, in the fact that they all have a common father, God Himself (v. 10).[1] Though "father" (אָב, *'āb*) is not inherently a covenant term, it is so used here, as the reference to covenant at the end of v. 10 makes clear. This precludes any possibility that the prophet is advocating the modern notion of the universal fatherhood of God. The idea of covenant fatherhood first originates in the Exodus narrative where YHWH commands Moses to return to Pharaoh with the message, "Israel is My son, My first born . . . let My son go that he may serve Me" (Ex. 4:22-23). Isaiah explicitly refers to YHWH as the father of Israel: "You, O YHWH, are our father, our redeemer from of old is Your name" (Isa. 63:16). Here there is an obvious connection between YHWH as Father and His redemption of Israel.

Malachi goes on, however, to describe YHWH as the Creator of His people in common. Again Isaiah provides the same image and, in fact, juxtaposes the notions of father and Creator exactly as does Malachi.[2] "O YHWH," he says, "You are our father; we are the clay, and You our potter. We all are the work of Your hand" (Isa. 64:8). Both prophets agree, then, that the people of YHWH are His uniquely in that He both created and redeemed them, making them His chosen son. Jeremiah adds his word, for the prophet records YHWH's asseveration, "I am a father to Israel, and Ephraim is My firstborn" (Jer. 31:9). It is well known, of course, that the Jeremiah passage is embedded in an undisputed covenant context.

Against that background Malachi's denunciatory query takes on heightened poignancy. If the people of Judah were one, elected and redeemed by one God who deigned to be their common Father, how could they abuse one another as they did? Such abuse, he says, constituted a most serious breach of the "covenant of the fathers," an

---

1. Thus Pieter A. Verhoef, *The Books of Haggai and Malachi*, NICOT (Grand Rapids: Eerdmans, 1987), 265-66, contra Baldwin who, with many others, understands the father to be Abraham; Joyce G. Baldwin, *Haggai, Zechariah, Malachi*, TOTC (London: Tyndale, 1972), 237. This is ruled out by the parallel, "Did not one God create us?" Cf. George W. Harrison, "Covenant Unfaithfulness in Malachi 2:1-16," *CTR* 2 (1987): 69. Ogden takes the father to be Levi and the covenant violation of vv. 10-16 to be the rupture of the covenant of Levi of the previous passage. To support this he must take the divorce motif figuratively and must interpret Judah as the priests of Judah, the "wife of your youth" as Israel in her early days, and "godly offspring" (v. 15) as the Levitical descent ("The Use of Figurative Language in Malachi 2:10-16," *BT* 39 [1988]: 223-30). Although there is indeed a great deal of figurative language, especially *double entendre*, throughout, the fact that the passage on the whole reflects a broader perspective than the cultic alone and that Ezra and Nehemiah had to deal with the issue of literal divorce just a few years after Malachi leads one to conclude that literal divorce is in view here.
2. Theodore Laetsch, *Minor Prophets* (St. Louis: Concordia, 1956), 524-25.

obvious reference in context to the Sinaitic covenant.³ One should recall that the quintessence of that covenant was to love YHWH with all the heart, soul, and mind (Deut. 6:4-5) and to love one's fellow as himself (Lev. 19:18; cf. Luke 10:27). The covenant could become profaned as much by violating the second part as by violating the first.

The prophet is not dealing in generalities here, as the continuation of his accusation shows. Judah—and, indeed, Israel and Jerusalem as well—has dealt treacherously as a sacred community by undertaking action whose net result would lead to the disintegration of the people as an elect nation more quickly and surely than anything else she could do, namely, by intermarriage with the pagans.⁴

The reference to Israel and Jerusalem as well as Judah is to underscore the pervasiveness of this abhorrent practice.⁵ Zechariah used the same formula to describe the completeness of the persecution and scattering of the chosen nation by the four horns in his second vision (Zech. 1:19). As a cliché, then, the statement has nothing to say one way or the other about the historical existence of Israel in Malachi's own day. The point is that the whole nation has been treacherous in marrying outside the strict parameters of the covenant stipulations.

The Torah texts are replete with prohibitions against this practice (Ex. 34:15-16; Deut. 7:3; cf. Josh. 23:12), and these same passages point out the dire consequences that follow such compromise. Nevertheless, intermarriage with pagans was persistently undertaken even at the highest levels of Israelite society, as the sordid record of Solomon in this respect attests (1 Kings 11:1-8). The reason for enjoining against it was not any sense of ethnic or racial superiority but because by elective design YHWH had chosen one man, Abraham, through whom He would mediate His saving work to the world. The channel thus must be limited to the offspring of Abraham, a limitation that was synonymous with Israel. The issue, then, was theological and not biological, for whenever illicit marriage was condoned

---

3. McKenzie and Wallace lean to the view that this is the patriarchal covenant but concede that the reference is ambiguous ("Covenant Themes in Malachi," *CBQ* 45 [1983]: 552).
4. See Stefan Schreiner, "Mischehen-Ehebruch-Ehescheidung. Betrachtungen zu Mal 2:10-16," *ZAW* 91 (1979): 207-28; Clemens Locher, "Altes und Neues zu Maleachi 2:10-16," in *Melanges Dominique Barthelemy*, ed. P. Casetti et al. (Göttingen: Vandenhoeck & Ruprecht, 1981), 241-71.
5. Keil correctly points out that Jerusalem is singled out because it was the capital of the whole nation. Syntactically one could make a case for the inclusion of Jerusalem as an epexegetical element, that is, "abomination has been committed in Israel, specifically in Jerusalem (the cultic center)" (*Biblical Commentary on the Old Testament. The Twelve Minor Prophets* [Edinburgh: T. & T. Clark, 1871], 2:449).

there was an accompanying moral and spiritual defection, a predictable drift toward idolatry. A glance at the passages cited above will make crystal clear this connection between physical, illicit intermarriage and spiritual declension.

As we pointed out in the Introduction, Malachi was not alone among postexilic spokesmen in dealing with this problem. It was the single biggest social and religious concern of the great priestly scribe Ezra. He no sooner arrived in Jerusalem in 458 B.C., possibly a decade or so after Malachi's provenence, than he was met by a delegation of leaders who complained that the people, including the priests and Levites, had not separated themselves from surrounding neighbors but had, to the contrary, entered into marriage with them. As they put it, "The holy seed have mingled themselves with the peoples of the lands" (Ezra 9:2). Ezra was so distraught with this information that he fell upon his face in a prayer of confession and asked whether the nation was about to repeat the sins of their preexilic fathers by joining in affinity with "the people that do these abominations" (9:14).[6]

His intercession provoked a spirit of repentance among the guilty. They put themselves at Ezra's disposal to do what he thought best (10:1-4). His counsel, after much deliberation and soul-searching, was that they must divorce these foreigners whom they had married (10:11-12), something they complied with at once (v. 17). There is no clear biblical precedent for Ezra's edict, so one must assume either that he used his own best judgment, perhaps even wrongly, or that he ruled as a "second Moses," one who enjoyed divine revelation and sanction for his policy.[7]

Before this is pursued, it is necessary to see how the same problem was handled by Nehemiah. He arrived in Judah thirteen years after Ezra to find that whatever reforms Ezra had achieved had failed to find solid anchorage, for intermarriage once more became a leading issue, especially in the latter part of his governorship. At the conclusion of his prayer of covenant renewal, Nehemiah and the people resolved to adhere faithfully to YHWH's covenant expectations, including the injunction against mixed marriage (Neh. 10:30). This took place early in his tenure (2:1; cf. 6:15; 9:1), and the pledge to

---

6. One should note that Malachi, like Ezra, describes such intermarriage as an "abomination" (תּוֹעֵבָה).

7. Williamson says regarding Ezra's approach: "He taught, and the community accepted, an interpretation of the law according to its 'spirit,' as he understood it. We may not agree with certain aspects of Ezra's interpretation, but his motivation and method here remain ones we would still acknowledge as valid today"; (*Ezra, Nehemiah*, WBC [Waco, Tex.: Word, 1985], 16:160).

refrain from such marriage seems to suggest that it had not been resumed since the Ezra reforms. The occasion for its resumption may have been Nehemiah's return to Susa in 432, for when he came back from there later on, he found a wholesale abandonment of the covenant pledge and the renewal of mixed marriages (Neh. 13:23-24).

The remedy this time was not as severe as that of Ezra. Nehemiah did not command divorce but issued a stern warning about what would happen were the practice to continue (v. 13). It was this very sin, he reminded them, that brought about Solomon's downfall (v. 14). Whether Nehemiah refrained from following Ezra's policy because he considered it nonauthoritative or unworkable or neither cannot be known. It may be that he was more persuaded by the message of Malachi than the practice of Ezra, a message that appears to forbid divorce at all (Mal. 2:16). This will be considered presently.

It is necessary first to return to Malachi 2:11 where the prophet makes clear that the abomination he has in mind is that of mixed marriage. His use of the word "abomination" (תּוֹעֵבָה, tôʿēbâ) is deliberate, for this frequently is the term used to describe such covenant breach (1 Kings 11:5, 7), especially by Ezra (9:1, 11, 14). The marriage itself, Malachi says, is to the "daughter of a foreign god." This metonymy does not imply something like sacred prostitution but only that Jewish men were marrying women who themselves worshiped pagan deities. In putting it this way, however, the prophet graphically and cleverly unites these prohibited marriages with one of the principal reasons for their impropriety, namely, that they tend to idolatry.[8] Marriage to a pagan spouse is tantamount to the embracing of a pagan god.

In v. 11 the difficult phrase, literally to be rendered "for Judah (has) profaned the holiness of YHWH which He loved," must be considered. The word "holiness" (קֹדֶשׁ, qōdeš) is an abstract masculine noun with the base meaning "apartness" or the like. Here it functions as an adjective and clearly refers to someone or something that is holy to YHWH, an object of His love. That it is YHWH who is the subject of "loved" is apparent from the proximity of the divine name to the relative clause containing the verb.

As for the thing loved, its identity must be determined by its relationship to the rest of the line in which it is mentioned.[9] Though

---

8. Baldwin's comment is cogent: "Since a married couple must come to a common understanding in order to live happily together, one or other partner had to compromise on the matter of religion" (*Haggai, Zechariah, Malachi*, 238).

9. The prevailing views are that the "holy thing" is (1) the sanctuary, that is, the Temple, or (2) the people of YHWH. See respectively, Theophane Chary,

the language is not poetic, v. 11 can be viewed as containing essentially synonymous ideas in a more or less parallel arrangement:

> Judah has profaned the holy thing of YHWH that He loves,
> and has married the daughter of a foreign god.

Here Judah is viewed as the collective of individuals who are guilty of the profanation. Whatever they have done must be set opposite the second line, that is, the marriage to a devotee of a pagan god. Since such marriage is a violation of the Mosaic covenant, it follows that the holy thing that has been profaned is the covenant itself or at least that statute which forbids such illicit relationships. Confirmation of this interpretation may be found in a close look now at all of v. 11, which consists of four ideas in what might be called "alternating parallelism," viz:

A Judah has acted treacherously
  B Abomination has been committed in Israel
A′ Judah has profaned the holy thing of YHWH
  B′ (Judah) has married the daughter of a foreign god.

Verse 10 has already shown conclusively that to act treacherously (נִבְגַד, *nibgad*)[10] is to profane (חַלֵּל, *ḥallēl*) the covenant. Now v. 11 says that Judah has acted treacherously (בָּגְדָה, *bāgĕdâ*) and has profaned (חִלֵּל, *hillēl*) the holy thing of YHWH. It is reasonable to conclude that to act treacherously here means to profane or "secularize" the covenant so that it is eviscerated of its authority.

Having contemplated the sins of his people, especially their blatant disregard of the covenant prohibitions against mixed marriage, Malachi utters an imprecative urging YHWH to cut off from the covenant community any who are guilty of the charges he has leveled. Excommunication from covenant faith and fellowship is clearly in mind as the expression "from the tents of Jacob" implies (v. 12). This harks back to Israel's nomadic days in the wilderness, for it was then and there that such a penalty was first promulgated and invoked (cf. Ex. 12:15, 19; 31:14; Lev. 7:20, 21, 25, 27; 19:8; 20:18; 22:3; Num. 9:13; 15:31; 19:13, 20; etc.).

The cryptic phrase "him who is awake and him who answers" is

Aggée-Zacharie, Malachie (Paris: Librairie Lecoffre, 1969), 257; Laetsch, *Minor Prophets*, 525.
10. This verb, not common to begin with (43 times), occurs five times in Malachi, all in this passage (2:10, 11, 14, 15, 16). It means "to act treacherously" (BDB, 93), in the Malachi context to undertake divorce of one's wife in order to marry the "daughter of a foreign god" (v. 11). Thus, to act treacherously is tantamount to violating the marriage covenant and, by extension, the covenant between YHWH and Israel. See S. Erlandsson, *TDOT*, 1:470-73, s.v. בגד.

patently an idiom, but one whose original meaning is uncertain. It appears to be a merism expressing totality. That is, every last man will be cut off, from him who is already awake to him who responds to the wakeup call. It may mean something like the awake and the asleep, who together make up all of mankind (cf. a similar kind of figure, "the quick and the dead").[11] The totality in mind includes even those who present offerings to YHWH (v. 12*b*), but they are specifically defined as hypocritical worshipers in v. 13. That is, even though covenant breakers make their pious pilgrimages to the sacrificial altar, they will be cut off, for their very behavior betrays the insincerity of their religious exercises.

The prophet describes this show of devotion in the cynical and grandiose terms of covering the altar with tears and of loud weeping and groaning. Coming in vain to present their offerings, these infidels, in their frustration at having their shallow pretenses exposed, exhibit the strongest emotion. They fail to see that YHWH's displeasure and lack of positive response are not because offerings are not being made but because they are offered by people who have broken covenant with Him and who refuse to do anything about it. Just as YHWH had not "received with favor" (לֹא אֶרְצֶה, *lō' 'erṣê*) the offerings of the priests (1:10), so now He will not "receive with favor" (לָקַחַת רָצוֹן, *lāqaḥat rāṣôn*) the offerings of the people.

Additional Notes

2:12 For עֵר, "awake," the LXX reads ἕως (= עַד), "unto," "until." The resulting idea is "until he is humbled," taking עָנָה as "to be humble" rather than "to answer." The Syr. and Tg. Neb. take the phrase as "his son and his son's son" whereas Vg. understands it as referring to teacher and pupil. BHS proposes עֵד, "witness," to be rendered here perhaps as "he who witnesses and he who answers," a reading that, as Richard D. Patterson (by private communication) notes, ties in with הֵעִיד in v. 14. The MT, by its very difficulty, appears to be correct and to suggest a merism of totality.

B. THE ILLUSTRATION OF THE COVENANT (2:14-16)

Translation

¹⁴Yet you ask, "Why?" Because YHWH has been a witness between you and the wife of your youth against whom you have acted

---

11. Keil, *The Twelve Minor Prophets*, 2:449-50; John M. P. Smith, *A Critical and Exegetical Commentary on Malachi*, ICC (Edinburgh: T. & T. Clark, 1912), 58. For a host of other suggestions, see Beth Glazier-McDonald, *Malachi: The Divine Messenger*, SBL Series 98 (Atlanta: Scholars Press, 1987), 94-99.

treacherously, though she is your companion and wife by covenant. ¹⁵No one does (this) who has (even) a remnant of the Spirit in him. What (did) that one (do) when seeking offspring of God? Be attentive then to your (own) spirit, for one should not be *treacherous to the wife of your youth. ¹⁶*"I hate divorce," says YHWH, God of Israel, "and him who covers his garment with violence," says YHWH of hosts. "Take heed therefore to your spirit, and do not be treacherous."

Exegesis and Exposition

The reason for YHWH's rejection of the offerings mentioned in v. 13 is the reverse side of the coin introduced in vv. 10-11—the divorce of their wives by the men of Judah. We call this the reverse side of the coin, for the obverse was their marriage to the daughters of foreign gods. The impression one gets is that many had divorced their Jewish wives precisely in order to marry pagans. This, Malachi says, is to act treacherously (v. 14). The same verb (בָּגַד, *bāgad*) has been used several times now by the prophet, and a careful analysis of its use clarifies the whole issue that concerned the prophet here. In v. 10, as already noted, treachery was synonymous with breaking the covenant, in this case the stipulations of the Mosaic covenant prohibiting intermarriage with the heathen nations. Verse 11 cements this connection by associating treachery with the profanation of the holy (covenant) that YHWH loves. Treachery in v. 14, therefore, must also relate to covenant violation, and indeed it does, as v. 16 puts beyond doubt. This time, however, the covenant is not that of Moses but the marriage covenant that bound husband and wife together.

Such a covenant, though not attested formally in the OT,¹² is a legally binding arrangement as YHWH's role as witness intimates. For the Jew to desert his wife and to marry another, particularly a foreigner, is not only morally odious but legally prohibited. It is because YHWH witnessed the pledges of mutual loyalty between husband and wife that He is able now to speak of its violation and to explain it as the cause for His rejection of hypocritical gestures of worship. The wife of one's youth, the prophet goes on to say, is not someone lightly to be put aside but is indeed a "companion," a "con-

---

12. See, however, Job 7:13; Prov. 2:17; Ezek. 16:8. De Vaux draws attention to the marriage contracts of the Jewish community of Elephantine in the fifth century B.C. (*Ancient Israel, Its Life and Institutions* [London: Darton, Longman & Todd, 1961], 33). It is not unreasonable that such contracts (or "covenants") were already in vogue in Palestine as early as Malachi's time. In fact, the existence of divorce documents (Deut. 24:1-3; Jer. 3:8) almost certainly demands marriage documents.

sort" (חֲבֶרְת, *ḥăberet*) inextricably linked to her husband by a covenant pledge.[13]

The monstrous evil of such a course of action is illustrated in v. 15, a difficult passage. The first clause (lit., "and not one has done, and a remnant of the Spirit to him") appears to introduce a proverbial truth to the effect that the behavior of these wicked men who reject their wives of a lifetime would never be true of one who has even a little part of God's Spirit within him.[14] Pre-Christian theology may not allow this to refer to a personal Holy Spirit in a full Trinitarian sense, but this is not necessary anyway. All that is being affirmed is that a godly man would never do what these men have done.

As an example the prophet turns obliquely to Abraham, for "the one" who was "seeking offspring of God" quite clearly refers to the patriarch.[15] What he did in his original efforts to secure offspring is not at all commendable, as the Genesis narrative reveals. Rather than wait for the promise of YHWH to come to pass in a monogamous relationship with Sarah, Abraham instead took Hagar as surrogate and by her bore Ishmael (Gen. 16:1-6). The result, of course, was disastrous.

Though the analogy is not perfect, inasmuch as Abraham did not, in fact, divorce Sarah and the matter of idolatry was not at issue, it is close enough for Malachi to make the point that such an approach by even a godly patriarch was an act of covenant unfaithfulness. Sarah deserved better even though she was party to the illicit arrangement and, in fact, first entertained the idea. And Abraham's treachery *vis à*

---

13. The parallelism between הֲבֶרְתֶּךָ ("your companion") and אֵשֶׁת בְּרִיתֶךָ ("the wife of your covenant") makes it clear that this is no ordinary companion but one inextricably bound by formal covenant, a fact supported by the cognate verb חָבַר (*ḥābar*), "to unite, be joined" (BDB, 287). As for "wife of your youth," Morgenstern plausibly argues that this refers to the first and only wife ("Jerusalem—485 B.C.," *HUCA* 28 [1957]: 33-34).
14. Other interpretations are: (1) those with spiritual insight will not violate marriage because they seek to procreate citizens for the kingdom of God (Verhoef, *The Books of Haggai and Malachi*, 277); (2) God made a single being with both flesh (revocalizing שְׁאָר, "remnant," to שְׁאֵר, "flesh") and spirit for the purpose of giving them godly offspring (Baldwin, *Haggai, Zechariah and Malachi*, 240); (3) the subject is God and "the one" is the object and equal to the "one flesh" of Gen. 2:24, a view that attributes the Spirit to God as His creative power (Walter C. Kaiser, Jr., *Malachi. God's Unchanging Love* [Grand Rapids: Baker, 1984], 71-72).
15. This is the view of most Jewish and earlier Christian scholars. See Keil, *The Twelve Minor Prophets*, 2:452-55; C. Von Orelli, *The Twelve Minor Prophets* (Edinburgh: T. & T. Clark, 1893), 395-96; F. Hitzig, *Die Zwölf kleinen Propheten* (Leipzig: S. Hirzel, 1881), 424. For other passages where Abraham is called "the one," see Isa. 51:2; Ezek. 33:24.

vis Sarah did not end there, for on two other occasions he had at least
partially lied about her, alleging her to be his sister rather than his
wife (Gen. 12:11-20; 20:2-18).

No wonder Malachi sees in Abraham a fit model of the principle
he is trying to establish. Do not emulate the great ancestor, he says,
but instead "be attentive to your own spirit" lest you commit a similar sin against your wife. Then, in the event there be any lingering
doubt as to the sin in question, YHWH Himself speaks forth: "I hate
divorce" (v. 16). And with the divorce He hates the one who covers his
garments with the violence that attends the breakup of the marriage.
The seriousness with which YHWH views the matter is reinforced by
a repetition of the exhortation already given in v. 15*b*: "take heed
therefore to your spirit and do not be treacherous" (v. 16*b*).[16]

Two aspects of v. 16 must be addressed separately, that of the
prohibition of divorce in light of the policies of Ezra and Nehemiah,
and the enigmatic reference to covering the garment with violence.
As noted earlier Ezra, when confronted with the issue of mixed marriages, unequivocally called upon his fellow Jews who had entered
such relationships to sever them at once. This they did without recorded protest (Ezra 9-10). Nehemiah, dealing with a recurrence of
the problem, advised only that such practice be avoided in the future.
There is no hint that he commended divorce at all.

These varying attitudes toward divorce (Malachi anti; Ezra pro;
Nehemiah non-committal?) have figured in the whole problem of the
chronological order of the figures who espoused these various viewpoints. It is impossible here to reopen that entire conundrum, especially as regards the Ezra-Nehemiah priority, but a few comments at
least may be helpful. First, it is frequently asserted that because Ezra
was a figure of such towering prominence and influence, a reputation
sustained by both Scripture and tradition, his rulings must be seen as
authoritative for the community. If this is the case, the only way to
account for the positions taken by both Malachi and Nehemiah is to
postulate that Ezra was last in succession. Having seen the failure of
the accommodating policies of Malachi and Nehemiah, he adopted a
hardline approach that would forever end the problem by divorce.[17]

Malachi's attitude seems most adamant of all against divorce, even
compared to Nehemiah, so Malachi, it appears, preceded Nehemiah.
The prophet had stated flatly that YHWH hates divorce. Encouraged

16. The phrase "take heed to your spirit" is common in covenant contexts (Ex.
23:13, 21; 34:12; Deut. 4:15, 23; 6:12; 8:11; 11:16; 12:13; 15:9; etc.). Its use
with בְּנַ in v. 16 clearly puts the passage in the realm of covenant violation. See McKenzie and Wallace, "Covenant Themes in Malachi," 552.
17. Jacob M. Myers, *Ezra-Nehemiah*, AB 14 (Garden City, N.Y.: Doubleday,
1965), xlv, 85.

by this and perverting it to their own benefit, those who had undertaken mixed marriages would have an excuse not to break them off, for if YHWH hates divorce, there is little they can do to disentangle themselves from their admittedly illicit relationships. Nehemiah, seeing this cynical reaction to the prophet, dared not countermand his oracular word, but he would at least command that the people cease and desist from such behavior in the future. Ezra, by virtue of his priestly authority and prestige, could, especially after enough time had elapsed, issue a mandate that divorce was not only possible under such circumstances but must be actively prosecuted, Malachi's word to the contrary notwithstanding.[18]

This scenario makes good sense provided one is willing to make a concession or two, primarily in the area of Malachi's prophetic authority and the possibility of its contravention by the priestly authority of Ezra.[19] But this is an enormous concession, for it pits two men of God in direct conflict and supposes that the one can overturn the teaching of the other without jeopardizing the credibility of either or, worse still, of YHWH who presumably inspired each to his own course of action. Such a possibility exists, of course, if one can tolerate an evolutionary understanding of the history of Israel's religion. But the scholar who is persuaded that both Malachi and Ezra reflect the mind and will of God cannot dispose of the problem that easily.

The answer appears not to lie in the direction of rearranging the order of the canonical witnesses. The tradition of the Ezra-Nehemiah sequence is too well established to be easily overthrown and the priority of Malachi to both is, as has been argued (pp. 377-78), most defensible. Thus Malachi abjures divorce, Ezra is its champion, and Nehemiah neither advocates it nor speaks out against it. What is to be made of this?

What critical scholars especially appear to have overlooked is that Malachi and Ezra are addressing two totally different kinds of marriage and divorce. Malachi, in the course of chastising his brethren for the mixed marriages, implies that these marriages have come about at the cost of divorcing their own Jewish wives. It is this divorce that prompts YHWH to say, "I hate divorce." One cannot de-

---

18. Cf. Glazier-McDonald, *Malachi: The Divine Messenger*, 15-16; Myers, *Ezra-Nehemiah*, 217-18; H. H. Rowley, "The Chronological Order of Ezra and Nehemiah," in *The Servant of the Lord and Other Essays on the Old Testament* (London: Lutterworth, 1952), 155-54. The reconstruction I have developed is not that of any of these scholars alone but derives from a consensus held by them and others to a greater or lesser extent.
19. Thus Joel F. Drinkard, Jr., says, "After Ezra's legislation was enacted, it would have been very difficult for Malachi's position to be held" ("The Socio-Historical Setting of Malachi," *RevExp* 84 [1987]: 388).

duce from this statement that a universal principle is being articulated. To the contrary, the word of YHWH here is limited to the horrible travesty of covenant-breaking expressed by the breakup of Jewish marriages. YHWH has no word here beyond that. Ezra, on the other hand, speaks not specifically to the problem of Jewish divorce that made illicit intermarriage possible, but to that mixed marriage itself. His thrust is exclusively that those who have entered *those kinds of marriages* must terminate them. There is thus no real contradiction at all. YHWH hates divorce between His covenant people but, in Ezra's situation at least, demands it when it involves a bonding between His people and the pagan world.[20]

One cannot extrapolate from Ezra's edict a principle for Christian or even general behavior regarding marriage and divorce.[21] The OT offers no legislation about the matter where believer and unbeliever are linked in marriage, and the NT, if anything, commends the notion that though such marriages are not to be undertaken in the first place (2 Cor. 6:14-18), once effected they should not be ended by divorce (1 Cor. 7:12-17). "From the beginning," Jesus said, "[divorce] was not so" (Matt. 19:3-9). Ezra's action was to meet a peculiar exigency in a crucial era in the life of the postexilic community. To argue normative policy from it is to go far beyond the evidence of a comprehensive biblical theology.

As for "him who covers his garment with violence" (v. 16a), its connection to the condemnation of divorce locates its meaning within that framework. The language is clearly figurative, probably a metonymy of effect for cause, built in turn on a metaphor. The metaphor "garment" pertains to the outside appearance, for, to quote the modern aphorism, "the clothes make the man." It is true that externals often betray internals either by giving unwarranted credibility to situations that do not deserve it or, conversely, by exposing innate corruption for what it is. The divorce of God's people is tantamount to their wearing garments that expose their perfidy for all to see.

The metonymy speaks of the condition brought about by the violence of divorce. They do not wear garments covered by violence but, as it were, violence has clothed them with garments that advertise to

---

20. Williamson says, "It is thus evident that in the circumstances [of Ezra] the divorce of foreign wives was considered the lesser of the two evils" *(Ezra Nehemiah*, 160-61). It is difficult to believe, however, that Ezra was advocating an evil of any degree. Dumbrell correctly notes that Malachi is condemning the divorce of Jewish wives that was required in order to undertake pagan marriages ("Malachi and the Ezra-Nehemiah Reforms," *RTR* 35 [1976]: 48).
21. William A. Heth and Gordon J. Wenham, *Jesus and Divorce. The Problem with the Evangelical Consensus* (Nashville: Thomas Nelson, 1984), 162-64.

society that they have broken covenant with the wives of their youth. Divorce is always violent and always leaves its emotional and spiritual scars.[22] The existence of divorce and the presence of those responsible for it are both abhorrent in the eyes of YHWH—thus He says in His own words.

Additional Notes

2:15 For the MT יִבְגֹּד, "one should (not) be treacherous," most ancient versions read תִּבְגֹּד, "you should (not) be treacherous." This seems to be a reasonable effort at grammatical harmony but an unnecessary resort given the penchant of Hebrew not to insist on such leveling, especially where suffixes are concerned.

2:16 One might expect, with the majority of scholars, to find שָׂנֵאתִי, "I hate," for the MT "he hates," and thus my translation renders it. However, again one must allow for fluidity in such grammatical forms, especially in the absence of MSS and versions to the contrary. Moreover, the phrase in question could be taken as an indirect, and not direct, quotation. Malachi would then be the speaker: "YHWH the God of Israel says that He hates divorce," etc. See David Clyde Jones, "A Note on the LXX of Malachi 2:16," *JBL* 109 (1990): 683-85.

---

22. Cf. Pss. 73:6; 109:18; Lam. 4:14; T. Chary, *Aggée-Zacharie, Malachie*, 262-63.

4
Resistance to YHWH
(2:17–3:21 [EB 4:3])

To this point the thrust of Malachi's message has been twofold. He has condemned the priests of Judah for trivializing the cult both by their illicit practice and their indifferent attitude. And he has scolded the population at large for its failure to adhere to YHWH's covenant, particularly in the realm of mixed marriage and illegal divorce. Now his focus becomes more expanded as he addresses a number of seemingly miscellaneous matters that may fall under the general umbrella of resistance to YHWH. There is clearly a pattern of presentation consisting of three causes of the people's resistance—self-deceit (2:17–3:5), selfishness (3:6-12), and self-sufficiency (3:13-21 [EB 4:3]) —each of which embraces a statement of the problem and a concomitant promise of either weal or woe.[1]

---

1. Coming at it from the angle of concentricity, Wendland describes the unit as "Dispute Four" in which A-B = B'-A':
   (A) Warning—the day of judgment is coming (2:17–3:2a)
       (B) Means—purification of the people (3:2b-3a)
       (B') Result—pleasing offerings (3:3b-4)
   (A') Warning—the day of judgment is coming (3:5)
       Ernst Wendland, "Linear and Concentric Patterns in Malachi," *BT* 36 (1985): 117. This structural way of looking at the passage is not at all in conflict with the pseudo-dialogical, disputational form I am suggesting.

A. RESISTANCE THROUGH SELF-DECEIT (2:17–3:5)

1. THE PROBLEM (2:17)

Translation

¹⁷You have wearied YHWH with your words. But you say, "How have we wearied Him?" Inasmuch as you say, "Everyone who does evil is good in the sight of YHWH, and He delights in them," or, "Where is the God of justice?"

Exegesis and Exposition

In the present section, which deals with self-deceit, the problem occurs in 2:17 and the promise in 3:1-5. In anthropomorphic language Malachi says that YHWH is worn out from the words of the people, words that betray an abysmal self-deception. To carry out his disputation schema the prophet contrives a series of interrogations and responses in which YHWH's accusation is invariably met with a questioning response, "How have we done thus and so?" This in turn elicits a specification of the charges in such unambiguous speech that the accused themselves are rendered speechless.

Following the charge that the people have wearied YHWH and their predictable but hypocritical "How?" the prophet lists two specifications: (1) the people claim that those who do evil are good in YHWH's opinion, and (2) they allege that the God of justice is nowhere to be found. The first indictment shows a topsy-turvy sense of morals and ethics in which criteria of right and wrong are so perverted as to be absolutely in reverse: they call good evil and evil good. Isaiah knew of such distorted perspective in his own day and railed against it. "Woe to them who call evil good, and good evil," he said, and "who put darkness for light, and light for darkness; who put bitter for sweet, and sweet for bitter. Woe to them who are wise in their own opinion, and prudent in their own sight" (Isa. 5:20-21). Such a view of God as an indulgent, nondiscriminating being who winks at iniquity is, of course, a totally sub-biblical concept.

The second indictment—that Judah has lost sight of a God of justice—is an outgrowth of the first. The people had obviously been sinning against God, as Malachi's message has consistently affirmed. The fact that they had done so with a minimum of negative reaction had lulled them into a spirit of serene self-deception about the principle of sin and punishment. If they had lived as they had and had been essentially none the worse for it, could there be a God of justice? This attitude and these words made Him weary, so YHWH replies with a promise (3:1-5).

428

2. THE PROMISE (3:1-5)

Translation

¹"Behold, I am about to send My messenger, who will make the way clear before Me. Indeed, the Lord whom you are seeking will suddenly come to His Temple; and the messenger of the covenant in whom you delight is coming," says YHWH of hosts. ²"Who can bear up under the day of His coming? Who can keep standing when He appears? For He will be like a refiner's fire, like a washerman's soap. ³He will act like a refiner and purifier of silver and will purify the Levites and refine them like gold and silver. Then they will offer YHWH a righteous offering. ⁴And the offering of Judah and Jerusalem will be pleasing to YHWH as in former days, as in years of old. ⁵I will come to you in judgment and will be a speedy witness against the sorcerers, the adulterers, those who swear falsely, those who cheat the wage-earner of wages, (who oppress) the widow and orphan, and those who turn aside the alien and do not fear Me," says YHWH of hosts.

Exegesis and Exposition

In wake of the problem expressed in 2:17 there now follows a promise that addresses both aspects of the people's grand self-delusion. That promise is that YHWH is about to send (so the *futur instans*[2] use of the participle שֹׁלֵחַ [*šōlēaḥ*]) His messenger. This one will prepare the way for the coming of YHWH Himself.

The construction of v. 1 is of interest both as a literary device and as a clue to its meaning. The word "messenger" (מַלְאָךְ, *mal'āk*) occurs twice, once at the beginning of the verse and again near the end. Although the word is not exegetically significant, perhaps one should note in passing that the noun in its first occurrence is with the pronominal suffix "my," מַלְאָכִי, that is, *mal'ākî* or Malachi. As suggested in the Introduction, this may be a play on the name of the prophet himself, or it may be purely coincidental. More to the point, the double use of the term suggests that the same messenger is in view throughout the passage. Enveloped within the double occurrence is the reference to YHWH, here described with the epithet הָאָדוֹן (*hā'ād-ôn*), "the Lord." Thus the messenger of YHWH comes to prepare the way for Adon, a messenger further identified as the "messenger of the covenant."[3]

---

2. GKC, 116p.
3. This interpretation goes against the vast majority of commentators and is therefore offered with great tentativeness. Even so, it does seem to fit the context of the whole passage better. Its major weakness is that it departs

One immediately thinks of a similar promise in Isaiah 40:3-5. There a voice proclaims, "Prepare in the wilderness the way of YHWH." The verb translated "prepare" there (פָּנָה, *pānâ*) is the very one we translate "make (the way) clear" here in Malachi. As the parallel in Isaiah 40:3*b* makes evident, to "make clear" is to "make smooth" or "level." In both Isaiah and Malachi this is to be taken metaphorically to speak of the removal of obstacles to His coming.[4]

Whereas Isaiah refers to the Lord as YHWH, Malachi speaks of him as Adon. Even though one ought not to exaggerate the difference in name choice, it may well be that Isaiah is focusing on the covenant name inasmuch as the historical and eschatological thrust of this entire section of the book (esp. chaps. 40-55) is on covenant restoration. Malachi, on the other hand, is addressing a people who have despised the covenant and who therefore have no real right to its claims or blessings.[5] This prophet may, then, be employing irony in proposing that the people are indeed not looking for their covenant Lord but, as they have already phrased it, "Where is the God of justice (2:17)?" If they want the God of justice, He will come as Adon, the Lord and Master.[6]

The NT identifies the messenger of Malachi 3:1 as John the Baptist (Matt. 11:10; Mark 1:2), making it clear that the messenger, in their view, is not deity. Indeed, he is not even an angel, but a man, a prophet, perhaps like Malachi himself. Malachi later elaborates on the identity of the messenger by referring to him as "Elijah the prophet" (4:5).[7] Whether, as in later Jewish tradition, Malachi looked

---

from the nearly unanimous Christian tradition that views the second messenger as identical to the Lord. For an approach that is cognizant of the ambiguities present in the text, see Joyce G. Baldwin, *Haggai, Zechariah, Malachi* (London: Tyndale, 1972), 242-43. Dumbrell says that a case can be made for this identification on the assumption that the prophecy is anonymous. What authorship of the book has to do with the matter is not plain ("Malachi and the Ezra-Nehemiah Reforms," *RTR* 35 [1976]: 48).

4. P.-E. Bonnard, *Le Second Isaïe*, Études Bibliques (Paris: Librairie Lecoffre, 1972), 87-88.
5. J. R. Villalón understands this covenant to be the one with Levi mentioned in 2:4, 5, 8 and the messenger of the covenant to be Elijah ("Sources Vétéro-Testamentaires de la Doctrine Qumranienne des Deux Messies," *RevQ* 8 [1972]: 60). Although Elijah no doubt is the messenger, the covenant, in light of the Isaiah parallels, would seem to be the Sinaitic, prefiguring the New.
6. O. Eissfeldt, *TDOT* 1:62, s.v. אָדוֹן: "It is used to emphasize Yahweh's rule over all the world." One should note that whereas the coming of YHWH in Isa. 40:3 is to bring salvation, the coming of Adon in Mal. 3:1 is for judgment. See Steven L. McKenzie and Howard N. Wallace, "Covenant Themes in Malachi," *CBQ* 45 (1983): 554.
7. That the messenger of 3:1 and Elijah of 4:5 are one and the same is ac-

forward to the literal Elijah cannot be known,[8] but Jesus Himself, in the same context in which Mal. 3:1 is cited, says that Elijah to come is none other than John the Baptist (Matt. 11:14; cf. 17:10-13; Mark 9:11-13; Luke 1:17). The Christological significance of Mal. 3:1 thus becomes immediately evident, for if John the Baptist came to prepare the way for Jesus, then the Adon of Malachi can be none other than the Messiah.[9] This may also explain why Adon is used rather than YHWH, for in the passage YHWH speaks, thus distinguishing Himself, at least functionally, from Adon.

Though not totally without distant eschatological import (cf. Mal. 4:5, "the great and terrible day of YHWH"), the passage at hand is fundamentally to be connected to the first advent. The promise is that the way having been prepared, the Lord will come to His Temple (cf. Matt. 3:1-3; 21:12-17; Luke 2:41-51). The messenger who prepares the way does so as a covenant spokesman, one who reminds his hearers that the long-awaited ("whom you are seeking") one has come to establish the kingdom of God as the ultimate expression of the ancient covenant promises (Matt. 11:11-13).[10]

The description of the messenger of the covenant as the "one in whom you delight" is somewhat problematic. In fact, most scholars identify this messenger with the Adon because it seems difficult to conceive of the messenger himself as the object of delight. Moreover, the parallel phrases, "the Adon whom you are seeking" and "the mes-

---

cepted by most scholars. See Pieter A. Verhoef, *The Books of Haggai and Malachi*, NICOT (Grand Rapids: Eerdmans, 1987), 340.

8. For the Jewish (and other ancient) traditions on Elijah redivivus and messianic forerunner, see Joseph Coppens, *Le Messianisme et sa Relève Prophétique* (Gembloux: J. Duculot, 1974), 129-32; Walter C. Kaiser, Jr., "The Promise of the Arrival of Elijah in Malachi and the Gospels," *GTJ* 3 (1982): 222-23. For an objection to this "early Jewish evidence" see Joseph A. Fitzmyer, "More About Elijah Coming First," *JBL* 104 (1985): 295-96.

9. R. T. France argues that Adon here is not a divine epithet but that it is synonymous with both "my messenger" and the "messenger of the covenant." He therefore distinguishes between Adon and YHWH (and Jesus); *Jesus and the Old Testament* (London: Tyndale, 1971), 91-92. This seems difficult to sustain in light of the NT understanding of the messenger as a forerunner of Jesus the Lord, but his argument that the messengers themselves do the refining and purifying of vv. 2-3 seems most compatible with my own position. For a rebuttal of France and affirmation of the Adon-Messiah equation, see D. A. Carson, "Matthew," in *EBC*, ed. Frank E. Gaebelein (Grand Rapids: Zondervan, 1984), 8:264.

10. In the immediate setting the one they are seeking could be "the God of justice" in 2:17. In this case the viewpoint is not messianic at all but merely time bound to the question concerning God's whereabouts as judge. Thus Robert C. Dentan, "The Book of Malachi," *IB* 6 (New York: Abingdon, 1956), 1137. However, the passage as it stands, without the additions alleged by Dentan and other scholars, is clearly messianic and eschatological in its overall import.

senger in whom you delight" appear to make this equation conclusive. Nevertheless, for the following reasons it seems best to see the two messengers mentioned in this verse as one and the same and distinct from the Lord.

First, the uses of the technical term מַלְאָךְ in such close juxtaposition would lead one immediately to suppose that they refer to the same individual.[11]

Second, YHWH (or Adon) is never described elsewhere as a messenger, though the phrase "Angel of YHWH" does serve as a synonym for YHWH and frequently so (cf. Judg. 6:19-24; 13:2-14; etc.). Here, however, "Angel of YHWH" does not occur but "messenger (or angel) of the covenant." The missing "of YHWH" certainly militates against this being YHWH.

Third, "messenger of the covenant" is a phrase occurring only here. This compounds the problem of its meaning, but the context in general would indicate that this is not a messenger of whom the covenant speaks but one who comes bearing the covenant message. That is, it is a subjective genitive. In this case the messenger is not the Adon, but one who comes to proclaim the covenant message of the Adon.[12]

Fourth, on the basis of the whole passage (vv. 1-5) and its NT fulfillment, it seems beyond question that the messenger here is human, not divine, and that his ministry can (and did) embrace all the elements of the passage. The objection that one cannot interpret an OT passage on the basis of NT fulfillment, citation, allusion, or otherwise fails to appreciate the wholistic nature of biblical revelation and the part that a comprehensive biblical theology and canonical wit-

---

11. France, *Jesus and the Old Testament*, 91.
12. "Messenger of" never occurs elsewhere in the objective genitive sense, that is, in the sense in which the messenger himself is the content of or subordinate to the message. Cf. Prov. 16:14; Mal. 2:7. The latter passage is particularly instructive because it occurs in Malachi and provides an apt parallel to 3:1. The priest is the messenger of YHWH in that he proclaims the instruction of YHWH (2:7a), and the messenger of the covenant is such because he proclaims the covenant. Van Selms, in fact, argues that Elijah himself is the messenger of the covenant, a role he ties to 2:7 inasmuch as Elijah functioned as a priest on occasion. He also connects Elijah to the "book of remembrance" (3:16) by suggesting that Elijah was the scribe (or recorder, *mazkir*) whose task was to keep notes for YHWH the king. The messenger of the covenant, then, will come to make his report to the king, one inscribed in the book of remembrance ("The Inner Cohesion of the Book of Malachi," *OTWSA* 13-14 [1970-71]: 36-38). Even though his identification of the messenger of the covenant with Elijah (and hence with "my messenger") is in line with my own thesis, it seems that the suggestion of Elijah as *mazkir*, particularly with reference to the "book of remembrance," has little to commend it.

ness must play in proper hermeneutical method. For the Christian, in fact, this appreciation is not an option but a *sine qua non*.

Having established on the basis of the witness of the gospels that John the Baptist was the predicted messenger of Mal. 3:1a, it is necessary now to see if he qualifies as the messenger of 3:1c.[13] That one is "desired" by the people, the prophet says, but surely the prophet is speaking irony here, for their question of 2:17 betrays their cynicism. They no more desire the messenger than they seek the Lord.

John's message was certainly attractive to those who came to hear him, but he understood full well that their "desire" for him was superficial. In fact, he called the curious religious leaders "offspring of vipers" who were in need of repentance (Matt. 3:7-8). He then announced the coming of the Lord, who would thoroughly sweep His threshing floor, gather the wheat for storage, and burn the chaff with unquenchable fire (Matt. 3:12). John therefore brought an unpopular message, one that crushed his hearers with its convicting power and knocked out from under their feet the hypocritical religiosity on which they depended (Mal. 3:2). He was a veritable "refiner's fire" and "washerman's soap" among his own generation, for his message drove a wedge between those who believed and repented and those who closed up their hearts to the overtures of covenant grace (Matt. 3:6; cf. vv. 7-8; 11:7-11).

Most specifically, John's message and ministry were directed to the religious leadership of Judaism, an element that could easily be accommodated under the loosely defined rubric of "Levite."[14] Malachi's messenger, the prophet says, will refine and purify the Levites in particular until those who are purged of their dross meet the standards for ministry to YHWH (3:3). Obviously the cleansing and refining are not done by the messenger as such but by the message he proclaims. In the NT frame of reference it is the gospel message that accomplishes this work of sifting and separating (Matt. 3:12).

The effects of John's personal ministry in terms of these specific results are not easy to determine. That the message he proclaimed produced these results in the ministry of Jesus and the apostles cannot be denied. Many of the priests and other religious leaders believed (cf. John 3:1; 19:39; Acts 6:7) and in that important sense became purified and qualified to serve as priests of a new order. Then

---

13. Dumbrell states, "The actions of the messenger of Mal. 3:1-5 very much foreshadow the ministry of John" ("Malachi and the Ezra-Nehemiah Reforms," 48).
14. John M. P. Smith, *A Critical and Exegetical Commentary on the Book of Malachi*, ICC (Edinburgh: T. & T. Clark, 1912), 64. In the context of Mal. 1:6–2:9, "Levites" appears to be a general term for priests here. See McKenzie and Wallace, "Covenant Themes in Malachi," 554.

and only then could they offer up to YHWH a "righteous offering" (Mal. 3:3), one that is reminiscent of those of old which, when offered by men of faith, were pleasing to him (v. 4).[15]

As for the question, "Where is the God of justice?" (2:17), the answer is "I will come to you in judgment" (3:5). The agent of purification who announced the coming of the Lord now gives way to the Lord, to YHWH, who will come as Judge.[16] The shift from the "he" of the first phase of the messianic coming (eight occurrences of "he" or "his" in vv. 1-4) to the "I" of the second phase lends support to the thesis that the work of the messenger is distinct from that of the Lord.[17] The refining and purification, moreover, appear to have special relevance to the priests and Levites, whereas the judgment breaks those narrow bounds to encompass all of society. Finally, although it is difficult to establish within the passage itself, it seems clear from a full (NT) analysis that the setting of vv. 1-4 is primarily first advent whereas that of v. 5 is more distant.[18] The message of John the Baptist was one of purging and perfecting within the covenant

---

15. In the NT sense of sacrifice this would refer to the offering of oneself (Rom. 12:1; 1 Cor. 6:20) or of one's praises (Heb. 13:15) or other "spiritual" sacrifices (1 Peter 2:5). Cf. Theodore Laetsch, *Minor Prophets* (St. Louis: Concordia, 1956), 536.

16. This shift from purification to judgment is noted by Dennis E. Johnson, who links the fire imagery implicit in 3:5 to that of 4:1 ("Fire in God's House: Imagery from Malachi 3 in Peter's Theology of Suffering [1 Pet. 4:12-19]," *JETS* 29 [1986]: 288-89).

17. At the very least, if vv. 2-4 speak of the work of Adon, he cannot be the same as YHWH, for YHWH, as speaker in both vv. 1 and 5, sets Himself off in v. 5 from the preceding agent. Although one could argue from a Christian theological perspective that Adon is the Son and YHWH the Father, it is unlikely that Malachi understood it that way. He would be more apt to see Adon as an epithet of YHWH and therefore to distinguish Him from the messenger of the covenant, who as actor in vv. 2-4, is himself distinguished from YHWH. Moreover, Adon is not a messianic epithet but one reserved for use in combination with YHWH or one of the other divine names. See Walther Eichrodt, *Theology of the Old Testament* (London: SCM, 1961), 1:203-4. Cf. Zech. 4:14; 6:5 where YHWH is described as "the Adon of the whole earth," suggestive of His capacity as sovereign.

18. The distinction "messianic" and "eschatological" is, in any event, artificial, for messianic hope in the OT always lies within the eschatological realm. Thus, even in our passage phrases such as "suddenly come to His Temple" (v. 1) and "the day of His coming" (v. 2) are eschatological terms. However, from the vantage point of fulfillment, vv. 1-4 took place already in the coming of Christ, whereas v. 5 still awaits the Parousia. Alden argues that only v. 1 pertains to the first advent ("Malachi," in *EBC*, ed. Frank E. Gaebelein [Grand Rapids: Zondervan, 1985] 7:719) and that vv. 2-5 are yet to be fulfilled. This is valid if Adon and the messenger of the covenant are one and the same but if, as I propose, the messenger of the covenant is the same as "my messenger," vv. 1-4 are all first advent inasmuch as they would all be fulfilled in John the Baptist.

fellowship so as to isolate a godly remnant therein (Matt. 3:10-11a). The message of YHWH is one of judgment with no hopeful note of repentance or salvation (Matt. 3:11b-12).

The catalogue of religious and social wrongs enumerated by the prophet (v. 5) does not necessarily correspond to specific items already mentioned by him (though compare sorcery[19] to "foreign god," 2:11, and adultery to mixed marriage, also 2:11) but is a rather formulaic list descriptive of apostate people of any time and place.[20] This is clear from the summary statement, "and do not fear me." Those who wonder if there is justice will discover ruefully in the day of God's wrath that indeed there is. Self-deceit will then be exposed, and those who find comfort in it will be judged accordingly.

B. RESISTANCE THROUGH SELFISHNESS (3:6-12)

1. THE PROBLEM (3:6-9)

Translation

⁶"Since, I, YHWH, do not change, you, O sons of Jacob, have not perished. ⁷From the days of your fathers you have turned aside from my statutes and have not kept them. Return to Me, and I will return to you," says YHWH of hosts. "But you say, 'How should we return?' ⁸Can a man *rob God? You indeed are *robbing Me, but you say, 'How are we *robbing You?' *In tithes and contributions. ⁹You are cursed with the curse because you are *robbing Me—this entire nation."

Exegesis and Exposition

Just as the people were resisting YHWH and His covenant claims on them through a perverse self-deception and inverted sense of righteousness, so they express resistance in flagrant self-centeredness and acquisitiveness. Though this may be demonstrated in any number of ways, their withholding of tribute to YHWH their sovereign Lord is the case in point in the present pericope.

Malachi continues his rhetorical pattern of disputation by leveling an accusation against the people (v. 7a), by recording their super-

---

19. The term here, the piel ptc. of כָּשַׁף, means "practicers of sorcery," that is, of divination. Cf. G. André, *TWAT* 4:3/4: cols. 375-81, s.v. כָּשַׁף.
20. There does appear to be a "descending" order in the list: (1) outright paganism (sorcery); (2) syncretism (adultery); (3) sin against YHWH and a brother (swear falsely; cf. Lev. 19:12; Ex. 20:16); (4) sin against the helpless of Israel (wage earner, widow, orphan); and (5) sin against the alien. Cf. Beth Glazier-McDonald, *Malachi: The Divine Messenger*, SBL Series 98 (Atlanta: Scholars Press, 1987), 159-68.

cilious question as to how to rectify the problem (v. 7*b*), and then by specifying once more what it is (v. 8). The form is more complicated this time[21] because there is a double accusation: "You have turned aside from my statutes" and "You are robbing me." There is also a double question: "How should we return?" and "How are we robbing You?" but only a single specification—"in tithes and contributions." The first specification is, however, implicit in the first allegation—"You have turned aside from My statutes *and have not kept them*." This is so specific as not to warrant the naive questions that are otherwise raised. Also added to the pattern is a self-standing introductory statement of principle (v. 6) and a concluding word as to the results of the present problem (v. 9).

The introductory particle כִּי (*kî*) in v. 6 may be understood in a variety of ways. If it is taken in a causal sense ("because, since"), it can refer either to the previous paragraph,[22] thereby granting the guilty of that section some figment of hope inasmuch as YHWH's covenant pledge is inalterable, or it can introduce the next paragraph, providing the same basis for His dealings with them as with the fathers in the past. The latter is by far to be preferred because the final verb (כָּלָה, *kālâ*) is in the perfect, "have not perished," the only translation the verb sequence allows. Therefore, the verse provides a general theological affirmation that the nation has not perished because YHWH Himself never changes. He always remains true to His covenant commitments.[23] The perfect tenses in v. 7*a*, followed by participles (v. 8) to bring the action to the present, favors the connection of v. 6 to vv. 7 ff. as well. The causal sense of כִּי is quite suitable to this.[24]

A second possibility is that כִּי is asseverative, to be rendered "indeed," "surely," or the like.[25] This is in line with the overall thrust of

---

21. Wendland's structural analysis—though approaching the passage in a rhetorical-critical rather than form-critical fashion—is very helpful. He perceives a concentric pattern for vv. 6-12 as follows:

    (A) Introduction: a divine promise (6)
        (B) Appeal—repent (7)
            (C) Indictment (8)
                (D) Verdict: Curse (9*a*)
            (C') Indictment (9*b*)
        (B') Promise—blessings on those who repent (10-11)
    (A') Conclusion: a messianic vision (12)

    E. Wendland, "Linear and Concentric Patterns in Malachi," 118; cf. E. Ray Clendenen, "The Structure of Malachi: A Textlinguistic Study," *CTR* 2 (1987): 14.
22. Ralph L. Smith, *Micah-Malachi*, EBC (Waco, Tex.: Word, 1984), 332.
23. Or, "For I, the Lord, have not gone back on My word." For support of this nuance of שָׁנִיתִי, see Nahum M. Waldman, "Some Notes on Malachi 3:6; 3:13; and Psalm 42:11," *JBL* 93 (1974): 544.
24. For this causal force of כִּי, see GKC, 158b.
25. Verhoef, *The Books of Haggai and Malachi*, 299.

the passage, but the conjunction prefixed to אַתֶּם (’attem), "you," weakens this likelihood unless the asseverative also carries a causal nuance such as, "Indeed, I, YHWH, do not change, *so* you," etc. Any other rendering of the *waw* conjunctive would be extremely problematic.[26] It is better on the whole to take the וְ . . . כִּי (*kî . . . wě*, "since . . . therefore") as a cause-result construction, as the translation proposes.

The changelessness of YHWH here has to do with covenant fidelity, as the "statutes" (v. 7) and "the curse" (v. 9) suggest. These two terms give His immutability a framework, for it is the very fickleness and faithlessness of the covenant people *vis à vis* the covenant that are at issue here, a changeableness on their part that must be contrasted with the steadfastness of YHWH. They have "turned aside" (סוּר, *sûr*) from His statutes from the time of the early ancestors, refusing to keep them. To keep (שָׁמַר, *šāmar*) the statutes (חֻקִּים, *ḥuqqîm*) is a fundamental duty of the vassal in the covenant contract (cf. Deut. 11:32; 26:17; etc.).

The utter dependability of YHWH, however, means that those who have turned aside have someone to whom they can come back. "Return (שׁוּבוּ, *šûbû*) to Me," He says, "and I will return (אָשׁוּבָה, *’āšûbâ*) to you." This appeal for and expression of genuine repentance will inevitably be met by YHWH's willingness to forgive, for His covenant word is as firmly established as He is. But Malachi's generation has hardened itself to such a gracious invitation because they see no need to return in the first place. "How should we return?" is not an earnest entreaty for information but a self-serving declaration of innocence.[27] The people, in effect, are saying, "What need do we have to return since we never turned away to begin with?"

At this point the specific charge is made: A return is absolutely

---

26. Many scholars obviate this problem with the *waw* by construing the verb כָּלָה as "cease," "stop," or the like. This allows it to be synonymous to שָׁנָה ("change") and for the line to be rendered, "I, YHWH, have not changed, but you, O sons of Jacob, have not stood firm." Thus Wilhelm Rudolph, *Haggai–Sacharja 1-8–Sacharja 9-14–Maleachi*, KAT (Gütersloh: Verlaghaus Gerd Mohn, 1976), 281. This takes *waw* as the coordinate rather than subordinate conjunction. In its favor additionally is the inconstancy of Israel revealed in v. 7. But כָּלָה with this meaning is difficult to establish. Cf. BDB, 477-78; KBL, 437-38. Another suggestion is that כָּלָה here means "come to an end"—a well-attested meaning—and that the comparison is thus made between the immutability of YHWH as covenant-maker and His people as covenant partners: "I, YHWH, do not change and you, sons of Jacob, do not come to an end." See Baldwin, *Haggai, Zechariah, Malachi*, 245. If, as we argue, v. 6 goes with 7 ff. and not vv. 1-5, this interpretation seems unlikely because it immediately seems to be contradicted by v. 7.
27. Laetsch, *Minor Prophets*, 539.

essential because you, the people, have robbed God. With this allegation flung in their faces their hollow pretenses to innocence are ripped away, and their query as to how or why they must return is answered. For a man to rob God seems preposterous, and this is the effect of the rhetorical question of v. 8*a*. But it is not preposterous, for Israel has done it (and was doing it, as the participle emphasizes). Even the feeble rejoinder "How are we robbing you?" is nothing but a last gasp effort to maintain a facade of nonculpability. This facade, too, is demolished by the unambiguous response of YHWH: "Tithes and contributions!" There are not even verbs or other qualifiers to soften the impact of the words (v. 8*b*).

"Tithes" (מַעֲשֵׂר, *maʿăśēr*)[28] refers primarily to the presentation of a tenth of one's goods to YHWH as a tribute of thanks for His blessing (Gen. 14:20; 28:22). It was used in the tabernacle and Temple administration to provide for the material welfare of the priests and Levites (Num. 18:21, 26) and, if enjoyed at all by the donor, it must be shared within the holy precincts (Deut. 12:17-18) with the Levites and others in need (Deut. 14:26-27; 26:12). The tithe, then, had a social dimension in that it provided for those who had no other means of support.

The "contributions" are the gifts "offered up" (תְּרוּמָה, *tĕrûmâ*, from רוּם, *rûm*, "to be high").[29] These are the same in material as the tithes and serve the same function, namely, to meet the needs of the disadvantaged and otherwise dependent (cf. Lev. 22:12; Num. 5:9), particularly the priests and Levites. The major differences between the two kinds of gifts are: (1) that the tithe was a mandatory tenth, whereas the "contribution" was voluntary; and (2) the "contribution" seems to have been used exclusively to meet the needs of the clergy, whereas the tithes served a broader social function.

Because the people have robbed God by withholding these gifts, they have already suffered "the curse" (v. 9). The article on "curse" (בַּמְּאֵרָה, *bammĕʾērâ*) reveals it to be a specific judgment applicable to this kind of covenant violation. What form it took cannot be determined with certainty.[30] The use of the same word in Mal. 2:2 shows it to be most serious indeed, for there the curse comes if God's glory is not sought, a curse that results in the overturning of all blessing. Whatever it is, it is already having its deleterious effect across the board and nationwide (v. 9).

---

28. E. E. Carpenter, *ISBE*, 4:861-64, s.v. "tithe."
29. Jacob Milgrom, "The *Šôq Hattĕrûmâ*: A Chapter in Cultic History," in *Studies in Cultic Theology and Terminology* (Leiden: Brill, 1983), 159-70; and "Akkadian Confirmation of the Meaning of the Term *Tĕrûmâ*, 171-72.
30. Van Hoonacker, in line with the Vg, takes the curse to be poverty. Because the people have defrauded YHWH, he has reduced them to penury (*Les Douze Petits Prophètes* [Paris: Librairie Victor Lecoffre, 1908], 734-35). This cannot be wide of the mark, as vv. 10-12 make clear.

Additional Notes

3:8 For the four occurrences in vv. 8, 9 of קָבַע, "to rob" (BDB, 867), the LXX presupposes the metathesized form עָקַב, "to deceive" (KBL, 820). Admittedly קבע is a rare word, occurring elsewhere only in Prov. 23:23. There, however, it clearly is a synonym of גָּזַל in v. 22, as the parallel, chiastic structure of the passage indicates. Moreover, in speaking of the matter of tithes and contributions one would hardly use the verb "deceive." Theft or robbery seems to be required in the nature of the case.

The absolute state of הַמַּעֲשֵׂר וְהַתְּרוּמָה has led *BHS*, with the Syr., Tg. Neb. and the Vg to prefix each noun with בְּ, thus "in" or "by tithes and contributions." However, the impact of YHWH's indictment is heightened by the present form of the text, and the MT, for that reason alone, is superior.

2. THE PROMISE (3:10-12)

Translation

¹⁰Bring the entire tithe into the storehouse so that there may be food in My house, and test Me now in this," says YHWH of hosts, "if I will not open to you the windows of heaven and pour out for you a blessing until there is no room for it. ¹¹ Then I will rebuke the devourer for you so that it will no longer corrupt the produce of the ground, nor will the vine in the field lose its fruit (before harvest)," says YHWH of hosts. ¹²"All nations will call you happy, for you indeed will be a delightful land," says YHWH of hosts.

Exegesis and Exposition

The proper response to the problem of selfishness, is, of course, generosity and altruism. This is no less the case when one robs God, as Malachi's fellow countrymen were doing. Therefore, the instruction is straightforward and unambiguous—"bring the whole tithe." This must be placed in the Temple storehouse (בֵּית הָאוֹצָר, *bêt hāʾôṣār*), which was like a warehouse for the collection of commodities presented by the people in accordance with the tithing laws referred to above (cf. v. 8). From here the goods presumably were distributed to the priests and Levites as a part of their remuneration and, separately, to the indigent elements of the society.

Nehemiah refers to these facilities as a לִשְׁכָּה גְדוֹלָה (*liškâ gĕdôlâ*), "a great chamber" (Neh. 13:5), a place whose function was to house offertory grains, frankincense, Temple vessels, and the tithes of grain, wine, and oil. These were to be allocated to the Levites, singers, porters, and priests (v. 6). Nehemiah relates that the system had broken down, however, with the result that the Levites and singers had had to go to the fields to collect their own food supplies (v. 10). He then brought about measures to enforce the proper payment of the tithes (v. 12). The concern for tithing articulated by Malachi remained unaddressed until the force of Nehemiah's leadership gave it embodiment decades later.

The blessing in the tithe was not just in the sense of obedience to the divine mandate, but it took tangible form in YHWH's reciprocation. "Give to Me, and I will give to you," He said in effect. In fact, the comparatively miserly giving of a tenth would result in a blessing in kind so immense that it would overflow the capacity of the people to receive it (Mal. 3:10). It is not inappropriate to apply this to spiritual and other immaterial blessings, but the prophet speaks of the bounties of harvest. YHWH will rebuke the "devourer," a term so general (אֹכֵל, 'ōkēl, lit. "the eater") that it can apply to any scourge of the harvest whether it be an animal, pest, or adverse climate. As a result the produce of the field and the fruit of the vine will come to full maturity in their proper time (v. 11).

When such evidence of blessing comes to pass, all the nations will call Judah happy (v. 12). It will be clear to them that everything is in balance, that Judah's God has returned favor for obedience, that those who honor their God are in turn honored by Him. Judah will be a delightful land. The ambiguous nature of the genitive construction in this last line (אֶרֶץ חֵפֶץ, 'ereṣ ḥēpeṣ, lit. "land of delight") makes it possible for it to be understood either as a land that causes delight, that is, to its inhabitants and others, or as a land in which one finds delight, that is, by YHWH as the focus of His blessing.[31] The parallelism with the previous line favors the latter interpretation.

C. RESISTANCE THROUGH SELF-SUFFICIENCY (3:13-21 [EB 4:3])

1. THE PROBLEM (3:13-15)

Translation

[13]"Your words against Me have been hard," says YHWH, "but you ask, 'What have we spoken against You?' [14]You have said, 'It is useless serving God. What profit is there that we have kept His charge and have walked like mourners before YHWH of hosts? [15]Now, therefore, we consider the arrogant to be happy; indeed, those who practice evil are built up. In fact, those who test God escape.'"

---

31. Dentan, "The Book of Malachi," 1140.

Exegesis and Exposition

The third attitude of resistance to YHWH on the part of the post-exilic Jewish community was expressed in its assertion of self-sufficiency. This is most surprising in that historical context, for if anything should have been obvious, it was that the very existence of that community depended on the prevenient grace and power of YHWH alone. All the self-effort in the world could not accomplish their release and return from Babylonia. Nor could they view the remarkable rebuilding of the Temple and the renewal of the state as anything but a supernatural work of their God.

Malachi's contemporaries soon forgot all that, however, and began to entertain the notion that the success and prosperity that had attended their efforts were of their own making. Indeed, it seemed that serving God had nothing to do with it. In fact, those among them who repudiated the sovereign claims of YHWH appeared to be happiest and most successful. This spirit, then, leads to the final exchange of accusation and response in the book. This time, however, the question by the accused is not "How?" (בַּמֶּה, *bammâ*) as in 1:2, 6, 7; 2:17; 3:7, 8. Rather, it is "What?" (מָה, *mâ*). The reason, of course, is that the accusation does not concern response to an affirmation by YHWH (cf. 1:2) or a question that He has posed (1:6) or even a complaint He has made in which He registers personal grievance (2:17). In this case YHWH merely refers to words spoken to Him without immediately elaborating on their effect. The people's response, then, can only be, "What are the words?"[32]

The words are "hard" (חָזַק, *ḥāzaq*), that is, perverse or cynical (BDB, p. 304), words "against" YHWH.[33] The accusation has now

---

32. Wendland appears to sense this difference without articulating it in so many words. Once more his concentric patterning is helpful in delimiting the boundaries of the whole passage.
   (A) Objection—YHWH is unjust: "serve God" + "doers of wickedness" (13-15)
       (B) Justice: YHWH "hears" those who "fear" Him (16)
       (B′) Blessing: YHWH will spare His "treasure" (17)
   (A′) Refutation—YHWH is just: "serve God" + "the wicked" (18)
                                                    plus
   (X) Fate of the wicked: "day" + "wicked" + "ablaze" + "YHWH of Hosts" (1)
       (Y) Future of the God-fearing (2)
   (X′) Fate of the wicked: "wicked" + "ashes" + "day" + "YHWH of Hosts" (3)
   Wendland, "Linear and Concentric Patterns in Malachi," 119.
33. Waldman, on the basis of Akkadian parallels, offers the bold but quite convincing translation, "your words have been too much for me," that is,

been reversed, for it is the people who lay charge against Him. Pretending to be oblivious of this massive hubris, they ask YHWH to specify the words in question. What have they said that has been so offensive (v. 13)? The very fact that words have been spoken against Him points to the heart of the problem—God has appeared to become unnecessary and, indeed, the object of contempt and scorn.

This is evident in their conclusion that it is useless (שָׁוְא, *šāw'*, lit. "emptiness, vanity") to serve God. All their devotion to covenant requirement, which is clearly implicit in their prideful statement "we have kept His charge" (שָׁמַרְנוּ מִשְׁמַרְתּוֹ, *šāmarnû mišmartô*), has gained them no profit. Even their displays of public devotion and self-effacing piety, manifested in their "walking about like mourners," has yielded no dividends.[34] It has not really paid to serve YHWH (v. 14). So much for the benefits to be gained by the godly who seek to impress their evil compatriots with the rewarding life of covenant commitment.

To make matters worse, they say, those evil ones whose lives are an antithesis to everything YHWH desires enjoy life at its best. By observing how it goes with the arrogant, the impartial observer can only conclude that they are happy, that is, prosperous and satisfied (v. 15). The doers of evil (thus the participle עֹשֵׂה, *'ōśê*), those who make it their everyday pursuit, are built up. They seem to know nothing of the disintegrating tragedies of human experience where everything falls apart. Instead, they are affirmed and vindicated in all their ways. They even go so far as to put God to the test[35] and come away scot-free, escaping both His censure and His punishment.

All these, then, are the words spoken against YHWH. They are words of complaint that the evil of this world seem to be as well off or more so than the righteous, a common complaint in the wisdom tradition especially (Job 9:22-24; 21:7-20; cf. Ps. 73:1-14; Jer. 5:26-27;

---

more than YHWH will tolerate ("Some Notes on Malachi 3:6; 3:13; and Psalm 42:11," 546).

34. This is clearly an expression of hypocritical deference to YHWH. So C. F. Keil, *Biblical Commentary on the Old Testament. The Twelve Minor Prophets* (Edinburgh: T. & T. Clark, 1871), 2:465.

35. There is an interesting contrast of the use of the verb בָּחַן here and in v. 10. In the earlier passage YHWH urges the people to test Him in regard to His willingness and ability to pour out His blessings in response to their devotion. Now, He says, His interrogators are upset that He will do nothing to those who test Him. The difference clearly is one of attitude. In v. 10 the idea is to put God to the test in light of His promise to bless (cf. Ex. 4:1-9; Judg. 6:36-40; 1 Kings 18:22-23; Isa. 7:10-11). In v. 15 it is to put God to the test in an act of defiant testing of His patience (Ps. 95:9). Cf. M. Tsevat, *TDOT*, 2:69-72, s.v. בחן; J. M. P. Smith, *A Commentary on Malachi*, 77.

12:1; Hab. 1:4). But in making this complaint, those who do so have only a short-range view of God's ways among men. The self-sufficiency of the sinner will turn out to be hollow in the day when YHWH comes to establish true equity. That day is the theme of the promise in 3:16–4:3.

2. THE PROMISE (3:16-21 [EB 4:3])

Translation

16*Then those who revered YHWH spoke to each other, and YHWH heard and heeded. (Now a book of remembrance was written before Him for those who revere YHWH and esteem His name.) 17"They will be mine," says YHWH of hosts, "in the day when I prepare (My own) possession. I will spare them as one spares his son who serves him. 18Then once more you will discern between the righteous and the wicked, between the one who serves God and the one who does not. 19For indeed the day is coming, burning like a furnace, and all the arrogant and evildoers will be chaff. The coming day will burn them, says YHWH of hosts, "so that it will not leave them root or branch. 20But for you who revere My name, the sun of righteousness will rise with healing in its wings, and you will go forth and skip about like calves from the stall. 21You will tread down the wicked, for they will be ashes under the soles of your feet on the day which I am preparing," says YHWH of hosts.

Exegesis and Exposition

The words of rebuke by YHWH (v. 13) and those of the people in support of their spirit of self-sufficiency (vv. 14-15) are followed now by a positive response by some who repent (v. 16) and a promise by YHWH of blessing (vv. 17-18, 20-21 [EB 4:2-3]) and of judgment (v. 19 [EB 4:1]).

The present passage serves as a conclusion not only to vv. 13-15, however, but to the entire section 2:17–3:15. It explains what happens to those who resist the saving overtures of YHWH and, happily, to those who do not but who turn to Him in faith and repentance. This appears to have come about in Malachi's own time, but the principle of divine response to human behavior is not limited to that era. The tone of the passage suggests that it summarizes the dynamics of the divine-human relationship for all time. Those who turn to Him God blesses, but those who do not will face inevitable judgment.

The words of the prophet did not fall altogether on stony ground, for he reports that certain ones, "fearing YHWH," spoke to one another in such a way that YHWH heard, forgave, and remembered (v. 16). To fear God is to revere Him, to recognize and confess His awesome sovereignty. Malachi uses the verb "to fear" frequently, both as an appeal (1:6; 2:5; 3:20 [EB 4:2]) and as a description of human response (2:5; 3:5). It is not overstating the case to say that the term in his lexicon is a synonym for covenant stance.[36] When he calls his congregation to covenant fidelity, he does so in terms of their fearing YHWH. When he chides them for covenant disloyalty, he says they no longer fear Him.

Thus, those fearing gave evidence of their renewed commitment by talking to one another, presumably in the sense of a mutual confession and corporate repentance. They discussed with one another the meaning of Malachi's message and together agreed that it correctly pinpointed their sinful condition and called for their radical reformation.[37] Whatever they said among themselves was favorably received by YHWH. He "gave attention" (וַיַּקְשֵׁב, *wayyaqšēb*) and "heard" (וַיִּשְׁמָע, *wayyišmaʿ*). This hendiadys construction means that YHWH paid the closest heed to what was said. So moved was He by the sincerity of the repentance He heard that He recorded their names in His "book of remembrance."

The use of participles in v. 16b and the whole tenor of the passage suggest that this sentence should be constructed parenthetically as a word of explanation. That is, YHWH did not just then originate a book of remembrance specifically in response to the repentance of Malachi's converts. Such a book had always existed, one that listed the "fearers of YHWH" (יִרְאֵי יְהוָה, *yirʾê YHWH*) and "the thinkers of His name" (חֹשְׁבֵי שְׁמוֹ, *ḥošĕbê šĕmô*). Though the book (more correctly, scroll) is obviously metaphorical of YHWH's omniscient recall, it appears elsewhere in the OT in a similar capacity. Moses, pleading on behalf of his people, begged YHWH to expunge his name from "the book you have written" if his people were condemned to extinction (Ex. 32:32). Isaiah spoke of those "written unto life" (4:3), and Daniel referred to the ultimate deliverance of God's people, "everyone found written in the book" (12:1). The NT also speaks of a "book of life," a record of names of those destined to eternal bliss (Rev. 20:12-15).

Malachi's term "book of remembrance" (סֵפֶר זִכָּרוֹן, *sēper zikkārôn*) is unique to him. It conveys, in highly anthropomorphic language, the idea of a divine ledger in which the names of God's covenant children are recorded for posterity.[38] There is not a chance that even one name can ever be forgotten in such a system. Therefore, when the

---

36. The verb יְרָא and its cognates are very much at home in OT covenant contexts. Cf. Deut. 6:2, 13, 24; 10:12–11:17; 31:12-13; Jer. 32:39, 40; H. F. Fuhs, *TWAT* 3:6/7; cols. 869-93, esp. 886-88, s.v. יְרָא.
37. Baldwin, *Haggai, Zechariah, Malachi*, 249: "They begin to encourage each other to renewed faith."
38. Chary rightly connects this record to Isa. 65:6 and Neh. 13:14 and sug-

day comes for YHWH to prepare His "possession," all those whose names appear in the record will be called forth to make up this happy host.

The "possession" (סְגֻלָּה, sĕgullâ) is a technical expression of the people of YHWH as His treasure or property, one rightly His by virtue of redemption. The word first occurs in Ex. 19:5 in the context of the offer of a covenant relationship by YHWH to Israel.[39] YHWH says, "If you will obey My voice and keep My covenant, you will become My own possession (sĕgullâ) among all people, though all the earth is mine." Israel thus is God's special property, for He chose her and she in turn acceded (Ex. 19:8). The same concept occurs in Deuteronomy 7:6; 14:2; 26:18.

Malachi is clearly looking to an eschatological day of new covenant, as both the term "possession" and the phrase "in the day" (3:17) or "the day comes" (3:19 [EB 4:1]) attest. Just as YHWH had prepared a possession through exodus and covenant in days of old, He will do the same in the day to come. The parallels between the two times of redemption are further strengthened in v. 17b, where YHWH says He will spare His people as one who spares the son who serves him. YHWH had referred to Israel in Egyptian bondage as His son (Ex. 4:22-23) and had instructed Moses to command Pharaoh to let the people go that they might serve Him (cf. Ex. 7:16; 8:1, 20; 9:1, 13; 10:3, 11, 24).[40] When Pharaoh refused to the end, his land and family suffered the death of the first-born sons. Only the sons of Israel, covered by the Passover blood, were "spared" (Ex. 12:23-27). Though the verb employed by Malachi (חָמַל, ḥāmal) is not used in the Passover account, the effect is the same. So also in the future Day of YHWH He will spare His own choice possession just as one spares his own son who serves him; indeed, just as He Himself spared Israel His son who was redeemed to serve Him.

The covenant perspective continues in v. 18 with the sharp distinction between those who serve God and those who do not. The servants are the liege vassals of the Great King, made such by the election and redemption of YHWH already described in v. 17. Those who do not serve Him are those who stand outside the pale of the covenant relationship. Or, to put it in other terms as Malachi himself does, those who serve God are the righteous and those who do not are

---

gests that the book contains not only names but deeds as well (*Aggée-Zacharie, Malachie* [Paris: Librairie Lecoffre, 1969], 273).

39. H. Wildberger, *THAT*, 2:cols. 142-44, s.v. סְגֻלָּה; Moshe Weinfeld, *Deuteronomy and the Deuteronomic School* (Oxford: Clarendon, 1972), 226; Moshe Greenberg, "Hebrew Segullā: Akkadian Sikiltu," *JAOS* 71 (1951): 172-74.

40. A. Deissler, *Zwölf Propheten III. Zefanja, Haggai, Sacharja, Maleachi* (Wurzburg: Echter, 1988), 335.

the wicked. The distinction between the two may have become blurred to the point of no essential difference at all in the day of the prophet, but the day will come when such lines of demarcation will be crystal clear. Then the prevailing opinion that the arrogant are happy, the evil-doers are built up, and the ones who test God go unscathed (3:15) will be exposed for the grand self-deception that it truly is.[41]

The means by which the differences between the righteous and wicked will be clarified will be fearful indeed, and herein lies the promise of judgment in response to the problem of self-sufficiency outlined in vv. 13-15. The same day that will bring about the reconstitution of God's son, the covenant nation (v. 17), will bring also the burning of a furnace,[42] a fire that will consume the wicked as so much chaff (v. 19 [EB 4:1]). The words used here to describe these, the "arrogant" (זֵדִים, *zēdîm*) and "evildoers" (עֹשֵׂה רִשְׁעָה, *'ōśê riš'â*), are the very ones (in reverse order) the prophet employed in v. 15 to speak of those who appeared to prosper despite their sinfulness. The point is thus most apparent. Because the evil seem to enjoy the favor of YHWH in this world and in this age, it may be difficult to distinguish between them and the righteous or, in any event, to consider such distinctions meaningful (v. 14). However, in "that day" the fire will clarify these matters and as it refines and purifies precious metals, allowing the dross to be exposed (cf. Mal. 3:2-3), so it will burn away the false and the hypocritical, leaving the righteous to stand vindicated.

Again, the righteous are described as "you who fear My name" (v. 20 [EB 4:2]; cf. 3:16). To them (that is, on their behalf, hence "for you") "the sun of righteousness will rise with healing in its wings." This complex metaphor serves as a radical contrast to the violent destruction of the previous verse.[43] In keeping with the notion of

---

41. Van Hoonacker, *Les Douze Petits Prophètes*, 739.
42. Though the word תַּנּוּר frequently means "pottery kiln" (cf. James L. Kelso, *The Ceramic Vocabulary of the Old Testament*, *BASOR* Supp. Studies 5-6 [New Haven, Conn.: American Schools of Oriental Research, 1948], 8-9, 10, 31-32), it must mean "furnace" or "incinerator" here, as the burning of the קַשׁ (*qaš*, "stubble") makes clear. As Elliger says, "Restlose Vernichtung ist der Sinn"; "the sense is that of complete annihilation" (*Die Propheten Nahum, Habakuk, Zephanja, Haggai, Sacharja, Maleachi*, ATD [Göttingen: Vandenhoeck & Ruprecht, 1982], 215).
43. For a full discussion of the imagery here, see Glazier-McDonald, *Malachi: The Divine Messenger*, 233-40. Though "sun" is nowhere else a messianic epithet, Zecharias the priest (and father of John the Baptist) appears to appropriate the imagery of Malachi as a part of his blessing on his son, the forerunner of Jesus (Luke 1:76-79). For a helpful discussion of the NT use of this text in Malachi, see Walter C. Kaiser, Jr., *Malachi. God's Unchanging Love* (Grand Rapids: Baker, 1984), 105-6.

"day" as a time of YHWH's eschatological intervention, that day of wrath and judgment for the wicked will be for the godly a cloudless day heralded by the rising of the sun as an instrument of blessing (cf. 2 Sam. 23:4). Isaiah speaks of it as a day when the sun will be seven times more brilliant than usual, a time when YHWH will "bind up the hurt of his people and heal the blow of their wound" (Isa. 30:26). In that day, the same prophet says, "the glory of YHWH will rise upon you" (60:1) so that "nations will come to your light and kings to the brightness of your rising" (60:3). What is burning fire to the godless will be glowing warmth and healing to the righteous.

The healing brought by the rejuvenating "wings"[44] of the sun (perhaps its rays or effects) certainly includes recovery from literal and physical ailments, but it should not be limited to these. The human condition is one of pervasive sickness as was that of biblical Israel, a sickness traceable to and inextricably linked to sin. Thus the suffering of the servant, for example, was to produce a healing and one synonymous with victory over transgression and iniquity (Isa. 53:5). The demonstration of that healing in Malachi's message is the renewal of strength and spirit that will energize the healed to "skip about like calves from the stall." It takes little imagination to envision these frisky young animals gamboling about in absolute freedom after confinement in a narrow stall. Filled with the fervor of youth and wholeness, they kick their heels high in the sheer exhilaration of their happy state. So it will be in the day of YHWH's healing grace.

The closing bracket of the unit draws attention once more to the wicked (v. 21 [EB 4:3]). The remnant of YHWH, having been delivered and renewed, will take up their covenant privilege of dominion and as the agents of the sovereign will tread down the wicked. The verb עָסַס (*ʿāsas*, "tread down") occurs only here, but its cognate noun (עָסִיס, *ʿasîs*), which means "sweet wine" (BDB, 779), puts its meaning beyond

---

44. Chary draws attention to similar imagery from the ancient Near East, including the Egyptian disk of the sun from which "hands" extend to the divine protege, the ideogram for which is the *ankh* sign meaning "life." The winged sun is also common in Assyrian art, examples of which are the disk of Shalmaneser III (*ANEP*, #351) and a figure of the god Aššur (*ANEP*, #536) (*Aggée-Zacharie, Malachie*, 275). Although there no doubt was a common fund of such imagery in the ancient Near East, a deposit from which the authors of the OT occasionally drew, there is enough inner-biblical support for the winged sun of Malachi as an apt metaphor for blessing as not to require any cross-cultural borrowing. Moreover, the "wing" here, in common with the usual use of כָּנָף in figurative speech in the OT (Num. 15:38; 1 Sam. 15:27; 24:5, 6, 12; Jer. 2:34; Hag. 2:12; Zech. 8:23), may refer to a pocket or fold in the garment. Perhaps, then, the sun rises with healing in its "pouch" or "bag." Cf. Verhoef, *The Books of Haggai and Malachi*, 331.

question. The normal verb for treading down in conquest or dominion is דָּרַךְ (*dārak*). This is not used here perhaps because the figure of a calf dancing about (v. 20 [EB 4:2]) has influenced the choice of a synonym. One can imagine the calf crushing the grapes much more readily than standing with its foot on the neck or back of a defeated foe.[45]

In any case, the picture is still one of dominion. The wicked, who have already been incinerated by the furnace of divine wrath (v. 19 [EB 4:1]), will be but mounds of ashes beneath the triumphant feet of God's saints. This will come to pass, He repeats, on the day He is preparing, that is, the day of perfecting His own possession (cf. 3:17).

Though it is tempting to see something of the full-blown NT doctrine of hell in this passage, to do so is to step outside the imagery here and to be theologically premature. Nevertheless, the idea of a day of judgment in which the wicked will be consumed is clearly in view. Isaiah had, in fact, preceded Malachi in looking to such a day when he says in YHWH's words, "They will go forth and look on the dead bodies of those who have transgressed against Me, for their worm shall not die, nor shall their fire be quenched. They shall be an abhorrence to everyone" (Isa. 66:24; cf. Matt. 3:12; Mark 9:48). One cannot, therefore, take "ashes" (אֵפֶר, *'ēper*) exclusively figuratively either, as some scholars do.[46] It is indeed used that way in other places (cf. Job 13:12; Isa. 44:20; Ezek. 28:18), but here the burning of the wicked (3:19 [EB 4:1]) that leaves "neither root nor branch" can hardly tolerate metaphorical speech. The fire and ashes no doubt speak only of death, but it is real death, nonetheless, and not just some kind of subjugation or humiliation.[47]

On this somber note Malachi's record of conflict between YHWH and His people of the postexilic community comes to an end. Priest and people alike had sinned in sacrilege and rebellion. They had resisted the pleadings of divine love through the prophet, choosing to continue in their selfish and independent ways. But as was true throughout biblical history, all was not lost, for there was a remnant

---

45. The Apocalypse of John describes the day of God's triumphant wrath in identical imagery. An angel will cast the fruit of the vineyard into the winepress where it will be trodden under foot, producing not juice but blood (Rev. 14:19-20). Then when the King of kings comes to assert His dominion, He will "rule [the nations] with a rod of iron" and "tread the winepress" of the wrath of God (Rev. 19:15). Clearly, to tread the winepress is synonymous with the imposition and exercise of dominion. The same Greek verb is used in both places (πατέω).

46. Thus, e.g. C. von Orelli, *The Twelve Minor Prophets* (Edinburgh: T. & T. Clark, 1897), 403.

47. Dentan weakens the imagery by referring to the scene only as "the defeat of the wicked" ("The Book of Malachi," 1143).

that heard and heeded. With them there could always be a new beginning and a promise of ultimate success in the redeeming purposes of
God. In the day of His restitution the godly who responded positively
to Malachi, as well as those of all ages, will stand vindicated and
triumphant upon the ashes of the unrepentant.

Additional Notes

3:16 Because the MT does not indicate what the people said to one
another, the LXX and Syr. have presupposed זאת or the like and render,
"Thus the fearers of YHWH spoke," etc. It is hardly likely, however, that
God-fearers said what is recorded in vv. 13-15 (or in 16*b* ff.). Moreover,
the gist of what they said may be inferred from YHWH's response: He
entered the names of the God-fearers into His book of remembrance.
They must have spoken words of exhortation to repentance.

5
Restoration through YHWH (3:22-24 [EB 4:4-6])

Many scholars, following the Greek version, place v. 22 after vv. 23-24, presumably to allow the book to end on a more positive note (see Introduction, pp. 385-86). Others argue that vv. 23-24 are an addition to the original composition, the uncomfortable juxtaposition between vv. 22 and 23 and the unexpected reintroduction of the "Day of YHWH" theme being principal reasons. The MT tradition knows nothing but the present arrangement, however. As for the work ending on the bleak notion of curse, conditions in Malachi's day, only exacerbated in the accounts of Ezra and Nehemiah, give real justification for the prophet's handling of the material. A grand and glorious day is indeed coming, but it will be a day of blessing only for those who are ready for it. For those who are not—and there must have been many such in Malachi's hearing—it is a day of unmitigated tragedy. To fail to repent and to make peace with God is to leave oneself open to the curse with which the book ends.[1]

---

1. Laetsch compares Malachi's ending with that of Isaiah and Acts and suggests that it shares with them a final appeal to the people to forsake their wickedness and in true repentance to turn to the Lord (*The Minor Prophets* [St. Louis: Concordia, 1956], 547). As Pierce notes, "The situation has worsened to the point of extreme pessimism" ("A Thematic Development of the Haggai/Zechariah/Malachi Corpus," *JETS* 27 [1984]: 410).

Translation

²²"Remember the law of My servant Moses, which I commanded him at Horeb for all Israel—statutes and ordinances. ²³Behold, I am about to send you Elijah the prophet before the great and terrible day of YHWH comes. ²⁴He will turn the hearts of the fathers toward their children and the hearts of the children toward their fathers, lest I come and smite the earth with a curse."

Exegesis and Exposition

The reference to Elijah is very much at home here, for it and Mal. 3:1 provide an enveloping structure to all of chapter 3 (+ 4 in the EB). The messenger who prepares the way for YHWH is none other than Elijah, as both Jewish and Christian exegetical tradition affirm. How he fulfills that role will be addressed presently.

I have argued throughout this commentary on Malachi that the prophet is inordinately preoccupied with the motif of covenant. It is most appropriate, then, that the concluding promise of eschatological restoration should be rooted in and conditioned upon the covenant.[2] The appeals Malachi has made to his generation repeatedly can be boiled down to the injunction of v. 22 (EB 4:4): "Remember the law of My servant Moses." This is all YHWH requires of His redeemed people, but nothing less will do.

To remember is to do.[3] There is no abstract reflection here but a command to bear in mind and to put into effect. This is the very exhortation Moses himself made, especially in the great pareneses of Deuteronomy. "Remember YHWH your God," he said, "that He may establish His covenant which He swore to your fathers" (Deut. 8:18). They must remember, too, that they had been slaves in Egypt and inasmuch as YHWH had redeemed them, they were to obey His commands (15:15). Then, as though to preclude their thinking of Torah as an overgeneralized statement of vague principle, YHWH specifies the requirements of covenant fealty—the statutes (חֻקִּים, *ḥuqqîm*) and ordinances (מִשְׁפָּטִים, *mišpāṭîm*). So the remembering must be grounded in identifiable, discrete propositions, the stipulation texts of the covenant codes. Only when God's people meet these conditions of covenant compliance can they expect the long-anticipated restoration.

Lest the whole process appear to be merely *quid pro quo*, restoration for blind obedience, YHWH promises to send the prophet Elijah to prepare for the Day of YHWH (vv. 23-24 [EB 5:4-6]). It will be his

---

2. Pieter A. Verhoef, *The Books of Haggai and Malachi*, NICOT (Grand Rapids: Eerdmans, 1987), 338-39.
3. H. Eising, *TDOT*, s.v. זָכַר.

task to preach a message of reconciliation that will draw father to children and children to father (cf. Luke 1:17). To "turn the heart" (הֵשִׁיב לֵב, hēšîb lēb) is an expression in Hebrew that shows, grammatically, divine initiative at work.[4] It is YHWH who causes hearts to turn and change (cf. 1 Sam. 10:6, 9). It is true, of course, that lēb in Hebrew psychology means fundamentally the mind, the rational power of man. But this does not at all undercut the need for divine prevenience in effecting change in human relationships.

The fact that only fathers and children are named does not limit the scope of the passage. Clearly these are just examples of the whole network of human relationships. Sin has so effectively disrupted the wholeness and happiness of societal life that no amount of good intentions or merely mechanical adherence to even the gracious provisions of Torah can patch things up again. What is needed is a redeeming word from YHWH, mediated through a prophet like Elijah. That word, faithfully proclaimed, will accomplish a healing, reconciling result.[5] When that occurs covenant is kept, at least on the horizontal axis, and if on that axis certainly on the vertical as well, because it is one integrated whole. Without that contravening message there would be no hope, for it would be impossible to keep the covenant without the divine energy that that word imparts. Instead Israel, and indeed the whole earth, would be consigned to the ban like a heathen nation.

The ban (חֵרֶם, ḥērem) was the judgment of God on places, things, and hopelessly unrepentant people that resulted in the extermination of living beings and the destruction or appropriation by YHWH of the rest.[6] Were God's people at last to remain in unbelief and rebellion, they must suffer the fate of those placed under ḥērem, for they, too, would be under His everlasting curse. The whole earth would suffer similarly, for without the mediatorial ministry of Israel, the kingdom of priests, the program of YHWH for universal redemption would collapse and the design for a universal kingdom come to an end.

In what sense should one understand the coming of Elijah? The answers to this question are varied. The OT record reveals that he did not die but was translated bodily into heaven (2 Kings 2:11). His coming thus could be more easily explained and made possible without the impediment of death. His very ascension perhaps was for the purpose of his later eschatological appearance as forerunner of the coming of YHWH. Jewish tradition from earliest times viewed it in

---

4. Verhoef, *The Books of Haggai and Malachi*, 343.
5. Robert L. Alden, "Malachi," in *EBC*, ed. Frank E. Gaebelein (Grand Rapids: Zondervan, 1955), 7:724.
6. N. Lohfink, *TDOT*, 5:180-99 (esp. p. 198), s.v. חָרַם.

this way,[7] as even the NT suggests. When the Jewish masses learned of the ministry of John the Baptist in the wilderness, they went out to him and inquired as to his identity. Was he the Messiah, they wondered, or Elijah, or the prophet, that is, the prophet of Deuteronomy 18? To each of these his answer was no. But the very question reflects anticipation of a coming Elijah.

Jesus, in an apparent contradiction of John's own testimony, clearly identified John as Elijah (Matt. 11:14), but in a highly nuanced way. John's inquisitors had wondered if he was not actually Elijah in the flesh returned to earth. This he was not, as he made clear in his reply. But he was, however, an Elijah figure, one who came in the spirit and power of Elijah. This is why Jesus qualified His assessment of the Elijah-John identification by saying, "If you are willing to receive him, this is Elijah who is to come." That is, John stands in fulfillment of the promise of Malachi concerning the coming of Elijah but only in the sense that he announced the coming of Christ, just as the messenger would come to announce the coming of Adon (Mal. 3:1).

Jesus touched on this point again in the transfiguration narrative (Matt. 17:1-13; cf. Mark 9:2-13; Luke 9:28-36). When Jesus appeared on the mountain in glory, He was accompanied by Moses and Elijah, the same two figures mentioned by Malachi. In later discussion with His disciples about His resurrection, they reminded Him that before the messianic manifestation could come to pass Elijah must first appear. Jesus agreed that Elijah must restore all things, but then announced that Elijah had already come, only to be rejected. They then understood that Jesus once more was connecting Elijah with John the Baptist.

As argued previously, however, in connection with Mal. 3:1, the messenger of the covenant there and John the Baptist are one and the same. Jesus established this linkage (Matt. 11:10-11) and went on to make the further linkage between John and Elijah in the same passage (Matt. 11:14). But Mal. 3:1-6, as we saw, has eschatological as well as messianic overtones. This suggests that the messenger (and thus also Elijah) has an eschatological identification and role as well. There is still a sense, then, in which Elijah is yet to come.[8] This is put beyond question by Mal. 3:23 (EB 4:5), which locates Elijah's coming

---

7. For various traditions to this effect, see Louis Ginzberg, *The Legends of the Jews* (Philadelphia: Jewish Publication Society of America, 1968), 6:316-42 *passim*.

8. As Kaiser notes, the day of YHWH here "embraces both advents" ("The Promise of the Arrival of Elijah in Malachi and the Gospels," *GTJ* 3 [1982]: 229).

in the setting of "the great and terrible day of YHWH," a description freighted with eschatological language.

It is likely, then, that the historical Elijah is not in view but instead an antitype Elijah who, like John, will announce the coming of YHWH in a day yet future.[9] But the fact that he may not be the historical Elijah cannot mitigate against the literalness of the figure himself any more than it could against the literalness of the historical John the Baptist.

Why Elijah is mentioned and not someone else may have to do with his place as a prophet *non pareil*.[10] Moses appears in Mal. 3:21 (EB 4:4) in connection with the law; Elijah appears in the next verse, perhaps in connection with the prophets. Thus the whole canon of Malachi's day is represented, attesting univocally to the certainty of YHWH's coming salvation. This sublime act of final redemption is confirmed by the word of two witnesses (Deut. 19:15), just as its anticipatory revelation in the Transfiguration of our Lord was accompanied by the same two witnesses, Moses and Elijah (Matt. 17:3). The great and terrible day of YHWH is a certainty, as both law and prophecy declare. But it will be a day of salvation for those of Israel, who, by the message of grace preached by Elijah, are thereby made capable of adhering to the covenant of Moses to which YHWH likewise elected them by grace.

9. Kaiser, "The Promise of the Arrival of Elijah in Malachi and the Gospels," 230.
10. Moreover, as Baldwin points out, the reference to Horeb ties the two together, for Moses received the law there and Elijah received a new sense of prophetic vocation on the same mountain (*Haggai, Zechariah, Malachi* [London: Tyndale, 1972], 252). Gerald L. Keown suggests that Elijah, as a powerful defender of Yahwistic faith, is frequently associated with the purifying qualities of fire and for that reason appears in the Malachi judgment passages ("Messianism in the Book of Malachi," *RevExp* 84 [1987]: 445-46).

Selected Index of Subjects

Index of Authors

Selected Index of Scripture

6:1-3	326	3:12	36
6:3, 8-15	131	4:1-5	22
9:10	195	4:3	131
11:3	386	4:4	117
11:30	202	4:5	63
21:1	133, 330	4:6	63, 370, 371, 372
27:15	194, 202	4:7-23	371
28:2	242	4:12	116, 372
28:4, 5, 6	107, 315	4:15-16	372
29:3-5	40	4:24	4, 22
		5:1-5	51
2 Chronicles		5:1-2	9, 16, 45, 62, 63
6:6	107, 134	5:1	12, 19, 62, 94
14:11	152	5:2	20, 131, 325
16:9	143	5:3	10, 116
21:14-15	358	5:6-17	9
24:20-22	95	5:9	10, 116
26:5	95	5:13-17	45, 63
29:1	387	5:14	7
34:21	294	5:16	161
35:6	386	6:1-12	63
35:25	323	6:4	26
36:19-20	117	6:6-15	45
36:22-23	6, 32, 189	6:6-12	189
		6:7-8	117
Ezra		6:9-12	401
1:1-4	6, 189, 401	6:12	221
1:1	4, 105, 146	6:13	63
1:5-11	7	6:14-15	62, 117
1:8	8	6:14	12, 19, 62, 94
2	10	6:15	4, 9, 161, 371
2:1-2, 21-35, 36-58,		6:16	206
64-65, 66-67, 70	117	6:22	189
2:2	131	7:1-10	376
2:28	208	7:6	189, 372
2:36, 62	195	7:10	402
2:59	195, 216	7:11-26	189, 372
3:1-7	8	7:15	221
3:2	7, 20, 131, 325	7:21, 23-26	373
3:6	4, 51	7:25	402
3:8–4:5	44	8:1-14	117
3:8-13	22, 36, 51	8:31-32	118
3:8-10	8, 62, 161	8:31	4
3:8-9	131	9:1-4	373
3:8	4, 7, 20, 44, 131, 225, 325	9:1	373, 415
		9:2	414
3:10	142, 161	9:5–10:44	373
3:11	51, 162	9:8	273

9:9	189
9:14	30, 373, 414, 415
10:1-4	374, 414
10:9	4
10:11-12	414
10:17	4, 414
10:18	20, 131

Nehemiah

1:1	4
1:3	116
2:1	4, 414
2:8	189
2:9–6:19	116
2:9	376
3:1	95, 131, 357
3:15	357
5:1-5	373
5:14	4
5:15	297
6:15	4, 414
7	10
7:1-2	373
7:4	118, 222
7:7	131
7:32	208
7:73–9:38	373
8:2	363
8:9	402
9:1-38	363
9:1-10	76
9:1	4, 414
9:8	96
9:11	348
9:13, 14	96
9:29	214
9:36-37	373
9:38	363
10:28-39	373
10:29	363
10:30	414
11:1-2	118, 222
11:23	189
12:1	7, 131, 325
12:7	131
12:10-16	63
12:10	30, 95, 131
12:12-16	95

12:16	76, 94
12:26	20, 131
13:4-5	374
13:4	95
13:5	437
13:6-7	371
13:6	4, 437
13:10, 12	438
13:13	415
13:14	415, 442
13:23-27	374
13:23-24	415

Esther

1:1	370
8:11	216
9:2	216
9:19	116

Job

1:6-12	330
1:6-7	132
1:6	187
1:7	104, 163, 173
1:8	23, 132
1:9-11	132
2:1	187
2:2-3	104
2:2	163, 173
2:4-5	132
9:13	280
9:22-24	440
10:10	351
13:12	446
15:32	356
16:20	132
19:3	235
19:7	356
21:7-20	440
28:12	280
28:26	268
33:23	132
38:4	212
38:25	268
42:10	260

Psalms

2:2-3	222

11:5	314, 336	14:16-21	69, 83, 84, 398
11:6, 9	336, 338	14:16	72, 88, 127, 233, 306
11:8	338		
11:12-13	75	**Malachi**	
11:15-17	334	1:1	21, 239, 377, 386, 387
11:16	314, 338	1:2-5	374, 380, 381, 386
11:17	84	1:2	378, 380, 381, 439
12:1-9	68, 73, 82, 83,	1:4	375
	343, 346, 347	1:5	311, 384
12:1	205, 239, 311, 377,	1:6–2:9	380, 431
	385, 386, 387	1:6-14	375, 380, 402, 403
12:3	82, 263	1:6	378, 380, 402, 403,
12:4	263		407, 439, 442
12:6	82, 263	1:7	378, 439
12:7-9	252	1:8	375, 378, 403
12:7-8	88	1:11-14	379
12:7	72, 263	1:11	377, 384
12:9	82, 263	1:12	384, 402
12:10–13:1	69, 82, 83	1:14	402, 403
12:10	82, 88, 328, 330,	2:1-9	380
	336, 339	2:1	402, 403
12:11	75, 263	2:2	379, 401, 436
12:12-14	328	2:3	378
13:1-6	309, 321	2:4	384, 428
13:1	82, 88	2:5-9	402
13:2-6	69, 83	2:5	428, 442
13:7-9	69, 82, 83, 309, 310	2:6	378
13:7	82, 285, 305	2:7-9	375
13:9	82, 88, 274	2:7	46, 378, 379, 430
14:1-15	69, 73, 82, 83, 84	2:8	428
14:1-8	72, 183, 309	2:10	378, 380, 384, 418
14:1-2, 3-5	82	2:11-12	379, 382
14:4-6	72	2:11	376, 415, 418
14:4-5	160	2:13	375
14:4	183, 282	2:15	378
14:5	78	2:16	415
14:6-8	82	2:17–3:5	380, 380, 425
14:7-14	84	2:17	378, 380, 384, 439
14:9-15	40	3:1	316, 378, 379, 387,
14:9-11	127, 309		388, 407, 450, 452
14:9-10	82	3:2-3	444
14:9	78, 88, 126, 183,	3:2	378
	233, 306, 310	3:5	442
14:10-11	82	3:6-12	380, 381, 425
14:10	82, 222	3:6	378, 379
14:11	183	3:7-10	375
14:12-15	82	3:7	378, 381, 439
14:14	123	3:8	378, 381, 439

Selected Index of Hebrew Words